Musical Instrument Auction Price Guide

2000 edition

STRING LETTER PUBLISHING

String Letter Publishing, Inc.
PO Box 767
San Anselmo, California 94979
(415) 485-6946

Editor: Jessamyn Reeves-Brown
Consulting Editor: Mary VanClay
Assistant Editor: Marsha Gonick

Design Director: Eliza Homelsky

Production Director: Ellen Richman
Production Coordinator: Judy Zimola
Production Assistant: Donna Yuen

Marketing Manager: Jen Fujimoto

The Publishers wish to thank Abby Baker and Peter Horner of Bonhams, Emma Sully and Kerry Keane of Christie's, Clare Roberts and Philip Scott of Phillips, Cindy Tashjian and David Bonsey of Skinner, and Tim Ingles of Sotheby's for their kind assistance in providing photographs for this guide. Photos on page 262, courtesy of Bonhams; photos on pages 125 and 260, courtesy of Christies; photos on pages 123, 124, 261, and 264, courtesy of Phillips; photos on pages 128, 129, 259, 265, and 266, courtesy of Skinner; and photos on pages 126, 127, 130, 260, and 263, courtesy of Sotheby's. Center back-cover photo, courtesy of Phillips; other back-cover photos, and front-cover photos at top and at bottom center and right, courtesy of Sotheby's; all other front-cover photos, courtesy of Skinner.

The Publishers assume no responsibility for errors or omissions in the material contained in this guide.

ISBN 1-890-490-23-7

TABLE OF CONTENTS

Introduction   v

Great Expectations   1

AUCTION ACTIVITY:
1999 INSTRUMENT SALES

Sales Included in this Guide   6

Directory of Auction Houses   7

A Key to the Item-by-Item Listings   8

Item-by-Item Listings   9

FIVE-YEAR SUMMARY:
SALES BY ITEM AND MAKER

How to Read the Summary by Item and Maker   69

Summary by Item and Maker   71

INTRODUCTION

This guide offers descriptions and prices of musical instruments and bows offered at auction by identifiable makers at 22 sales held in the United States and England during 1999. (For a complete list of sales, see page 6.)

It is emphatically not a guide to the playing qualities of these instruments, nor to their physical condition. Nor does the guide generally reflect "retail prices," since many items bought at auction are subsequently resold.

The guide is divided into three sections. The first section presents a report on stringed-instrument sales in 1999, reprinted from *Strings* magazine. The second section contains auction results in the Item-by-Item Listings. It provides the details on each item: where it was offered, lot number, where and when made, low and high estimated prices, the specifics of the most recent certificate—if any—with which the item was offered, and the actual selling price shown in four currencies. The first currency is U.S. dollars, followed by pounds sterling, deutsche marks, and yen. The order of currencies is fixed, regardless of the currency in which the sale was conducted.

The third section contains the Summary by Item and Maker, which briefly encapsulates the offerings of the last five years in four currencies. The summary is subdivided alphabetically by item, from Accordion to Zither-Banjo. Within each subdivision, you will find an alphabetical list of makers whose work appeared at auction, along with the barest of facts: how many items by that maker were offered, how many sold, and what were the lowest, highest, and average selling prices. If no items were sold, you will find no price information. If no items were offered by a particular maker, you will simply not find that maker's name.

Please note that all the basic information in this guide was supplied by the auction houses themselves, and it mirrors whatever inconsistencies or ambiguities you will find in the catalogs and the salesrooms. To cite one such example, you may find bows stamped "A. Vigneron," with no attempt to lump them with bows by Joseph Arthur Vigneron or his son, André. Although authorities may tell us that it was the father who used this stamp, while his son used a stamp reading "André Vigneron," we are not prepared to second-guess the auction houses who offered these bows under the sobriquet "A. Vigneron."

At the same time, we have attempted to clear up merely stylistic inconsistencies. For example, Italian forms of proper names are used rather than Latin forms; thus Hieronymus Amati II is listed as Amati, Girolamo (II).

Let the reader then be wary. When in doubt, first refer, if possible, to the catalog of the auction house itself. If the catalog is unavailable to you, contact the auction house directly, using the directory of names and addresses on page 7 of this guide, and request further clarification.

GREAT EXPECTATIONS

by Mary VanClay

Any turnover of a decade, much less a century or millennium, is inevitably accompanied by loud declarations that society is heading into a bright new era. Of course, such predictions aren't always justified by the mere trick of a changing calendar.

As 2000 rolled in, however, the world of musical-instrument sales really did seem to be shaking off some of the ghosts of its past, and to be publicly embracing (if reluctantly, in places) new ways of doing business.

Most of the dealers and auction-house experts we spoke to confidently told *Strings* that the market is in fine fettle. It has taken most of the '90s for many observers to be so certain; auctions of the 1980s saw unprecedented increases in prices paid, until the euphoria ended in a terrible crash—at least in the fine-paintings market. Instrument auctions paralleled the unprecedented growth in prices; but even though a corresponding price drop never actually came, the inevitable slowdown turned much of the next decade into an exercise in psychological recovery. Sales of good-quality instruments chugged along at a reasonable pace, but the era of high excitement ("speculative buying," in the words of one expert), was over.

However, 1999 was a banner year for most of those interviewed, with more and more players appearing in shops and auction houses looking for instruments and bows. "Because of all the Y2K fears, I was somewhat worried in the beginning [of the year]," admits Robert Cauer, a violin dealer in Los Angeles and current president of the American Federation of Violin and Bow Makers. "That fear was totally unfounded."

Experts at the auction houses concur. "It's been an amazing year!" exclaims Tim Ingles, instrument expert at Sotheby's in London. For Ingles, the highlight of 1999 was Sotheby's November sale of the late Yehudi Menuhin's instrument and bow collection. "That was the highlight of the decade, let alone 1999," he volunteers. "Musicians like Menuhin come along once every generation, and it was an extraordinary honor to have the collection." Ingles considers the bows to have been the most interesting, citing in particular three François Tourte violin bows that sold, with buyer's premium, for £30,418 ($49,185), £37,030 ($59,878), and £42,205 ($68,245) as lots 57, 58, and 59.

A bow was also the top pick of Kerry Keane, now head of the musical instruments department at Christie's in both London and New York (Keane was formerly Skinner's resident expert in Boston, as well as a maker and dealer in his own right). "The highlight for me, though it probably wasn't the most expensive thing Christie's sold, was an exquisite Joseph Henry cello bow [November sale, lot 181]," he says. "It was ca. 1860 and came from a private musician in England who was absolutely flabbergasted when I gave him a presale estimate of £8,000–£12,000. Its hammer price was £17,000 [with buyer's premium, $31,671]. He was darned happy! It went to a musician."

David Bonsey, now heading the musical-instruments department at Skinner, also said bows sold well in 1999, as well as cellos. "We had two Sartory cello bows," he says of the November sale, "both in fine condition. Both sold for around retail prices [$13,225 and $15,870, with buyer's premium, for lots 97 and 106 respectively]. The market for Sartorys is still really, really strong."

For Peter Horner, the expert at Bonhams in London, the November sale of lot 74, a Gennaro Gagliano cello, was the highlight, setting a world record for the maker. "It came from a private family," he says, "and the hammer price was £220,000 [with buyer's premium, $409,860]."

"We marketed the instrument very well," he adds. "We achieved a magnificent price by careful planning. It went to a player."

Over at Phillips, instrument expert Philip Scott sums it up this way: "The year began with promise and finished up brilliantly, in spite of the strong pound. The Joseph Rocca violin that we sold in November [as lot 127] made the very high price—an auction record—of £160,000 with the buyer's premium [$238,464]. It was a collector who bought it; the two Nicolo Gaglianos in that sale also went to collectors, who were outbidding the traders and everyone else."

Scott pegged the individual collectors as the high rollers this year. But several of the top items listed by the other auction-house experts went to players. And Scott himself agreed that "players are entering the market in quite a strong way."

"I myself have spent the last 13 years trying to make players comfortable with the auction process," Christie's Keane says emphatically. "Auction houses aren't ever in the position to offer all the services that a retail venue can offer, and we'd be fooling ourselves if we said we could. But if you've got specialists in the [musical-instruments] department who are trained, then you can, as a consumer, feel confident in the condition report you get. And I see, more and more, that musicians may be willing to trade condition for price." Players can sometimes afford to outbid dealers, Keane points out, because they don't have to turn around and make a profit on their purchase.

Dealers don't seem worried that they're losing business to the auction houses, however. "They exist, that is a fact of life," Cauer says philosophically of the auctions. "As long as I'm doing the way I'm doing now, I won't gripe about it!"

Richard Ward, of Ifshin Violins in Berkeley, California, says he's also heard from the auction houses that players are more interested in buying and selling in that venue, but he hasn't seen any corresponding drop in customers at the dealers'. "There's a demand for instruments now," he says. "Music schools keep growing, and there are many new ones. I talk to the players auditioning for the symphony here [in the San Francisco Bay Area], and the competition is incredibly intense. They need every edge they can get: the best instrument they can get, and the best adjustment. They're looking for old instruments, and there's a finite supply but more and more demand. The results are obvious."

James McKean, *Strings'* corresponding editor and a maker and dealer in New York City, agrees that demand is high and notes that he is "amazed" at the prices being paid for modern Italian instruments, which get increasing attention as older instruments become rarer. In nearby Philadelphia at William Moennig & Son, partner Philip Kass also notes that the "hot spots continue to be Italian instruments and French bows."

McKean, however, adds that high-end contemporary instruments are also in great demand. "I have seen a drastic shift in attitude in the past ten years. People are not only willing to look at new instruments, they ask for them."

There's been a change of attitude about the student-instrument lines as well: China is increasingly a player in that market. Robert Cauer says that, only a few years ago, products from Chinese workshops were universally scoffed at by U.S. dealers, who preferred to sell better-quality student instruments from long-established regions such as Mittenwald. "But I don't think Germany is laughing anymore," says Cauer. "It's less expensive for me, as a dealer, to get instruments of similar quality from a Chinese wholesaler than direct from a German workshop."

Another major change currently under way is the rise in on-line instrument auctions. Will the Internet be the instrument marketplace of the future? Opinions vary widely. Nearly everyone discounted direct, person-to-person sales made on sites such as eBay. "I've been watching eBay for a long time," notes Todd French, who heads the instrument department at Butterfield & Butterfield in Los Angeles. "The market has really slowed down there as far as musical instruments are concerned. People are feeling burned by inexperienced sellers."

But the auction houses themselves are flirting, to varying degrees, with on-line sales. That's no surprise coming from Butterfield & Butterfield, since the house was recently acquired by eBay. But others are joining in as well. Sotheby's, for instance, has taken full-page ads announcing its on-line auction presence (at www.sothebys.com) in major newspapers. Tim Ingles is quick to note that live Internet bidding may become more important for some Sotheby's departments than for musical instruments. "For the upper end of the market, I don't feel that the Web is a suitable way of selling," he says honestly. Instrument sales are, he explains, "very much a live experience, very touchy-feely, very physical. And the concern is that you spoil the atmosphere in the saleroom because you have to wait for something like eight seconds for the Internet bid to come through, so you don't get that amazing bustle that makes an instrument sale so special.

"But," he adds, "it will be very interesting to see how things progress."

Skinner will include on-line bidding starting with its first sale of 2000, on May 7. Bidders will be able to place offers on-line at skinner.lycos.com before the sale, then up their offers by telephone during the live sale itself. "I still have serious doubts about buying things totally on-line," concedes Bonsey. "I think that we're going the right way in combining on-line capability with the live viewings and the regular auction. Violins are tactile things, and it's really important that players see and feel and hear them."

Christie's, for its part, currently has on-line viewing of instruments but no Internet bidding. For Bonhams and Phillips, it's not even in the works. "You're never going to replace the theater of an auction with a screen," says Phillips' Scott. He predicts that, ultimately, the Internet will simply provide another method of bidding, as the phone and fax have already done.

But some businesses are banking on more of a sea change. November saw the first sale by Tarisio, an instruments-only auction house based in Boston. It could be argued that Tarisio is really something more like an on-line dealership; it is run by experienced dealers and does not actually exist as a physical building. (And it's no secret that, for these reasons, personnel at some of the traditional auction houses aren't pleased that Tarisio is known as one, as well.) Christopher Reuning, of Reuning & Son Violins in Boston, and Dmitry Gindin, of Gindin & Gindin in New York City, are the dealers who launched Tarisio; they collect the instruments, provide the market expertise, and work with Jason Price, who is the company's Web expert. Because it has no auction-house infrastructure to support, the trio charges low commission rates. It began assembling instruments from private consigners during the summer, and, in November, Tarisio staged a live viewing for three days in Boston, just as Skinner's traditional sale was going on across the street. Afterward it took offers on-line at www.tarisio.com from numerous bidders all around the country. The sale's highlight was a 1760 violin made by Ferdinand Gagliano, with the original scroll by Joseph Gagliano, which went for $65,000. "That's a pretty good sign that people are willing to trust the Internet," remarks Price.

"And," adds fellow owner Christopher Reuning, "we reached a much broader market because of its being on-line than we would have otherwise." Reuning touts on-line auctions as the "wave of the future," citing the fact that such a format is more accessible to the general public and cuts down on the intimidation factor so famous in auction rooms. But everyone, Tarisio included, agrees that the sales must incorporate live viewings if buyers are to be comfortable with on-line bidding.

It's too early to tell whether the Internet will ultimately take over instrument auctions or simply provide yet another way to place a bid. Either way, it does provide an opportunity for more players to research their options, both at auction and at retail. And, says Reuning, "anything that opens up the market, and gives players more information and more options, is a positive thing for the market in general."

—*Mary VanClay*

Auction Activity

1999
instrument
sales

SALES INCLUDED IN THIS GUIDE

The bracketed code is shorthand that consists of a letter (or letters) denoting the auction house, followed by a number for the month in which the sale took place. (This year Sotheby's held two sales on November 16; the sale encoded here as S11M dealt strictly with the late Lord Yehudi Menuhin's collection.) You will find these codes used throughout the detailed item-by-item listings later in the guide.

House	Place	Code	Date	Rate of Exchange
Bonhams	Knightsbridge	[B2]	2/9/99	$1.64
Phillips	London	[P2]	2/16/99	$1.63
Phillips	London	[P3]	3/15/99	$1.62
Bonhams	Knightsbridge	[B3]	3/16/99	$1.62
Sotheby's	London	[S3]	3/16/99	$1.62
Christie's	South Kensington	[C3]	3/17/99	$1.63
Butterfields'	Los Angeles and Elgin, Illinois	[Bf4]	4/19/99	$1.00
Bonhams	Knightsbridge	[B5]	5/6/99	$1.64
Skinner	Boston	[Sk5]	5/9/99	$1.00
Phillips	London	[P5]	5/10/99	$1.63
Phillips	London	[P6]	6/14/99	$1.61
Sotheby's	London	[S6]	6/15/99	$1.59
Bonhams	Knightsbridge	[B6]	6/15/99	$1.59
Phillips	London	[P9]	9/20/99	$1.62
Butterfields'	Los Angeles	[Bf10]	10/18/99	$1.00
Sotheby's	London	[S10]	10/27/99	$1.65
Skinner	Boston	[Sk11]	11/7/99	$1.00
Phillips	London	[P11]	11/15/99	$1.62
Sotheby's	London	[S11M]	11/16/99	$1.62
Sotheby's	London	[S11]	11/16/99	$1.62
Christie's	South Kensington	[C11]	11/17/99	$1.62
Bonhams	Knightsbridge	[B11]	11/17/99	$1.62

DIRECTORY OF AUCTION HOUSES

These are the firms in the United States and England that regularly conduct sales of musical instruments, particularly stringed instruments and bows.

Bonhams
Montpelier St.
Knightsbridge
London SW7 1HH, England
Telephone: (44) 171 393 3900
Fax: (44) 171 393 3905
Web site: www.bonhams.com
Specialist: Peter Horner

Butterfield & Butterfield
7601 Sunset Blvd.
Los Angeles, CA 90046, USA
Telephone: (323) 850-7500
Fax: (323) 850-5843
Web site: www.butterfields.com
Specialist: Todd French

Christie's
85 Old Brompton Rd.
London SW7 3LD, England
Telephone: (44) 171 321 3472
Fax: (44) 171 321 3321
Web site: www.christies.com
Specialist: Kerry K. Keane
Contact: Caroline Gill

219 E. 67th St.
New York, NY 10021, USA
Telephone: (212) 606-0562
Fax: (212) 744-9946
Specialist: Kerry K. Keane
Contact: Genevieve Wheeler

Phillips
101 New Bond St.
London W1Y 0AS, England
Telephone: (44) 171 629 6602
Fax: (44) 171 468 8227
Web site: www.phillips-auctions.com
Specialist: Philip Scott
Contact: Mary Jane Potter

406 E. 79th St.
New York, NY 10021, USA
Telephone: (212) 570-4830
Fax: (212) 570-2207
Contact: Karen Cangelosi

Skinner
357 Main St.
Bolton, MA 01740, USA
Telephone: (978) 779-6241
Fax: (978) 779-5144
Web site: www.skinnerinc.com
Specialist: David Bonsey

Sotheby's
34-35 New Bond St.
London W1A 2AA, England
Telephone: (44) 171 293 5034
Fax: (44) 171 293 5942
Web site: www.sothebys.com
Specialist: Tim Ingles
Contact: Paul Hayday

1334 York Ave.
New York, NY 10021, USA
Telephone: (212) 606-7938
Fax: (212) 774-5310
Contact: Katherine Paculba

A KEY TO THE ITEM-BY-ITEM LISTINGS

1. Name of Maker   2. Sale/Lot   3. Item   4. Where/When Made

GUADAGNINI, LORENZO [P11/154] Fine and Handsome Violin w/case: Piacenza,
1742 (W. E. Hill & Sons, London, June 1933)   122,960/184,440
$304,326   £198,000   DM480,942   ¥57,370,500

5. Certificate   6. Estimated Prices ($)   7. Selling Prices

1. Name. An "attributed" work signals an attribution made, or agreed to, by the auction house; when "ascribed," a traditional ascription is acknowledged but not necessarily agreed with.

2. The lot number assigned by the auctioneer is preceded by an initial to identify the house (B Bonhams; Bf Butterfields'; C Christie's; P Phillips; S Sotheby's; Sk Skinner) followed by a number for the sale. If there were two sales at one house during the same month, the numbers for the month and day are both used to identify the sale.

3. A description of the item as it appears in the sale catalog. When the item is sold with accessories or when additional items are part of the same lot, a brief itemization appears here. This is also the place where defects or repairs, as reported in the sale catalog, are noted.

4. Place and date of manufacture, if known.

5. If sold with a certificate attesting to its provenance or identity, the most recent issuer is indicated in parentheses, along with the place and date of issuance.

6. Low and high estimated prices (in dollars) are separated by a slash (/). This is the price range within which the item was expected to sell, in the opinion of the auctioneers. On occasion, no estimate is made—most often involving an important instrument by a famous maker. In these cases, only the selling price appears in the tables.

7. The actual selling price includes the buyer's premium, at Bonhams, Christie's, Phillips, and Sotheby's: 15 percent on the first £30,000 of the hammer price and 10 percent on the amount above; and at Butterfields' and Skinner, 15 percent on the first $50,000 plus 10 percent on the amount above. Prices are given in four currencies, converted from local currency at their value on the day sold. You may determine the auction house at which the sale took place from the "Sale" information in "2" above. An unsold item is recorded as "NS." These listings do not provide details on size, weight, color, etc., which often help to identify or distinguish particular items. You are advised to consult the catalogs published prior to the sales, which may be obtained directly from the auctioneers.

ACCORDION

SCANDALLI [P2/13] Good Piano Accordion w/case
489/815 NS

SOPRANI, PAOLO [P2/14] Piano Accordion w/box
163/326
$225   £138   DM393   ¥26,572

AEOLA

WHEATSTONE & CO., C. [S10/55] Forty-Eight
Button Aeola w/case: London, 1919   330/494
$1,851   £1,124   DM3,438   ¥193,015

BANJELE

SMECK, ROY [B5/34] Banjele w/case   33/49
$75   £46   DM137   ¥9,108

BANJO

BACON & DAY [Sk11/31] American Tenor Banjo
w/case: Groton, Connecticut   800/1,000
$1,455   £900   DM2,746   ¥153,913

BARNES & MULLINS [B5/33] Five-String Banjo
w/case: London   164/246
$217   £132   DM394   ¥26,184

CONTESSA [Bf10/8108] Banjo   300/400 NS

DOBSON CO. [Sk11/21] Five-String Banjo: New
York, c. 1900   200/300
$231   £143   DM437   ¥24,486

FAIRBANKS CO., A.C. [Bf10/8109] Banjo
700/900 NS

GIBSON CO. [Sk11/30] Tenor Banjo w/case:
Kalamazoo, Michigan   3,000/4,000
$4,893   £3,029   DM9,236   ¥517,706

GRETSCH [Sk11/26] Tenor Banjo w/case: c. 1930
600/800 NS

VEGA COMPANY [Sk11/17] Tenor Banjo w/case:
c. 1930   350/450
$562   £348   DM1,061   ¥59,466

VEGA COMPANY [Sk11/28] "Vegaphone
Professional" Model Tenor Banjo w/case: Boston,
1932   350/450
$529   £327   DM998   ¥55,968

VEGA COMPANY [Sk11/32] "Vegaphone
Professional" Model Tenor Banjo w/case: Boston,
c. 1930   250/350
$596   £369   DM1,124   ¥63,025

WEYMANN CO. [Sk11/29] Plectrum Banjo w/case:
Philadelphia, Pennsylvania   400/600
$529   £327   DM998   ¥55,968

BANJOLIN

RELIANCE [B2/41] Banjolin   49/66
$94   £58   DM163   ¥10,762

BARITONE

LYON & HEALY [Bf10/8065] B-Flat Baritone:
Chicago, c. 1925   400/600 NS

MARCEAU & CO. [Bf10/8068] B-Flat Baritone:
Paris, c. 1910   700/900 NS

SAPORETTI & CAPPARELI [Bf10/8064] B-Flat
Baritone: Florence, c. 1920   400/600 NS

BASSET HORN

ALBERT, E. [B5/22] Rosewood Basset Horn: c. 1870
820/1,148
$943   £575   DM1,714   ¥113,844

BASSOON

BILTON, R. [Bf4/2769] Nine-Key Bassoon missing
crook   800/1,200 NS

BIZEY, CHARLES [S10/124] Baroque Racket
Bassoon: Paris, c. 1720   16,479/24,719 NS

DUPRE, PAUL [Sk5/11] Modern French Bassoon
w/case: Paris   250/350
$633   £386   DM1,145   ¥76,368

LAFLEUR, J.R. & SON [P11/11] Bassoon w/case
486/648
$471   £291   DM895   ¥49,523

MILHOUSE, WILLIAM [S10/25] Eight-Keyed
Pearwood Bassoon: London, second quarter 19th C.
1,154/1,648 NS

MILHOUSE, WILLIAM & W. WHEATCROFT
[S10/104] Composite Eight-Keyed Bassoon: England,
late 18th C.   989/1,318 NS

SCHREIBER & SOHNE, W. [Sk5/10] Contemporary
German Bassoon w/case: Nauheim   150/250
$863   £526   DM1,561   ¥104,138

BUGLE

COUESNON & CO. [Bf10/8066] Bugle: Paris,
c. 1905   400/600 NS

MILLENS, J. [Bf10/8076] Two-Valve Bugle: Paris,
c. 1935   550/750 NS

SAURLE, MICHAEL [S10/80] Six-Keyed Bugle with
later mouthpiece: Munich, c. 1835   1,648/2,472
$2,615   £1,587   DM4,856   ¥272,631

THIBOUVILLE-LAMY, J. [Bf10/8067] Bugle: Paris,
c. 1905   400/600 NS

CAVAQUINHO

D'ATHOUGUIA, RUFINO FELIX [P11/15]
Cavaquinho: Madeira, 1850   648/810
$1,028   £635   DM1,953   ¥108,049

CHAMBER BASS

POLLMAN [P2/143D] Good Contemporary Five-String Chamber Bass in immediate playing condition, w/wheeled case   6,520/7,335
$7,123   £4,370   DM12,455   ¥841,444

POLLMAN [P2/143M] Good Contemporary Five-String Chamber Bass in immediate playing condition, w/wheeled case   7,335/8,150
$7,123   £4,370   DM12,455   ¥841,444

CLARINET

ALBERT, E. [B2/25] Bass Clarinet w/original case
                                                              328/492
$981   £598   DM1,692   ¥111,922

ALBERT, E. [B5/19] Boxwood Boehm-System Clarinet   82/115
$415   £253   DM754   ¥50,091

BERNAREGGI [Sk5/8] Six-Keyed Clarinet: Barcelona
                                                              250/350
$374   £228   DM676   ¥45,127

BILTON, RICHARD [S10/3] Six-Keyed Boxwood Clarinet in C, w/case, 2 four-keyed flutes: London, c. 1825   659/989
$762   £462   DM1,415   ¥79,419

BILTON, RICHARD (workshop of) [C11/2] Eight-Keyed Boxwood and Ivory Clarinet w/period mouthpiece: London   324/486 NS

BOOSEY & CO. [B2/19] Rosewood Small-System Clarinet w/original case   164/246
$321   £196   DM553   ¥36,590

CLEMENT & CO. [B5/20] Six-Keyed Boxwood Clarinet: London, c. 1810   820/1,148
$905   £552   DM1,645   ¥109,290

FLEISCHMANN, ANTON [Bf4/2778] Five-Keyed Clarinet in A: Baden, c. 1800   500/800
$331   £206   DM608   ¥38,997

GEROCK & WOLF [Sk5/7] English Boxwood Six-Keyed Clarinet: London, 19th C.   500/700
$460   £281   DM833   ¥55,540

HAWKES & SON [B2/20] Clarinet w/case, another clarinet   131/197
$94   £58   DM163   ¥10,762

HAWKES & SONS [B5/21] Clarinet w/case, matching clarinet   98/131
$104   £63   DM188   ¥12,523

HAWKES & SONS [B5/23] Bass Clarinet w/case: London   492/820
$528   £322   DM960   ¥63,753

HEROUARD PERE ET FILS [P2/3] Boxwood and Ivory Clarinet in good condition: c. 1840
                                                              326/489 NS

KEY [B2/21] Six-Keyed Boxwood Clarinet: c. 1830
                                                              492/656
$943   £575   DM1,627   ¥107,617

KRUSPE, C. [S10/122] Ten-Keyed Boxwood Clarinet in high E-flat: Erfurt, third quarter 19th C.   330/494
$392   £238   DM728   ¥40,895

LEBLANC [P6/6] Bass Clarinet w/case   644/966 NS

LEBLANC, GEORGES [S10/17] Boehm-System Contrabass Metal Clarinet: Paris, first half 20th C.
                                                            1,318/1,977
$2,287   £1,388   DM4,247   ¥238,453

LOT, ISADORE [Bf4/2766] Twelve-Keyed Rosewood Clarinet in B-Flat, w/case: La Couture, late 19th C.
                                                              500/800
$397   £247   DM730   ¥46,797

MARTIN BROS. [Sk5/15] French Clarinet w/case: Paris   300/400 NS

MILHOUSE [S10/117] Five-Keyed Boxwood Clarinet in C: London, c. 1805   1,154/1,648
$3,051   £1,852   DM5,665   ¥318,069

NOBLET [P3/14] Boehm-System Clarinet in good condition, w/box, clarinet: Paris   648/729 NS

PRESTON, JOHN [S10/109] Eight-Keyed Boxwood Clarinet in B-flat: London, c. 1830   659/989 NS

RUDALL, CARTE & CO. [B5/18] Rosewood Simple-System Clarinet w/case   131/197
$151   £92   DM274   ¥18,215

WOOD & IVY [S10/100] Six-Keyed Boxwood Clarinet in C: London, c. 1840   577/824 NS

CONCERTINA

CHIDLEY, ROCK [B2/28] Forty-Eight-Button English-System Concertina w/case   246/328 NS

CHIDLEY, ROCK [S10/56] Forty-Eight-Button English Concertina w/case: London, mid 19th C.
                                                              412/577
$872   £529   DM1,619   ¥90,877

JEFFRIES, CHARLES [S10/54] Thirty-Button Anglo-German-System Concertina w/case: London, early 20th C.   1,648/2,472
$3,923   £2,381   DM7,284   ¥408,946

LACHENAL [B2/29] Forty-Eight-Button Concertina w/case   131/197
$472   £288   DM814   ¥53,809

LACHENAL [B2/30] Seventy-Eight-Button Duet-System Concertina   656/984
$1,037   £633   DM1,790   ¥118,379

LACHENAL [B5/24] Forty-Eight-Button English-System Concertina w/case   98/164
$207   £127   DM377   ¥25,046

LACHENAL & CO. [C11/5] Thirty-Button English Concertina w/fitted box   324/486
$782   £483   DM1,473   ¥82,699

LACHENAL & CO. [P2/12] Treble Concertina w/box   326/489
$975   £598   DM1,704   ¥115,145

LACHENAL & CO. [S10/58] Forty-Eight-Button English Concertina w/case, 30-button concertina in case: London, late 19th C. 330/494
$1,634   £991   DM3,033   ¥170,295

LACHENAL & CO. [S10/61] Thirty-Button Anglo-German System Concertina w/case: London, early 20th C. 494/824
$1,634   £991   DM3,033   ¥170,295

WHEATSTONE, C. [B2/31] Sixty-Four-Button English-System Concertina w/case 328/492
$1,358   £828   DM2,343   ¥154,968

WHEATSTONE, C. [P6/8] Treble Concertina 644/805 NS

WHEATSTONE, CHARLES [S10/57] Forty-Eight-Button English Concertina w/case: London, 1854 494/824
$697   £423   DM1,295   ¥72,702

WHEATSTONE & CO., C. [P6/9] Treble Concertina w/case: London 644/805 NS

WHEATSTONE & CO., C. [S10/51] Fifty-Six-Button English Concertina w/case: London, 1924 989/1,318
$2,615   £1,587   DM4,856   ¥272,631

WHEATSTONE & CO., C. [S10/52] Miniature English Concertina w/case: London, 1933 1,154/165
$2,069   £1,256   DM3,843   ¥215,734

WHEATSTONE & CO., C. [S10/53] Fifty-Seven-Button McCann Duet Concertina w/case: London, 1916 989/1,318
$1,308   £794   DM2,428   ¥136,315

WHEATSTONE & CO., C. [S10/59] Forty-Eight-Button English Concertina w/case: London, 1925 412/577
$1,198   £727   DM2,224   ¥124,857

WHEATSTONE & CO., C. [S10/60] Sixty-Two-Button Duet Concertina w/case: London, 1926 659/989
$1,634   £991   DM3,033   ¥170,295

CORNET

BESSON & CO. [P2/2] Attractive Compact Brass Three-Cylinder-Valve Soprano Cornet in overall good condition: London 326/489
$337   £207   DM590   ¥39,858

BESSON & CO. [Sk5/4] Silver-Plated Cornet w/case: London 150/250
$98   £60   DM177   ¥11,802

BOSTON MUSICAL INSTRUMENT MANUFAC-TURER [Sk5/3] Silver-Plated Cornet w/case: early 20th C. 250/350
$288   £175   DM520   ¥34,713

COURTURIER, ERNST ALBERT [Bf4/2789] Cornet: La Porte, Indiana, 1923 500/700
$463   £288   DM852   ¥54,596

DISTIN, HENRY [Sk5/2] Silver-Plated Coronet w/case, multiple mouthpieces, mute: Williamsport, Pennsylvania, c. 1900 300/500
$863   £526   DM1,561   ¥104,138

GLASS [B2/32] Three-Keyed Brass Pocket Cornet w/trumpet 164/246
$283   £173   DM488   ¥32,285

HILLYARD, W. [P11/12] Silver-Plated Three-Cylinder Valve Military-Band Cornet w/case 648/810 NS

MARCEAU & CO. [Bf10/8078] E-Flat Cornet w/case: Paris, c. 1910 1,000/1,200 NS

CRUMHORN

GUNTHER [Bf10/8083] Tenor Crumhorn 700/900 NS

CYMBALUM

SCHUNDA, JOSEF V. [S10/41] Cymbalum: Budapest, c. 1900 659/989 NS

DOUBLE BASS

GILKES, WILLIAM [B6/28] English Four-String Double Bass: London, 1840 31,800/39,750 NS

MONTAGNANA, DOMENICO [S3/83] Double Bass: Venice, c. 1747 405,000/567,000
$251,910 £155,500   DM452,505   ¥29,742,485

PRENTICE, RONALD [S3/82] Five-String Double Bass: Ash Priors, 1975 6,480/9,720 NS

PRENTICE, RONALD [S11/222] Five-String Double Bass: Ash Priors, 1975 4,536/5,670
$6,521   £4,025   DM12,357   ¥688,557

STANLEY, ROBERT [B6/29] Four-String Double Bass: Manchester 9,540/12,720 NS

WILFER, E. (ascribed to) [P5/128] German Four-String Double Bass in immediate playing condition, w/nickel bow: Mohrendorf, c. 1900 1,141/1,304
$2,062   £1,265   DM3,732   ¥248,813

DOUBLE BASS BOW

BRYANT, P.W. [P11/136] Silver Double Bass Bow with full hair 1,458/1,620
$2,251   £1,389   DM4,275   ¥236,456

FETIQUE, VICTOR [S6/136] Silver Double Bass Bow with repaired head: Paris, c. 1900 1,908/2,385 NS

LA MAY [Bf4/2751] Double Bass Bow 700/900 NS

LEE, JOHN NORWOOD [Bf4/2753] Silver French Double Bass Bow 1,500/2,000 NS

PECATTE, CHARLES [Bf4/2755] Very Fine and Rare Double Bass Bow in a fine state of preservation (Bernard Millant, January 2, 1988) 10,000/14,000 NS

PFRETZSCHNER, H.R. [Bf4/2752] Double Bass Bow 2,500/3,000 NS

PFRETZSCHNER, H.R. [Bf4/2754] German Silver Double Bass Bow 1,200/1,600 NS

PFRETZSCHNER, H.R. [S3/149] Silver Double Bass Bow: Markneukirchen 810/1,134
$1,453   £897   DM2,610   ¥171,569

THIBOUVILLE-LAMY, J. [P11/135] Good French Silver Double Bass Bow with full hair: c. 1930

			1,620/1,944
$2,571	£1,587	DM4,883	¥270,123

TUBBS, JAMES [P11/139] Part-Silver Double Bass Bow 2,430/2,916 NS

EDEOPHONE

LACHENAL & CO. [S10/50] Forty-Eight-Button Edeophone w/case: London, early 20th C. 989/1,318

$2,397	£1,455	DM4,451	¥249,912

FIFE

GEROCK, CHRISTOPHER [S10/121] Boxwood Fife: London, early 19th C. 198/264 NS

HOLLINGS, WILLIAM [S10/14] Fife: London, c. 1875 198/297 NS

FLUGELHORN

ANSINGH & CO., D. [Bf10/8081] Fine Flugelhorn w/mouthpiece: The Netherlands, c. 1885
1,200/1,500 NS

FLUTE

ASTOR & CO. [S10/127] Eight-Keyed Boxwood Flute w/alternate flageolet head joint: London, c. 1820 824/1,154

$1,198	£727	DM2,224	¥124,857

BARLASSINA, GIUSEPPE [Bf4/2788] Metal Boehm-System Flute w/case: Milan, c. 1920 800/1,200 NS

BILTON [B5/14] Eight-Keyed English Boxwood Flute w/case: London, c. 1826 820/1,148 NS

BILTON, RICHARD [S10/19] Four-Keyed Boxwood Flute: London, c. 1830 412/494

$436	£265	DM809	¥45,438

BILTON, RICHARD [S10/125] Eight-Keyed Rosewood Flute: London, c. 1835 412/494

$762	£462	DM1,415	¥79,419

BONN, G.W. [S10/15] Four-Keyed Rosewood Flute: London, c. 1850 494/824 NS

BUTLER [B5/11] Rosewood Flute w/case 164/246

$189	£115	DM343	¥22,769

CAHUSAC [B2/13] One-Keyed Stained Boxwood Flute missing a key: London 492/656

$566	£345	DM976	¥64,570

CAHUSAC, THOMAS (SR.) [S10/28A] One-Keyed Boxwood Flute: London, late 18th C. 824/1,154

$1,198	£727	DM2,224	¥124,857

CLEMENTI & CO. [S10/18] Seven-Keyed Rosewood Flute: London, c. 1825 1,648/2,472

$1,961	£1,190	DM3,642	¥204,473

D'ALMAINE & CO. [S10/126] Six-Keyed Rosewood Flute w/case: London, c. 1840 494/659

$872	£529	DM1,619	¥90,877

DROUET, LOUIS [S10/9] Eight-Keyed Ivory Flute: London, c. 1820 2,472/3,296

$2,833	£1,719	DM5,261	¥295,350

DROUET, LOUIS [S10/102] Eight-Keyed Ebony Flute: London, 1820 659/989

$785	£476	DM1,457	¥81,789

EMBACH, LUDWIG [S10/130] Stained Boxwood One-Keyed Flute now converted to a four-keyed flute: Amsterdam, c. 1825 494/824

$610	£370	DM1,133	¥63,614

FIRTH & HALL [Bf4/2781] One-Keyed Flute: New York, c. 1825 400/600

$265	£165	DM487	¥31,198

FLORIO, PIETRO GRASSI [S10/21] One-Keyed Boxwood Flute with later brass key, w/case: London, c. 1775 1,648/2,472

$1,961	£1,190	DM3,642	¥204,473

GAUTROT (AINE) [S10/2] Five-Keyed Blackwood Flute: Paris, c. 1845 165/247

$370	£224	DM686	¥38,524

GOULDING & D'ALMAINE [S10/113] Composite One-Keyed Boxwood Flute: London, c. 1825 198/297

$262	£159	DM486	¥27,263

GRENSER, H. & WIESNER [S10/129] Seven-Keyed Blackwood Flute in F: Dresden, c. 1820
1,318/1,977 NS

GRENSER, JOHANN HEINRICH [S10/119] Four-Keyed Ebony Flute: Dresden, c. 1800
4,120/5,768 NS

HALL & SON, WILLIAM [Bf4/2780] Eight-Keyed Flute: New York, c. 1855 600/900

$397	£247	DM730	¥46,797

HEROUARD FRERES [S10/7] Six-Keyed Rosewood Flute w/case: La Couture, second quarter 19th C.
1,318/1,977 NS

HUELLER, G.H. [Bf4/2777] Nine-Keyed Flute w/case, six-keyed piccolo: Schoenick, c. 1930
700/1,000

$463	£288	DM852	¥54,596

JULLIOT, DJALMA [Bf4/2783] Silver Boehm-System Flute w/case 1,600/2,000 NS

LEROUX (AINE) [S10/5] Five-Keyed Rosewood Flute: Mirecourt, second quarter 19th C. 494/494

$587	£357	DM1,091	¥61,243

MAYBRICK, WILLIAM [S10/111] One-Keyed Boxwood Flute missing key: Liverpool, c. 1820
198/297 NS

MONZANI [B2/15] Seven-Keyed Rosewood Flute with two later keys: London 656/984 NS

MONZANI [B5/9] Seven-Keyed Rosewood Flute with two later nickel keys 410/574 NS

MONZANI [B5/10] Fine Silver-Mounted Ivory Flute w/case: London, 1827 4,920/8,200 NS

MONZANI & CO. [P3/16] Handsome Ebony and Ivory Conical-Bore Flute w/box: London, 1829
1,296/1,458 NS

MONZANI & CO. [P9/7] Eight-Silver-Keyed
Conical-Bore Patent Concert Flute: London, c. 1820
567/648 NS

MONZANI & CO. [P11/10] Handsome Ebony and
Ivory Conical-Bore Flute w/box: 1829   648/810
$857   £529   DM1,628   ¥90,041

MONZANI & CO. [S10/26] Eight-Keyed Rosewood
Flute w/case: London, c. 1815   824/1,154 NS

MONZANI & CO. [S10/103] Eight-Keyed Rosewood Flute: London, 1825/26   494/824
$610   £370   DM1,133   ¥63,614

MONZANI & CO. [S10/112] Eight-Keyed Ebony
Flute w/case: London, 1819   989/1,318 NS

MONZANI & CO. [S10/115] Eight-Keyed Rosewood Flute: London, 1813   494/824 NS

MONZANI & CO. [S10/118] Seven-Keyed Ivory
Flute w/case: London, c. 1815   3,296/4,944
$3,923   £2,381   DM7,284   ¥408,946

NEUZIL, JOHANN [Bf4/2775] Six-Keyed Flute in F:
Pisek, Czech Republic, c. 1850   600/800 NS

NOBLET BROS. [S10/8] Five-Keyed Rosewood Flute:
Paris, c. 1830   659/989
$762   £462   DM1,415   ¥79,419

PFAFF, FRANZ [S10/10] Six-Keyed Boxwood Flute:
Kaiserslautern, c. 1845   1,648/2,472 NS

PFAFF, JOHN [Bf4/2782] Eight-Keyed Flute:
Philadelphia, c. 1860   500/700
$331   £206   DM608   ¥38,997

POTTER, RICHARD [Bf4/2779] Six-Keyed Flute:
London, c. 1795   600/900
$1,124   £699   DM2,068   ¥132,591

POTTER, RICHARD [S10/110] Five-Keyed Boxwood Flute: London, 1782   659/989
$1,503   £912   DM2,790   ¥156,664

POTTER, WILLIAM HENRY [S10/22] Six-Keyed
Blackwood Flute: London, c. 1800   494/824
$697   £423   DM1,295   ¥72,702

POTTER, WILLIAM HENRY [S10/128] Six-Keyed
Boxwood Flute: London, c. 1810   494/659
$785   £476   DM1,457   ¥81,789

PROWSE, THOMAS [S10/20] Seven-Keyed Rosewood Flute: London, c. 1840   412/577
$436   £265   DM809   ¥45,438

PRUNIER [S10/13] Twelve-Keyed Rosewood Flute
w/case: Paris, late 19th C.   989/1,318 NS

RITTERSHAUSEN, E. [Bf4/2786] Metal Boehm-
System Flute: Berlin, c. 1920   800/1,200 NS

RUDALL, CARTE & CO. [B2/12] Handmade Silver
1867-System Flute w/case: 1874   164/328
$245   £150   DM423   ¥27,980

RUDALL, CARTE & CO. [B5/8] Handmade Silver
1867-System Flute: 1874   164/328
$170   £104   DM308   ¥20,492

RUDALL, CARTE & CO. [B5/13] Blackwood
Boehm-System Flute w/case   164/328
$396   £242   DM720   ¥47,815

RUDALL, CARTE & CO. [Bf4/2784] Boehm-System
Flute: London, c. 1884   600/1,000
$397   £247   DM730   ¥46,797

RUDALL, CARTE & CO. [S10/101] Cocuswood
Combined Carte- and Boehm-System Flute w/2 cases,
flute: London, c. 1930   494/824
$1,090   £661   DM2,023   ¥113,596

RUDALL, CARTE & CO. [S10/114] Eight-Keyed
Rosewood Flute w/case: London, c. 1875   989/1,318
$4,359   £2,645   DM8,093   ¥454,385

RUDALL & ROSE [S10/6] Eight-Keyed Blackwood
Flute: London, c. 1840   824/1,154
$1,787   £1,084   DM3,318   ¥186,298

RUDALL, ROSE, CARTE & CO. [Bf4/2785] Metal
Boehm-System Flute w/case: London, c. 1865 500/90
$331   £206   DM608   ¥38,997

RUDALL, ROSE, CARTE & CO. [S10/23] Eight-
Keyed Rosewood Flute: London, c. 1860   659/989
$3,487   £2,116   DM6,475   ¥363,508

SICCAMA, ABEL [S10/4] Rosewood Siccama-System
Diatonic Flute: London, c. 1850   577/824
$610   £370   DM1,133   ¥63,614

SIMPSON, JOHN [S10/1] Eight-Keyed Boxwood
Flute: London, c. 1830   824/1,154
$1,198   £727   DM2,224   ¥124,857

STRASSER, MARIGAUX, LEMAIRE [B5/12] Silver
Boehm-System Flute w/case: Paris, c. 1940   410/574
$453   £276   DM822   ¥54,645

WILLIS, JOHN [S10/12] Eight-Keyed Rosewood
Flute: London, c. 1820   1,648/2,472 NS

WOOD & IVY [S10/16] Six-Keyed Rosewood Flute:
London, c. 1840   412/577
$544   £330   DM1,010   ¥56,699

FRENCH HORN

BOOSEY & HAWKES [B5/26] French Horn w/case
131/197
$170   £104   DM308   ¥20,492

MILLEREAU [S10/87] French Horn: Paris, c. 1890
1,318/1,977 NS

MILLEREAU [S10/90] French Horn w/case,
mute, mouthpiece, valves, crook: Paris, c. 1890
494/824 NS

GUITAR

BAY STATE [Bf4/2760] Brazilian Hardwood Parlor
Guitar w/case: c. 1920   800/1,200
$1,323   £823   DM2,433   ¥155,989

BERTET, JOSEPH R. (attributed to) [S10/42] Five-
Course Guitar w/case: Paris, 1762   1,318/1,977
$1,787   £1,084   DM3,318   ¥186,298

BERWIND, J. [Sk11/19] Good American Guitar
w/original wooden case: Philadelphia, c. 1880
1,000/1,500 NS

BORREGUERO, MODESTO [B5/42] Spanish Guitar
w/case 984/1,312
$1,320 £805 DM2,399 ¥159,382

CARPIO, RICARDO SANCHIS [B5/43] Spanish
Guitar w/case: Valencia, 1973 492/656
$754 £460 DM1,371 ¥91,075

CONTRERAS, M.G. [B5/49] Spanish Flamenco
Guitar w/case: c. 1990 328/492
$377 £230 DM685 ¥45,538

CONTRERAS, MANUEL [C11/12] Seven-String
Classical Guitar w/case 1,296/1,944
$1,304 £805 DM2,455 ¥137,832

D'ANGELICO, JOHN [Sk11/11] Fine American
Archtop Guitar w/case: New York, 1935
8,000/12,000
$9,258 £5,730 DM17,474 ¥979,444

DOBRO [Sk11/16] Resonator Guitar w/case: c. 1980
300/500
$463 £287 DM874 ¥48,972

FABRICATORE, GENNARO [P2/6] Italian Guitar
with applied foliate decoration: Napoli, 1847
815/978
$712 £437 DM1,245 ¥84,144

FAVILLA GUITARS [Sk11/6] American Classical
Guitar w/case 250/350
$165 £102 DM312 ¥17,490

FRIEDERICH, DANIEL [S10/36] Concert Guitar
w/case: Paris, 1971 6,592/8,240
$7,628 £4,629 DM14,164 ¥795,173

GIBSON CO. [Bf4/2758] L1 Robert Johnson Model
Guitar w/case: 1927 1,000/1,500
$992 £617 DM1,825 ¥116,992

GIBSON CO. [Bf4/2761] ES175 Guitar w/case: 1954
1,800/2,500 NS

GIBSON CO. [Bf4/2762] L-Series Guitar w/case:
c. 1930 700/900
$1,058 £658 DM1,947 ¥124,791

GIBSON CO. [Bf10/8062] L7 Archtop Guitar w/case:
1948 600/900
$978 £587 DM1,760 ¥7,595

GIBSON CO. [Sk11/9] Early American Archtop
Guitar w/original case: Kalamazoo, Michigan,
c. 1921 1,600/1,800
$1,984 £1,228 DM3,744 ¥209,881

GIBSON CO. [Sk11/34] American Style L-4 Archtop
Guitar: Kalamazoo, Michigan, 1935 300/500
$992 £614 DM1,873 ¥105,001

GRETSCH [Sk11/10] American Archtop Guitar
w/case: c. 1935 1,200/1,400
$1,455 £900 DM2,746 ¥153,913

GRIMSHAW, EMIL [B5/41] Guitar w/case 492/656
$604 £368 DM1,097 ¥72,860

GUADAGNINI, CARLO (ascribed to) [Sk11/37]
Italian Guitar w/period wooden case: Turin, 1814
1,600/1,800
$1,190 £737 DM2,247 ¥125,928

HOWE, ELIAS [Sk11/18] American Guitar w/case:
Boston, c. 1880 600/800 NS

LARSON BROS. [Sk11/33] American Guitar:
Chicago, c. 1900 200/300
$397 £246 DM749 ¥41,976

MARTIN [C3/459] OO-21 Acoustic Guitar w/case:
1975 652/978
$1,312 £805 DM2,326 ¥155,148

MARTIN & CO., C.F. [Bf4/2756] OOO-18 Guitar
w/case 1,500/2,000
$1,852 £1,152 DM3,407 ¥218,384

MARTIN & CO., C.F. [Bf4/2763] O-17 Mahogany
Guitar w/case 700/1,200
$727 £452 DM1,338 ¥85,794

MARTIN & CO., C.F. [Sk11/5] American Guitar
w/original wooden case: Nazareth, Pennsylvania,
before 1898 500/700
$992 £614 DM1,872 ¥104,940

MARTIN & CO., C.F. [Sk11/13] American Style I-21
Guitar w/original wooden case: Nazareth,
Pennsylvania, c. 1865 1,000/1,500
$860 £532 DM1,623 ¥90,948

MARTIN & CO., C.F. [Sk11/14] American Style O-
18 Guitar w/soft case: Nazareth, Pennsylvania, 1946
600/800
$794 £491 DM1,498 ¥83,952

MAST, BLAISE [S10/37] Guitar w/case: Mirecourt,
c. 1820 2,472/3,296
$2,615 £1,587 DM4,856 ¥272,631

NATIONAL [Sk11/15] Duolian Resonator Guitar
w/case: 1937 700/900
$1,587 £982 DM2,995 ¥167,905

NATIONAL [Sk11/7] Early Style 2$^1/_2$ Square-Neck
Resonator Guitar w/3 period resonator cones: 1927
1,600/1,800
$1,852 £1,146 DM3,495 ¥195,889

NATIONAL [Sk11/8] Good Style O Resonator
Guitar w/original case: 1933 2,000/2,500
$3,968 £2,456 DM7,489 ¥419,762

PANORMO [C11/8] Good English Guitar w/original
case: London, 1839 2,592/2,916
$7,079 £4,370 DM13,329 ¥748,231

PANORMO, JOSEPH [P3/20] Good English Guitar
with minor restorable blemishes: 1825 810/891 NS

PETITJEAN (L'AINE) [S10/38] Guitar: Mirecourt,
c. 1810 1,154/1,648
$1,416 £859 DM2,629 ¥147,576

RAMIREZ [Bf4/2757] 1A Flamenco Cypress Guitar
w/case: Madrid, 1968 2,250/2,750 NS

RAMIREZ, MANUEL [B5/50] Nine-Stringed Spanish
Guitar w/case: Madrid, c. 1906 1,968/2,460 NS

RICKENBACKER [Bf10/8106] "Electro" Lap-Steel
Guitar   250/400
$150   £90   DM269   ¥1,162

RIDOUT, MAGGIE [B5/51] Modern Classical Guitar
w/case   246/328
$396   £242   DM720   ¥47,815

RODRIGUEZ (SR.), MANUEL [B5/48] Spanish
Guitar w/case: Madrid, 1984   1,312/1,968
$2,263   £1,380   DM4,112   ¥273,226

VINACCIA, GENNARO & ACHILLE [S10/44]
Guitar w/case: Naples, 1890   1,071/1,318
$1,416   £859   DM2,629   ¥147,576

HARP

BLAZDELL, A. [P11/18] English Gothic Concert
Harp   1,620/2,430
$2,142   £1,323   DM4,069   ¥225,103

ERARD [C3/462] Double-Action Pedal Harp
                                           2,445/3,260
$4,499   £2,760   DM7,976   ¥531,935

ERARD, SEBASTIAN [P11/17] Attractive Grecian
Patent Concert Harp   3,240/4,050
$8,570   £5,290   DM16,277   ¥900,411

ERAT, J. [P2/7] Regency Harp in good condition:
London   1,630/1,956
$1,969   £1,208   DM3,443   ¥232,600

STUMPFF, J.A. [P6/12] Regency Grecian Eight-Pedal
Patent Harp: London   644/966
$2,129   £1,323   DM3,994   ¥255,930

HARP-LUTE

BARRY [S10/45] Harp-Lute: London, c. 1815
                                             494/824
$654   £397   DM1,214   ¥68,158

HARPSICHORD

BRITSEN, JORIS [S10/74] Two-Manual Harpsichord: Antwerp, 1680   115,353/164,790 NS

SHUDI, BURKAT & JOHN BROADWOOD
[S10/68] Two-Manual Harpsichord: London, 1773
                                   131,832/197,748
$200,879 £121,900   DM373,002   ¥20,941,201

HELICON

DE CART FRERES, FERDINAND & LOUIS
[S10/84] Helicon w/tenor horn: Lierre, early 20th C.
                                             330/494
$392   £238   DM728   ¥40,895

DE CART FRERES, FERDINAND & LOUIS
[S10/85] Helicon: Lierre, early 20th C.   330/494
$523   £317   DM971   ¥54,526

HORN

BLIGHT, J. [S10/92] Baritone Horn in B-flat/C:
London, mid 19th C.   4,120/5,768 NS

MILLEREAU [S10/91] Tenor Horn w/alto horn,
euphonium, valves: Paris, first quarter 20th C.
                                             330/494
$413   £251   DM767   ¥43,068

PERCIVAL, THOMAS [S10/81] Boxwood
Foxhunting Horn: London, second quarter 19th C.
                                             247/412
$436   £265   DM809   ¥45,438

SCHOPPER, ROBERT [S10/82] Alto Horn: Leipzig,
c. 1910   330/494 NS

LUTE

GOLD, PERL [B2/46] Eight-Course Lute w/case
                                             492/820
$566   £345   DM976   ¥64,570

HARWOOD, IAN [B2/45] Modern Seven-Course
Lute   131/164
$660   £403   DM1,139   ¥75,332

HOLMES, HENRY H. [B2/44] Modern Eight-Course
Lute w/case   492/820 NS

HOLMES, HENRY H. [B5/37] Modern Eight-Course
Lute w/case   328/492
$264   £161   DM480   ¥31,876

SPRIGGS, G.W. [B2/47] Nine-Course Lute w/case:
1962   492/820
$528   £322   DM911   ¥60,266

MANDO-CELLO

GIBSON CO. [Bf4/2759] K-2 Mando-Cello w/case:
1918   1,800/2,250 NS

MANDOLIN

CALACE, RAFFAELE [S10/39] Mandolin w/case:
Naples, 1904   2,307/2,966
$2,615   £1,587   DM4,856   ¥272,631

CIANI, RAPHAEL [Sk11/24] Italian Bowl-Back
Mandolin w/case   200/300
$363   £225   DM686   ¥38,448

EMBERGHER, LUIGI [S10/35] Mandolin w/case:
Rome, 1937   4,120/5,768
$7,846   £4,761   DM14,568   ¥817,892

FABRICATORE, GIOVANNI [Bf4/2764] Mandolin
Naples, 1780, w/case   1,500/2,000
$1,455   £905   DM2,677   ¥171,588

GIBSON CO. [Sk11/12] American Style A-3
Mandolin w/case: Kalamazoo, Michigan, c. 1914
                                           800/1,200
$1,455   £900   DM2,746   ¥153,913

GIBSON CO. [Sk11/20] American Style A-1
Mandolin w/case: Kalamazoo, Michigan, c. 1917
                                             400/600
$860   £532   DM1,623   ¥90,948

GIBSON CO. [Sk11/25] American Mandolin:
Kalamazoo, Michigan, c. 1915   700/800 NS

SILVESTRI, CARMINE [P11/16] Neapolitan
Mandolin w/similar mandolin: 1896   567/648
$1,028   £635   DM1,953   ¥108,049

VINACCIA, GIOVANNI [S10/34] Mandolin: Naples,
1765   3,296/4,944
$9,153   £5,555   DM16,996   ¥954,208

VINACCIA, GIUSEPPE [S10/31] Mandolin w/case:
Naples, 1898   659/989
$1,482   £899   DM2,752   ¥154,491

WASHBURN [Sk11/4] American Bowl-Back
Mandolin w/case   200/300
$132   £82   DM250   ¥13,992

MANDOLIN-LYRE

CALACE, RAFFAELE [Sk11/35] Neapolitan
Mandolin-Lyre w/case: 1907   300/500
$463   £287   DM875   ¥49,033

MELLOPHONE

PEPPER, J.W. [Bf10/8071] Silver-Plated Mellophone
w/extra slides for tuning to F: Philadelphia, c. 1915
    600/800 NS

MUSETTE

MARTIN BROS. [S10/24] Blackwood Musette
w/bombarde, bamboo flute: Paris, late 19th C.
    412/577
$436   £265   DM809   ¥45,438

OBOE

BUFFET CRAMPON & CO. [B2/16] Rosewood
Full-Thumbplate-Model Oboe w/case: Paris   164/246
$490   £299   DM846   ¥55,961

BUTHOD & THIBOUVILLE [B5/17] Boxwood
Oboe: Paris, c. 1860   98/131
$943   £575   DM1,714   ¥113,844

MILHOUSE, WILLIAM [S10/116] Two-Keyed
Boxwood Oboe: London, c. 1800   1,648/2,472
$3,705   £2,248   DM6,879   ¥386,227

NOBLET [P3/15] Oboe in good condition, w/case:
Paris   972/1,053 NS

REIST, H. [S10/106] Three-Keyed Boxwood Oboe:
Trachselwald/Sumiswald, c. 1750   494/824
$4,795   £2,910   DM8,903   ¥499,823

WARD & SONS [B5/16] Rosewood Oboe w/case:
Liverpool, c. 1875   131/164
$207   £127   DM377   ¥25,046

OBOE D'AMORE

OBERLENDER, JOHANN WILHELM (I) [S10/108]
Three-Keyed Boxwood Oboe d'Amore: Nuremberg,
c. 1725   29,662/41,198
$54,484   £33,063   DM101,168   ¥5,679,807

OCTAVIN

ADLER & CO., OSCAR [Bf4/2771] Octavin:
Markneukirchen, c. 1900   2,000/2,500
$1,852   £1,152   DM3,407   ¥218,384

OPHICLEIDE

HENRI [S10/89] Nine-Keyed Bass Ophicleide: Dijon,
mid 19th C.   1,154/1,648
$1,308   £794   DM2,428   ¥136,315

ORGAN

SNETZLER, JOHN [S10/75] Bureau Organ: London,
1751   57,677/74,156
$69,550   £42,205   DM129,143   ¥7,250,397

PIANO

BEYER, ADAM [Bf4/2800] Square Piano: London,
1784   2,500/4,000
$1,190   £740   DM2,190   ¥140,390

BEYER, ADAM [S10/77] Square Piano: London,
1795   2,472/4,120
$2,615   £1,587   DM4,856   ¥272,631

BROADWOOD, JOHN & SONS [S10/76] Square
Piano: London, 1818   989/1,318
$326   £198   DM605   ¥33,980

CHALLEN & HOLLIS [S10/62] Upright Piano:
London, c. 1840   577/824 NS

CLEMENTI & CO. [S10/63] Square Piano: London,
c. 1820   989/1,318
$2,833   £1,719   DM5,261   ¥295,350

KIRCKMAN, JACOB & ABRAHAM [Bf4/2801]
Fine Square Piano: London, 1779   4,500/6,000 NS

KLEIN, F.A. [S10/67] Lyre Piano: Berlin, c. 1835
    8,240/11,535 NS

PLEYEL [C3/465] Square Piano from the collection
of Rudolph Nureyev   1,630/2,445 NS

ROLOFF, H. [S10/66] Obliquely Strung "Dog
Kennel" Piano: Neubrandenburg, c. 1840
    9,887/13,183 NS

WACHTL, JOSEPH & JACOB BLEYER [S10/72]
Double-Giraffe Piano: Vienna, c. 1805
    13,183/19,775 NS

PIANOFORTE

BROADWOOD, JOHN & SONS [S10/70] Grand
Pianoforte: London, 1804   5,768/7,416
$13,076   £7,935   DM24,280   ¥1,363,154

SCHANZ, JOHANN [S10/69] Grand Pianoforte:
Vienna, c. 1820   16,479/24,719
$33,780   £20,499   DM62,724   ¥3,521,480

STODART, M. & W. [S10/65] Grand Pianoforte:
London, c. 1800   6,592/9,887
$9,153   £5,555   DM16,996   ¥954,208

TOMKISON, THOMAS [C3/463] Square Pianoforte
with detached legs and pedals   978/1,304
$1,687   £1,035   DM2,991   ¥199,476

PICCOLO

LOT, LOUIS [P3/13] Attractive Rosewood Boehm-
System Piccolo in immediate playing condition,
w/case: Paris, c. 1890   810/891 NS

LOT, LOUIS [P11/9] Attractive Rosewood Boehm-
System Piccolo w/case: Paris, c. 1890   810/891
$771   £476   DM1,465   ¥81,037

RUDALL, CARTE & CO. [B5/7] Blackwood Boehm-
System Piccolo w/case   49/66
$94   £58   DM171   ¥11,384

POCHETTE

WORLE, MATHIAS [Sk11/40] Fine and Rare
Tyrolian Pochette   4,000/5,000
$9,919   £6,140   DM18,722   ¥1,049,404

RAUSCHPFEIFE

GUNTHER [Bf10/8084] Tenor Rauschpfeife
                                    700/900 NS

SAXOPHONE

BUESCHER [B5/29] Tenor Saxophone w/case
                                    492/820
$566   £345   DM1,028   ¥68,307

CONN, C.G. [Sk5/5] 20th-Century American Alto
Saxophone w/2 cases, matching saxophone: Elkhart
                                    200/300
$316   £193   DM572   ¥38,184

COUESNON & CO. [B2/34] Alto Saxophone w/case
                                    492/656
$472   £288   DM814   ¥53,809

FOOTE [B5/27] Alto Saxophone w/case   492/820
$377   £230   DM685   ¥45,538

GRAFTON [C11/7] Brass and Lucite Alto Saxophone
w/case   1,134/1,620 NS

SELMER, HENRI [B5/28] Alto Saxophone w/case:
Paris   820/1,148
$1,792   £1,093   DM3,256   ¥216,304

THIBOUVILLE-LAMY, J. [C11/6] Alto Saxophone
w/case   486/810
$559   £345   DM1,052   ¥59,071

SOUSAPHONE

DE PRINS GEBRUDER [S10/94] Sousaphone:
Antwerp, first half 20th C.   330/494
$392   £238   DM728   ¥40,895

SPINET

BARTON (ascribed to) [P2/15] Attractive English
Spinet: c. 1730
                                13,040/16,300 NS

BARTON (ascribed to) [P11/20] Attractive English
Spinet: c. 1730   11,340/12,960 NS

HITCHCOCK, JOHN [S10/64] Spinet: London, third
quarter 18th C.   13,183/19,775
$20,704   £12,564   DM38,444   ¥2,158,327

TAROGATO

MOGYOROSSY, G.Y. [S10/123] Rosewood
Tarogato: Budapest, early 20th C.   494/659
$785   £476   DM1,457   ¥81,789

TROMBONE

BUNDY [B5/25] Brass Trombone w/case   82/131
$141   £86   DM257   ¥17,077

TROMPE DE CHASSE

RAOUX, MARCEL-AUGUSTE [S10/93] Helical
Trompe de Chasse: Paris, second quarter 19th C.
                                  3,296/4,944 NS

SCHMIDT, JOHANN JACOB [S10/95] Trompe de
Chasse: Nürnberg, second quarter 18th C.
                                  6,592/9,887 NS

TRUMPET

CALICCHIO, DOMINIC [Bf10/8079] Important
Trumpet: Los Angeles, c. 1977   2,000/2,500
$1,495   £897   DM2,691   ¥11,616

CONN, C.G. [Bf10/8070] Victor-Model Trumpet in
excellent condition, w/triple case: Indiana, c. 1956
                                    500/700 NS

CONN, C.G. [Sk5/1] American Trumpet w/case:
Elkhart, Indiana, c. 1935   300/500
$489   £298   DM885   ¥59,012

COUESNON [Bf10/8080] Piccolo Trumpet: Paris,
c. 1960   1,000/1,400 NS

COURTURIER, ERNST ALBERT [Bf10/8074]
Conical-Bore Trumpet: La Porte, Indiana, c. 1920
                                    600/800 NS

JAY CO., H.B. [Bf10/8072] Trumpet w/case: c. 1920
                                    800/1,200 NS

MIRAFONE [Bf10/8069] Bass Trumpet w/case,
mouthpiece: Sun Valley, California, c. 1955
                                    800/1,000 NS

WHITE & CO., H.N. [Bf10/8073] Silver-Plated One-
Valve Marching Trumpet in B-flat: Cleveland, c. 1930
                                    600/800 NS

WHITE & CO., H.N. [Bf10/8077] B-Flat Trumpet:
Cleveland, c. 1935   800/1,200 NS

TUBA

HALARI [S10/83] Tuba: Paris, third quarter 19th C.
                                    330/494 NS

SUDRE, FRANCOIS [S10/96] Tuba w/trompe de
chasse: Paris, first half 20th C.   330/494 NS

UKULELE

KAMAKA [Bf10/8107] Ukulele			125/175
$92	£55	DM166	¥715

MARTIN & CO., C.F. [B5/38] Good Ukulele
			656/984
$905	£552	DM1,645	¥109,290

MARTIN & CO., C.F. [Sk11/2] American Ukulele
w/original case: c. 1930   300/500
$1,587	£982	DM2,995	¥167,905

MARTIN & CO., C.F. [Sk11/3] American Ukulele
w/case: c. 1920   300/400
$1,256	£778	DM2,371	¥132,924

MARTIN & CO., C.F. [Sk11/27a] American Tenor
Ukulele w/case   300/500
$661	£409	DM1,248	¥69,960

UNION PIPES

REID, ROBERT [S10/120] Set of Union Pipes: North
Shields, c. 1830 and later   494/824
$1,198	£727	DM2,224	¥124,857

VIOL

COLETTI, A. [B11/86] Viola d'Amore: Vienna, 1918
3,240/4,860 NS

EBERLE, JOHANN ULRICH [S10/49] Viola
d'Amore of festoon outline, w/double case, bow:
Prague, 1749   23,071/29,662
$30,511	£18,515	DM56,654	¥3,180,692

EBERLE, TOMASO [Sk5/25] Rare Viola d'Amore
w/case, bow: Naples, 1772   8,000/12,000
$7,188	£4,384	DM13,009	¥867,819

GUGGENBERGER, ANTON [P2/22] Fine and
Handsome Viola d'Amore in good condition, w/case:
Vienna, 1961   3,260/4,075 NS

GUGGENBERGER, ANTON [P3/22] Fine and
Handsome Viola d'Amore in immediate playing condition, w/case: Vienna, 1961   2,430/2,916 NS

GUGGENBERGER, ANTON [P11/21] Fine and
Handsome Viola d'Amore in immediate playing condition, w/case: Vienna, 1961   3,240/4,050 NS

ROSE, ROGER [Bf10/8060] Good Treble Viol
w/case, bow: Haslemere, Surrey, 1978   2,000/3,000
$2,300	£1,380	DM4,140	¥17,871

ROSE, ROGER [Bf10/8061] Good Bass Viola da
Gamba w/case, bow: Haslemere, Surrey, 1977
3,500/4,500 NS

STIEBER, ERNST [Sk11/46] German Viola da
Gamba w/soft case   1,800/2,200
$529	£327	DM998	¥55,968

VIOL BOW

DOLMETSCH, ARNOLD [Sk5/230] Ivory Viol Bow
600/800 NS

VIOLA

ACOULON, ALFRED [S6/155] Viola w/case: Paris or
Mirecourt, c. 1910   3,180/3,975 NS

ANTONIAZZI, ROMEO [Sk11/90] Fine Italian
Viola w/case: Cremona, 1910   32,000/36,000
$39,675	£24,559	DM74,887	¥4,197,615

ANTONIAZZI, ROMEO (workshop of) [S3/135]
Viola w/case: Milan, c. 1910   16,200/24,300 NS

AUDINOT, PIERRE M. [S6/150] Viola w/case, cover,
bow: Paris, 1955 (Louis Monnin, Geneva, November
2, 1996)   6,360/9,540
$7,314	£4,600	DM13,754	¥884,304

BAILLY, PAUL [C3/201] Good French Viola
9,780/13,040 NS

BANKS, BENJAMIN [B11/82] Viola in pieces
(unglued)   3,240/4,860
$7,079	£4,370	DM13,329	¥748,231

BANKS, JAMES & HENRY [B11/85] Very Fine
English Viola: c. 1803   11,340/16,200
$13,041	£8,050	DM24,553	¥1,378,321

BEDER, ANTON [Bf10/8053] Viola w/case, bow
400/600
$288	£173	DM518	¥2,234

BEDOCCHI, MARIO [B6/51] Italian Viola: Reggio,
1954   7,950/11,130 NS

BEDOCCHI, MARIO [B11/94] Italian Viola: Reggio,
1954   6,480/9,720 NS

BERTOLAZZI, GIACINTO [Sk11/203] Modern
Viola: Milan, 1945   2,500/3,500
$3,042	£1,883	DM5,741	¥321,817

BIRD, RICHMOND HENRY (attributed to) [P2/43]
Good English Viola in immediate playing condition,
w/case: Liverpool, 1934   1,304/1,467
$1,537	£943	DM2,688	¥181,575

BRADSHAW, B.L. [C11/105] English Viola w/case,
bow   1,296/1,620 NS

BRAY, E. [P5/152] Viola in immediate playing condition, w/3 bows in cases: Middlesborough, 1909
652/734
$469	£288	DM850	¥56,647

BRETON [C3/439] French Viola   815/1,141
$562	£345	DM997	¥66,492

BRIGGS, JAMES WILLIAM [Sk11/88] Good Scottish
Viola w/case: Glasgow, 1908   3,500/5,000
$6,084	£3,766	DM11,483	¥643,634

BRYANT, GEORGE E. [Sk11/205] American Viola:
Lowell, Massachusetts, 1899   1,800/2,200
$3,174	£1,965	DM5,991	¥335,809

BUTHOD, CHARLES LOUIS [S6/153] Viola:
Mirecourt, c. 1880   2,385/3,180
$2,560	£1,610	DM4,814	¥309,506

CANDI, CESARE [P2/21] Fine and Handsome Italian
Viola in immediate playing condition, w/case: Genoa,
1923 (Claude Lebet, La Chaux-de-Fonds,
Switzerland, April 14, 1997)   14,670/16,300 NS

CANDI, CESARE [P3/49] Fine and Handsome Italian Viola in immediate playing condition, w/case: Genoa, 1923 (Claude Lebet, La Chaux-de-Fonds, Switzerland, April 14, 1997)   13,770/14,580 NS

CASTELLI, CESARE [S3/131] Viola w/case: Ascoli Piceno, 1966   1,944/2,592 NS

CASTELLI, CESARE [S6/161] Viola w/case: Ascoli Piceno, 1966   1,272/1,908 NS

CAVANI, GIOVANNI (ascribed to) [C11/102] Viola   4,050/5,670 NS

CAVANI, VINCENZO [Sk5/21] Contemporary Italian Viola w/case: 1965   4,000/6,000
$6,900   £4,209   DM12,489   ¥833,106

CONIA, STEFANO [Sk5/19] Contemporary Italian Viola: Cremona, 1973   4,000/5,000
$3,738   £2,280   DM6,765   ¥451,266

CONTINO, ALFREDO (workshop of) [Sk5/17] Good Viola: Naples, 1920   5,000/7,000
$8,050   £4,911   DM14,571   ¥971,957

CUYPERS, JOHANNES [P11/88] Fine and Handsome Viola with minor restored blemishes, w/case: The Hague, 1787   14,580/16,200
$17,140   £10,580   DM32,555   ¥1,800,822

DARCHE, HILAIRE [P6/58] Fine and Handsome Viola in fine condition: Brussels, 1908   16,100/19,320 NS

DARCHE, HILAIRE [P11/70] Fine and Handsome Viola in fine condition: Brussels, 1908   9,720/11,340 NS

DERACHE, PAUL [Sk11/340] French Viola w/case: Lyon   600/800
$1,257   £778   DM2,372   ¥132,985

DERAZEY, HONORE [B3/48] Fine French Viola: Mirecourt, 1860 (W.E. Hill & Sons)   9,720/12,960
$10,247   £6,325   DM18,406   ¥1,209,783

EBERLE, J.U. (ascribed to) [B6/54] Fine Viola   10,335/13,515 NS

EBERLE, J.U. (ascribed to) [B11/90] Fine Viola   10,530/13,770 NS

EDLER, ERNEST [Sk5/24] American Viola w/case, bow: Boston, 1940   1,500/1,700
$1,380   £842   DM2,498   ¥166,621

EMERY, JULIAN [P9/22] Good Viola in immediate playing condition, w/case: Corsley, England, 1981   2,268/2,916 NS

ERDESZ, OTTO [S11M/35] Viola with the upper treble bout cut away, w/correspondence between maker and Yehudi Menuhin: Budapest, c. 1977   4,043/5,660
$4,705   £2,910   DM8,918   ¥497,728

ERDESZ, OTTO [S11M/36] Viola w/photocopy correspondence between maker and Yehudi Menuhin: Budapest, c. 1977   4,528/5,660 NS

ERICAN, MARTIN [Sk5/30] Contemporary Italian Viola: Piacenza, 1960   4,000/6,000
$3,738   £2,280   DM6,765   ¥451,266

FERET-MARCOTTE [B11/89] Viola   2,268/2,916
$2,422   £1,495   DM4,560   ¥255,974

FIORI BROTHERS (attributed to) [Sk11/68] Italian Viola w/case   10,000/12,000 NS

GAILLARD, CHARLES [P11/94] Fine and Handsome French Viola in restored playing condition, w/case: c. 1860 (W.E. Hill & Sons, Havenfields, September 8, 1989)   12,960/14,580
$16,068   £9,919   DM30,520   ¥1,688,270

GAILLARD, CHARLES [P11/104] Fine and Handsome French Viola in immediate playing condition, w/case: Paris, 1861   4,860/5,670
$7,284   £4,497   DM13,836   ¥765,349

GALIMBERTI, LUIGI [B3/46] Italian Viola: 1929   11,340/16,200 NS

GAND, GUILLAUME CHARLES LOUIS [S3/130] Viola w/case: Versailles, 1841 (Jean Fritsch, Paris, May 17, 1969)   11,340/16,200
$12,668   £7,820   DM22,756   ¥1,495,731

GAND & BERNARDEL FRERES [S6/151] Viola: Paris, 1884   19,080/23,850 NS

GAND & BERNARDEL FRERES [S11/337] Viola: Paris, 1877 (Joseph Vedral, The Hague, 1953)   12,960/19,440 NS

GOFFRILLER, MATTEO (ascribed to) [S6/157] Viola w/case, cover, bow: Italy, c. 1800 (Emil Herrmann, New York, October 1, 1935)   12,720/19,080
$54,855   £34,500   DM103,155   ¥6,632,280

HARDIE, THOMAS [B11/93A] Very Fine Scottish Viola: Edinburgh, 1828 (Edward Withers, Ltd., London, December 15, 1994)   24,300/29,160 NS

HARRILD, PAUL V. [S3/142] Viola: Newark, 1984   3,240/4,050 NS

HARRIS, CHARLES [B3/51] Viola: Addenbury, Oxen, 1824   2,430/3,240
$2,795   £1,725   DM5,020   ¥329,941

HARRIS, RICHARD [B3/49] Viola with a carved leaf motif on the upper back: Oxfordshire, 1869   4,860/8,100 NS

HARRIS, RICHARD [B11/83] Viola   4,860/8,100
$5,216   £3,220   DM9,821   ¥551,328

HILL, JOSEPH [P2/27] Viola with restorations, w/case: London, 1779   4,075/4,890 NS

HILL, JOSEPH [S11/343] Viola: London, c. 1770   7,290/9,720 NS

HILL, W.E. & SONS [B3/50] Very Fine English Viola: London, 1895   19,440/24,300 NS

HILL, W.E. & SONS [P3/71] Good English Viola in good condition: London, 1973   4,050/4,860 NS

HOFMANN, MAX [S3/140] Viola w/case: Mittenwald, 1977   2,430/3,240
$2,795   £1,725   DM5,020   ¥329,941

HOFNER, KARL [Sk5/33] Child's German Viola w/case, bow: Bubenreuth, 1963   250/350
$144   £88   DM260   ¥17,356

19

HOMOLKA, FERDINAND AUGUST [S6/158] Viola
w/case: Prague, 1859   3,180/4,770
$4,754   £2,990   DM8,940   ¥574,798

JACQUOT, CHARLES [P3/79] Fine and Handsome
French Viola in immediate playing condition, w/case:
Paris, c. 1860   8,100/9,720 NS

JACQUOT, CHARLES [P5/35] Fine and Handsome
French Viola in immediate playing condition, w/case:
Paris, c. 1860   6,520/8,150 NS

KENNEDY, T. (attributed to) [P6/23] Good English
Viola in immediate playing condition: London,
c. 1810   2,415/3,220
$2,342   £1,455   DM4,393   ¥281,523

KLOTZ, AEGIDIUS (I) [Sk11/377] Viola w/case:
Mittenwald, 1670 (Dario D'Attili, Dumont, New
Jersey, February 8, 1991)   5,000/6,000
$5,290   £3,275   DM9,985   ¥559,682

KLOTZ, AEGIDIUS (II) [B11/87] German Viola:
Mittenwald, 1772   3,240/4,860
$5,589   £3,450   DM10,523   ¥590,709

KLOTZ FAMILY (MEMBER OF) [Sk11/385] Viola
w/case: Mittenwald   4,000/6,000 NS

LANARO, UMBERTO [Bf4/2839] Italian Viola
w/case: Padua, 1982   4,500/6,500 NS

LANDOLFI, CARLO FERDINANDO [C3/204] Very
Fine Italian Viola: 1768 (W.E. Hill & Sons, London,
March 17, 1947)   81,500/114,100
$131,541   £80,700   DM233,223   ¥15,553,311

LANTNER, FERDINAND [P11/115] Good Viola in
immediate playing condition, w/case: Prague, 1882
                                        1,944/2,430
$4,928   £3,042   DM9,359   ¥517,736

LEONI, GUIDO [S3/139] Viola w/case: San
Benedetto del Tronto, 1966   1,620/24,300
$1,490   £920   DM2,677   ¥175,968

LOVERI BROTHERS [Sk11/69] Viola w/case:
Naples, 1942 (Dario D'Attili, Dumont, New Jersey,
October 6, 1982)   4,000/6,000
$3,968   £2,456   DM7,489   ¥419,762

LYE, HENRY [B6/48] Viola   795/1,113 NS

MARAVIGLIA, GUIDO [C11/109] Italian Viola
                                        1,620/2,268
$2,422   £1,495   DM4,560   ¥255,974

MATTER, ANITA [P9/63] Good Contemporary
Viola in immediate playing condition: Malmo, 1983
                                        1,620/1,944
$1,863   £1,150   DM3,508   ¥198,605

MELLONI, SETTIMO [Sk5/26] Modern Italian Viola
w/case: Ferrara, 1925   3,000/4,000
$2,990   £1,824   DM5,412   ¥361,013

MILLOSLAVSKI, JOSEPH [P3/36] Good Russian
Viola with minor restorable table blemishes: Moscow,
1975   1,944/2,430 NS

MILLOSLAVSKI, JOSEPH [P5/55] Good Russian
Viola with minor restorable table blemishes: Moscow,
1975   1,141/1,304 NS

MOZZANI, LUIGI [S3/136] Viola w/case: Bologna,
c. 1935 (Hieronymus Köstler, Stuttgart, September
10, 1998)   6,480/8,100
$7,079   £4,370   DM12,717   ¥835,850

NEBEL, MARTIN [Sk5/27] Contemporary American
Viola: Philadelphia, 1967   2,000/2,500 NS

NEBEL, MARTIN [Sk11/207] Contemporary
American Viola: Philadelphia, 1967   1,200/1,400
$1,587   £982   DM2,995   ¥167,905

NIX, CHARLES WILLIAM [P9/83] Viola or small-
size violoncello, w/case, bow: Worth, Sussex, 1928
                                        1,296/1,458 NS

ORNATI, GIUSEPPE [B6/53] Very Fine Italian Viola
in an exceptional state of preservation: Milan, 1921
(Etienne Vatelot, Paris, 1980)   39,750/55,650
$40,227   £25,300   DM76,153   ¥4,821,927

PANORMO, VINCENZO [S3/129] Viola w/case,
cover: London, c. 1800   35,640/45,360 NS

PANORMO, VINCENZO (attributed to) [S3/134]
Viola: England, early 19th C.   24,300/32,400 NS

PFRETZSCHNER, CARL FRIEDRICH [P3/80] Fine
and Handsome German-School Viola in immediate
playing condition, w/case: Markneukirchen, c. 1790
                                        6,480/7,290
$7,452   £4,600   DM13,340   ¥878,922

PINEIRO, HORACIO [Sk5/23] Fine Contemporary
Viola: Buenos Aires, 1974   3,000/4,000
$4,715   £2,876   DM8,534   ¥569,289

RACZ, LORAND [P9/26] Fine and Handsome Viola
in immediate playing condition, w/case: Den Haag,
1950   3,240/4,050
$3,726   £2,300   DM7,015   ¥397,210

RACZ, LORAND [S6/156] Viola w/case: The Hague,
1950   4,770/7,950 NS

RINALDI, GIOFREDO BENEDETTO (ascribed to)
[P11/102] Interesting Viola in immediate playing condition, w/case (Hans Schmidta, Mittenwald, February
10, 1971)   12,150/13,770 NS

ROSSI, STELIO [Sk11/201] Modern Italian Viola:
Sienna, 1954   2,800/3,200
$5,819   £3,602   DM10,983   ¥615,650

ROST, FRANZ GEORG [C11/100] Good Modern
English Viola w/case, bow: London, 1938
                                        6,480/8,100 NS

ROTH, ERNST HEINRICH [P6/172] Viola in good
condition: 1982   644/805
$681   £423   DM1,278   ¥81,898

ROTH, ERNST HEINRICH (workshop of)
[Sk11/209] German Viola: Bubenreuth-Erlangen
                                        800/1,200
$1,323   £819   DM2,496   ¥139,921

SANAVIA, LEONE [Sk11/378] Viola: Venice
                                        6,000/7,000
$7,605   £4,707   DM14,354   ¥804,604

SCHLOSSER, HERMANN [B5/84] German Viola
                                        656/984
$754   £460   DM1,371   ¥91,075

SCOLARI, GIORGIO [S11/342] Viola w/case:
Cremona, 1975 (maker's, March 17, 1975)
4,860/6,480 NS

SDERCI, IGINO [B3/52] Viola: 1973
8,100/11,340 NS

SDERCI, IGINO [B6/55] Viola   6,360/9,540
$8,777   £5,520   DM16,615   ¥1,052,057

SGARBI, GIUSEPPE [B6/50] Italian Viola: Rome,
c. 1882 (Carlson Cacciatori Neumann, Cremona,
1997)   39,750/55,650 NS

SIMONAZZI, AMADEO [P3/62] Good Italian Viola
in good condition: Santa Vittoria, Emilia, 1965
11,340/12,150 NS

SIMONAZZI, AMADEO [P5/14] Good Italian Viola
in immediate playing condition: Santo Vittoria,
Emilia, 1965   4,890/5,705 NS

SIMONAZZI, AMADEO [P9/33] Good Italian Viola
in immediate playing condition, w/case: Santo
Vittoria, Emilia, 1965   3,240/4,050
$4,099   £2,530   DM7,717   ¥436,931

SIMONAZZI, AMADEO [P11/112] Fine and Handsome Italian Viola in immediate playing condition,
w/case: 1958   7,290/8,100 NS

SIMONAZZI, AMADEO [S6/154] Viola w/case:
Santa Vittoria, Emilia, 1958   12,720/15,900 NS

SIRLETO BROTHERS [Sk5/28] Contemporary
Italian Viola w/case: Naples, 1985   2,800/3,200
$4,600   £2,806   DM8,326   ¥555,404

SMITH, BERT [S3/138] Viola: Coniston, 1966
3,240/4,860
$3,353   £2,070   DM6,024   ¥395,929

SOFFRITTI, ETTORE [C11/104] Good Modern
Italian Viola w/case: Ferrara, 1905   6,480/8,100
$14,904   £9,200   DM28,060   ¥1,575,224

STYLES, HAROLD LEICESTER [P2/80] Good Viola
in immediate playing condition, w/case: Bath, 1970
815/1,141
$487   £299   DM852   ¥57,572

THOMSON, GEORGE [P6/74] Viola in immediate
playing condition: Glasgow, 1862   805/966
$959   £596   DM1,799   ¥115,280

VATELOT, ETIENNE [S11M/34] Viola: Paris, 1977
3,234/4,851
$16,039   £9,919   DM30,401   ¥1,696,801

VETTORI, PAULO (attributed to) [P11/31] Good
Viola in immediate playing condition, w/case:
Florence, 1983   1,620/2,430
$4,071   £2,513   DM7,732   ¥427,695

VUILLAUME, NICOLAS FRANCOIS [Bf10/8054]
Fine Viola: Brussels, 1863   6,000/8,000
$5,463   £3,278   DM9,833   ¥42,444

WARD, ROD [Sk5/34] Contemporary English Viola:
1984   200/300
$288   £175   DM520   ¥34,713

WHEDBEE, WILLIAM [Bf4/2838] Good American
Viola w/case: Chicago, 1992   6,500/7,500 NS

WHEDBEE, WILLIAM [Bf10/8051] Good American
Viola w/case: Chicago, 1992   5,500/6,500 NS

WILKINSON, JOHN [P3/54] English Viola in immediate playing condition, w/case: London, c. 1940
3,240/4,050
$7,079   £4,370   DM12,673   ¥834,976

WILLER, JOANNES MICHAEL [S11/338] Viola
w/case: Prague, 1802   2,268/2,916 NS

ZANI, ALDO [B6/47] Italian Viola: 1965
9,540/12,720 NS

VIOLA BOW

BALINT, GEZA [Sk11/132] Silver Viola Bow with
baleen wrap   600/800
$529   £327   DM998   ¥55,968

BRISTOW, S.E. [P9/110] Silver Viola Bow with full
hair: England   729/810
$745   £460   DM1,403   ¥79,442

BRISTOW, STEPHEN [S6/214] Silver Viola Bow:
London, c. 1980   1,272/1,590 NS

BRYANT, PERCIVAL WILFRED [C11/158] Silver
Viola Bow   1,296/1,944 NS

BRYANT, PERCIVAL WILFRED [C11/166] Silver
Viola Bow with damage to back of head   405/567
$1,118   £690   DM2,105   ¥118,142

BULTITUDE, ARTHUR RICHARD [C11/67] Gold
Viola Bow   2,430/2,754
$3,353   £2,070   DM6,314   ¥354,425

COCKER, L. [P3/177] Good Silver Viola Bow
567/648
$653   £403   DM1,169   ¥77,001

CUNIOT-HURY [B6/21A] Silver Viola Bow
1,908/2,385
$2,743   £1,725   DM5,192   ¥328,768

DODD, J. [B6/17] Silver Viola Bow with later frog
and button   2,862/3,975
$3,291   £2,070   DM6,231   ¥394,521

DOLLING, MICHAEL [C3/261] Silver Viola Bow
652/978 NS

DURRSCHMIDT, OTTO [C3/63] Silver Viola Bow
652/978
$750   £460   DM1,329   ¥88,656

ENGLISH, CHRIS [Sk11/147] Silver Viola Bow
600/800
$596   £369   DM1,124   ¥63,025

FETIQUE, VICTOR [S11/195] Silver Viola Bow for J.
Tournier & Fils: Paris, c. 1925 (Jean-François Raffin,
Paris, March 17, 1997)   4,860/8,100 NS

FINKEL, JOHANNES S. [S6/106] Gold and Ivory
Viola Bow: Brienz, c. 1975   2,544/3,180
$2,743   £1,725   DM5,158   ¥331,614

HILL, W.E. & SONS [B11/51] Silver Viola Bow
3,240/4,860
$3,540   £2,185   DM6,664   ¥374,116

HILL, W.E. & SONS [B11/58] Silver and Tortoiseshell Viola Bow   4,050/5,670
$4,658   £2,875   DM8,769   ¥492,258

HILL, W.E. & SONS [C3/20] Silver Viola Bow
                                          1,630/2,445
$1,500   £920   DM2,659   ¥177,312

HILL, W.E. & SONS [P3/133] Good Viola Bow with
full hair: London   3,240/4,050 NS

HILL, W.E. & SONS [P6/111] Silver and Ivory Viola
Bow with skillful repair at head: London   644/805
$1,405   £873   DM2,636   ¥168,914

HILL, W.E. & SONS [S11/281] Silver Viola Bow:
London, c. 1930   1,296/1,944
$2,049   £1,265   DM3,884   ¥216,404

HILL, W.E. & SONS [S11/325] Gold Viola Bow:
London, 1960   2,916/4,050
$5,962   £3,680   DM11,298   ¥629,538

HILL, W.E. & SONS [S11M/53] Chased Gold Viola
Bow: London, 1970   2,264/2,911
$4,705   £2,910   DM8,918   ¥497,728

HILL, W.E. & SONS [Sk5/191] Silver Viola Bow
                                    1,800/2,200 NS

HILL, W.E. & SONS [Sk5/201] Silver Viola Bow
                                          1,800/2,200
$1,840   £1,122   DM3,330   ¥222,162

LAMY, ALFRED JOSEPH [S11/302] Silver Viola
Bow: Paris, c. 1900   4,860/6,480
$16,767   £10,350   DM31,775   ¥1,770,575

LAPIERRE, MARCEL [C3/12] Silver Viola Bow
                                       652/978 NS

LEE, JOHN NORWOOD [Sk11/146] Gold and Ivory
Viola Bow with baleen wrap: Chicago   800/1,000
$794   £491   DM1,498   ¥83,952

LOTTE, FRANCOIS [S11/275] Silver Viola Bow
w/bow: Mirecourt, c. 1950   486/810
$838   £517   DM1,587   ¥88,443

MAIRE (workshop of) [Sk11/144] Nickel Viola Bow
                                          3,000/3,500
$3,571   £2,210   DM6,740   ¥377,785

MALINE, GUILLAUME [C11/162] Interesting Silver
Viola Bow   3,564/4,212
$4,099   £2,530   DM7,717   ¥433,187

METTAL, WALTER [C3/219] Silver Viola Bow
                                             326/489
$450   £276   DM798   ¥53,193

MOINIER, A. [S11/264] Silver Viola Bow:
Mirecourt, c. 1960   810/1,134 NS

MORIZOT, LOUIS [B11/52] Silver Viola Bow (J.F.
Raffin, Paris, 1997)   2,430/3,240
$2,608   £1,610   DM4,911   ¥275,664

NURNBERGER, ALBERT [B3/27] Silver Viola Bow
                                    2,430/3,240 NS

NURNBERGER, ALBERT [B5/65] Silver Viola Bow
                                          1,312/1,968
$1,509   £920   DM2,742   ¥182,151

NURNBERGER, ALBERT [C11/161] Silver Viola
Bow   1,296/1,944
$1,769   £1,092   DM3,331   ¥186,972

OUCHARD, JEAN-CLAUDE [S6/225] Silver Viola
Bow: Mirecourt, c. 1970   1,113/1,590
$2,194   £1,380   DM4,126   ¥265,291

OUCHARD, JEAN-CLAUDE [S11/199] Silver Viola
Bow: Mirecourt, c. 1970   1,134/1,620 NS

PECCATTE, FRANCOIS [S6/218] Nickel Viola Bow:
Paris, c. 1850   5,565/7,155 NS

PECCATTE, FRANCOIS [S11/317] Nickel Viola
Bow: Paris, c. 1850   2,916/4,050
$5,589   £3,450   DM10,592   ¥590,192

PECCATTE, FRANCOIS [Sk11/157] Fine Nickel
Viola Bow (Jean-François Raffin, Paris, May 1993)
                                   45,000/50,000 NS

PFRETZSCHNER, H.R. [C3/10] Silver Viola Bow
                                    1,630/1,956 NS

PFRETZSCHNER, H.R. [S11/278] Silver Viola Bow
w/viola bow: Markneukirchen, c. 1900   1,620/2,430
$2,049   £1,265   DM3,884   ¥216,404

RAUM, WILHELM [C3/262] Silver Viola Bow
                                       652/815 NS

SALCHOW, WILLIAM [C3/31] Silver Viola Bow
                                             978/1,304
$1,125   £690   DM1,994   ¥132,984

STAGG, JOHN W. [S6/227] Gold Viola Bow for
Machold: Bristol, c. 1990   954/1,272 NS

THIBOUVILLE-LAMY, J. [P2/102] Silver Viola Bow
(Jean-François Raffin, Paris, March 26, 1996)
                                             978/1,141
$1,219   £748   DM2,132   ¥144,027

THIBOUVILLE-LAMY, J. (workshop of) [C11/157]
Nickel Viola Bow (Jean-François Raffin, Paris, June
14, 1998)   810/972 NS

TUBBS, J. [B3/19] Fine Silver Viola Bow
                                          8,100/11,340
$10,805   £6,670   DM19,410   ¥1,275,771

TUBBS, JAMES [B11/59] Silver Viola Bow
                                          4,860/8,100
$7,079   £4,370   DM13,329   ¥748,231

TUBBS, JAMES [B11/61] Silver Viola Bow
                                          4,860/8,100
$7,079   £4,370   DM13,329   ¥748,231

TUBBS, JAMES [S6/210] Silver Viola Bow: London,
c. 1900   4,770/6,360
$8,228   £5,175   DM15,473   ¥994,842

TUBBS, JAMES (attributed to) [P11/149] Silver Viola
Bow with full hair   2,916/3,240 NS

VOIGT, ARNOLD [B11/48] Silver Viola Bow
                                          1,620/2,430
$1,584   £978   DM2,981   ¥167,368

VUILLAUME, GUSTAVE [S11/316] Silver Viola
Bow: Nancy, c. 1930   970/1,294
$1,925   £1,190   DM3,648   ¥203,616

VUILLAUME, GUSTAVE EUGENE [S11/316] Silver
Viola Bow: Nancy, c. 1930   972/1,296
$1,677   £1,035   DM3,177   ¥177,057

WEICHOLD, R. [B11/50] Gold Viola Bow
                                      1,620/3,240
$1,863   £1,150   DM3,508   ¥196,903

WILSON, GARNER [P6/110] Silver Viola Bow
                                        644/805
$894   £555   DM1,677   ¥107,491

WILSON, GARNER [S3/170] Silver Viola Bow: Bury
St. Edmunds, c. 1975   1,620/24,300 NS

WILSON, GARNER [S6/211] Gold and Tortoiseshell
Viola Bow: Bury St. Edmunds, c. 1980   1,590/2,385
$2,377   £1,495   DM4,470   ¥287,399

WURLITZER, REMBERT [C3/18] Silver Viola Bow
                                      978/1,304 NS

VIOLIN

ACHNER, PHILIP (attributed to) [P3/104]
Mittenwald Violin with minor restorable blemishes,
w/case, 2 bows: c. 1780   4,860/5,670 NS

ACOULON, A. (attributed to) [P5/32] Good
Mirecourt Violin in good condition, w/case, bow:
c. 1910   1,060/1,141 NS

ACOULON, A. (attributed to) [P9/40] Good
Mirecourt Violin in good condition, w/case, bow:
c. 1910   810/972
$2,049   £1,265   DM3,858   ¥218,466

ACOULON, ALFRED (attributed to) [P2/65] Good
French Violin with old table restoration, w/case:
Mirecourt, c. 1920   815/978
$1,219   £748   DM2,132   ¥144,027

ALBANI, MATTHIAS [S6/181] Violin w/case, cover,
2 bows: Bolzano, 1702   7,950/11,130
$8,411   £5,290   DM15,817   ¥1,016,950

ALBANI, MATTHIAS [S11/367] Violin w/case:
Bolzano, 1694   6,480/9,720
$7,825   £4,830   DM14,828   ¥826,268

ALBERT, J. [Sk11/292] American Violin w/case, bow:
Philadelphia   800/1,200
$661   £409   DM1,248   ¥69,960

ALEKSA, JOHN [S6/270] Violin: Indiana, 1983
                                  2,862/3,975 NS

ALTAVILLA, ARMANDO [S3/26] Violin after Joseph
Gagliano, w/case, cover: Naples, c. 1930 6,480/9,720
$8,942   £5,520   DM16,063   ¥1,055,810

AMATI, ANTONIO & GIROLAMO [C3/154] Very
Fine Italian Violin (W.E. Hill & Sons, London,
October 28, 1958)   97,800/130,400
$142,299   £87,300   DM252,297   ¥16,825,329

AMATI, DOM NICOLO [B11/121] Italian Violin:
Bologna, 1719   19,440/24,300 NS

AMATI, DOM NICOLO [S11M/99] Violin: Bologna,
c. 1730   24,255/32,340
$34,216   £21,160   DM64,855   ¥3,619,841

AMATI, NICOLO [S3/94] Violin w/case: Cremona,
c. 1640   113,400/145,800
$207,360   £128,000   DM372,480   ¥24,482,560

AMEDO, SIMONAZZI [B3/116] Italian Violin: 1920
                                  9,720/16,200 NS

AMEDO, SIMONAZZI [B6/117] Italian Violin:
Emilia, 1920   7,155/10,335
$7,314   £4,600   DM13,846   ¥876,714

ANCIAUME, BERNARD [C3/88] French Violin
                                      815/1,304 NS

ANDERSON, A. [P2/211] Violin w/case, bow:
Edinburgh, 1932   244/326
$300   £184   DM524   ¥35,429

ANTONIAZZI, GAETANO (attributed to) [C3/138]
Italian Violin w/case (Dykes & Sons, London,
January 14, 1915)   11,410/14,670
$56,235   £34,500   DM99,705   ¥6,649,185

ANTONIAZZI, ROMEO [B11/137] Fine Italian
Violin: Cremona, 1911   16,200/24,300
$18,630   £11,500   DM35,075   ¥1,969,030

ANTONIAZZI, ROMEO [P11/68] Fine and Handsome Italian Violin in immediate playing condition,
w/case, 2 bows: Milan, 1908   19,440/24,300
$25,709   £15,870   DM48,832   ¥2,701,233

ANTONIAZZI, ROMEO (attributed to) [Bf4/2830]
Fine Italian Violin w/case: c. 1930 10,000/15,000 NS

APPARUT, GEORGES (workshop of) [C11/189]
French Violin   972/1,296
$1,583   £977   DM2,980   ¥167,282

ARDERN, JOB [B6/78] English Violin
                                  3,180/4,770 NS

ARDERN, JOB [B11/101] English Violin
                                      1,620/2,430
$1,584   £978   DM2,981   ¥167,368

ARTHUR & JOHNSON [Sk5/244] Contemporary
American Violin   1,400/1,600
$1,150   £702   DM2,082   ¥138,851

ATKINSON, WILLIAM [B2/126] Violin: c. 1926
                                      1,968/2,460
$1,886   £1,150   DM3,255   ¥215,234

ATKINSON, WILLIAM [P6/72] Good English Violin
in immediate playing condition, w/German violin, 2
cases: Tottenham, 1907   1,932/2,415
$3,194   £1,984   DM5,991   ¥383,895

AUDINOT, NESTOR [S11/149] Violin after Guarneri
del Gesù: Paris, 1893   9,720/12,960
$18,630   £11,500   DM35,305   ¥1,967,305

AUDINOT, VICTOR [S3/100] Violin w/case:
Mirecourt, c. 1910   8,100/11,340
$9,315   £5,750   DM16,733   ¥1,099,803

BAADER & CO., J.A. [Sk5/344] Mittenwald Violin:
1926   400/600
$403   £246   DM729   ¥48,598

BADALASSI, PIERO [B3/72] Violin: Pisa, 1949
                                  8,100/11,340 NS

BADARELLO, CARLO [B11/110] Violin: Turin,
1927   3,240/4,860
$5,962   £3,680   DM11,224   ¥630,090

BAILLY, CHARLES [S6/48] Violin w/case: Mirecourt,
1947 (maker's, March 14, 1949)   2,385/3,180
$2,926   £1,840   DM5,502   ¥353,722

BAILLY, CHARLES (workshop of) [Sk5/43] French
Violin w/case: 1912   1,800/2,200
$2,760   £1,684   DM4,996   ¥333,242

BAILLY, JENNY [P2/19] Violin with minor table
restoration and regluing: Paris, c. 1930
                                       1,141/1,304 NS

BAILLY, JENNY [P5/141] Violin with minor table
restoration and regluing: Paris, c. 1930   652/815
$450   £276   DM814   ¥54,286

BAILLY, JENNY (attributed to) [P9/72] French Violin
in immediate playing condition: c. 1930   648/810
$1,211   £748   DM2,280   ¥129,093

BAILLY, PAUL [B6/64] Good Violin (Etienne Vatelot,
1996)   7,950/11,130 NS

BAILLY, PAUL [P3/73] Fine and Handsome Violin:
Paris, c. 1900   6,480/8,100
$7,079   £4,370   DM12,673   ¥834,976

BAILLY, PAUL [P11/80] Good French Violin in
immediate playing condition, w/case: c. 1900
                                       6,480/7,290
$8,570   £5,290   DM16,277   ¥900,411

BAILLY, PAUL [S3/17] Violin w/case: London, 1888
                                       4,860/8,100
$5,962   £3,680   DM10,709   ¥703,874

BAILLY, PAUL [Sk11/381] Good French Violin
w/case: Paris, 1886   5,000/6,000
$7,935   £4,912   DM14,977   ¥839,523

BAILLY, PAUL (attributed to) [P5/20] Good French
Violin in good condition: Paris, 1906   4,564/5,216
$5,249   £3,220   DM9,499   ¥633,342

BAILLY, PAUL (attributed to) [P11/33] French Violin
in immediate playing condition: c. 1880
                                       2,430/3,240 NS

BALESTRIERI, TOMMASO [S6/185] Violin:
Mantua, c. 1765 (Kenneth Warren & Son, Ltd.,
Chicago, October 8, 1979)   50,880/60,420 NS

BALTZERSON, PETER E. [Sk5/64] American Violin:
Boston, 1926   1,400/1,600 NS

BANKS, BENJAMIN [B6/73] English Violin
                                       3,180/4,770
$2,926   £1,840   DM5,538   ¥350,686

BANKS, BENJAMIN [S11/386] Violin w/case, cover,
2 bows: Salisbury, 1775   2,430/3,240
$2,981   £1,840   DM5,649   ¥314,769

BARBE, F. (attributed to) [P9/187] French Violin
w/violin: c. 1880   810/972
$1,118   £690   DM2,105   ¥119,163

BARBE FAMILY [P6/71] French Violin or small viola
with minor old button restoration, otherwise in good
condition, w/case: c. 1840   1,288/1,932 NS

BARTON, GEORGE [P2/200] Old English Violin
with restorable blemishes: London, c. 1790   489/652
$600   £368   DM1,049   ¥70,858

BARZONI, FRANCOIS [P9/12] Good French Violin
in good condition, w/case, bow   972/1,134
$1,453   £897   DM2,736   ¥154,912

BAUER, JEAN [Sk5/163] Good Contemporary
French Violin: Angers, 1971   3,000/4,000
$5,405   £3,297   DM9,783   ¥652,600

BELLAROSA, VITTORIO [C3/98] Italian Violin
                                       16,300/19,560 NS

BELTRAMI, GIUSEPPE [B11/180] Violin: Cremona,
1888   3,240/4,860 NS

BERINI, MARCUS [Sk11/322] German Violin
w/case: c. 1970   700/900 NS

BERNADELL, ERNEST [B6/81] Violin
                                       6,360/9,540 NS

BERNARDEL (attributed to) [P5/12] French Violin of
quality: Paris, 1875   1,956/2,445
$2,249   £1,380   DM4,071   ¥271,432

BERNARDEL, AUGUST SEBASTIEN & ERNEST
AUGUST [Bf4/2834] Good French Violin w/case:
Paris, c. 1855   17,000/22,500 NS

BERNARDEL, AUGUST SEBASTIEN & ERNEST
AUGUST [Bf10/8024] Good French Violin w/case:
Paris, c. 1859   15,000/20,000 NS

BERNARDEL, AUGUST SEBASTIEN PHILIPPE
[Bf10/8035] Fine French Violin: Paris, 1843 (Etienne
Vatelot, March 28, 1995)   14,000/18,000 NS

BERNARDEL, LEON [Sk11/84] Modern French
Violin w/case: Paris   4,000/6,000
$4,893   £3,029   DM9,236   ¥517,706

BERNARDEL, LEON (attributed to) [P9/185] French
Violin in good condition   648/810
$1,118   £690   DM2,105   ¥119,163

BERNARDEL FAMILY (attributed to) [P11/111]
French Violin in good condition: Paris, c. 1860
                                       1,944/2,430
$2,999   £1,852   DM5,697   ¥315,144

BETTS [B2/91] English Violin: London, c. 1820
                                       328/492
$717   £437   DM1,237   ¥81,789

BETTS, JOHN [P6/20] Good English Violin in
immediate playing condition, w/case, bow: London,
c. 1800   2,415/2,898 NS

BETTS, JOHN [P9/15] Good English Violin in
immediate playing condition, w/case, bow: London,
c. 1800   1,620/2,430
$3,540   £2,185   DM6,664   ¥377,350

BIANCHI, NICOLO [S6/67] Violin: Genoa, 1873
                                       7,950/11,130
$5,851   £3,680   DM11,003   ¥707,443

BIGNAMI, OTELLO [C3/160] Italian Violin: Bolgna,
1982   8,150/9,780 NS

BIGNAMI, OTELLO [Sk11/397] Italian Violin: 1982
                                       14,000/16,000 NS

24

BIRD, RICHMOND HENRY [P2/39] Good English
Violin in immediate playing condition, w/case: 1925
1,630/1,956
$1,782   £1,093   DM3,115   ¥210,457

BIRD, RICHMOND HENRY [P3/61] Good English
Violin with minor table blemish: 1927
1,944/2,430 NS

BIRD, RICHMOND HENRY [P5/54] Good English
Violin with minor table blemish: 1927
1,141/1,304 NS

BIRD, RICHMOND HENRY [P11/30] Good English
Violin with minor table blemish, otherwise in good
condition: 1927   1,134/1,296
$1,822   £1,125   DM3,461   ¥191,435

BIRD, RICHMOND HENRY [S11/251] Violin
w/case, bow: Wolverhampton, c. 1910   4,050/4,860
$4,099   £2,530   DM7,767   ¥432,807

BISIACH, CARLO [Bf4/2817] Very Fine Violin in a
remarkable state of preservation, w/case: Florence,
1934   30,000/35,000 NS

BISIACH, CARLO [S3/95] Violin w/case, cover:
Florence, 1937   29,160/40,500 NS

BISIACH, CARLO [S6/183] Violin after Stradivari,
c. 1715, w/case: Florence, 1948   23,850/31,800
$21,942   £13,800   DM41,262   ¥2,652,912

BISIACH, CARLO [S11/243] Violin w/case, cover:
Florence, 1937   22,680/29,160 NS

BISIACH, LEANDRO [P11/62] Good Italian Violin
in immediate playing condition: Milan, 1910 (D.R.
Hill & Son, September 22, 1999)   32,400/40,500
$47,134   £29,095   DM89,525   ¥4,952,260

BISIACH, LEANDRO (attributed to) [B6/100] Violin
7,950/11,130
$8,228   £5,175   DM15,577   ¥986,303

BISIACH, LEANDRO (attributed to) [P11/90] Italian
Violin in immediate playing condition, w/case: Milan,
1910   19,440/24,300 NS

BISIACH FAMILY [P3/87] Fine and Handsome
Italian Violin in good condition: c. 1900
24,300/29,160
$29,808   £18,400   DM53,360   ¥3,515,688

BITTERER, JOSEPH [Bf10/8100] Good Violin in
nearly perfect condition, w/case, bow   800/1,200
$460   £276   DM828   ¥3,574

BLANCHARD, PAUL [B11/154] Fine French Violin
(Vatelot, Paris, December 11, 1989)
16,200/24,300 NS

BLANCHARD, PAUL [P11/77] Fine and Handsome
French Violin in immediate playing condition, w/case:
Lyon, 1912   9,720/12,960
$18,211   £11,241   DM34,589   ¥1,913,373

BLANCHARD, PAUL [S6/56] Violin w/case: Lyon,
1891 (Etienne Vatelot, Paris, December 11, 1989)
11,130/14,310 NS

BLANCHARD, PAUL [S11/150] Violin w/case, cover:
Lyon, 1898   12,960/19,440 NS

BLANCHI, ALBERTO [P3/66] Good Violin in immediate playing condition: Nice, 1932   10,530/11,340
$11,923   £7,360   DM21,344   ¥1,406,275

BLONDELET, EMILE (workshop of) [C11/173]
Violin   1,296/1,944
$1,490   £920   DM2,806   ¥157,522

BLONDELET, H. EMILE [P5/33] Good French
Violin in good condition: Paris, 1921
1,304/1,467 NS

BLONDELET, H. EMILE [P6/69] Good French
Violin in immediate playing condition, w/case: Paris,
1924   1,610/1,932 NS

BLONDELET, H. EMILE [P9/13] Good French
Violin in good condition: Paris, 1921   891/972
$1,155   £713   DM2,175   ¥123,135

BLONDELET, H. EMILE [P9/16] Good French
Violin with minor restorable blemishes, w/case, bow:
Paris, 1922   1,296/1,944
$1,490   £920   DM2,806   ¥158,884

BLYTH, WILLIAMSON [Sk5/105] Scottish Violin:
Edinburgh, 1806   2,200/2,400 NS

BLYTH, WILLIAMSON [Sk11/333] Scottish Violin:
Edinburgh, 1806   1,200/1,400 NS

BOCQUAY, JACQUES (attributed to) [P5/18] Old
French Violin of quality: c. 1750   3,260/4,075 NS

BOCQUAY, JACQUES (attributed to) [P9/31] Old
French Violin: c. 1750   1,620/2,430 NS

BOSSI, GIUSEPPE [B3/110] Italian Violin: 1929
4,860/8,100 NS

BOSSI, GIUSEPPE [B6/120] Italian Violin: 1929
1,590/2,385 NS

BOTTURI, BENVENUTO [S6/70] Violin w/case:
Brescia, 1934 (Max Möller, Amsterdam, June 10,
1966)   12,720/15,900 NS

BOTTURI, BENVENUTO [S11/372] Violin w/case:
Brescia, 1934   6,480/9,720
$8,942   £5,520   DM16,946   ¥944,306

BOULANGEOT, EMILE (workshop of) [C11/72]
French Violin w/case   1,620/2,430
$2,049   £1,265   DM3,858   ¥216,593

BOULANGIER, CHARLES [B3/82] Fine Violin:
London, 1884   6,480/9,720
$7,825   £4,830   DM14,055   ¥923,834

BOULANGIER, CHARLES [P3/105] Violin in good
condition, w/case: London, 1892 (Ralph P. Powell,
Smethwick, England, January 2, 1962)
1,620/2,430 NS

BOULANGIER, CHARLES [S3/9] Violin w/case:
London, 1881 (J. & A. Beare, London, July 31, 1946)
5,670/8,100
$15,836   £9,775   DM28,445   ¥1,869,664

BOULLANGIER, CHARLES (FILS) [P5/51] Violin in
immediate playing condition, w/case: London, 1892
(Ralph P. Powell, Smethwick, January 2, 1962)
1,630/1,956
$1,725   £1,058   DM3,121   ¥208,098

BOYES, ARNOLD [S6/193] Violin: Leeds, 1974
2,385/3,180 NS

BRETON BREVETE [C3/326] French Violin 326/489
$187   £115   DM332   ¥22,164

BRIGGS, JAMES WILLIAM [B2/141] Good Scottish
Violin: Glasgow, 1897   4,920/8,200
$5,092   £3,105   DM8,787   ¥581,132

BROWN, J. [P6/80] Good English Violin in immediate playing condition: Huddersfield   966/1,127 NS

BROWN, J. [P9/10] Good English Violin in immediate playing condition: Huddersfield   810/972
$932   £575   DM1,754   ¥99,303

BROWN, JAMES [S6/83] Violin w/case: London,
c. 1820 (D.R. Hill, Great Missenden, April 15, 1994)
1,590/2,385
$1,829   £1,150   DM3,439   ¥221,076

BRUET, NICOLAS [B11/115] French Violin:
Mirecourt, c. 1850   810/1,134 NS

BRUGERE, P. [B3/74] Violin: 1911   3,240/4,860
$3,353   £2,070   DM6,024   ¥395,929

BRUNO, CARLO [S3/33] Violin w/case: Turin, 1908
3,240/4,860 NS

BUCHSTETTER, GABRIEL DAVID [Sk5/372] South
German Violin w/case: Regensburg   1,800/2,200
$1,380   £842   DM2,498   ¥166,621

CALCAGNI, BERNARDO [S11/242] Violin with
later sides: Genoa, 1729 (W.E. Hill & Sons, London,
February 8, 1946)   24,300/32,400
$22,356   £13,800   DM42,366   ¥2,360,766

CAMILLI, CAMILLO [B3/69] Fine Italian Violin:
Mantua, 1741 (Jacques Français, 1972)
97,200/113,400 NS

CAMILLI, CAMILLO [B6/95] Fine Italian Violin:
Mantua, 1741 (Jacques Français, 1972)
95,400/111,300 NS

CAMILLI, CAMILLO [S6/265] Violin w/case:
Mantua, c. 1745   47,700/63,600
$45,713   £28,750   DM85,963   ¥5,526,900

CAMILLI, CAMILLO (attributed to) [Bf4/2823]
Good Italian Violin w/case, 2 bows: Mantua, c. 1750
(Emil Herrmann, January 13, 1930)
14,000/18,000 NS

CAMILLI, CAMILLO (attributed to) [Bf10/8041]
Good Italian Violin w/case, 2 bows: Mantua, c. 1750
10,000/15,000
$13,800   £8,280   DM24,840   ¥107,226

CAPELA, ANTONIO [B11/153] Violin: Portugal,
1982   6,480/9,720
$5,589   £3,450   DM10,523   ¥590,709

CAPICCHIONI, MARINO [Bf10/8040] Fine
Modern Italian Violin w/case: Rimini, 1956 (Prof.
Dott. Carlo Carfagna, November 16, 1991)
9,000/15,000
$13,800   £8,280   DM24,840   ¥107,226

CAPICCHIONI, MARINO [S11M/32] Violin w/cor-
respondence between maker and Yehudi Menuhin:
Rimini, 1961   19,404/29,106
$59,878   £37,030   DM113,497 ¥6,334,722

CAPICCHIONI, MARINO (attributed to) [Sk5/66]
Modern Italian Violin w/case (Giorgio Foschi, Milan,
September 16, 1980)   8,000/12,000
$12,650   £7,717   DM22,897   ¥1,527,361

CARBONARE, ALAIN [S11M/33] Violin: Mirecourt,
1993   4,851/6,468
$5,988   £3,703   DM11,350   ¥633,472

CARCASSI, LORENZO [B3/62] Italian Violin:
Florence, 1762 (W.E. Hill & Sons) 32,400/48,600 NS

CARCASSI, LORENZO [B6/85] Italian Violin:
Florence, 1762 (W.E. Hill & Sons) 28,620/39,750 NS

CARCASSI, LORENZO [B11/179] Italian Violin:
Florence, 1762 (W.E. Hill & Sons, London, August 7,
1981)   24,300/32,400
$26,082   £16,100   DM49,105   ¥2,756,642

CARCASSI, LORENZO & TOMMASO [B6/112]
Fine Italian Violin: Florence, 1778   31,800/47,700
$36,570   £23,000   DM69,230   ¥4,383,570

CARCASSI, LORENZO & TOMMASO [Bf4/2819]
Fine Italian Violin w/case: Florence, c. 1780 (Dario
D'Attili, June 12, 1984)   30,000/40,000 NS

CARCASSI, LORENZO & TOMMASO [S3/128]
Violin w/case: Florence, 1787 (W.E. Hill & Sons,
London, September 15, 1891)   40,500/48,600 NS

CARCASSI, LORENZO & TOMMASO [S11/254]
Violin w/case: Florence, 1787 (W.E. Hill & Sons,
London, September 15, 1891)   29,160/40,500
$29,808   £18,400   DM56,488   ¥3,147,688

CARCASSI, LORENZO & TOMMASO [S11/371]
Violin w/case: Florence, 1765 (L.P. Balmforth & Son,
Leeds, December 1970)   40,500/56,700
$55,890   £34,500   DM105,915 ¥5,901,915

CARCASSI, VINCENZO [S6/176] Violin: Florence,
c. 1795 (Jacques Français, New York, June 13, 1997)
39,750/47,700
$32,913   £20,700   DM61,893   ¥3,979,368

CARESSA, ALBERT [P3/77] Good French Violin in
immediate playing condition: Paris, 1924
5,670/6,480 NS

CARESSA, ALBERT [P5/38] Good French Violin in
immediate playing condition: Paris, 1924
3,260/4,890
$3,749   £2,300   DM6,785   ¥452,387

CARLETTI, CARLO [S6/268] Violin w/case, bow:
Pieve di Cento, first half 20th C. (Antonio Citella, La
Haye, February 17, 1927)   6,360/9,540 NS

CARLETTI, CARLO [S11/347] Violin w/case, bow:
Pieve di Cento, first half 20th C. (Antonio Citella, La
Haye, February 17, 1927)   4,536/5,670
$10,247   £6,325   DM19,418   ¥1,082,018

CARTWRIGHT, CHARLES D. [Sk5/286] American
Violin w/case, 2 bows: Berlin, Massachusetts 400/600
$690   £421   DM1,249   ¥83,311

CASTAGNERI, ANDREA [S6/190] Violin w/case, 2
bows: Paris, c. 1745   6,360/9,540
$6,400   £4,025   DM12,035   ¥773,766

CASTAGNINO, GIUSEPPE [S11/158] Violin w/case:
Chiavari, 1947 (Giuseppe Lucci, Rome, undated)
                                            6,480/8,100
$14,904   £9,200   DM28,244   ¥1,573,844

CATENARI, ENRICO [P3/58] Fine, Handsome, and
Rare Italian Violin in good condition: Turin, c. 1680
(J. & A. Beare, London, June 10, 1987)
                                         64,800/72,900 NS

CAUSSIN, F. (attributed to) [P11/72] Violin with
minor restorable blemishes, w/case: c. 1860
                                            4,050/4,860
$4,713   £2,910   DM8,953   ¥495,226

CAUSSIN, F.N. [B11/95] French Violin: c. 1860
                                            2,916/4,050
$2,422   £1,495   DM4,560   ¥255,974

CAUSSIN, FRANCOIS [S6/64] Violin w/case, bow:
Rouvres-la-Chetive, c. 1850   4,770/6,360 NS

CAUSSIN, FRANCOIS (attributed to) [P3/26] Good
French Violin in immediate playing condition, w/case:
c. 1870   810/972
$2,049   £1,265   DM3,669   ¥241,704

CAVALLI, ARISTIDE [B5/154] Italian Violin
                                            3,280/4,920
$3,395   £2,070   DM6,169   ¥409,839

CAVANI, G. [B11/124] Italian Violin with later scroll:
Spilamberto (Eric Blot, Cremona, October 30, 1997)
                                         12,960/19,440 NS

CAVANI, GIOVANNI [Sk11/71] Italian Violin:
Modena, 1936   8,000/10,000 NS

CAVANI, VINCENZO [Sk5/44] Italian Violin:
Spilamberto, 1969   6,000/8,000 NS

CELONIATO, GIOVANNI FRANCESCO [S3/123]
Violin w/case: Turin, c. 1720 (W.E. Hill & Sons,
London, June 16, 1939)   45,360/56,700 NS

CELONIATO, GIOVANNI FRANCESCO [S11/362]
Violin w/case: Turin, c. 1720 (W.E. Hill & Sons,
London, June 16, 1939)   32,400/48,600
$33,534   £20,700   DM63,549   ¥3,541,149

CERUTI, ENRICO [S6/75] Violin: Cremona, 1831
(W.E. Hill & Sons, London, November 14, 1950)
                                         44,520/55,650
$61,851   £38,900   DM116,311   ¥7,478,136

CERUTI, GIOVANNI BATTISTA (attributed to)
[S6/196] Violin w/case: probably Italy, c. 1800
                                            3,975/5,565
$7,680   £4,830   DM14,442   ¥928,519

CHANOT, FRANCOIS [C11/37] Rare Guitar-Shaped
Violin in its original setup, w/case: 1820
                                            3,240/4,860 NS

CHANOT, GEORGES [C11/79] Fine English Violin
w/case, bow: London, 1878 (Max Möller, Amsterdam, December 10, 1951)   12,960/19,440
$18,630   £11,500   DM35,075   ¥1,969,030

CHANOT, GEORGES [Sk5/39] Good French Violin
w/case, bow: Paris, 1822   15,000/17,000
$24,150   £14,732   DM43,712   ¥2,915,871

CHANOT, GEORGES (attributed to) [P3/76] Violin
with restored table blemishes: Paris, 1835
                                            6,480/7,290 NS

CHANOT, GEORGES (II) [S6/59] Violin after
Guarneri del Gesù: Paris, 1856   11,130/15,900
$10,971   £6,900   DM20,631   ¥1,326,456

CHAPPUY, AUGUSTINE [Sk11/384] French Violin
w/case, bow: Paris, 1750   5,000/6,000 NS

CHAPPUY, N.A. (attributed to) [P11/71] Good
French Violin with restorable blemishes, otherwise in
playing condition, w/case, bow: c. 1770 1,620/2,025
$2,142   £1,323   DM4,069   ¥225,103

CHAPPUY, NICOLAS [P11/114] Fine French Violin
in immediate playing condition, w/case: Paris, 1763
                                            1,620/2,430
$3,214   £1,984   DM6,104   ¥337,654

CHAPPUY, NICOLAS AUGUSTIN [P6/51] Good
French Violin with minor cleaning required, otherwise
in good condition: Paris, 1784   1,288/1,449
$4,258   £2,645   DM7,988   ¥511,860

CHERPITEL, GEORGE [C11/249] Violin w/case
                                            972/1,296 NS

CHERPITEL, LOUIS [Bf4/2822] Good French Violin
w/case: Mirecourt, 1925   4,000/5,500 NS

CHERPITEL, LOUIS [Bf10/8023] Good French
Violin w/case: Mirecourt, 1925   4,000/5,500 NS

CHERPITEL, N.E. (attributed to) [P11/103] French
Violin of quality, w/case, bow: c. 1870 1,296/1,458
$2,999   £1,852   DM5,697   ¥315,144

CHIOCCHI, GAETANO (attributed to) [C3/144]
Italian Violin w/case (John L. Rossi, New York,
October 20, 1994)   8,150/13,040
$12,184   £7,475   DM21,603   ¥1,440,657

CHIPOT, PAUL [C11/93] French Violin   1,944/2,916
$4,844   £2,990   DM9,120   ¥511,948

CHIPOT-VUILLAUME [C3/95] French Violin w/case
                                            978/1,304
$1,125   £690   DM1,994   ¥132,984

CHIPOT-VUILLAUME [P2/42] Good French Violin
in good condition: c. 1890   1,304/1,467
$1,537   £943   DM2,688   ¥181,575

CICILIATI, ALESSANDRO [B3/99A] Violin: 1993
                                            4,860/8,100
$5,216   £3,220   DM9,370   ¥615,889

CLAUDOT, ALBERT [Sk5/78] French Violin: c. 1926
                                            3,000/4,000
$4,945   £3,016   DM8,950   ¥597,059

CLEMENT, JEAN LAMBERT (attributed to)
[S11/381] Violin: Paris or Mirecourt, c. 1835
                                            3,240/4,860
$4,099   £2,530   DM7,767   ¥432,807

COCKCROFT, W. [P5/136] Good Violin in immediate playing condition, w/case, violin: Rochdale, 1851
652/815
$825   £506   DM1,493   ¥99,525

COLIN, JEAN BAPTISTE [P9/54] Mirecourt Violin with old restorations, now in playing condition, w/case: 1895   1,134/1,296
$2,049   £1,265   DM3,858   ¥218,466

COLLIN-MEZIN [C11/73] French Violin w/period case: 1884   2,916/3,888
$4,658   £2,875   DM8,769   ¥492,258

COLLIN-MEZIN (attributed to) [P2/44] French Violin with minor table blemish, w/case: 1949
1,630/1,956 NS

COLLIN-MEZIN (attributed to) [P5/53] French Violin in immediate playing condition, w/case: 1949
1,141/1,304
$2,249   £1,380   DM4,071   ¥271,432

COLLIN-MEZIN, CH.J.B. [B11/126] Violin (Etienne Vatelot, Paris, August 29, 1996)   6,480/9,720 NS

COLLIN-MEZIN, CH.J.B. [B11/140] Violin: 1903
2,430/4,050 NS

COLLIN-MEZIN, CH.J.B. [C3/120] French Violin w/case, 2 bows: Paris, 1922   1,304/1,956
$1,780   £1,092   DM3,156   ¥210,461

COLLIN-MEZIN, CH.J.B. [C3/156] French Violin: Paris, 1892   3,260/4,075
$3,374   £2,070   DM5,982   ¥398,951

COLLIN-MEZIN, CH.J.B. [C11/96] French Violin w/case: 1896   2,916/3,564
$5,216   £3,220   DM9,821   ¥551,328

COLLIN-MEZIN, CH.J.B. [P3/75] Good Violin in good condition, w/case: Paris, 1884   2,430/2,916
$5,403   £3,335   DM9,672   ¥637,218

COLLIN-MEZIN, CH.J.B. [P6/19] French Violin in immediate playing condition: w/3 bows: Paris, 1887
1,932/2,093
$3,088   £1,918   DM5,793   ¥371,210

COLLIN-MEZIN, CH.J.B. [P6/42] Good French Violin in immediate playing condition: Paris, 1912
2,415/2,898
$2,768   £1,719   DM5,192   ¥332,709

COLLIN-MEZIN, CH.J.B. [P6/59] Good French Violin in immediate playing condition, w/case, bow: Paris, 1892   4,025/4,830
$5,323   £3,306   DM9,985   ¥639,826

COLLIN-MEZIN, CH.J.B. [S3/8] Violin w/case: Paris, 1892   4,860/6,480
$5,589   £3,450   DM10,040   ¥659,882

COLLIN-MEZIN, CH.J.B. [S6/50] Violin w/case, bow: Paris, 1884   4,770/6,360 NS

COLLIN-MEZIN, CH.J.B. [S6/187] Violin: Paris, 1888   3,975/5,565 NS

COLLIN-MEZIN, CH.J.B. [Sk5/56] French Violin w/case: 1894   2,800/3,200
$3,335   £2,034   DM6,036   ¥402,668

COLLIN-MEZIN, CH.J.B. (attributed to) [P9/23] Good French Violin in immediate playing condition: Paris, 1940   1,620/2,025
$1,863   £1,150   DM3,508   ¥198,605

COLLIN-MEZIN, CH.J.B. (workshop of) [C11/31] French Violin   1,620/1,944
$1,677   £1,035   DM3,157   ¥177,213

COLLIN-MEZIN, CH.J.B. (workshop of) [C11/82] French Violin   1,296/1,944 NS

COLLIN-MEZIN, CH.J.B. (workshop of) [Sk5/374] French Violin w/case: Mirecourt, 1928   1,400/1,600
$2,760   £1,684   DM4,996   ¥333,242

COLLIN-MEZIN, CH.J.B. (FILS) [P9/42] Good French Violin in immediate playing condition: Paris, 1882   1,134/1,296
$2,422   £1,495   DM4,560   ¥258,186

COLLIN-MEZIN, CH.J.B. (FILS) (attributed to) [P2/86] Good French Violin with minor restorable blemishes, w/violin: 1911   652/815
$1,407   £863   DM2,460   ¥166,171

COLLINS, GLEN [S11M/29] Violin after the "Lord Wilton" Guarneri del Gesù: London, 1992 (maker's, March 3, 1992)   9,702/12,936
$27,800   £17,193   DM52,695   ¥2,941,121

COLLINS, GLEN [S11M/91] Violin after the "d'Egville" Guarneri del Gesù, w/letter from Yehudi Menuhin to owner of the "d'Egville": London, 1987
6,468/9,702
$27,800   £17,193   DM52,695   ¥2,941,121

COMBS, JOHN [Sk5/37] American Violin w/case: Brooklyn, 1895   400/600
$230   £140   DM416   ¥27,770

COMSTOCK, WILMER E. [Sk5/176] American Violin   1,400/1,600 NS

CONE, GEORGES & FILS [S3/5] Violin: Lyon, 1939
2,916/4,050
$3,353   £2,070   DM6,024   ¥395,929

CONIA, STEFANO [S3/125] Violin: Tatabánya, 1971   1,944/2,592 NS

CONTINO, ALFREDO [B3/112] Italian Violin (Rene Morel)   16,200/19,440
$16,767   £10,350   DM30,119   ¥1,979,645

CONTINO, ALFREDO [C11/24] Modern Italian Violin w/case, bow: Naples, 1921   9,720/12,960
$22,356   £13,800   DM42,090   ¥2,362,836

COURTIER, LOUIS [Bf4/2811] French Violin: Mirecourt, 1928   1,700/2,250 NS

COUTURIEUX, M. [C11/193] French Violin w/case
810/97
$932   £575   DM1,754   ¥98,452

CRASKE, GEORGE [B11/118A] Violin: London, c. 1870   4,860/6,480 NS

CRASKE, GEORGE [B11/123A] Violin   6,480/9,720
$6,521   £4,025   DM12,276   ¥689,161

CRASKE, GEORGE [C3/131] English Violin w/case,
2 bows   4,075/5,705
$7,498   £4,600   DM13,294   ¥886,558

CRASKE, GEORGE [P9/20] Good Violin in immediate playing condition, w/case, bow: c. 1840
                                          4,860/5,670
$5,403   £3,335   DM10,172   ¥575,955

CRASKE, GEORGE [S3/13] Violin w/case: Stockport,
c. 1850   2,916/4,050
$6,521   £4,025   DM11,713   ¥769,862

CUNAULT, GEORGES [B6/107] Violin
                                          6,360/9,540 NS

CUNIN, ALBERT (attributed to) [P5/26] Good
French Violin in immediate playing condition, w/case:
Mirecourt, 1889   1,304/1,956
$1,594   £978   DM2,885   ¥192,363

CURTIN, JOSEPH [S11M/94] Violin w/correspon-
dence between maker and Yehudi Menuhin: Ann
Arbor, 1993   12,936/19,404
$25,662   £15,870   DM48,642   ¥2,714,881

CUTHBERT, ROBERT [S6/189] Violin w/case, bow:
London, 1685   4,770/7,950
$9,143   £5,750   DM17,193   ¥1,105,380

CUYPERS, J.T. (attributed to) [P6/44] Dutch Violin
requiring minor regluing   3,220/4,830 NS

CUYPERS, J.T. (attributed to) [P11/27] Dutch Violin
requiring minor regluing   648/972
$857   £529   DM1,628   ¥90,041

CUYPERS, JOHANNES [C3/206] Dutch Violin
w/case: 1787   24,450/32,600 NS

CUYPERS, JOHANNES [P11/59] Good Violin in
immediate playing condition, w/case, 3 bows: The
Hague, 1805   19,440/29,160 NS

CUYPERS, JOHANNES [P11/131] Fine and Handsome Dutch Violin in immediate playing condition,
w/case: The Hague, 1783   24,300/32,400
$32,137   £19,838   DM61,040   ¥3,376,541

CUYPERS FAMILY (MEMBER OF) (ascribed to)
[P11/92] Violin in immediate playing condition,
w/case: c. 1810   4,050/4,860
$10,284   £6,348   DM19,533   ¥1,080,493

D'ARIA, VINCENZO [B3/115] Violin: Naples, 1943
                                          4,860/8,100
$11,178   £6,900   DM20,079   ¥1,319,763

DAILEY, ISRAEL A. [Sk5/174] American Violin:
Weymouth   1,200/1,400
$1,150   £702   DM2,082   ¥138,851

DALL'AGLIO, GIUSEPPE [Bf4/2818] Very Fine
Violin w/case: Mantua, 1809   30,000/40,000 NS

DALL'AGLIO, GIUSEPPE [Bf10/8050] Very Fine
Violin w/case: Mantua, 1809   30,000/40,000 NS

DALL'AGLIO, GIUSEPPE (ascribed to) [S11/247]
Violin: Probably Mantua, c. 1920   8,100/11,340
$26,082   £16,100   DM49,427   ¥2,754,227

DARCHE, HILAIRE [P6/57] Fine and Handsome
Violin in immediate playing condition: Brussels, 1922
                                          8,050/9,660 NS

DARCHE, HILAIRE [P11/67] Fine and Handsome
Violin in immediate playing condition: Brussels, 1922
                                          4,860/5,670
$6,427   £3,968   DM12,208   ¥675,308

DARCHE, HILAIRE [C3/161] Good Belgian Violin
w/case: 1911   8,150/11,410
$7,498   £4,600   DM13,294   ¥886,558

DARTE, A. [P11/79] Violin in good condition:
Mirecourt   1,377/1,458
$2,785   £1,719   DM5,290   ¥292,634

DAY, WILLIAM [B11/167] Violin: 1863
                                          810/1,134 NS

DAY, WILLIAM [P6/166] English Violin with minor
blemishes, in good condition: Newcastle 644/966 NS

DEARLOVE, MARK [P3/101] Violin in good condition: Leeds, c. 1850   3,240/4,050
$5,403   £3,335   DM9,672   ¥637,218

DE BARBIERI, PAOLO [Bf4/2828] Very Fine Violin:
Genoa, 1928   16,000/20,000 NS

DEBLAYE, ALBERT [C11/74] French Violin w/case:
1924   1,944/2,268
$2,795   £1,725   DM5,261   ¥295,355

DEBLAYE, ALBERT [C11/77] Violin   1,944/2,268
$2,981   £1,840   DM5,612   ¥315,045

DECONET, MICHAEL [Bf4/2833] Good Venetian
Violin: Venice, c. 1760 (J.R. Carlisle, May 12, 1945)
                                      15,000/25,000 NS

DEGANI, EUGENIO [B3/70] Fine Italian Violin:
Venice, 1896   29,160/40,500
$34,466   £21,275   DM61,910   ¥4,069,269

DEGANI, EUGENIO [P6/46] Good Italian Violin in
immediate playing condition, w/case: Venice, 1893
                                     16,100/19,320
$25,551   £15,870   DM47,927   ¥3,071,162

DEGANI, EUGENIO [S6/58] Violin w/case:
Montagnana, 1887   23,850/31,800 NS

DEGANI, EUGENIO [S11/152] Violin w/case:
Venice, 1898   24,300/32,400
$29,808   £18,400   DM56,488   ¥3,147,688

DEGANI, GIULIO [Bf4/2820] Very Fine Violin
w/case: Venice, 1906 (Carlo Vettori, Florence, 1994)
                                     20,000/25,000 NS

DEL BUSSETTO, GIOVANNI MARIA [S11M/95]
Violin: Cremona, c.1680 (Peter Biddulph, London,
September 30, 1999)   113,190/161,700
$248,250 £153,525   DM470,554   ¥26,263,522

DENNIS, JESSE [C3/101] English Violin: London
                                          1,956/2,445 NS

DERAZEY, H. [B6/90] French Violin: Mirecourt,
c. 1870   6,360/9,540 NS

DERAZEY, H. [B11/119] French Violin: Mirecourt,
c. 1870   4,860/8,100
$5,589   £3,450   DM10,523   ¥590,709

DERAZEY, H. [P11/109] Good French Violin with restorable blemishes, w/case: c. 1860   3,240/4,050
$3,214   £1,984   DM6,104   ¥337,654

DERAZEY, HONORE [C3/112] French Violin w/case, bow   2,445/3,260
$2,624   £1,610   DM4,653   ¥310,295

DERAZEY, HONORE [S6/65] Violin w/case: Mirecourt, c. 1850 (W.E. Hill & Sons, London, November 22, 1948)   7,950/11,130
$16,457   £10,350   DM30,947   ¥1,989,684

DERAZEY, JUSTIN [S6/51] Violin: Mirecourt, c. 1880   3,975/5,565 NS

DERAZEY, JUSTIN [S6/278] Violin: Mirecourt, c. 1890   3,180/4,770
$4,754   £2,990   DM8,940   ¥574,798

DERAZEY, JUSTIN (workshop of) [C11/92] French Violin   2,268/2,592 NS

DERAZEY FAMILY (MEMBER OF) [P2/31] French Violin with minor worm restoration: c. 1870 (Gilles Chancereul, Paris, May 27, 1997)   3,260/4,890
$3,936   £2,415   DM6,883   ¥465,008

DE RUB, A. [B6/62] Violin: Viterbo, 1766
15,900/23,850 NS

DE RUB, A. [B11/109] Violin with later scroll: Rome, c. 1750 (J. & A. Beare, March 31, 1998)
16,200/24,300 NS

DE RUB, ANGELO [P3/48] Fine Violin in good condition: Viterbo, c. 1760 (W.E. Hill & Son)
19,440/21,060 NS

DESIATO, GIUSEPPE (attributed to) [B6/115] Violin
3,975/5,565
$4,023   £2,530   DM7,615   ¥482,193

DESIDERI, PIETRO PAOLO [S11/357] Violin w/child's violin, case, bow: Ripatransone, c. 1795 (W.E. Hill & Sons, London, July 21, 1892)
3,240/4,860
$13,041   £8,050   DM24,714   ¥1,377,114

DICONET, MICHAEL (attributed to) [P6/13] Interesting Small-Size Violin w/case: 1785   1,610/1,932
$3,620   £2,248   DM6,790   ¥435,081

DIDCZENKO, DIMITRO [Sk5/159] Violin: Warsaw
4,000/5,000 NS

DIEUDONNE, A. (attributed to) [P5/23] French Violin in good condition: 1934   1,956/2,445 NS

DIEUDONNE, A. (attributed to) [P9/37] French Violin in good condition: 1934   1,296/1,458
$1,863   £1,150   DM3,508   ¥198,605

DIEUDONNE, AMEDEE [C3/132] French Violin: Mirecourt, 1934   978/1,304 NS

DIEUDONNE, AMEDEE [C11/25] French Violin w/case, bow (maker's, 1934)   2,430/3,240
$3,540   £2,185   DM6,664   ¥374,116

DIEUDONNE, AMEDEE [S6/69] Violin: Mirecourt, 1948   2,862/3,975 NS

DIEUDONNE, AMEDEE [Sk5/180] French Violin w/case: Mirecourt, 1929   2,000/3,000
$2,990   £1,824   DM5,412   ¥361,013

DIEUDONNE, AMEDEE (attributed to) [P3/44] Good French Violin: 1934   1,620/1,944
$2,981   £1,840   DM5,336   ¥351,569

DIEUDONNE, AMEDEE (attributed to) [P9/27] Good French Violin in immediate playing condition: 1934   2,430/2,916
$2,236   £1,380   DM4,209   ¥238,326

DOBBIE, WILLIAM [P2/24] Good Violin requiring minor regluing, w/case, bow: Stirling, Scotland, 1912
815/978
$937   £575   DM1,639   ¥110,716

DOTSCH, MICHAEL [B3/61] Fine Violin after Guarneri del Gesù: Berlin, 1934   6,480/9,720
$10,247   £6,325   DM18,406   ¥1,209,783

DOTSCH, MICHAEL (attributed to) [Bf4/2812] Fine Violin w/case   5,000/8,000
$4,298   £2,673   DM7,909   ¥506,964

DUCHENE, NICOLAS (ascribed to) [Bf4/2826] French Violin: c. 1900   2,000/3,000 NS

DUERER, WILHELM [C3/308] German Violin
326/489 NS

DUERER, WILHELM [Sk5/357] German Violin w/case, bow: 1902   250/350
$518   £316   DM937   ¥62,483

DUKE, RICHARD [B3/57] English Violin: London, c. 1780 (W.E. Hill & Sons)   6,480/9,720
$7,452   £4,600   DM13,386   ¥879,842

DUKE, RICHARD [B11/148] Violin: London, 1767
1,296/1,944 NS

DUKE, RICHARD (workshop of) [Sk11/76] English Violin w/case: London, c. 1800 (Horst L. Kloss, Needham, Massachusetts, April 28, 1996)
2,000/3,000
$3,571   £2,210   DM6,740   ¥377,785

DVORAK, JAN BAPTISTA [S11/376] Violin w/case: Prague, 1876   4,050/5,670 NS

EBERLE, JOHANN ULRICH [S3/34] Violin w/case, 2 bows, cover: Prague, 1757   4,050/5,670
$4,099   £2,530   DM7,362   ¥483,913

EBERLE, JOHANN ULRICH [S11M/96] Violin: Prague, c. 1765   6,468/9,702
$9,623   £5,951   DM18,241   ¥1,018,080

EBERLE, JOHANN ULRICH [Sk5/61] Bohemian Violin w/case, bow: Prague   2,800/3,200
$2,990   £1,824   DM5,412   ¥361,013

EBERLE, TOMASO [S3/20] Violin w/case, bow: Naples, c. 1780   29,160/40,500
$30,740   £18,975   DM55,217   ¥3,629,348

EBERLE, TOMASO [Sk11/91] Fine Violin w/case: Naples, c. 1780 (Kenneth Warren & Son, Chicago, July 5, 1979)   16,000/18,000
$26,450   £16,373   DM49,924   ¥2,798,410

EBERLE, TOMASO (attributed to) [Bf4/2813] Violin
w/case: c. 1810   1,800/2,500
$2,513   £1,563   DM4,623   ¥296,379

ECKLAND, DONALD [Sk11/67] Good American
Violin w/case: Miami, 1978   3,000/5,000
$4,364   £2,701   DM8,238   ¥461,738

EHRICKE, CHARLES [Sk5/162] American Violin
w/case   1,800/2,200 NS

ELLIOT, WILLIAM [P6/65] Violin   966/1,127
$1,150   £714   DM2,157   ¥138,202

ERDESZ, OTTO [S11M/31] Violin after J.B.
Guadagnini: Budapest, mid 20th C.   4,043/5,660 NS

ERDESZ, OTTO [Sk5/79] Contemporary American
Violin w/case   2,800/3,200
$3,738   £2,280   DM6,765   ¥451,266

EVANS & CO., GEORGE [S10/43] Stroh Violin
w/case, bow: London, second quarter 20th C.
                                    494/659
$1,743   £1,058   DM3,237   ¥181,754

EWAN, D. [P2/207] Violin w/case, cornet: Cowden-
beath, Scotland, 1906   163/244
$225   £138   DM393   ¥26,572

FABRIS, LUIGI (attributed to) [B6/96] Interesting
Violin (E.R. Voigt & Son, 1968)   7,950/11,130
$8,777   £5,520   DM16,615   ¥1,052,057

FAGNOLA, ANNIBALE [B3/77] Fine Italian Violin
after Pressenda: Turin, 1929   40,500/56,700
$55,890   £34,500   DM100,395   ¥6,598,815

FAGNOLA, ANNIBALE [C3/164] Fine Italian Violin:
1925 (Kenneth Warren & Son, Ltd., Chicago,
December 9, 1997)   57,050/65,200 NS

FAGNOLA, ANNIBALE (ascribed to) [C11/184]
Italian Violin w/case   8,100/11,340
$18,630   £11,500   DM35,075   ¥1,969,030

FAGNOLA, ANNIBALE (attributed to) [P6/21]
Violin with minor restorable blemishes: Turin, 1898
                                    4,830/6,440
$12,350   £7,671   DM23,165   ¥1,484,395

FANTIN, DOMENICO [S11M/88] Violin: Varese,
1969   2,264/2,911
$5,988   £3,703   DM11,350   ¥633,472

FARINA, ERMINIO [S3/121] Violin w/case: Milan,
c. 1910   16,200/22,680
$17,699   £10,925   DM31,792   ¥2,089,625

FARLEY, CHARLES E. [Sk11/265] American Violin
w/case: 1886   800/1,000
$529   £327   DM998   ¥55,968

FENDT, BERNARD SIMON (attributed to) [S3/4]
Violin w/case: England, c. 1840   4,860/8,100
$11,178   £6,900   DM20,079   ¥1,319,763

FETIQUE, EMILE (attributed to) [P11/78] French
Violin in immediate playing condition: Paris, 1876
                                    2,430/2,916
$5,570   £3,439   DM10,580   ¥585,267

FICKER, JOHANN GOTTLOB [P11/28] Good
Violin with restorable blemishes, w/case, bow:
Markneukirchen, c. 1760   1,944/2,430
$3,856   £2,381   DM7,325   ¥405,185

FICKER, JOHANN GOTTLOB [S3/105] Violin
w/case, cover: Markneukirchen, 1795
                                    3,240/4,860 NS

FICKER, JOHANN GOTTLOB [S11/240] Violin
w/case, cover: Markneukirchen, 1795   2,268/2,916
$2,236   £1,380   DM4,237   ¥236,077

FIKER, JOHANN CHRISTIAN [Sk11/380] Good
Violin w/case: Markneukirchen   4,000/6,000
$3,968   £2,456   DM7,489   ¥419,762

FIORINI, GIUSEPPE [P11/61] Good Violin in immediate playing condition, w/case: Munich, 1892
                                    24,300/32,400
$47,134   £29,095   DM89,525   ¥4,952,260

FLEURY, BENOIT [Sk11/78] French Violin: Paris,
late 18th C.   14,000/15,000 NS

FORSTER, W. [B11/131] English Violin: London,
1773   3,240/4,860 NS

FORSTER, WILLIAM [B3/84] Fine English Violin:
London, C. 1780   8,100/11,340 NS

FORSTER, WILLIAM [P2/28] Violin with some
varnish loss on table, w/case, bow: London,
c. 1790 (Phillips Son & Neale, August 21, 1979)
                                    2,445/3,260 NS

FORSTER, WILLIAM [P6/66] Violin with some
varnish loss on table, otherwise in good condition,
w/case, bow: London, c. 1790 (Phillips Son & Neale,
August, 21, 1979)   2,737/3,220 NS

FORSTER, WILLIAM (III) [S3/12] Violin w/case:
London, c. 1810 (W.E. Hill & Sons, London, January
9, 1924)   4,050/5,670 NS

FRANOT, P. [P3/119] Violin in good condition,
w/violin: Mirecourt, c. 1870   1,620/1,944
$1,267   £782   DM2,268   ¥149,417

FREYMADL, SEBASTIAN [S6/66] Violin w/case,
bow: Cremona, 1986   3,180/4,770 NS

FURBER, JOHN [P3/98] Good English Violin in
good condition: London, 1817   3,240/4,050
$3,353   £2,070   DM6,003   ¥395,515

GADDA, GAETANO [Sk5/55] Good Modern Italian
Violin: Mantua   12,000/14,000
$10,925   £6,664   DM19,774   ¥1,319,085

GADDA, GAETANO (attributed to) [P6/32] Good
Violin in immediate playing condition, w/case:
Mantua, 1930 (Mario Gadda, September 30, 1995)
                                    12,880/14,490 NS

GADDA, GAETANO (attributed to) [P11/96] Good
Italian Violin in immediate playing condition, w/case:
Mantua, 1930 (Mario Gadda, September 30, 1995)
                                    8,100/9,720
$10,284   £6,348   DM19,533   ¥1,080,493

GAFFINO, ANDREA [S11M/39] Violin w/correspondence between maker and Yehudi Menuhin:
Bienne, 1993   2,426/4,043
$8,982   £5,555   DM17,025   ¥950,208

GAFFINO, GIUSEPPE (attributed to) [Bf10/8039]
French Violin: Paris, late 18th C.   5,000/7,000 NS

GAGGINI, PIETRO (attributed to) [B11/170] Violin:
Nice, 1933   1,620/2,430
$2,049   £1,265   DM3,858   ¥216,593

GAGLIANO (workshop of) [S3/30] Violin w/case,
cover: Naples, early 19th C.   29,160/40,500 NS

GAGLIANO, ALESSANDRO [S6/88] Violin w/case,
bow: Naples, c. 1720   39,750/55,650
$121,317 £76,300   DM228,137   ¥14,667,912

GAGLIANO, ALESSANDRO [S6/205] Violin w/case,
cover, bow: Naples, c. 1730 (J. & A. Beare, London,
April 18, 1975)   44,520/55,650
$61,851   £38,900   DM116,311   ¥7,478,136

GAGLIANO, ALESSANDRO [Sk11/70] Fine and
Rare Italian Violin w/case: Naples, 1709 (William
Lewis & Son, April 1946)   75,000/100,000
$230,575 £142,726   DM435,210 ¥24,394,835

GAGLIANO, GIUSEPPE [Bf10/8045] Fine Italian
Violin w/case, bow: Naples, c. 1770 (Kenneth Warren
& Son, May 18, 1999)   35,000/45,000 NS

GAGLIANO, GIUSEPPE [Bf10/8049] Very Fine
Violin w/case, bow: Naples, 1768 (Kenneth Warren
& Son, July 31, 1999)   40,000/60,000
$54,050   £32,430   DM97,290   ¥419,969

GAGLIANO, NICOLA [C11/70] Good Neapolitan
Violin: c. 1765 (Rudolph Wurlitzer Co., New York,
February 1, 1946)   92,340/105,300 NS

GAGLIANO, NICOLA [P11/121] Fine Violin in good
condition: Naples, 1782 (W.E. Hill & Sons, London,
June 22, 1931)   97,200/113,400
$146,246   £90,275   DM277,776   ¥15,365,708

GAGLIANO, NICOLA [P11/132] Fine and Handsome Italian Violin in immediate playing condition,
w/case: Naples, 1731 (Max Möller, Amsterdam,
October 1958)   129,600/145,800
$156,492   £96,600   DM297,238   ¥16,442,286

GAGLIANO, NICOLA [S3/36] Violin w/case:
Naples, 1744   97,200/129,600
$141,426   £87,300   DM254,043   ¥16,697,871

GAGLIANO, NICOLA [S6/80] Violin w/case, cover,
bow: Naples, 1780 (J. & A. Beare, London, March 6,
1936)   111,300/143,100
$163,293 £102,700   DM307,073   ¥19,743,048

GAGLIANO, NICOLA [S11/255] Violin w/case:
Naples, c. 1770   48,600/64,800 NS

GAGLIANO, RAFFAELE & ANTONIO (II)
[Bf4/2804] Italian Violin: Naples, c. 1840
                                     19,000/22,500 NS

GAGLIANO FAMILY (MEMBER OF) [C11/98]
Italian Violin w/case: c. 1820   17,820/21,060 NS

GAIBISSO, GIOVANNI BATTISTA [B6/67] Violin
                                       9,540/12,720
$10,971   £6,900   DM20,769   ¥1,315,071

GAIDA, GIOVANNI [C3/149] Fine Violin
                                      19,560/24,450
$20,620   £12,650   DM36,559   ¥2,438,035

GAIDA, GIOVANNI [C11/34] Fine Violin (W.E. Hill
& Sons, London, December 23, 1969) 16,200/24,300
$18,630   £11,500   DM35,075   ¥1,969,030

GAIDA, SILVIO (attributed to) [C11/85] Modern
Italian Violin w/case   12,960/19,440 NS

GAILLARD, CHARLES [S6/198] Violin: Paris, 1867
                                       3,180/4,770 NS

GAND, CHARLES FRANCOIS [Sk5/82] Good
French Violin: Paris, 1843 (Bernard Millant, Paris,
May 8, 1988)   16,000/18,000
$23,000   £14,030   DM41,630   ¥2,777,020

GAND BROS. [P6/52] Fine and Handsome French
Violin in immediate playing condition, w/case: Paris,
1866   12,880/14,490
$15,969   £9,919   DM29,955   ¥1,919,477

GAND FAMILY (MEMBER OF) [S11/377] Violin
w/case: Paris, late 19th C.   4,860/8,100
$5,589   £3,450   DM10,592   ¥590,192

GAND & BERNARDEL [S11/160] Violin w/case:
Paris, 1890   6,480/9,720
$7,452   £4,600   DM14,122   ¥786,922

GAND & BERNARDEL (workshop of) [C11/99]
Good 7/8-Size Violin: c. 1880   3,240/4,860
$3,353   £2,070   DM6,314   ¥354,425

GAND & BERNARDEL FRERES [P11/76] Fine and
Handsome French Violin in immediate playing condition, w/case   14,580/19,440
$19,282   £11,903   DM36,624   ¥2,025,925

GARTNER, EUGEN [Sk5/41] German Violin:
Stuttgart, 1898   1,800/2,200
$1,380   £842   DM2,498   ¥166,621

GEISSENHOF, FRANZ [C3/145] Austrian Violin
w/case: Vienna, 1802   4,890/6,520
$5,624   £3,450   DM9,971   ¥664,919

GEMUNDER, AUGUST [S3/2] Violin w/case: New
York, c. 1875   1,620/2,430
$3,167   £1,955   DM5,689   ¥373,933

GEMUNDER, GEORGE (SR.) [C11/28] Good
American Violin w/case, bow: Astoria, 1886
                                       6,804/7,452
$13,973   £8,625   DM26,306   ¥1,476,773

GERMAIN, EMILE [S11/139] Violin w/case: Paris,
1898   4,050/5,670
$7,825   £4,830   DM14,828   ¥826,268

GERMAIN, LOUIS JOSEPH (attributed to)
[Sk11/254] Violin   3,500/4,000
$3,968   £2,456   DM7,489   ¥419,762

GIANOTTI, ALFREDO [Sk5/378] Contemporary
Italian Violin: Milan, 1975   2,500/3,500
$4,830   £2,946   DM8,742   ¥583,174

GIBSON CO. [Sk11/308] American Violin w/case, bow: Kalamazoo, Michigan 600/800
$794   £491   DM1,498   ¥83,952

GIRARDI, MARIO [C11/30] Modern Italian Violin w/case   4,860/6,480 NS

GIUDICI, CARLO [Bf4/2808] Good Violin w/case: Varese, 1928   3,500/4,500 NS

GLAESEL, EDMUND [Sk11/227] Modern German Violin w/case: Markneukirchen, 1950   1,400/1,600
$2,513   £1,555   DM4,743   ¥265,849

GLIER & SOHN, C.G. [S11/141] Violin: Markneukirchen, early 20th C.   1,944/2,592
$1,863   £1,150   DM3,531   ¥196,731

GLIER, ROBERT [Sk11/217] American Violin w/case: 1896   1,300/1,500 NS

GLIGA, VASILE [S11M/25] Violin: Reghin, 1995   647/970
$961   £595   DM1,822   ¥101,710

GOFFRILLER, MATTEO (ascribed to) [S6/76] Violin w/case: mid 18th C. (Jacques Français, New York, April 22, 1999)   23,850/31,800
$21,942   £13,800   DM41,262   ¥2,652,912

GOFFRILLER, MATTEO (ascribed to) [S11/148] Violin: Venice or Bolgna, c. 1720 (Hamma & Co., Stuttgart, January 11, 1948)   48,600/64,800
$55,890   £34,500   DM105,915   ¥5,901,915

GOLL, CAROLUS [S11/138] Violin w/case, bow: Brno, 1897   3,240/4,860
$7,452   £4,600   DM14,122   ¥786,922

GONZALEZ, FERNANDO SOLAR [P3/81] Good Spanish Violin in good condition, w/case: Madrid, 1968   3,240/4,050 NS

GOTTI, ANSELMO [Sk5/60] Modern Italian Violin w/case: Ferrara, 1949   7,000/9,000
$16,100   £9,821   DM29,141   ¥1,943,914

GOULDING [P2/81] English Violin with minor restorable blemishes: London, c. 1790   652/815
$975   £598   DM1,704   ¥115,145

GOULDING [P3/31] English Violin requiring some regluing and lacking fingerboard: London, c. 1790   1,134/1,215
$1,639   £1,012   DM2,935   ¥193,363

GRAGNANI, ANTONIO [S6/175] Violin w/case, cover, bow: Livorno, 1786   31,800/47,700
$61,851   £38,900   DM116,311   ¥7,478,136

GRAGNANI, ANTONIO [S11/364] Violin w/case: Livorno, c. 1780   19,440/25,920
$29,808   £18,400   DM56,488   ¥3,147,688

GRANCINO, FRANCESCO (attributed to) [B6/70] Fine Violin (J. van der Geest)   12,720/19,080 NS

GRANCINO, GIOVANNI [B11/112] Very Fine Italian Violin: Milan, 1687 (W.E. Hill & Sons, London, December 21, 1903)   81,000/113,400
$83,835   £51,750   DM157,838   ¥8,860,635

GRANCINO, GIOVANNI [S11M/37] Violin: Milan, c. 1695   64,680/97,020
$207,340 £128,225   DM393,010   ¥21,935,451

GRANDJON, JULES (FILS) (attributed to) [S3/3] Violin: Paris or Mirecourt, late 19th C.   1,620/2,430
$2,049   £1,265   DM3,681   ¥241,957

GRANDJON, JULES (FILS) (attributed to) [Sk11/390] French Violin: Paris, c. 1900 4,000/5,000
$4,761   £2,947   DM8,986   ¥503,714

GRATER & SON, T. [B2/140] Violin: 1927 328/492
$660   £403   DM1,139   ¥75,332

GUADAGNINI, ANTONIO [B11/164] Fine and Rare Italian Violin: Turin, 1864 (Peter Biddulph, London, 1999)   40,500/56,700
$40,986   £25,300   DM77,165   ¥4,331,866

GUADAGNINI, GIUSEPPE (attributed to) [P11/95] Italian Violin with restored table blemishes, w/case: Pavia, c. 1800   24,300/32,400
$32,137   £19,838   DM61,040   ¥3,376,541

GUARNERI, ANDREA [B11/146] Fine Italian Violin: Cremona, 1674 (Peter Biddulph, London, June 1999)   48,600/81,000 NS

GUARNERI, ANDREA [S11/151] Violin: Cremona, 1673 (Hamma & Co., Stuttgart, October 23, 1975)   129,600/162,000
$141,426 £87,300   DM268,011   ¥14,934,411

GUARNERI, ANDREA [S11/378] Violin: Cremona, c. 1695 (Bein & Fushi, Chicago, February 28, 1986)   113,400/145,800
$162,339 £100,395   DM307,711   ¥17,174,573

GUARNERI, ANDREA (attributed to) [B11/159] Fine Italian Violin (Hamma & Co., Stuttgart, August 12, 1949)   24,300/32,400
$44,712   £27,600   DM84,180   ¥4,725,672

GUARNERI, GIUSEPPE (FILIUS ANDREAE) [S3/99] Violin w/case: Cremona, 1697 (Etienne Vatelot, Paris, February 18, 1988)   324,000/405,000 NS

GUARNERI, GIUSEPPE (FILIUS ANDREAE) (ascribed to) [Bf10/8042] Good Violin: c. 1790   3,000/5,000
$4,600   £2,760   DM8,280   ¥35,742

GUARNERI, PIETRO (OF MANTUA) [S3/31] Violin w/case, cover: Mantua, 1699 (W.E. Hill & Sons, London, January 3, 1900)   64,800/97,200
$64,800   £40,000   DM116,400   ¥7,650,800

GUARNERI, PIETRO (OF VENICE) [B11/129] Very Fine Italian Violin with later Italian scroll: Venice, 1729 (Rembert Wurlitzer, New York, March 24, 1953)   NS

GUASTALLA, DANTE & ALFREDO [S3/1] Violin w/case: Reggiolo Emiliano, 1926   4,860/6,480
$13,414   £8,280   DM24,095   ¥1,583,716

GUERRA, EVASIO EMILE [S3/28] Violin after an inlaid Stradivari, w/case: Turin, 1941 17,820/22,680
$14,904   £9,200   DM26,772   ¥1,759,684

GUERSAN, LOUIS [Bf10/8020] French Violin: c. 1746   5,000/8,000
$4,600   £2,760   DM8,280   ¥35,742

GUIDANTE, FLORENO (ascribed to) [Bf4/2831]
Good English Violin w/case   2,500/3,500
$2,645   £1,645   DM4,867   ¥311,978

GUILLAMI, JUAN [S11/252] Violin w/case:
Barcelona, c. 1760 (W.E. Hill & Sons, London,
November 22, 1944)   9,720/12,960
$14,531   £8,970   DM27,538   ¥1,534,498

GUINDON, H. [Sk11/279] American Violin w/case:
1973   200/300
$298   £184   DM562   ¥31,513

HARDIE, MATTHEW & SON [S3/98] Violin w/case,
cover: Edinburgh, 1822   4,050/5,670
$5,216   £3,220   DM9,370   ¥615,889

HARRIS, HENRY [Sk5/298] American Violin:
Mercer, Maine, 1893   800/1,200
$805   £491   DM1,457   ¥97,196

HARRIS, J.E. [Sk11/387] English Violin: Gateshead,
1924   10,000/12,000 NS

HART & SON [S3/27] Violin w/case: London, 1894
                                     2,430/3,240
$4,285   £2,645   DM7,697   ¥505,909

HART & SON [S6/274] Violin: London, 1899
                                     1,590/2,385
$1,609   £1,012   DM3,026   ¥194,547

HAWKES & SON [B2/117] Violin: 1893   656/984
$943   £575   DM1,627   ¥107,617

HEBERLEIN, ALBERT (JR.) [Bf4/2825] Good
Violin w/case, 2 bows: Markneukirchen, c. 1920
                                     1,500/2,250
$3,306   £2,056   DM6,084   ¥389,972

HEBERLEIN, ALBERT AUGUST (JR.) [C3/127]
German Violin w/case: 1915   1,304/1,956
$1,874   £1,150   DM3,324   ¥221,640

HEBERLEIN FAMILY (MEMBER OF) [S11/365]
Child's Violin w/child's violin, case: Markneukirchen,
1913   1,620/2,430 NS

HEINICKE, MATHIAS [B11/123] Violin: Schönbach,
1907   3,240/4,860
$3,353   £2,070   DM6,314   ¥354,425

HEL, JOSEPH [B11/151] Fine Violin: Lille, 1885
                                    12,960/19,440
$13,041   £8,050   DM24,553   ¥1,378,321

HEL, JOSEPH [C3/113] French Violin w/case: Lille,
1896   4,890/6,520
$5,249   £3,220   DM9,306   ¥620,591

HEL, JOSEPH [P3/103] Fine and Handsome French
Violin with post repair on the back: Lille, 1903
                                     3,240/4,050
$3,540   £2,185   DM6,337   ¥417,488

HEL, PIERRE [P6/49] Fine and Handsome French
Violin in immediate playing condition, w/case: Lille,
1903   8,855/9,660
$11,711   £7,274   DM21,967   ¥1,407,616

HEL, PIERRE JEAN HENRI [S11/250] Violin
w/case: Lille, 1920   9,720/12,960
$15,836   £9,775   DM30,009   ¥1,672,209

HELLMER, JOHANN GEORG (attributed to)
[P3/55] Violin in good condition, w/case: c. 1760
                                     6,480/7,290 NS

HELLMER, JOHANN GEORG (attributed to)
[P5/34] Violin in immediate playing condition,
w/case: c. 1760   2,445/2,934
$3,187   £1,955   DM5,767   ¥384,529

HENRY, CHARLES [S6/86] Violin w/case: Paris,
1835   6,360/7,950 NS

HEYLIGERS, MATHIJS [C3/97] Violin (maker's,
Cremona, December 10, 1987)   4,075/4,890 NS

HILL, JOSEPH [Sk5/47] Eighteenth-Century English
Violin: London   2,000/2,500
$3,565   £2,175   DM6,453   ¥430,438

HILL, W.E. & SONS [P3/64] Good Violin in good
condition: London, 1912   5,670/6,480
$5,962   £3,680   DM10,672   ¥703,138

HILL, W.E. & SONS [P11/75] Fine and Handsome
Violin in immediate playing condition: London, 1885
                                     7,290/8,100
$9,855   £6,084   DM18,719   ¥1,035,473

HILL, W.E. & SONS [S11/145] Violin after the
"Messiah" Stradivari: London, 1900   9,720/12,960
$16,767   £10,350   DM31,775   ¥1,770,575

HILL, W.E. & SONS (workshop of) [P11/46] Violin
with minor table restoration, w/case: London, 1913
                                     1,296/1,458
$2,251   £1,389   DM4,275   ¥236,456

HJORTH, A. [B11/150] Danish Violin: Copenhagen,
1819   3,240/4,860 NS

HOFFMANN, EDUARD [Sk11/276] American
Violin w/case, bow: Philadelphia, 1933 1,200/1,400
$1,058   £655   DM1,997   ¥111,936

HOFMANN, G. WILLIAM [P11/84] Fine and
Handsome Violin in immediate playing condition:
Dublin, 1926   1,620/2,430
$3,214   £1,984   DM6,104   ¥337,654

HORNSTEINER [B2/123] Violin: c. 1800   492/820
$490   £299   DM846   ¥55,961

HUDSON, GEORGE WULME [B11/133] Violin:
London, 1927   4,860/8,100
$8,942   £5,520   DM16,836   ¥945,134

HUDSON, GEORGE WULME [Sk5/67] Good
English Violin: London   5,000/7,000
$9,200   £5,612   DM16,652   ¥1,110,808

HUMBERT [P9/80] Mirecourt Violin in good condition: c. 1930   810/891
$1,211   £748   DM2,280   ¥129,093

HURE, HARRY [Sk5/373] American Violin:
Brooklyn, 1921   1,200/1,400 NS

HURE, HARRY [Sk11/222] American Violin:
Brooklyn, 1921   800/1,200
$794   £491   DM1,498   ¥83,952

JACOBS, HENDRIK [C3/151] Fine Dutch Violin
w/case (Lyon & Healy)   22,820/29,340
$24,369   £14,950   DM43,206   ¥2,881,314

JACOBS, HENDRIK [P6/43] Violin in immediate
playing condition, w/case: Amsterdam 12,880/14,490
$17,460   £10,845   DM32,750   ¥2,098,628

JACOBS, HENDRIK [Sk5/68] Dutch Violin:
Amsterdam, c.1690   6,000/8,000
$11,500   £7,015   DM20,815   ¥1,388,510

JACQUOT, CHARLES [P3/78] French Violin with
restored blemishes, w/case: Nancy, 1838 3,564/4,536
$3,726   £2,300   DM6,670   ¥439,461

JACQUOT, CHARLES [S6/178] Violin w/case, bow:
Paris, c. 1860   3,975/5,565
$4,571   £2,875   DM8,596   ¥552,690

JACQUOT, CHARLES [S11/361] Violin w/case, bow:
Paris, 1866   8,100/11,340
$8,942   £5,520   DM16,946   ¥944,306

JACQUOT, FERNAND [Bf10/8037] Good French
Violin: Nancy, 1914   3,000/4,000
$5,175   £3,105   DM9,315   ¥40,210

JAY, HENRY (ascribed to) [P3/97] English Violin
with restorable blemishes: London, c.1760
                                     1,944/2,268
$2,702   £1,668   DM4,837   ¥318,705

JOHNSON, JOHN [B11/111] Fine Violin: London,
1759   6,480/9,720
$5,962   £3,680   DM11,224   ¥630,090

JOMBAR, PAUL [S11/236] Violin: Paris, c. 1920
                                     4,860/6,480 NS

JUZEK, JOHN (workshop of) [Sk5/358] Czech Violin
w/case   200/300
$431   £263   DM781   ¥52,069

KAGANSKY, VALERY [S11M/87] Violin: New York,
1987   2,426/4,043
$2,994   £1,852   DM5,675   ¥316,736

KAUL, PAUL [P6/55] Fine and Handsome French
Violin in immediate playing condition
                                     8,050/9,660 NS

KAUL, PAUL [P11/107] Fine and Handsome French
Violin in immediate playing condition 6,480/8,100
$8,998   £5,555   DM17,091   ¥945,431

KAUL, PAUL [S11M/30] Violin: Paris, 1933
                                     6,468/9,702
$8,554   £5,290   DM16,214   ¥904,960

KENNEDY, THOMAS [P3/88] Good English Violin:
London, 1813   8,100/8,910 NS

KENNEDY, THOMAS [S3/32] Violin w/case, bow:
London, 1813 (Violinateljé Gefle, Gävle, April 16,
1997)   8,100/11,340 NS

KENNEDY, THOMAS [S11/137] Violin w/case:
London, c. 1850   4,860/8,100
$5,962   £3,680   DM11,298   ¥629,538

KENNEDY, THOMAS (attributed to) [P6/62] Good
English Violin in immediate playing condition,
w/case: London, c. 1860   2,415/3,220 NS

KENNEDY, THOMAS (attributed to) [P9/25] Good
English Violin in immediate playing condition,
w/case: London, c. 1860   1,458/1,539
$2,236   £1,380   DM4,209   ¥238,326

KLOTZ, AEGIDIUS (I) (attributed to) [C3/90]
German Violin   3,260/4,890
$3,374   £2,070   DM5,982   ¥398,951

KLOTZ, AEGIDIUS (II) [Bf10/8028] Fine Bavarian
Violin: Mittenwald, 1799   4,000/6,000 NS

KLOTZ, AEGIDIUS (II) [Sk5/51] Mittenwald Violin
w/case, bow: 1770   2,500/3,500
$2,530   £1,543   DM4,579   ¥305,472

KLOTZ, AEGIDIUS (II) (attributed to) [Bf10/8022]
Fine Bohemian Violin w/case: c. 1770
                                     3,000/5,000 NS

KLOTZ, GEORG (II) [S3/127] Violin w/case, silver
bow: Mittenwald, 1764   5,670/7,290 NS

KLOTZ, GEORG (II) [S11/146] Violin w/case, cover,
2 bows: Mittenwald, 1773 (Kenneth Warren & Son,
Ltd., Chicago, February 14, 1980)   4,050/5,670 NS

KLOTZ, GEORG (II) [S11/379] Violin with possibly
later head, w/case, bow: Mittenwald, 1764
                                     4,050/5,670 NS

KLOTZ, GEORG (II) [S11M/98] Violin: Mittenwald,
1790   6,468/9,702
$19,246   £11,903   DM36,481   ¥2,036,161

KLOTZ, JOHANN CARL [B6/109] German Violin
                                     2,385/3,180 NS

KLOTZ, JOSEPH [B3/93A] German Violin:
Mittenwald, C. 1790   5,670/8,100
$6,521   £4,025   DM11,713   ¥769,862

KLOTZ, JOSEPH [S11/368] Violin: Mittenwald,
c. 1790   3,240/4,860 NS

KLOTZ, MICHAEL [B11/128] Violin: c. 1780
                                     6,480/9,720 NS

KLOTZ, SEBASTIAN [B11/168] Violin: Mittenwald,
1763   4,860/8,100
$27,945   £17,250   DM52,613   ¥2,953,545

KLOTZ, SEBASTIAN [S6/49] Violin w/case:
Mittenwald, 1751 (L.P. Balmforth & Son, Leeds,
September 10, 1955)   3,975/5,565 NS

KLOTZ, SEBASTIAN [S11/352] Violin: Mittenwald,
c. 1750   2,916/4,050 NS

KLOTZ FAMILY (MEMBER OF) [B2/96] Violin
                                     1,312/1,968 NS

KLOTZ FAMILY (MEMBER OF) [C3/71] German
Violin   1,467/1,956 NS

KLOTZ FAMILY (MEMBER OF) [C11/258]
Mittenwald Violin w/case, bow   2,430/4,050
$2,608   £1,610   DM4,911   ¥275,664

KLOTZ FAMILY (MEMBER OF) [Sk11/337] Violin
w/case: Mittenwald, 18th C.   1,200/1,400
$1,323   £819   DM2,496   ¥139,921

KNOPF, W. [B11/34] Silver Violin   1,296/1,944
$1,397   £863   DM2,631   ¥147,677

KNORR, ALBERT [Sk5/35] German Violin w/case, bow 600/800
$1,495   £912   DM2,706   ¥180,506

KOCH, FRANZ JOSEPH [P9/21] Good German Violin in immediate playing condition, w/case, 2 bows
1,620/2,430
$2,608   £1,610   DM4,911   ¥278,047

KONYA, ISTVAN [S6/275] Violin: Tatabanya, 1971
954/1,272 NS

KRELL, ALBERT [Sk11/309] American Violin w/case: Cincinnati, c. 1875   1,000/1,200 NS

KRINER, HANS B. [Sk5/294] Mittenwald Violin: 1954   1,000/1,500
$1,380   £842   DM2,498   ¥166,621

KRUMBHOLZ, LORENZ [C3/109] Dutch Violin w/case: 1942   1,304/1,956
$1,687   £1,035   DM2,991   ¥199,476

KRUMBHOLZ, LORENZ [C3/143] Dutch Violin w/case: The Hague, 1940   3,260/4,890 NS

KRUMBHOLZ, LORENZ [C11/32] Dutch Violin w/case   2,916/3,564
$5,216   £3,220   DM9,821   ¥551,328

KUCHARSKI, B. [Sk11/342] American Violin: Mission, Texas, 1946   2,000/4,000 NS

KULIK, JOHANN [P6/37] Violin in immediate playing condition, w/case: Prague, c. 1860   4,025/4,830
$5,323   £3,306   DM9,985   ¥639,826

KULIK, JOHANN [P11/106] Good Violin in immediate playing condition, w/case: Prague, 1835 (Vladimir Pilar, Czech Republic, September 23, 1997)
3,240/4,860
$4,071   £2,513   DM7,732   ¥427,695

KUNTZE-FECHNER, MARTIN [B11/158] German Violin: Brussels, 1910   3,240/4,860
$7,452   £4,600   DM14,030   ¥787,612

KUNZE, WILHELM PAUL [P9/67] Violin in good condition   1,296/1,458 NS

KUNZE, WILHELM PAUL [P11/51] Violin in good condition   486/648
$1,179   £728   DM2,240   ¥123,904

KUNZE, WILHELM PAUL [S11/385] Violin: The Hague, 1923   4,050/5,670
$4,658   £2,875   DM8,826   ¥491,826

LABERTE [P9/180] Good French Violin in immediate playing condition, w/case, 2 bows: c. 1900
648/810 NS

LABERTE, MARC (workshop of) [Sk11/305] French Violin: Mirecourt, c. 1920   2,000/2,500
$2,645   £1,637   DM4,992   ¥279,841

LABERTE-HUMBERT BROS. [C3/114] French Violin w/case, 2 bows: Mirecourt, 1924   978/1,304
$1,312   £805   DM2,326   ¥155,148

LABERTE-HUMBERT BROS. [P5/24] Mirecourt Violin in good condition: c. 1930   1,141/1,304 NS

LABERTE-MAGNIE [P5/65] Good Mirecourt Violin in good condition: c. 1930   1,141/1,304 NS

LAJOS, KONYA [P3/46] Good Contemporary Violin in good condition, w/case: Tatabanya, Hungary, 1996 (maker's, September 1997)   1,944/2,430 NS

LAMBERT [B6/82] Fine French Violin: Paris, c. 1770
4,770/7,950
$4,754   £2,990   DM9,000   ¥569,864

LANDOLFI, CARLO FERDINANDO [Sk5/77] Interesting Violin w/case (William Lewis & Son, Lincolnwood, June 29, 1971)   12,000/14,000
$13,800   £8,418   DM24,978   ¥1,666,212

LANDOLFI, PIETRO ANTONIO [Bf10/8033] Fine Italian Violin w/case, bow: Milan, c. 1755 (O.H. Bryant, September 29, 1936)   25,000/35,000 NS

LANGONET, EUGENE [Sk11/343] French Violin: Nantes, 1927   2,000/3,000
$3,703   £2,292   DM6,989   ¥391,777

LANTNER, FERDINAND MARTIN [P6/88] Good Violin in good condition: Prague, c. 1880
1,288/1,610
$1,235   £767   DM2,316   ¥148,440

LARCHER, JEAN (attributed to) [P5/4] French Violin of quality: 1930   978/1,141 NS

LARCHER, JEAN (attributed to) [P9/73] French Violin   810/972 NS

LASSI, FRANCESCO [S6/282] Violin: Faenza, 1942
2,226/2,862
$2,194   £1,380   DM4,126   ¥265,291

LAURENT, EMILE [Sk5/42] Belgian Violin w/case: Brussels, 1904   5,500/6,500 NS

LECCI, G. (attributed to) [B6/68] Good Violin: Genova   7,155/10,335 NS

LECHI [B5/100] Violin   820/1,312
$754   £460   DM1,371   ¥91,075

LECHLEITNER, CHRISTIAN (attributed to) [P11/89] Violin with some old restorations: 1794
1,944/2,430
$2,571   £1,587   DM4,883   ¥270,123

LEIDOLFF, JOHANN CHRISTOPH [Sk11/307] Violin w/case, bow: Vienna, 1757   2,500/2,800 NS

LEONORI, PAOLO [B11/183] Violin: Rome, 1982
3,240/4,860
$5,962   £3,680   DM11,224   ¥630,090

LONDERO, RAFFAELE [P3/93] Good Modern Italian Violin in good condition, w/case: Tortona, 1951 (André Levi, Paris, March 5, 1990)
9,720/10,530 NS

LONGIARU, GIOVANNI [Sk11/64] Good Modern Violin: New York, 1925   2,500/3,500
$3,042   £1,883   DM5,741   ¥321,817

LONGMAN [B2/134] Violin   328/492
$245   £150   DM423   ¥27,980

LONGMAN & BRODERIP [P2/163] English Violin with original neck lengthened from the block: London, c. 1790   815/978
$3,281   £2,013   DM5,737   ¥387,603

LORENZ FAMILY (attributed to) [P2/52] German Violin in good condition: Klingenthal, c. 1870
1,304/1,467 NS

LOTT, JOHN FREDERICK (PERE) (attributed to) [P11/58] English Violin with restored blemishes: London, c. 1820   2,430/2,916
$3,856   £2,381   DM7,325   ¥405,185

LOWENDALL, LOUIS [P2/203] Violin in good condition, w/case, bow: Berlin, c. 1900   489/652
$525   £322   DM918   ¥62,001

LOWENDALL, LOUIS (workshop of) [C11/257] German Violin   972/1,296
$1,118   £690   DM2,105   ¥118,142

LUCCA, ANTONIO [B11/165] Violin: 1919
4,860/8,100
$5,216   £3,220   DM9,821   ¥551,328

LUCCI, GIUSEPPE [Sk5/65] Modern Italian Violin: Rome, 1979   12,000/14,000
$10,925   £6,664   DM19,774   ¥1,319,085

LUFF, WILLIAM H. [P11/26] Good Violin in immediate playing condition: London, 1989   3,240/4,050
$5,142   £3,174   DM9,766   ¥540,247

LUFF, WILLIAM H. [S11/238] Violin w/case: London, 1992   2,916/4,050
$3,167   £1,955   DM6,002   ¥334,442

LUPOT, NICOLAS [P6/50] French Violin in immediate playing condition, w/case: Orleans, c. 1790
4,025/4,830
$31,938   £19,838   DM59,909   ¥3,838,953

LUPOT, NICOLAS [S6/272] Violin w/case: Paris, 1798   87,450/111,300 NS

LUPOT, NICOLAS [S11/157] Violin w/case: Paris, 1798   64,800/97,200 NS

LUPOT, NICOLAS (attributed to) [C3/159] Fine French Violin w/case (Max Möller, Amsterdam, April 3, 1939)   24,450/29,340 NS

LUPOT, NICOLAS (attributed to) [P11/86] French Violin in immediate playing condition, w/case: c. 1820 (Max Möller, Antwerp, April 3, 1939)
19,440/24,300 NS

LUTHER, ANDREAS [Sk11/324] Tyrolean Violin w/case: 1920   600/800 NS

LUTZ, LOUIS (attributed to) [P11/47] French Violin with old table repairs, now in playing condition: Paris, 1896   810/972 NS

LYON, U. [C11/246] American Violin   648/972 NS

MALAGUTI, ERMINIO [Sk11/355] Modern Italian Violin: Milan, 1957   2,600/2,800
$3,439   £2,128   DM6,490   ¥363,793

MALINE FAMILY (MEMBER OF) [Sk11/79] French Violin: Mirecourt, c. 1870   3,000/3,500 NS

MANGENOT, PAUL [B3/58] Violin 2,430/4,050 NS

MANGENOT, PAUL [B5/121] Violin   1,312/1,968
$1,603   £978   DM2,913   ¥193,535

MANGENOT, PAUL [C11/88] Violin   1,620/1,944
$2,608   £1,610   DM4,911   ¥275,664

MANGENOT, PAUL [C11/230] French Violin
810/972
$1,304   £805   DM2,455   ¥137,832

MARCHAND, EUGENE [C3/139] French Violin w/case: Paris, 1912   6,520/9,780
$7,123   £4,370   DM12,629   ¥842,230

MARCHETTI, ENRICO [S3/16] Violin: Turin, c. 1890 (L.P. Balmforth & Son, Leeds, March 10, 1952)   16,200/24,300
$17,699   £10,925   DM31,792   ¥2,089,625

MARCHETTI, ENRICO [Sk5/106] Italian Violin w/case: Turin, 1927   4,000/5,000
$5,290   £3,227   DM9,575   ¥638,715

MARDULA, FRANCISZEK & STANISLAW [Sk5/287] Polish Violin w/case: Zakopane, 1989
800/1,200
$690   £421   DM1,249   ¥83,311

MARIANI, ANTONIO [S6/273] Violin: Pesaro, 1669 (Dario D'Attili, New Jersey, October 22, 1991)
23,850/31,800 NS

MARISSAL, O. (workshop of) [P9/82] Good French Violin in good condition, w/violin: 1934   648/729
$969   £598   DM1,824   ¥103,275

MARISSAL, OLIVIER [P5/8] Good French Violin in good condition, w/violin: 1934   978/1,141 NS

MAST, JEAN LAURENT (attributed to) [P3/27] Violin or Small Viola with original neck: c. 1770
972/1,134 NS

MAST, JOSEPH LAURENT [S3/112] Violin: France, early 19th C.   1,296/1,944 NS

MAST, JOSEPH LAURENT [S11/246] Violin w/bow by James Tubbs: France, early 19th C.   1,134/1,620
$1,118   £690   DM2,118   ¥118,038

MAUCOTEL, CHARLES [C11/75] Good English Violin w/case: London, 1858   8,910/10,530 NS

MAUCOTEL, CHARLES [S3/90] Violin w/case: mid 19th C. (W.E. Hill & Sons, London, January 18, 1948)   12,960/16,200
$13,041   £8,050   DM23,426   ¥1,539,724

MAUCOTEL, CHARLES [S6/177] Violin after Guarneri del Gesù, w/case: London, 1858
9,540/12,720 NS

MAYSON, WALTER H. [Sk11/251] English Violin w/case, bow: Manchester, 1878   1,400/1,600
$1,719   £1,064   DM3,245   ¥181,897

MELZL, JOHANN GEORG [S3/110] Violin w/case, 2 bows: Straubing, 1855   405/567
$1,024   £632   DM1,839   ¥120,883

MENNESSON, EMILE (attributed to) [P9/18] Good French Violin in immediate playing condition
1,458/1,620
$1,770   £1,093   DM3,332   ¥188,675

MERMILLOT, MAURICE [B11/108] Fine French
Violin: Paris, 1884   8,100/11,340
$8,942   £5,520   DM16,836   ¥945,134

MERMILLOT, MAURICE [Bf4/2802] Good French
Violin: Paris, 1882   4,000/6,000 NS

MERMILLOT, MAURICE [C11/183] French Violin:
1896   12,960/16,200
$11,178   £6,900   DM21,045   ¥1,181,418

MERMILLOT, MAURICE [S11/374] Violin: Paris,
1900   4,860/6,480 NS

MESSON, E. [C11/38] French Violin   1,620/2,430
$1,677   £1,035   DM3,157   ¥177,213

MICELLI, CARLO [Bf10/8099] Violin w/case: 1920
                                                400/600
$230   £138   DM414   ¥1,787

MILLANT, ROGER & MAX [Bf4/2807] Fine French
Violin: Paris, 1960   6,500/8,000 NS

MILTON, LOUIS [P11/246] Good Violin in good
condition, w/case, bow: Bedford, England, 1925
                                             972/1,134
$2,142   £1,323   DM4,069   ¥225,103

MIREMONT, CLAUDE AUGUSTIN [B3/114] Fine
French Violin: Paris, 1872   12,960/16,200 NS

MIREMONT, CLAUDE AUGUSTIN [S6/45] Violin
w/case: Paris, 1874   3,975/5,565
$8,228   £5,175   DM15,473   ¥994,842

MIREMONT, CLAUDE AUGUSTIN [S11/241]
Violin after Guarneri del Gesù, w/case, 2 bows: Paris,
1872   9,720/12,960 NS

MIREMONT, CLAUDE AUGUSTIN [Sk11/60]
French Violin w/case: Paris, 1874   12,000/15,000
$17,193   £10,642   DM32,451   ¥1,818,967

MODAUDO, G. [B11/177] Violin: Catania, 1920
                                          2,430/3,240 NS

MOINEL & CHERPITEL [S3/11] Violin: Paris, 1929
                                             3,564/4,536
$3,726   £2,300   DM6,693   ¥439,921

MONTAGNANA, DOMENICO [B3/90] Very Fine
and Important Violin: Venice, 1742 (Max Möller,
Amsterdam)   356,400/421,200 NS

MONZANI (attributed to) [B3/99] Violin
                                          2,430/3,240 NS

MONZANI (attributed to) [B6/86] Violin
                                          1,590/2,385 NS

MOUGENOT, GEORGES [C3/106] French Violin
w/case: 1928   2,445/3,260
$2,812   £1,725   DM4,985   ¥332,459

MOUGENOT, GEORGES [S6/82] Violin: Brussels,
1891   3,975/5,565
$4,388   £2,760   DM8,252   ¥530,582

MOUGENOT, LEON [B3/78] French Violin:
Mirecourt   2,430/3,240
$2,422   £1,495   DM4,350   ¥285,949

MOUGENOT, LEON [C3/83] French Violin w/case
                                          2,445/3,260 NS

MOUGENOT, LEON (attributed to) [P5/21] Violin
in good condition: 1912   1,304/1,467
$2,062   £1,265   DM3,732   ¥248,813

MOUGENOT, LEON (attributed to) [P9/69] Violin
                                                648/810
$932   £575   DM1,754   ¥99,303

MOYA, HIDALGO [P11/55] Violin in immediate
playing condition, w/case, 1916 edition of *Violin
Tone and Violin Makers*: 1919   1,944/2,430
$2,999   £1,852   DM5,697   ¥315,144

MOZZANI, LUIGI [B3/89] Violin: 1921
                                          6,480/9,720 NS

MOZZANI, LUIGI [S6/71] Violin w/case: Pieve di
Cento, 1916   4,770/6,360 NS

MOZZANI, LUIGI [S11/143] Violin w/case, cover:
Cento, 1917   3,240/4,860
$7,452   £4,600   DM14,122   ¥786,922

MUTTI, VITTORIO [Bf4/2824] Italian Violin w/case:
Mantua, c. 1940   1,500/2,000 NS

NEUDORFER, ALFRED [C3/193] Bohemian Violin
w/case   1,630/1,956
$1,218   £747   DM2,159   ¥143,969

NEUNER, MATHIAS [C11/180] Mittenwald Violin
w/case   1,296/1,944
$2,236   £1,380   DM4,209   ¥236,284

NEUNER & HORNSTEINER [P2/78] Good Violin
in good condition: Mittenwald, c. 1880   652/815
$975   £598   DM1,704   ¥115,145

NEUNER & HORNSTEINER [P2/144] Violin with
minor restorable blemishes: Mittenwald, c. 1880
                                                652/815
$750   £460   DM1,311   ¥88,573

NEUNER & HORNSTEINER [P2/147] Small-Size
Violin with minor bass-bar and rib repair:
Mittenwald, c. 1880   652/815 NS

NEUNER & HORNSTEINER [P2/150] Violin with
pegbox requiring restoration: Mittenwald, c. 1870
                                                652/815 NS

NEUNER & HORNSTEINER [P3/212] Good Small-
Size Violin: Mittenwald, c. 1880   648/729
$857   £529   DM1,534   ¥101,076

NEUNER & HORNSTEINER [P3/220] Good Violin
with three minor table cracks: Mittenwald, c. 1900
                                                648/810
$373   £230   DM667   ¥43,946

NEUNER & HORNSTEINER [P5/135] Small-Size
Mittenwald Violin with minor bass-bar and rib repair,
w/violin by same makers: c. 1880   489/652
$562   £345   DM1,018   ¥67,858

NEUNER & HORNSTEINER [P11/38] Good Violin
in immediate playing condition, w/case, bow:
Mittenwald, 1890   810/972
$1,671   £1,032   DM3,174   ¥175,580

NEUNER & HORNSTEINER [S11M/28] Violin:
Mittenwald, c. 1890   647/970
$4,919   £3,042   DM9,323   ¥520,352

NICOLAS [P11/34] Good French Violin in good condition: c. 1790   1,620/1,944
$2,999   £1,852   DM5,697   ¥315,144

NICOLAS, DIDIER (L'AINE) [B11/104] Violin
1,620/2,430 NS

NICOLAS, DIDIER (L'AINE) [C3/74] French Violin
w/case   1,956/2,934
$2,249   £1,380   DM3,988   ¥265,967

NICOLAS, DIDIER (L'AINE) [C3/84] French Violin
w/case, bow (W.E. Hill & Sons, London, January 6,
1930)   3,260/4,890 NS

NICOLAS, DIDIER (L'AINE) [C3/118] French Violin
(Jean-Jacques Rampal, Paris, December 10, 1998)
2,282/2,934 NS

NICOLAS, DIDIER (L'AINE) [C11/232] French
Violin w/case   972/1,296
$1,304   £805   DM2,455   ¥137,832

NICOLAS, DIDIER (L'AINE) [P3/39] Good French
Violin with well-restored old worm blemishes, w/case:
Mirecourt, c. 1790   810/891
$1,118   £690   DM2,001   ¥131,838

NICOLAS, DIDIER (L'AINE) [S3/101] Violin
w/another violin: Mirecourt, c. 1820   2,592/3,888 NS

NICOLAS, DIDIER (L'AINE) [Sk5/49] Good French
Violin w/case: Mirecourt, c. 1800   3,000/4,000
$4,888   £2,981   DM8,846   ¥590,117

NOEBE, LOUIS [P11/120] Good German Violin in
immediate playing condition, w/case: 1893
1,620/2,430
$2,785   £1,719   DM5,290   ¥292,634

NOSEK, VACLAV [Bf10/8029] Good Violin: Trest,
Czechoslovakia, c. 1940   3,000/4,000 NS

ODDONE, CARLO GIUSEPPE (ascribed to) [P3/74]
Violin with minor restorable blemishes: c. 1900
4,050/4,860 NS

OLIVIER & BISCH (attributed to) [P5/62] French
Violin in good condition: c. 1920   489/652
$525   £322   DM950   ¥63,334

OMOND, JAMES [P11/116] Violin in immediate
playing condition: Stromness, Scotland, 1905
2,430/2,916 NS

ORNATI, GIUSEPPE [B11/138] Very Fine Violin:
Milan, 1920   29,160/40,500
$40,986   £25,300   DM77,165   ¥4,331,866

ORNATI, GIUSEPPE [S6/179] Violin: Milan, c. 1920
(Jacques Français, New York, November 13, 1998)
28,620/39,750 NS

OTTO, CARL AUGUST [Sk5/370] German Violin
w/case, 2 bows: Ludwigslust, 1856   2,000/3,000
$2,645   £1,613   DM4,787   ¥319,357

PAJEOT (FILS) (workshop of) [C11/231] French
Violin   810/1,134
$932   £575   DM1,754   ¥98,452

PANORMO, JOSEPH [B11/142] Very Fine and Rare
Violin: London, 1808 (P. Biddulph, London, 1999)
24,300/32,400
$40,986   £25,300   DM77,165   ¥4,331,866

PANORMO, VINCENZO (attributed to) [B6/83]
Violin   7,155/10,335 NS

PARKER, DANIEL [S6/68] Violin w/bow
12,720/15,900
$13,714   £8,625   DM25,789   ¥1,658,070

PARMEGGIANI, ROMOLA [B11/143] Violin
9,720/12,960 NS

PAWLIKOWSKI, JAN [Bf10/8052] Modern Violin
w/case, bow: Krakow, 1985   2,000/2,500
$1,725   £1,035   DM3,105   ¥13,403

PEDRAZZINI, GIUSEPPE [B3/96] Violin: Milan,
1910 (W.E. Hill & Sons)   29,160/40,500 NS

PEDRAZZINI, GIUSEPPE [B3/102] Very Fine Violin:
Milan, 1922 (Paul Voigt, 1968)   29,160/40,500
$31,671   £19,550   DM56,891   ¥3,739,329

PEDRAZZINI, GIUSEPPE [B11/117] Fine Violin:
Milan, 1925   29,160/40,500
$29,808   £18,400   DM56,120   ¥3,150,448

PEDRAZZINI, GIUSEPPE [P6/38] Good Italian
Violin in immediate playing condition, w/case, 2
bows: Milan, 1948   9,660/11,270
$12,775   £7,935   DM23,964   ¥1,535,581

PEDRAZZINI, GIUSEPPE [S3/21] Violin w/case:
Milan, 1914   29,160/40,500 NS

PEDRAZZINI, GIUSEPPE [S3/88] Violin w/case,
bow: Milan, 1915   32,400/48,600 NS

PEDRAZZINI, GIUSEPPE [S11/147] Violin w/case,
bow: Milan, 1915   25,920/32,400 NS

PEDRAZZINI, GIUSEPPE [S11/245] Violin w/double
case: Milan, 1920   16,200/24,300 NS

PELLACANI, GIUSEPPE [C11/171] Fine Modern
Italian Violin w/case: Mantua (Horacio Piñero, New
York, April 25, 1989)   19,440/22,680 NS

PELLACANI, GIUSEPPE (ascribed to) [S6/197]
Violin w/case: probably Italy, c. 1965 (Primavera-
Capellini, Cremona, April 1, 1996)   2,385/3,180 NS

PEROTTI, ENEA [B3/87] Violin: 1924
2,916/4,050 NS

PERRY, THOMAS [P3/107] Good Violin in good
condition, w/case, bow: Dublin, 1772 1,620/1,944 NS

PERRY, THOMAS [P5/45] Good Violin in immediate
playing condition, w/case, bow: Dublin, 1772
1,304/1,467
$1,219   £748   DM2,207   ¥147,124

PETERNELLA, JAGO [Sk5/53] Good Violin w/case:
1944   6,000/8,000 NS

PETERSON, P.A. [C11/178] American Violin:
Chicago, 1914   648/972 NS

PIEROTTE, JULES [C11/191] French Violin 648/972
$559   £345   DM1,052   ¥59,071

PILAT, PAUL [S11/159] Violin w/case, cover, bow:
Budapest, 1895   6,480/8,100
$6,707   £4,140   DM12,710   ¥708,230

PILAT, PAUL [Sk11/379] Good Hungarian Violin
w/case: Budapest   12,000/15,000
$11,903   £7,368   DM22,466   ¥1,259,285

PILLEMENT, FRANCOIS [P3/123] French Violin in
good condition: Mirecourt, c. 1800   972/1,134
$1,267   £782   DM2,268   ¥149,417

POGGI, ANSALDO (attributed to) [Bf10/8030]
Violin w/case   2,000/3,000
$1,725   £1,035   DM3,105   ¥13,403

POIROT, AINE [S3/111] Violin: Mirecourt, early
19th C.   1,944/2,592 NS

POLLASTRI, GAETANO (ascribed to) [S3/92] Violin
w/case, cover: c. 1950 (Giuseppe Lucci, Rome,
September 14, 1985)   16,200/22,680 NS

POLLASTRI, GAETANO (ascribed to) [S11/248]
Violin w/case, cover: Reggio Emilia or Lazio, c. 1950
(Giuseppe Lucci, Rome, September 14, 1985)
                                          6,480/9,720
$6,521   £4,025   DM12,357   ¥688,557

POLLASTRI, GAETANO (attributed to) [S11/161]
Violin w/case: Italy, mid 20th C.   9,720/12,960
$8,384   £5,175   DM15,887   ¥885,287

POSCH, ANTON [B11/114] Violin: Vienna, 1721
                                          4,860/6,480
$5,216   £3,220   DM9,821   ¥551,328

POSTACCHINI, ANDREA (attributed to) [S6/85]
Violin: North Italy, c. 1830   3,180/4,770
$4,388   £2,760   DM8,252   ¥530,582

POSTIGLIONE, VINCENZO [C11/39] Good
Modern Neapolitan Violin w/case: 1893
                                        25,920/32,400
$31,671   £19,550   DM59,628   ¥3,347,351

POSTIGLIONE, VINCENZO [S11/165] Violin
w/case, 2 bows: Naples, c. 1890   24,300/32,400 NS

POSTIGLIONE, VINCENZO [Sk5/54] Neapolitan
Violin: 1907   10,000/12,000
$10,350   £6,314   DM18,734   ¥1,249,659

POUZOL, EMILE (attributed to) [P11/29] French
Violin in good condition: 1921   972/1,296
$1,971   £1,217   DM3,744   ¥207,095

PRAGA, EUGENIO [B11/155] Very Fine Italian
Violin: Genoa, 1901   25,920/32,400
$48,438   £29,900   DM91,195   ¥5,119,478

PRIER, PETER PAUL [S11M/97] Violin: Salt Lake
City, 1986   4,851/6,468
$5,988   £3,703   DM11,350   ¥633,472

PROKOP, LADISLAV [P11/97] Fine and Handsome
Violin in immediate playing condition, w/case
                                          4,860/5,670
$6,856   £4,232   DM13,022   ¥720,329

PUGLISI, REALE [S11/153] Violin w/case, cover, 2
bows: Catania, 1913   4,860/6,480
$4,658   £2,875   DM8,826   ¥491,826

PYNE, GEORGE [B2/110] English Violin: London,
1917   3,280/4,920
$3,772   £2,300   DM6,509   ¥430,468

PYNE, GEORGE [B11/116] English Violin
                                        4,050/5,670 NS

PYNE, GEORGE [P3/41] Good English Violin in
immediate playing condition: London, 1891
                                        4,860/5,670 NS

PYNE, GEORGE [P5/27] Good English Violin in
immediate playing condition: London, 1891
                                        4,075/4,890 NS

PYNE, GEORGE [S3/93] Violin w/case: London,
1882   2,268/2,916
$2,236   £1,380   DM4,016   ¥263,953

QUAN, SHEN FEI ZHENG [S11M/27] Violin
w/case: Beijing, 1981   970/1,294
$2,138   £1,323   DM4,053   ¥226,240

RADIGHIERI, OTELLO [Sk5/107] Contemporary
Italian Violin: Modena, 1996   1,800/2,200
$2,185   £1,333   DM3,955   ¥263,817

RAMIREZ, MANUEL (ascribed to) [P3/56] Violin in
good condition, w/case: Madrid, c. 1910 4,860/5,670
$7,638   £4,715   DM13,674   ¥900,895

RAVIZZA, CARLO [Sk11/86] Modern Violin: Milan,
1958   2,500/3,500
$4,893   £3,029   DM9,236   ¥517,706

RAVIZZA, CARLO (attributed to) [P11/57] Italian
Violin in immediate playing condition: Milan, 1942
                                          3,240/4,050
$6,642   £4,100   DM12,615   ¥697,818

RICHARD, ALEXANDER [Sk11/311] American
Violin w/case, bow: Springfield, Massachusetts, 1906
                                        800/1,200 NS

RICHARDSON, ARTHUR [B11/160] English Violin:
Crediton, 1926   3,240/4,860
$5,216   £3,220   DM9,821   ¥551,328

RICHARDSON, ARTHUR [B11/173] English Violin:
Crediton, 1919   3,240/4,860
$6,521   £4,025   DM12,276   ¥689,161

RICHARDSON, ARTHUR [S6/55] Violin w/case:
Crediton, 1927   3,180/4,770
$3,474   £2,185   DM6,533   ¥420,044

RICHELME, ANTOINE MARIUS [P11/64] Good
French Violin in immediate playing condition, w/case,
2 bows: Marseille, 1870   3,240/4,050 NS

RIEGER, PAUL [C11/233] German Violin w/case,
bow   1,134/1,458
$1,677   £1,035   DM3,157   ¥177,213

ROBINSON, WILLIAM [B11/171] Violin: Liverpool,
1929   3,240/4,860 NS

ROBINSON, WILLIAM [P2/40] Good Violin in playing condition, w/case: Plumstead, London, 1956
                                          1,304/1,467
$1,500   £920   DM2,622   ¥177,146

ROBINSON, WILLIAM [P11/32] Violin in immediate playing condition, w/case: Plumstead, London, 1922   1,620/1,944
$1,714   £1,058   DM3,255   ¥180,082

ROBINSON, WILLIAM [Sk5/63] English Violin: London, 1928   2,500/3,500
$4,600   £2,806   DM8,326   ¥555,404

ROCCA, ENRICO (ascribed to) [B6/87] Interesting Violin   4,770/7,950 NS

ROCCA, JOSEPH [P11/127] Good Italian Violin in immediate playing condition: Turin, 1843   97,200/113,400
$238,464 £147,200   DM452,934   ¥25,054,912

ROCCA, JOSEPH (attributed to) [P11/134] Interesting Italian Violin in immediate playing condition, w/case: Turin, 1845   24,300/32,400
$25,709   £15,870   DM48,832   ¥2,701,233

ROCKWELL, JOSEPH H. [Sk5/168] American Violin w/case, bow: Providence, 1911   1,200/1,400 NS

ROCKWELL, JOSEPH H. [Sk11/296] American Violin w/case, bow: Providence, 1911   800/1,200 NS

ROMBOUTS, PIETER (attributed to) [P11/60] Good Dutch Violin in immediate Baroque playing condition, w/case: c. 1700   7,290/8,910 NS

ROTH, ERNST HEINRICH [P6/40] Fine and Handsome Violin in immediate playing condition: Markneukirchen, 1930   3,220/4,830
$6,388   £3,968   DM11,982   ¥767,791

ROTH, ERNST HEINRICH [Sk5/45] Good Violin w/case, 2 bows: Markneukirchen, 1924 1,800/2,200
$4,140   £2,525   DM7,493   ¥499,864

ROTH, ERNST HEINRICH [Sk11/238] German Violin w/case: 1925   1,800/2,200
$2,910   £1,801   DM5,492   ¥307,825

ROTH, ERNST HEINRICH [Sk11/382] Modern German Violin w/case: Neukirchen, 1925   4,000/6,000
$3,968   £2,456   DM7,489   ¥419,762

ROTH, ERNST HEINRICH (workshop of) [C11/241] German Violin   648/972
$1,118   £690   DM2,105   ¥118,142

ROTH & LEDERER [C3/270] German Violin
978/1,304 NS

ROTH & LEDERER [C11/239] German Violin
486/810 NS

ROUMEN, L.W. (attributed to) [P11/100] Violin in immediate Baroque playing condition, w/case: c. 1820   3,240/4,050
$4,285   £2,645   DM8,139   ¥450,205

ROVATTI, LUIGI [C11/172] Good Violin
4,536/5,184
$5,216   £3,220   DM9,821   ¥551,328

ROVESCALLI, A. [B11/176] Violin: Milan, 1920
6,480/9,720
$5,589   £3,450   DM10,523   ¥590,709

RUGGIERI, FRANCESCO [S6/81] Violin with later head, w/case: Cremona, 1680   22,260/28,620 NS

RUGGIERI, FRANCESCO (ascribed to) [S11/363] Violin w/case, cover: North Italy, c. 1700 (Emil Herrmann, Berlin, September 1936)
40,500/56,700 NS

RUGGIERI, FRANCESCO (attributed to) [S3/89] Violin w/case, cover: North Italy, c. 1700 (Emil Herrmann, Berlin, September 1936)
61,560/72,900 NS

RUSHWORTH & DREAPER [B3/111A] English Violin: Liverpool, 1929   1,296/1,944
$2,608   £1,610   DM4,685   ¥307,945

RUZIEKA, JOSEPHUS (attributed to) [P11/43] Violin in immediate playing condition: Opava, 1913   810/972
$2,357   £1,455   DM4,476   ¥247,613

SALOMON [P6/53] Good French Violin in immediate playing condition: Paris, c. 1760   5,635/7,245
$6,388   £3,968   DM11,982   ¥767,791

SALOMON, JEAN BAPTISTE DESHAYES [S11/359] Violin: Paris, c. 1760 (Colin Nicholls, Northolt, July 8, 1999)   8,100/11,340 NS

SALSEDO, LUIGI [S6/52] Violin w/case: Italy, c. 1925   3,180/4,770
$2,743   £1,725   DM5,158   ¥331,614

SANNINO, VINCENZO [B11/103] Violin: Naples, 1901   29,160/40,500
$63,342 £39,100   DM119,255   ¥6,694,702

SANNINO, VINCENZO [Bf4/2821] Fine Italian Violin: c. 1927 (Kenneth Warren and Son, August 27, 1971)   25,000/30,000 NS

SANNINO, VINCENZO [Bf10/8048] Fine Italian Violin: c. 1927 (Kenneth Warren & Son, August 27, 1971)   20,000/25,000 NS

SANNINO, VINCENZO [C3/153] Good Italian Violin: Naples, 1911   32,600/40,750 NS

SANNINO, VINCENZO [S6/74] Violin after Ferdinand Gagliano, w/case: Naples, c. 1930 (Andreas Woywood, London, November 25, 1994)
28,620/34,980 NS

SANNINO, VINCENZO [Sk11/59] Fine Violin w/case: Naples, 1911   50,000/55,000 NS

SANNINO, VINCENZO [Sk11/75] Fine Neapolitan Violin: Naples, 1905   25,000/30,000
$29,095 £18,010   DM54,917   ¥3,078,251

SARFATI, GERARDO [S6/199] Violin: Mirecourt, c. 1935 (maker's)   2,385/3,180 NS

SCARAMPELLA, GIUSEPPE [B3/105] Very Fine and Rare Italian Violin after Guarneri del Gesù: Florence, 1884   40,500/56,700
$48,438 £29,900   DM87,009   ¥5,718,973

SCARAMPELLA, STEFANO [B3/63] Fine Violin: Mantua, 1903 (Hans Weisshaar) 48,600/64,800 NS

SCARAMPELLA, STEFANO [B6/84] Fine Violin: Mantua, 1903 (Peter Biddulph, London)
39,750/55,650
$40,227   £25,300   DM76,153   ¥4,821,927

SCARAMPELLA, STEFANO [S11/154] Child's Violin w/case, bow: Mantua, early 20th C.
6,480/9,720
$13,973   £8,625   DM26,479   ¥1,475,479

SCARAMPELLA, STEFANO (attributed to) [P11/63] Italian Violin in immediate playing condition, w/case: Mantua, 1899   3,240/4,860
$4,713   £2,910   DM8,953   ¥495,226

SCHMITT, LUCIEN [C11/83] Violin w/case: Grenoble, 1936   4,050/4,860
$4,658   £2,875   DM8,769   ¥492,258

SCHONFELDER, JOHANN GEORG [Sk5/57] Saxon Violin w/case: Neukirchen, c. 1780
1,400/1,600 NS

SCHONFELDER, JOHANN GEORG [Sk11/295] Saxon Violin w/case: Neukirchen, c. 1780   600/800
$1,058   £655   DM1,997   ¥111,936

SCHWAICHER, LEOPOLD (attributed to) [P9/70] Violin: c. 1800   1,053/1,134
$1,118   £690   DM2,105   ¥119,163

SCHWEITZER, JOHANN BAPTISTE (attributed to) [Bf4/2809] Violin w/case: c. 1830   1,200/1,800
$794   £494   DM1,460   ¥93,593

SEBASTIEN, JEAN [Bf10/8027] French Violin in need of some restoration   1,200/1,800 NS

SERAPHIN, SANTO [S3/104] Violin w/case: Venice, 1736 (J. & A. Beare, London, April 23, 1998)
81,000/113,400
$118,260   £73,000   DM212,430   ¥13,962,710

SERAPHIN, SANTO [S11M/100] Violin after the Amati brothers: Venice, 1739   113,190/161,700
$135,747   £83,950   DM257,307   ¥14,361,327

SERDET, PAUL [B11/98] Violin: Paris, 1902
3,240/4,860 NS

SERDET, PAUL [C3/148] French Violin: Paris, 1901 (Jean-Christophe Graff, Strasbourg, September 19, 1997)   6,520/9,780 NS

SGARABOTTO, GAETANO (attributed to) [Bf4/2814] Fine Violin w/case: Probably Milan, c. 1940   6,000/8,000
$11,241   £6,992   DM20,684   ¥1,325,905

SHEARER, THOMAS [Sk11/338] Scottish Violin: Backbrea Kilsyth, 1906   800/1,000
$661   £409   DM1,248   ¥69,960

SIEGA, ETTORE & SON [S11/163] Violin w/case: Venice, 1931   6,480/9,720
$7,825   £4,830   DM14,828   ¥826,268

SILVESTRE, HIPPOLYTE CHRETIEN [P11/133] Good French Violin in immediate playing condition, w/case: Lyon, 1877   12,150/13,770 NS

SILVESTRE, PIERRE [Bf10/8026] Fine French Violin w/case: Lyon, 1835   17,000/22,500
$9,775   £5,865   DM17,595   ¥75,952

SILVESTRE, PIERRE (attributed to) [Sk11/61] French Violin w/case (Jacques Français, New York, July 1977)   16,000/18,000
$26,450   £16,373   DM49,924   ¥2,798,410

SILVESTRE, PIERRE & HIPPOLYTE [S11/360] Violin after Guarneri del Gesù, w/case: Lyon, 1835
6,480/9,720
$7,825   £4,830   DM14,828   ¥826,268

SILVESTRE & MAUCOTEL [B11/161] Three-Quarter-Size Violin: Paris, 1910   3,240/4,860
$5,589   £3,450   DM10,523   ¥590,709

SILVESTRE & MAUCOTEL [S3/22] Violin w/case: Paris, 1903   6,480/9,720 NS

SIMONAZZI, AMADEO [P11/113] Good Italian Violin in immediate playing condition, w/case: 1955
6,480/7,290
$11,141   £6,877   DM21,161   ¥1,170,534

SIMONAZZI, AMADEO [S6/78] Violin w/case: Gualtieri, 1955   9,540/12,720 NS

SIMONIN, CHARLES [B3/98] Violin   3,240/4,860
$3,167   £1,955   DM5,689   ¥373,933

SIMONIN, CHARLES (attributed to) [P3/100] French Violin in immediate playing condition, w/case: c. 1850   6,480/7,290 NS

SMITH, BERT [S3/107] Violin w/case: Coniston, 1970   2,430/3,240
$2,236   £1,380   DM4,016   ¥263,953

SMITH, THOMAS (attributed to) [P2/32] English Violin in good condition, w/case: c. 1770
3,260/4,890
$3,936   £2,415   DM6,883   ¥465,008

SMITH, THOMAS (attributed to) [P6/18] English Violin: London, c. 1770   1,610/2,415
$2,129   £1,323   DM3,994   ¥255,930

SMITH, THOMAS (attributed to) [P6/31] English Violin in immediate Baroque playing condition: London, c. 1760   3,220/4,025 NS

SMITH, THOMAS (attributed to) [P9/35] English Violin in immediate Baroque playing condition: London, c. 1760   2,430/3,240
$1,863   £1,150   DM3,508   ¥198,605

SOFFRITTI, ETTORE [S3/97] Violin w/case: North Italy, c. 1920   19,440/25,920 NS

SPIDLEN, FRANTISEK F. [P11/98] Good Violin in immediate playing condition, w/case: Prague, 1913
5,670/6,480 NS

SPIDLEN, OTAKAR FRANTISEK [S6/44] Violin w/case: Prague, 1946   3,975/5,565
$6,948   £4,370   DM13,066   ¥840,089

SPIDLEN, PREMYSL OTAKAR [S3/113] Violin w/case, cover: Prague, 1955   4,050/5,670 NS

STADLMANN, JOHANN JOSEPH [S3/23] Violin w/case: Vienna, 1774   3,240/4,860
$3,726   £2,300   DM6,693   ¥439,921

STADLMANN, JOHANN JOSEPH (attributed to) [P2/59] Violin with old restorations back and front, w/case: Vienna 1,467/1,956 NS

STADLMANN, MICHAEL IGNAZ [B3/88] Violin: Vienna, c. 1790 4,860/8,100
$5,216 £3,220 DM9,370 ¥615,889

STEPHANINI [B3/107] Violin 12,960/19,440 NS

STEPHANINI [B6/97] Violin: Milan, 1948
9,540/12,720 NS

STIEBER, ERNST [C3/134] German Violin w/case: Markneukirchen, 1925 978/1,304
$2,812 £1,725 DM4,985 ¥332,459

STORIONI, LORENZO [S3/124] Violin w/case, cover, 2 bows: Cremona, c. 1790 64,800/81,000
$70,146 £43,300 DM126,003 ¥8,281,991

STRADIVARI, ANTONIO [S11/249] Violin with later 18th-C. Italian head, w/case, cover: Cremona, c. 1705 (Max Möller & Zoon, Amsterdam, June 23, 1962) 259,200/324,000 NS

STROBL, MICHAEL [S3/7] Violin w/case: Berlin, 1948 5,670/7,290 NS

SZEPESSY, BELA [Sk5/40] English Violin: London, 1902 7,000/9,000
$8,050 £4,911 DM14,571 ¥971,957

TENUCCI, EUGEN [S6/60] Violin: Zurich, 1930
3,180/3,975
$3,657 £2,300 DM6,877 ¥442,152

TERRANA, GERLANDO [B11/132] Violin: Naples, 1951 9,720/12,960 NS

TESTORE, CARLO ANTONIO [B3/101] Fine Violin: Milan, c. 1770 56,700/72,900
$65,205 £40,250 DM117,128 ¥7,698,618

TESTORE, CARLO ANTONIO [C3/162] Italian Violin with scroll by another hand (J. & A. Beare, London, December 18, 1998) 29,340/40,750
$31,866 £19,550 DM56,500 ¥3,767,872

TESTORE, CARLO ANTONIO [S11/370] Violin: Milan, c. 1735 (W.E. Hill & Sons, London, September 12, 1946) 22,680/29,160
$52,164 £32,200 DM98,854 ¥5,508,454

TESTORE, CARLO GIUSEPPE [S6/184] Violin, possibly composite, w/case: Milan, early 18th C.
28,620/39,750
$72,345 £45,500 DM136,045 ¥8,746,920

THIBOUVILLE-LAMY, J. [C11/201] Mirecourt Violin 486/648
$894 £552 DM1,684 ¥94,513

THIBOUVILLE-LAMY, J. [C11/204] Half-Size Violin
486/648
$1,118 £690 DM2,105 ¥118,142

THIBOUVILLE-LAMY, J. [P2/45] Good French Violin in good condition, w/case, 2 bows: Paris, c. 1900 978/1,141
$1,407 £863 DM2,460 ¥166,171

THIBOUVILLE-LAMY, J. [P2/73] Good French Violin in immediate playing condition: Paris, c. 1900
978/1,141 NS

THIBOUVILLE-LAMY, J. [P2/159] Good Violin in good condition, w/violin: Mirecourt, c. 1910
978/1,141
$1,125 £690 DM1,967 ¥132,860

THIBOUVILLE-LAMY, J. [P2/206] Violin in good condition: Mirecourt, c. 1900 326/408 NS

THIBOUVILLE-LAMY, J. [P2/214] Violin w/small-size violin: Mirecourt, c. 1900 163/326
$244 £150 DM428 ¥28,883

THIBOUVILLE-LAMY, J. [P3/213] Good Violin in good condition: Mirecourt, c. 1900 648/729
$745 £460 DM1,334 ¥87,892

THIBOUVILLE-LAMY, J. [P3/216] Good Violin in good condition: Mirecourt, c. 1900 810/891 NS

THIBOUVILLE-LAMY, J. [P3/226] Good French Violin in good condition, w/case: c. 1900
648/729 NS

THIBOUVILLE-LAMY, J. [P5/40] Good French Violin in immediate playing condition, w/case, 2 bows: c. 1910 978/1,304 NS

THIBOUVILLE-LAMY, J. [P5/66] Good French Violin in immediate playing condition: c. 1900
652/815 NS

THIBOUVILLE-LAMY, J. [P5/131] Mirecourt Violin in good condition, w/violin by same maker: c. 1900
815/978 NS

THIBOUVILLE-LAMY, J. [P5/167] Good French Violin in good condition, w/case: c. 1900 489/571
$657 £403 DM1,189 ¥79,266

THIBOUVILLE-LAMY, J. [P6/84] Good French Violin in immediate playing condition: c. 1900
966/1,127
$1,746 £1,084 DM3,275 ¥209,863

THIBOUVILLE-LAMY, J. [P6/158] Good French Violin in immediate playing condition: c. 1900
805/966
$1,235 £767 DM2,316 ¥148,440

THIBOUVILLE-LAMY, J. [P9/183] Good French Violin in immediate playing condition: Paris, c. 1900
648/810
$838 £518 DM1,578 ¥89,372

THIBOUVILLE-LAMY, J. [P9/231] Mirecourt Violin in good condition, w/violin: c. 1900 648/729
$838 £518 DM1,578 ¥89,372

THIBOUVILLE-LAMY, J. [P9/234] Mirecourt Violin in good condition: c. 1900 324/405
$373 £230 DM702 ¥39,721

THIBOUVILLE-LAMY, J. [P11/249] Violin in immediate playing condition, w/case: Mirecourt, c. 1900
810/972
$900 £555 DM1,709 ¥94,543

THIBOUVILLE-LAMY, J. [P11/250] French Violin in immediate playing condition: c. 1900 486/648
$751 £463 DM1,426 ¥78,884

THIBOUVILLE-LAMY, J. [P11/255] Good Mirecourt Violin in immediate playing condition: c. 1900
810/972
$1,028   £635   DM1,953   ¥108,049

THIBOUVILLE-LAMY, J. [P11/266] French Violin in good condition: c. 1900   486/567
$857   £529   DM1,628   ¥90,041

THIBOUVILLE-LAMY, J. [S3/29] Violin w/case, 2 bows: Mirecourt, c. 1900   1,296/1,944
$1,304   £805   DM2,343   ¥153,972

THIBOUVILLE-LAMY, J. [Sk5/371] French Violin
1,800/2,200 NS

THIBOUVILLE-LAMY, JEROME [S6/204] Child's Violin w/case, child's bow: Mirecourt, c. 1920
636/954 NS

THIR, JOHANN GEORG [B11/141] German Violin: Vienna, 1763   3,240/4,860
$3,353   £2,070   DM6,314   ¥354,425

THOMPSON, CHARLES & SAMUEL [C11/87] English Violin: London, 1783   1,944/2,268
$1,863   £1,150   DM3,508   ¥196,903

THOMPSON, CHARLES & SAMUEL [P2/176] English Violin with restorable blemishes: c. 1770
326/489
$337   £207   DM590   ¥39,858

THOUVENEL, CHARLES [P9/34] Mirecourt Violin: c. 1780   648/729
$559   £345   DM1,052   ¥59,581

TILLER, C.W. (attributed to) [P5/52] Violin in immediate playing condition, w/case, bow: Bournemouth, 1920   652/815
$450   £276   DM814   ¥54,286

TIMTONE [Sk5/293] American Violin: Baltimore, c. 1930   400/500
$1,150   £702   DM2,082   ¥138,851

TOBIN, RICHARD [S3/18] Violin w/case: London, c. 1820 (W.E. Hill & Sons, London, January 16, 1943)   11,340/16,200
$13,414   £8,280   DM24,095   ¥1,583,716

TOMASHOV, DANIEL [C3/133] Good Violin: Moscow, 1910   6,520/9,780 NS

TONONI, CARLO [S6/180] Violin: Venice, 1729 (Jacques Français, New York, November 13, 1998)
87,450/111,300
$51,198   £32,200   DM96,278   ¥6,190,128

TONONI, GIOVANNI [S6/87] Violin w/case, cover: Bologna, c. 1700 (W.E. Hill & Sons, London, May 5, 1920)   23,850/39,750
$43,884   £27,600   DM82,524   ¥5,305,824

TONONI, JOANNES (attributed to) [Sk5/177] Italian Violin w/case: Bologna, c. 1696 (Kenneth Warren & Son, Chicago, May 13, 1974)   8,000/12,000
$9,200   £5,612   DM16,652   ¥1,110,808

TRAPANI, RAFFAELE [P3/59] Fine, Handsome, and Rare Italian Violin in immediate playing condition, w/case: Naples, c. 1830   35,640/40,500
$35,397   £21,850   DM63,365   ¥4,174,880

TRAPP, HERMANN [Sk5/300] Bohemian Violin w/case, bow: Wildstein   800/1,200 NS

TRAUTNER, HANS [P9/28] Good German Violin with minor restorable blemishes, w/case, bow: Ansbach, 1928   1,944/2,430
$4,285   £2,645   DM8,067   ¥456,791

TURCSAK, TIBOR GABOR [S11M/90] Violin: Budapest, 1991   1,294/1,940
$2,780   £1,719   DM5,270   ¥294,112

VAN HOOF, ALPHONS [S3/19] Violin w/case, bow: Antwerp, 1928   4,860/8,100
$4,658   £2,875   DM8,366   ¥549,901

VAN HOOF, ALPHONS [S6/73] Violin w/case: Antwerp, 1929   5,565/7,155
$6,400   £4,025   DM12,035   ¥773,766

VATELOT, MARCEL [S11/140] Violin w/case: Paris, 1942   3,564/4,212 NS

VAUTRIN, JOSEPH [B11/130] Violin: Chaumont, 1933   2,430/4,050
$2,795   £1,725   DM5,261   ¥295,355

VAUTRIN, JOSEPH [S6/200] Violin: Chaumont, 1933   2,862/3,975 NS

VAVRA, JAN BAPTISTA [C3/77] Czech Violin w/case   3,260/4,075 NS

VENTAPANE, LORENZO [B3/83] Fine Violin: Naples, c. 1800 (Rene A. Morel)   48,600/64,800 NS

VENTAPANE, LORENZO [B6/102] Italian Violin: Naples, c. 1800 (Rene A. Morel)   39,750/47,700 NS

VENTAPANE, LORENZO [S6/264] Violin w/case: Naples, c. 1820 (L.P. Balmforth & Son, Leeds, July 24, 1948)   44,520/55,650
$51,198   £32,200   DM96,278   ¥6,190,128

VENTAPANE, LORENZO [S6/61] Violin w/case, 2 bows: Naples, 1820 (W.E. Hill & Sons, London, June 15, 1956)   23,850/31,800 NS

VENTURINI, LUCIANO [C3/107] Italian Violin: Venice, 1985   1,956/2,934 NS

VICKERS, J.E. [P2/188] Contemporary Violin in good condition, w/case   326/489
$375   £230   DM656   ¥44,287

VINACCIA, GENNARO [Sk11/62] Fine Violin: Naples, 1759   25,000/35,000
$31,740   £19,647   DM59,909   ¥3,358,092

VINCENT, ALFRED [B6/56] Violin   3,975/5,565
$4,571   £2,875   DM8,654   ¥547,946

VINCENT, ALFRED [P3/89] Good English Violin in good condition: London, c. 1930   4,050/4,860 NS

VINCENT, ALFRED [P3/90] Good English Violin in good condition: 1940   4,860/5,670
$5,030   £3,105   DM9,005   ¥593,272

VINCENT, ALFRED [P5/37] Good English Violin in immediate playing condition: London, c. 1930
3,260/4,075 NS

VINCENT, ALFRED [S3/14] Violin: London, 1927
3,240/4,860
$5,962   £3,680   DM10,709   ¥703,874

VINCENT, ALFRED [S6/72] Violin: London, 1924
3,180/4,770
$2,926   £1,840   DM5,502   ¥353,722

VINCENT, ALFRED [S11/346] Violin w/double case:
London, c. 1930   3,240/4,860
$4,844   £2,990   DM9,179   ¥511,499

VOIGT, ARNOLD [P2/156] Good Violin in good
condition, w/case, 2 bows: Markneukirchen, c. 1900
408/571
$1,012   £621   DM1,770   ¥119,574

VOIGT, JOHANN CHRISTIAN (II) [Sk5/38] Saxon
Violin w/case, bow: Markneukirchen, c. 1810
400/600
$1,035   £631   DM1,873   ¥124,966

VRANCKO, JULIUS [P6/16] Violin with very minor
rib worm: 1954   805/966
$1,385   £860   DM2,598   ¥166,466

VUILLAUME, JEAN BAPTISTE [C11/86] Good
French Violin w/case: Paris   45,360/55,080
$48,438   £29,900   DM91,195   ¥5,119,478

VUILLAUME, JEAN BAPTISTE [P11/125] Violin in
playing condition: Paris, c. 1860 (Roland
Baumgartner, Basel, June 12, 1999)   9,720/11,340
$14,140   £8,729   DM26,858   ¥1,485,678

VUILLAUME, JEAN BAPTISTE [P11/126] Fine and
Handsome French Violin in immediate playing condi-
tion, w/case: Paris, 1867 (William E. Hill & Sons,
London, 1946)   64,800/81,000
$84,767   £52,325   DM161,004   ¥8,906,238

VUILLAUME, JEAN BAPTISTE [S3/25] Violin
w/case: Paris, 1848 (W.E. Hill & Sons, London,
September 20, 1940)   64,800/81,000
$95,094   £58,700   DM170,817   ¥11,227,549

VUILLAUME, JEAN BAPTISTE [S11/162] Violin
after c.-1716 Stradivari, w/case: Paris, 1862
72,900/89,100
$102,222   £63,100   DM193,717   ¥10,794,517

VUILLAUME, JEAN BAPTISTE [Sk5/48] French
Violin w/case: Paris, c. 1850   35,000/45,000
$31,050   £18,941   DM56,201   ¥3,748,977

VUILLAUME, JEAN BAPTISTE (attributed to)
[P11/101] French Violin in immediate playing condition, w/case: Paris, 1827   12,960/19,440 NS

VUILLAUME, NICHOLAS & J.B. [P3/67] Good
French Violin with minor restored table blemishes,
w/case: c. 1860 (W.E. Hill & Sons, London, February
22, 1943)   24,300/32,400
$20,493   £12,650   DM36,685   ¥2,417,036

VUILLAUME, NICOLAS [S3/35] Violin: Mirecourt,
c. 1860 (Daniel Schranz, Thun, June 1, 1994)
5,670/7,290
$5,589   £3,450   DM10,040   ¥659,882

VUILLAUME, NICOLAS [S3/96] "St. Cécile" Violin
w/case, bow: Mirecourt, 1844   3,240/4,860
$6,334   £3,910   DM11,378   ¥747,866

VUILLAUME, NICOLAS [S11/348] Violin:
Mirecourt, c. 1850   2,430/3,240
$4,844   £2,990   DM9,179   ¥511,499

WAGNER & GEORGE [S11/155] Violin after
Guarneri del Gesù, w/case, cover: Chicago, 1913
4,050/5,670
$4,099   £2,530   DM7,767   ¥432,807

WALMSLEY, P. (attributed to) [P5/13] English Violin
of quality, w/silver bow, case: London, c. 1760
1,304/1,467
$2,062   £1,265   DM3,732   ¥248,813

WAMSLEY, PETER [B11/182] Violin: London,
c. 1750   810/1,134
$1,025   £633   DM1,929   ¥108,297

WAMSLEY, PETER [S11/239] Violin w/case, 2 bows:
London, 1749   3,240/4,860 NS

WARD, ROBERT [C11/175a] English Violin
972/1,296 NS

WELLBY, CHARLES [P3/120] Good Violin in good
condition, w/case: Edinburgh, 1892   1,296/1,377 NS

WHEELER, A.H. [Sk5/308] American Violin w/case,
bow: Brookline, 1925 (John A. Gould & Sons,
Boston, November 2, 1959)   800/1,200
$805   £491   DM1,457   ¥97,196

WHITE, ASA WARREN [Sk5/75] American Violin
w/case: Boston   2,500/3,500
$2,645   £1,613   DM4,787   ¥319,357

WHITE, ASA WARREN [Sk5/167] American Violin
w/case: Boston, 1886   1,800/2,200
$1,840   £1,122   DM3,330   ¥222,162

WIDHALM, LEOPOLD [C3/142] German Violin
with original neck and in Classical condition
4,890/6,520 NS

WIDHALM, LEOPOLD [S6/47] Violin w/case:
Nuremberg, 1783 (L.P. Balmforth & Son, Leeds,
September 14, 1949)   4,770/6,360 NS

WIDHALM, MARTIN LEOPOLD (attributed to)
[P3/28] Violin with restorable blemishes, w/case, bow:
Nurnberg, c. 1780   1,944/2,430
$3,540   £2,185   DM6,337   ¥417,488

WIEBE, DAVID [S11M/89] Violin: David City, 1981
1,617/2,426
$4,705   £2,910   DM8,918   ¥497,728

WILKANOWSKI, WILLIAM [Sk11/249] American
Violin w/case, bow: Brooklyn, c. 1925
1,800/2,200 NS

WILKINSON (attributed to) [P11/99] English Violin
in good condition: c. 1760   2,268/2,592
$3,428   £2,116   DM6,511   ¥360,164

WILKINSON, JOHN (ascribed to) [P5/22] Interesting
English Violin in good condition, w/case, 2 bows:
London, c. 1940   1,141/1,304
$1,594   £978   DM2,885   ¥192,363

WITHERS, JOSEPH [P11/83] English Violin in good
condition: London, 1896   4,050/4,860
$5,356   £3,306   DM10,173   ¥562,757

WOLFF BROS. [P2/184] Good German Violin in
good condition, w/case: 1890   652/815
$712   £437   DM1,245   ¥84,144

WOLFF BROS. [S6/54] Violin w/case, violin:
Kreuznach, 1892   1,272/1,908
$3,291   £2,070   DM6,189   ¥397,937

WOOD, WILLIAM HOWARD [Sk11/213]
Contemporary American Violin w/case, 2 bows: 1975
    600/800
$1,125   £696   DM2,123   ¥118,993

WORNLE, GEORG (attributed to) [C3/69] German
Violin w/case   3,260/4,075
$2,812   £1,725   DM4,985   ¥332,459

WOULDHAVE, JOHN [Sk5/170] English Violin
w/case: North Shields, 1868   1,000/1,500 NS

WOULDHAVE, JOHN [Sk11/294] English Violin
w/case: North Shields, 1868   800/1,200
$728   £451   DM1,374   ¥77,017

ZANOLI, GIACOMO [Bf4/2816] Fine Italian Violin:
Verona, c. 1745 (Dario D'Attili, October 10, 1995)
    37,500/42,500 NS

ZANOLI, GIACOMO [Bf10/8046] Fine Italian
Violin: Verona, c. 1745 (Dario D'Attili, October 10,
1995)   37,500/42,500
$28,750   £17,250   DM51,750   ¥223,388

VIOLIN BOW

ACKERMANN, GOTTFRIED [S11M/66] Nickel
Violin Bow w/note from maker to Yehudi Menuhin:
Switzerland, late 20th C.   809/1,132
$1,389   £859   DM2,633   ¥146,958

ADAM, J.D. [B11/4] Nickel Violin Bow (Bernard
Millant, Paris, 1993)   9,720/12,960
$10,247   £6,325   DM19,291   ¥1,082,967

ADAM FAMILY (attributed to) [P5/74] Silver Violin
Bow with full hair, w/violoncello bow   652/815
$2,062   £1,265   DM3,732   ¥248,813

ALLEN, SAMUEL [S6/253] Silver Violin Bow for
W.E. Hill: London, c. 1885   2,385/3,180
$3,657   £2,300   DM6,877   ¥442,152

AMES, ROBERT [Sk5/152] Gold and Tortoiseshell
Violin Bow   2,000/3,000
$2,415   £1,473   DM4,371   ¥291,587

BAILLY, CHARLES [S6/90] Silver Violin Bow:
Mirecourt, early 20th C.   1,272/1,908
$1,646   £1,035   DM3,095   ¥198,968

BAUSCH (workshop of) [Sk11/94] Silver Violin Bow
    1,800/2,200 NS

BAUSCH, L. [Sk5/226] Silver Violin Bow   300/400
$403   £246   DM729   ¥48,598

BAUSCH, LUDWIG [B3/25] Silver Violin Bow:
c. 1860   648/810
$894   £552   DM1,606   ¥105,581

BAUSCH, LUDWIG [Sk5/147] Silver Violin Bow
    800/1,200
$805   £491   DM1,457   ¥97,196

BAZIN [B2/57] Silver Violin Bow   1,148/1,640 NS

BAZIN [B5/55] Silver Violin Bow   820/1,148 NS

BAZIN [Bf4/2731] Silver Violin Bow   2,000/2,750
$2,381   £1,481   DM4,380   ¥280,780

BAZIN [C3/64] Nickel Violin Bow   326/652
$600   £368   DM1,064   ¥70,925

BAZIN [S11M/67] Silver Violin Bow: Mirecourt,
c. 1900   970/1,294
$5,346   £3,306   DM10,134   ¥565,600

BAZIN, CHARLES [B6/8] Silver Violin Bow
    1,590/2,385
$1,463   £920   DM2,769   ¥175,343

BAZIN, CHARLES [Bf10/8011] Fine Gold and
Tortoiseshell Violin Bow lacking hair   3,000/4,000
$2,875   £1,725   DM5,175   ¥22,339

BAZIN, CHARLES [C11/54] Silver Violin Bow
    1,620/1,944 NS

BAZIN, CHARLES (II) [S3/45] Silver and Ivory
Violin Bow with damaged head: Mirecourt, c. 1930
    648/972
$559   £345   DM1,004   ¥65,988

BAZIN, CHARLES (II) [S11/313] Silver Violin Bow:
Mirecourt, mid 20th C.   972/1,296 NS

BAZIN, CHARLES ALFRED [Sk5/155] Silver Violin
Bow   800/1,200
$1,955   £1,193   DM3,539   ¥236,047

BAZIN, CHARLES NICHOLAS [C3/15] Silver Violin
Bow without hair   1,956/2,445
$1,500   £920   DM2,659   ¥177,312

BAZIN, CHARLES NICHOLAS [S3/153] Silver
Violin Bow: France, c. 1890   810/1,134
$6,521   £4,025   DM11,713   ¥769,862

BAZIN, LOUIS [B6/10A] Silver and Ebony Violin
Bow   477/795
$878   £552   DM1,662   ¥105,206

BAZIN, LOUIS [B11/38] Silver Violin Bow (J.F.
Raffin, Paris, 1998)   1,296/1,944
$3,167   £1,955   DM5,963   ¥334,735

BAZIN, LOUIS [C11/45] Silver Violin Bow (Bernard
Millant, Paris, March 16, 1999)   1,620/2,430
$2,422   £1,495   DM4,560   ¥255,974

BAZIN, LOUIS [C11/167] Nickel Violin Bow with
minor damage to the tip   324/486
$838   £517   DM1,577   ¥88,521

BAZIN, LOUIS [P2/94] French Nickel Violin Bow
lacking hair: c. 1940 (Jean-François Raffin, Paris,
June 10, 1998)   978/1,141
$1,125   £690   DM1,967   ¥132,860

BAZIN, LOUIS (II) [S11/280] Silver Violin Bow:
Mirecourt, c. 1950   1,296/1,944
$1,396   £862   DM2,646   ¥147,462

BAZIN, LOUIS (II) [S11/303] Nickel Violin Bow:
Mirecourt, c. 1950   1,134/1,620
$1,118   £690   DM2,118   ¥118,038

BAZIN, LOUIS (workshop of) [Bf10/8008] Silver
Violin Bow   400/600
$374   £224   DM673   ¥2,904

BERNARDEL, LEON [S11/290] Silver Violin Bow:
Paris, c. 1920   1,296/1,944 NS

BOURGUIGNON, MAURICE [S6/221] Silver
Violin Bow with minor damage to stick: Brussels,
early 20th C.   795/1,113
$878   £552   DM1,650   ¥106,116

BOVIS, FRANCOIS [S6/116] Silver Violin Bow: Nice,
c. 1900   636/954
$878   £552   DM1,650   ¥106,116

BRUGERE FAMILY [S3/64] Silver Violin Bow with
later adjuster: Paris, early 20th C.   1,296/1,944
$1,769   £1,092   DM3,178   ¥208,867

BRYANT, PERCIVAL WILFRED [S11/311] Silver
Violin Bow: Brighton, c. 1960   972/1,296
$1,210   £747   DM2,293   ¥127,789

BULTITUDE, ARTHUR RICHARD [C3/6] Silver and
Tortoiseshell Violin Bow   1,956/2,445
$1,874   £1,150   DM3,324   ¥221,640

BULTITUDE, ARTHUR RICHARD [Sk11/143]
Silver Violin Bow with baleen wrap   1,600/1,800
$2,381   £1,474   DM4,493   ¥251,857

CALLIER, FRANK [Sk11/162] Nickel Violin Bow
                                            400/600
$331   £205   DM625   ¥35,041

CARESSA, ALBERT [S3/72] Silver Violin Bow with
later adjuster, w/bow box for 6 bows: Paris, c. 1910
                                          972/1,296
$1,024   £632   DM1,839   ¥120,883

CHANOT, G.A. [B11/36] Nickel Violin Bow
                                        810/1,134 NS

CHANOT & CHARDON [B11/9] Silver Violin Bow
                                        1,296/1,944
$1,490   £920   DM2,806   ¥157,522

CHANOT & CHARDON [S6/235] Nickel Violin
Bow with later adjuster: Paris, c. 1870 1,113/1,590
$914   £575   DM1,719   ¥110,538

CHIPOT-VUILLAUME [S11/197] Silver Violin Bow
with repaired head: Mirecourt, late 19th C.
                                          567/729 NS

CLARK, JULIAN B. [B11/26] Snakewood Violin Bow
in Baroque style   567/729 NS

COLLENOT, LOUIS [S6/113] Silver Violin Bow with
repaired head: Reims, early 20th C.   636/954
$1,463   £920   DM2,751   ¥176,861

COLLIN-MEZIN, CH.J.B. (II) [S11/298] Silver
and Ivory Violin Bow: Mirecourt, c. 1900
                                        1,620/2,430 NS

CUNIOT-HURY, EUGENE [S6/114] Silver Violin
Bow: Mirecourt, c. 1900 (Jean-François Raffin, Paris,
June 17, 1998)   954/1,272
$1,371   £862   DM2,577   ¥165,711

DARBEY, GEORGE [B3/7] Silver Violin Bow
                                        810/1,134
$838   £518   DM1,506   ¥98,982

DARBEY, GEORGE [P6/98] Engraved Gold Violin
Bow   1,288/1,610
$2,555   £1,587   DM4,793   ¥307,116

DODD, JAMES [Bf4/2734] Silver Violin Bow
                                        1,200/2,000
$1,852   £1,152   DM3,407   ¥218,384

DODD, JAMES [S6/118] Silver Violin Bow: London,
c. 1830   1,908/2,544
$1,829   £1,150   DM3,439   ¥221,076

DODD, JOHN [Bf4/2726] Fine Silver and Ivory
Violin Bow in a nearly perfect state of condition
                                        5,000/6,000
$6,613   £4,113   DM12,167   ¥779,944

DODD, JOHN [S3/39] Silver Violin Bow with damaged head: Kew, c. 1810   648/972
$651   £402   DM1,170   ¥76,891

DODD, JOHN [S11/182] Silver Violin Bow with
damaged handle: London, early 19th C. 1,620/2,430
$1,677   £1,035   DM3,177   ¥177,057

DODD, JOHN [S11/319] Ebony Violin Bow with repaired stick: London, early 19th C.   1,296/1,944 NS

DODD, JOHN KEW [Bf4/2727] Fine Silver and
Ivory Violin Bow   3,000/4,000
$2,116   £1,316   DM3,893   ¥249,582

DODD FAMILY [S3/182] Gold and Tortoiseshell
Violin Bow with repaired stick, w/bow box: London,
mid 19th C.   1,296/1,620 NS

DOLLING, HEINZ [S3/40] Silver Violin Bow w/2
bows   648/972
$1,304   £805   DM2,343   ¥153,972

DOLLING, HEINZ [S11M/79] Silver Violin Bow
                                          323/485
$1,175   £727   DM2,228   ¥124,334

DUGAD, ANDRE [S3/62] Silver Violin Bow: Paris,
mid 20th C.   1,620/2,430 NS

DURRSCHMIDT, OTTO [B2/48] Gold Violin Bow
                                          656/984
$604   £368   DM1,041   ¥68,875

FETIQUE, MARCEL [B11/5] Silver and Ivory Violin
Bow   4,860/6,480 NS

FETIQUE, V. [B6/7A] Silver Violin Bow 2,385/3,180
$2,743   £1,725   DM5,192   ¥328,768

FETIQUE, VICTOR [B3/26] Silver Violin Bow: Paris
(Jean-François Raffin)   3,240/4,860
$3,540   £2,185   DM6,358   ¥417,925

FETIQUE, VICTOR [Bf4/2728] Silver "Exhibition"
Violin Bow   5,000/7,000 NS

FETIQUE, VICTOR [Bf4/2732] Exceptionally Fine
"Exhibition" Violin Bow in a remarkable state of
preservation   9,000/12,000
$11,241   £6,992   DM20,684   ¥1,325,905

FETIQUE, VICTOR [Bf4/2744] Fine Silver Violin
Bow for Albert Caressa   3,000/4,000
$4,298   £2,673   DM7,909   ¥506,964

FETIQUE, VICTOR [C3/1] Silver Violin Bow
                                          3,260/4,075
$3,374   £2,070   DM5,982   ¥398,951

FETIQUE, VICTOR [C3/42] Silver Violin Bow
                                          2,934/3,586
$5,249   £3,220   DM9,306   ¥620,591

FETIQUE, VICTOR [C11/40] Silver Violin Bow
                                          4,050/4,860
$5,589   £3,450   DM10,523   ¥590,709

FETIQUE, VICTOR [C11/43] Good Gold Violin
Bow   9,720/11,340 NS

FETIQUE, VICTOR [S3/184] Silver Violin Bow with
damaged stick: Paris, c. 1920   1,620/2,268
$1,677   £1,035   DM3,012   ¥197,964

FETIQUE, VICTOR [S6/97] Silver Violin Bow with
repaired stick and head: Paris, c. 1910
                                      1,908/2,544 NS

FETIQUE, VICTOR [S6/243] Silver Violin Bow:
Paris, early 20th C.   2,862/3,975
$2,743   £1,725   DM5,158   ¥331,614

FETIQUE, VICTOR [S6/260] Silver Violin Bow:
Paris, c. 1910   2,862/3,975
$2,743   £1,725   DM5,158   ¥331,614

FETIQUE, VICTOR [S11/176] Silver Violin Bow:
Paris, c. 1925 (Kenneth Warren & Son, Ltd., Chicago,
December 30, 1998)   4,860/6,480
$6,334   £3,910   DM12,004   ¥668,884

FETIQUE, VICTOR [S11/267] Silver Violin Bow:
Paris, c. 1920   4,050/5,670 NS

FETIQUE, VICTOR [S11/299] Silver Exhibition
Violin Bow with repaired head: Paris, 1908
                                      1,620/2,430
$2,236   £1,380   DM4,237   ¥236,077

FETIQUE, VICTOR [Sk5/143] Silver Violin Bow
                                      2,000/2,500
$2,415   £1,473   DM4,371   ¥291,587

FETIQUE, VICTOR (attributed to) [C11/159] Silver
Violin Bow (Jean-François Raffin, Paris, April 17,
1999)   3,240/4,860
$4,844   £2,990   DM9,120   ¥511,948

FINKEL, JOHANNES S. [S11M/54] Gold and
Tortoiseshell Violin Bow engraved "Yehudi Menuhin"
on the ferrule: Brienz, 1977   2,426/3,234
$8,126   £5,026   DM15,403   ¥859,712

FINKEL, SIEGFRIED [S11/277] Gold Violin Bow:
Brienz, c. 1960   1,296/1,944
$1,304   £805   DM2,471   ¥137,711

FONCLAUSE, JOSEPH [S11/322] Silver Violin Bow
with later frog: Paris, c. 1840   3,240/4,860
$3,353   £2,070   DM6,355   ¥354,115

FORSTER, WILLIAM (II) [S11/193] Ivory Violin
Bow with swan head: London, late 18th C.
                                      3,240/4,860 NS

FRANCAIS, EMILE [Bf4/2743] Silver Violin Bow
                                      1,200/1,800
$1,323   £823   DM2,433   ¥155,989

FRITSCH, JEAN [S11/265] Nickel Violin Bow with
later frog and adjuster: Paris, mid 20th C.   972/1,296
$932   £575   DM1,765   ¥98,365

GERMAIN, EMILE [S3/38] Silver Violin Bow: Paris,
early 20th C.   1,620/2,430
$9,315   £5,750   DM16,733   ¥1,099,803

GEROME, ROGER [C3/2] Gold and Tortoiseshell
Violin Bow   1,630/2,445
$1,125   £690   DM1,994   ¥132,984

GEROME, ROGER [C3/30] Gold and Tortoiseshell
Violin Bow   1,630/2,445
$1,218   £747   DM2,159   ¥143,969

GEROME, ROGER [Sk5/134] Gold and Ebony
Violin Bow   1,200/1,400
$2,185   £1,333   DM3,955   ¥263,817

GILLET, LOUIS [S11/260] Silver Violin Bow for
George Dupuy: Paris, c. 1900   972/1,296
$1,677   £1,035   DM3,177   ¥177,057

GOTZ, CONRAD [S3/148] Gold Violin Bow
                                      810/1,134
$745   £460   DM1,339   ¥87,984

HART & SON [S11M/78] Silver Violin Bow:
London, c. 1910   566/728
$2,352   £1,455   DM4,459   ¥248,864

HENRY, EUGENE [S6/133] Nickel Violin Bow: Paris,
c. 1880   954/1,272
$914   £575   DM1,719   ¥110,538

HENRY, JOSEPH [Bf4/2724] Silver Violin Bow with
later ebony adjuster   2,000/3,000
$2,645   £1,645   DM4,867   ¥311,978

HENRY, JOSEPH [P6/94] Nickel Violin Bow lacking
hair (Jean-François Raffin, Paris, December 2, 1996)
                                      3,220/4,025 NS

HENRY, JOSEPH [P9/91] Nickel Violin Bow without
hair (Jean-François Raffin, Paris, December 2, 1996)
                                      1,620/2,430 NS

HENRY, JOSEPH [Sk11/141] Fine French Silver
Violin Bow with baleen wrap and later adjuster
(Willam Salchow, New York, September 28, 1999)
                                      6,000/8,000
$14,548   £9,005   DM27,458   ¥1,539,126

HERRMANN, A. [Sk5/192] Silver Violin Bow
                                      600/800
$1,035   £631   DM1,873   ¥124,966

HERRMANN, EMIL [Bf4/2729] Silver Violin Bow
                                      1,200/1,800
$1,323   £823   DM2,433   ¥155,989

HILL, W.E. & SONS [B3/6] Silver Violin Bow
                                      1,944/2,430
$3,167   £1,955   DM5,689   ¥373,933

HILL, W.E. & SONS [B3/20] Silver Violin Bow:
c. 1920   2,430/3,240
$2,795   £1,725   DM5,020   ¥329,941

HILL, W.E. & SONS [B5/63] Silver and Tortoiseshell Violin Bow   328/492 NS

HILL, W.E. & SONS [B11/18] Silver Violin Bow
1,944/2,430
$3,167   £1,955   DM5,963   ¥334,735

HILL, W.E. & SONS [B11/19] Gold and Tortoiseshell Violin Bow   3,240/4,860
$3,540   £2,185   DM6,664   ¥374,116

HILL, W.E. & SONS [B11/28] Silver Violin Bow
1,944/2,430
$2,981   £1,840   DM5,612   ¥315,045

HILL, W.E. & SONS [B11/31] Gold Violin Bow
4,050/5,670
$3,540   £2,185   DM6,664   ¥374,116

HILL, W.E. & SONS [B11/37] Silver Violin Bow
1,944/2,430
$4,471   £2,760   DM8,418   ¥472,567

HILL, W.E. & SONS [B11/42] Silver Violin Bow without hair   1,620/3,240
$2,608   £1,610   DM4,911   ¥275,664

HILL, W.E. & SONS [B11/45] Silver Violin Bow
1,296/1,944
$3,540   £2,185   DM6,664   ¥374,116

HILL, W.E. & SONS [Bf4/2720] Silver Violin Bow
1,800/2,250
$3,306   £2,056   DM6,084   ¥389,972

HILL, W.E. & SONS [C3/7] Silver Violin Bow
1,956/2,934
$2,812   £1,725   DM4,985   ¥332,459

HILL, W.E. & SONS [C3/43] Silver Violin Bow with partial hair   1,141/1,467
$1,593   £977   DM2,824   ¥188,297

HILL, W.E. & SONS [C3/58] Gold and Tortoiseshell Violin Bow with repair   815/1,630
$1,405   £862   DM2,491   ¥166,133

HILL, W.E. & SONS [C3/61] Gold and Tortoiseshell Violin Bow   3,260/4,075
$3,749   £2,300   DM6,647   ¥443,279

HILL, W.E. & SONS [C11/44] Silver Violin Bow without hair   972/1,296
$2,236   £1,380   DM4,209   ¥236,284

HILL, W.E. & SONS [C11/52] Silver and Tortoise-shell Violin Bow   2,592/3,240
$2,795   £1,725   DM5,261   ¥295,355

HILL, W.E. & SONS [C11/56] Silver Violin Bow
1,620/2,430
$3,167   £1,955   DM5,963   ¥334,735

HILL, W.E. & SONS [C11/58] Gold Violin Bow
1,620/2,430
$3,353   £2,070   DM6,314   ¥354,425

HILL, W.E. & SONS [C11/151] Silver Violin Bow with tinsel wrap but without hair   810/1,134
$2,049   £1,265   DM3,858   ¥216,593

HILL, W.E. & SONS [C11/153] Silver Violin Bow
1,134/1,458
$1,863   £1,150   DM3,508   ¥196,903

HILL, W.E. & SONS [P3/131] Silver Violin Bow with full hair: London   1,944/2,430
$2,906   £1,794   DM5,203   ¥342,780

HILL, W.E. & SONS [P3/136] Good Silver Violin Bow with full hair: London   1,620/2,430
$1,863   £1,150   DM3,335   ¥219,731

HILL, W.E. & SONS [P3/139] Good Silver Violin Bow: London   1,944/2,430
$2,236   £1,380   DM4,002   ¥263,677

HILL, W.E. & SONS [P3/140] Small-Size Silver Violin Bow with skillful repair at head: London
810/972 NS

HILL, W.E. & SONS [P3/164] Good Silver Violin Bow: London   1,296/1,458
$1,584   £978   DM2,836   ¥186,866

HILL, W.E. & SONS [P3/166] Good Violin Bow: London   1,134/1,215
$1,304   £805   DM2,335   ¥153,811

HILL, W.E. & SONS [P3/167] Silver Violin Bow in playing condition: London   810/891 NS

HILL, W.E. & SONS [P3/179] Silver and Ivory Violin Bow with some possible restoration: London
810/972 NS

HILL, W.E. & SONS [P5/69] Silver Violin Bow
978/1,141
$1,125   £690   DM2,036   ¥135,716

HILL, W.E. & SONS [P5/80] Silver Violin Bow with minor head blemish: London   652/815
$750   £460   DM1,357   ¥90,477

HILL, W.E. & SONS [P5/103] Small-Size Silver Violin Bow with skillful repair at head   571/652 NS

HILL, W.E. & SONS [P5/104] Silver Violin Bow with restored stick, in playing condition: London
652/734 NS

HILL, W.E. & SONS [P6/90] Good Silver Violin Bow: London   1,932/2,415
$3,833   £2,381   DM7,189   ¥460,674

HILL, W.E. & SONS [P6/91] Good Silver Violin Bow: London   1,610/1,932
$1,916   £1,190   DM3,595   ¥230,337

HILL, W.E. & SONS [P6/92] Silver Violin Bow with full hair, some wear at hand position: London
1,610/1,932
$1,598   £992   DM2,997   ¥192,059

HILL, W.E. & SONS [P6/96] Silver Violin Bow: London   1,610/1,932
$2,129   £1,323   DM3,994   ¥255,930

HILL, W.E. & SONS [P6/121] Silver Violin Bow with full hair, w/silver violin bow: London   725/886
$1,385   £860   DM2,598   ¥166,466

HILL, W.E. & SONS [P6/128] Violin Bow with minor head repair, w/violin bow stick: London
805/966
$4,258   £2,645   DM7,988   ¥511,860

HILL, W.E. & SONS [P9/92] Good Silver Violin Bow
with full hair: London   1,944/2,430
$2,888   £1,783   DM5,437   ¥307,838

HILL, W.E. & SONS [P11/128] Gold Violin Bow
with full hair: London   3,240/4,860 NS

HILL, W.E. & SONS [P11/147] Silver Violin Bow
with full hair: London   2,430/3,240
$3,642   £2,248   DM6,918   ¥382,675

HILL, W.E. & SONS [P11/152] Octagonal Gold and
Tortoiseshell Violin Bow with some wear at thumb
position: London   1,620/2,430
$3,428   £2,116   DM6,511   ¥360,164

HILL, W.E. & SONS [P11/153] Octagonal Gold
Presentation Violin Bow with some wear: London
                                           2,025/2,430
$3,964   £2,447   DM7,530   ¥416,538

HILL, W.E. & SONS [P11/162A] Good Silver Violin
Bow with full hair and restored head: London
                                               486/648
$1,071   £661   DM2,035   ¥112,551

HILL, W.E. & SONS [P11/162B] Silver Violin Bow
with full hair: London   1,296/1,944
$2,785   £1,719   DM5,290   ¥292,634

HILL, W.E. & SONS [S3/37] Gold Violin Bow:
London, c. 1920   2,430/3,240
$4,099   £2,530   DM7,362   ¥483,913

HILL, W.E. & SONS [S3/61] Silver Violin Bow
w/bow: London, c. 1940   810/1,134 NS

HILL, W.E. & SONS [S3/71] Chased Gold Violin
Bow: London, 1976   2,430/3,240
$2,981   £1,840   DM5,354   ¥351,937

HILL, W.E. & SONS [S3/147] Silver Violin Bow:
London, c. 1920   1,134/1,620
$2,049   £1,265   DM3,681   ¥241,957

HILL, W.E. & SONS [S3/160] Silver Violin Bow:
London, c. 1930   972/1,296
$1,863   £1,150   DM3,347   ¥219,961

HILL, W.E. & SONS [S3/163] Silver Violin Bow:
London, c. 1950   1,296/1,944
$1,490   £920   DM2,677   ¥175,968

HILL, W.E. & SONS [S3/186] Silver Violin Bow:
London, 1933   1,620/2,430
$2,422   £1,495   DM4,350   ¥285,949

HILL, W.E. & SONS [S6/102] Silver and Tortoiseshell
Violin Bow w/silver violin bow: London, c. 1920
                                        1,272/1,590 NS

HILL, W.E. & SONS [S6/141] Silver Violin Bow:
London, c. 1930   1,113/1,590
$1,829   £1,150   DM3,439   ¥221,076

HILL, W.E. & SONS [S6/223] Silver Violin Bow:
London, 1929   1,272/1,908
$1,646   £1,035   DM3,095   ¥198,968

HILL, W.E. & SONS [S6/228] Silver Violin Bow:
London, c. 1930   1,113/1,590
$1,371   £862   DM2,577   ¥165,711

HILL, W.E. & SONS [S6/230] Silver Violin Bow:
London, mid 20th C.   1,113/1,590 NS

HILL, W.E. & SONS [S6/239] Silver Violin Bow:
London, mid 20th C.   1,590/2,385
$2,377   £1,495   DM4,470   ¥287,399

HILL, W.E. & SONS [S6/241] Silver Violin Bow:
London, c. 1930   1,272/1,908
$1,280   £805   DM2,407   ¥154,753

HILL, W.E. & SONS [S6/249] Silver and Tortoiseshell
Violin Bow: London, early 20th C.   1,908/2,544
$3,657   £2,300   DM6,877   ¥442,152

HILL, W.E. & SONS [S11/166] Silver and Ivory
Violin Bow w/bow box: London, c. 1930 2,430/3,240
$3,540   £2,185   DM6,708   ¥373,788

HILL, W.E. & SONS [S11/180] Gold Violin Bow:
London, 1970   1,944/2,916 NS

HILL, W.E. & SONS [S11/183] Silver Violin Bow:
London, c. 1930   1,296/1,944
$2,608   £1,610   DM4,943   ¥275,423

HILL, W.E. & SONS [S11/203] Gold Violin Bow:
London, c. 1970   2,430/3,240
$2,795   £1,725   DM5,296   ¥295,096

HILL, W.E. & SONS [S11/258] Silver Violin Bow:
London, c. 1920 (Bearden Violin Shop, St. Louis,
June 11, 1976)   1,944/2,430
$2,049   £1,265   DM3,884   ¥216,404

HILL, W.E. & SONS [S11/262] Silver Violin Bow:
London, c. 1930   1,944/2,592
$3,726   £2,300   DM7,061   ¥393,461

HILL, W.E. & SONS [S11/288] Silver Violin Bow:
London, 1949   1,944/2,592
$2,981   £1,840   DM5,649   ¥314,769

HILL, W.E. & SONS [S11/300] Silver Violin Bow
w/bow: London, c. 1940   486/810
$745   £460   DM1,412   ¥78,692

HILL, W.E. & SONS [S11/304] Silver Violin Bow:
London, c. 1920   486/810
$522   £322   DM989   ¥55,085

HILL, W.E. & SONS [S11/315] Silver Violin Bow
w/bow by John Dodd: London, 1929   972/1,296
$2,608   £1,610   DM4,943   ¥275,423

HILL, W.E. & SONS [S11M/71] Chased Gold Violin
Bow with repaired stick: London, c. 1920   647/970
$813   £503   DM1,540   ¥85,971

HILL, W.E. & SONS [Sk5/116] Silver Violin Bow
                                           1,200/1,400
$1,265   £772   DM2,290   ¥152,736

HILL, W.E. & SONS [Sk5/149] Silver Violin Bow
                                           1,600/1,800
$3,220   £1,964   DM5,828   ¥388,783

HILL, W.E. & SONS [Sk5/189] Silver Violin Bow
                                           1,600/1,800
$2,645   £1,613   DM4,787   ¥319,357

HOYER, C.A. [S11/194] Silver Violin Bow w/bow
                                        1,134/1,620 NS

HOYER, OTTO [Bf4/2733] Silver Violin Bow
600/900
$1,124   £699   DM2,068   ¥132,591

HOYER, OTTO A. [S6/261] Silver and Ivory Violin
Bow   954/1,272
$1,097   £690   DM2,063   ¥132,646

HOYER, OTTO A. [Sk5/139] Silver Violin Bow
800/1,200
$1,495   £912   DM2,706   ¥180,506

HOYER, OTTO A. (workshop of) [Sk11/169] Silver
Violin Bow   400/500
$661   £409   DM1,248   ¥69,960

HURY, CUNIOT [C3/19] Silver Violin Bow
1,304/1,956
$1,312   £805   DM2,326   ¥155,148

HURY, CUNIOT [P9/136] Silver Violin Bow with full
hair, w/violin bow   1,053/1,215
$1,826   £1,127   DM3,437   ¥194,633

HUSSON, AUGUST [S6/138] Silver Violin Bow:
Paris, c. 1900   2,862/3,498
$3,474   £2,185   DM6,533   ¥420,044

HUSSON, CHARLES CLAUDE [B5/64] Silver French
Violin Bow   984/1,312 NS

HUSSON, CHARLES CLAUDE [Bf10/8000] Silver
Violin Bow   1,500/2,000
$1,495   £897   DM2,691   ¥11,616

JOMBAR, PAUL [S3/47] Silver Violin Bow: Paris,
c. 1920   3,240/4,860
$4,099   £2,530   DM7,362   ¥483,913

JOMBAR, PAUL [S6/119] Silver Violin Bow: Paris,
c. 1930   2,862/3,975 NS

JOMBAR, PAUL [S11/167] Silver Violin Bow: Paris,
early 20th C.   1,296/1,944 NS

KARON, JAN [Sk11/159] Gold and Tortoiseshell
Violin Bow   400/600
$794   £491   DM1,498   ¥83,952

KITTEL (attributed to) [P11/146] Silver Violin Bow
with full hair   8,910/12,150 NS

KITTEL, NICOLAUS (ascribed to) [S11M/65] Gold
and Tortoiseshell Violin Bow with later tortoiseshell
frog: St. Petersburg, mid 19th C. (Kenneth Warren &
Son, Ltd., Chicago, December 20, 1980)
19,404/29,106 NS

KITTEL, NICOLAUS (attributed to) [S11M/63] Gold
and Tortoiseshell Violin Bow w/label in Yehudi
Menuhin's hand: St. Petersburg, mid 19th C.
16,170/24,255
$94,837   £58,650   DM179,762   ¥10,033,256

KITTEL, NICOLAUS (attributed to) [S11M/64]
Silver Violin Bow with repaired head: St. Petersburg,
mid 19th C.   9,702/12,936
$20,316   £12,564   DM38,508   ¥2,149,281

KNOPF, H. [B3/10] Silver Violin Bow: c. 1880
1,296/1,620
$1,304   £805   DM2,343   ¥153,972

KNOPF, HEINRICH [S3/57] Silver Violin Bow:
Berlin, c. 1880   1,620/2,430
$1,677   £1,035   DM3,012   ¥197,964

KOLSTEIN, SAMUEL [S11M/69] Silver Violin Bow:
New York, c. 1960   323/485
$534   £330   DM1,012   ¥56,462

KOLSTEIN, SAMUEL [S11M/72] Silver Violin Bow:
New York, c. 1960   323/485
$534   £330   DM1,012   ¥56,462

KOLSTEIN, SAMUEL [S11M/76] Gold Violin Bow:
New York, c. 1987 (maker's, June 18, 1987)
970/1,294
$1,711   £1,058   DM3,243   ¥180,992

LABERTE [P2/111] French Silver Violin Bow lacking
hair: c. 1950 (Jean-François Raffin, Paris, June 10,
1998)   978/1,141
$1,125   £690   DM1,967   ¥132,860

LABERTE [P3/169] Nickel Violin Bow with full hair,
w/violin bow (Jean-François Raffin, Paris, June 14,
1998)   810/972
$745   £460   DM1,334   ¥87,892

LABERTE, MARC [S3/165] Silver Violin Bow:
Mirecourt, c. 1900   648/972 NS

LABERTE, MARC [S6/209] Silver Violin Bow:
Mirecourt, c. 1930   954/1,272
$1,097   £690   DM2,063   ¥132,646

LAFLEUR, JOSEPH RENE [C3/37] Silver Violin Bow
(Jean-François Raffin, Paris, March 31, 1993)
6,520/8,150 NS

LAMBERT, N. [S6/207] Silver Violin Bow: France,
mid 20th C.   954/1,272
$1,646   £1,035   DM3,095   ¥198,968

LAMY, A. [P11/140] Silver Violin Bow with full hair:
Paris   4,860/5,670
$6,427   £3,968   DM12,208   ¥675,308

LAMY, A. [P11/144] Good Silver Violin Bow with
full hair: Paris   4,860/5,670
$6,427   £3,968   DM12,208   ¥675,308

LAMY, A. [Sk5/137] Silver Violin Bow with later frog
and adjuster   2,800/3,200 NS

LAMY, A. [Sk5/141] Silver Violin Bow
3,000/4,000 NS

LAMY, ALFRED [Bf4/2745] Fine Silver Violin Bow
4,000/5,000 NS

LAMY, ALFRED [C3/59] Silver Violin Bow
3,260/4,890
$3,749   £2,300   DM6,647   ¥443,279

LAMY, ALFRED [Sk5/220] Silver Violin Bow
800/1,200
$920   £561   DM1,665   ¥111,081

LAMY, ALFRED JOSEPH [Bf10/8013] Very Fine
Silver Violin Bow: Paris (Jean-François Raffin, May
25, 1998)   8,000/11,000
$4,887   £2,932   DM8,797   ¥37,972

LAMY, ALFRED JOSEPH [C3/34] Silver Violin Bow
with replacement frog and adjuster   2,934/3,586
$3,374   £2,070   DM5,982   ¥398,951

LAMY, ALFRED JOSEPH [S3/42] Silver Violin Bow:
Paris, c. 1900   1,944/2,916
$2,981   £1,840   DM5,354   ¥351,937

LAMY, ALFRED JOSEPH [S3/168] Silver Violin
Bow: Paris, c. 1910   4,860/6,480
$10,247   £6,325   DM18,406   ¥1,209,783

LAMY, ALFRED JOSEPH [S3/178] Silver Violin
Bow: Paris, c. 1900   4,860/6,480
$10,805   £6,670   DM19,410   ¥1,275,771

LAMY, ALFRED JOSEPH [S3/181] Silver Violin
Bow: Paris, c. 1885 (Etienne Vatelot, Paris, June 14,
1996)   5,670/7,290
$10,433   £6,440   DM18,740   ¥1,231,779

LAMY, ALFRED JOSEPH [S6/94] Silver Violin Bow:
Paris, c. 1885   1,908/2,544
$4,023   £2,530   DM7,565   ¥486,367

LAMY, ALFRED JOSEPH [S6/143] Silver Violin
Bow: Paris, c. 1890   5,565/7,155 NS

LAMY, ALFRED JOSEPH [S6/219] Silver Violin
Bow: Paris, c. 1900 (Jean-François Raffin, Paris,
March 8, 1999)   3,975/5,565 NS

LAMY, ALFRED JOSEPH [S11/170] Silver Violin
Bow: Paris, c. 1910   3,240/4,860
$4,099   £2,530   DM7,767   ¥432,807

LAMY, ALFRED JOSEPH [S11/178] Silver Violin
Bow: Paris, c. 1890   4,860/6,480
$4,658   £2,875   DM8,826   ¥491,826

LAMY, ALFRED JOSEPH [S11/192] Silver Violin
Bow: Paris, c. 1890   4,536/5,670
$7,825   £4,830   DM14,828   ¥826,268

LAMY, ALFRED JOSEPH [Sk5/128] Silver Violin
Bow (Kenneth Warren & Son, Chicago, October 10,
1992)   3,000/4,000 NS

LAMY FAMILY (MEMBER OF) [B3/11] Silver
Violin Bow   2,916/4,050 NS

LA PIERRE [Sk5/229] Nickel Violin Bow   400/600
$633   £386   DM1,145   ¥76,368

LAUXERROIS, JEAN-PAUL [S3/151] Silver Violin
Bow: Paris, c. 1960   1,296/1,944
$1,453   £897   DM2,610   ¥171,569

LEE, JOHN NORWOOD [S11M/60] Gold and
Tortoiseshell Violin Bow w/letter from Bein & Fushi
to Yehudi Menuhin: Chicago, c. 1980 (Bein & Fushi,
Chicago, January 30, 1982)   1,940/2,587
$2,352   £1,455   DM4,459   ¥248,864

LENOBLE, AUGUSTE [C3/25] Gold Violin Bow
                                             6,520/9,780
$7,498   £4,600   DM13,294   ¥886,558

LOTTE, FRANCOIS [Bf4/2741] Silver Violin Bow
                                             800/1,200
$1,256   £781   DM2,311   ¥148,122

LOTTE, ROGER-FRANCOIS [S6/122] Silver Violin
Bow: Mirecourt, c. 1970 (Jean-François Raffin, Paris,
June 15, 1998)   795/954
$822   £517   DM1,546   ¥99,388

LOTTE, ROGER-FRANCOIS [S11/274] Silver Violin
Bow: Mirecourt, c. 1960   972/1,296 NS

LUPOT, F. (attributed to) [B11/30] Fine Silver Violin
Bow with later button   8,100/11,340 NS

MAIRE (workshop of) [C3/29] Nickel Violin Bow
(Paul Childs, Montrose, December 4, 1997)
                                             2,934/3,586
$2,999   £1,840   DM5,318   ¥354,623

MAIRE, NICOLAS [S6/130] Silver Violin Bow
w/bow box: Paris, c. 1860 (Rudolph Wurlitzer Co.,
New York, March 22, 1948)   11,130/14,310
$13,165   £8,280   DM24,757   ¥1,591,747

MAIRE, NICOLAS [Sk5/113] Fine Nickel Violin Bow
                                             5,000/7,000
$5,750   £3,508   DM10,408   ¥694,255

MALINE (workshop of) [S6/117] Nickel Violin Bow:
Paris or Mirecourt, mid 19th C. (Jean-François
Raffin, Paris, December 11, 1997)   954/1,272
$4,388   £2,760   DM8,252   ¥530,582

MALINE, GUILLAUME [S11/332] Nickel Violin
Bow: Mirecourt, c. 1840   3,240/4,860
$6,521   £4,025   DM12,357   ¥688,557

MARTIN, J. (attributed to) [P3/138] Good Silver
Violin Bow with full hair   2,430/3,240 NS

MARTIN, J. (attributed to) [P5/85] Good Silver
Violin Bow with full hair   1,223/1,304
$1,782   £1,093   DM3,224   ¥214,982

MARTIN, JEAN JOSEPH [C3/3] Silver Violin Bow
                                         1,630/2,445 NS

MARTIN, JEAN JOSEPH [S6/120] Nickel Violin
Bow: Paris, c. 1890 (Bernard Millant, Paris, January
8, 1999)   2,385/3,180
$5,486   £3,450   DM10,316   ¥663,228

MILLANT, ROGER [S6/146] Silver Violin Bow:
Paris, c. 1950   2,385/3,180
$1,829   £1,150   DM3,439   ¥221,076

MILLANT, ROGER & MAX [B6/7] Silver and
Ebony Violin Bow   795/1,113
$878   £552   DM1,662   ¥105,206

MILLANT, ROGER & MAX [B6/12A] Silver Violin
Bow   795/1,113
$823   £518   DM1,558   ¥98,630

MILLANT, ROGER & MAX [S11/257] Silver Violin
Bow: Paris   2,430/3,240 NS

MORIZOT, L. [P11/179] Silver Violin Bow without
hair: c. 1940   1,296/1,458
$1,671   £1,032   DM3,174   ¥175,580

MORIZOT, L. [P11/198] White Gold Violin Bow
with full hair and head repair   810/972
$1,071   £661   DM2,035   ¥112,551

MORIZOT, LOUIS [B6/12] Silver Violin Bow
                                         1,908/2,385 NS

MORIZOT, LOUIS [Bf4/2721] Silver Violin Bow
1,500/2,000 NS

MORIZOT, LOUIS [Bf4/2735] Silver Violin Bow
1,700/2,250
$1,984   £1,234   DM3,650   ¥233,983

MORIZOT, LOUIS [S3/51] Silver Violin Bow:
Mirecourt, c. 1930   972/1,296
$1,583   £977   DM2,843   ¥186,871

MORIZOT, LOUIS [S3/56] Silver Violin Bow:
Mirecourt, c. 1930   2,268/2,916
$2,236   £1,380   DM4,016   ¥263,953

MORIZOT, LOUIS (attributed to) [Sk5/138] French
Silver Violin Bow (William Salchow, New York, April
12, 1988)   1,400/1,600
$1,495   £912   DM2,706   ¥180,506

MORIZOT, LOUIS (II) [S3/63] Nickel Violin Bow:
Mirecourt, mid 20th C.   972/1,296
$1,453   £897   DM2,610   ¥171,569

MORIZOT, LOUIS (II) [S6/224] Silver Violin Bow:
Mirecourt, c. 1930   2,385/3,180
$4,571   £2,875   DM8,596   ¥552,690

MORIZOT, LOUIS (II) [S11/184] Silver Violin Bow:
Mirecourt, c. 1950   1,620/2,430 NS

MORIZOT, LOUIS (II) [S11/273] Silver Violin Bow:
Mirecourt, c. 1930   1,134/1,620 NS

MORIZOT FAMILY [C11/146] Silver Violin Bow
1,296/1,944
$1,490   £920   DM2,806   ¥157,522

MORIZOT FAMILY [Sk5/124] Nickel Violin Bow
1,400/1,600
$1,265   £772   DM2,290   ¥152,736

MORIZOT FAMILY [Sk5/222] Nickel Violin Bow
400/600
$748   £456   DM1,353   ¥90,253

MORIZOT FRERES [Sk11/117] Silver Violin Bow
2,500/3,000 NS

MORIZOT (FRERES), LOUIS [C3/44] Silver Violin
Bow (Jean-François Raffin, Paris, June 10, 1998)
978/1,304
$1,312   £805   DM2,326   ¥155,148

MULLER, FRIEDRICH KARL [S11M/80] Gold
Violin Bow w/violin bow stamped "Y.M." and
"J.P.M.": Bubenreuth, second half of 20th C.
323/485
$1,925   £1,190   DM3,648   ¥203,616

NURNBERGER [Sk11/140] Silver Violin Bow
1,000/1,200
$1,125   £696   DM2,123   ¥118,993

NURNBERGER, ALBERT [B11/22] Gold Violin Bow
2,430/3,240
$2,608   £1,610   DM4,911   ¥275,664

NURNBERGER, ALBERT [B11/44] Silver Violin
Bow   1,620/2,430 NS

NURNBERGER, ALBERT [Bf4/2719] Silver Violin
Bow   800/1,200
$1,587   £987   DM2,920   ¥187,187

NURNBERGER, ALBERT [C3/241] Silver Violin
Bow   326/489
$525   £322   DM931   ¥62,059

NURNBERGER, ALBERT [C3/243] Silver Violin
Bow   326/489
$562   £345   DM997   ¥66,492

NURNBERGER, ALBERT [C3/250] Silver Violin
Bow   489/652
$600   £368   DM1,064   ¥70,925

NURNBERGER, ALBERT [Sk5/156] Silver Violin
Bow   600/800
$748   £456   DM1,353   ¥90,253

NURNBERGER, ALBERT [Sk11/107] Silver Violin
Bow without hair   800/1,200
$1,323   £819   DM2,496   ¥139,921

NURNBERGER, CHRISTIAN ALBERT [S3/53]
Gold Violin Bow: c. 1980   1,296/1,944
$1,677   £1,035   DM3,012   ¥197,964

NURNBERGER, KARL ALBERT [S3/48] Silver
Violin Bow: Markneukirchen, mid 20th C.
1,296/1,944
$1,583   £977   DM2,843   ¥186,871

NURNBERGER, KARL ALBERT [S3/69] Silver
Portrait Violin Bow: Markneukirchen   2,268/2,916
$2,795   £1,725   DM5,020   ¥329,941

NURNBERGER, KARL ALBERT [S6/208] Silver
Violin Bow: France, mid 20th C.   1,113/1,590
$1,097   £690   DM2,063   ¥132,646

NURNBERGER, KARL ALBERT [S6/229] Silver
Violin Bow: Markneukirchen   1,113/1,590 NS

NURNBERGER, KARL ALBERT [S6/256] Silver
Violin Bow   1,272/1,908
$1,280   £805   DM2,407   ¥154,753

NURNBERGER, KARL ALBERT [S11/287] Silver
Violin Bow: Markneukirchen, c. 1950   1,296/1,944
$2,049   £1,265   DM3,884   ¥216,404

NURNBERGER, KARL ALBERT [S11/327] Silver
Violin Bow: Markneukirchen, c. 1930   972/1,296
$1,769   £1,092   DM3,352   ¥186,808

OUCHARD, BERNARD [S11/330] Silver Violin
Bow: Probably Geneva, c. 1970   2,430/3,240
$3,540   £2,185   DM6,708   ¥373,788

OUCHARD, E. [B11/25] Silver Violin Bow (Paul
Childs, Montrose)   4,860/8,100 NS

OUCHARD, EMILE [B6/23A] Silver Violin Bow
636/954
$2,011   £1,265   DM3,808   ¥241,096

OUCHARD, EMILE [B11/21] Silver Violin Bow
1,620/3,240
$1,584   £978   DM2,981   ¥167,368

OUCHARD, EMILE (FILS) [P11/157] Good Silver
Violin Bow with full hair   1,620/2,430
$6,856   £4,232   DM13,022   ¥720,329

OUCHARD, EMILE A. [S11/168] Silver and Ivory
Violin Bow: Paris, c. 1940   2,430/3,240
$11,178   £6,900   DM21,183   ¥1,180,383

OUCHARD, EMILE A. [S11/190] Silver Violin Bow:
Paris, c. 1940   2,268/2,916
$2,981   £1,840   DM5,649   ¥314,769

OUCHARD, EMILE A. [S11/310] Silver Violin Bow:
Paris, mid 20th C.   1,944/2,916
$4,099   £2,530   DM7,767   ¥432,807

OUCHARD, EMILE A. [S11/323] Silver Violin Bow:
Paris, c. 1940   1,944/2,592
$8,942   £5,520   DM16,946   ¥944,306

OUCHARD, EMILE [Sk5/111] Silver Violin Bow
(Jean-François Raffin, Paris, January 28, 1998)
                                             1,800/2,200
$1,955   £1,193   DM3,539   ¥236,047

OUCHARD, EMILE FRANCOIS [S3/183] Silver
Violin Bow: Mirecourt, c. 1920   1,620/2,430
$2,049   £1,265   DM3,681   ¥241,957

OUCHARD, EMILE FRANCOIS [S6/98] Silver
Violin Bow: Mirecourt, c. 1930   2,226/2,862
$2,194   £1,380   DM4,126   ¥265,291

OUCHARD, EMILE FRANCOIS [S6/213] Silver
Violin Bow: Mirecourt, c. 1920   1,908/2,385 NS

OUCHARD, EMILE FRANCOIS [S11/259] Gold
and Tortoiseshell Violin Bow: Mirecourt, c. 1910
                                             1,296/1,944
$9,688   £5,980   DM18,359   ¥1,022,999

OUCHARD, EMILE FRANCOIS [S11/289] Silver
Violin Bow: Mirecourt, c. 1890   1,620/2,430
$1,677   £1,035   DM3,177   ¥177,057

PAJEOT [B6/26] Silver Violin Bow (J. Roda, 1966)
                                             3,180/4,770
$6,217   £3,910   DM11,769   ¥745,207

PAJEOT, E. [B11/41] Silver Violin Bow (J. Roda,
1966)   5,670/7,290 NS

PAJEOT, ETIENNE [S6/217] Silver Violin Bow: Paris,
c. 1830   3,975/5,565
$3,657   £2,300   DM6,877   ¥442,152

PAJEOT, LOUIS SIMON [S6/149] Nickel Violin Bow
with later ebony frog and adjuster: probably
Mirecourt, c. 1800 (Jean-François Raffin, Paris,
January 9, 1998)   1,908/2,862 NS

PAJEOT, LOUIS SIMON [S6/220] Silver Violin Bow:
Mirecourt, c. 1800   4,770/6,360
$10,971   £6,900   DM20,631   ¥1,326,456

PAJEOT, LOUIS SIMON [S11M/47] Gold and Ivory
Violin Bow with a stellar motif set in mastic:
Mirecourt, c. 1800   9,702/12,936
$13,900   £8,596   DM26,348   ¥1,470,560

PATIGNY, PIERRE [S11M/55] Gold and Tortoiseshell Violin Bow: Brussels, c. 1980   1,132/1,617
$4,277   £2,645   DM8,107   ¥452,480

PATIGNY, PIERRE [S11M/61] Chased-Gold and
Blonde-Tortoiseshell Violin Bow: Brussels, second half
of the 20th C.   1,617/2,426
$5,560   £3,439   DM10,539   ¥588,224

PECATTE, CHARLES [B6/14] Silver Violin Bow
                                             4,770/7,950
$4,571   £2,875   DM8,654   ¥547,946

PECCATTE, CHARLES [S6/246] Silver Violin Bow
with later ebony frog and adjuster: Paris, c. 1900
                                             3,975/5,565
$5,486   £3,450   DM10,316   ¥663,228

PECCATTE, DOMINIQUE [S11/294] Silver Violin
Bow with repaired stick: Paris, mid 19th C. (Rembert
Wurlitzer, New York, June 6, 1961)   16,200/24,300
$18,630   £11,500   DM35,305   ¥1,967,305

PECCATTE, FRANCOIS [S11M/56] Gold and Tortoiseshell Violin Bow: Paris, c. 1840   12,936/19,404
$27,800   £17,193   DM52,695   ¥2,941,121

PECCATTE FAMILY (MEMBER OF) [S3/68] Silver
Violin Bow: Paris, c. 1870   9,720/12,960
$15,836   £9,775   DM28,445   ¥1,869,664

PERSOIS [Bf10/8012] Very Fine and Rare Silver
Violin Bow in a fine state of preservation
                                     8,000/14,000 NS

PERSOIS [C3/53] Gold Violin Bow
                                     35,860/45,640 NS

PERSOIS, JEAN-PIERRE-MARIE [Sk11/124] Fine
Gold Violin Bow with tinsel wrap: Paris
                                             45,000/50,000
$56,868   £35,201   DM107,337   ¥6,016,582

PFRETZSCHNER [B3/4] Gold and Ebony Violin
Bow   3,240/4,050 NS

PFRETZSCHNER, G.A. [Bf10/8006] Chased Silver
and Ebony Violin Bow   400/600
$460   £276   DM828   ¥3,574

PFRETZSCHNER, H.R. [B5/59] Silver Violin Bow
with damaged head   328/492 NS

PFRETZSCHNER, H.R. [B11/27] Silver Violin Bow
                                     1,620/2,430 NS

PFRETZSCHNER, H.R. [B11/32] Gold Violin Bow
                                             3,240/4,050
$3,353   £2,070   DM6,314   ¥354,425

PFRETZSCHNER, H.R. [C11/60] Gold Violin Bow
                                             972/1,296
$745   £460   DM1,403   ¥78,761

PFRETZSCHNER, H.R. [C11/170] Nickel Violin
Bow   324/486
$373   £230   DM702   ¥39,381

PFRETZSCHNER, H.R. [S11/318] Silver Violin Bow
w/bow: Markneukirchen, c. 1900   972/1,296
$1,304   £805   DM2,471   ¥137,711

PFRETZSCHNER, H.R. [Sk5/145] Silver Violin Bow
                                             800/1,200
$920   £561   DM1,665   ¥111,081

PFRETZSCHNER, H.R. [Sk5/227] Silver Violin Bow
                                             300/400
$690   £421   DM1,249   ¥83,311

PFRETZSCHNER, HERMANN RICHARD [S6/212]
Silver Violin Bow: Markneukirchen, early 20th C.
                                             954/1,272
$1,736   £1,092   DM3,265   ¥209,926

PFRETZSCHNER, W. [B11/20] Silver Violin Bow
with later nickel button   648/972 NS

PFRETZSCHNER, W.A. [C3/247] Silver Violin Bow
without hair 326/489
$280 £172 DM497 ¥33,150

PFRETZSCHNER, W.A. [Sk5/146] Engraved Gold
and Ebony Violin Bow 1,500/2,000
$1,610 £982 DM2,914 ¥194,391

PFRETZSCHNER, WILHELM AUGUST [S6/99]
Silver Violin Bow: Markneukirchen, c. 1920
954/1,272 NS

POIRSON [B6/5] Silver Violin Bow 2,385/3,180 NS

POIRSON, JUSTIN [S6/240] Silver Violin Bow: Paris,
c. 1900 1,113/1,590
$1,829 £1,150 DM3,439 ¥221,076

POIRSON, JUSTIN (attributed to) [Sk5/119] Silver
Violin Bow (Jean-François Raffin, Paris, March 17,
1997) 1,800/2,200
$2,185 £1,333 DM3,955 ¥263,817

PRAGER, GUSTAV [C3/224] Silver Violin Bow
489/652
$412 £253 DM731 ¥48,761

PRELL, HERMAN WILHELM [B5/52] Silver Violin
Bow 328/492
$415 £253 DM754 ¥50,091

PRELL, HERMAN WILHELM [Sk5/195] Silver
Violin Bow 800/1,200 NS

PRELL, HERMAN WILHELM [Sk11/123] Silver and
Tortoiseshell Violin Bow 800/1,200
$661 £409 DM1,248 ¥69,960

RAU, AUGUST [B11/40] Silver Violin Bow
972/1,620 NS

RAU, AUGUST [B11/46] Silver Violin Bow
972/1,620
$1,118 £690 DM2,105 ¥118,142

RAU, AUGUST [C3/57] Gold Violin Bow w/case
1,304/1,630
$1,687 £1,035 DM2,991 ¥199,476

RAU, AUGUST [C3/245] Silver Violin Bow with
partial hair 326/489
$375 £230 DM665 ¥44,328

REICHEL [B2/49] Nickel Violin Bow 164/246
$226 £138 DM391 ¥25,828

RICHAUME, ANDRE [S11/169] Silver and Tortoiseshell Violin Bow w/bow: Paris, c. 1940 1,620/2,430
$7,825 £4,830 DM14,828 ¥826,268

ROLLAND, BENOIT [S11M/77] Silver Spiccato-
Model Violin Bow engraved "Y.M." on the ferrule:
Paris, c. 1994 970/1,294
$1,175 £727 DM2,228 ¥124,334

ROLLAND, S. [S11M/62] Gold and Tortoiseshell
Violin Bow: Paris, c. 1980 2,426/3,234 NS

SANDNER, A.L. [C11/65] Silver Violin Bow
486/810 NS

SARTORY, E. [B3/13] Very Fine Gold Violin Bow:
Paris (Jean-François Raffin) 22,680/25,920 NS

SARTORY, E. [B3/14] Extremely Fine Silver Violin
Bow in an exceptional state of preservation
1,620/19,440
$18,630 £11,500 DM33,465 ¥2,199,605

SARTORY, E. [P11/145] Good Silver Violin Bow with
full hair: Paris, c. 1930 (Bernard Millant, Paris, June
16, 1999) 8,100/9,720
$10,712 £6,613 DM20,347 ¥1,125,514

SARTORY, EUGENE [B6/15] Silver Violin Bow
7,950/11,130 NS

SARTORY, EUGENE [Bf4/2722] Fine Silver Violin
Bow lacking hair 5,000/7,000 NS

SARTORY, EUGENE [C3/24] Silver Violin Bow
6,520/8,150
$12,184 £7,475 DM21,603 ¥1,440,657

SARTORY, EUGENE [C3/38] Silver Violin Bow
6,520/9,780
$7,873 £4,830 DM13,959 ¥930,886

SARTORY, EUGENE [C3/52] Silver Violin Bow
8,150/11,410 NS

SARTORY, EUGENE [C11/49] Silver Violin Bow
6,480/9,720
$11,178 £6,900 DM21,045 ¥1,181,418

SARTORY, EUGENE [C11/164] Silver Violin Bow
6,480/9,720
$10,247 £6,325 DM19,291 ¥1,082,967

SARTORY, EUGENE [P3/84] Silver Violin Bow with
full hair: Paris 7,290/8,100
$8,384 £5,175 DM15,008 ¥988,787

SARTORY, EUGENE [P3/85] Silver Violin Bow: Paris
4,860/6,480
$6,148 £3,795 DM11,006 ¥725,111

SARTORY, EUGENE [S3/55] Silver Violin Bow without lapping or hair, w/German violin bow: Paris,
c. 1930 2,916/4,050
$7,825 £4,830 DM14,055 ¥923,834

SARTORY, EUGENE [S3/177] Silver Violin Bow with
later ebony frog: Paris, c. 1910 4,050/5,670
$10,805 £6,670 DM19,410 ¥1,275,771

SARTORY, EUGENE [S6/125] Silver Violin Bow:
Paris, c. 1920 3,975/5,565
$3,657 £2,300 DM6,877 ¥442,152

SARTORY, EUGENE [S6/206] Silver Violin Bow:
Paris, c. 1920 3,180/4,770
$7,680 £4,830 DM14,442 ¥928,519

SARTORY, EUGENE [S6/263] Silver Violin Bow:
Paris, c. 1930 4,770/6,360 NS

SARTORY, EUGENE [S11/175] Silver Violin Bow:
Paris, c. 1920 6,480/9,720
$7,079 £4,370 DM13,416 ¥747,576

SARTORY, EUGENE [S11/295] Silver Violin Bow:
Paris, c. 1910 (Paul Childs, Montrose, July 3, 1997)
9,720/12,960
$11,178 £6,900 DM21,183 ¥1,180,383

SARTORY, EUGENE [S11/306] Silver Violin Bow:
Paris, c. 1900   6,480/9,720
$10,805   £6,670   DM20,477   ¥1,141,037

SARTORY, EUGENE [Sk5/109] Silver Violin Bow
lacking adjuster   5,000/7,000
$8,338   £5,086   DM15,091   ¥1,006,670

SARTORY, EUGENE [Sk5/118] Silver Violin Bow
with replacement frog and adjuster (Paul Childs,
Montrose, September 23, 1998)   4,000/6,000
$5,463   £3,332   DM9,887   ¥659,542

SARTORY, EUGENE [Sk5/125] Silver Violin Bow
                                          5,000/7,000
$9,488   £5,787   DM17,172   ¥1,145,521

SARTORY, EUGENE [Sk5/133] Silver Violin Bow
                                          1,800/2,200
$3,220   £1,964   DM5,828   ¥388,783

SARTORY, EUGENE [Sk5/185] Silver Violin Bow
with damaged head   600/800
$2,760   £1,684   DM4,996   ¥333,242

SARTORY, EUGENE [Sk11/112] Silver Violin Bow:
Paris   10,000/12,000 NS

SCHUBERT, PAUL [S11M/73] Silver Child's Violin
Bow with repaired stick: Markneukirchen, c. 1925
                                             129/194
$149   £92   DM282   ¥15,738

SCHUSTER, ADOLPH CURT [S11/292] Silver Violin
Bow w/viola bow: Markneukirchen, c. 1930
                                           972/1,296
$1,490   £920   DM2,824   ¥157,384

SCHUSTER, GOTHARD [C11/42] Silver Violin Bow
                                           810/1,134
$1,210   £747   DM2,278   ¥127,901

SEIFERT, LOTHAR [P11/143] Gold and Engraved
Violin Bow with full hair, w/violin case 2,430/3,240
$2,999   £1,852   DM5,697   ¥315,144

SERDET, PAUL [Bf10/8007] Silver Violin Bow: Paris
                                             600/900
$575   £345   DM1,035   ¥4,468

SILVESTRE & MAUCOTEL [S3/154] Silver Violin
Bow: Paris, c. 1910   1,620/2,430
$2,422   £1,495   DM4,350   ¥285,949

SIMON, PAUL [Sk5/182] Fine Silver Violin Bow
                                   14,000/16,000 NS

SIMON, PIERRE [S11/321] Silver Violin Bow: Paris,
c. 1850   4,860/6,480
$8,570   £5,290   DM16,240   ¥904,960

SIMON BROS. [S3/159] Nickel Violin Bow: France,
c. 1850   1,296/1,944 NS

SMITH, THOMAS [S11M/50] Ivory Violin Bow with
fluted stick and swan head: London, c. 1780
                                         3,234/4,851
$4,063   £2,513   DM7,702   ¥429,856

STOHR, H.A. [B5/61] Silver Violin Bow   164/246
$207   £127   DM377   ¥25,046

STOSS, ARNOLD [Sk11/100] Gold Violin Bow
                                         1,200/1,400
$1,323   £819   DM2,496   ¥139,921

SUSS, CARL [Bf10/8003] Chased Silver and Ebony
Violin Bow lacking hair   500/700
$632   £379   DM1,138   ¥4,911

THIBOUVILLE-LAMY, J. [P3/168] Nickel Violin
Bow with full hair: Mirecourt (Jean-François Raffin,
Paris, June 14, 1998)   810/972 NS

THIBOUVILLE-LAMY, J. [P11/176] Good Mirecourt
Violin Bow with full hair   810/972
$965   £596   DM1,833   ¥101,394

THIBOUVILLE-LAMY, JEROME [C11/148] Silver
Violin Bow   1,296/1,944 NS

THIBOUVILLE-LAMY, JEROME [P5/90] Nickel
Violin Bow with full hair: Mirecourt (Jean-François
Raffin, Paris, June 14, 1998)   652/815 NS

THIBOUVILLE-LAMY, JEROME [S6/100] Silver
Violin Bow: Mirecourt, c. 1910   954/1,272
$1,371   £862   DM2,577   ¥165,711

THIBOUVILLE-LAMY, JEROME [S11/283] Silver
Violin Bow: Mirecourt, c. 1930   1,620/2,430
$1,677   £1,035   DM3,177   ¥177,057

THOMA, ARTHUR [S3/49] Silver Violin Bow: Bad
Brambach, 20th C.   648/972 NS

THOMA, ARTHUR [S11/196] Gold Violin Bow
w/bow: Brambach, c. 1935   1,296/1,944 NS

THOMA, MATHIAS [P9/94] Gold Violin Bow with
full hair   1,296/1,458
$1,304   £805   DM2,455   ¥139,024

THOMASSIN [C11/163] Silver Violin Bow (Jean-
François Raffin, Paris, April 17, 1999)
                                   3,240/4,050 NS

THOMASSIN (attributed to) [P5/84] Good Silver
Violin Bow with full hair   1,141/1,304 NS

THOMASSIN, C. [C11/149] Nickel Violin Bow
                                         1,944/2,268
$2,981   £1,840   DM5,612   ¥315,045

THOMASSIN, CLAUDE [Bf4/2739] Violin Bow
                                         2,000/3,000
$2,381   £1,481   DM4,380   ¥280,780

THOMASSIN, CLAUDE [C3/33] Silver Violin Bow
with partial hair: Paris   1,304/1,630
$4,874   £2,990   DM8,641   ¥576,263

THOMASSIN, CLAUDE [S11/171] Silver Violin
Bow: Paris, c. 1920   1,620/2,430
$4,099   £2,530   DM7,767   ¥432,807

THOMASSIN, CLAUDE [Sk5/129] Silver Violin Bow
(Paul Childs, Montrose, September 24, 1998)
                                         2,200/2,600
$3,220   £1,964   DM5,828   ¥388,783

THOMASSIN, CLAUDE [Sk5/183] Silver Violin Bow
                                   1,800/2,200 NS

TOURTE, FRANCOIS XAVIER [S11M/57] Gold
Violin Bow engraved "R. Kreutzer" on the ferrule,
w/mahogany bow box: Paris, c. 1790   6,468/9,702
$49,185   £30,418   DM93,230   ¥5,203,522

TOURTE, FRANCOIS XAVIER [S11M/58] Gold
Violin Bow with later ebony frog and adjuster: Paris,
c. 1800   12,936/19,404
$59,878   £37,030   DM113,497   ¥6,334,722

TOURTE, FRANCOIS XAVIER [S11M/59] Gold and
Tortoiseshell Violin Bow with later frog: Paris,
c. 1810   24,255/32,340
$68,245   £42,205   DM129,358   ¥7,220,009

TOURTE, LOUIS (PERE) [S11/271] Silver Violin
Bow with later frog and adjuster: Paris, c. 1780
6,480/9,720
$5,589   £3,450   DM10,592   ¥590,192

TOURTE, LOUIS (PERE) [S11M/48] Violin Bow
with repair to mortice: Paris, c. 1760   9,702/12,936
$20,316   £12,564   DM38,508   ¥2,149,281

TOURTE, XAVIER (ascribed to) [C11/66] Silver
Violin Bow with replacement adjuster (R. & M.
Millant-Deroux, Paris, June 26, 1962)
3,564/4,860 NS

TOURTE FAMILY (ascribed to) [P3/82] Violin Bow
or Viola Bow   12,960/16,200 NS

TUBBS, ALFRED [B3/8] Rare Silver Violin Bow
2,430/3,240
$2,608   £1,610   DM4,685   ¥307,945

TUBBS, EDWARD [Sk5/123] Silver Violin Bow
1,200/1,400
$1,840   £1,122   DM3,330   ¥222,162

TUBBS, J. [B3/12] Silver Violin Bow   3,240/4,860 NS

TUBBS, J. [B3/23] Silver Violin Bow   3,240/4,860
$3,353   £2,070   DM6,024   ¥395,929

TUBBS, J. [B5/53] Silver Violin Bow   1,640/2,460 NS

TUBBS, J. [B11/8] Silver Violin Bow   3,240/4,860
$2,981   £1,840   DM5,612   ¥315,045

TUBBS, JAMES [B2/60] Silver Violin Bow
2,460/3,280 NS

TUBBS, JAMES [B11/10] Silver Violin Bow
3,240/4,860
$3,167   £1,955   DM5,963   ¥334,735

TUBBS, JAMES [B11/16] Silver Violin Bow
3,240/4,860
$3,353   £2,070   DM6,314   ¥354,425

TUBBS, JAMES [B11/35] Silver Violin Bow
4,050/5,670
$7,079   £4,370   DM13,329   ¥748,231

TUBBS, JAMES [B11/39] Silver Violin Bow
3,240/4,860
$6,707   £4,140   DM12,627   ¥708,851

TUBBS, JAMES [Bf4/2740] Silver Violin Bow for
Georges Adolphe Chanot   2,500/3,000 NS

TUBBS, JAMES [C3/55] Silver Violin Bow
2,445/3,260
$2,249   £1,380   DM3,988   ¥265,967

TUBBS, JAMES [C3/68] Silver Violin Bow
4,564/5,705 NS

TUBBS, JAMES [C11/46] Good Engraved Silver
Violin Bow   4,860/6,480
$5,589   £3,450   DM10,523   ¥590,709

TUBBS, JAMES [C11/142] Gold Violin Bow
3,240/4,860 NS

TUBBS, JAMES [C11/145] Good Silver Violin Bow
4,536/5,184
$5,962   £3,680   DM11,224   ¥630,090

TUBBS, JAMES [P3/129] Silver Violin Bow
1,944/2,430 NS

TUBBS, JAMES [P5/87] Silver Violin Bow with later
frog   1,630/1,956 NS

TUBBS, JAMES [P11/148] Fine Early Silver Violin
Bow without hair: London   3,240/4,050
$4,499   £2,777   DM8,546   ¥472,716

TUBBS, JAMES [P11/160] Violin Bow with full hair:
London, c. 1890   2,916/3,240
$3,750   £2,315   DM7,123   ¥394,028

TUBBS, JAMES [S3/43] Silver Violin Bow w/wooden
bow box: London, c. 1890   2,430/3,240
$5,403   £3,335   DM9,705   ¥637,885

TUBBS, JAMES [S3/58] Silver Violin Bow: London,
c. 1890   2,916/4,050
$4,844   £2,990   DM8,701   ¥571,897

TUBBS, JAMES [S3/67] Chased Gold Violin Bow
w/bow box: London, c. 1890   11,340/16,200
$14,531   £8,970   DM26,103   ¥1,715,692

TUBBS, JAMES [S3/179] Silver Violin Bow: London,
c. 1890   3,240/4,860
$3,726   £2,300   DM6,693   ¥439,921

TUBBS, JAMES [S6/91] Silver Violin Bow: London,
c. 1875   1,590/2,385
$2,011   £1,265   DM3,782   ¥243,184

TUBBS, JAMES [S6/132] Silver Violin Bow: London,
c. 1900   2,862/3,975 NS

TUBBS, JAMES [S6/142] Silver Violin Bow: London,
c. 1895   3,975/5,565
$4,388   £2,760   DM8,252   ¥530,582

TUBBS, JAMES [S6/247] Silver Violin Bow: London,
c. 1890   1,590/2,385
$1,646   £1,035   DM3,095   ¥198,968

TUBBS, JAMES [S11/179] Silver Violin Bow:
London, c. 1890   3,240/4,860 NS

TUBBS, JAMES [S11/201] Silver Violin Bow:
London, c. 1890   4,050/5,670
$4,099   £2,530   DM7,767   ¥432,807

TUBBS, JAMES [S11/270] Silver Violin Bow:
London, c. 1900   2,916/4,050
$3,167   £1,955   DM6,002   ¥334,442

TUBBS, JAMES [S11/279] Silver Violin Bow with
possibly damaged stick: London, c. 1890
3,240/4,860 NS

TUBBS, JAMES [S11/293] Chased Gold Violin Bow:
London, c. 1900   9,720/12,960
$9,315   £5,750   DM17,653   ¥983,653

TUBBS, JAMES [S11M/44] Silver Violin Bow:
London, c. 1860   3,234/4,851
$7,485   £4,629   DM14,187   ¥791,840

TUBBS, T. (attributed to) [B11/23] Silver Violin Bow
                                   1,296/1,944
$1,397   £863   DM2,631   ¥147,677

TUBBS, THOMAS [Sk11/110] Transitional Ebony
Violin Bow with baleen wrap (William Salchow, New
York, September 28, 1999)   1,200/1,400
$2,248   £1,392   DM4,244   ¥237,865

VAN DER MEER, KAREL [S3/54] Silver Violin
Bow w/matching bow: Amsterdam or Bussum, early
20th C.   810/1,134
$2,236   £1,380   DM4,016   ¥263,953

VAN DER MEER, KAREL [S6/148] Silver Violin
Bow with damaged stick and repaired head: Amsterdam, c. 1900   159/239
$91   £57   DM170   ¥10,958

VEDRAL, JOSEPH [S11/186] Silver Violin Bow: The
Hague   648/972
$1,118   £690   DM2,118   ¥118,038

VICKERS, J.E. [P2/125] Violin Bow w/violoncello
bow   163/244
$244   £150   DM428   ¥28,883

VIGNERON, A. [B6/6] Nickel Violin Bow: Paris
                                   1,272/1,908
$1,280   £805   DM2,423   ¥153,425

VIGNERON, A. [B6/24] Silver Violin Bow lacking
hair   3,975/5,565
$4,023   £2,530   DM7,615   ¥482,193

VIGNERON, A. [B11/6] Silver Violin Bow
                                   6,480/9,720
$7,079   £4,370   DM13,329   ¥748,231

VIGNERON, A. [B11/12] Silver Violin Bow (J.F.
Raffin, Paris, November 1, 1998)   3,240/4,860
$3,726   £2,300   DM7,015   ¥393,806

VIGNERON, A. [B11/47] Silver Violin Bow without
hair   4,050/5,670 NS

VIGNERON, A. [C11/152] Good Gold and Tortoiseshell Violin Bow   11,340/14,580 NS

VIGNERON, A. [C11/156] Silver Violin Bow with
later adjuster   3,240/4,860
$7,079   £4,370   DM13,329   ¥748,231

VIGNERON, JOSEPH ARTHUR [C3/8] Silver Violin
Bow with partial hair, formerly owned by Eugene
Ysaÿe   2,934/3,586
$7,873   £4,830   DM13,959   ¥930,886

VIGNERON, JOSEPH ARTHUR [C3/54] Silver
Violin Bow   4,564/5,705
$4,686   £2,875   DM8,309   ¥554,099

VIGNERON, JOSEPH ARTHUR [S3/52] Silver
Violin Bow with later silver overlaid adjuster: Paris,
c. 1890   2,916/4,050
$3,167   £1,955   DM5,689   ¥373,933

VIGNERON, JOSEPH ARTHUR [S3/157] Silver
Violin Bow: Paris, c. 1880   4,050/5,670 NS

VIGNERON, JOSEPH ARTHUR [S3/174] Silver
Violin Bow: Paris, c. 1890   972/1,296
$1,210   £747   DM2,174   ¥142,879

VIGNERON, JOSEPH ARTHUR [S6/93] Silver
Violin Bow: Paris, c. 1900   2,385/3,180
$3,291   £2,070   DM6,189   ¥397,937

VIGNERON, JOSEPH ARTHUR [S11/189] Silver
Violin Bow: Paris, c. 1890   4,860/6,480
$11,551   £7,130   DM21,889   ¥1,219,729

VIGNERON, JOSEPH ARTHUR [S11M/51] Silver
Violin Bow: Paris, c. 1890   4,043/5,660
$11,762   £7,274   DM22,294   ¥1,244,320

VIGNERON, JOSEPH ARTHUR [Sk5/127] Silver
Violin Bow   3,000/4,000
$4,600   £2,806   DM8,326   ¥555,404

VIGNERON, JOSEPH ARTHUR (attributed to)
[S3/173] Silver Violin Bow   1,620/2,430
$2,049   £1,265   DM3,681   ¥241,957

VOIRIN, F.N. [B11/3] Silver Violin Bow
                                   8,100/11,340
$12,110   £7,475   DM22,799   ¥1,279,870

VOIRIN, F.N. [B11/7] Silver Violin Bow
                                   6,480/9,720 NS

VOIRIN, F.N. [C11/55] Silver Violin Bow
                                   5,508/6,480 NS

VOIRIN, F.N. [P6/102] Silver Violin Bow with full
hair, w/case: Paris   4,830/6,440
$5,962   £3,703   DM11,183   ¥716,605

VOIRIN, F.N. [Sk5/153] Silver Violin Bow (Rudolph
Wurlitzer, New York, September 15, 1934)
                                   2,800/3,200
$8,913   £5,437   DM16,132   ¥1,076,095

VOIRIN, FRANCOIS NICOLAS [C3/28] Silver
Violin Bow   3,260/4,075 NS

VOIRIN, FRANCOIS NICOLAS [P11/142] Good
Gold Violin Bow with later adjuster: Paris, c. 1880
(Bernard Millant, Paris, June 16, 1999)
                                   9,720/11,340 NS

VOIRIN, FRANCOIS NICOLAS [S3/169] Silver
Violin Bow: Paris, c. 1870   4,860/8,100
$8,942   £5,520   DM16,063   ¥1,055,810

VOIRIN, FRANCOIS NICOLAS [S3/175] Silver
Violin Bow with repaired stick: Paris, c. 1880
                                   1,134/1,620
$1,528   £943   DM2,744   ¥180,368

VOIRIN, FRANCOIS NICOLAS [S3/180] Silver
Violin Bow w/2 silver violin bows, 1 stick damaged:
Paris, c. 1875   3,240/4,050 NS

VOIRIN, FRANCOIS NICOLAS [S6/104] Gold
Violin Bow with later adjuster: Paris, c. 1870
                                   3,180/4,770
$3,657   £2,300   DM6,877   ¥442,152

VOIRIN, FRANCOIS NICOLAS [S6/255] Silver
Violin Bow: Paris, c. 1870   2,862/3,975 NS

VOIRIN, FRANCOIS NICOLAS [S11/177] Silver
Violin Bow w/bow box: Paris, c. 1870   6,480/9,720
$7,079   £4,370   DM13,416   ¥747,576

VOIRIN, FRANCOIS NICOLAS [S11/286] Silver
Violin Bow with replacement adjuster: Paris, c. 1870
                                       1,620/2,430
$3,540   £2,185   DM6,708   ¥373,788

VOIRIN, FRANCOIS NICOLAS [S11M/40] Gold
Violin Bow w/label in Yehudi Menuhin's hand: Paris,
1870   9,702/12,936
$42,770   £26,450   DM81,069   ¥4,524,802

VOIRIN, FRANCOIS NICOLAS [S11M/41] Gold
and Ivory Violin Bow: Paris, c. 1870   9,702/12,936
$22,454   £13,886   DM42,561   ¥2,375,521

VOIRIN, FRANCOIS NICOLAS [S11M/42] Gold
and Tortoiseshell Violin Bow with repaired head:
Paris, c. 1870   4,851/6,468
$14,969   £9,258   DM28,374   ¥1,583,681

VOIRIN, FRANCOIS NICOLAS [S11M/49] Silver
Violin Bow: Paris, c. 1870   6,468/9,702
$14,969   £9,258   DM28,374   ¥1,583,681

VOIRIN, FRANCOIS NICOLAS [Sk11/142] Silver
Violin Bow (Willam Salchow, New York, September
28, 1999)   6,000/8,000
$7,935   £4,912   DM14,977   ¥839,523

VOIRIN, FRANCOIS NICOLAS [Sk11/145] Silver
Violin Bow (William Salchow, New York, September
28, 1999)   6,000/8,000 NS

VOIRIN, FRANCOIS NICOLAS [Sk11/157a] Silver
Violin Bow   6,000/8,000
$8,596   £5,321   DM16,225   ¥909,483

VOIRIN, J. [B3/5] Silver Violin Bow   4,860/8,100 NS

VOIRIN, JOSEPH [S6/254] Silver Violin Bow: Paris,
c. 1860   1,590/3,180
$2,560   £1,610   DM4,814   ¥309,506

VOIRIN, JOSEPH [S11/188] Silver Violin Bow: Paris,
c. 1860   1,296/1,944
$1,304   £805   DM2,471   ¥137,711

VUILLAUME (workshop of) [S6/92] Silver Violin
Bow: Paris, c. 1870   1,272/1,908
$2,560   £1,610   DM4,814   ¥309,506

VUILLAUME, JEAN BAPTISTE [C11/64] Silver
Violin Bow   6,156/6,804 NS

VUILLAUME, JEAN BAPTISTE [S6/238] Silver
Violin Bow: Paris, c. 1850   3,975/5,565 NS

VUILLAUME, JEAN BAPTISTE [S11/191] Silver
Picture Violin Bow: Paris, c. 1870   4,860/6,480
$9,688   £5,980   DM18,359   ¥1,022,999

VUILLAUME, JEAN BAPTISTE (workshop of)
[Sk5/114] Silver Violin Bow   2,800/3,200
$3,220   £1,964   DM5,828   ¥388,783

VUILLAUME, JEAN BAPTISTE (workshop of)
[Sk5/126] Silver Violin Bow   3,000/4,000
$2,990   £1,824   DM5,412   ¥361,013

WEICHOLD, R. [B11/24] Silver Violin Bow
                                        810/1,134
$1,025   £633   DM1,929   ¥108,297

WEICHOLD, RICHARD [S11/329] Silver Violin
Bow: Dresden, c. 1890   648/972
$782   £483   DM1,483   ¥82,627

WEICHOLD, RICHARD [Sk11/152] Silver Violin
Bow   400/600
$992   £614   DM1,873   ¥105,001

WEIMER, CARL [S11M/74] Silver Violin Bow
                                        404/566
$898   £555   DM1,702   ¥95,021

WERNER, EMIL [C3/32] Gold Violin Bow
                                        815/1,304
$1,687   £1,035   DM2,991   ¥199,476

WERRO, HENRY [S11/198] Silver Violin Bow: Bern,
mid 20th C.   486/810 NS

WILSON, GARNER [P9/102] Gold Violin Bow
                                        1,296/1,458
$1,751   £1,081   DM3,297   ¥186,689

WILSON, GARNER [P11/192] Silver Violin Bow
with full hair   648/810
$965   £596   DM1,833   ¥101,394

WILSON, GARNER [S6/140] Gold Violin Bow: Bury
St. Edmunds, c. 1995 (maker's, July 28, 1995)
                                        1,272/1,590
$1,553   £977   DM2,921   ¥187,818

WITHERS, GEORGE & SONS [B6/3] Silver Violin
Bow   1,590/2,385
$1,829   £1,150   DM3,461   ¥219,179

WURLITZER, REMBERT [S11/285] Silver Violin
Bow: New York, c. 1950   648/972
$651   £402   DM1,234   ¥68,770

VIOLONCELLO

ALBERTI, FERDINANDO (attributed to) [Bf4/2836]
Good Child's Violoncello   1,200/1,800
$1,852   £1,152   DM3,407   ¥218,384

APPARUT, GEORGES (workshop of) [P3/200] Fine
and Handsome French Violoncello of good quality
and condition: Mirecourt, 1929   7,290/8,100
$9,315   £5,750   DM16,675   ¥1,098,653

BAADER, J.A. (attributed to) [P9/154] Violoncello in
playing condition, w/cover: Mittenwald, c. 1930
                                        648/810
$2,608   £1,610   DM4,911   ¥278,047

BANDINI, MARIO [S3/74] Violoncello: Ravenna,
1981   5,670/8,100
$5,589   £3,450   DM10,040   ¥659,882

BARBE, F.J. [B11/69] Fine French Violoncello:
c. 1840 (J. & A. Beare, London, March 24, 1995)
                                        40,500/56,700
$46,575   £28,750   DM87,688   ¥4,922,575

BARRETT, JOHN [B3/34A] Fine English Violoncello:
London, 1731   19,440/24,300 NS

BERNARDEL, GUSTAVE (workshop of) [Sk5/89]
Good French Violoncello w/case: Paris, 1892
15,000/20,000
$20,700　　£12,627　　DM37,467　　¥2,499,318

BETTS [B6/34] Fine English Violoncello: London,
1791　　　　　　　　　　　　　23,850/31,800
$23,771　　£14,950　　DM45,000　　¥2,849,321

BETTS, JOHN [S3/80] Violoncello: London, c. 1780
3,240/4,860
$3,353　　£2,070　　DM6,024　　¥395,929

BOUSSU, JOSEPH BENOIT [Sk5/83] Rare Flemish
Violoncello: Brussels, 1752 (Ivo Loerakker, Montreal,
January 30, 1981)　　　　　　　20,000/30,000
$20,700　　£12,627　　DM37,467　　¥2,499,318

CALCAGNI, BERNARDO [P3/184] Fine and
Handsome Italian Violoncello in good condition:
Genoa, c. 1750　　　　　　　　19,440/24,300
$34,466　　£21,275　　DM61,698　　¥4,065,014

CARCASSI, LORENZO & TOMMASO [S11/230]
Violoncello w/case: Florence, 1769　97,200/129,600
$153,900　　£95,000　　DM291,650　　¥16,251,650

CATENI, PIETRO [S6/172] Violoncello w/bow, case:
Livorno, c. 1800 (Dario D'Attili, New Jersey,
November 16, 1994)　　　　　63,600/95,400 NS

CAVALLI, ARISTIDE [C3/181] Italian Violoncello
w/case, bow: Cremona, 1923　　　　6,520/8,150
$14,059　　£8,625　　DM24,926　　¥1,662,296

CHARDON & FILS [P3/191] Good French Violoncello in immediate playing condition, w/cover: Paris,
1921　　　　　　　　　　　12,960/16,200 NS

CHARDON & FILS [P5/106] Good French
Violoncello in immediate playing condition, w/cover:
Paris, 1921　　　　　　　　　8,150/13,040
$9,373　　£5,750　　DM16,963　　¥1,130,968

CHARETTE, PIERRE [Sk5/99] Contemporary
Canadian Violoncello: Montreal, 1982　1,400/1,600
$2,300　　£1,403　　DM4,163　　¥277,702

COSTA, FELIX MORI (attributed to) [Sk5/90]
Milanese Violoncello w/case: c. 1810 (Dario D'Attili,
Dumont, October 9, 1989)　　　　60,000/80,000
$57,500　　£35,075　　DM104,075　　¥6,942,550

CUISSET, A. [B2/74] Good Belgian Violoncello
4,100/5,740
$4,715　　£2,875　　DM8,136　　¥538,085

CUYPERS, JOHANNES [P11/208] Rare Violoncello
in playing condition　　　　　29,160/35,640 NS

DEARLOVE, WILLIAM [P3/202] English Violoncello with restorable rib and table blemishes, w/case,
2 bows: Leeds, c. 1870　　　　　2,430/3,240 NS

DEARLOVE, WILLIAM [P6/145] English Violoncello in immediate playing condition, w/case, 2 bows:
Leeds, c. 1870　　　　　　　　1,610/2,415
$2,768　　£1,719　　DM5,192　　¥332,709

DOLLING, AUGUST [S3/87] Violoncello w/case,
bow: Erfurt, 1915　　　　　　　4,050/5,670
$4,658　　£2,875　　DM8,366　　¥549,901

DUKE, RICHARD (attributed to) [P11/215] English
Violoncello with skillful old restorations: London,
c. 1780　　　　　　　　　　　4,860/6,480
$7,284　　£4,497　　DM13,836　　¥765,349

DYKES, GEORGE L. (workshop of) [Sk5/92] English
Violoncello　　　　　　　　　2,800/3,200
$5,463　　£3,332　　DM9,887　　¥659,542

ELLERSIECK, ALBERT [S3/77] Violoncello
2,430/3,240
$4,844　　£2,990　　DM8,701　　¥571,897

FORSTER, WILLIAM [Bf10/8058] Good English
Violoncello bearing two original additional f-hole
cutouts in the center bouts, which have been filled,
w/soft case, bow: London, 1793　　25,000/35,000
$26,450　　£15,870　　DM47,610　　¥205,517

GAGLIANO, GENNARO [B11/74] Very Fine and
Important Violoncello: Naples, 1741 (W.E. Hill &
Sons, London, April 13, 1920)
$409,860　£253,000　　DM771,650　　¥43,318,660

GALIMBERTI, LUIGI [Bf10/8057] Fine Italian
Violoncello in immediate playing condition: Milan,
1953　　　　　　　　　　　　20,000/25,000
$20,700　　£12,420　　DM37,260　　¥160,839

GALLA, ANTON [S11/219] Violoncello w/cover:
Brno, c. 1930　　　　　　　　3,240/4,860
$3,353　　£2,070　　DM6,355　　¥354,115

GAND BROS. [P11/207] Fine and Handsome French
Violoncello in immediate playing condition, w/cover:
Paris, c. 1860　　　　　　　　35,640/45,360 NS

GEISSENHOF, FRANZ (attributed to) [C11/122]
Viennese Violoncello w/case: 1806　8,100/11,340
$13,973　　£8,625　　DM26,306　　¥1,476,773

GLENISTER, WILLIAM [P11/216] English Violoncello in immediate playing condition, w/cover:
London, 1924　　　　　　　　3,240/4,050
$4,285　　£2,645　　DM8,139　　¥450,205

HAMMIG, W.H. [B3/45] German Violoncello:
Leipzig, 1885　　　　　　　　6,480/9,720
$7,825　　£4,830　　DM14,055　　¥923,834

HARRIS, CHARLES [P3/193] English Violoncello,
well-restored, w/cover: Adderbury, Oxon., c. 1830
4,860/5,670
$4,285　　£2,645　　DM7,671　　¥505,380

HEINICKE, MATHIAS [P9/141] Fine and Handsome
Violoncello in immediate playing condition, w/bow:
Wildstein　　　　　　　　　　6,480/8,100
$7,452　　£4,600　　DM14,030　　¥794,420

HILL, LOCKEY [B11/76] English Violoncello:
London, c. 1780　　　　　　11,340/16,200 NS

HILL, WILLIAM EBSWORTH [P11/211] Fine and
Handsome English Violoncello in immediate playing
condition: London, c. 1860　　32,400/40,500 NS

JORIO, VINCENZO [B6/41] Rare Italian Violoncello: Naples, c. 1840 (J.&A. Beare, London, 1995)
47,700/63,600 NS

JUZEK, JOHN [Sk11/47] Czech Violoncello w/soft
case: Prague　　　　　　　　1,200/1,400
$2,777　　£1,719　　DM5,242　　¥293,833

JUZEK, JOHN [Sk11/48] Czech Violoncello: Prague
800/1,200
$1,455   £900   DM2,746   ¥153,913

JUZEK, JOHN [Sk11/55] Czech Violoncello w/bow:
Prague, 1969   600/800 NS

KAUL, PAUL [S3/84] Violoncello w/case, 2 bows:
Nantes, 1908   16,200/22,680
$18,630   £11,500   DM33,465   ¥2,199,605

KENNEDY, THOMAS [B6/35] English Violoncello:
London, 1823   28,620/39,750
$32,913   £20,700   DM62,307   ¥3,945,213

KENNEDY, THOMAS [P11/212] Good English
Violoncello with restorable blemishes, w/cover:
London, 1843   12,150/13,770
$15,426   £9,522   DM29,299   ¥1,620,740

KENNEDY, THOMAS [S11/233] Violoncello w/case:
London, 1814   19,440/25,920
$22,356   £13,800   DM42,366   ¥2,360,766

KLOZ, JOSEPH [S3/79] Violoncello w/case:
Mittenwald, 1778   16,200/24,300 NS

KRUMBHOLZ, LORENZ [C3/199] Dutch
Violoncello w/case   8,150/11,410 NS

LABERTE [P11/220] Mirecourt Violoncello in immediate playing condition, w/case, bow: c. 1900
6,480/9,720 NS

LAJOS, KONYA [P3/196] Good Violoncello in good
condition, w/cover: Tatabanya, Hungary, 1996
(maker's, June 1998)   4,050/4,860
$4,658   £2,875   DM8,338   ¥549,326

LANG, BENEDIKT [C3/169] German Violoncello
w/case, 2 bows: Mittenwald, 1981   1,630/2,445 NS

LONGMAN, LUKEY & CO. [S6/167] Violoncello:
London, c. 1770   6,360/9,540
$6,400   £4,025   DM12,035   ¥773,766

MAGNIERE, GABRIEL [B11/63] French Violoncello:
Mirecourt, 1899   3,240/4,860
$2,981   £1,840   DM5,612   ¥315,045

MERLIN, JOSEPH [P11/210] Fine and Handsome
English Violoncello in immediate playing condition,
w/case: London, c. 1780   12,960/14,580
$27,852   £17,193   DM52,901   ¥2,926,335

MOUGENOT, LEON [C3/196] French Violoncello:
1926   1,956/2,934
$5,624   £3,450   DM9,971   ¥664,919

NEUNER & HORNSTEINER [P2/142] Violoncello
with minor restorable blemishes, w/violin, 2 violin
bows: Mittenwald, 1912   1,630/2,445
$3,374   £2,070   DM5,900   ¥398,579

NEUNER & HORNSTEINER [P9/157] Mittenwald
Violoncello requiring minor regluing, w/bow: c. 1880
1,296/1,458
$3,726   £2,300   DM7,015   ¥397,210

PANORMO, VINCENZO (attributed to) [C3/203]
Fine Violoncello w/case   32,600/48,900
$59,821   £36,700   DM106,063   ¥7,073,191

POGGI, ANSALDO [C3/207] Fine Italian Violoncello: Bolgna, 1931 (Peter Biddulph, London, April
18, 1997)   61,940/73,350
$59,821   £36,700   DM106,063   ¥7,073,191

POSCH, ANTON [Bf4/2837] Fine Violoncello
w/case, bow: Vienna, 1723 (Douglas Bearden Violin
Shop, October 23, 1968)   18,000/22,500
$17,193   £10,694   DM31,634   ¥2,027,855

PRENTICE, RONALD [P2/135] Good Contemporary English Violoncello in immediate playing condition, w/case: 1978   2,445/3,260 NS

PRENTICE, RONALD [P5/116] Good Contemporary English Violoncello in immediate playing condition, w/case: 1978   1,956/2,445
$3,374   £2,070   DM6,107   ¥407,148

REITER, JOHANN [S11/231] Violoncello w/cover:
Mittenwald, 1879   6,480/9,720 NS

RICHARDSON, ARTHUR [P3/197] Good Violoncello with minor restored table blemishes: Crediton,
Devon, 1926   4,860/6,480
$5,403   £3,335   DM9,672   ¥637,218

SANNINO, VINCENZO [Sk11/89] Fine Violoncello:
Naples, 1898   70,000/80,000 NS

SCAPPIO, FRANCESCO [S11/212] Violoncello
w/cover, bow: Italy, late 19th C.   4,050/5,670
$11,178   £6,900   DM21,183   ¥1,180,383

SCARAMPELLA, GIUSEPPE (ascribed to) [S11/224]
Violoncello w/case: North Italy, mid 20th C. (Max
Möller B.V., Amsterdam, April 19, 1977)
16,200/24,300 NS

SCARAMPELLA, STEFANO (ascribed to) [S6/173]
Violoncello: probably Mantua, c. 1930 (Walter
Hamma, Stuttgart, June 14, 1985)   12,720/19,080
$14,628   £9,200   DM27,508   ¥1,768,608

SCARAMPELLA, STEFANO (attributed to) [C3/208]
Good Violoncello w/case   32,600/48,900 NS

SMITH, THOMAS [S11/214] Violoncello: London,
1757   4,860/6,480
$10,247   £6,325   DM19,418   ¥1,082,018

SMITH, THOMAS (attributed to) [P3/192] Attractive
English Violoncello with minor restored blemishes:
London, c. 1770   9,720/10,530 NS

SMITH, THOMAS (attributed to) [P5/111] Attractive
English Violoncello in immediate playing condition:
London, c. 1770   5,705/6,520
$8,060   £4,945   DM14,588   ¥972,632

STRADIVARI, ANTONIO [C3/205] Important
Italian "Segelman Ex-Hart" Violoncello: Cremona,
1692   978,000/1,304,000
$898,945 £551,500DM1,593,835   ¥106,290,595

THIBOUVILLE-LAMY, J. [P2/141] Violoncello with
minor worm and some table restoration, w/cover:
Mirecourt, c. 1920   815/1,141
$937   £575   DM1,639   ¥110,716

THIBOUVILLE-LAMY, J. [P5/110] French Violoncello in immediate playing condition, w/case: c. 1900
2,445/2,934
$2,812   £1,725   DM5,089   ¥339,290

THIBOUVILLE-LAMY, J. [P5/112] French Violoncello with restorable neck repair, w/case, 2 bows:
c. 1900   1,141/1,304
$1,594   £978   DM2,885   ¥192,363

THIBOUVILLE-LAMY, J. [P11/224] French
Violoncello requiring some restoration, otherwise in
playing condition, w/cover: c. 1910   810/972
$1,500   £926   DM2,849   ¥157,572

THIBOUVILLE-LAMY, JEROME [S6/171]
Violoncello w/bow, cover: Mirecourt, c. 1890
                                       1,272/1,908
$1,280   £805   DM2,407   ¥154,753

TOMASSINI, DOMENICO [Bf10/8055] Fine
Modern Italian Violoncello in immediate playing condition: Viterbo, 1971   18,000/22,000 NS

VUILLAUME, SEBASTIAN [B6/42] Very Fine French
Violoncello (Peter Biddulph, London)
                                47,700/63,600 NS

WAMSLEY, PETER [B3/35] Violoncello: London,
1740   8,100/11,340
$8,384   £5,175   DM15,059   ¥989,822

WEERTMAN, ROELOF [Sk5/86] American
Violoncello w/case, bow: Cape Cod, 1973
                                  6,000/8,000 NS

WHITE, ASA WARREN [Sk5/97] American
Violoncello w/bow: Boston, 1874   600/800
$1,725   £1,052   DM3,122   ¥208,277

ZANI, ALDO [Bf10/8056] Fine Italian Violoncello in
nearly perfect and immediate playing condition,
w/case: Cesena, 1972   20,000/25,000 NS

ZIMMERMANN, JULIUS HEINRICH (attributed
to) [P3/189] Good German Violoncello in good condition, w/case: Berlin, 1919   4,050/4,536 NS

ZIMMERMANN, JULIUS HEINRICH (attributed
to) [P5/114] Good German Violoncello in immediate
playing condition, w/case: Leipzig, Berlin, 1919
                                      3,586/4,075
$4,124   £2,530   DM7,464   ¥497,626

VIOLONCELLO BOW

ADAM, JEAN DOMINIQUE (attributed to) [S6/237]
Violoncello Bow: France, mid 19th C.
                                  4,452/5,565 NS

BAUSCH [B6/4] Silver and Ebony Violoncello Bow
                                      1,272/1,590
$2,011   £1,265   DM3,808   ¥241,096

BAUSCH, LUDWIG [C11/129] Silver Violoncello
Bow   1,296/1,944
$2,049   £1,265   DM3,858   ¥216,593

BAZIN (attributed to) [P3/156] Silver Violoncello
Bow requiring rehairing   1,944/2,430
$2,236   £1,380   DM4,002   ¥263,677

BAZIN, CHARLES NICHOLAS [S11/204] Silver
Violoncello Bow for Silvestre & Maucotel: Paris or
Mirecourt, c. 1920   2,916/4,050
$3,167   £1,955   DM6,002   ¥334,442

BAZIN, LOUIS [C3/21] Silver Violoncello Bow
                                  3,260/4,890 NS

BAZIN, LOUIS (II) [S11/282] Silver Violoncello Bow:
Mirecourt, c. 1950   1,620/2,430
$1,677   £1,035   DM3,177   ¥177,057

BERNARDEL, GUSTAVE [Sk11/115] Silver Violoncello Bow   1,400/1,600
$1,984   £1,228   DM3,744   ¥209,881

BULTITUDE, ARTHUR RICHARD [B3/30] Gold
and Tortoiseshell Violoncello Bow with a golden rose
set in the frog   1,944/2,430
$2,049   £1,265   DM3,681   ¥241,957

BULTITUDE, ARTHUR RICHARD [S11/261] Gold
and Tortoiseshell Violoncello Bow w/bow box:
Hawkhurst, 1977   3,240/4,860 NS

BULTITUDE, ARTHUR RICHARD [S11/284] Gold
and Tortoiseshell Violoncello Bow w/bow box:
Hawkhurst, 1966   3,564/4,536 NS

BULTITUDE, ARTHUR RICHARD [S11/297] Gold
and Tortoiseshell Violoncello Bow: Hawkhurst, 1961
                                  2,916/4,050 NS

BUTHOD, CHARLES [C3/65] Silver Violoncello
Bow   652/978
$787   £483   DM1,396   ¥93,089

COLAS, PROSPER [C3/67] Silver Violoncello Bow
                                  1,304/1,956 NS

COLAS, PROSPER [S6/134] Nickel Violoncello Bow:
Paris, c. 1900   954/1,272
$475   £299   DM894   ¥57,480

COLAS, PROSPER [Sk5/211] Silver Violoncello Bow
                                      600/800
$1,380   £842   DM2,498   ¥166,621

DODD [B6/16] Silver Violoncello Bow with later frog
and button   3,180/4,770
$3,291   £2,070   DM6,231   ¥394,521

DODD, J. [B11/57] Silver and Ivory Violoncello Bow
                                  2,916/4,050 NS

DODD, JAMES [S6/111] Violoncello Bow with
minor damage to head: London, early 19th C.
                                      1,272/1,908
$1,371   £862   DM2,577   ¥165,711

DODD, JOHN [C3/51] Silver Violoncello Bow
                                      6,520/8,150
$7,498   £4,600   DM13,294   ¥886,558

EURY, NICOLAS [Sk11/92] Fine Silver Violoncello
Bow (Pierre Vidoudez, Geneva, March 1979)
                                40,000/45,000 NS

FETIQUE, MARCEL (attributed to) [C11/136] Silver
Violoncello Bow   4,050/5,670 NS

FETIQUE, VICTOR [B3/17] Silver Violoncello Bow:
Paris   6,480/9,720
$7,452   £4,600   DM13,386   ¥879,842

FETIQUE, VICTOR [S6/244] Silver Violoncello Bow:
Paris, c. 1920   2,862/3,975
$2,743   £1,725   DM5,158   ¥331,614

FETIQUE, VICTOR (ascribed to) [C11/133] Silver Violoncello Bow (Jean-François Raffin, Paris, July 3, 1999)   810/972
$1,210   £747   DM2,278   ¥127,901

FORSTER, WILLIAM (II) [S11/324] Transitional Ivory Violoncello Bow: London, c. 1800 1,944/2,916
$2,422   £1,495   DM4,590   ¥255,750

GRUNKE [B2/63] Silver Violoncello Bow
                                              1,312/1,640 NS

GRUNKE [B5/68] Silver Violoncello Bow
                                              820/1,148 NS

HEL, PIERRE [C3/23] Silver Violoncello Bow
                                              4,890/6,520 NS

HENDERSON, F.V. [Sk11/109] Gold and Mountain Mahogany Violoncello Bow   1,600/1,800 NS

HENRY, EUGENE [S6/95] Silver Violoncello Bow: Paris, c. 1880   1,908/2,544 NS

HENRY, JOSEPH [C11/181] Fine Silver Violoncello Bow: Paris, c. 1860   12,960/19,440
$31,671   £19,550   DM59,628   ¥3,347,351

HILL, W.E. & SONS [B6/23] Silver Violoncello Bow
                                              1,272/1,908
$1,280   £805   DM2,423   ¥153,425

HILL, W.E. & SONS [Bf10/8017] Silver Violoncello Bow   2,750/3,500
$2,875   £1,725   DM5,175   ¥22,339

HILL, W.E. & SONS [P2/97] Silver Violoncello Bow with minor head blemish: London   652/815
$712   £437   DM1,245   ¥84,144

HILL, W.E. & SONS [P3/155] Good Silver Violon-cello Bow w/case: London   1,296/1,620 NS

HILL, W.E. & SONS [P3/173] Good Silver Violon-cello Bow with full hair: London   1,296/1,458
$1,528   £943   DM2,735   ¥180,179

HILL, W.E. & SONS [P5/96] Good Silver Violoncello Bow w/case: London   1,141/1,467 NS

HILL, W.E. & SONS [P6/107] Silver Violoncello Bow   966/1,127 NS

HILL, W.E. & SONS [P9/113] Good Silver Violon-cello Bow w/case: London   810/972
$671   £414   DM1,263   ¥71,498

HILL, W.E. & SONS [P9/129] Silver Violoncello Bow   648/810
$932   £575   DM1,754   ¥99,303

HILL, W.E. & SONS [P11/151] Violoncello Bow with full hair: London   810/972
$1,243   £767   DM2,360   ¥130,560

HILL, W.E. & SONS [S6/126] Silver Violoncello Bow: London, 1931   2,862/3,975
$4,754   £2,990   DM8,940   ¥574,798

HILL, W.E. & SONS [S6/231] Gold and Tortoiseshell Fleur-de-Lys Violoncello Bow: London, 1966
                                              4,770/5,565
$5,120   £3,220   DM9,628   ¥619,013

HILL, W.E. & SONS [Sk11/102] Silver and Tortoise-shell Violoncello Bow with baleen wrap 4,000/5,000
$5,290   £3,275   DM9,985   ¥559,682

HUSSON, CHARLES CLAUDE [P3/135] Good Nickel Violoncello Bow with full hair (Jean-François Raffin, Paris, June 9, 1998)   1,944/2,430
$2,236   £1,380   DM4,002   ¥263,677

LABERTE [P3/174] Nickel Violoncello Bow with full hair (Jean-François Raffin, Paris, June 14, 1998)
                                              810/891
$782   £483   DM1,401   ¥92,287

LAFLEUR, JACQUES [S3/66] Silver Violoncello Bow w/bow box: Paris, c. 1820 (William Moennig & Son, Philadelphia, April 4, 1985)   19,440/25,920 NS

LAMY, A. [B11/55] Silver Violoncello Bow with later frog and button   2,430/3,240 NS

LAMY, ALFRED [C3/41] Silver Violoncello Bow
                                              3,260/4,890
$3,562   £2,185   DM6,315   ¥421,115

LAMY, ALFRED [S6/236] Silver Violoncello Bow: Paris, c. 1890   3,975/5,565 NS

LAMY, ALFRED JOSEPH [C3/27] Silver Violoncello Bow   9,780/14,670 NS

LAMY, ALFRED JOSEPH [C3/39] Silver Violoncello Bow   9,780/13,040 NS

LAMY, ALFRED JOSEPH [C3/49] Silver Violoncello Bow   4,890/6,520
$5,249   £3,220   DM9,306   ¥620,591

LAMY, ALFRED JOSEPH [C11/128] Silver Violon-cello Bow (Jean-François Raffin, Paris, June 13, 1999)   3,240/4,860
$3,726   £2,300   DM7,015   ¥393,806

LAMY, ALFRED JOSEPH [S6/127] Gold and Tortoiseshell Violoncello Bow: Paris, c. 1890
                                              12,720/19,080
$16,457   £10,350   DM30,947   ¥1,989,684

LAMY, ALFRED JOSEPH [S6/135] Silver Violoncello Bow: Paris, c. 1910   3,180/4,770
$2,743   £1,725   DM5,158   ¥331,614

LAMY, ALFRED JOSEPH [S6/245] Gold Violoncello Bow: Paris, c. 1900   3,180/4,770
$5,851   £3,680   DM11,003   ¥707,443

LAMY, ALFRED JOSEPH [S11/331] Silver Violon-cello Bow: Paris, c. 1900   2,430/3,240
$2,236   £1,380   DM4,237   ¥236,077

LAMY, ALFRED JOSEPH [Sk5/203] Good Silver Violoncello Bow (Peter Paul Prier, Salt Lake City, May 12, 1993)   5,000/7,000
$5,175   £3,157   DM9,367   ¥624,830

LAPIERRE, MARCEL [Sk5/208] Nickel Violoncello Bow   300/500
$575   £351   DM1,041   ¥69,426

LOTTE, FRANCOIS [Sk11/154] Silver Violoncello Bow   500/700
$860   £532   DM1,624   ¥91,009

63

MALINE, GUILLAUME [S3/166] Silver Violoncello
Bow w/bow box: Paris, c. 1840   9,720/12,960 NS

MALINE, GUILLAUME [S6/222] Silver Violoncello
Bow with later adjuster: Mirecourt, c. 1840
3,180/4,770 NS

MARTIN, JEAN JOSEPH [S11/269] Silver Violoncello Bow with later adjuster: Paris or Mirecourt,
c. 1890   4,050/5,670
$6,521   £4,025   DM12,357   ¥688,557

MARTIN, JEAN JOSEPH [Sk11/93] Silver Violoncello Bow   3,500/4,000
$5,687   £3,520   DM10,734   ¥601,658

MILLANT, ROGER & MAX [S6/147] Silver Violoncello Bow: Paris, c. 1950   2,385/3,180
$2,560   £1,610   DM4,814   ¥309,506

MILLANT, ROGER & MAX [S6/252] Gold Violoncello Bow   6,360/7,950
$10,971   £6,900   DM20,631   ¥1,326,456

MORIZOT, LOUIS [Bf4/2747] Silver Violoncello
Bow   2,000/3,000
$2,248   £1,398   DM4,137   ¥265,181

MORIZOT (FRERES), LOUIS [P2/93] French Silver
Violoncello Bow: c. 1950 (Jean-François Raffin, Paris,
June 14, 1998)   1,630/1,956 NS

NEUDORFER, RODOLF (II) [S11/268] Silver
Violoncello Bow: Switzerland, c. 1970   648/972
$894   £552   DM1,695   ¥94,431

NEUVEVILLE, P.C. [S3/50] Silver Violoncello Bow:
Switzerland, c. 1960   972/1,296 NS

NURNBERGER [B3/31] Silver Violoncello Bow
4,050/4,860 NS

NURNBERGER, A. [B11/54] Silver Violoncello Bow
3,240/4,860
$3,353   £2,070   DM6,314   ¥354,425

NURNBERGER, ALBERT [C3/267] Silver Violoncello Bow   326/489
$937   £575   DM1,662   ¥110,820

NURNBERGER, ALBERT [Sk5/205] Silver Violoncello Bow   800/1,200
$690   £421   DM1,249   ¥83,311

NURNBERGER, ALBERT [Sk5/212] Silver Violoncello Bow   600/800
$863   £526   DM1,561   ¥104,138

OUCHARD, EMILE FRANCOIS [S6/232] Gold
Violoncello Bow: Mirecourt, c. 1930   3,975/4,770
$4,023   £2,530   DM7,565   ¥486,367

OUCHARD, EMILE FRANCOIS [S11/326] Silver
Violoncello Bow with repaired stick: Mirecourt,
c. 1920   2,430/3,240 NS

PAJEOT, ETIENNE [S6/234] Nickel Violoncello
Bow: Paris, c. 1830   5,565/7,155
$8,228   £5,175   DM15,473   ¥994,842

PANORMO (ascribed to) [P6/93] Part-Silver Violoncello Bow with full hair: c. 1840   2,415/2,898NS

PANORMO (ascribed to) [P9/112] Part-Silver
Violoncello Bow with full hair: c. 1840   1,296/1,458
$2,142   £1,323   DM4,034   ¥228,396

PANORMO (attributed to) [P11/177] Ivory Violoncello Bow with full hair   1,215/1,296
$2,364   £1,459   DM4,490   ¥248,396

PECCATTE, CHARLES [B2/65] Silver Violoncello
Bow with later button   1,640/2,460
$1,792   £1,093   DM3,092   ¥204,472

PECCATTE, CHARLES (attributed to) [C11/130]
Good Silver Violoncello Bow missing some pearl from
eye: c. 1910   4,860/6,480 NS

PECCATTE, CHARLES & AUGUSTE LENOBLE
(workshop of) [S11/205] Silver Violoncello Bow:
Paris, 1875 (Paul Childs, Montrose, September, 15,
1998)   4,860/5,670
$5,589   £3,450   DM10,592   ¥590,192

PECCATTE, DOMINIQUE [B11/62] Fine Silver
Violoncello Bow with frog possibly by another hand
(J.F. Raffin, Paris, April 1999)   19,440/24,300
$22,356   £13,800   DM42,090   ¥2,362,836

PECCATTE, DOMINIQUE [S11/307] Silver
Violoncello Bow: Paris, c. 1860   12,960/19,440 NS

PFRETZSCHNER (workshop of) [Sk5/206] Silver
Violoncello Bow   800/1,200
$489   £298   DM885   ¥59,012

PFRETZSCHNER, H.R. [Sk5/210] Silver Violoncello
Bow   800/1,200
$1,495   £912   DM2,706   ¥180,506

SARTORY, E. [P6/95] Silver Violoncello Bow requiring rehairing: Paris   4,025/5,635
$12,775   £7,935   DM23,964   ¥1,535,581

SARTORY, EUGENE [Bf4/2748] Very Fine Silver
Violoncello Bow   11,000/15,000
$19,838   £12,339   DM36,501   ¥2,339,833

SARTORY, EUGENE [C3/40] Silver Violoncello Bow
11,410/16,300 NS

SARTORY, EUGENE [C11/137] Silver Violoncello
Bow   7,290/8,910
$13,041   £8,050   DM24,553   ¥1,378,321

SARTORY, EUGENE [Sk5/203A] Silver Violoncello
Bow   10,000/15,000
$17,825   £10,873   DM32,263   ¥2,152,191

SARTORY, EUGENE [Sk11/97] Silver Violoncello
Bow without wrap   6,000/8,000
$13,225   £8,186   DM24,962   ¥1,399,205

SARTORY, EUGENE [Sk11/106] Silver Violoncello
Bow: Paris   14,000/16,000
$15,870   £9,824   DM29,955   ¥1,679,046

SEIFERT, LOTHAR [Bf10/8015] Fine Gold and
Tortoiseshell Violoncello Bow in a nearly perfect state
of preservation   3,250/3,750 NS

SIMON, PAUL [Bf4/2750] Fine Silver Violoncello
Bow   3,000/4,000
$4,959   £3,085   DM9,125   ¥584,958

SIMON, PAUL [S3/167] Silver Violoncello Bow
w/bow box: Paris, c. 1840   4,860/6,480
$7,452   £4,600   DM13,386   ¥879,842

TAYLOR, DAVID [P3/152] Engraved Gold
Commemorative Violoncello Bow: England (maker's)
2,430/2,916 NS

TAYLOR, MALCOLM [P5/78] Engraved Gold
Commemorative Violoncello Bow with Prince of
Wales feathers inset: England (maker's)
1,630/2,445 NS

TAYLOR, MALCOLM [P9/97] Engraved Gold
Commemorative Violoncello Bow: England (maker's)
1,134/1,215
$1,304   £805   DM2,455   ¥139,024

THOMASSIN (attributed to) [P3/127] Good Silver
Violoncello Bow with full hair   1,620/1,944 NS

THOMASSIN, VICTOR [S11/185] Silver Violoncello
Bow: London, c. 1920   3,240/4,860 NS

TUBBS, JAMES (attributed to) [P3/154] Silver
Presentation Violoncello Bow: c. 1886   1,620/2,430
$1,714   £1,058   DM3,068   ¥202,152

VAN HEMERT, KEES [Sk5/213] Silver Dutch
Violoncello Bow   600/800
$575   £351   DM1,041   ¥69,426

VICKERS, J.E. [C11/138] Silver and Ivory Violoncello Bow   324/486
$782   £483   DM1,473   ¥82,699

VIGNERON, A. [Bf4/2746] Silver Violoncello Bow
3,500/4,500
$4,298   £2,673   DM7,909   ¥506,964

VIGNERON, ANDRE [B3/21] Silver Violoncello
Bow   1,296/1,944 NS

VIGNERON, JOSEPH ARTHUR [C3/60] Silver
Violoncello Bow   4,890/8,150
$5,624   £3,450   DM9,971   ¥664,919

VIGNERON, JOSEPH ARTHUR [S6/144] Silver
Violoncello Bow: Paris, c. 1890   3,975/5,565
$4,023   £2,530   DM7,565   ¥486,367

VIGNERON, JOSEPH ARTHUR [S6/233] Silver
Violoncello Bow: Paris, c. 1900   4,770/7,950
$6,948   £4,370   DM13,066   ¥840,089

VOIRIN, FRANCOIS NICOLAS [B6/20] Silver and
Ebony Violoncello Bow with later button
2,385/3,180 NS

VOIRIN, FRANCOIS NICOLAS [Bf4/2749] Fine
Silver Violoncello Bow with silver tip, probably later
(Jean-François Raffin, May 25, 1998)   5,000/7,000
$6,613   £4,113   DM12,167   ¥779,944

VOIRIN, FRANCOIS NICOLAS [C3/22] Silver
Violoncello Bow   4,890/5,705
$6,561   £4,025   DM11,632   ¥775,738

VOIRIN, FRANCOIS NICOLAS [C3/36] Silver
Violoncello Bow   4,890/6,520
$7,498   £4,600   DM13,294   ¥886,558

VOIRIN, FRANCOIS NICOLAS [S6/107] Silver
Violoncello Bow: Paris, c. 1875   3,180/4,770 NS

VOIRIN, FRANCOIS NICOLAS [S6/145] Silver
Violoncello Bow: Paris, c. 1870   4,770/6,360 NS

VOIRIN, FRANCOIS NICOLAS [S6/250] Silver
Violoncello Bow: Paris, c. 1860   1,590/2,385 NS

VOIRIN, FRANCOIS NICOLAS [S11/308] Silver
Violoncello Bow: Paris, c. 1870   3,240/4,860
$3,353   £2,070   DM6,355   ¥354,115

VOIRIN, FRANCOIS NICOLAS [S11/309] Silver
Violoncello Bow: Paris, c. 1870   7,290/8,910 NS
$3,849   £2,381   DM7,296   ¥407,232

VOIRIN, FRANCOIS NICOLAS [Sk5/204] Silver
Violoncello Bow   1,200/1,400
$748   £456   DM1,353   ¥90,253

VUILLAUME, JEAN BAPTISTE [C11/132] Silver
Violoncello Bow with possibly later adjuster (Rembert
Wurlitzer, New York, February 8, 1917)
6,156/6,804 NS

VUILLAUME, JEAN BAPTISTE [S6/128] Silver
Violoncello Bow: Paris, c. 1860 (Bernard Millant,
Paris, October 12, 1993)   10,335/11,925
$13,714   £8,625   DM25,789   ¥1,658,070

VUILLAUME, JEAN BAPTISTE [S11/296] Silver
Violoncello Bow: Paris, c. 1860 (Bernard Millant,
Paris, January 13, 1998)   9,720/11,340
$11,178   £6,900   DM21,183   ¥1,180,383

WANKA, HERBERT [C3/66] Silver Violoncello Bow
1,304/1,630 NS

WATSON, W.D. [B3/18] Gold Violoncello Bow:
London   2,592/2,916
$2,981   £1,840   DM5,354   ¥351,937

WEICHOLD, R. [B2/64] Silver Violoncello Bow
656/984 NS

WEICHOLD, R. [B5/66] Silver Violoncello Bow
492/820 NS

WERNER, KARL [Sk11/99] Gold and Tortoiseshell
Violoncello Bow   1,600/1,800
$1,190   £737   DM2,247   ¥125,928

WILSON, GARNER [C3/13] Silver Violoncello Bow
978/1,304 NS

WITHERS, GEORGE & SONS [P2/116] Part-Silver
Violoncello Bow: London   489/652
$487   £299   DM852   ¥57,572

YAKQUSHKIN [B2/62] Silver Violoncello Bow
492/820
$415   £253   DM716   ¥47,351

ZITHER-BANJO

HUNT, H.H. [B5/32] Five-String Zither Banjo w/case
66/82
$104   £63   DM188   ¥12,523

WINDSOR, A.O. [B5/31] Five-String Zither Banjo
w/case   98/131
$85   £52   DM154   ¥10,246

Five-Year Summary

sales by
item and
maker

HOW TO READ THE SUMMARY
BY ITEM AND MAKER

Beginning on the next page, you will find the five-year Summary by Item and Maker, with monetary values expressed in dollars, deutsche marks, pounds sterling, and yen. This section summarizes the more detailed data found in the first part of the guide (the Item-by-Item Listings) and combines it with auction information from the preceding four years. Hence you will find a brief overview of the items offered from 1995 through 1999, arranged alphabetically by item—viola, violin, violoncello, etc.—and, within each item category, by maker. Items that have been offered as being "attributed to" or "ascribed to" a particular maker are shown separately from those identified as "by" that maker. (You may find inconsistencies in the way names have been given—a first initial in one case, a full name in the next. These problems have been raised and discussed in the Introduction.)

In the second column, you will find a numeric count of the items by that maker that were offered at auction during the 1995–1999 period. To the immediate right is the count of those items that were actually sold. If none sold, you will see a zero here. (If you are looking for information on a particular maker and cannot find the name, it is because no items by that maker were offered at auction during this period.)

In the next three columns are monetary values. First is the lowest sale price of an item by that maker, then the highest, and finally the average. If only one item was sold, you will find the same number in all three columns. Please use extreme caution in assessing these monetary values. From a purely statistical point of view, they are almost completely unreliable. Nonetheless, they can be construed, within narrow limits, as reflective of the current market. This is also a good place to repeat what was said earlier: this guide does not reflect upon the playing qualities or the physical condition of the items offered at auction. The only way to assess these factors is through personal experience.

Maker	Items Bid	Sold	Selling Prices Low	High	Avg

ACCORDION

CASALI	1	0			
SCANDALLI	2	0			
SOPRANI, PAOLO	2	1	$225	$225	$225
			DM393	DM393	DM393
			£138	£138	£138
			¥26,572	¥26,572	¥26,572

ÆOLA

WHEATSTONE & CO., C.	4	4	$1,061	$2,252	$1,704
			DM1,561	DM4,016	DM2,872
			£690	£1,380	£1,043
			¥112,580	¥294,809	¥196,030

ARPANETTA

KARP, JOHANN	1	1	$11,836	$11,836	$11,836
			DM19,679	DM19,679	DM19,679
			£7,130	£7,130	£7,130
			¥1,378,514	¥1,378,514	¥1,378,514

BAGPIPES

COULLIE, THOMAS	1	1	$2,720	$2,720	$2,720
			DM4,074	DM4,074	DM4,074
			£1,610	£1,610	£1,610
			¥302,744	¥302,744	¥302,744
HEDWORTH, WILLIAM	1	1	$2,332	$2,332	$2,332
			DM3,492	DM3,492	DM3,492
			£1,380	£1,380	£1,380
			¥259,495	¥259,495	¥259,495
HENDERSON, PETER	1	1	$2,181	$2,181	$2,181
			DM3,080	DM3,080	DM3,080
			£1,380	£1,380	£1,380
			¥194,631	¥194,631	¥194,631
LAWRIE, R.G.	1	1	$778	$778	$778
			DM1,312	DM1,312	DM1,312
			£483	£483	£483
			¥95,568	¥95,568	¥95,568
REID, ROBERT	5	4	$1,149	$5,440	$3,242
			DM1,936	DM8,149	DM4,844
			£713	£3,220	£1,961
			¥141,076	¥605,489	¥356,816
ROBERTSON	1	1	$6,765	$6,765	$6,765
			DM10,122	DM10,122	DM10,122
			£4,025	£4,025	£4,025
			¥754,607	¥754,607	¥754,607
ROBERTSON (attributed to)	1	0			

BANDURRIA

ANDRADE, JOAO MIGUEL	1	1	$324	$324	$324
			DM538	DM538	DM538
			£195	£195	£195
			¥37,701	¥37,701	¥37,701

Maker	Items Bid	Sold	Selling Prices Low	High	Avg

BANJEAURINE

HAYNES CO., JOHN C. — 1 / 0

BANJELE

SMECK, ROY — 1 / 1
$75 / $75 / $75
DM137 / DM137 / DM137
£46 / £46 / £46
¥9,108 / ¥9,108 / ¥9,108

BANJO

ABBOTT, J. — 2 / 1
$164 / $164 / $164
DM287 / DM287 / DM287
£98 / £98 / £98
¥20,954 / ¥20,954 / ¥20,954

BACON BANJO CO. — 1 / 1
$431 / $431 / $431
DM649 / DM649 / DM649
£262 / £262 / £262
¥48,205 / ¥48,205 / ¥48,205

BACON & DAY — 5 / 4
$144 / $1,455 / $687
DM243 / DM2,746 / DM1,234
£86 / £900 / £419
¥17,538 / ¥153,913 / ¥78,032

BARNES & MULLINS — 2 / 1
$217 / $217 / $217
DM394 / DM394 / DM394
£132 / £132 / £132
¥26,184 / ¥26,184 / ¥26,184

CHAMBERLAIN, J. — 1 / 1
$501 / $501 / $501
DM897 / DM897 / DM897
£299 / £299 / £299
¥58,156 / ¥58,156 / ¥58,156

CONTESSA — 1 / 0

DALLAS, D.E. — 2 / 1
$212 / $212 / $212
DM312 / DM312 / DM312
£138 / £138 / £138
¥22,516 / ¥22,516 / ¥22,516

DALLAS, J.E. — 1 / 1
$348 / $348 / $348
DM534 / DM534 / DM534
£230 / £230 / £230
¥37,082 / ¥37,082 / ¥37,082

DANIELS, J. — 1 / 1
$159 / $159 / $159
DM234 / DM234 / DM234
£104 / £104 / £104
¥16,887 / ¥16,887 / ¥16,887

DOBSON, E.C. — 1 / 1
$150 / $150 / $150
DM221 / DM221 / DM221
£98 / £98 / £98
¥15,949 / ¥15,949 / ¥15,949

DOBSON, E.D.W.G. — 1 / 1
$345 / $345 / $345
DM583 / DM583 / DM583
£207 / £207 / £207
¥42,090 / ¥42,090 / ¥42,090

DOBSON, GEORGE — 1 / 1
$230 / $230 / $230
DM389 / DM389 / DM389
£138 / £138 / £138
¥28,060 / ¥28,060 / ¥28,060

Maker	Items		Selling Prices		
	Bid	Sold	Low	High	Avg
DOBSON CO.	1	1	$231	$231	$231
			DM437	DM437	DM437
			£143	£143	£143
			¥24,486	¥24,486	¥24,486
DORE BROS.	1	0			
EPIPHONE	1	1	$690	$690	$690
			DM1,166	DM1,166	DM1,166
			£414	£414	£414
			¥84,180	¥84,180	¥84,180
ESSEX, CLIFFORD	5	3	$373	$556	$448
			DM653	DM937	DM782
			£230	£345	£276
			¥45,069	¥68,263	¥55,246
FAIRBANKS CO., A.C.	2	1	$3,163	$3,163	$3,163
			DM5,345	DM5,345	DM5,345
			£1,898	£1,898	£1,898
			¥420,834	¥420,834	¥420,834
FAIRBANKS & COLE	4	3	$173	$374	$249
			DM249	DM632	DM391
			£113	£224	£156
			¥17,466	¥45,598	¥27,813
GIBSON CO.	2	2	$2,070	$4,893	$3,482
			DM3,115	DM9,236	DM6,176
			£1,257	£3,029	£2,143
			¥231,385	¥517,706	¥374,545
GRETSCH	1	0			
GREY & SONS, JOHN	2	1	$604	$604	$604
			DM1,098	DM1,098	DM1,098
			£368	£368	£368
			¥76,228	¥76,228	¥76,228
HANDEL, J.T.C.	1	1	$141	$141	$141
			DM208	DM208	DM208
			£92	£92	£92
			¥15,011	¥15,011	¥15,011
HAYNES CO., JOHN C.	2	1	$150	$150	$150
			DM253	DM253	DM253
			£90	£90	£90
			¥18,239	¥18,239	¥18,239
JEDSON	2	2	$338	$380	$359
			DM573	DM674	DM623
			£207	£230	£219
			¥39,226	¥52,645	¥45,935
LANGE, WILLIAM L.	3	3	$201	$1,725	$786
			DM303	DM2,596	DM1,183
			£122	£1,047	£477
			¥22,496	¥192,821	¥87,840
LOCKE, G.S.	1	1	$316	$316	$316
			DM534	DM534	DM534
			£190	£190	£190
			¥38,583	¥38,583	¥38,583
LUDWIG	3	2	$460	$748	$604
			DM787	DM1,279	DM1,033
			£272	£442	£357
			¥57,123	¥92,825	¥74,974
LYON & HEALY	1	1	$132	$132	$132
			DM240	DM240	DM240
			£81	£81	£81
			¥16,675	¥16,675	¥16,675

Maker	Items		Selling Prices		
	Bid	Sold	Low	High	Avg
MANSFIELD, E.B.	1	1	$518	$518	$518
			DM875	DM875	DM875
			£311	£311	£311
			¥63,135	¥63,135	¥63,135
MORRISON, JAMES A.	1	1	$460	$460	$460
			DM777	DM777	DM777
			£276	£276	£276
			¥56,120	¥56,120	¥56,120
RELIANCE	1	1	$143	$143	$143
			DM203	DM203	DM203
			£90	£90	£90
			¥12,722	¥12,722	¥12,722
SHELTONE	1	1	$112	$112	$112
			DM196	DM196	DM196
			£69	£69	£69
			¥13,521	¥13,521	¥13,521
SIMSON & CO., J.K.	2	1	$130	$130	$130
			DM179	DM179	DM179
			£81	£81	£81
			¥10,834	¥10,834	¥10,834
SLINGERLAND (attributed to)	1	0			
STEWART, S.S.	5	3	$271	$611	$459
			DM472	DM980	DM727
			£161	£397	£293
			¥34,512	¥69,519	¥52,189
TEMLETT, W.	2	2	$223	$637	$430
			DM331	DM937	DM634
			£144	£414	£279
			¥24,118	¥67,548	¥45,833
THOMPSON & ODELL	2	2	$201	$230	$216
			DM340	DM346	DM343
			£121	£140	£130
			¥24,553	¥25,709	¥25,131
TURNER, JOHN ALVEY	2	2	$209	$290	$249
			DM371	DM506	DM438
			£127	£173	£150
			¥28,955	¥36,977	¥32,966
TURNER, WILLIAM	1	0			
VEGA COMPANY	13	11	$115	$5,980	$1,127
			DM166	DM8,647	DM1,753
			£75	£3,906	£722
			¥11,644	¥605,475	¥119,369
WARD & SON	1	1	$168	$168	$168
			DM247	DM247	DM247
			£109	£109	£109
			¥17,825	¥17,825	¥17,825
WEAVER	1	1	$196	$196	$196
			DM315	DM315	DM315
			£115	£115	£115
			¥24,175	¥24,175	¥24,175
WELTTON	1	1	$132	$132	$132
			DM240	DM240	DM240
			£81	£81	£81
			¥16,675	¥16,675	¥16,675
WEYMANN CO.	1	1	$529	$529	$529
			DM998	DM998	DM998
			£327	£327	£327
			¥55,968	¥55,968	¥55,968

Maker	Items Bid	Sold	Low	Selling Prices High	Avg
WILKES, F.C.	1	1	$180 DM275 £115 ¥20,073	$180 DM275 £115 ¥20,073	$180 DM275 £115 ¥20,073
WINDER, J.G.	1	1	$262 DM456 £161 ¥31,693	$262 DM456 £161 ¥31,693	$262 DM456 £161 ¥31,693
WINDSOR	1	1	$1,880 DM3,183 £1,150 ¥217,920	$1,880 DM3,183 £1,150 ¥217,920	$1,880 DM3,183 £1,150 ¥217,920

BANJO-GUITAR

Maker	Items Bid	Sold	Low	Selling Prices High	Avg
VEGA COMPANY	1	1	$1,035 DM1,771 £612 ¥128,526	$1,035 DM1,771 £612 ¥128,526	$1,035 DM1,771 £612 ¥128,526

BANJO-MANDOLIN

| TIERI | 1 | 1 | $86 DM148 £51 ¥10,711 | $86 DM148 £51 ¥10,711 | $86 DM148 £51 ¥10,711 |

BANJOLELE

| DALLAS, J.E. | 1 | 1 | $151 DM275 £92 ¥19,057 | $151 DM275 £92 ¥19,057 | $151 DM275 £92 ¥19,057 |
| FORMBY, GEORGE | 1 | 1 | $289 DM519 £172 ¥33,408 | $289 DM519 £172 ¥33,408 | $289 DM519 £172 ¥33,408 |

BANJOLIN

| RELIANCE | 1 | 1 | $94 DM163 £58 ¥10,762 | $94 DM163 £58 ¥10,762 | $94 DM163 £58 ¥10,762 |

BARITONE

BUNDY	1	1	$184 DM328 £112 ¥25,561	$184 DM328 £112 ¥25,561	$184 DM328 £112 ¥25,561
LYON & HEALY	1	0			
MARCEAU & CO.	1	0			
SAPORETTI & CAPPARELI	1	0			

Maker	Items		Selling Prices		
	Bid	Sold	Low	High	Avg

BASS GUITAR

Maker	Bid	Sold	Low	High	Avg
FENDER	3	2	$525	$972	$748
			DM911	DM1,685	DM1,298
			£322	£575	£449
			¥60,823	¥123,550	¥92,186
GIBSON CO.	1	1	$806	$806	$806
			DM1,399	DM1,399	DM1,399
			£495	£495	£495
			¥93,406	¥93,406	¥93,406
GOODFELLOW CO.	1	0			
GRETSCH	1	0			
HOFNER	4	2	$18	$70	$44
			DM27	DM108	DM68
			£12	£46	£29
			¥1,920	¥7,679	¥4,799
HOFNER, KARL	2	1	$700	$700	$700
			DM1,213	DM1,213	DM1,213
			£414	£414	£414
			¥88,956	¥88,956	¥88,956
JOURDAN	1	0			
RICKENBACKER	1	0			

BASSET HORN

Maker	Bid	Sold	Low	High	Avg
ALBERT, E.	1	1	$943	$943	$943
			DM1,714	DM1,714	DM1,714
			£575	£575	£575
			¥113,844	¥113,844	¥113,844

BASSOON

Maker	Bid	Sold	Low	High	Avg
ADLER & CO., OSCAR	1	1	$2,051	$2,051	$2,051
			DM3,590	DM3,590	DM3,590
			£1,265	£1,265	£1,265
			¥247,877	¥247,877	¥247,877
BESSON & CO.	1	1	$288	$288	$288
			DM476	DM476	DM476
			£173	£173	£173
			¥33,689	¥33,689	¥33,689
BILTON	2	0			
BILTON, R.	1	0			
BIZEY, CHARLES	1	0			
BOOSEY & CO.	1	0			
BUCHNER, F.	1	1	$3,259	$3,259	$3,259
			DM6,037	DM6,037	DM6,037
			£1,955	£1,955	£1,955
			¥435,242	¥435,242	¥435,242
BUFFET CRAMPON & CO.	2	2	$262	$463	$363
			DM467	DM781	DM624
			£161	£288	£224
			¥35,248	¥56,886	¥46,067
CABART	1	1	$425	$425	$425
			DM636	DM636	DM636
			£253	£253	£253
			¥47,432	¥47,432	¥47,432

Maker	Items		Selling Prices		
	Bid	Sold	Low	High	Avg
CHAPPELL, S.A.	1	1	$254	$254	$254
			DM360	DM360	DM360
			£161	£161	£161
			¥26,243	¥26,243	¥26,243
CRAMPON & CO.	1	1	$351	$351	$351
			DM498	DM498	DM498
			£225	£225	£225
			¥35,675	¥35,675	¥35,675
CUVILLIER (ascribed to)	1	1	$271	$271	$271
			DM405	DM405	DM405
			£161	£161	£161
			¥30,184	¥30,184	¥30,184
DE LUIGI, GIACOMO	1	1	$1,527	$1,527	$1,527
			DM2,539	DM2,539	DM2,539
			£920	£920	£920
			¥177,873	¥177,873	¥177,873
DUPRE, PAUL	1	1	$633	$633	$633
			DM1,145	DM1,145	DM1,145
			£386	£386	£386
			¥76,368	¥76,368	¥76,368
FELCHLIN, JOSEF KARL	1	1	$993	$993	$993
			DM1,650	DM1,650	DM1,650
			£598	£598	£598
			¥115,617	¥115,617	¥115,617
GALANDER	1	0			
HASENEIER, H.F.	1	1	$1,121	$1,121	$1,121
			DM1,955	DM1,955	DM1,955
			£690	£690	£690
			¥135,827	¥135,827	¥135,827
HAWKES & SON	3	3	$168	$509	$331
			DM177	DM719	DM443
			£104	£322	£207
			¥12,813	¥45,414	¥28,180
HECKEL	6	4	$1,845	$14,098	$6,425
			DM2,764	DM23,871	DM10,930
			£1,092	£8,625	£3,924
			¥205,340	¥1,634,403	¥772,850
HIRSBRUNNER FAMILY (MEMBER OF)	2	2	$1,622	$3,054	$2,338
			DM2,697	DM5,078	DM3,887
			£977	£1,840	£1,409
			¥188,893	¥355,746	¥272,319
HOLLER	1	1	$1,196	$1,196	$1,196
			DM1,836	DM1,836	DM1,836
			£782	£782	£782
			¥130,545	¥130,545	¥130,545
KOHLERT & SONS	1	1	$672	$672	$672
			DM989	DM989	DM989
			£437	£437	£437
			¥71,301	¥71,301	¥71,301
KOHLERT'S SOHNE, V.	1	1	$382	$382	$382
			DM635	DM635	DM635
			£230	£230	£230
			¥44,468	¥44,468	¥44,468
LAFLEUR	1	1	$279	$279	$279
			DM383	DM383	DM383
			£173	£173	£173
			¥23,217	¥23,217	¥23,217

Maker	Items		Selling Prices		
	Bid	Sold	Low	High	Avg
LAFLEUR, J.R. & SON	1	1	$471	$471	$471
			DM895	DM895	DM895
			£291	£291	£291
			¥49,523	¥49,523	¥49,523
LARSHOF, JACOB GEORG	1	1	$1,635	$1,635	$1,635
			DM2,317	DM2,317	DM2,317
			£1,035	£1,035	£1,035
			¥167,353	¥167,353	¥167,353
LINTON MANUFACTURING CO.	1	1	$147	$147	$147
			DM217	DM217	DM217
			£96	£96	£96
			¥15,623	¥15,623	¥15,623
LUDWIG, FRANZ	1	1	$1,527	$1,527	$1,527
			DM2,539	DM2,539	DM2,539
			£920	£920	£920
			¥177,873	¥177,873	¥177,873
MILHOUSE, WILLIAM	7	3	$751	$1,749	$1,406
			DM1,339	DM2,857	DM2,271
			£460	£1,035	£843
			¥98,270	¥200,107	¥164,333
MILHOUSE, WILLIAM & W. WHEATCROFT	1	0			
PARKER, JOHN	1	1	$725	$725	$725
			DM1,206	DM1,206	DM1,206
			£437	£437	£437
			¥84,490	¥84,490	¥84,490
RUDALL, CARTE & CO.	1	0			
SAVARY	1	0			
SAVARY, J.N. (JEUNE)	2	1	$789	$789	$789
			DM1,337	DM1,337	DM1,337
			£483	£483	£483
			¥91,527	¥91,527	¥91,527
SAVARY, JEAN NICHOLAS	2	0			
SCHREIBER	4	4	$1,266	$1,671	$1,469
			DM1,944	DM2,565	DM2,255
			£828	£1,093	£960
			¥138,224	¥182,379	¥160,301
SCHREIBER & SOHNE, W.	1	1	$863	$863	$863
			DM1,561	DM1,561	DM1,561
			£526	£526	£526
			¥104,138	¥104,138	¥104,138
TAYLOR, R.	1	0			
TRIEBERT	1	1	$1,055	$1,055	$1,055
			DM1,620	DM1,620	DM1,620
			£690	£690	£690
			¥115,187	¥115,187	¥115,187
TRIEBERT & SONS, GUILLAUME	2	2	$458	$1,689	$1,074
			DM762	DM3,012	DM1,887
			£276	£1,035	£656
			¥53,362	¥221,107	¥137,234
WOOD & IVY	2	0			

BUGLE

Maker	Bid	Sold	Low	High	Avg
BESSON, FONTAINE	1	0			

Maker	Items		Selling Prices		
	Bid	Sold	Low	High	Avg
CLEMENTI & CO.	1	1	$4,025	$4,025	$4,025
			DM6,802	DM6,802	DM6,802
			£2,415	£2,415	£2,415
			¥535,607	¥535,607	¥535,607
COUESNON & CO.	1	0			
EBERSOHN, J.F.	1	1	$2,908	$2,908	$2,908
			DM4,107	DM4,107	DM4,107
			£1,840	£1,840	£1,840
			¥259,508	¥259,508	¥259,508
FIRTH, HALL & POND	1	1	$3,163	$3,163	$3,163
			DM5,345	DM5,345	DM5,345
			£1,898	£1,898	£1,898
			¥420,834	¥420,834	¥420,834
HIGHAM, JOSEPH	1	1	$161	$161	$161
			DM246	DM246	DM246
			£104	£104	£104
			¥15,917	¥15,917	¥15,917
LOGIER, JOHN BERNHARD	1	1	$3,163	$3,163	$3,163
			DM5,345	DM5,345	DM5,345
			£1,898	£1,898	£1,898
			¥420,834	¥420,834	¥420,834
MILLENS, J.	1	0			
PACE, CHARLES	2	0			
SANDBACH, W.	1	1	$1,183	$1,183	$1,183
			DM1,692	DM1,692	DM1,692
			£748	£748	£748
			¥118,842	¥118,842	¥118,842
SAURLE, MICHAEL	2	1	$2,615	$2,615	$2,615
			DM4,856	DM4,856	DM4,856
			£1,587	£1,587	£1,587
			¥272,631	¥272,631	¥272,631
THIBOUVILLE-LAMY, J.	1	0			
WHITE & CO., H.N.	1	0			

BUGLET

Maker	Items		Selling Prices		
	Bid	Sold	Low	High	Avg
KEAT & SONS, H.	1	0			

CAVAQUINHO

Maker	Items		Selling Prices		
	Bid	Sold	Low	High	Avg
D'ATHOUGUIA, RUFINO FELIX	1	1	$1,028	$1,028	$1,028
			DM1,953	DM1,953	DM1,953
			£635	£635	£635
			¥108,049	¥108,049	¥108,049

CECILIUM

Maker	Items		Selling Prices		
	Bid	Sold	Low	High	Avg
DE GROMBARD, ARTHUR QUENTIN	1	0			

CHAMBER BASS

Maker	Items		Selling Prices		
	Bid	Sold	Low	High	Avg
BAJONI, LUIGI	1	1	$62,186	$62,186	$62,186
			DM87,004	DM87,004	DM87,004
			£38,900	£38,900	£38,900
			¥5,259,786	¥5,259,786	¥5,259,786

Maker	Items		Selling Prices		
	Bid	Sold	Low	High	Avg
DOLLING, HERMANN (JR.)	1	1	$5,257	$5,257	$5,257
			DM9,119	DM9,119	DM9,119
			£3,105	£3,105	£3,105
			¥666,364	¥666,364	¥666,364
GILKES, SAMUEL	1	0			
HILL, JOSEPH (ascribed to)	1	0			
PALLOTTA, PIETRO (attributed to)	1	0			
POLLMAN	1	1	$7,123	$7,123	$7,123
			DM12,455	DM12,455	DM12,455
			£4,370	£4,370	£4,370
			¥841,444	¥841,444	¥841,444
SCHULZ, AUGUST (attributed to)	1	1	$2,927	$2,927	$2,927
			DM4,154	DM4,154	DM4,154
			£1,840	£1,840	£1,840
			¥271,676	¥271,676	¥271,676

CHURCH BASS

Maker	Items		Selling Prices		
	Bid	Sold	Low	High	Avg
PRENTISS, HENRY	1	1	$1,265	$1,265	$1,265
			DM1,827	DM1,827	DM1,827
			£806	£806	£806
			¥109,739	¥109,739	¥109,739
PRESCOTT, ABRAHAM	1	1	$690	$690	$690
			DM998	DM998	DM998
			£451	£451	£451
			¥69,863	¥69,863	¥69,863

CITTERN

Maker	Items		Selling Prices		
	Bid	Sold	Low	High	Avg
BRODERIP & WILKINSON	1	1	$730	$730	$730
			DM1,219	DM1,219	DM1,219
			£437	£437	£437
			¥88,707	¥88,707	¥88,707
LIESSEM, R.	1	1	$867	$867	$867
			DM1,303	DM1,303	DM1,303
			£518	£518	£518
			¥96,545	¥96,545	¥96,545
RUTHERFORD	1	1	$1,252	$1,252	$1,252
			DM1,882	DM1,882	DM1,882
			£748	£748	£748
			¥139,454	¥139,454	¥139,454

CLARINET

Maker	Items		Selling Prices		
	Bid	Sold	Low	High	Avg
ALBERT, E.	2	2	$415	$981	$698
			DM754	DM1,692	DM1,223
			£253	£598	£426
			¥50,091	¥111,922	¥81,007
ALBERT, EUGENE A.	1	1	$764	$764	$764
			DM1,270	DM1,270	DM1,270
			£460	£460	£460
			¥88,936	¥88,936	¥88,936
AMMANN, ULRICH	2	1	$6,491	$6,491	$6,491
			DM10,792	DM10,792	DM10,792
			£3,910	£3,910	£3,910
			¥755,959	¥755,959	¥755,959
ASTOR & CO.	1	0			

Maker	Items Bid	Sold	Selling Prices Low	High	Avg
ASTOR & CO., GEORGE	1	1	$2,363	$2,363	$2,363
			DM3,337	DM3,337	DM3,337
			£1,495	£1,495	£1,495
			¥210,850	¥210,850	¥210,850
BARFOOT, CHARLES SMITH	1	1	$472	$472	$472
			DM669	DM669	DM669
			£299	£299	£299
			¥48,347	¥48,347	¥48,347
BAUMANN	1	1	$1,680	$1,680	$1,680
			DM2,793	DM2,793	DM2,793
			£1,012	£1,012	£1,012
			¥195,660	¥195,660	¥195,660
BERNAREGGI	1	1	$374	$374	$374
			DM676	DM676	DM676
			£228	£228	£228
			¥45,127	¥45,127	¥45,127
BETTONEY, H.	1	1	$259	$259	$259
			DM437	DM437	DM437
			£161	£161	£161
			¥31,856	¥31,856	¥31,856
BILTON	5	3	$460	$1,725	$882
			DM676	DM2,915	DM1,429
			£276	£1,035	£537
			¥48,785	¥229,546	¥109,940
BILTON, RICHARD	3	3	$618	$762	$673
			DM873	DM1,415	DM1,142
			£391	£462	£415
			¥55,145	¥83,529	¥72,698
BILTON, RICHARD (workshop of)	1	0			
BOOSEY & CO.	6	3	$94	$321	$223
			DM167	DM553	DM360
			£58	£196	£138
			¥12,284	¥36,590	¥25,039
BOOSEY & HAWKES	17	15	$74	$3,452	$648
			DM125	DM4,891	DM973
			£46	£2,185	£416
			¥9,102	¥353,301	¥69,858
BRAUN	1	1	$587	$587	$587
			DM945	DM945	DM945
			£345	£345	£345
			¥72,526	¥72,526	¥72,526
BRONSEL, T.	1	1	$201	$201	$201
			DM375	DM375	DM375
			£127	£127	£127
			¥23,758	¥23,758	¥23,758
BUESCHER	3	3	$77	$230	$154
			DM128	DM409	DM259
			£46	£140	£97
			¥9,338	¥31,952	¥19,325
BUFFET	1	1	$82	$82	$82
			DM116	DM116	DM116
			£52	£52	£52
			¥8,435	¥8,435	¥8,435
BUFFET CRAMPON & CO.	5	2	$218	$1,055	$637
			DM309	DM1,763	DM1,036
			£138	£632	£385
			¥22,494	¥128,290	¥75,392

| Maker | Items | | Selling Prices | | |
	Bid	Sold	Low	High	Avg
BUTLER, GEORGE	1	1	$291	$291	$291
			DM412	DM412	DM412
			£184	£184	£184
			¥29,752	¥29,752	¥29,752
CHRISTIANI	1	1	$576	$576	$576
			DM1,070	DM1,070	DM1,070
			£345	£345	£345
			¥77,087	¥77,087	¥77,087
CLEMENT & CO.	1	1	$905	$905	$905
			DM1,645	DM1,645	DM1,645
			£552	£552	£552
			¥109,290	¥109,290	¥109,290
CLEMENTI & CO.	3	2	$348	$417	$382
			DM534	DM591	DM563
			£230	£264	£247
			¥37,082	¥42,687	¥39,884
CONN, C.G.	1	0			
CONN, USA	1	1	$278	$278	$278
			DM468	DM468	DM468
			£173	£173	£173
			¥34,131	¥34,131	¥34,131
CRAMPON & CO.	1	1	$242	$242	$242
			DM424	DM424	DM424
			£150	£150	£150
			¥29,295	¥29,295	¥29,295
D'ALMAINE & CO.	1	1	$699	$699	$699
			DM1,048	DM1,048	DM1,048
			£414	£414	£414
			¥77,849	¥77,849	¥77,849
DAVIS	1	1	$52	$52	$52
			DM80	DM80	DM80
			£35	£35	£35
			¥5,562	¥5,562	¥5,562
DISTIN, HENRY	1	1	$133	$133	$133
			DM221	DM221	DM221
			£80	£80	£80
			¥15,467	¥15,467	¥15,467
DISTIN & CO.	1	1	$800	$800	$800
			DM1,229	DM1,229	DM1,229
			£529	£529	£529
			¥85,288	¥85,288	¥85,288
ELKHART	1	1	$132	$132	$132
			DM240	DM240	DM240
			£81	£81	£81
			¥16,675	¥16,675	¥16,675
FINGERHUTH, CHRISTIAN	1	1	$1,240	$1,240	$1,240
			DM2,062	DM2,062	DM2,062
			£747	£747	£747
			¥144,425	¥144,425	¥144,425
FLEISCHMANN, ANTON	1	1	$331	$331	$331
			DM608	DM608	DM608
			£206	£206	£206
			¥38,997	¥38,997	¥38,997
GARRETT, RICHARD	1	1	$581	$581	$581
			DM824	DM824	DM824
			£368	£368	£368
			¥59,503	¥59,503	¥59,503

Maker	Items		Selling Prices		
	Bid	Sold	Low	High	Avg
GAUTROT (AINE)	1	0			
GEROCK & WOLF	2	2	$460	$632	$546
			DM833	DM893	DM863
			£281	£403	£342
			¥53,968	¥55,540	¥54,754
GILMER & CO.	1	1	$131	$131	$131
			DM233	DM233	DM233
			£81	£81	£81
			¥17,624	¥17,624	¥17,624
GOODLAD & CO.	1	1	$283	$283	$283
			DM515	DM515	DM515
			£173	£173	£173
			¥35,732	¥35,732	¥35,732
GOULDING	1	1	$846	$846	$846
			DM1,432	DM1,432	DM1,432
			£518	£518	£518
			¥98,064	¥98,064	¥98,064
GOULDING & CO.	2	2	$383	$730	$557
			DM710	DM1,219	DM965
			£230	£437	£334
			¥51,205	¥88,707	¥69,956
GOULDING & D'ALMAINE	2	1	$635	$635	$635
			DM900	DM900	DM900
			£402	£402	£402
			¥65,001	¥65,001	¥65,001
GOULDING D'ALMAINE POTTER	1	1	$542	$542	$542
			DM766	DM766	DM766
			£345	£345	£345
			¥46,258	¥46,258	¥46,258
GRAFTON	1	1	$502	$502	$502
			DM903	DM903	DM903
			£299	£299	£299
			¥58,075	¥58,075	¥58,075
GREEN, J.	1	1	$546	$546	$546
			DM789	DM789	DM789
			£348	£348	£348
			¥47,387	¥47,387	¥47,387
GRETSCH	2	1	$163	$163	$163
			DM232	DM232	DM232
			£104	£104	£104
			¥16,871	¥16,871	¥16,871
HALL & SON, WILLIAM	1	1	$230	$230	$230
			DM409	DM409	DM409
			£140	£140	£140
			¥31,952	¥31,952	¥31,952
HASENEIER, H.F.	1	1	$1,431	$1,431	$1,431
			DM2,379	DM2,379	DM2,379
			£862	£862	£862
			¥166,659	¥166,659	¥166,659
HAWKES & SON	4	3	$94	$391	$290
			DM163	DM717	DM505
			£58	£242	£176
			¥10,762	¥46,018	¥34,045
HAWKES & SONS	1	1	$104	$316	$528
			DM188	DM574	DM960
			£63	£193	£322
			¥12,523	¥38,138	¥63,753

Maker	Items		Selling Prices		
	Bid	Sold	Low	High	Avg
HEROUARD	1	1	$245	$245	$245
			DM347	DM347	DM347
			£157	£157	£157
			¥24,893	¥24,893	¥24,893
HEROUARD PERE ET FILS	1	0			
JEHRING FAMILY (MEMBER OF)	1	0			
KEY	1	1	$943	$943	$943
			DM1,627	DM1,627	DM1,627
			£575	£575	£575
			¥107,617	¥107,617	¥107,617
KEY, THOMAS	2	1	$480	$480	$480
			DM681	DM681	DM681
			£304	£304	£304
			¥49,155	¥49,155	¥49,155
KLEMM & BRO.	1	1	$920	$920	$920
			DM1,555	DM1,555	DM1,555
			£552	£552	£552
			¥122,424	¥122,424	¥122,424
KOHLER & SON	1	1	$1,336	$1,336	$1,336
			DM2,222	DM2,222	DM2,222
			£805	£805	£805
			¥155,639	¥155,639	¥155,639
KOHLERT, VINCENZ FERARIUS	1	0			
KRUSPE, C.	2	1	$392	$392	$392
			DM728	DM728	DM728
			£238	£238	£238
			¥40,895	¥40,895	¥40,895
LAFLEUR, J.R. & SON	1	1	$546	$546	$546
			DM781	DM781	DM781
			£345	£345	£345
			¥54,850	¥54,850	¥54,850
LEBLANC	2	0			
LEBLANC, GEORGES	3	1	$2,287	$2,287	$2,287
			DM4,247	DM4,247	DM4,247
			£1,388	£1,388	£1,388
			¥238,453	¥238,453	¥238,453
LEDUC	1	1	$58	$58	$58
			DM102	DM102	DM102
			£35	£35	£35
			¥7,988	¥7,988	¥7,988
LEWIN BROS.	2	0			
LINTON MANUFACTURING CO.	1	0			
LOT, ISADORE	1	1	$397	$397	$397
			DM730	DM730	DM730
			£247	£247	£247
			¥46,797	¥46,797	¥46,797
MARTIN	1	1	$161	$161	$161
			DM226	DM226	DM226
			£101	£101	£101
			¥13,657	¥13,657	¥13,657
MARTIN BROS.	3	1	$575	$575	$575
			DM972	DM972	DM972
			£345	£345	£345
			¥76,515	¥76,515	¥76,515

Maker	Items		Selling Prices		
	Bid	Sold	Low	High	Avg
MEINEL, CLEMENS	1	1	$764	$764	$764
			DM1,270	DM1,270	DM1,270
			£460	£460	£460
			¥88,936	¥88,936	¥88,936
METZLER & CO.	4	4	$247	$496	$358
			DM376	DM825	DM584
			£150	£299	£217
			¥22,716	¥57,809	¥40,915
MEYER, KARL	1	1	$176	$176	$176
			DM284	DM284	DM284
			£104	£104	£104
			¥21,758	¥21,758	¥21,758
MILHOUSE	1	1	$3,051	$3,051	$3,051
			DM5,665	DM5,665	DM5,665
			£1,852	£1,852	£1,852
			¥318,069	¥318,069	¥318,069
MILLER, GEORGE	2	2	$816	$2,673	$1,744
			DM1,222	DM4,444	DM2,833
			£483	£1,610	£1,047
			¥90,823	¥311,277	¥201,050
MOLLENHAUER, JOHANN ANDREAS	1	1	$438	$438	$438
			DM729	DM729	DM729
			£264	£264	£264
			¥51,042	¥51,042	¥51,042
MONNIG GEBRUDER	1	1	$1,718	$1,718	$1,718
			DM2,857	DM2,857	DM2,857
			£1,035	£1,035	£1,035
			¥200,107	¥200,107	¥200,107
NICHOLSON, CHARLES	1	1	$151	$151	$151
			DM275	DM275	DM275
			£92	£92	£92
			¥19,057	¥19,057	¥19,057
NOBLET	1	0			
NOBLET, N.	1	0			
ORSI, ROMEO	1	0			
PAN-AMERICAN	1	0			
PASK, JOHN	1	1	$611	$611	$611
			DM1,016	DM1,016	DM1,016
			£368	£368	£368
			¥71,149	¥71,149	¥71,149
PAYNE, GEORGE	1	1	$509	$509	$509
			DM719	DM719	DM719
			£322	£322	£322
			¥45,414	¥45,414	¥45,414
PEACHEY, G.	1	1	$385	$385	$385
			DM579	DM579	DM579
			£230	£230	£230
			¥42,909	¥42,909	¥42,909
POTTER, HENRY	3	2	$309	$353	$331
			DM437	DM486	DM461
			£196	£219	£207
			¥29,408	¥31,867	¥30,637
POTTER, SAMUEL	1	1	$461	$461	$461
			DM762	DM762	DM762
			£276	£276	£276
			¥53,903	¥53,903	¥53,903

Maker	Items Bid	Sold	Selling Prices Low	High	Avg
PRESTON, JOHN	1	0			
PURDAY	1	0			
RAMPONE, AGOSTINO	1	1	$1,336	$1,336	$1,336
			DM2,222	DM2,222	DM2,222
			£805	£805	£805
			¥155,639	¥155,639	¥155,639
REILLY, J.	1	1	$492	$492	$492
			DM756	DM756	DM756
			£322	£322	£322
			¥53,754	¥53,754	¥53,754
ROTTENBURGH, G.A.	1	1	$1,128	$1,128	$1,128
			DM1,863	DM1,863	DM1,863
			£690	£690	£690
			¥139,676	¥139,676	¥139,676
ROUSTAGNEQ	1	1	$1,718	$1,718	$1,718
			DM2,857	DM2,857	DM2,857
			£1,035	£1,035	£1,035
			¥200,107	¥200,107	¥200,107
RUDALL, CARTE & CO.	2	2	$151	$226	$188
			DM274	DM382	DM328
			£92	£138	£115
			¥18,215	¥26,150	¥22,183
SCHENKELAARS, H.	1	0			
SCHUSTER & CO., G.	1	1	$1,107	$1,107	$1,107
			DM1,841	DM1,841	DM1,841
			£667	£667	£667
			¥128,958	¥128,958	¥128,958
SELMER	6	4	$161	$525	$337
			DM227	DM934	DM544
			£101	£322	£215
			¥14,277	¥70,495	¥38,807
SELMER, HENRI	6	4	$168	$5,814	$1,714
			DM177	DM8,238	DM2,469
			£104	£3,680	£1,078
			¥12,813	¥595,034	¥177,376
SELMER BUNDY	2	1	$115	$115	$115
			DM205	DM205	DM205
			£70	£70	£70
			¥15,976	¥15,976	¥15,976
STIEGLER, MAX	1	1	$1,127	$1,127	$1,127
			DM1,591	DM1,591	DM1,591
			£713	£713	£713
			¥100,559	¥100,559	¥100,559
THIBOUVILLE	1	1	$230	$230	$230
			DM409	DM409	DM409
			£140	£140	£140
			¥31,952	¥31,952	¥31,952
THIBOUVILLE-LAMY, J.	3	3	$61	$316	$150
			DM94	DM563	DM260
			£40	£193	£93
			¥6,489	¥43,933	¥19,841
TOMSCHIK, MARTIN	1	0			
TRIEBERT	1	1	$180	$180	$180
			DM275	DM275	DM275
			£115	£115	£115
			¥20,073	¥20,073	¥20,073

Maker	Items		Selling Prices		
	Bid	Sold	Low	High	Avg
UHLMANN, JOHANN TOBIAS	1	1	$1,431	$1,431	$1,431
			DM2,379	DM2,379	DM2,379
			£862	£862	£862
			¥166,659	¥166,659	¥166,659
WHITELY	1	1	$805	$805	$805
			DM1,360	DM1,360	DM1,360
			£483	£483	£483
			¥107,121	¥107,121	¥107,121
WILLIAMS, E.G.	1	1	$800	$800	$800
			DM1,129	DM1,129	DM1,129
			£506	£506	£506
			¥71,365	¥71,365	¥71,365
WINNEN, JEAN	1	1	$311	$311	$311
			DM466	DM466	DM466
			£184	£184	£184
			¥34,599	¥34,599	¥34,599
WOLF & CO., ROBERT	1	1	$509	$509	$509
			DM719	DM719	DM719
			£322	£322	£322
			¥45,414	¥45,414	¥45,414
WOOD, JAMES	1	1	$232	$232	$232
			DM417	DM417	DM417
			£138	£138	£138
			¥26,804	¥26,804	¥26,804
WOOD, JAMES & SON	1	1	$125	$125	$125
			DM206	DM206	DM206
			£75	£75	£75
			¥14,599	¥14,599	¥14,599
WOOD & IVY	4	3	$649	$1,380	$907
			DM975	DM2,332	DM1,462
			£391	£828	£552
			¥61,633	¥183,637	¥106,955
WREDE, H.	1	1	$319	$319	$319
			DM567	DM567	DM567
			£196	£196	£196
			¥42,801	¥42,801	¥42,801
WURLITZER, FRITZ	1	0			
YAMAHA	1	0			

CLAVICHORD

Maker	Items		Selling Prices		
	Bid	Sold	Low	High	Avg
DOLMETSCH, ARNOLD	1	1	$2,544	$2,544	$2,544
			DM3,604	DM3,604	DM3,604
			£1,610	£1,610	£1,610
			¥260,327	¥260,327	¥260,327
GOUGH, HUGH PERCIVAL HENRY	1	1	$1,222	$1,222	$1,222
			DM1,960	DM1,960	DM1,960
			£794	£794	£794
			¥139,037	¥139,037	¥139,037
HERZ, ERIC	1	1	$2,185	$2,185	$2,185
			DM3,341	DM3,341	DM3,341
			£1,437	£1,437	£1,437
			¥230,299	¥230,299	¥230,299
PALAZZI, NICOLA	1	1	$11,658	$11,658	$11,658
			DM17,462	DM17,462	DM17,462
			£6,900	£6,900	£6,900
			¥1,297,476	¥1,297,476	¥1,297,476

Maker	Items		Selling Prices		
	Bid	Sold	Low	High	Avg

CLAVIOLINE

SELMER, HENRI	1	0			

COMPAGNON

THIBOUVILLE-LAMY, J.	1	1	$382	$382	$382
			DM547	DM547	DM547
			£242	£242	£242
			¥38,395	¥38,395	¥38,395

CONCERTINA

Maker	Bid	Sold	Low	High	Avg
BOSTOCK	1	1	$2,513	$2,513	$2,513
			DM3,759	DM3,759	DM3,759
			£1,495	£1,495	£1,495
			¥280,283	¥280,283	¥280,283
CASE, GEORGE	3	2	$160	$544	$352
			DM264	DM815	DM539
			£98	£322	£210
			¥19,787	¥60,549	¥40,168
CHIDLEY, ROCK	6	2	$380	$872	$626
			DM674	DM1,619	DM1,146
			£230	£529	£380
			¥52,645	¥90,877	¥71,761
CRABB, HENRY	2	2	$807	$2,905	$1,856
			DM1,497	DM5,169	DM3,333
			£483	£1,783	£1,133
			¥107,922	¥390,243	¥249,082
JEFFRIES	6	6	$1,055	$4,481	$3,352
			DM1,959	DM7,843	DM5,591
			£632	£2,910	£2,085
			¥141,214	¥568,331	¥403,921
JEFFRIES, CHARLES	15	15	$178	$4,660	$3,266
			DM252	DM8,159	DM5,460
			£112	£2,875	£2,002
			¥15,832	¥563,356	¥377,270
JONES	1	1	$1,710	$1,710	$1,710
			DM2,613	DM2,613	DM2,613
			£1,093	£1,093	£1,093
			¥190,696	¥190,696	¥190,696
JONES, GEORGE	3	2	$1,220	$1,783	$1,501
			DM2,175	DM3,179	DM2,677
			£748	£1,093	£920
			¥159,688	¥233,391	¥196,540
JONES, WILLIAM H.	1	1	$1,215	$1,215	$1,215
			DM2,118	DM2,118	DM2,118
			£748	£748	£748
			¥147,145	¥147,145	¥147,145
LACHENAL	49	37	$59	$1,482	$473
			DM95	DM2,499	DM768
			£35	£920	£296
			¥7,253	¥182,034	¥53,781
LACHENAL, LOUIS	4	2	$261	$321	$291
			DM275	DM476	DM375
			£161	£207	£184
			¥19,931	¥34,730	¥27,331

Maker	Items		Selling Prices		
	Bid	Sold	Low	High	Avg
LACHENAL & CO.	20	14	$93	$1,634	$803
			DM156	DM3,033	DM1,349
			£58	£991	£491
			¥11,377	¥196,540	¥91,559
METZLER & CO.	1	1	$80	$80	$80
			DM117	DM117	DM117
			£52	£52	£52
			¥8,444	¥8,444	¥8,444
PARISH, THOMAS	1	1	$261	$261	$261
			DM401	DM401	DM401
			£173	£173	£173
			¥27,811	¥27,811	¥27,811
PEAKE, J.	2	1	$151	$151	$151
			DM225	DM225	DM225
			£98	£98	£98
			¥16,400	¥16,400	¥16,400
VICKERS	1	1	$508	$508	$508
			DM819	DM819	DM819
			£299	£299	£299
			¥62,856	¥62,856	¥62,856
VICKERS, J.J. & SONS	1	1	$1,521	$1,521	$1,521
			DM2,325	DM2,325	DM2,325
			£978	£978	£978
			¥150,324	¥150,324	¥150,324
WHEATSTONE, C.	38	28	$145	$2,846	$702
			DM253	DM5,054	DM1,148
			£86	£1,725	£433
			¥18,489	¥394,835	¥80,805
WHEATSTONE, C. (attributed to)	2	1	$783	$783	$783
			DM825	DM825	DM825
			£483	£483	£483
			¥59,793	¥59,793	¥59,793
WHEATSTONE, CHARLES	1	1	$697	$697	$697
			DM1,295	DM1,295	DM1,295
			£423	£423	£423
			¥72,702	¥72,702	¥72,702
WHEATSTONE & CO., C.	33	26	$200	$4,963	$1,158
			DM283	DM8,252	DM1,912
			£126	£2,990	£711
			¥18,530	¥578,087	¥126,420
WOODWARD	1	1	$72	$72	$72
			DM110	DM110	DM110
			£46	£46	£46
			¥8,029	¥8,029	¥8,029

CONTRABASSOON

Maker	Items		Selling Prices		
HECKEL	3	0			
MONNIG, FRITZ	1	1	$5,263	$5,263	$5,263
			DM8,912	DM8,912	DM8,912
			£3,220	£3,220	£3,220
			¥610,177	¥610,177	¥610,177

CORNET

Maker	Items		Selling Prices		
ANTON (SR.), EBERHARD	1	0			

| Maker | Items | | Selling Prices | | |
	Bid	Sold	Low	High	Avg
BESSON	3	3	$123	$1,049	$445
			DM189	DM1,744	DM720
			£81	£632	£271
			¥13,438	¥122,191	¥49,762
BESSON & CO.	4	4	$98	$466	$325
			DM177	DM698	DM532
			£60	£276	£196
			¥11,802	¥51,899	¥38,232
BOOSEY & CO.	4	2	$85	$805	$445
			DM140	DM1,360	DM750
			£52	£483	£267
			¥10,476	¥107,121	¥58,799
BOOSEY & HAWKES	3	2	$97	$457	$277
			DM149	DM702	DM425
			£63	£299	£181
			¥10,559	¥49,914	¥30,236
BOSTON MUSICAL INSTRUMENT MANUFACTURER	1	1	$288	$288	$288
			DM520	DM520	DM520
			£175	£175	£175
			¥34,713	¥34,713	¥34,713
CONN, C.G.	1	1	$748	$748	$748
			DM1,331	DM1,331	DM1,331
			£449	£449	£449
			¥99,403	¥99,403	¥99,403
CONN, USA	1	1	$690	$690	$690
			DM1,166	DM1,166	DM1,166
			£414	£414	£414
			¥91,818	¥91,818	¥91,818
CORTON	2	0			
COURTURIER, ERNST ALBERT	1	1	$463	$463	$463
			DM852	DM852	DM852
			£288	£288	£288
			¥54,596	¥54,596	¥54,596
DISTIN, HENRY	4	3	$805	$1,243	$1,024
			DM1,231	DM1,788	DM1,509
			£530	£805	£667
			¥84,847	¥126,176	¥105,511
DUPONT, M.	1	1	$92	$92	$92
			DM164	DM164	DM164
			£56	£56	£56
			¥12,781	¥12,781	¥12,781
GLASS	1	1	$283	$283	$283
			DM488	DM488	DM488
			£173	£173	£173
			¥32,285	¥32,285	¥32,285
GLASSL, EGIDIUS	1	1	$802	$802	$802
			DM1,333	DM1,333	DM1,333
			£483	£483	£483
			¥93,383	¥93,383	¥93,383
GRAVES, J.G.	1	1	$113	$113	$113
			DM206	DM206	DM206
			£69	£69	£69
			¥14,293	¥14,293	¥14,293
HAWKES & SON	1	1	$256	$256	$256
			DM478	DM478	DM478
			£161	£161	£161
			¥30,237	¥30,237	¥30,237

Maker	Items Bid	Sold	Selling Prices Low	High	Avg
HILLYARD, W.	1	0			
HULLER, EMMANUEL	1	1	$1,145	$1,145	$1,145
			DM1,904	DM1,904	DM1,904
			£690	£690	£690
			¥133,405	¥133,405	¥133,405
KOHLER	2	2	$1,789	$2,738	$2,263
			DM3,344	DM5,118	DM4,231
			£1,127	£1,725	£1,426
			¥211,662	¥323,972	¥267,817
LAFLEUR, J.R. & SON	3	0			
LYON & HEALY	1	1	$916	$916	$916
			DM1,524	DM1,524	DM1,524
			£552	£552	£552
			¥106,724	¥106,724	¥106,724
MARCEAU & CO.	1	0			
MORITZ, C.W.	1	0			
OLDS & SON	1	1	$690	$690	$690
			DM1,166	DM1,166	DM1,166
			£414	£414	£414
			¥91,818	¥91,818	¥91,818
SCHUSTER & CO., G.	1	1	$690	$690	$690
			DM1,166	DM1,166	DM1,166
			£414	£414	£414
			¥91,818	¥91,818	¥91,818
STAR	1	1	$1,265	$1,265	$1,265
			DM2,238	DM2,238	DM2,238
			£764	£764	£764
			¥164,324	¥164,324	¥164,324
THIBOUVILLE-LAMY, J.	2	1	$150	$150	$150
			DM261	DM261	DM261
			£92	£92	£92
			¥18,110	¥18,110	¥18,110
WHITE & CO., H.N.	1	1	$115	$115	$115
			DM176	DM176	DM176
			£76	£76	£76
			¥12,121	¥12,121	¥12,121
WOODS & CO.	2	1	$77	$77	$77
			DM116	DM116	DM116
			£46	£46	£46
			¥8,624	¥8,624	¥8,624
WURLITZER CO., RUDOLPH	1	1	$144	$144	$144
			DM256	DM256	DM256
			£86	£86	£86
			¥19,116	¥19,116	¥19,116

CORNOPEAN

Maker	Bid	Sold	Low	High	Avg
KOHLER, JOHN	1	1	$6,217	$6,217	$6,217
			DM9,313	DM9,313	DM9,313
			£3,680	£3,680	£3,680
			¥691,987	¥691,987	¥691,987

CRUMHORN

Maker	Bid	Sold
GUNTHER	1	0

Maker	Items		Selling Prices		
	Bid	Sold	Low	High	Avg

CYMBALUM

| SCHUNDA, JOSEF V. | 2 | 0 | | | |

DOUBLE BASS

BERGONZI, NICOLO	1	1	$124,369	$124,369	$124,369
			DM215,166	DM215,166	DM215,166
			£76,300	£76,300	£76,300
			¥14,191,800	¥14,191,800	¥14,191,800
CUNE, RENE	1	1	$4,520	$4,520	$4,520
			DM6,946	DM6,946	DM6,946
			£2,990	£2,990	£2,990
			¥482,063	¥482,063	¥482,063
DERAZEY, JUSTIN	1	1	$13,530	$13,530	$13,530
			DM20,243	DM20,243	DM20,243
			£8,050	£8,050	£8,050
			¥1,509,214	¥1,509,214	¥1,509,214
FENDT, BERNARD SIMON	1	1	$36,708	$36,708	$36,708
			DM66,009	DM66,009	DM66,009
			£21,850	£21,850	£21,850
			¥4,243,926	¥4,243,926	¥4,243,926
GARIMBERTI, FERDINANDO	1	1	$17,621	$17,621	$17,621
			DM26,012	DM26,012	DM26,012
			£11,500	£11,500	£11,500
			¥1,873,362	¥1,873,362	¥1,873,362
GILKES, WILLIAM	1	0			
HAMMIG, JOHANN CHRISTIAN	1	0			
HAWKES & SON	1	1	$8,304	$8,304	$8,304
			DM11,559	DM11,559	DM11,559
			£5,175	£5,175	£5,175
			¥700,571	¥700,571	¥700,571
HERRMANN, KARL (workshop of)	1	0			
MONTAGNANA, DOMENICO	1	1	$251,910	$251,910	$251,910
			DM452,505	DM452,505	DM452,505
			£155,500	£155,500	£155,500
			¥29,742,485	¥29,742,485	¥29,742,485
PILLEMENT, FRANCOIS	2	1	$12,617	$12,617	$12,617
			DM21,345	DM21,345	DM21,345
			£7,935	£7,935	£7,935
			¥1,563,195	¥1,563,195	¥1,563,195
POLLMAN	2	2	$4,420	$8,746	$6,583
			DM6,525	DM15,163	DM10,844
			£2,875	£5,175	£4,025
			¥470,856	¥1,111,952	¥791,404
PRENTICE, RONALD	3	2	$6,521	$7,499	$7,010
			DM12,357	DM14,210	DM13,284
			£4,025	£4,629	£4,327
			¥688,557	¥791,840	¥740,199
STANLEY, ROBERT	1	0			
VILLA, LUIGI	3	3	$5,377	$9,218	$6,786
			DM8,984	DM15,401	DM11,337
			£3,220	£5,520	£4,063
			¥653,628	¥1,120,505	¥824,816
WILFER, E. (ascribed to)	1	1	$2,062	$2,062	$2,062
			DM3,732	DM3,732	DM3,732
			£1,265	£1,265	£1,265
			¥248,813	¥248,813	¥248,813

Maker	Items		Selling Prices		
	Bid	Sold	Low	High	Avg

DOUBLE BASS BOW

Maker	Bid	Sold	Low	High	Avg
BAILEY, G.E.	1	1	$1,019	$1,019	$1,019
			DM1,718	DM1,718	DM1,718
			£633	£633	£633
			¥125,148	¥125,148	¥125,148
BRYANT, P.W.	1	1	$2,251	$2,251	$2,251
			DM4,275	DM4,275	DM4,275
			£1,389	£1,389	£1,389
			¥236,456	¥236,456	¥236,456
BRYANT, PERCIVAL WILFRED	4	4	$1,944	$2,437	$2,073
			DM2,872	DM4,216	DM3,341
			£1,207	£1,495	£1,308
			¥207,124	¥278,070	¥229,205
BULTITUDE, ARTHUR RICHARD	1	1	$1,475	$1,475	$1,475
			DM2,054	DM2,054	DM2,054
			£920	£920	£920
			¥124,704	¥124,704	¥124,704
DEVOIVRE, JEROME	1	0			
FETIQUE, VICTOR	4	3	$2,766	$5,991	$4,481
			DM3,851	DM8,844	DM6,934
			£1,725	£3,910	£2,837
			¥233,820	¥636,943	¥468,504
HILL, W.E. & SONS	1	1	$387	$387	$387
			DM578	DM578	DM578
			£230	£230	£230
			¥43,120	¥43,120	¥43,120
LA MAY	1	0			
LAPIERRE	2	0			
LAPIERRE, MARCEL	2	2	$1,687	$2,875	$2,281
			DM2,919	DM4,327	DM3,623
			£1,035	£1,745	£1,390
			¥192,510	¥321,368	¥256,939
LEE, JOHN NORWOOD	1	0			
LENOBLE, AUGUSTE	1	1	$3,998	$3,998	$3,998
			DM5,647	DM5,647	DM5,647
			£2,530	£2,530	£2,530
			¥356,824	¥356,824	¥356,824
LOTTE, FRANCOIS	1	1	$1,018	$1,018	$1,018
			DM1,633	DM1,633	DM1,633
			£661	£661	£661
			¥115,864	¥115,864	¥115,864
MORIZOT, LOUIS	2	1	$1,840	$1,840	$1,840
			DM3,180	DM3,180	DM3,180
			£1,137	£1,137	£1,137
			¥233,192	¥233,192	¥233,192
MORIZOT, LOUIS (II)	1	1	$1,828	$1,828	$1,828
			DM3,382	DM3,382	DM3,382
			£1,092	£1,092	£1,092
			¥243,614	¥243,614	¥243,614
PECATTE, CHARLES	1	0			
PFRETZSCHNER, H.R.	4	2	$778	$1,453	$1,116
			DM1,145	DM2,610	DM1,877
			£506	£897	£702
			¥82,559	¥171,569	¥127,064

Maker	Items Bid	Sold	Selling Prices Low	High	Avg
RAU, AUGUST	1	1	$1,344	$1,344	$1,344
			DM2,246	DM2,246	DM2,246
			£805	£805	£805
			¥163,407	¥163,407	¥163,407
TARR, THOMAS	1	1	$1,089	$1,089	$1,089
			DM1,533	DM1,533	DM1,533
			£690	£690	£690
			¥111,319	¥111,319	¥111,319
TEMPLE, WILLIAM	1	1	$271	$271	$271
			DM382	DM382	DM382
			£172	£172	£172
			¥27,749	¥27,749	¥27,749
THIBOUVILLE-LAMY, J.	1	1	$2,571	$2,571	$2,571
			DM4,883	DM4,883	DM4,883
			£1,587	£1,587	£1,587
			¥270,123	¥270,123	¥270,123
THOMASSIN, CLAUDE	1	1	$792	$792	$792
			DM1,169	DM1,169	DM1,169
			£517	£517	£517
			¥84,220	¥84,220	¥84,220
TUBBS, JAMES	1	0			
ULLMANN, GIORGIO	1	1	$881	$881	$881
			DM1,301	DM1,301	DM1,301
			£575	£575	£575
			¥93,668	¥93,668	¥93,668
VICKERS, J.E.	4	3	$291	$364	$333
			DM416	DM639	DM525
			£184	£230	£207
			¥29,253	¥46,084	¥37,302
WANKA, HERBERT	1	1	$1,139	$1,139	$1,139
			DM1,718	DM1,718	DM1,718
			£690	£690	£690
			¥129,030	¥129,030	¥129,030
WERNER, ERICH	1	1	$528	$528	$528
			DM961	DM961	DM961
			£322	£322	£322
			¥66,699	¥66,699	¥66,699

DULCIMER

| EBBLEWHITE | 1 | 0 | | | |

EDEOPHONE

LACHENAL & CO.	7	5	$782	$2,397	$1,447
			DM1,300	DM4,451	DM2,422
			£471	£1,455	£880
			¥91,063	¥249,912	¥161,646

ENGLISH HORN

ALBERT, JACQUES	1	1	$820	$820	$820
			DM864	DM864	DM864
			£506	£506	£506
			¥62,640	¥62,640	¥62,640
BOOSEY & HAWKES	1	1	$739	$739	$739
			DM1,134	DM1,134	DM1,134
			£483	£483	£483
			¥80,631	¥80,631	¥80,631

Maker	Items		Selling Prices		
	Bid	Sold	Low	High	Avg
FORNARI, ANDREAS	2	0			
HOWARD	1	1	$1,091	$1,091	$1,091
			DM1,674	DM1,674	DM1,674
			£713	£713	£713
			¥119,026	¥119,026	¥119,026
LOREE, F.	1	1	$993	$993	$993
			DM1,650	DM1,650	DM1,650
			£598	£598	£598
			¥115,617	¥115,617	¥115,617
LOUIS	2	2	$1,091	$1,196	$1,143
			DM1,674	DM1,836	DM1,755
			£713	£782	£748
			¥119,026	¥130,545	¥124,785
TRIEBERT & SONS, GUILLAUME	3	3	$3,054	$9,759	$6,774
			DM5,078	DM17,402	DM11,955
			£1,840	£5,980	£4,140
			¥355,746	¥1,277,507	¥871,984
ZIEGLER, I.	1	1	$3,818	$3,818	$3,818
			DM6,348	DM6,348	DM6,348
			£2,300	£2,300	£2,300
			¥444,682	¥444,682	¥444,682

EPINETTE DES VOSGES

LAMBERT, A.	1	1	$476	$476	$476
			DM792	DM792	DM792
			£287	£287	£287
			¥55,489	¥55,489	¥55,489

EUPHONIUM

BESSON	2	1	$457	$457	$457
			DM702	DM702	DM702
			£299	£299	£299
			¥49,914	¥49,914	¥49,914
BOOSEY & HAWKES	2	2	$457	$563	$510
			DM702	DM864	DM783
			£299	£368	£334
			¥49,914	¥61,433	¥55,673

FIFE

ADLEF	1	1	$112	$112	$112
			DM153	DM153	DM153
			£69	£69	£69
			¥9,287	¥9,287	¥9,287
GEROCK, CHRISTOPHER	1	0			
HAWKES & SON	1	0			
HOLLINGS, WILLIAM	1	0			
MILHOUSE, WILLIAM	1	1	$191	$191	$191
			DM317	DM317	DM317
			£115	£115	£115
			¥22,234	¥22,234	¥22,234
SIMPSON	1	1	$142	$142	$142
			DM253	DM253	DM253
			£86	£86	£86
			¥19,742	¥19,742	¥19,742

Maker	Items		Selling Prices		
	Bid	Sold	Low	High	Avg
WOLF & FIGG	1	1	$113	$113	$113
			DM174	DM174	DM174
			£75	£75	£75
			¥12,052	¥12,052	¥12,052

FLAGEOLET

Maker	Items		Selling Prices		
	Bid	Sold	Low	High	Avg
BAINBRIDGE, WILLIAM	8	8	$243	$3,271	$1,230
			DM360	DM4,620	DM1,807
			£161	£2,070	£766
			¥25,957	¥291,947	¥120,532
BAINBRIDGE & WOOD	4	4	$529	$3,627	$1,468
			DM813	DM6,031	DM2,443
			£345	£2,185	£894
			¥57,956	¥422,448	¥171,021
BUHNER & KELLER	1	1	$955	$955	$955
			DM1,587	DM1,587	DM1,587
			£575	£575	£575
			¥111,171	¥111,171	¥111,171
BUTHOD & THIBOUVILLE	1	1	$938	$938	$938
			DM1,673	DM1,673	DM1,673
			£575	£575	£575
			¥122,837	¥122,837	¥122,837
CARD, W.	1	1	$289	$289	$289
			DM519	DM519	DM519
			£172	£172	£172
			¥33,408	¥33,408	¥33,408
CLEMENTI & CO.	1	1	$981	$981	$981
			DM1,386	DM1,386	DM1,386
			£621	£621	£621
			¥87,584	¥87,584	¥87,584
HASTRICK	3	2	$635	$763	$699
			DM900	DM1,081	DM991
			£402	£483	£443
			¥65,001	¥78,098	¥71,550
LAMBERT, JEAN NICOLAS	1	1	$955	$955	$955
			DM1,587	DM1,587	DM1,587
			£575	£575	£575
			¥111,171	¥111,171	¥111,171
LAUSSEDAT	1	0			
MARGUERITAT	1	1	$1,240	$1,240	$1,240
			DM2,062	DM2,062	DM2,062
			£747	£747	£747
			¥144,425	¥144,425	¥144,425
PROWSE & CO., KEITH	2	2	$363	$712	$538
			DM513	DM1,267	DM890
			£230	£437	£334
			¥32,439	¥95,672	¥64,055
SATZGER	1	0			
SIMPSON	1	1	$533	$533	$533
			DM766	DM766	DM766
			£345	£345	£345
			¥54,075	¥54,075	¥54,075
SIMPSON, JOHN	3	2	$237	$955	$596
			DM444	DM1,587	DM1,015
			£150	£575	£362
			¥28,078	¥111,171	¥69,624

Maker	Items Bid	Sold	Low	Selling Prices High	Avg
FLUGELHORN					
ANSINGH & CO., D.	1	0			
BESSON & CO.	1	1	$575	$575	$575
			DM972	DM972	DM972
			£345	£345	£345
			¥76,515	¥76,515	¥76,515
LOW, JACOB	1	1	$1,909	$1,909	$1,909
			DM3,174	DM3,174	DM3,174
			£1,150	£1,150	£1,150
			¥222,341	¥222,341	¥222,341
OTTO, FRANZ	1	1	$916	$916	$916
			DM1,524	DM1,524	DM1,524
			£552	£552	£552
			¥106,724	¥106,724	¥106,724
SCHUSTER & CO.	1	1	$633	$633	$633
			DM1,069	DM1,069	DM1,069
			£380	£380	£380
			¥84,167	¥84,167	¥84,167
FLUTE					
ADLER, F.O.	1	1	$186	$186	$186
			DM256	DM256	DM256
			£115	£115	£115
			¥15,478	¥15,478	¥15,478
ALEXANDER GEBRUDER	1	1	$458	$458	$458
			DM762	DM762	DM762
			£276	£276	£276
			¥53,362	¥53,362	¥53,362
ARMSTRONG CO.	2	1	$354	$354	$354
			DM522	DM522	DM522
			£230	£230	£230
			¥37,668	¥37,668	¥37,668
ARMSTRONG, W.T.	1	0			
ARTILEY	1	0			
ASTOR & CO.	2	2	$764	$1,198	$981
			DM1,270	DM2,224	DM1,747
			£460	£727	£593
			¥88,936	¥124,857	¥106,897
BACON & HART	1	0			
BAINBRIDGE & WOOD	3	2	$224	$2,294	$1,259
			DM391	DM3,524	DM1,958
			£138	£1,495	£817
			¥27,165	¥251,144	¥139,154
BARLASSINA, GIUSEPPE	1	0			
BERCIOUX, EUGENE	1	1	$1,783	$1,783	$1,783
			DM3,179	DM3,179	DM3,179
			£1,093	£1,093	£1,09
			¥233,391	¥233,391	¥233,391
BERNAREGGI, FRANCISCO	1	1	$1,454	$1,454	$1,454
			DM2,059	DM2,059	DM2,059
			£920	£920	£920
			¥148,758	¥148,758	¥148,758
BEUKERS, WILLEM	2	0			

| Maker | Items | | Selling Prices | | |
	Bid	Sold	Low	High	Avg
BILTON	4	2	$219	$351	$285
			DM409	DM498	DM454
			£138	£225	£182
			¥25,918	¥35,675	¥30,796
BILTON, RICHARD	5	3	$436	$762	$593
			DM809	DM1,415	DM1,015
			£265	£462	£365
			¥45,438	¥79,419	¥58,920
BLESSING	1	1	$209	$209	$209
			DM321	DM321	DM321
			£138	£138	£138
			¥22,249	¥22,249	¥22,249
BOEHM & MENDLER	2	2	$11,658	$13,151	$12,404
			DM17,462	DM18,667	DM18,064
			£6,900	£8,437	£7,669
			¥1,297,476	¥1,337,720	¥1,317,598
BOIE, FRIEDRICH	1	1	$1,314	$1,314	$1,314
			DM2,343	DM2,343	DM2,343
			£805	£805	£805
			¥171,972	¥171,972	¥171,972
BONN, G.W.	1	0			
BONNEVILLE	2	0			
BOOSEY & CO.	4	3	$307	$583	$418
			DM434	DM873	DM607
			£196	£345	£257
			¥26,213	¥64,874	¥42,759
BOOSEY & HAWKES	12	7	$74	$205	$147
			DM125	DM344	DM218
			£46	£127	£91
			¥9,102	¥25,030	¥16,015
BUFFET	3	2	$156	$309	$233
			DM240	DM556	DM398
			£104	£184	£144
			¥16,687	¥35,738	¥26,213
BUFFET CRAMPON & CO.	2	1	$1,577	$1,577	$1,577
			DM2,239	DM2,239	DM2,239
			£1,012	£1,012	£1,012
			¥160,457	¥160,457	¥160,457
BUTLER	1	1	$189	$189	$189
			DM343	DM343	DM343
			£115	£115	£115
			¥22,769	¥22,769	¥22,769
BUTLER, GEORGE	1	1	$103	$103	$103
			DM184	DM184	DM184
			£63	£63	£63
			¥13,512	¥13,512	¥13,512
BUTTON & CO.	1	1	$134	$134	$134
			DM201	DM201	DM201
			£80	£80	£80
			¥14,998	¥14,998	¥14,998
CABART	8	2	$103	$195	$149
			DM108	DM286	DM197
			£63	£127	£95
			¥7,830	¥20,640	¥14,235
CAHUSAC	4	2	$566	$1,128	$847
			DM976	DM1,910	DM1,443
			£345	£690	£518
			¥64,570	¥130,752	¥97,661

| Maker | Items | | Selling Prices | | |
	Bid	Sold	Low	High	Avg
CAHUSAC, THOMAS	4	3	$120	$816	$486
			DM203	DM1,222	DM742
			£75	£483	£301
			¥14,790	¥90,823	¥53,745
CAHUSAC, THOMAS (SR.)	2	2	$1,198	$2,544	$1,871
			DM2,224	DM3,594	DM2,909
			£727	£1,610	£1,168
			¥124,857	¥227,070	¥175,963
CLEMENTI & CO.	5	3	$318	$1,961	$1,075
			DM554	DM3,642	DM1,844
			£196	£1,190	£661
			¥38,484	¥204,473	¥109,099
COLAS, PROSPER	1	0			
COLLARD & COLLARD	1	1	$618	$618	$618
			DM873	DM873	DM873
			£391	£391	£391
			¥55,145	¥55,145	¥55,145
COLONIEU, MARIUS HENRY	3	1	$264	$264	$264
			DM480	DM480	DM480
			£161	£161	£161
			¥33,350	¥33,350	¥33,350
CONN, USA	1	1	$485	$485	$485
			DM841	DM841	DM841
			£287	£287	£287
			¥61,668	¥61,668	¥61,668
COUESNON	1	0			
CRONE, GOTTLEIB	1	0			
CUVILLIER	1	1	$1,145	$1,145	$1,145
			DM1,904	DM1,904	DM1,904
			£690	£690	£690
			¥133,405	¥133,405	¥133,405
D'ALMAINE & CO.	4	3	$179	$872	$453
			DM326	DM1,619	DM794
			£109	£529	£278
			¥22,630	¥90,877	¥48,346
D'ALMAINE, GOULDING	2	2	$135	$498	$317
			DM236	DM923	DM580
			£81	£299	£190
			¥17,256	¥66,566	¥41,911
DALE, COCKERILL & CO.	1	1	$1,362	$1,362	$1,362
			DM1,924	DM1,924	DM1,924
			£862	£862	£862
			¥121,574	¥121,574	¥121,574
DODD	1	1	$72	$72	$72
			DM110	DM110	DM110
			£46	£46	£46
			¥8,029	¥8,029	¥8,029
DOLLING FAMILY (MEMBER OF)	1	1	$840	$840	$840
			DM1,397	DM1,397	DM1,397
			£506	£506	£506
			¥97,830	¥97,830	¥97,830
DROUET	1	1	$2,113	$2,113	$2,113
			DM3,529	DM3,529	DM3,529
			£1,265	£1,265	£1,265
			¥256,782	¥256,782	¥256,782

Maker	Items		Selling Prices		
	Bid	Sold	Low	High	Avg
DROUET, LOUIS	6	5	$622	$6,217	$2,752
			DM931	DM9,313	DM4,382
			£368	£3,680	£1,640
			¥69,199	¥691,987	¥301,189
DUBOIS & COUTURIER	2	1	$573	$573	$573
			DM952	DM952	DM952
			£345	£345	£345
			¥66,702	¥66,702	¥66,702
ELKHART	5	0			
EMBACH, LUDWIG	2	1	$610	$610	$610
			DM1,133	DM1,133	DM1,133
			£370	£370	£370
			¥63,614	¥63,614	¥63,614
EULER, AUGUST ANTON	1	1	$618	$618	$618
			DM875	DM875	DM875
			£391	£391	£391
			¥63,222	¥63,222	¥63,222
FIRTH & HALL	1	1	$265	$265	$265
			DM487	DM487	DM487
			£165	£165	£165
			¥31,198	¥31,198	¥31,198
FIRTH, HALL & POND	3	3	$230	$489	$357
			DM409	DM747	DM559
			£138	£322	£230
			¥30,585	¥51,514	¥39,875
FISCHER, CARL	1	1	$115	$115	$115
			DM205	DM205	DM205
			£70	£70	£70
			¥15,976	¥15,976	¥15,976
FLORIO, PIETRO GRASSI	1	1	$1,961	$1,961	$1,961
			DM3,642	DM3,642	DM3,642
			£1,190	£1,190	£1,190
			¥204,473	¥204,473	¥204,473
FRENCH, G.	1	1	$283	$283	$283
			DM418	DM418	DM418
			£184	£184	£184
			¥30,127	¥30,127	¥30,127
FREYER, JOHANN GOTTLIEB	1	1	$2,471	$2,471	$2,471
			DM3,796	DM3,796	DM3,796
			£1,610	£1,610	£1,610
			¥270,462	¥270,462	¥270,462
FREYER & MARTIN	2	0			
GARRETT	1	1	$230	$230	$230
			DM385	DM385	DM385
			£138	£138	£138
			¥28,013	¥28,013	¥28,013
GAUTROT (AINE)	2	1	$370	$370	$370
			DM686	DM686	DM686
			£224	£224	£224
			¥38,524	¥38,524	¥38,524
GEDNEY, CALEB	1	1	$5,451	$5,451	$5,451
			DM7,723	DM7,723	DM7,723
			£3,450	£3,450	£3,450
			¥557,844	¥557,844	¥557,844
GEHRING	1	1	$6,706	$6,706	$6,706
			DM10,302	DM10,302	DM10,302
			£4,370	£4,370	£4,370
			¥734,112	¥734,112	¥734,112

Maker	Items		Selling Prices		
	Bid	Sold	Low	High	Avg
GEMEINHARDT	3	2	$212	$309	$260
			DM381	DM556	DM468
			£126	£184	£155
			¥24,473	¥35,738	¥30,106
GEROCK, CHRISTOPHER	6	3	$324	$872	$677
			DM538	DM1,232	DM985
			£195	£552	£425
			¥37,701	¥85,536	¥67,030
GLIER, JOHANN WILHELM	1	1	$1,909	$1,909	$1,909
			DM3,174	DM3,174	DM3,174
			£1,150	£1,150	£1,150
			¥222,341	¥222,341	¥222,341
GODEFROY, CLAIR	3	3	$2,181	$5,088	$3,582
			DM3,080	DM7,208	DM5,513
			£1,380	£3,220	£2,223
			¥194,631	¥520,655	¥372,447
GODEFROY, CLAIR (AINE)	5	3	$676	$2,291	$1,434
			DM1,205	DM3,809	DM2,412
			£414	£1,380	£866
			¥88,443	¥266,809	¥170,297
GOLDING & CO.	2	1	$169	$169	$169
			DM243	DM243	DM243
			£109	£109	£109
			¥17,124	¥17,124	¥17,124
GOODLAD, JOHN DUNKIN	1	1	$381	$381	$381
			DM539	DM539	DM539
			£241	£241	£241
			¥38,968	¥38,968	¥38,968
GOODLAD & CO.	1	1	$840	$840	$840
			DM1,397	DM1,397	DM1,397
			£506	£506	£506
			¥97,830	¥97,830	¥97,830
GOOZMAN, J.P.	1	0			
GOTTFRIED, AUGUST LEHNHOLD	1	1	$327	$327	$327
			DM463	DM463	DM463
			£207	£207	£207
			¥33,471	¥33,471	¥33,471
GOULDING & CO.	5	3	$291	$691	$460
			DM504	DM975	DM682
			£172	£437	£287
			¥36,958	¥61,633	¥46,500
GOULDING & D'ALMAINE	2	2	$262	$836	$549
			DM486	DM1,181	DM833
			£159	£529	£344
			¥27,263	¥74,609	¥50,936
GOULDING D'ALMAINE POTTER	4	3	$535	$955	$690
			DM821	DM1,587	DM1,099
			£322	£575	£422
			¥51,902	¥111,171	¥75,109
GRENSER, CARL AUGUSTIN (I)	4	2	$2,362	$9,994	$6,178
			DM3,347	DM14,159	DM8,753
			£1,495	£6,325	£3,910
			¥241,733	¥1,022,715	¥632,224
GRENSER, H. & WIESNER	1	0			
GRENSER, JOHANN HEINRICH	3	0			
GREVE, ANDREAS	1	0			
HALE, JOHN	1	0			

| Maker | Items | | Selling Prices | | |
	Bid	Sold	Low	High	Avg
HALL, WILLIAM	1	1	$288	$288	$288
			DM512	DM512	DM512
			£173	£173	£173
			¥38,232	¥38,232	¥38,232
HALL & SON, WILLIAM	1	1	$397	$397	$397
			DM730	DM730	DM730
			£247	£247	£247
			¥46,797	¥46,797	¥46,797
HAMMIG, PHILIP	2	1	$1,999	$1,999	$1,999
			DM2,832	DM2,832	DM2,832
			£1,265	£1,265	£1,265
			¥204,543	¥204,543	¥204,543
HANN, RICHARD	1	0			
HARRIS	1	1	$437	$437	$437
			DM625	DM625	DM625
			£276	£276	£276
			¥43,880	¥43,880	¥43,880
HAWKES & SON	4	3	$210	$409	$306
			DM299	DM562	DM392
			£135	£253	£191
			¥21,405	¥34,051	¥26,078
HAYNES & CO.	3	3	$1,265	$2,185	$1,648
			DM2,187	DM3,777	DM2,849
			£782	£1,350	£1,019
			¥160,320	¥276,916	¥208,902
HAYNES CO., WILLIAM S.	3	3	$863	$2,070	$1,514
			DM1,319	DM3,685	DM2,488
			£567	£1,242	£956
			¥90,908	¥275,269	¥178,623
HEROUARD FRERES	2	1	$691	$691	$691
			DM975	DM975	DM975
			£437	£437	£437
			¥61,633	¥61,633	¥61,633
HILL, HENRY	1	1	$488	$488	$488
			DM870	DM870	DM870
			£299	£299	£299
			¥63,875	¥63,875	¥63,875
HILL, HENRY LOCKEY	1	1	$836	$836	$836
			DM1,181	DM1,181	DM1,181
			£529	£529	£529
			¥74,609	¥74,609	¥74,609
HUELLER, G.H.	1	1	$463	$463	$463
			DM852	DM852	DM852
			£288	£288	£288
			¥54,596	¥54,596	¥54,596
HUSSON & BUTHOD	1	1	$300	$300	$300
			DM535	DM535	DM535
			£184	£184	£184
			¥39,308	¥39,308	¥39,308
INGRAM, THOMAS WILLIAM	1	0			
JACOBS, HENDRIK	1	1	$30,728	$30,728	$30,728
			DM57,040	DM57,040	DM57,040
			£18,400	£18,400	£18,400
			¥4,111,296	¥4,111,296	¥4,111,296
JAMES, TREVOR J.	5	1	$130	$130	$130
			DM219	DM219	DM219
			£81	£81	£81
			¥15,928	¥15,928	¥15,928

Maker	Items		Selling Prices		
	Bid	Sold	Low	High	Avg
JULLIOT, DJALMA	2	0			
KAUFFMANN, ANDREW	2	1	$1,606	$1,606	$1,606
			DM2,447	DM2,447	DM2,447
			£1,035	£1,035	£1,035
			¥178,124	¥178,124	¥178,124
KEY, THOMAS	1	1	$945	$945	$945
			DM1,339	DM1,339	DM1,339
			£598	£598	£598
			¥96,693	¥96,693	¥96,693
KING MUSICAL INSTRUMENT CO.	1	0			
KLINGSON	1	0			
KNOCHENHAUER, AUGUST T.A.	1	1	$2,544	$2,544	$2,544
			DM3,604	DM3,604	DM3,604
			£31,610	£31,610	£31,610
			¥8260,327	¥8260,327	¥8260,327
KOCH, FRANZ JOSEPH	1	1	$2,907	$2,907	$2,907
			DM4,119	DM4,119	DM4,119
			£31,840	£31,840	£31,840
			¥8297,517	¥8297,517	¥8297,517
KOCH, S.	2	2	$1,260	$4,009	$2,635
			DM1,926	DM6,665	DM4,296
			£3805	£32,415	£31,610
			¥8140,513	¥8466,916	¥8303,714
KOHLER, JOHN	1	0			
KUSDER, HENRY	1	1	$3,284	$3,284	$3,284
			DM5,904	DM5,904	DM5,904
			£31,955	£31,955	£31,955
			¥8379,720	¥8379,720	¥8379,720
LAFLEUR, J.R. & SON	2	1	$817	$817	$817
			DM1,157	DM1,157	DM1,157
			£3517	£3517	£3517
			¥883,596	¥883,596	¥883,596
LAMY, J.T.	1	0			
LANGLOIS, A.M.	2	1	$678	$678	$678
			DM1,033	DM1,033	DM1,033
			£3437	£3437	£3437
			¥875,208	¥875,208	¥875,208
LAWSON	3	2	$699	$878	$789
			DM1,048	DM1,460	DM1,254
			£414	£529	£472
			¥77,849	¥102,277	¥90,063
LEBLANC	1	0			
LEBRET	2	1	$816	$816	$816
			DM1,222	DM1,222	DM1,222
			£483	£483	£483
			¥90,823	¥90,823	¥90,823
LEBRET, LOUIS LEON JOSEPH	1	1	$382	$382	$382
			DM635	DM635	DM635
			£230	£230	£230
			¥44,468	¥44,468	¥44,468
LEROUX (AINE)	4	2	$509	$587	$548
			DM719	DM1,091	DM905
			£322	£357	£339
			¥45,414	¥61,243	¥53,329

Maker	Items		Selling Prices		
	Bid	Sold	Low	High	Avg
LEWISCH, M.	1	1	$509	$509	$509
			DM721	DM721	DM721
			£322	£322	£322
			¥52,065	¥52,065	¥52,065
LOT, LOUIS	5	4	$967	$9,694	$4,048
			DM1,686	DM16,971	DM6,819
			£575	£5,980	£2,516
			¥123,257	¥1,171,781	¥480,720
LUVONI, UBALDO	2	1	$612	$612	$612
			DM916	DM916	DM916
			£362	£362	£362
			¥68,070	¥68,070	¥68,070
MAHILLON, C.	1	1	$535	$535	$535
			DM889	DM889	DM889
			£322	£322	£322
			¥62,255	¥62,255	¥62,255
MARTIN, A.	1	0			
MARTIN, JEAN-FRANCOIS	1	1	$690	$690	$690
			DM978	DM978	DM978
			£437	£437	£437
			¥70,660	¥70,660	¥70,660
MARTIN BROS.	2	1	$1,943	$1,943	$1,943
			DM2,910	DM2,910	DM2,910
			£1,150	£1,150	£1,150
			¥216,246	¥216,246	¥216,246
MATEKI	1	1	$2,452	$2,452	$2,452
			DM4,461	DM4,461	DM4,461
			£1,495	£1,495	£1,495
			¥309,674	¥309,674	¥309,674
MAYBRICK, WILLIAM	1	0			
MCNEILL, JOHN	1	1	$618	$618	$618
			DM873	DM873	DM873
			£391	£391	£391
			¥55,145	¥55,145	¥55,145
METZLER	5	3	$128	$178	$152
			DM228	DM272	DM243
			£78	£115	£97
			¥16,694	¥19,792	¥17,730
METZLER, VALENTIN	3	1	$407	$407	$407
			DM610	DM610	DM610
			£241	£241	£241
			¥45,318	¥45,318	¥45,318
METZLER & CO.	4	3	$112	$432	$305
			DM200	DM770	DM494
			£69	£265	£188
			¥15,106	¥56,505	¥34,189
MILHOUSE, WILLIAM	3	3	$400	$1,565	$849
			DM566	DM2,603	DM1,331
			£253	£943	£521
			¥40,909	¥182,320	¥94,244
MILLHOUSE	2	1	$327	$327	$327
			DM463	DM463	DM463
			£207	£207	£207
			¥33,741	¥33,741	¥33,741
MILLIGAN	1	1	$400	$400	$400
			DM665	DM665	DM665
			£241	£241	£241
			¥46,595	¥46,595	¥46,595

Maker	Items Bid	Sold	Selling Prices Low	High	Avg
MOLLENHAUER & SONS, J.	2	1	$261	$261	$261
			DM275	DM275	DM275
			£161	£161	£161
			¥19,931	¥19,931	¥19,931
MONZANI	5	2	$773	$895	$834
			DM1,288	DM1,567	DM1,427
			£460	£552	£506
			¥92,363	¥108,164	¥100,264
MONZANI, TEBALDO	3	1	$858	$858	$858
			DM1,427	DM1,427	DM1,427
			£517	£517	£517
			¥99,957	¥99,957	¥99,957
MONZANI & CO.	21	16	$285	$3,923	$1,033
			DM411	DM7,284	DM1,695
			£184	£2,381	£639
			¥25,951	¥466,877	¥109,938
MURAMATSU	1	0			
NAUST	1	1	$26,098	$26,098	$26,098
			DM45,692	DM45,692	DM45,692
			£16,100	£16,100	£16,100
			¥3,154,795	¥3,154,795	¥3,154,795
NEDDERMANN, JOHANN ADOPH	2	1	$764	$764	$764
			DM1,270	DM1,270	DM1,270
			£460	£460	£460
			¥88,936	¥88,936	¥88,936
NEUZIL, JOHANN	1	0			
NICHOLSON, CHARLES	1	1	$1,933	$1,933	$1,933
			DM2,892	DM2,892	DM2,892
			£1,150	£1,150	£1,150
			¥215,602	¥215,602	¥215,602
NOBLET BROS.	1	1	$762	$762	$762
			DM1,415	DM1,415	DM1,415
			£462	£462	£462
			¥79,419	¥79,419	¥79,419
OPPENHEIM, H.	1	1	$802	$802	$802
			DM1,333	DM1,333	DM1,333
			£483	£483	£483
			¥93,383	¥93,383	¥93,383
OTTEN, JOHN	2	2	$282	$394	$338
			DM502	DM703	DM602
			£173	£242	£207
			¥36,851	¥51,592	¥44,221
OTTO, JOHANN GEORG	1	0			
PAN-AMERICAN	1	0			
PARKER, JOHN	1	1	$618	$618	$618
			DM873	DM873	DM873
			£391	£391	£391
			¥55,145	¥55,145	¥55,145
PAXMAN BROS.	1	0			
PFAFF, FRANZ	1	0			
PFAFF, JOHN	1	1	$331	$331	$331
			DM608	DM608	DM608
			£206	£206	£206
			¥38,997	¥38,997	¥38,997
PHILLIPS	1	0			
PHIPPS & CO.	1	0			

Maker	Items		Selling Prices		
	Bid	Sold	Low	High	Avg
POTTER	6	2	$332	$336	$334
			DM471	DM494	DM483
			£213	£219	£216
			¥33,772	¥35,650	¥34,711
POTTER, HENRY	1	1	$224	$224	$224
			DM391	DM391	DM391
			£138	£138	£138
			¥27,165	¥27,165	¥27,165
POTTER, RICHARD	7	7	$763	$3,353	$1,607
			DM1,078	DM5,151	DM2,613
			£483	£2,185	£1,012
			¥68,121	¥367,056	¥177,052
POTTER, WILLIAM HENRY	18	13	$102	$894	$561
			DM172	DM1,457	DM909
			£63	£552	£342
			¥12,515	¥99,473	¥60,483
PROSER	3	2	$773	$1,107	$940
			DM1,157	DM1,841	DM1,499
			£460	£667	£564
			¥86,241	¥128,958	¥107,599
PROWSE, JOSEPH	1	1	$509	$509	$509
			DM719	DM719	DM719
			£322	£322	£322
			¥45,414	¥45,414	¥45,414
PROWSE, THOMAS	8	8	$327	$1,093	$646
			DM463	DM1,846	DM1,010
			£207	£656	£394
			¥33,471	¥145,379	¥72,581
PROWSE & CO., KEITH	1	1	$601	$601	$601
			DM1,071	DM1,071	DM1,071
			£368	£368	£368
			¥78,616	¥78,616	¥78,616
PRUNIER	1	0			
RITTERSHAUSEN, E.	1	0			
ROBINSON	1	1	$149	$149	$149
			DM204	DM204	DM204
			£92	£92	£92
			¥12,382	¥12,382	¥12,382
ROESSLER, HEINZ	2	1	$469	$469	$469
			DM837	DM837	DM837
			£288	£288	£288
			¥61,419	¥61,419	¥61,419
RUDALL, CARTE & CO.	53	36	$85	$4,963	$822
			DM143	DM8,252	DM1,366
			£52	£2,990	£505
			¥9,806	¥578,087	¥89,842
RUDALL & ROSE	13	12	$442	$4,880	$2,001
			DM653	DM8,701	DM3,262
			£288	£2,990	£1,236
			¥47,074	¥638,754	¥226,774
RUDALL, ROSE, CARTE & CO.	9	9	$331	$3,487	$1,311
			DM608	DM6,475	DM2,177
			£206	£2,116	£813
			¥38,997	¥368,512	¥146,010
SAX, CHARLES JOSEPH	1	1	$1,544	$1,544	$1,544
			DM2,187	DM2,187	DM2,187
			£977	£977	£977
			¥157,975	¥157,975	¥157,975

Maker	Items		Selling Prices		
	Bid	Sold	Low	High	Avg
SCHAEFFER, EVETTE	1	1	$840	$840	$840
			DM1,397	DM1,397	DM1,397
			£506	£506	£506
			¥97,830	¥97,830	¥97,830
SCHMIDT	1	1	$945	$945	$945
			DM1,335	DM1,335	DM1,335
			£598	£598	£598
			¥84,340	¥84,340	¥84,340
SCHOTT, B. (FILS)	1	1	$573	$573	$573
			DM952	DM952	DM952
			£345	£345	£345
			¥66,702	¥66,702	¥66,702
SCHUCHART	1	1	$1,352	$1,352	$1,352
			DM2,431	DM2,431	DM2,431
			£805	£805	£805
			¥156,355	¥156,355	¥156,355
SCHUCHART, CHARLES	2	2	$727	$3,453	$2,090
			DM1,027	DM4,877	DM2,952
			£460	£2,185	£1,323
			¥64,877	¥308,166	¥186,521
SCHUCHART, JOHN JUST	1	0			
SEIDEL, AUGUST	1	1	$363	$363	$363
			DM515	DM515	DM515
			£230	£230	£230
			¥37,190	¥37,190	¥37,190
SELMER	1	0			
SICCAMA, ABEL	6	3	$305	$1,145	$687
			DM508	DM1,904	DM1,182
			£184	£690	£415
			¥35,575	¥133,405	¥77,531
SIMPSON	1	1	$4,235	$4,235	$4,235
			DM6,507	DM6,507	DM6,507
			£2,760	£2,760	£2,760
			¥463,650	¥463,650	¥463,650
SIMPSON, JOHN	2	2	$350	$1,198	$774
			DM524	DM2,224	DM1,374
			£207	£727	£467
			¥38,924	¥124,857	¥81,891
STANESBY, THOMAS	2	2	$9,706	$14,536	$12,121
			DM14,911	DM20,594	DM17,753
			£6,325	£9,200	£7,763
			¥1,062,530	¥1,487,585	¥1,275,058
STARK	1	1	$473	$473	$473
			DM667	DM667	DM667
			£299	£299	£299
			¥42,170	¥42,170	¥42,170
STRASSER, MARIGAUX, LEMAIRE	1	1	$453	$453	$453
			DM822	DM822	DM822
			£276	£276	£276
			¥54,645	¥54,645	¥54,645
SZEPESSY, BELA	1	1	$8,818	$8,818	$8,818
			DM16,336	DM16,336	DM16,336
			£5,290	£5,290	£5,290
			¥1,177,713	¥1,177,713	¥1,177,713
THIBOUVILLE, MARTIN (L'AINE)	1	1	$764	$764	$764
			DM1,270	DM1,270	DM1,270
			£460	£460	£460
			¥88,936	¥88,936	¥88,936

| Maker | Items | | Selling Prices | | |
	Bid	Sold	Low	High	Avg
THIBOUVILLE-LAMY, J.	2	2	$54	$436	$245
			DM77	DM618	DM348
			£35	£276	£155
			¥5,624	¥44,628	¥25,126
THORSEN, NIELS CHRISTENSEN	1	1	$960	$960	$960
			DM1,604	DM1,604	DM1,604
			£575	£575	£575
			¥116,719	¥116,719	¥116,719
THURGOOD, G.J.	1	1	$1,636	$1,636	$1,636
			DM2,310	DM2,310	DM2,310
			£1,035	£1,035	£1,035
			¥145,973	¥145,973	¥145,973
TULOU, JEAN-LOUIS	3	1	$756	$756	$756
			DM1,158	DM1,158	DM1,158
			£483	£483	£483
			¥84,293	¥84,293	¥84,293
UEBEL	1	1	$189	$189	$189
			DM279	DM279	DM279
			£123	£123	£123
			¥20,144	¥20,144	¥20,144
VAN GULIK, D.	1	1	$1,090	$1,090	$1,090
			DM1,545	DM1,545	DM1,545
			£690	£690	£690
			¥111,569	¥111,569	¥111,569
WALLIS, JOSEPH & SON	2	1	$472	$472	$472
			DM669	DM669	DM669
			£299	£299	£299
			¥48,347	¥48,347	¥48,347
WALLIS, JOSEPH & SONS	1	1	$763	$763	$763
			DM1,078	DM1,078	DM1,078
			£483	£483	£483
			¥68,121	¥68,121	¥68,121
WARREN, I.	1	1	$836	$836	$836
			DM1,181	DM1,181	DM1,181
			£529	£529	£529
			¥74,609	¥74,609	¥74,609
WELSH, THOMAS	1	1	$526	$526	$526
			DM937	DM937	DM937
			£322	£322	£322
			¥68,789	¥68,789	¥68,789
WHEATSTONE, C.	1	1	$237	$237	$237
			DM444	DM444	DM444
			£150	£150	£150
			¥28,078	¥28,078	¥28,078
WHITAKER & CO.	1	0			
WILLIAMS, E.G.	1	1	$329	$329	$329
			DM493	DM493	DM493
			£195	£195	£195
			¥36,668	¥36,668	¥36,668
WILLIS, JOHN	3	0			
WOOD, JAMES & SON	1	1	$1,049	$1,049	$1,049
			DM1,744	DM1,744	DM1,744
			£632	£632	£632
			¥122,191	¥122,191	¥122,191

Maker	Items		Selling Prices		
	Bid	Sold	Low	High	Avg
WOOD & IVY	4	2	$381	$544	$462
			DM538	DM1,010	DM774
			£241	£330	£286
			¥33,990	¥56,699	¥45,345
WYLDE, HENRY	3	2	$535	$2,332	$1,433
			DM816	DM3,492	DM2,154
			£345	£1,380	£863
			¥59,375	¥259,495	¥159,435
XAVER, FRANZ	1	1	$1,541	$1,541	$1,541
			DM2,316	DM2,316	DM2,316
			£920	£920	£920
			¥171,636	¥171,636	¥171,636
XAVER, FRANZ (attributed to)	1	0			
YAMAHA	6	5	$247	$1,075	$553
			DM423	DM1,733	DM903
			£150	£633	£333
			¥30,284	¥132,964	¥67,020

FLUTE D'AMORE

Maker	Items		Selling Prices		
MONZANI, TEBALDO	1	1	$1,635	$1,635	$1,635
			DM2,317	DM2,317	DM2,317
			£1,035	£1,035	£1,035
			¥167,353	¥167,353	¥167,353
MONZANI & CO.	1	1	$1,817	$1,817	$1,817
			DM2,574	DM2,574	DM2,574
			£1,150	£1,150	£1,150
			¥185,948	¥185,948	¥185,948

FLUTE/PICCOLO

Maker	Items		Selling Prices		
NICHOLSON	2	1	$224	$224	$224
			DM236	DM236	DM236
			£138	£138	£138
			¥17,084	¥17,084	¥17,084

FRENCH HORN

Maker	Items		Selling Prices		
BOOSEY & HAWKES	2	1	$170	$170	$170
			DM308	DM308	DM308
			£104	£104	£104
			¥20,492	¥20,492	¥20,492
DALLAS	1	0			
GREY & SONS, JOHN	1	0			
KNOPF	2	0			
MAHILLON, C.	1	1	$496	$496	$496
			DM825	DM825	DM825
			£299	£299	£299
			¥57,809	¥57,809	¥57,809
MILLEREAU	1	0			
STOWASSER, ADOLF	1	0			

GALOUBET

Maker	Items		Selling Prices		
LONG	1	1	$1,069	$1,069	$1,069
			DM1,777	DM1,777	DM1,777
			£644	£644	£644
			¥124,511	¥124,511	¥124,511

Maker	Items		Selling Prices		
	Bid	Sold	Low	High	Avg

GIRAFFENFLUGEL

SCHEHL, KARL	2	0			

GLOCKENSPIEL

PREMIER	1	1	$282	$282	$282
			DM477	DM477	DM477
			£173	£173	£173
			¥32,688	¥32,688	¥32,688

GUITAR

ABBOTT	1	1	$750	$750	$750
			DM1,302	DM1,302	DM1,302
			£460	£460	£460
			¥86,889	¥86,889	¥86,889
ALBERTINI, ALFREDO	1	0			
ARAM, KEVIN	1	1	$3,749	$3,749	$3,749
			DM6,509	DM6,509	DM6,509
			£2,300	£2,300	£2,300
			¥434,447	¥434,447	¥434,447
ARIA	1	1	$124	$124	$124
			DM182	DM182	DM182
			£81	£81	£81
			¥13,134	¥13,134	¥13,134
AUBRY, JACQUES	1	0			
BARRY	1	1	$1,336	$1,336	$1,336
			DM2,222	DM2,222	DM2,222
			£805	£805	£805
			¥155,639	¥155,639	¥155,639
BAY STATE	1	1	$1,323	$1,323	$1,323
			DM2,433	DM2,433	DM2,433
			£823	£823	£823
			¥155,989	¥155,989	¥155,989
BERNABE, PAULINO	2	0			
BERTET, JOSEPH R. (attributed to)	2	1	$1,787	$1,787	$1,787
			DM3,318	DM3,318	DM3,318
			£1,084	£1,084	£1,084
			¥186,298	¥186,298	¥186,298
BERWIND, J.	2	1	$1,380	$1,380	$1,380
			DM2,332	DM2,332	DM2,332
			£828	£828	£828
			¥168,360	¥168,360	¥168,360
BODY, HANS	3	1	$118	$118	$118
			DM167	DM167	DM167
			£75	£75	£75
			¥12,184	¥12,184	¥12,184
BOOSEY & CO.	1	1	$1,456	$1,456	$1,456
			DM2,181	DM2,181	DM2,181
			£862	£862	£862
			¥162,090	¥162,090	¥162,090
BORREGUERO, MODESTO	1	1	$1,320	$1,320	$1,320
			DM2,399	DM2,399	DM2,399
			£805	£805	£805
			¥159,382	¥159,382	¥159,382

Maker	Items		Selling Prices		
	Bid	Sold	Low	High	Avg
BOUCHET, ROBERT	3	3	$26,476	$30,912	$28,847
			DM42,465	DM55,568	DM49,525
			£17,193	£18,400	£17,614
			¥3,012,470	¥3,706,508	¥3,430,936
BOULLANGIER, CHARLES (attributed to)	3	1	$280	$280	$280
			DM295	DM295	DM295
			£173	£173	£173
			¥21,355	¥21,355	¥21,355
BOULLANGIER, G.	1	1	$168	$168	$168
			DM248	DM248	DM248
			£109	£109	£109
			¥17,888	¥17,888	¥17,888
BURNS	2	1	$1,125	$1,125	$1,125
			DM1,953	DM1,953	DM1,953
			£690	£690	£690
			¥130,334	¥130,334	¥130,334
BUTLER	1	1	$89	$89	$89
			DM137	DM137	DM137
			£58	£58	£58
			¥8,843	¥8,843	¥8,843
CAMACHO, RODOLFO	1	0			
CAMACHO, VICENTE	2	1	$1,635	$1,635	$1,635
			DM2,317	DM2,317	DM2,317
			£1,035	£1,035	£1,035
			¥167,353	¥167,353	¥167,353
CARPIO, RICARDO SANCHIS	1	1	$754	$754	$754
			DM1,371	DM1,371	DM1,371
			£460	£460	£460
			¥91,075	¥91,075	¥91,075
CHIQUITA	1	1	$1,125	$1,125	$1,125
			DM1,953	DM1,953	DM1,953
			£690	£690	£690
			¥130,334	¥130,334	¥130,334
COLUMBIAN	2	2	$131	$225	$178
			DM228	DM391	DM309
			£81	£138	£109
			¥15,206	¥26,067	¥20,636
CONDE, HERMANOS	2	0			
CONTRERAS, M.G.	1	1	$377	$377	$377
			DM685	DM685	DM685
			£230	£230	£230
			¥45,538	¥45,538	¥45,538
CONTRERAS, MANUEL	7	2	$1,304	$1,845	$1,575
			DM2,455	DM3,200	DM2,827
			£805	£1,092	£949
			¥137,832	¥234,638	¥186,235
DANELECTRO	1	0			
D'ANGELICO	1	0			
D'ANGELICO, JOHN	3	1	$9,258	$9,258	$9,258
			DM17,474	DM17,474	DM17,474
			£5,730	£5,730	£5,730
			¥979,444	¥979,444	¥979,444
DEL PILAR, GUILLERMO	1	0			
DE SOTO Y SOLARES, MANUEL	2	2	$297	$909	$603
			DM409	DM1,283	DM846
			£184	£575	£380
			¥24,765	¥81,096	¥52,930

Maker	Items		Selling Prices		
	Bid	Sold	Low	High	Avg
DITSON, OLIVER	1	1	$690	$690	$690
			DM996	DM996	DM996
			£440	£440	£440
			¥59,858	¥59,858	¥59,858
DOBRO	6	5	$403	$1,062	$652
			DM582	DM1,909	DM1,091
			£263	£632	£404
			¥40,753	¥122,753	¥73,718
DREAPER	2	1	$487	$487	$487
			DM846	DM846	DM846
			£299	£299	£299
			¥56,478	¥56,478	¥56,478
DUBOIS (FILS)	1	1	$1,817	$1,817	$1,817
			DM2,574	DM2,574	DM2,574
			£1,150	£1,150	£1,150
			¥185,948	¥185,948	¥185,948
EPIPHONE	4	3	$546	$1,052	$715
			DM790	DM1,493	DM1,069
			£328	£675	£453
			¥55,308	¥107,024	¥76,325
ESPINOSA, JULIAN	1	1	$580	$580	$580
			DM1,042	DM1,042	DM1,042
			£345	£345	£345
			¥67,009	¥67,009	¥67,009
ESTRUCH, JUAN	1	0			
FABRICATORE, GENNARO	4	3	$712	$1,010	$887
			DM1,245	DM1,627	DM1,462
			£437	£598	£537
			¥84,144	¥112,448	¥101,735
FABRICATORE, GIOVANNI BATTISTA	2	1	$1,783	$1,783	$1,783
			DM2,875	DM2,875	DM2,875
			£1,035	£1,035	£1,035
			¥209,875	¥209,875	¥209,875
FAVILLA, HERK (workshop of)	1	1	$288	$288	$288
			DM433	DM433	DM433
			£175	£175	£175
			¥32,137	¥32,137	¥32,137
FAVILLA GUITARS	1	1	$165	$165	$165
			DM312	DM312	DM312
			£102	£102	£102
			¥17,490	¥17,490	¥17,490
FENDER	13	10	$289	$4,910	$1,070
			DM433	DM6,969	DM1,659
			£172	£3,150	£671
			¥32,247	¥499,445	¥114,916
FERNANDEZ, ARCANGEL	2	1	$5,377	$5,377	$5,377
			DM8,984	DM8,984	DM8,984
			£3,220	£3,220	£3,220
			¥653,628	¥653,628	¥653,628
FISCHER, CARL	2	1	$535	$535	$535
			DM889	DM889	DM889
			£322	£322	£322
			¥62,255	¥62,255	¥62,255
FLEESON, MARTIN	1	0			
FLETA, IGNACIO	3	1	$26,432	$26,432	$26,432
			DM39,018	DM39,018	DM39,018
			£17,250	£17,250	£17,250
			¥2,810,042	¥2,810,042	¥2,810,042

Maker	Items		Selling Prices		
	Bid	Sold	Low	High	Avg
FLETA & SONS, IGNACIO	2	2	$19,090	$20,645	$19,867
			DM31,740	DM36,812	DM34,276
			£11,500	£12,650	£12,075
			¥2,223,410	¥2,702,420	¥2,462,915
FRIEDERICH, DANIEL	2	2	$7,628	$12,719	$10,173
			DM14,164	DM18,020	DM16,092
			£4,629	£8,050	£6,339
			¥795,173	¥1,301,637	¥1,048,405
FRITH, STEPHEN	1	0			
FUSSINGER, J.T.	1	1	$1,166	$1,166	$1,166
			DM1,746	DM1,746	DM1,746
			£690	£690	£690
			¥129,748	¥129,748	¥129,748
GARCIA, ENRIQUE	2	0			
GARCIA, JOAQUIN	1	0			
GIBSON, WILLIAM	1	1	$1,049	$1,049	$1,049
			DM1,744	DM1,744	DM1,744
			£632	£632	£632
			¥122,191	¥122,191	¥122,191
GIBSON CO.	38	29	$184	$9,644	$1,797
			DM328	DM13,689	DM2,825
			£112	£6,187	£1,120
			¥7,595	¥980,974	¥188,154
GOUDOT	1	0			
GRETSCH	6	5	$1,455	$6,561	$4,190
			DM2,746	DM11,391	DM7,319
			£900	£4,025	£2,572
			¥153,913	¥760,282	¥482,607
GRIMSHAW, EMIL	1	1	$604	$604	$604
			DM1,097	DM1,097	DM1,097
			£368	£368	£368
			¥72,860	¥72,860	¥72,860
GRUMMIT	1	0			
GUADAGNINI, CARLO (ascribed to)	1	1	$1,190	$1,190	$1,190
			DM2,247	DM2,247	DM2,247
			£737	£737	£737
			¥125,928	¥125,928	¥125,928
GUADAGNINI, FRANCESCO (ascribed to)	1	1	$1,610	$1,610	$1,610
			DM2,755	DM2,755	DM2,755
			£952	£952	£952
			¥199,930	¥199,930	¥199,930
GUILD	1	0			
HAGSTROM	1	0			
HAMER	1	0			
HANDEL, J.T.C.	2	0			
HAUSER, HERMANN	3	1	$13,122	$13,122	$13,122
			DM22,782	DM22,782	DM22,782
			£8,050	£8,050	£8,050
			¥1,520,565	¥1,520,565	¥1,520,565
HAUSER, HERMANN (II)	1	1	$21,146	$21,146	$21,146
			DM31,214	DM31,214	DM31,214
			£13,800	£13,800	£13,800
			¥2,248,034	¥2,248,034	¥2,248,034
HAYNES CO., JOHN C.	1	0			
HENRY, NICOLAS	1	0			

Maker	Items		Selling Prices		
	Bid	Sold	Low	High	Avg
HENSE, DIETER	1	1	$675	$675	$675
			DM1,214	DM1,214	DM1,214
			£402	£402	£402
			¥78,080	¥78,080	¥78,080
HERNANDEZ, MANUEL & VICTORIANO AGUADO	1	1	$18,354	$18,354	$18,354
			DM32,994	DM32,994	DM32,994
			£10,925	£10,925	£10,925
			¥2,121,963	¥2,121,963	¥2,121,963
HERNANDEZ, SANTOS	3	1	$1,762	$1,762	$1,762
			DM2,601	DM2,601	DM2,601
			£1,150	£1,150	£1,150
			¥187,336	¥187,336	¥187,336
HERNANDEZ, SOBRINOS SANTOS	1	0			
HOFNER	6	2	$44	$134	$89
			DM68	DM201	DM134
			£29	£80	£54
			¥4,799	¥14,998	¥9,899
HOFNER, KARL	2	2	$244	$412	$328
			DM423	DM716	DM570
			£150	£253	£201
			¥28,239	¥47,789	¥38,014
HOPF, DIETER	1	0			
HOWE, ELIAS	1	0			
HOWELL, T.	1	1	$2,037	$2,037	$2,037
			DM3,267	DM3,267	DM3,267
			£1,323	£1,323	£1,323
			¥231,728	¥231,728	¥231,728
HUSSON, BUTHOD & THIBOUVILLE	3	1	$619	$619	$619
			DM911	DM911	DM911
			£403	£403	£403
			¥65,672	¥65,672	¥65,672
IBANEZ	1	1	$428	$428	$428
			DM652	DM652	DM652
			£276	£276	£276
			¥47,500	¥47,500	¥47,500
JONES, A.H.	1	1	$382	$382	$382
			DM588	DM588	DM588
			£253	£253	£253
			¥40,790	¥40,790	¥40,790
JONES, EDWARD B.	1	0			
KIMBARA	1	1	$112	$112	$112
			DM195	DM195	DM195
			£69	£69	£69
			¥13,033	¥13,033	¥13,033
KONO, MASARU	1	1	$967	$967	$967
			DM1,329	DM1,329	DM1,329
			£598	£598	£598
			¥80,485	¥80,485	¥80,485
LACOTE	3	1	$1,273	$1,273	$1,273
			DM1,873	DM1,873	DM1,873
			£828	£828	£828
			¥135,096	¥135,096	¥135,096
LACOTE, RENE (attributed to)	1	0			
LARSON (workshop of)	1	0			

| Maker | Items | | Selling Prices | | |
	Bid	Sold	Low	High	Avg
LARSON BROS.	2	1	$397	$397	$397
			DM749	DM749	DM749
			£246	£246	£246
			¥41,976	¥41,976	¥41,976
LEVIN GOLIATH	1	1	$412	$412	$412
			DM716	DM716	DM716
			£253	£253	£253
			¥47,789	¥47,789	¥47,789
LIESSEM, R.	1	0			
LION, ARTHUR	1	1	$374	$374	$374
			DM665	DM665	DM665
			£228	£228	£228
			¥51,921	¥51,921	¥51,921
LONGMAN & BRODERIP	3	2	$1,145	$5,727	$3,436
			DM1,904	DM9,522	DM5,713
			£690	£3,450	£2,070
			¥133,405	¥667,023	¥400,214
LUTZEMBERGER	1	0			
MACCAFERRI	1	1	$233	$233	$233
			DM329	DM329	DM329
			£146	£146	£146
			¥20,638	¥20,638	¥20,638
MAIRE, FRANCAIS	1	1	$1,360	$1,360	$1,360
			DM2,037	DM2,037	DM2,037
			£805	£805	£805
			¥151,372	¥151,372	¥151,372
MANN	1	0			
MANZANERO, FELIX	1	0			
MARCHAL	2	1	$590	$590	$590
			DM822	DM822	DM822
			£368	£368	£368
			¥49,882	¥49,882	¥49,882
MARCHAL, PIERRE PAUL	1	0			
MARCHAND	1	1	$713	$713	$713
			DM1,272	DM1,272	DM1,272
			£437	£437	£437
			¥93,356	¥93,356	¥93,356
MARTIN	6	4	$537	$5,637	$2,368
			DM821	DM8,309	DM3,518
			£345	£3,680	£1,541
			¥53,055	¥601,202	¥248,740
MARTIN, CHRISTIAN FREDERICK	3	2	$2,070	$2,622	$2,346
			DM3,115	DM3,928	DM3,521
			£1,257	£1,552	£1,404
			¥231,385	¥291,838	¥261,611
MARTIN, E.	1	0			
MARTIN & CO., C.F.	28	27	$345	$16,100	$3,101
			DM590	DM27,209	DM5,207
			£204	£9,660	£1,861
			¥42,842	¥1,964,200	¥373,402
MARZAL, JESUS	1	0			
MAST, BLAISE	2	1	$2,615	$2,615	$2,615
			DM4,856	DM4,856	DM4,856
			£1,587	£1,587	£1,587
			¥272,631	¥272,631	¥272,631

Maker	Items		Selling Prices		
	Bid	Sold	Low	High	Avg
MAST, JOSEPH LAURENT	1	1	$1,360	$1,360	$1,360
			DM2,037	DM2,037	DM2,037
			£805	£805	£805
			¥151,372	¥151,372	¥151,372
MATHIEU, MARESCHAL	1	0			
MOITESSIER, LOUIS	1	0			
MONTRON (attributed to)	1	0			
MONZINO, ANTONIO	1	1	$690	$690	$690
			DM1,166	DM1,166	DM1,166
			£414	£414	£414
			¥84,180	¥84,180	¥84,180
MOSELEY, SEMI	1	1	$288	$288	$288
			DM512	DM512	DM512
			£175	£175	£175
			¥39,940	¥39,940	¥39,940
MUSSER, D.	1	1	$6,748	$6,748	$6,748
			DM11,716	DM11,716	DM11,716
			£4,140	£4,140	£4,140
			¥782,005	¥782,005	¥782,005
NADERMAN, JEAN-HENRI	1	0			
NATIONAL	17	14	$259	$11,500	$2,823
			DM443	DM16,606	DM4,555
			£153	£7,327	£1,761
			¥32,132	¥997,625	¥292,322
PADILLA, JUAN ROMAIN	1	1	$103	$103	$103
			DM108	DM108	DM108
			£63	£63	£63
			¥7,830	¥7,830	¥7,830
PANORMO	2	2	$2,050	$7,079	$4,565
			DM2,160	DM13,329	DM7,744
			£31,265	£34,370	£32,818
			¥8156,601	¥8748,231	¥8452,416
PANORMO, JOSEPH	1	0			
PANORMO, LOUIS	15	14	$828	$4,582	$2,319
			DM1,484	DM7,618	DM3,653
			£3495	£32,760	£31,429
			¥896,180	¥8533,618	¥8260,083
PERFUMO, JUAN	1	1	$1,595	$1,595	$1,595
			DM2,845	DM2,845	DM2,845
			£3978	£3978	£3978
			¥8208,823	¥8208,823	¥8208,823
PETERSEN, HAROLD	6	3	$264	$360	$323
			DM390	DM550	DM492
			£3172	£3230	£3203
			¥828,169	¥840,147	¥835,903
PETITJEAN (L'AINE)	3	1	$1,416	$1,416	$1,416
			DM2,629	DM2,629	DM2,629
			£3859	£3859	£3859
			¥8147,576	¥8147,576	¥8147,576
PIRETTI, ENRICO	1	0			
PONS FAMILY (MEMBER OF)	1	1	$3,109	$3,109	$3,109
			DM4,656	DM4,656	DM4,656
			£1,840	£1,840	£1,840
			¥345,994	¥345,994	¥345,994

Maker	Items Bid	Sold	Selling Prices Low	High	Avg
PRESTON, JOHN	2	1	$638 DM1,138 £391 ¥83,529	$638 DM1,138 £391 ¥83,529	$638 DM1,138 £391 ¥83,529
RAMIREZ	2	1	$1,217 DM1,870 £805 ¥129,786	$1,217 DM1,870 £805 ¥129,786	$1,217 DM1,870 £805 ¥129,786
RAMIREZ, JOSE	7	5	$881 DM1,298 £575 ¥93,938	$2,899 DM5,210 £1,725 ¥335,047	$1,910 DM3,047 £1,173 ¥210,413
RAMIREZ, JOSE (workshop of)	1	1	$1,840 DM2,769 £1,117 ¥205,675	$1,840 DM2,769 £1,117 ¥205,675	$1,840 DM2,769 £1,117 ¥205,675
RAMIREZ, JOSE (I)	1	0			
RAMIREZ, JOSE (III)	5	1	$2,999 DM5,207 £1,840 ¥347,558	$2,999 DM5,207 £1,840 ¥347,558	$2,999 DM5,207 £1,840 ¥347,558
RAMIREZ, MANUEL	3	1	$4,229 DM6,243 £2,760 ¥449,607	$4,229 DM6,243 £2,760 ¥449,607	$4,229 DM6,243 £2,760 ¥449,607
RAUCHE, MICHAEL	1	0			
REGAL CO.	1	1	$259 DM461 £158 ¥35,946	$259 DM461 £158 ¥35,946	$259 DM461 £158 ¥35,946
RHOUDLOFF, H.	1	1	$1,527 DM2,539 £920 ¥177,873	$1,527 DM2,539 £920 ¥177,873	$1,527 DM2,539 £920 ¥177,873
RICKENBACKER	3	3	$150 DM269 £90 ¥1,162	$4,686 DM8,136 £2,875 ¥543,059	$1,824 DM3,171 £1,119 ¥206,025
RIDOUT, MAGGIE	1	1	$396 DM720 £242 ¥47,815	$396 DM720 £242 ¥47,815	$396 DM720 £242 ¥47,815
ROCA, ALEJANDRO & BROS.	1	0			
RODRIGUEZ (SR.), MANUEL	1	1	$2,263 DM4,112 £1,380 ¥273,226	$2,263 DM4,112 £1,380 ¥273,226	$2,263 DM4,112 £1,380 ¥273,226
ROMANILLOS, JOSE	2	1	$8,435 DM14,645 £5,175 ¥977,506	$8,435 DM14,645 £5,175 ¥977,506	$8,435 DM14,645 £5,175 ¥977,506
ROUDHLOFF, D. & A.	1	0			
ROUDHLOFF, D. & A. (attributed to)	1	1	$1,519 DM2,634 £897 ¥192,505	$1,519 DM2,634 £897 ¥192,505	$1,519 DM2,634 £897 ¥192,505
RUBIO, DAVID	1	0			

Maker	Items		Selling Prices		
	Bid	Sold	Low	High	Avg
RUBIO, JOSE	1	0			
SALOMON (attributed to)	1	0			
SCHERZER	1	0			
SCHMIDT & MAUL	1	1	$748	$748	$748
			DM1,279	DM1,279	DM1,279
			£442	£442	£442
			¥92,825	¥92,825	¥92,825
SELMER	1	1	$7,890	$7,890	$7,890
			DM11,200	DM11,200	DM11,200
			£5,062	£5,062	£5,062
			¥802,600	¥802,600	¥802,600
SELMER, HENRI	1	1	$21,252	$21,252	$21,252
			DM38,203	DM38,203	DM38,203
			£12,650	£12,650	£12,650
			¥2,457,010	¥2,457,010	¥2,457,010
SEMPLE, TREVOR	1	0			
SENSIER	2	1	$73	$73	$73
			DM103	DM103	DM103
			£46	£46	£46
			¥7,498	¥7,498	¥7,498
SILVERTONE	3	2	$104	$345	$224
			DM184	DM614	DM399
			£63	£210	£137
			¥14,378	¥47,927	¥31,153
SIMPLICIO, FRANCISCO	2	2	$4,639	$5,163	$4,901
			DM6,941	DM7,189	DM7,065
			£2,760	£3,220	£2,990
			¥436,465	¥517,445	¥476,955
SIMPLICIO, FRANCISCO & MIGUEL	2	1	$3,816	$3,816	$3,816
			DM5,406	DM5,406	DM5,406
			£2,415	£2,415	£2,415
			¥390,491	¥390,491	¥390,491
SMALLMAN, GREG	1	0			
STAUFFER (attributed to)	1	0			
STAUFFER, ANTON	1	0			
STAUFFER, JOHANN GEORG	2	1	$1,456	$1,456	$1,456
			DM2,082	DM2,082	DM2,082
			£920	£920	£920
			¥146,267	¥146,267	¥146,267
STROMBERG, CHARLES AND ELMER	1	1	$10,350	$10,350	$10,350
			DM17,709	DM17,709	DM17,709
			£6,122	£6,122	£6,122
			¥1,285,263	¥1,285,263	¥1,285,263
STROMBERG, ELMER	1	1	$18,400	$18,400	$18,400
			DM31,096	DM31,096	DM31,096
			£11,040	£11,040	£11,040
			¥2,244,800	¥2,244,800	¥2,244,800
TAYMAR	2	1	$200	$200	$200
			DM283	DM283	DM283
			£127	£127	£127
			¥20,620	¥20,620	¥20,620
THIBOUVILLE-LAMY, J.	1	1	$562	$562	$562
			DM976	DM976	DM976
			£345	£345	£345
			¥65,167	¥65,167	¥65,167

Maker	Items Bid	Sold	Selling Prices Low	High	Avg
THOMSON	1	1	$934	$934	$934
			DM1,629	DM1,629	DM1,629
			£575	£575	£575
			¥113,189	¥113,189	¥113,189
VEGA COMPANY	3	3	$345	$2,990	$1,275
			DM583	DM5,053	DM2,154
			£207	£1,794	£765
			¥42,090	¥364,780	¥155,499
VELASQUEZ, JOSE LUIS	1	1	$115	$115	$115
			DM205	DM205	DM205
			£70	£70	£70
			¥15,976	¥15,976	¥15,976
VENTAPANE, PASQUALE	1	0			
VILLA, LUIGI	1	0			
VINACCIA, GAETANO	1	0			
VINACCIA, GENNARO & ACHILLE	2	1	$1,416	$1,416	$1,416
			DM2,629	DM2,629	DM2,629
			£859	£859	£859
			¥147,576	¥147,576	¥147,576
VOX	1	1	$562	$562	$562
			DM976	DM976	DM976
			£345	£345	£345
			¥65,167	¥65,167	¥65,167
WASHBURN	1	0			
WOODFIELD, PHILIP	1	0			
YAMAHA	1	1	$811	$811	$811
			DM1,459	DM1,459	DM1,459
			£483	£483	£483
			¥93,813	¥93,813	¥93,813
ZEMAITIS, A.G. (TONY)	1	0			

GUITAR-HARP

Maker	Bid	Sold	Low	High	Avg
LEVIEN, MORDAUNT	1	1	$485	$485	$485
			DM726	DM726	DM726
			£287	£287	£287
			¥53,967	¥53,967	¥53,967

GUITAR-LUTE

Maker	Bid	Sold	Low	High	Avg
HAUSER, HERMANN	1	1	$1,093	$1,093	$1,093
			DM1,846	DM1,846	DM1,846
			£656	£656	£656
			¥133,285	¥133,285	¥133,285

GUITARRA

Maker	Bid	Sold	Low	High	Avg
ANDRADE, JOAO MIGUEL	1	1	$182	$182	$182
			DM337	DM337	DM337
			£109	£109	£109
			¥24,322	¥24,322	¥24,322

HARP

Maker	Bid	Sold	Low	High	Avg
BANKS, BENJAMIN	1	1	$1,431	$1,431	$1,431
			DM2,379	DM2,379	DM2,379
			£862	£862	£862
			¥166,659	¥166,659	¥166,659

Maker	Items		Selling Prices		
	Bid	Sold	Low	High	Avg
BLAZDELL, A.	1	1	$2,142	$2,142	$2,142
			DM4,069	DM4,069	DM4,069
			£1,323	£1,323	£1,323
			¥225,103	¥225,103	¥225,103
DELVEAU	1	1	$3,864	$3,864	$3,864
			DM6,440	DM6,440	DM6,440
			£2,300	£2,300	£2,300
			¥461,817	¥461,817	¥461,817
ERARD	1	1	$4,499	$4,499	$4,499
			DM7,976	DM7,976	DM7,976
			£2,760	£2,760	£2,760
			¥531,935	¥531,935	¥531,935
ERARD, J.	1	1	$1,076	$1,076	$1,076
			DM1,668	DM1,668	DM1,668
			£644	£644	£644
			¥122,560	¥122,560	¥122,560
ERARD, SEBASTIAN	18	18	$1,738	$8,570	$3,989
			DM2,466	DM16,277	DM6,486
			£1,093	£5,290	£2,465
			¥161,308	¥900,411	¥440,705
ERARD, SEBASTIAN & PIERRE	10	10	$1,728	$12,751	$5,436
			DM2,829	DM21,252	DM9,248
			£1,035	£7,590	£3,283
			¥171,044	¥1,523,996	¥650,863
ERARD & CIE.	2	1	$4,200	$4,200	$4,200
			DM6,983	DM6,983	DM6,983
			£2,530	£2,530	£2,530
			¥489,150	¥489,150	¥489,150
ERAT, I. & I.	2	1	$3,003	$3,003	$3,003
			DM5,354	DM5,354	DM5,354
			£1,840	£1,840	£1,840
			¥393,079	¥393,079	¥393,079
ERAT, J.	2	1	$1,969	$1,969	$1,969
			DM3,443	DM3,443	DM3,443
			£1,208	£1,208	£1,208
			¥232,600	¥232,600	¥232,600
GROSJEAN, SCHWIESO & CO.	1	1	$2,012	$2,012	$2,012
			DM2,856	DM2,856	DM2,856
			£1,265	£1,265	£1,265
			¥186,777	¥186,777	¥186,777
HOLDERNESSE, CHARLES	2	2	$1,336	$6,217	$3,777
			DM2,222	DM9,313	DM5,767
			£805	£3,680	£2,243
			¥155,639	¥691,987	¥423,813
LIGHT, EDWARD	3	2	$661	$1,013	$837
			DM1,015	DM1,807	DM1,411
			£437	£621	£529
			¥70,455	¥132,664	¥101,560
MOFFAT, J.W.	1	0			
MORLEY, JOHN	2	0			
MUIR CO.	1	0			
MUIR WOOD & CO.	1	1	$2,820	$2,820	$2,820
			DM4,658	DM4,658	DM4,658
			£1,725	£1,725	£1,725
			¥349,190	¥349,190	¥349,190

Maker	Items		Selling Prices		
	Bid	Sold	Low	High	Avg

NADERMANN, HENRY	1	1	$9,603 DM16,043 £5,750 ¥1,167,193	$9,603 DM16,043 £5,750 ¥1,167,193	$9,603 DM16,043 £5,750 ¥1,167,193
NADERMAN FAMILY (MEMBER OF)	1	0			
PLEYEL, WOLFE, LYON & CO.	1	1	$3,271 DM4,634 £2,070 ¥334,707	$3,271 DM4,634 £2,070 ¥334,707	$3,271 DM4,634 £2,070 ¥334,707
RENAULT & CHATELAIN	1	1	$5,036 DM7,045 £3,150 ¥425,921	$5,036 DM7,045 £3,150 ¥425,921	$5,036 DM7,045 £3,150 ¥425,921
SCHWIESO, J.	2	2	$1,427 DM2,025 £897 ¥132,442	$3,018 DM4,342 £1,955 ¥306,427	$2,222 DM3,184 £1,426 ¥219,434
SEROUET, E.	1	1	$1,032 DM1,841 £633 ¥135,121	$1,032 DM1,841 £633 ¥135,121	$1,032 DM1,841 £633 ¥135,121
STUMPFF, J.A.	1	1	$2,129 DM3,994 £1,323 ¥255,930	$2,129 DM3,994 £1,323 ¥255,930	$2,129 DM3,994 £1,323 ¥255,930
STUMPFF, J.C.	1	0			
VENTURA, A.B. (attributed to)	1	1	$2,291 DM3,809 £1,380 ¥266,809	$2,291 DM3,809 £1,380 ¥266,809	$2,291 DM3,809 £1,380 ¥266,809

HARP-LUTE

BARRY	2	1	$654 DM1,214 £397 ¥68,158	$654 DM1,214 £397 ¥68,158	$654 DM1,214 £397 ¥68,158
CLEMENTI & CO.	1	0			
LIGHT, EDWARD	1	1	$840 DM1,397 £506 ¥97,830	$840 DM1,397 £506 ¥97,830	$840 DM1,397 £506 ¥97,830

HARPSICHORD

BACKERS, AMERICUS	2	1	$67,565 DM120,474 £41,400 ¥8,844,282	$67,565 DM120,474 £41,400 ¥8,844,282	$67,565 DM120,474 £41,400 ¥8,844,282
BRITSEN, JORIS	1	0			
DOWD, WILLIAM	1	1	$18,400 DM32,550 £11,110 ¥2,390,160	$18,400 DM32,550 £11,110 ¥2,390,160	$18,400 DM32,550 £11,110 ¥2,390,160
FRY, E.V.	1	1	$3,672 DM5,495 £2,185 ¥409,644	$3,672 DM5,495 £2,185 ¥409,644	$3,672 DM5,495 £2,185 ¥409,644

Maker	Items Bid	Sold	Selling Prices Low	High	Avg
HERZ, ERIC	1	1	$2,300	$2,300	$2,300
			DM3,517	DM3,517	DM3,517
			£1,513	£1,513	£1,513
			¥242,420	¥242,420	¥242,420
KIRCKMAN, JACOB & ABRAHAM	1	1	$173,512	$173,512	$173,512
			DM259,903	DM259,903	DM259,903
			£102,700	£102,700	£102,700
			¥19,311,708	¥19,311,708	¥19,311,708
PLEYEL	1	1	$5,345	$5,345	$5,345
			DM8,887	DM8,887	DM8,887
			£3,220	£3,220	£3,220
			¥622,555	¥622,555	¥622,555
RUCKERS, ANDREAS	1	1	$141,410	$141,410	$141,410
			DM200,346	DM200,346	DM200,346
			£89,500	£89,500	£89,500
			¥14,471,613	¥14,471,613	¥14,471,613
SHUDI, BURKAT & JOHN BROADWOOD	2	2	$104,746	$200,879	$152,813
			DM174,156	DM373,002	DM273,579
			£63,100	£121,900	£92,500
			¥12,199,754	¥20,941,201	¥16,570,478

HELICON

Maker	Items Bid	Sold	Selling Prices Low	High	Avg
DE CART FRERES, FERDINAND & LOUIS	3	2	$392	$523	$458
			DM728	DM971	DM850
			£238	£317	£278
			¥40,895	¥54,526	¥47,710

HORN

Maker	Items Bid	Sold	Selling Prices Low	High	Avg
BESSON	3	2	$97	$114	$106
			DM149	DM176	DM162
			£63	£75	£69
			¥10,559	¥12,479	¥11,519
BLIGHT, J.	1	0			
BOOSEY & CO.	1	1	$156	$156	$156
			DM255	DM255	DM255
			£92	£92	£92
			¥18,407	¥18,407	¥18,407
BOOSEY & HAWKES	2	2	$211	$457	$334
			DM324	DM702	DM513
			£138	£299	£219
			¥23,037	¥49,914	¥36,476
CERVENY & SOHNE, V.F.	1	1	$764	$764	$764
			DM1,270	DM1,270	DM1,270
			£460	£460	£460
			¥88,936	¥88,936	¥88,936
GROSS & BRAMBACH	1	1	$1,813	$1,813	$1,813
			DM3,014	DM3,014	DM3,014
			£1,092	£1,092	£1,092
			¥211,127	¥211,127	¥211,127
KNOPF	1	1	$324	$324	$324
			DM495	DM495	DM495
			£3207	£3207	£3207
			¥836,132	¥836,132	¥836,132
KOHLERT'S SOHNE, V.	1	1	$458	$458	$458
			DM762	DM762	DM762
			£3276	£3276	£3276
			¥853,362	¥853,362	¥853,362

NICOLA GAGLIANO
Fine and Handsome Italian Violin:
Naples, 1731
Phillips, November 15, 1999, Lot 132

JOSEPH ROCCA
Good Italian Violin: Turin, 1843
Phillips, November 15, 1999, Lot 127

ANTONIO & GIROLAMO AMATI
Very Fine Italian Violin
Christie's, March 17, 1999, Lot 154

NICOLO AMATI
Violin: Cremona, c. 1640
Sotheby's, March 16, 1999, Lot 94

DOMENICO MONTAGNANA
Double Bass: Venice, c. 1747
Sotheby's, March 16, 1999, Lot 83

JEAN BAPTISTE VUILLAUME
French Violin: Paris, c. 1850
Skinner, May 9, 1999, Lot 48

M. & W. STODART
Grand Pianoforte: London, c. 1800
Sotheby's, October 27, 1999, Lot 65

Maker	Items Bid	Sold	Selling Prices Low	High	Avg
KRETZSCHMANN, CHARLES	1	0			
LAPINI	1	1	$403 DM680 £3242 ¥853,561	$403 DM680 £3242 ¥853,561	$403 DM680 £3242 ¥853,561
MILLEREAU	1	1	$413 DM767 £3251 ¥843,068	$413 DM767 £3251 ¥843,068	$413 DM767 £3251 ¥843,068
MULLER, C.A.	1	1	$535 DM889 £3322 ¥862,255	$535 DM889 £3322 ¥862,255	$535 DM889 £3322 ¥862,255
PERCIVAL, THOMAS	1	1	$436 DM809 £3265 ¥845,438	$436 DM809 £3265 ¥845,438	$436 DM809 £3265 ¥845,438
PERINET, FRANCOIS	1	1	$1,189 DM1,711 £771 ¥120,768	$1,189 DM1,711 £771 ¥120,768	$1,189 DM1,711 £771 ¥120,768
POTTER, HENRY	3	0			
SCHOPPER, ROBERT	2	0			
WEBER, CARL AUGUST	1	1	$1,049 DM1,744 £632 ¥122,191	$1,049 DM1,744 £632 ¥122,191	$1,049 DM1,744 £632 ¥122,191
ZEDLITZ, EDUARD	1	1	$764 DM1,270 £460 ¥88,936	$764 DM1,270 £460 ¥88,936	$764 DM1,270 £460 ¥88,936

HURDY-GURDY

Maker	Bid	Sold	Low	High	Avg
COLSON, NICOLAS	1	1	$1,413 DM2,088 £920 ¥150,635	$1,413 DM2,088 £920 ¥150,635	$1,413 DM2,088 £920 ¥150,635
MASSETY	1	1	$4,543 DM6,436 £2,875 ¥464,870	$4,543 DM6,436 £2,875 ¥464,870	$4,543 DM6,436 £2,875 ¥464,870
PAJEOT (FILS)	1	1	$1,635 DM2,317 £1,035 ¥167,353	$1,635 DM2,317 £1,035 ¥167,353	$1,635 DM2,317 £1,035 ¥167,353

KIT

Maker	Bid	Sold	Low	High	Avg
PERRY	1	1	$2,332 DM4,043 £1,380 ¥291,180	$2,332 DM4,043 £1,380 ¥291,180	$2,332 DM4,043 £1,380 ¥291,180
PERRY, THOMAS	1	0			

LUTE

Maker	Bid	Sold	Low	High	Avg
BARRY	1	0			

Maker	Items Bid	Sold	Selling Prices Low	High	Avg
CHALLEN, CHRISTOPHER	1	1	$3,036 DM5,391 £1,840 ¥421,158	$3,036 DM5,391 £1,840 ¥421,158	$3,036 DM5,391 £1,840 ¥421,158
DOLMETSCH, ARNOLD	3	1	$1,267 DM1,335 £782 ¥96,808	$1,267 DM1,335 £782 ¥96,808	$1,267 DM1,335 £782 ¥96,808
GOFF, THOMAS	1	1	$1,457 DM2,183 £863 ¥162,185	$1,457 DM2,183 £863 ¥162,185	$1,457 DM2,183 £863 ¥162,185
GOLD, PERL	1	1	$566 DM976 £345 ¥64,570	$566 DM976 £345 ¥64,570	$566 DM976 £345 ¥64,570
GORRETT, JOHN	1	1	$526 DM891 £322 ¥61,018	$526 DM891 £322 ¥61,018	$526 DM891 £322 ¥61,018
GUGGENBERGER, ANTON	1	0			
HARWOOD, IAN	2	1	$660 DM1,139 £403 ¥75,332	$660 DM1,139 £403 ¥75,332	$660 DM1,139 £403 ¥75,332
HARWOOD, JOHN	2	1	$186 DM196 £115 ¥14,236	$186 DM196 £115 ¥14,236	$186 DM196 £115 ¥14,236
HAUSER, HERMANN	1	0			
HOLMES, HENRY H.	3	2	$264 DM480 £161 ¥31,876	$348 DM607 £207 ¥44,373	$306 DM543 £184 ¥38,124
JAKOB, RICHARD	1	0			
JORDAN, HANS	1	0			
KAROUBI, J.	1	0			
SPRIGGS, G.W.	1	1	$528 DM911 £322 ¥60,266	$528 DM911 £322 ¥60,266	$528 DM911 £322 ¥60,266
TIEFFENBRUCKER, WENDELIN ("VENERE")	1	0			
WHITEMAN, DAVID	1	1	$540 DM825 £345 ¥60,220	$540 DM825 £345 ¥60,220	$540 DM825 £345 ¥60,220

MANDO-CELLO

Maker	Bid	Sold	Low	High	Avg
GIBSON CO.	2	1	$1,380 DM2,361 £816 ¥171,368	$1,380 DM2,361 £816 ¥171,368	$1,380 DM2,361 £816 ¥171,368

Maker	Items Bid	Sold	Selling Prices Low	High	Avg
MANDOLA					
GARGANO, FRANCESCO	1	1	$368 DM552 £218 ¥40,993	$368 DM552 £218 ¥40,993	$368 DM552 £218 ¥40,993
MANDOLIN					
ABBOTT	1	1	$171 DM261 £109 ¥19,070	$171 DM261 £109 ¥19,070	$171 DM261 £109 ¥19,070
BOHMANN, JOSEPH	2	1	$115 DM205 £70 ¥15,976	$115 DM205 £70 ¥15,976	$115 DM205 £70 ¥15,976
CALACE, GIUSEPPE	2	2	$4,857 DM7,276 £2,875 ¥540,615	$14,092 DM20,774 £9,200 ¥1,503,004	$9,474 DM14,025 £6,038 ¥1,021,810
CALACE, NICOLA & RAFFAELLE	1	1	$2,363 DM3,337 £1,495 ¥210,850	$2,363 DM3,337 £1,495 ¥210,850	$2,363 DM3,337 £1,495 ¥210,850
CALACE, RAFFAELE	2	2	$1,534 DM2,841 £920 ¥204,820	$2,615 DM4,856 £1,587 ¥272,631	$2,074 DM3,849 £1,254 ¥238,725
CALACE & FIGLIO, RAFFAEL	2	2	$2,628 DM4,685 £1,610 ¥343,944	$3,378 DM6,024 £2,070 ¥442,214	$3,003 DM5,354 £1,840 ¥393,079
CAPONETTO, LUIGI	2	1	$168 DM177 £104 ¥12,813	$168 DM177 £104 ¥12,813	$168 DM177 £104 ¥12,813
CAPPIELLO, V. & G.	3	1	$113 DM201 £69 ¥14,740	$113 DM201 £69 ¥14,740	$113 DM201 £69 ¥14,740
CASELLA, M.	1	1	$782 DM1,202 £518 ¥83,434	$782 DM1,202 £518 ¥83,434	$782 DM1,202 £518 ¥83,434
CECCHERINI, UMBERTO	3	3	$154 DM254 £92 ¥17,968	$482 DM863 £288 ¥55,919	$308 DM519 £188 ¥35,333
CIANI, RAPHAEL	1	1	$363 DM686 £225 ¥38,448	$363 DM686 £225 ¥38,448	$363 DM686 £225 ¥38,448
DALLAS, J.E.	1	1	$230 DM338 £150 ¥24,392	$230 DM338 £150 ¥24,392	$230 DM338 £150 ¥24,392

Maker	Items		Selling Prices		
	Bid	Sold	Low	High	Avg
DEL PERUGIA, FERNANDO	2	2	$452	$1,212	$832
			DM801	DM1,955	DM1,378
			£278	£704	£491
			¥55,148	¥142,715	¥98,932
DE MEGLIO, GIOVANNI	6	6	$149	$657	$335
			DM157	DM1,171	DM541
			£92	£403	£207
			¥11,389	¥85,986	¥39,152
DE MEGLIO, VINCENZO	1	1	$343	$343	$343
			DM485	DM485	DM485
			£219	£219	£219
			¥29,297	¥29,297	¥29,297
DE MEGLIO & FIGLIO	4	4	$230	$710	$425
			DM426	DM1,015	DM640
			£138	£449	£267
			¥30,723	¥71,305	¥45,508
DOBRO	2	2	$287	$985	$636
			DM405	DM1,391	DM898
			£180	£618	£399
			¥25,444	¥87,359	¥56,401
EMBERGHER, LUIGI	2	2	$7,846	$8,018	$7,932
			DM13,331	DM14,568	DM13,949
			£4,761	£4,830	£4,796
			¥817,892	¥933,832	¥875,862
ESSEX, CLIFFORD	2	2	$241	$597	$419
			DM406	DM1,044	DM725
			£150	£368	£259
			¥29,581	¥72,110	¥50,845
FABRICATORE, GIOVANNI	1	1	$1,455	$1,455	$1,455
			DM2,677	DM2,677	DM2,677
			£905	£905	£905
			¥171,588	¥171,588	¥171,588
FANGA, LUIGI	1	0			
FERRARI & CO.	4	3	$321	$433	$368
			DM476	DM809	DM626
			£207	£273	£233
			¥34,730	¥51,197	¥43,054
GAROZZO, C.	1	1	$1,217	$1,217	$1,217
			DM1,870	DM1,870	DM1,870
			£805	£805	£805
			¥129,786	¥129,786	¥129,786
GIBSON CO.	27	24	$345	$3,335	$1,092
			DM590	DM5,636	DM1,788
			£204	£2,001	£672
			¥42,842	¥406,870	¥123,473
GRIMALDI, EMILIO	1	1	$4,504	$4,504	$4,504
			DM8,032	DM8,032	DM8,032
			£2,760	£2,760	£2,760
			¥589,619	¥589,619	¥589,619
HOWE, ELIAS	1	1	$518	$518	$518
			DM875	DM875	DM875
			£311	£311	£311
			¥63,135	¥63,135	¥63,135
IBANEZ	1	1	$707	$707	$707
			DM1,044	DM1,044	DM1,044
			£460	£460	£460
			¥75,337	¥75,337	¥75,337

Maker	Items Bid	Sold	Selling Prices Low	High	Avg
KAY	1	1	$92	$92	$92
			DM164	DM164	DM164
			£56	£56	£56
			¥12,781	¥12,781	¥12,781
LYON & HEALY	1	1	$150	$150	$150
			DM266	DM266	DM266
			£91	£91	£91
			¥20,769	¥20,769	¥20,769
MAGLIONI, GENNARO	1	1	$169	$169	$169
			DM286	DM286	DM286
			£104	£104	£104
			¥19,613	¥19,613	¥19,613
MANFREDI, GIUSEPPE	2	1	$2,137	$2,137	$2,137
			DM3,201	DM3,201	DM3,201
			£1,265	£1,265	£1,265
			¥237,871	¥237,871	¥237,871
MARTELLO, CARLOS	2	1	$400	$400	$400
			DM614	DM614	DM614
			£265	£265	£265
			¥42,644	¥42,644	¥42,644
MARTIN & CO., C.F.	2	2	$288	$403	$345
			DM486	DM689	DM586
			£173	£238	£206
			¥35,075	¥49,982	¥42,382
MEGLIO & FIGLIO	1	1	$445	$445	$445
			DM750	DM750	DM750
			£276	£276	£276
			¥54,610	¥54,610	¥54,610
MOLINARI, GIUSEPPE	1	1	$5,255	$5,255	$5,255
			DM9,370	DM9,370	DM9,370
			£3,220	£3,220	£3,220
			¥687,889	¥687,889	¥687,889
MONZINO, ANTONIO	1	1	$1,164	$1,164	$1,164
			DM2,075	DM2,075	DM2,075
			£713	£713	£713
			¥152,318	¥152,318	¥152,318
NAPOLI, DOMENICO BANONI	1	1	$891	$891	$891
			DM1,322	DM1,322	DM1,322
			£575	£575	£575
			¥96,474	¥96,474	¥96,474
PECORARO, P.	1	1	$675	$675	$675
			DM1,201	DM1,201	DM1,201
			£414	£414	£414
			¥90,637	¥90,637	¥90,637
PERRETTI, FRANCESCO & SON	3	2	$243	$371	$307
			DM374	DM625	DM499
			£161	£230	£196
			¥25,957	¥45,509	¥35,733
PRESBLER, GIUSEPPE	1	0			
PUGLISI, GIUSEPPE	3	2	$288	$2,440	$1,364
			DM433	DM4,350	DM2,392
			£175	£1,495	£835
			¥32,137	¥319,377	¥175,757
ROCCA, ENRICO	1	0			

| Maker | Items | | Selling Prices | | |
	Bid	Sold	Low	High	Avg
ROMANILLOS, JOSE	2	1	$1,079	$1,079	$1,079
			DM1,510	DM1,510	DM1,510
			£675	£675	£675
			¥91,269	¥91,269	¥91,269
SALVINO & CO., A.	1	1	$618	$618	$618
			DM1,111	DM1,111	DM1,111
			£368	£368	£368
			¥71,477	¥71,477	¥71,477
SILVESTRI, CARMINE	1	1	$1,028	$1,028	$1,028
			DM1,953	DM1,953	DM1,953
			£635	£635	£635
			¥108,049	¥108,049	¥108,049
STEWART, S.S.	1	1	$431	$431	$431
			DM729	DM729	DM729
			£259	£259	£259
			¥52,613	¥52,613	¥52,613
TONELLI, PIETRO	1	1	$231	$231	$231
			DM414	DM414	DM414
			£138	£138	£138
			¥26,841	¥26,841	¥26,841
VARANO, MICHELE	2	1	$446	$446	$446
			DM661	DM661	DM661
			£288	£288	£288
			¥48,237	¥48,237	¥48,237
VATIANI, PAOLO	1	1	$74	$74	$74
			DM125	DM125	DM125
			£46	£46	£46
			¥9,102	¥9,102	¥9,102
VEGA COMPANY	2	1	$518	$518	$518
			DM748	DM748	DM748
			£338	£338	£338
			¥52,397	¥52,397	¥52,397
VINACCIA, ANTONIO	2	2	$2,864	$9,927	$6,395
			DM4,761	DM16,505	DM10,633
			£1,725	£5,980	£3,853
			¥333,512	¥1,156,173	¥744,842
VINACCIA, GENNARO	1	0			
VINACCIA, GENNARO & ACHILLE	1	1	$3,997	$3,997	$3,997
			DM5,663	DM5,663	DM5,663
			£2,530	£2,530	£2,530
			¥409,086	¥409,086	¥409,086
VINACCIA, GIOVANNI	2	2	$2,724	$9,153	$5,939
			DM3,859	DM16,996	DM10,428
			£1,725	£5,555	£3,640
			¥281,175	¥954,208	¥617,691
VINACCIA, GIUSEPPE	2	2	$789	$1,482	$1,136
			DM1,337	DM2,752	DM2,044
			£483	£899	£691
			¥91,527	¥154,491	¥123,009
VINACCIA BROS.	2	2	$4,721	$6,537	$5,629
			DM6,689	DM9,262	DM7,975
			£2,990	£4,140	£3,565
			¥487,370	¥674,820	¥581,095
WASHBURN	3	3	$132	$316	$199
			DM250	DM563	DM360
			£82	£193	£122
			¥13,992	¥43,933	¥26,231

Maker	Items		Selling Prices		
	Bid	Sold	Low	High	Avg

MANDOLIN-LYRE

Maker	Bid	Sold	Low	High	Avg
CALACE, RAFFAELE	1	1	$463 DM875 £287 ¥49,033	$463 DM875 £287 ¥49,033	$463 DM875 £287 ¥49,033
CALACE FRATELLI	1	1	$1,035 DM1,749 £621 ¥126,270	$1,035 DM1,749 £621 ¥126,270	$1,035 DM1,749 £621 ¥126,270

MANDOLINO

Maker	Bid	Sold	Low	High	Avg
FONTANELLI, GIOVANNI GIUSEPPE	1	1	$2,496 DM4,025 £1,449 ¥293,825	$2,496 DM4,025 £1,449 ¥293,825	$2,496 DM4,025 £1,449 ¥293,825
NONEMACHER, CRISTIANO	1	1	$6,872 DM11,426 £4,140 ¥800,428	$6,872 DM11,426 £4,140 ¥800,428	$6,872 DM11,426 £4,140 ¥800,428

MARTINSHORN

Maker	Bid	Sold	Low	High	Avg
MARTIN, MAX BERNHARDT	1	0			

MELLOPHONE

Maker	Bid	Sold	Low	High	Avg
HOLTON & CO.	1	0			
PEPPER	1	0			
PEPPER, J.W.	1	0			
YORK	1	0			

MUSETTE

Maker	Bid	Sold	Low	High	Avg
MARTIN BROS.	1	1	$436 DM809 £265 ¥45,438	$436 DM809 £265 ¥45,438	$436 DM809 £265 ¥45,438

NORMAPHON

Maker	Bid	Sold	Low	High	Avg
WUNDERLICH	1	1	$5,463 DM9,232 £3,278 ¥726,895	$5,463 DM9,232 £3,278 ¥726,895	$5,463 DM9,232 £3,278 ¥726,895

OBOE

Maker	Bid	Sold	Low	High	Avg
ADLER, FREDERIC GUILLAUME	2	0			
ALBERT, J.	1	1	$97 DM143 £63 ¥10,320	$97 DM143 £63 ¥10,320	$97 DM143 £63 ¥10,320
ALBERT, JACQUES	1	1	$327 DM463 £207 ¥33,471	$327 DM463 £207 ¥33,471	$327 DM463 £207 ¥33,471
ANCIUTI, JOHANNES MARIA	1	0			

Maker	Items		Selling Prices		
	Bid	*Sold*	*Low*	*High*	*Avg*
ASTOR & CO., GEORGE	3	2	$407	$3,436	$1,922
			DM610	DM5,713	DM3,162
			£241	£2,070	£1,156
			¥45,318	¥400,214	¥222,766
BAHRMAN	1	1	$2,362	$2,362	$2,362
			DM3,347	DM3,347	DM3,347
			£1,495	£1,495	£1,495
			¥241,733	¥241,733	¥241,733
BAUER, JEAN	1	0			
BAUR, JAKOB	1	1	$2,907	$2,907	$2,907
			DM4,119	DM4,119	DM4,119
			£1,840	£1,840	£1,840
			¥297,517	¥297,517	¥297,517
BOOSEY & HAWKES	5	3	$317	$422	$358
			DM486	DM648	DM549
			£207	£276	£234
			¥34,556	¥46,075	¥39,035
BUFFET	2	2	$242	$2,628	$1,435
			DM255	DM4,685	DM2,470
			£150	£1,610	£880
			¥18,507	¥343,944	¥181,226
BUFFET CRAMPON & CO.	1	1	$490	$490	$490
			DM846	DM846	DM846
			£299	£299	£299
			¥55,961	¥55,961	¥55,961
BUISSON, F.	3	1	$334	$334	$334
			DM562	DM562	DM562
			£207	£207	£207
			¥40,958	¥40,958	¥40,958
BUTHOD & THIBOUVILLE	1	1	$943	$943	$943
			DM1,714	DM1,714	DM1,714
			£575	£575	£575
			¥113,844	¥113,844	¥113,844
CAHUSAC, THOMAS (SR.)	1	1	$3,634	$3,634	$3,634
			DM5,149	DM5,149	DM5,149
			£2,300	£2,300	£2,300
			¥371,896	¥371,896	¥371,896
COLLIER, THOMAS	1	0			
CRONE, JOHANN AUGUST	1	1	$1,999	$1,999	$1,999
			DM2,832	DM2,832	DM2,832
			£1,265	£1,265	£1,265
			¥204,543	¥204,543	¥204,543
DELUSSE, CHRISTOPHER	2	2	$3,754	$9,759	$6,756
			DM6,693	DM17,402	DM12,047
			£2,300	£5,980	£4,140
			¥491,349	¥1,277,507	¥884,428
ENGELHARD, JOHANN FRIEDRICH	1	0			
GEDNEY, CALEB	1	1	$3,529	$3,529	$3,529
			DM5,422	DM5,422	DM5,422
			£2,300	£2,300	£2,300
			¥386,375	¥386,375	¥386,375
GOLDE, CARL	2	1	$6,606	$6,606	$6,606
			DM9,895	DM9,895	DM9,895
			£3,910	£3,910	£3,910
			¥735,236	¥735,236	¥735,236

| Maker | Items | | Selling Prices | | |
---	Bid	Sold	Low	High	Avg
GRENSER, CARL AUGUSTIN (I)	2	2	$5,088	$18,768	$11,928
			DM7,208	DM33,465	DM20,336
			£3,220	£11,500	£7,360
			¥520,655	¥2,456,745	¥1,488,700
GRUNDMANN & FLOT	1	1	$826	$826	$826
			DM1,472	DM1,472	DM1,472
			£506	£506	£506
			¥108,097	¥108,097	¥108,097
GUERINI	1	0			
GULIELMINETTI	1	1	$2,137	$2,137	$2,137
			DM3,201	DM3,201	DM3,201
			£1,265	£1,265	£1,265
			¥237,871	¥237,871	¥237,871
HAWKES & CO.	1	1	$93	$93	$93
			DM156	DM156	DM156
			£58	£58	£58
			¥11,377	¥11,377	¥11,377
HAWKES & SON	2	1	$132	$132	$132
			DM203	DM203	DM203
			£86	£86	£86
			¥14,398	¥14,398	¥14,398
HECKEL	1	1	$827	$827	$827
			DM1,400	DM1,400	DM1,400
			£506	£506	£506
			¥95,885	¥95,885	¥95,885
HOE, JOHANN WOLFGANG	1	1	$10,686	$10,686	$10,686
			DM16,007	DM16,007	DM16,007
			£6,325	£6,325	£6,325
			¥1,189,353	¥1,189,353	¥1,189,353
HORAK & SOHN, W.	1	1	$1,909	$1,909	$1,909
			DM3,174	DM3,174	DM3,174
			£1,150	£1,150	£1,150
			¥222,341	¥222,341	¥222,341
HOWARTH	1	1	$535	$535	$535
			DM816	DM816	DM816
			£345	£345	£345
			¥59,375	¥59,375	¥59,375
HOWARTH & CO.	1	1	$336	$336	$336
			DM587	DM587	DM587
			£207	£207	£207
			¥40,562	¥40,562	¥40,562
HULLER, G.H.	1	1	$382	$382	$382
			DM635	DM635	DM635
			£230	£230	£230
			¥44,468	¥44,468	¥44,468
KATTOFEN, AMMON	1	1	$382	$382	$382
			DM635	DM635	DM635
			£230	£230	£230
			¥44,468	¥44,468	¥44,468
KOHLERT & SONS	1	1	$150	$150	$150
			DM267	DM267	DM267
			£92	£92	£92
			¥20,142	¥20,142	¥20,142
KRUSPE, FRIEDRICH WILHELM	1	1	$2,137	$2,137	$2,137
			DM3,201	DM3,201	DM3,201
			£1,265	£1,265	£1,265
			¥237,871	¥237,871	¥237,871

Maker	Items		Selling Prices		
	Bid	Sold	Low	High	Avg
LAFLEUR, J.R. & SON	1	1	$150	$150	$150
			DM267	DM267	DM267
			£92	£92	£92
			¥20,142	¥20,142	¥20,142
LOREE, F.	6	4	$818	$1,548	$1,261
			DM1,170	DM2,376	DM1,830
			£517	£1,012	£791
			¥82,196	¥168,940	¥130,941
LOREE, FRANCOIS	2	0			
LOUIS	4	2	$469	$719	$594
			DM663	DM1,006	DM835
			£299	£450	£375
			¥40,090	¥60,846	¥50,468
LUDWIG, FRANZ	2	2	$3,436	$4,582	$4,009
			DM5,713	DM7,618	DM6,665
			£2,070	£2,760	£2,415
			¥400,214	¥533,618	¥466,916
LUDWIG & MARTINKA	2	2	$1,456	$4,963	$3,210
			DM2,181	DM8,252	DM5,217
			£862	£2,990	£1,926
			¥162,090	¥578,087	¥370,089
METZLER & CO.	1	1	$363	$363	$363
			DM515	DM515	DM515
			£230	£230	£230
			¥37,190	¥37,190	¥37,190
MILHOUSE, RICHARD	1	1	$3,627	$3,627	$3,627
			DM6,031	DM6,031	DM6,031
			£2,185	£2,185	£2,185
			¥422,448	¥422,448	¥422,448
MILHOUSE, WILLIAM	3	3	$909	$3,705	$2,446
			DM1,287	DM6,879	DM4,006
			£575	£2,248	£1,516
			¥92,974	¥386,227	¥240,830
MOENNIG, OTTO	1	0			
MOLLENHAUER, CONRAD	1	0			
MONNIG, OTTO	2	2	$764	$802	$783
			DM1,270	DM1,333	DM1,301
			£460	£483	£472
			¥88,936	¥93,383	¥91,160
MONNIG GEBRUDER	4	1	$179	$179	$179
			DM295	DM295	DM295
			£109	£109	£109
			¥22,115	¥22,115	¥22,115
MORTON, ALFRED	1	1	$155	$155	$155
			DM231	DM231	DM231
			£92	£92	£92
			¥17,248	¥17,248	¥17,248
MORTON & SONS, A.	2	1	$180	$180	$180
			DM275	DM275	DM275
			£115	£115	£115
			¥20,073	¥20,073	¥20,073
NOBLET	1	0			
OMS	1	1	$8,160	$8,160	$8,160
			DM12,223	DM12,223	DM12,223
			£4,830	£4,830	£4,830
			¥908,233	¥908,233	¥908,233

Maker	Items		Selling Prices		
	Bid	Sold	Low	High	Avg
PANORMO, VINCENZO	1	0			
PARADIS	1	1	$86	$86	$86
			DM132	DM132	DM132
			£57	£57	£57
			¥9,091	¥9,091	¥9,091
PINDER, HEINRICH FRANZ EDUARD	1	1	$916	$916	$916
			DM1,524	DM1,524	DM1,524
			£552	£552	£552
			¥106,724	¥106,724	¥106,724
REICHENBACHER, ERNST	1	1	$1,943	$1,943	$1,943
			DM2,910	DM2,910	DM2,910
			£1,150	£1,150	£1,150
			¥216,246	¥216,246	¥216,246
REIST, H.	1	1	$4,795	$4,795	$4,795
			DM8,903	DM8,903	DM8,903
			£2,910	£2,910	£2,910
			¥499,823	¥499,823	¥499,823
RICHTERS, HENDRIK	1	1	$22,522	$22,522	$22,522
			DM40,158	DM40,158	DM40,158
			£13,800	£13,800	£13,800
			¥2,948,094	¥2,948,094	¥2,948,094
ROESSLER, HEINZ	1	1	$432	$432	$432
			DM770	DM770	DM770
			£265	£265	£265
			¥56,505	¥56,505	¥56,505
ROTTENBURGH, JOANNES HYACINTHUS (I)	1	1	$24,398	$24,398	$24,398
			DM43,505	DM43,505	DM43,505
			£14,950	£14,950	£14,950
			¥3,193,769	¥3,193,769	¥3,193,769
RUDALL, CARTE & CO.	3	2	$132	$334	$233
			DM223	DM562	DM392
			£81	£207	£144
			¥15,254	¥40,958	¥28,106
SATTLER, CARL WILHELM	1	1	$7,507	$7,507	$7,507
			DM13,386	DM13,386	DM13,386
			£4,600	£4,600	£4,600
			¥982,698	¥982,698	¥982,698
SCHLEGEL, JEREMIAS	2	1	$1,240	$1,240	$1,240
			DM2,062	DM2,062	DM2,062
			£747	£747	£747
			¥144,425	¥144,425	¥144,425
SELMER	1	1	$169	$169	$169
			DM286	DM286	DM286
			£104	£104	£104
			¥19,613	¥19,613	¥19,613
SHARPE, JOHN	2	2	$622	$1,527	$1,074
			DM931	DM2,539	DM1,735
			£368	£920	£644
			¥69,199	¥177,873	¥123,536
SIMPSON, JOHN	1	0			
STANESBY, THOMAS SR. AND JR.	1	1	$11,261	$11,261	$11,261
			DM20,079	DM20,079	DM20,079
			£6,900	£6,900	£6,900
			¥1,474,047	¥1,474,047	¥1,474,047

Maker	Items		Selling Prices		
	Bid	Sold	Low	High	Avg
STARK	1	1	$196	$196	$196
			DM319	DM319	DM319
			£115	£115	£115
			¥23,009	¥23,009	¥23,009
STEHLE	1	1	$1,049	$1,049	$1,049
			DM1,744	DM1,744	DM1,744
			£632	£632	£632
			¥122,191	¥122,191	¥122,191
THIBOUVILLE-LAMY, J.	1	1	$182	$182	$182
			DM260	DM260	DM260
			£115	£115	£115
			¥18,283	¥18,283	¥18,283
TRIEBERT	1	0			
TRIEBERT & SONS, GUILLAUME	1	1	$1,622	$1,622	$1,622
			DM2,697	DM2,697	DM2,697
			£977	£977	£977
			¥188,893	¥188,893	¥188,893
TRIEBERT & COUESNON	1	1	$1,454	$1,454	$1,454
			DM2,059	DM2,059	DM2,059
			£920	£920	£920
			¥148,758	¥148,758	¥148,758
UHLMANN, JOHANN TOBIAS	1	1	$2,291	$2,291	$2,291
			DM3,809	DM3,809	DM3,809
			£1,380	£1,380	£1,380
			¥266,809	¥266,809	¥266,809
WARD & SONS	1	1	$207	$207	$207
			DM377	DM377	DM377
			£127	£127	£127
			¥25,046	¥25,046	¥25,046
WEYGANDT, T.J.	1	1	$6,109	$6,109	$6,109
			DM10,157	DM10,157	DM10,157
			£3,680	£3,680	£3,680
			¥711,491	¥711,491	¥711,491

OBOE D'AMORE

Maker	Items		Selling Prices		
	Bid	Sold	Low	High	Avg
OBERLENDER, JOHANN WILHELM (I)	1	1	$54,484	$54,484	$54,484
			DM101,168	DM101,168	DM101,168
			£33,063	£33,063	£33,063
			¥5,679,807	¥5,679,807	¥5,679,807

OCTAVIN

Maker	Items		Selling Prices		
	Bid	Sold	Low	High	Avg
ADLER & CO., OSCAR	1	1	$1,852	$1,852	$1,852
			DM3,407	DM3,407	DM3,407
			£1,152	£1,152	£1,152
			¥218,384	¥218,384	¥218,384

OPHICLEIDE

Maker	Items		Selling Prices		
	Bid	Sold	Low	High	Avg
BONNEL	1	1	$2,064	$2,064	$2,064
			DM3,681	DM3,681	DM3,681
			£1,265	£1,265	£1,265
			¥270,242	¥270,242	¥270,242
HENRI	2	1	$1,308	$1,308	$1,308
			DM2,428	DM2,428	DM2,428
			£794	£794	£794
			¥136,315	¥136,315	¥136,315

Maker	Items		Selling Prices		
	Bid	Sold	Low	High	Avg

ORGAN

Maker	Bid	Sold	Low	High	Avg
HANCOCK, JAMES GRANGE	1	1	$16,353	$16,353	$16,353
			DM23,168	DM23,168	DM23,168
			£10,350	£10,350	£10,350
			¥1,673,533	¥1,673,533	¥1,673,533
SNETZLER, JOHN	1	1	$69,550	$69,550	$69,550
			DM129,143	DM129,143	DM129,143
			£42,205	£42,205	£42,205
			¥7,250,397	¥7,250,397	¥7,250,397
STUMPHLER, JOHANN STEPHAN					
(ascribed to)	1	0			
WILLIS, HENRY	1	0			

PHONO-FIDDLE

Maker	Bid	Sold	Low	High	Avg
EVANS & CO., GEORGE	1	1	$840	$840	$840
			DM1,397	DM1,397	DM1,397
			£506	£506	£506
			¥97,830	¥97,830	¥97,830
HOWSON, A.T.	6	5	$131	$447	$231
			DM228	DM783	DM389
			£81	£276	£143
			¥14,772	¥54,082	¥26,422
STROH, CHARLES	1	1	$687	$687	$687
			DM1,143	DM1,143	DM1,143
			£414	£414	£414
			¥80,043	¥80,043	¥80,043
STROVIOL	2	2	$180	$248	$214
			DM276	DM364	DM320
			£115	£161	£138
			¥20,070	¥26,269	¥23,169

PIANINO

Maker	Bid	Sold	Low	High	Avg
CHAPPELL	1	1	$13,600	$13,600	$13,600
			DM20,372	DM20,372	DM20,372
			£8,050	£8,050	£8,050
			¥1,513,722	¥1,513,722	¥1,513,722

PIANO

Maker	Bid	Sold	Low	High	Avg
ASTOR & HORWOOD	1	1	$909	$909	$909
			DM1,287	DM1,287	DM1,287
			£575	£575	£575
			¥92,974	¥92,974	¥92,974
BERNHARDT, P.	1	1	$6,756	$6,756	$6,756
			DM12,047	DM12,047	DM12,047
			£4,140	£4,140	£4,140
			¥884,428	¥884,428	¥884,428
BEYER, ADAM	2	2	$1,190	$2,615	$1,903
			DM2,190	DM4,856	DM3,523
			£740	£1,587	£1,164
			¥140,390	¥272,631	¥206,510
BLAND & WELLER	1	1	$999	$999	$999
			DM1,415	DM1,415	DM1,415
			£632	£632	£632
			¥102,191	¥102,191	¥102,191

Maker	Items		Selling Prices		
	Bid	Sold	Low	High	Avg
BLUTHNER	3	2	$1,618	$2,141	$1,879
			DM2,263	DM3,262	DM2,763
			£1,012	£1,380	£1,196
			¥136,836	¥237,498	¥187,167
BOSENDORFER	1	1	$387,500	$387,500	$387,500
			DM685,488	DM685,488	DM685,488
			£233,973	£233,973	£233,973
			¥50,336,250	¥50,336,250	¥50,336,250
BROADWOOD, JOHN	1	1	$2,104	$2,104	$2,104
			DM2,987	DM2,987	DM2,987
			£1,350	£1,350	£1,350
			¥214,048	¥214,048	¥214,048
BROADWOOD, JOHN & SONS	5	3	$326	$2,362	$1,678
			DM605	DM4,183	DM2,712
			£198	£1,495	£1,043
			¥33,980	¥307,093	¥194,269
CHALLEN & HOLLIS	3	0			
CLEMENTI, MUZIO	4	3	$464	$1,835	$1,123
			DM694	DM2,746	DM1,690
			£276	£1,092	£686
			¥51,744	¥204,728	¥125,074
CLEMENTI & CO.	2	1	$2,833	$2,833	$2,833
			DM5,261	DM5,261	DM5,261
			£1,719	£1,719	£1,719
			¥295,350	¥295,350	¥295,350
COLLARD & COLLARD	2	1	$2,291	$2,291	$2,291
			DM3,809	DM3,809	DM3,809
			£1,380	£1,380	£1,380
			¥266,809	¥266,809	¥266,809
EDWARDS, WILLIAM	1	1	$3,003	$3,003	$3,003
			DM5,354	DM5,354	DM5,354
			£1,840	£1,840	£1,840
			¥393,079	¥393,079	¥393,079
GANER, CHRISTOPHER	1	1	$916	$916	$916
			DM1,469	DM1,469	DM1,469
			£595	£595	£595
			¥104,177	¥104,177	¥104,177
GANER, CHRISTOPHER (attributed to)	1	1	$188	$188	$188
			DM335	DM335	DM335
			£115	£115	£115
			¥24,567	¥24,567	¥24,567
HAXBY, THOMAS	2	2	$1,240	$2,854	$2,047
			DM2,062	DM4,350	DM3,206
			£747	£1,840	£1,294
			¥144,425	¥316,664	¥230,544
KIRCKMAN, JACOB & ABRAHAM	2	0			
KLEIN, F.A.	2	0			
LONGMAN, JAMES	1	1	$1,641	$1,641	$1,641
			DM2,951	DM2,951	DM2,951
			£977	£977	£977
			¥189,763	¥189,763	¥189,763
LONGMAN & CO.	2	1	$1,240	$1,240	$1,240
			DM2,062	DM2,062	DM2,062
			£747	£747	£747
			¥144,425	¥144,425	¥144,425

Maker	Items		Selling Prices		
	Bid	Sold	Low	High	Avg
LONGMAN & BRODERIP	10	8	$960	$2,720	$1,775
			DM1,604	DM4,168	DM2,854
			£575	£1,610	£1,057
			¥116,719	¥302,744	¥203,871
LONGMAN, CLEMENTI & CO.	1	1	$1,408	$1,408	$1,408
			DM2,510	DM2,510	DM2,510
			£863	£863	£863
			¥184,256	¥184,256	¥184,256
MORNINGTON, ROBERT	1	0			
PHILLIPS, W.	1	1	$1,222	$1,222	$1,222
			DM1,960	DM1,960	DM1,960
			£794	£794	£794
			¥139,037	¥139,037	¥139,037
PLEYEL	1	0			
POHLMAN, JOHANNES	1	1	$1,689	$1,689	$1,689
			DM3,012	DM3,012	DM3,012
			£1,035	£1,035	£1,035
			¥221,107	¥221,107	¥221,107
PRESTON, THOMAS	2	1	$1,145	$1,145	$1,145
			DM1,904	DM1,904	DM1,904
			£690	£690	£690
			¥133,405	¥133,405	¥133,405
ROLFE, WILLIAM & SONS	2	0			
ROLOFF, H.	1	0			
STEINWAY & SONS	1	1	$2,877	$2,877	$2,877
			DM4,026	DM4,026	DM4,026
			£1,800	£1,800	£1,800
			¥243,383	¥243,383	¥243,383
STEINWEG, GROTRIAN	1	1	$3,156	$3,156	$3,156
			DM4,480	DM4,480	DM4,480
			£2,025	£2,025	£2,025
			¥321,072	¥321,072	¥321,072
STODART, M. & W.	1	1	$618	$618	$618
			DM1,111	DM1,111	DM1,111
			£368	£368	£368
			¥71,477	¥71,477	¥71,477
STODART, WILLIAM	1	0			
STODART, WILLIAM & SON	1	1	$6,606	$6,606	$6,606
			DM9,895	DM9,895	DM9,895
			£3,910	£3,910	£3,910
			¥735,236	¥735,236	¥735,236
WACHTL, JOSEPH & JACOB BLEYER	1	0			
WEBLEN, ALEXANDER	1	0			

PIANOFORTE

Maker	Items		Selling Prices		
	Bid	Sold	Low	High	Avg
BROADWOOD, JOHN	2	0			
BROADWOOD, JOHN & SONS	7	5	$1,909	$27,201	$11,308
			DM3,174	DM40,744	DM17,707
			£1,150	£16,100	£6,854
			¥222,341	¥3,027,444	¥1,216,386
COLLARD & COLLARD	1	1	$3,245	$3,245	$3,245
			DM5,396	DM5,396	DM5,396
			£1,955	£1,955	£1,955
			¥377,980	¥377,980	¥377,980

Maker	Items Bid	Sold	Selling Prices Low	High	Avg
CRISI, VINCENZO	1	1	$9,759	$9,759	$9,759
			DM17,402	DM17,402	DM17,402
			£5,980	£5,980	£5,980
			¥1,277,507	¥1,277,507	¥1,277,507
EHLERS, JOACHIM	1	0			
FIRTH & HALL	1	1	$920	$920	$920
			DM1,638	DM1,638	DM1,638
			£552	£552	£552
			¥122,342	¥122,342	¥122,342
GRAF, CONRAD	2	2	$26,275	$38,859	$32,567
			DM46,851	DM58,206	DM52,529
			£16,100	£23,000	£19,550
			¥3,439,443	¥4,324,920	¥3,882,182
HANCOCK, CRANG	1	1	$22,941	$22,941	$22,941
			DM35,245	DM35,245	DM35,245
			£14,950	£14,950	£14,950
			¥2,511,436	¥2,511,436	¥2,511,436
HAWKINS, JOHN ISAAC	1	1	$34,362	$34,362	$34,362
			DM57,132	DM57,132	DM57,132
			£20,700	£20,700	£20,700
			¥4,002,138	¥4,002,138	¥4,002,138
LONGMAN & BRODERIP	1	1	$17,830	$17,830	$17,830
			DM31,792	DM31,792	DM31,792
			£10,925	£10,925	£10,925
			¥2,333,908	¥2,333,908	¥2,333,908
LONGMAN, CLEMENTI & CO.	1	0			
SCHANZ, JOHANN	1	1	$33,780	$33,780	$33,780
			DM62,724	DM62,724	DM62,724
			£20,499	£20,499	£20,499
			¥3,521,480	¥3,521,480	¥3,521,480
STEIN, JOHANN ANDREAS	1	1	$76,872	$76,872	$76,872
			DM115,147	DM115,147	DM115,147
			£45,500	£45,500	£45,500
			¥8,555,820	¥8,555,820	¥8,555,820
STEIN, MATTHAUS ANDREAS	1	1	$27,201	$27,201	$27,201
			DM40,744	DM40,744	DM40,744
			£16,100	£16,100	£16,100
			¥3,027,444	¥3,027,444	¥3,027,444
STODART, M. & W.	2	1	$9,153	$9,153	$9,153
			DM16,996	DM16,996	DM16,996
			£5,555	£5,555	£5,555
			¥954,208	¥954,208	¥954,208
TOMKISON, THOMAS	1	1	$1,687	$1,687	$1,687
			DM2,991	DM2,991	DM2,991
			£1,035	£1,035	£1,035
			¥199,476	¥199,476	¥199,476

PICCOLO

Maker	Items Bid	Sold	Selling Prices Low	High	Avg
BESSON & CO.	1	1	$207	$207	$207
			DM342	DM342	DM342
			£127	£127	£127
			¥25,607	¥25,607	¥25,607
BUTLER	1	1	$150	$150	$150
			DM248	DM248	DM248
			£92	£92	£92
			¥18,623	¥18,623	¥18,623
GAND, CHARLES	1	0			

| Maker | Items | | Selling Prices | | |
	Bid	Sold	Low	High	Avg
GOULDING & CO.	1	1	$188	$188	$188
			DM335	DM335	DM335
			£115	£115	£115
			¥24,567	¥24,567	¥24,567
HAMMIG, PHILIP	1	1	$1,635	$1,635	$1,635
			DM2,317	DM2,317	DM2,317
			£1,035	£1,035	£1,035
			¥167,353	¥167,353	¥167,353
HAWKES & SON	1	1	$158	$158	$158
			DM167	DM167	DM167
			£98	£98	£98
			¥12,101	¥12,101	¥12,101
HAYNES CO., WILLIAM S.	1	1	$382	$382	$382
			DM635	DM635	DM635
			£230	£230	£230
			¥44,468	¥44,468	¥44,468
HAYNES & CO.	1	1	$748	$748	$748
			DM1,292	DM1,292	DM1,292
			£462	£462	£462
			¥94,734	¥94,734	¥94,734
JAHN, M.A.	1	0			
KING MUSICAL INSTRUMENT CO.	1	0			
KRUSPE, C.	1	0			
LEFT, JACK	1	0			
LOT, LOUIS	8	3	$414	$771	$589
			DM683	DM1,465	DM991
			£253	£476	£366
			¥51,215	¥81,037	¥63,918
MONZANI	1	1	$714	$714	$714
			DM1,087	DM1,087	DM1,087
			£460	£460	£460
			¥79,166	¥79,166	¥79,166
RITTERSHAUSEN, E.	1	1	$150	$150	$150
			DM221	DM221	DM221
			£98	£98	£98
			¥15,949	¥15,949	¥15,949
RUDALL, CARTE & CO.	10	6	$94	$317	$184
			DM171	DM486	DM294
			£58	£207	£117
			¥11,384	¥34,556	¥21,088
SELMER	1	0			
SKOUSBOE, HENNING ANDERSEN	1	1	$581	$581	$581
			DM824	DM824	DM824
			£368	£368	£368
			¥59,503	¥59,503	¥59,503
THIBOUVILLE-LAMY, J.	1	1	$56	$56	$56
			DM95	DM95	DM95
			£35	£35	£35
			¥6,538	¥6,538	¥6,538
WALLIS, JOSEPH	2	1	$725	$725	$725
			DM1,206	DM1,206	DM1,206
			£437	£437	£437
			¥84,490	¥84,490	¥84,490
YAMAHA	1	0			

Maker	Items		Selling Prices		
	Bid	Sold	Low	High	Avg

POCHETTE

Maker	Bid	Sold	Low	High	Avg
AMAN, GEORG	2	1	$4,880	$4,880	$4,880
			DM8,701	DM8,701	DM8,701
			£2,990	£2,990	£2,990
			¥638,754	¥638,754	¥638,754
BAADER, J. (workshop of)	1	1	$978	$978	$978
			DM1,471	DM1,471	DM1,471
			£593	£593	£593
			¥109,265	¥109,265	¥109,265
BETTS, JOHN	1	1	$642	$642	$642
			DM1,115	DM1,115	DM1,115
			£380	£380	£380
			¥81,444	¥81,444	¥81,444
BETTS, JOHN (attributed to)	1	0			
WORLE, MATHIAS	2	2	$4,888	$9,919	$7,403
			DM8,363	DM18,722	DM13,542
			£2,891	£6,140	£4,515
			¥606,930	¥1,049,404	¥828,167

QUINTON

Maker	Bid	Sold	Low	High	Avg
GUERSAN, LOUIS	2	2	$4,663	$4,673	$4,668
			DM6,985	DM8,106	DM7,545
			£2,760	£2,760	£2,760
			¥518,990	¥592,324	¥555,657

RACKET BASSOON

Maker	Bid	Sold	Low	High	Avg
BIZEY, CHARLES	1	0			

RAUSCHPFEIFE

Maker	Bid	Sold	Low	High	Avg
GUNTHER	1	0			

RECORDER

Maker	Bid	Sold	Low	High	Avg
AULOS	1	1	$35	$35	$35
			DM52	DM52	DM52
			£23	£23	£23
			¥3,753	¥3,753	¥3,753
DENNER, JOHANN CHRISTOPH	2	0			
EICHENTOPF, JOHANN HEINRICH	1	1	$20,645	$20,645	$20,645
			DM36,812	DM36,812	DM36,812
			£12,650	£12,650	£12,650
			¥2,702,420	¥2,702,420	¥2,702,420
GAHN, JOHANN B.	1	0			
HOHNER	1	1	$9	$9	$9
			DM13	DM13	DM13
			£6	£6	£6
			¥938	¥938	¥938
OBERLENDER, JOHANN WILHELM (I)	1	0			
RIPPERT, JEAN JACQUES	2	1	$17,181	$17,181	$17,181
			DM28,566	DM28,566	DM28,566
			£10,350	£10,350	£10,350
			¥2,001,069	¥2,001,069	¥2,001,069

Maker	Items		Selling Prices		
	Bid	Sold	Low	High	Avg
STANESBY, THOMAS	2	1	$40,801	$40,801	$40,801
			DM61,116	DM61,116	DM61,116
			£24,150	£24,150	£24,150
			¥4,541,166	¥4,541,166	¥4,541,166
STANESBY, THOMAS JR.	1	1	$20,999	$20,999	$20,999
			DM34,914	DM34,914	DM34,914
			£12,650	£12,650	£12,650
			¥2,445,751	¥2,445,751	¥2,445,751
VON HUENE, FRIEDRICH	1	1	$1,610	$1,610	$1,610
			DM2,866	DM2,866	DM2,866
			£966	£966	£966
			¥214,098	¥214,098	¥214,098

ROTHPHONE

Maker	Items		Selling Prices		
BOTTALI, A.M.	1	1	$2,291	$2,291	$2,291
			DM3,809	DM3,809	DM3,809
			£1,380	£1,380	£1,380
			¥266,809	¥266,809	¥266,809
BOTTALI FRATELLI, A.M.	2	2	$3,054	$6,109	$4,582
			DM5,078	DM10,157	DM7,618
			£1,840	£3,680	£2,760
			¥355,746	¥711,491	¥533,618

SARRUSOPHONE

Maker	Items		Selling Prices		
CONN, C.G.	1	0			
ORSI, ROMEO	1	0			
RAMPONE	1	1	$5,345	$5,345	$5,345
			DM8,887	DM8,887	DM8,887
			£3,220	£3,220	£3,220
			¥622,555	¥622,555	¥622,555

SAW

Maker	Items		Selling Prices		
FELDMANN, C.	1	1	$56	$56	$56
			DM94	DM94	DM94
			£34	£34	£34
			¥6,574	¥6,574	¥6,574
SANDVICKENS, JERNVERKS A.B.	1	1	$133	$133	$133
			DM221	DM221	DM221
			£80	£80	£80
			¥15,467	¥15,467	¥15,467

SAXHORN

Maker	Items		Selling Prices		
KLEMM & BRO.	1	1	$3,163	$3,163	$3,163
			DM5,345	DM5,345	DM5,345
			£1,898	£1,898	£1,898
			¥420,834	¥420,834	¥420,834
ZOEBISCH & SONS, C.A.	1	1	$802	$802	$802
			DM1,333	DM1,333	DM1,333
			£483	£483	£483
			¥93,383	¥93,383	¥93,383

SAXOPHONE

Maker	Items		Selling Prices		
BEAUGNIER	1	0			
BLESSING	2	0			

Maker	Items		Selling Prices		
	Bid	Sold	Low	High	Avg
BOOSEY & HAWKES	1	0			
BUESCHER	15	10	$149	$1,260	$528
			DM261	DM1,926	DM839
			£92	£805	£333
			¥18,027	¥140,513	¥60,210
BUFFET CRAMPON & CO.	1	0			
CABART	2	1	$338	$338	$338
			DM573	DM573	DM573
			£207	£207	£207
			¥39,226	¥39,226	¥39,226
COHN	2	2	$522	$695	$608
			DM801	DM1,069	DM935
			£345	£460	£403
			¥55,623	¥74,164	¥64,893
CONN, C.G.	14	12	$271	$981	$494
			DM314	DM1,784	DM823
			£161	£598	£304
			¥22,778	¥123,870	¥58,752
COUESNON	2	2	$616	$669	$642
			DM920	DM945	DM933
			£403	£414	£408
			¥55,720	¥67,192	¥61,456
COUESNON & CO.	1	1	$472	$472	$472
			DM814	DM814	DM814
			£288	£288	£288
			¥53,809	¥53,809	¥53,809
DUBOIS, RAYMOND	1	1	$259	$259	$259
			DM437	DM437	DM437
			£161	£161	£161
			¥31,856	¥31,856	¥31,856
ELKHART	1	1	$429	$429	$429
			DM657	DM657	DM657
			£276	£276	£276
			¥42,444	¥42,444	¥42,444
ELKHART BAND INSTRUMENT CO.	1	0			
FOOTE	1	1	$377	$377	$377
			DM685	DM685	DM685
			£230	£230	£230
			¥45,538	¥45,538	¥45,538
GRAFTON	13	11	$574	$2,141	$1,369
			DM810	DM3,262	DM2,089
			£360	£1,380	£851
			¥50,889	¥237,498	¥146,592
GUENOT	1	0			
HAWKES & SON	6	5	$130	$447	$279
			DM228	DM783	DM482
			£81	£276	£170
			¥15,774	¥54,082	¥34,947
HULLER, G.H.	1	1	$916	$916	$916
			DM1,524	DM1,524	DM1,524
			£552	£552	£552
			¥106,724	¥106,724	¥106,724
KEILWERTH, JULIUS	1	0			
KING MUSICAL INSTRUMENT CO.	1	0			

Maker	Items		Selling Prices		
	Bid	Sold	Low	High	Avg
LAFLEUR	3	1	$533	$533	$533
			DM766	DM766	DM766
			£345	£345	£345
			¥54,075	¥54,075	¥54,075
MARTIN BAND INSTRUMENT CO.	1	0			
OEHLER, OSKAR	2	0			
ORSI, ROMEO	1	0			
SAX, ADOLPHE	4	3	$940	$2,252	$1,388
			DM1,431	DM4,016	DM2,346
			£575	£1,380	£863
			¥103,199	¥294,809	¥168,989
SELMER	12	9	$336	$2,632	$1,422
			DM494	DM4,456	DM2,268
			£219	£1,610	£906
			¥35,650	¥305,089	¥158,800
SELMER, HENRI	5	3	$1,792	$2,260	$1,956
			DM2,574	DM3,473	DM3,101
			£1,093	£1,495	£1,246
			¥185,948	¥241,031	¥214,428
SELMER BUNDY	1	1	$150	$150	$150
			DM266	DM266	DM266
			£91	£91	£91
			¥20,769	¥20,769	¥20,769
STRASSER MARIGAUX	1	1	$161	$161	$161
			DM287	DM287	DM287
			£98	£98	£98
			¥22,366	¥22,366	¥22,366
STRASSER, MARIGAUX, LEMAIRE	1	1	$630	$630	$630
			DM963	DM963	DM963
			£403	£403	£403
			¥70,256	¥70,256	¥70,256
THIBOUVILLE-LAMY, J.	5	3	$155	$559	$374
			DM270	DM1,052	DM670
			£92	£345	£230
			¥19,721	¥59,071	¥42,950

SERPENT

Maker	Items		Selling Prices		
CRAMER, JOHN	1	0			
MONK, CHRISTOPHER	1	1	$1,009	$1,009	$1,009
			DM1,759	DM1,759	DM1,759
			£621	£621	£621
			¥122,244	¥122,244	¥122,244
PRETTY, F.	1	1	$2,922	$2,922	$2,922
			DM4,108	DM4,108	DM4,108
			£1,840	£1,840	£1,840
			¥260,783	¥260,783	¥260,783
PRETTY, F. (attributed to)	1	1	$2,056	$2,056	$2,056
			DM3,584	DM3,584	DM3,584
			£1,265	£1,265	£1,265
			¥249,015	¥249,015	¥249,015
PRETTY, ROBERT	1	1	$2,277	$2,277	$2,277
			DM4,043	DM4,043	DM4,043
			£1,380	£1,380	£1,380
			¥315,868	¥315,868	¥315,868

Maker	Items		Selling Prices		
	Bid	Sold	Low	High	Avg
WOLF & CO., ROBERT	1	1	$4,200	$4,200	$4,200
			DM6,983	DM6,983	DM6,983
			£2,530	£2,530	£2,530
			¥489,150	¥489,150	¥489,150

SOUSAPHONE

Maker	Bid	Sold	Low	High	Avg
BESSON	1	1	$805	$805	$805
			DM1,433	DM1,433	DM1,433
			£491	£491	£491
			¥111,831	¥111,831	¥111,831
DE PRINS GEBRUDER	2	1	$392	$392	$392
			DM728	DM728	DM728
			£238	£238	£238
			¥40,895	¥40,895	¥40,895

SPINET

Maker	Bid	Sold	Low	High	Avg
BARTON (ascribed to)	3	0			
BARTON, GEORGE	1	0			
HITCHCOCK, JOHN	1	1	$20,704	$20,704	$20,704
			DM38,444	DM38,444	DM38,444
			£12,564	£12,564	£12,564
			¥2,158,327	¥2,158,327	¥2,158,327
HITCHCOCK, THOMAS (YOUNGER)	2	1	$16,353	$16,353	$16,353
			DM23,168	DM23,168	DM23,168
			£10,350	£10,350	£10,350
			¥1,673,533	¥1,673,533	¥1,673,533
SHEAN, CHRISTIAN	1	0			
SISON, BENJAMIN	1	0			
SMITH, WILLIAM	1	1	$17,395	$17,395	$17,395
			DM26,027	DM26,027	DM26,027
			£10,350	£10,350	£10,350
			¥1,940,418	¥1,940,418	¥1,940,418
STEWART, N.	1	1	$9,894	$9,894	$9,894
			DM14,619	DM14,619	DM14,619
			£6,440	£6,440	£6,440
			¥1,054,447	¥1,054,447	¥1,054,447
WEBER, FERDINAND	1	1	$23,315	$23,315	$23,315
			DM34,924	DM34,924	DM34,924
			£13,800	£13,800	£13,800
			¥2,594,952	¥2,594,952	¥2,594,952

STRING QUARTET

Maker	Bid	Sold	Low	High	Avg
CANDI, ORESTE	1	1	$109,965	$109,965	$109,965
			DM154,112	DM154,112	DM154,112
			£69,000	£69,000	£69,000
			¥9,693,465	¥9,693,465	¥9,693,465

SUSAPHONE

Maker	Bid	Sold	Low	High	Avg
PAXMAN BROS.	1	0			

Maker	Items		Selling Prices		
	Bid	Sold	Low	High	Avg

SYMPHONIUM

WHEATSTONE, C.	1	1	$3,651	$3,651	$3,651
			DM5,610	DM5,610	DM5,610
			£2,415	£2,415	£2,415
			¥389,358	¥389,358	¥389,358

TAROGATO

MOGYOROSSY, G.Y.	2	1	$785	$785	$785
			DM1,457	DM1,457	DM1,457
			£476	£476	£476
			¥81,789	¥81,789	¥81,789

TIMPANI

HAWKES & SON	1	1	$505	$505	$505
			DM757	DM757	DM757
			£299	£299	£299
			¥56,224	¥56,224	¥56,224
HIGHAM, JOSEPH	1	0			

TIPLE

MARTIN & CO., C.F.	2	2	$259	$431	$345
			DM437	DM738	DM588
			£155	£255	£205
			¥31,568	¥53,553	¥42,560

TROMBONE

BESSON	3	3	$79	$106	$91
			DM122	DM156	DM138
			£52	£69	£59
			¥8,639	¥11,258	¥9,832
BOOSEY & CO.	1	1	$403	$403	$403
			DM680	DM680	DM680
			£242	£242	£242
			¥53,561	¥53,561	¥53,561
BOOSEY & HAWKES	4	4	$160	$334	$220
			DM270	DM513	DM350
			£98	£219	£142
			¥19,198	¥36,476	¥24,740
BUNDY	1	1	$141	$141	$141
			DM257	DM257	DM257
			£86	£86	£86
			¥17,077	¥17,077	¥17,077
BURGER, JULIUS MAX	1	1	$428	$428	$428
			DM712	DM712	DM712
			£258	£258	£258
			¥49,882	¥49,882	¥49,882
COUESNON	1	1	$335	$335	$335
			DM460	DM460	DM460
			£207	£207	£207
			¥27,860	¥27,860	¥27,860
COURTOIS, ANTOINE (FILS)	3	1	$485	$485	$485
			DM726	DM726	DM726
			£287	£287	£287
			¥53,967	¥53,967	¥53,967

Maker	Items		Selling Prices		
	Bid	Sold	Low	High	Avg
DE CART FRERES, FERDINAND & LOUIS	1	1	$840	$840	$840
			DM1,397	DM1,397	DM1,397
			£506	£506	£506
			¥97,830	¥97,830	¥97,830
FICKHERT, WILHELM	1	0			
HAWKES & SON	1	1	$84	$84	$84
			DM147	DM147	DM147
			£52	£52	£52
			¥10,187	¥10,187	¥10,187
LAFLEUR	1	1	$54	$54	$54
			DM82	DM82	DM82
			£35	£35	£35
			¥5,306	¥5,306	¥5,306
RIVIERE & HAWKES	1	0			
ROUSSEAU, A.F.	1	1	$611	$611	$611
			DM1,016	DM1,016	DM1,016
			£368	£368	£368
			¥71,149	¥71,149	¥71,149
RUDALL, CARTE & CO.	1	1	$188	$188	$188
			DM318	DM318	DM318
			£115	£115	£115
			¥21,792	¥21,792	¥21,792
SENECAUT, PIERRE	1	1	$878	$878	$878
			DM1,460	DM1,460	DM1,460
			£529	£529	£529
			¥102,277	¥102,277	¥102,277
VAN ENGELEN, H.	1	0			
WHITE & CO., H.N.	1	0			
ZELENKA, ANTONIN	1	1	$420	$420	$420
			DM698	DM698	DM698
			£253	£253	£253
			¥48,915	¥48,915	¥48,915

TROMPE DE CHASSE

Maker	Items		Selling Prices		
GAUTROT (AINE)	1	1	$916	$916	$916
			DM1,524	DM1,524	DM1,524
			£552	£552	£552
			¥106,724	¥106,724	¥106,724
RAOUX, MARCEL-AUGUSTE	1	0			
SCHMIDT, JOHANN JACOB	1	0			

TRUMPET

Maker	Items		Selling Prices		
BESSON	2	2	$281	$387	$334
			DM432	DM594	DM513
			£184	£253	£219
			¥30,716	¥42,235	¥36,476
BESSON, FONTAINE	1	1	$56	$56	$56
			DM95	DM95	DM95
			£35	£35	£35
			¥6,538	¥6,538	¥6,538
BOOSEY & HAWKES	1	1	$62	$62	$62
			DM95	DM95	DM95
			£40	£40	£40
			¥6,719	¥6,719	¥6,719

Maker	Items		Selling Prices		
	Bid	Sold	Low	High	Avg
CALICCHIO, DOMINIC	1	1	$1,495	$1,495	$1,495
			DM2,691	DM2,691	DM2,691
			£897	£897	£897
			¥11,616	¥11,616	¥11,616
CONN, C.G.	2	1	$489	$489	$489
			DM885	DM885	DM885
			£298	£298	£298
			¥59,012	¥59,012	¥59,012
COUESNON	1	0			
COURTURIER, ERNST ALBERT	2	1	$748	$748	$748
			DM1,263	DM1,263	DM1,263
			£449	£449	£449
			¥99,470	¥99,470	¥99,470
DE CLERCQ, L.	1	1	$535	$535	$535
			DM889	DM889	DM889
			£322	£322	£322
			¥62,255	¥62,255	¥62,255
HAWKES & SON	1	1	$74	$74	$74
			DM102	DM102	DM102
			£46	£46	£46
			¥6,191	¥6,191	¥6,191
HOLTON	1	1	$115	$115	$115
			DM166	DM166	DM166
			£73	£73	£73
			¥9,976	¥9,976	¥9,976
JAY CO., H.B.	1	0			
MAINZ, ALEXANDER	2	1	$1,173	$1,173	$1,173
			DM1,911	DM1,911	DM1,911
			£690	£690	£690
			¥138,055	¥138,055	¥138,055
MIRAFONE	1	0			
OTTO, FRANZ	1	1	$878	$878	$878
			DM1,460	DM1,460	DM1,460
			£529	£529	£529
			¥102,277	¥102,277	¥102,277
SCHULLER, LUHABEN	1	1	$1,635	$1,635	$1,635
			DM2,317	DM2,317	DM2,317
			£1,035	£1,035	£1,035
			¥167,353	¥167,353	¥167,353
WHITE & CO., H.N.	1	0			
WOLF, AUGUST	1	0			

TUBA

Maker	Items		Selling Prices		
BESSON & CO.	2	1	$188	$188	$188
			DM335	DM335	DM335
			£115	£115	£115
			¥24,567	¥24,567	¥24,567
BOOSEY & HAWKES	5	5	$158	$668	$429
			DM243	DM1,026	DM659
			£104	£437	£281
			¥17,278	¥72,951	¥46,843
HALARI	2	0			
SUDRE, FRANCOIS	2	0			

Maker	Items		Selling Prices		
	Bid	Sold	Low	High	Avg

UKULELE

Maker	Bid	Sold	Low	High	Avg
ALOHA	1	1	$288	$288	$288
			DM512	DM512	DM512
			£175	£175	£175
			¥39,940	¥39,940	¥39,940
GIBSON CO.	2	2	$179	$295	$237
			DM274	DM416	DM345
			£115	£185	£150
			¥17,685	¥26,151	¥21,918
KAMAKA	1	1	$92	$92	$92
			DM166	DM166	DM166
			£55	£55	£55
			¥715	¥715	¥715
KUMALAE	2	2	$150	$201	$175
			DM266	DM344	DM305
			£91	£119	£105
			¥20,769	¥24,991	¥22,880
MARTIN, CHRISTIAN FREDERICK	1	1	$138	$138	$138
			DM199	DM199	DM199
			£88	£88	£88
			¥11,972	¥11,972	¥11,972
MARTIN & CO., C.F.	6	6	$374	$1,587	$912
			DM632	DM2,995	DM1,679
			£224	£982	£559
			¥45,598	¥167,905	¥101,894

UNION PIPES

Maker	Bid	Sold	Low	High	Avg
REID, ROBERT	1	1	$1,198	$1,198	$1,198
			DM2,224	DM2,224	DM2,224
			£727	£727	£727
			¥124,857	¥124,857	¥124,857
ROBERTSON, HUGH	1	1	$7,636	$7,636	$7,636
			DM12,696	DM12,696	DM12,696
			£4,600	£4,600	£4,600
			¥889,364	¥889,364	¥889,364

VIELLE

Maker	Bid	Sold	Low	High	Avg
COLSON	1	0			

VIHUELA

Maker	Bid	Sold	Low	High	Avg
DOLMETSCH, ARNOLD	1	1	$999	$999	$999
			DM1,415	DM1,415	DM1,415
			£632	£632	£632
			¥102,191	¥102,191	¥102,191

VIOL

Maker	Bid	Sold	Low	High	Avg
CAPICCHIONI, MARINO	1	0			
CARLETTI, NATALE	1	0			
CASTAGNERI, ANDREA	2	1	$3,109	$3,109	$3,109
			DM4,656	DM4,656	DM4,656
			£1,840	£1,840	£1,840
			¥345,994	¥345,994	¥345,994
COLETTI, A.	1	0			

Maker	Items		Selling Prices		
	Bid	Sold	Low	High	Avg
CROSS, H. CHARLES (attributed to)	1	1	$839	$839	$839
			DM884	DM884	DM884
			£518	£518	£518
			¥64,064	¥64,064	¥64,064
EBERLE, JOHANN ULRICH	1	1	$30,511	$30,511	$30,511
			DM56,654	DM56,654	DM56,654
			£18,515	£18,515	£18,515
			¥3,180,692	¥3,180,692	¥3,180,692
EBERLE, JOHANN ULRICH (attributed to)	1	0			
EBERLE, TOMASO	1	1	$7,188	$7,188	$7,188
			DM13,009	DM13,009	DM13,009
			£4,384	£4,384	£4,384
			¥867,819	¥867,819	¥867,819
FIORINI, RAFFAELE	1	0			
GAGLIANO, FERDINAND	1	1	$10,322	$10,322	$10,322
			DM18,406	DM18,406	DM18,406
			£6,325	£6,325	£6,325
			¥1,351,210	¥1,351,210	¥1,351,210
GOLDT, JACOBUS HEINRICH	1	1	$46,764	$46,764	$46,764
			DM66,148	DM66,148	DM66,148
			£29,900	£29,900	£29,900
			¥4,748,389	¥4,748,389	¥4,748,389
GUGGENBERGER, ANTON	4	0			
JORDAN, HANS	1	1	$955	$955	$955
			DM1,587	DM1,587	DM1,587
			£575	£575	£575
			¥111,171	¥111,171	¥111,171
KESSLER, DIETRICH	1	1	$1,002	$1,002	$1,002
			DM1,795	DM1,795	DM1,795
			£598	£598	£598
			¥116,311	¥116,311	¥116,311
PIERRAY, CLAUDE	1	1	$38,157	$38,157	$38,157
			DM54,060	DM54,060	DM54,060
			£24,150	£24,150	£24,150
			¥3,904,910	¥3,904,910	¥3,904,910
ROSE, ROGER	2	1	$2,300	$2,300	$2,300
			DM4,140	DM4,140	DM4,140
			£1,380	£1,380	£1,380
			¥17,871	¥17,871	¥17,871
ROTA, JOANNES (attributed to)	1	0			
ROY, KARL	1	0			
SEELOS, JOHANN	1	1	$36,271	$36,271	$36,271
			DM60,306	DM60,306	DM60,306
			£21,850	£21,850	£21,850
			¥4,224,479	¥4,224,479	¥4,224,479
STEBER, ERNST	1	0			
STIEBER, ERNST	1	1	$529	$529	$529
			DM998	DM998	DM998
			£327	£327	£327
			¥55,968	¥55,968	¥55,968
UDALRICUS, JOHANNES (attributed to)	2	1	$822	$822	$822
			DM1,433	DM1,433	DM1,433
			£506	£506	£506
			¥99,606	¥99,606	¥99,606

Maker	Items Bid	Sold	Low	Selling Prices High	Avg
UEBEL, WOLFGANG	1	1	$1,043 DM1,603 £690 ¥111,245	$1,043 DM1,603 £690 ¥111,245	$1,043 DM1,603 £690 ¥111,245

VIOL BOW

BRYANT (attributed to)	1	1	$634 DM895 £403 ¥63,850	$634 DM895 £403 ¥63,850	$634 DM895 £403 ¥63,850
DOLMETSCH, ARNOLD	1	0			
TUBBS, JAMES (attributed to)	2	1	$809 DM1,449 £483 ¥93,944	$809 DM1,449 £483 ¥93,944	$809 DM1,449 £483 ¥93,944

VIOLA

ACOULON, ALFRED	1	0			
ALBANELLI, FRANCO	2	0			
AMATI, ANTONIO & GIROLAMO	1	0			
AMATI, DOM NICOLO	1	0			
ANTONIAZZI, ROMEO	3	1	$39,675 DM74,887 £324,559 ¥84,197,615	$39,675 DM74,887 £324,559 ¥84,197,615	$39,675 DM74,887 £324,559 ¥84,197,615
ANTONIAZZI, ROMEO (workshop of)	1	0			
ARASSI, ENZO	1	1	$5,175 DM7,788 £33,141 ¥8578,462	$5,175 DM7,788 £33,141 ¥8578,462	$5,175 DM7,788 £33,141 ¥8578,462
ARCANGELI, ULDERICO	1	0			
AREZIO, CLAUDIO	4	1	$4,397 DM6,751 £32,875 ¥8479,944	$4,397 DM6,751 £32,875 ¥8479,944	$4,397 DM6,751 £32,875 ¥8479,944
ARTMANN, GEORG VALENTIN	1	0			
ASHFORD, LAWRENCE	1	0			
ATKINSON, WILLIAM	1	1	$2,383 DM3,339 £31,495 ¥8210,025	$2,383 DM3,339 £31,495 ¥8210,025	$2,383 DM3,339 £31,495 ¥8210,025
AUDINOT, PIERRE M.	1	1	$7,314 DM13,754 £4,600 ¥884,304	$7,314 DM13,754 £4,600 ¥884,304	$7,314 DM13,754 £4,600 ¥884,304
AVERNA, GESUALDO	1	0			
AYERS, PAUL	1	0			
BADALASSI, PIERO (attributed to)	1	1	$3,319 DM4,622 £2,070 ¥280,584	$3,319 DM4,622 £2,070 ¥280,584	$3,319 DM4,622 £2,070 ¥280,584
BAILLY, PAUL	2	0			

| Maker | Items | | Selling Prices | | |
	Bid	Sold	Low	High	Avg
BANKS, BENJAMIN	1	1	$7,079	$7,079	$7,079
			DM13,329	DM13,329	DM13,329
			£4,370	£4,370	£4,370
			¥748,231	¥748,231	¥748,231
BANKS, JAMES & HENRY	1	1	$13,041	$13,041	$13,041
			DM24,553	DM24,553	DM24,553
			£8,050	£8,050	£8,050
			¥1,378,321	¥1,378,321	¥1,378,321
BANKS FAMILY (MEMBER OF)	2	0			
BARBIERI, BRUNO	9	2	$2,846	$5,175	$4,011
			DM5,123	DM7,483	DM6,303
			£1,725	£3,380	£2,553
			¥410,464	¥523,969	¥467,216
BARBIERI, ENZO	1	0			
BARBIERI, PAOLO	1	0			
BARGELLI, G.	2	0			
BARKER, J.	1	1	$1,585	$1,585	$1,585
			DM2,337	DM2,337	DM2,337
			£1,035	£1,035	£1,035
			¥169,088	¥169,088	¥169,088
BARNABETTI, GERONIMO	1	1	$2,131	$2,131	$2,131
			DM3,592	DM3,592	DM3,592
			£1,323	£1,323	£1,323
			¥261,674	¥261,674	¥261,674
BARTON, JOHN	1	1	$1,817	$1,817	$1,817
			DM2,567	DM2,567	DM2,567
			£1,150	£1,150	£1,150
			¥162,193	¥162,193	¥162,193
BARZONI, FRANCOIS	4	4	$1,252	$2,944	$1,982
			DM1,924	DM4,981	DM3,258
			£828	£1,852	£1,262
			¥133,494	¥364,746	¥227,699
BASTON, VICTOR	2	1	$466	$466	$466
			DM491	DM491	DM491
			£288	£288	£288
			¥35,591	¥35,591	¥35,591
BEARD, JOHN	1	0			
BEDER, ANTON	1	1	$288	$288	$288
			DM518	DM518	DM518
			£173	£173	£173
			¥2,234	¥2,234	¥2,234
BEDOCCHI, MARIO	2	0			
BELLAROSA, VITTORIO	1	0			
BERNARDEL, GUSTAVE	1	0			
BERNARDEL, GUSTAVE ADOLPHE	1	0			
BERTOLAZZI, GIACINTO	3	1	$3,042	$3,042	$3,042
			DM5,741	DM5,741	DM5,741
			£1,883	£1,883	£1,883
			¥321,817	¥321,817	¥321,817
BETTS	1	1	$15,159	$15,159	$15,159
			DM26,282	DM26,282	DM26,282
			£8,970	£8,970	£8,970
			¥1,892,670	¥1,892,670	¥1,892,670
BETTS, JOHN	3	3	$2,557	$11,064	$7,097
			DM3,595	DM15,406	DM9,928
			£1,610	£6,900	£4,447
			¥228,185	¥935,281	¥615,111

Maker	Items		Selling Prices		
	Bid	Sold	Low	High	Avg
BEYER, GEORGE W.	2	1	$690	$690	$690
			DM1,166	DM1,166	DM1,166
			£414	£414	£414
			¥84,180	¥84,180	¥84,180
BICKLE, PAUL	1	1	$785	$785	$785
			DM1,368	DM1,368	DM1,368
			£483	£483	£483
			¥95,079	¥95,079	¥95,079
BIGNAMI, OTELLO	2	0			
BIRD, RICHMOND HENRY (attributed to)	2	1	$1,537	$1,537	$1,537
			DM2,688	DM2,688	DM2,688
			£943	£943	£943
			¥181,575	¥181,575	¥181,575
BISIACH, LEANDRO	1	0			
BISSOLOTTI, TIZIANO	1	1	$1,955	$1,955	$1,955
			DM2,827	DM2,827	DM2,827
			£1,277	£1,277	£1,277
			¥197,944	¥197,944	¥197,944
BISSOLOTTI, VINCENZO	1	1	$2,070	$2,070	$2,070
			DM3,498	DM3,498	DM3,498
			£1,242	£1,242	£1,242
			¥275,455	¥275,455	¥275,455
BLANCHARD, PAUL	3	2	$5,532	$15,771	$10,651
			DM7,703	DM26,681	DM17,192
			£3,450	£9,919	£6,684
			¥467,641	¥1,953,994	¥1,210,817
BLANCHI, ALBERTO	2	0			
BOIANCIUC, ROMAN	1	1	$1,387	$1,387	$1,387
			DM2,485	DM2,485	DM2,485
			£828	£828	£828
			¥161,046	¥161,046	¥161,046
BOTTAJO, VINCENZO JOANNES	1	0			
BOUETTE, MAURICE	1	1	$3,353	$3,353	$3,353
			DM5,151	DM5,151	DM5,151
			£2,185	£2,185	£2,185
			¥367,056	¥367,056	¥367,056
BOULLANGIER, CHARLES	5	2	$7,951	$19,376	$13,663
			DM11,747	DM28,564	DM20,155
			£5,175	£12,650	£8,913
			¥847,323	¥2,066,631	¥1,456,977
BOULLANGIER, CHARLES (attributed to)	1	1	$3,129	$3,129	$3,129
			DM4,809	DM4,809	DM4,809
			£2,070	£2,070	£2,070
			¥333,736	¥333,736	¥333,736
BOURGUIGNON, MAURICE	1	0			
BOYES, ARNOLD	1	1	$1,708	$1,708	$1,708
			DM2,577	DM2,577	DM2,577
			£1,035	£1,035	£1,035
			¥193,545	¥193,545	¥193,545
BRADSHAW, B.L.	1	0			
BRAY, E.	1	1	$469	$469	$469
			DM850	DM850	DM850
			£288	£288	£288
			¥56,647	¥56,647	¥56,647

Maker	Items Bid	Sold	Selling Prices Low	High	Avg
BRETON	1	1	$562	$562	$562
			DM997	DM997	DM997
			£345	£345	£345
			¥66,492	¥66,492	¥66,492
BRETON BREVETE	2	2	$1,629	$4,073	$2,851
			DM2,613	DM6,533	DM4,573
			£1,058	£2,645	£1,852
			¥185,383	¥463,457	¥324,420
BRIGGS, JAMES WILLIAM	1	1	$6,084	$6,084	$6,084
			DM11,483	DM11,483	DM11,483
			£3,766	£3,766	£3,766
			¥643,634	¥643,634	¥643,634
BRUCKNER, WILHELM	1	1	$2,294	$2,294	$2,294
			DM3,524	DM3,524	DM3,524
			£1,495	£1,495	£1,495
			¥251,144	¥251,144	¥251,144
BRYANT, GEORGE E.	1	1	$3,174	$3,174	$3,174
			DM5,991	DM5,991	DM5,991
			£1,965	£1,965	£1,965
			¥335,809	¥335,809	¥335,809
BUCKMAN, GEORGE H.	1	1	$1,310	$1,310	$1,310
			DM2,347	DM2,347	DM2,347
			£782	£782	£782
			¥152,099	¥152,099	¥152,099
BUTHOD	3	1	$3,091	$3,091	$3,091
			DM5,557	DM5,557	DM5,557
			£1,840	£1,840	£1,840
			¥357,383	¥357,383	¥357,383
BUTHOD, CHARLES LOUIS	2	2	$2,560	$3,271	$2,916
			DM4,620	DM4,814	DM4,717
			£1,610	£2,070	£1,840
			¥291,947	¥309,506	¥300,726
CANDI, CESARE	3	0			
CAPELA, ANTONIO	7	4	$5,290	$7,475	$6,198
			DM7,639	DM12,633	DM9,352
			£3,370	£4,485	£3,890
			¥458,908	¥994,698	¥648,093
CAPELA, D.	1	0			
CAPELA, DOMINGOS	1	0			
CAPELLI, ALDO	1	0			
CAPICCHIONI, MARINO	3	2	$25,816	$27,209	$26,513
			DM35,946	DM47,173	DM41,560
			£16,100	£16,100	£16,100
			¥2,182,323	¥3,397,100	¥2,789,711
CARESSA & FRANCAIS	1	0			
CARLETTI, CARLO	4	2	$9,718	$19,550	$14,634
			DM14,358	DM28,269	DM21,314
			£6,325	£12,770	£9,548
			¥1,035,618	¥1,979,438	¥1,507,528
CARLETTI, GENUZIO	3	1	$4,664	$4,664	$4,664
			DM8,087	DM8,087	DM8,087
			£2,760	£2,760	£2,760
			¥582,360	¥582,360	¥582,360
CASINI, SERAFINO	1	0			
CASTELLI, CESARE	4	0			

Maker	Items		Selling Prices		
	Bid	Sold	Low	High	Avg
CASTELLO, PAOLO	1	1	$23,972	$23,972	$23,972
			DM33,379	DM33,379	DM33,379
			£14,950	£14,950	£14,950
			¥2,026,443	¥2,026,443	¥2,026,443
CAUSSIN FAMILY (MEMBER OF)	1	1	$3,992	$3,992	$3,992
			DM5,622	DM5,622	DM5,622
			£2,530	£2,530	£2,530
			¥408,170	¥408,170	¥408,170
CAVALAZZI, ANTONIO	1	0			
CAVALINI, DINO	1	0			
CAVANI, GIOVANNI	1	1	$23,000	$23,000	$23,000
			DM33,258	DM33,258	DM33,258
			£15,024	£15,024	£15,024
			¥2,328,750	¥2,328,750	¥2,328,750
CAVANI, GIOVANNI (ascribed to)	1	0			
CAVANI, VINCENZO	3	2	$6,900	$9,087	$7,993
			DM12,489	DM12,835	DM12,662
			£4,209	£5,750	£4,980
			¥810,963	¥833,106	¥822,034
CE, GIORGIO	1	1	$1,955	$1,955	$1,955
			DM2,827	DM2,827	DM2,827
			£1,277	£1,277	£1,277
			¥197,944	¥197,944	¥197,944
CERUTI, GIUSEPPE (ascribed to)	1	1	$14,610	$14,610	$14,610
			DM20,542	DM20,542	DM20,542
			£9,200	£9,200	£9,200
			¥1,298,792	¥1,298,792	¥1,298,792
CHADWICK, JOHN	1	1	$975	$975	$975
			DM1,378	DM1,378	DM1,378
			£621	£621	£621
			¥83,264	¥83,264	¥83,264
CHANOT, FRANCOIS	1	1	$2,300	$2,300	$2,300
			DM3,326	DM3,326	DM3,326
			£1,502	£1,502	£1,502
			¥232,875	¥232,875	¥232,875
CHANOT, JOSEPH ANTHONY (attributed to)	1	1	$5,375	$5,375	$5,375
			DM7,537	DM7,537	DM7,537
			£3,450	£3,450	£3,450
			¥543,040	¥543,040	¥543,040
CHEVRIER (attributed to)	3	0			
CHEVRIER, ANDRE	1	0			
COCKER, LAWRENCE	5	2	$1,660	$2,922	$2,291
			DM2,311	DM4,108	DM3,210
			£1,035	£1,840	£1,438
			¥140,292	¥259,758	¥200,025
COLLENOT, LOUIS	1	1	$2,471	$2,471	$2,471
			DM3,792	DM3,792	DM3,792
			£1,610	£1,610	£1,610
			¥270,496	¥270,496	¥270,496
COLLIN-MEZIN, CH.J.B.	3	2	$1,291	$5,163	$3,227
			DM1,797	DM7,189	DM4,493
			£805	£3,220	£2,013
			¥109,116	¥436,465	¥272,790

Maker	Items		Selling Prices		
	Bid	Sold	Low	High	Avg
COLLIN-MEZIN, CH.J.B. (attributed to)	1	1	$5,641	$5,641	$5,641
			DM9,317	DM9,317	DM9,317
			£3,450	£3,450	£3,450
			¥698,380	¥698,380	¥698,380
CONIA, STEFANO	5	2	$3,738	$5,762	$4,750
			DM6,765	DM9,626	DM8,195
			£2,280	£3,450	£2,865
			¥451,266	¥700,316	¥575,791
CONTAVALLI, PRIMO	1	1	$3,680	$3,680	$3,680
			DM6,219	DM6,219	DM6,219
			£2,208	£2,208	£2,208
			¥448,960	¥448,960	¥448,960
CONTIN, MARIO	1	1	$6,344	$6,344	$6,344
			DM9,364	DM9,364	DM9,364
			£4,140	£4,140	£4,140
			¥674,410	¥674,410	¥674,410
CONTINO, ALFREDO (workshop of)	1	1	$8,050	$8,050	$8,050
			DM14,571	DM14,571	DM14,571
			£4,911	£4,911	£4,911
			¥971,957	¥971,957	¥971,957
COOPER, HUGH W.	1	1	$2,582	$2,582	$2,582
			DM3,595	DM3,595	DM3,595
			£1,610	£1,610	£1,610
			¥218,232	¥218,232	¥218,232
COPELAND, JOSEPH N.	1	0			
COPLERE, JEAN	1	1	$1,495	$1,495	$1,495
			DM2,527	DM2,527	DM2,527
			£897	£897	£897
			¥182,390	¥182,390	¥182,390
CRASKE, GEORGE	8	7	$2,889	$10,592	$5,933
			DM5,177	DM14,893	DM8,931
			£1,725	£6,670	£3,733
			¥335,513	¥1,020,217	¥600,933
CRASKE, GEORGE (attributed to)	1	1	$4,748	$4,748	$4,748
			DM6,676	DM6,676	DM6,676
			£2,990	£2,990	£2,990
			¥423,773	¥423,773	¥423,773
CROSS, H. CHARLES	2	2	$466	$652	$559
			DM491	DM687	DM589
			£288	£403	£345
			¥35,591	¥49,827	¥42,709
CURLETTO, ANSELMO	1	0			
CURTIN, JOSEPH	1	0			
CUYPERS, JOHANNES	1	1	$17,140	$17,140	$17,140
			DM32,555	DM32,555	DM32,555
			£10,580	£10,580	£10,580
			¥1,800,822	¥1,800,822	¥1,800,822
DA FIESOLE, GIANPIERO	1	1	$4,180	$4,180	$4,180
			DM5,904	DM5,904	DM5,904
			£2,645	£2,645	£2,645
			¥373,043	¥373,043	¥373,043
DA FIESOLE, MINO	1	0			
DARCHE, HILAIRE	2	0			
DEARLOVE, MARK WILLIAM	1	1	$3,651	$3,651	$3,651
			DM5,610	DM5,610	DM5,610
			£2,415	£2,415	£2,415
			¥389,358	¥389,358	¥389,358

Maker	Items		Selling Prices		
	Bid	Sold	Low	High	Avg
DE BARBIERI, PAOLO	1	0			
DE JONG, MATTHIJS	1	0			
DELEPLANQUE, GERARD J.	1	1	$3,479	$3,479	$3,479
			DM5,205	DM5,205	DM5,205
			£2,070	£2,070	£2,070
			¥388,084	¥388,084	¥388,084
DERACHE, PAUL	1	1	$1,257	$1,257	$1,257
			DM2,372	DM2,372	DM2,372
			£778	£778	£778
			¥132,985	¥132,985	¥132,985
DERAZEY, HONORE	1	1	$10,247	$10,247	$10,247
			DM18,406	DM18,406	DM18,406
			£6,325	£6,325	£6,325
			¥1,209,783	¥1,209,783	¥1,209,783
DERAZEY, JUSTIN (workshop of)	1	1	$3,816	$3,816	$3,816
			DM5,391	DM5,391	DM5,391
			£2,415	£2,415	£2,415
			¥340,604	¥340,604	¥340,604
DEROUX, SEBASTIEN AUGUSTE	1	1	$7,728	$7,728	$7,728
			DM13,892	DM13,892	DM13,892
			£4,600	£4,600	£4,600
			¥893,458	¥893,458	¥893,458
DE SOUZA, COSMO	1	0			
DE VITOR, PIETRO PAOLO (attributed to)	1	1	$55,028	$55,028	$55,028
			DM83,042	DM83,042	DM83,042
			£33,350	£33,350	£33,350
			¥6,236,450	¥6,236,450	¥6,236,450
DEVONEY, FRANK	1	1	$2,462	$2,462	$2,462
			DM3,781	DM3,781	DM3,781
			£1,610	£1,610	£1,610
			¥268,769	¥268,769	¥268,769
DICKSON, JOHN (attributed to)	1	1	$4,710	$4,710	$4,710
			DM6,652	DM6,652	DM6,652
			£2,990	£2,990	£2,990
			¥474,313	¥474,313	¥474,313
DIDIER, MARIUS	2	0			
DIEUDONNE, AMEDEE	1	0			
DIGIUNI, LUIGI	4	2	$1,837	$3,769	$2,803
			DM3,089	DM6,679	DM4,884
			£1,150	£2,314	£1,732
			¥225,472	¥459,569	¥342,521
DOBBS, HARRY	2	1	$1,011	$1,011	$1,011
			DM1,415	DM1,415	DM1,415
			£633	£633	£633
			¥85,522	¥85,522	¥85,522
DODD, THOMAS	1	1	$21,379	$21,379	$21,379
			DM37,065	DM37,065	DM37,065
			£12,650	£12,650	£12,650
			¥2,669,150	¥2,669,150	¥2,669,150
DODDS, EDWARD	1	1	$5,499	$5,499	$5,499
			DM8,820	DM8,820	DM8,820
			£3,571	£3,571	£3,571
			¥625,667	¥625,667	¥625,667
DUKE, RICHARD	5	4	$1,944	$3,649	$3,037
			DM3,370	DM6,096	DM4,969
			£1,150	£2,185	£1,869
			¥247,101	¥443,533	¥355,024

Maker	Items Bid	Sold	Selling Prices Low	High	Avg
DVORAK, JAN BAPTISTA	1	0			
EBERLE, EUGENE	1	1	$7,682	$7,682	$7,682
			DM12,834	DM12,834	DM12,834
			£4,600	£4,600	£4,600
			¥933,754	¥933,754	¥933,754
EBERLE, J.U. (ascribed to)	2	0			
EDLER, ERNEST	2	1	$1,380	$1,380	$1,380
			DM2,498	DM2,498	DM2,498
			£842	£842	£842
			¥166,621	¥166,621	¥166,621
EMERY, JULIAN	5	0			
ENEL, CHARLES	1	0			
ERDESZ, OTTO	2	1	$4,713	$4,713	$4,713
			DM8,932	DM8,932	DM8,932
			£2,910	£2,910	£2,910
			¥497,728	¥497,728	¥497,728
ERICIAN, MARTIN	2	1	$3,738	$3,738	$3,738
			DM6,765	DM6,765	DM6,765
			£2,280	£2,280	£2,280
			¥451,266	¥451,266	¥451,266
EVE, J.C.	1	1	$2,336	$2,336	$2,336
			DM4,053	DM4,053	DM4,053
			£1,380	£1,380	£1,380
			¥296,162	¥296,162	¥296,162
FABIANI, ANTONIO (ascribed to)	1	0			
FAGNOLA, ANNIBALE	2	0			
FAGNOLA, ANNIBALE (workshop of)	1	0			
FAIRFAX, ANNELEEN	1	0			
FANTIN, DOMENICO	1	0			
FARLEY, CHARLES E.	1	1	$690	$690	$690
			DM998	DM998	DM998
			£451	£451	£451
			¥69,863	¥69,863	¥69,863
FAROTTI, CELESTE	1	1	$4,225	$4,225	$4,225
			DM7,843	DM7,843	DM7,843
			£2,530	£2,530	£2,530
			¥565,303	¥565,303	¥565,303
FAROTTO, CELESTE	5	4	$4,025	$6,613	$5,353
			DM5,812	DM10,235	DM8,419
			£2,564	£4,350	£3,339
			¥349,169	¥764,635	¥592,832
FENDT, BERNARD SIMON	2	0			
FENDT, BERNARD SIMON JR.	1	1	$13,800	$13,800	$13,800
			DM23,322	DM23,322	DM23,322
			£8,280	£8,280	£8,280
			¥1,683,600	¥1,683,600	¥1,683,600
FERET-MARCOTTE	1	1	$2,422	$2,422	$2,422
			DM4,560	DM4,560	DM4,560
			£1,495	£1,495	£1,495
			¥255,974	¥255,974	¥255,974
FERRONI, FERDINANDO	2	1	$2,645	$2,645	$2,645
			DM4,470	DM4,470	DM4,470
			£1,587	£1,587	£1,587
			¥322,690	¥322,690	¥322,690

Maker	Items Bid	Sold	Selling Prices Low	High	Avg
FICHTL, JOHANN ULRICH	1	1	$1,910 DM3,080 £1,109 ¥224,840	$1,910 DM3,080 £1,109 ¥224,840	$1,910 DM3,080 £1,109 ¥224,840
FIORI BROTHERS (attributed to)	1	0			
FIORINI, RAFFAELE	1	1	$59,606 DM87,988 £38,900 ¥6,336,849	$59,606 DM87,988 £38,900 ¥6,336,849	$59,606 DM87,988 £38,900 ¥6,336,849
FLETA, IGNACIO	1	1	$5,693 DM10,247 £3,450 ¥820,928	$5,693 DM10,247 £3,450 ¥820,928	$5,693 DM10,247 £3,450 ¥820,928
FLEURY, BENOIT	2	1	$15,902 DM23,495 £10,350 ¥1,694,647	$15,902 DM23,495 £10,350 ¥1,694,647	$15,902 DM23,495 £10,350 ¥1,694,647
FLORENTIN, N.	1	1	$1,380 DM2,077 £838 ¥154,256	$1,380 DM2,077 £838 ¥154,256	$1,380 DM2,077 £838 ¥154,256
FONTANA, ALFREDO	1	1	$2,126 DM3,181 £1,265 ¥237,162	$2,126 DM3,181 £1,265 ¥237,162	$2,126 DM3,181 £1,265 ¥237,162
FORSTER	3	1	$4,225 DM7,843 £2,530 ¥565,303	$4,225 DM7,843 £2,530 ¥565,303	$4,225 DM7,843 £2,530 ¥565,303
FORSTER, WILLIAM	4	4	$3,208 DM4,761 £2,070 ¥347,305	$18,453 DM25,688 £11,500 ¥1,556,824	$8,217 DM12,024 £5,118 ¥793,780
FORSTER, WILLIAM (workshop of)	1	1	$3,529 DM5,422 £2,300 ¥386,375	$3,529 DM5,422 £2,300 ¥386,375	$3,529 DM5,422 £2,300 ¥386,375
FORSTER, WILLIAM (II)	6	3	$5,410 DM9,728 £3,220 ¥625,421	$12,650 DM21,379 £7,590 ¥1,543,300	$9,649 DM15,480 £5,903 ¥1,093,970
FOSCHI, GIORGIO	1	0			
FOSCHINI, GIOVANNI	3	1	$3,887 DM6,739 £2,300 ¥494,201	$3,887 DM6,739 £2,300 ¥494,201	$3,887 DM6,739 £2,300 ¥494,201
GABRIELLI, GIOVANNI BATTISTA	1	1	$46,000 DM66,516 £30,047 ¥4,657,500	$46,000 DM66,516 £30,047 ¥4,657,500	$46,000 DM66,516 £30,047 ¥4,657,500
GABRIELLI, GIOVANNI BATTISTA (workshop of)	1	1	$30,360 DM45,816 £18,400 ¥3,440,800	$30,360 DM45,816 £18,400 ¥3,440,800	$30,360 DM45,816 £18,400 ¥3,440,800

Maker	Items		Selling Prices		
	Bid	Sold	Low	High	Avg
GADDA, GAETANO	1	1	$14,539	$14,539	$14,539
			DM20,535	DM20,535	DM20,535
			£9,200	£9,200	£9,200
			¥1,297,540	¥1,297,540	¥1,297,540
GADDA, MARIO	1	1	$7,166	$7,166	$7,166
			DM10,050	DM10,050	DM10,050
			£4,600	£4,600	£4,600
			¥724,054	¥724,054	¥724,054
GAGLIANO, ANTONIO	1	0			
GAGLIANO FAMILY (MEMBER OF)	1	0			
GAILLARD, CHARLES	2	2	$7,284	$16,068	$11,676
			DM13,836	DM30,520	DM22,178
			£4,497	£9,919	£7,208
			¥765,349	¥1,688,270	¥1,226,810
GALIMBERTI, LUIGI	1	0			
GALLA, ANTON	1	1	$4,832	$4,832	$4,832
			DM7,230	DM7,230	DM7,230
			£2,875	£2,875	£2,875
			¥539,005	¥539,005	¥539,005
GAND, GUILLAUME CHARLES LOUIS	1	1	$12,668	$12,668	$12,668
			DM22,756	DM22,756	DM22,756
			£7,820	£7,820	£7,820
			¥1,495,731	¥1,495,731	¥1,495,731
GAND & BERNARDEL	1	1	$18,288	$18,288	$18,288
			DM33,835	DM33,835	DM33,835
			£10,925	£10,925	£10,925
			¥2,437,258	¥2,437,258	¥2,437,258
GAND & BERNARDEL FRERES	2	0			
GARDINI, ATHOS	1	0			
GARIMBERTI, F.	1	0			
GARTNER, EUGEN	1	1	$7,360	$7,360	$7,360
			DM12,451	DM12,451	DM12,451
			£4,629	£4,629	£4,629
			¥911,864	¥911,864	¥911,864
GAVINIES, FRANCOIS	1	1	$13,739	$13,739	$13,739
			DM20,254	DM20,254	DM20,254
			£8,970	£8,970	£8,970
			¥1,465,429	¥1,465,429	¥1,465,429
GEISSENHOF, FRANZ	1	1	$14,719	$14,719	$14,719
			DM24,903	DM24,903	DM24,903
			£9,258	£9,258	£9,258
			¥1,823,728	¥1,823,728	¥1,823,728
GIANOTTI, ALFREDO	2	1	$6,325	$6,325	$6,325
			DM10,822	DM10,822	DM10,822
			£3,741	£3,741	£3,741
			¥785,439	¥785,439	¥785,439
GILBERT, JEFFREY J.	1	1	$2,867	$2,867	$2,867
			DM4,020	DM4,020	DM4,020
			£1,840	£1,840	£1,840
			¥289,622	¥289,622	¥289,622
GILKES, SAMUEL (attributed to)	1	1	$1,363	$1,363	$1,363
			DM2,364	DM2,364	DM2,364
			£805	£805	£805
			¥172,761	¥172,761	¥172,761
GIULIANI, R.G.	1	0			

Maker	Items		Selling Prices		
	Bid	Sold	Low	High	Avg
GLOOR, ADOLF	2	1	$860	$860	$860
			DM1,499	DM1,499	DM1,499
			£529	£529	£529
			¥104,134	¥104,134	¥104,134
GOFFRILLER, MATTEO (ascribed to)	1	1	$54,855	$54,855	$54,855
			DM103,155	DM103,155	DM103,155
			£34,500	£34,500	£34,500
			¥6,632,280	¥6,632,280	¥6,632,280
GOFTON, ROBERT	1	0			
GORRIE, ANDREW	1	1	$951	$951	$951
			DM1,350	DM1,350	DM1,350
			£598	£598	£598
			¥88,295	¥88,295	¥88,295
GOTTI, ANSELMO	1	1	$4,543	$4,543	$4,543
			DM6,417	DM6,417	DM6,417
			£2,875	£2,875	£2,875
			¥405,481	¥405,481	¥405,481
GOTZ, CONRAD	3	2	$658	$848	$753
			DM935	DM1,519	DM1,227
			£414	£506	£460
			¥61,127	¥98,417	¥79,772
GOULDING	2	0			
GOUVERNEL, PIERRE	2	1	$2,643	$2,643	$2,643
			DM3,902	DM3,902	DM3,902
			£1,725	£1,725	£1,725
			¥281,004	¥281,004	¥281,004
GRABNER, KARL HEINZ JOACHIM	1	1	$575	$575	$575
			DM831	DM831	DM831
			£376	£376	£376
			¥58,219	¥58,219	¥58,219
GRANDJON, JULES (FILS)	1	1	$4,383	$4,383	$4,383
			DM6,163	DM6,163	DM6,163
			£2,760	£2,760	£2,760
			¥389,637	¥389,637	¥389,637
GUADAGNINI, GIUSEPPE (ascribed to)	1	0			
GUASTALLA, DANTE (attributed to)	2	0			
GUERRA, ALBERTO	1	1	$6,762	$6,762	$6,762
			DM12,160	DM12,160	DM12,160
			£4,025	£4,025	£4,025
			¥781,776	¥781,776	¥781,776
GUERRA, ALBERTO (ascribed to)	3	2	$1,495	$1,495	$1,495
			DM2,606	DM2,606	DM2,606
			£920	£920	£920
			¥181,102	¥181,102	¥181,102
GUERSAN, LOUIS	1	1	$17,265	$17,265	$17,265
			DM24,386	DM24,386	DM24,386
			£10,925	£10,925	£10,925
			¥1,540,829	¥1,540,829	¥1,540,829
GUICCIARDI, GIANCARLO	1	1	$12,681	$12,681	$12,681
			DM17,910	DM17,910	DM17,910
			£8,050	£8,050	£8,050
			¥1,276,996	¥1,276,996	¥1,276,996
HAAHTI, NICOLIEN	2	1	$3,887	$3,887	$3,887
			DM5,743	DM5,743	DM5,743
			£2,530	£2,530	£2,530
			¥414,247	¥414,247	¥414,247

Maker	Items		Selling Prices		
	Bid	Sold	Low	High	Avg
HALLETT, L.C.	1	1	$863	$863	$863
			DM1,539	DM1,539	DM1,539
			£529	£529	£529
			¥113,010	¥113,010	¥113,010
HALLIDAY, R.L.	1	1	$1,091	$1,091	$1,091
			DM1,674	DM1,674	DM1,674
			£713	£713	£713
			¥119,026	¥119,026	¥119,026
HAMMOND, JOHN	1	0			
HARDIE, THOMAS	1	0			
HARRILD, PAUL V.	5	1	$1,478	$1,478	$1,478
			DM2,271	DM2,271	DM2,271
			£978	£978	£978
			¥157,597	¥157,597	¥157,597
HARRIS, CHARLES	5	3	$2,795	$4,225	$3,571
			DM5,020	DM7,059	DM6,160
			£1,725	£2,530	£2,147
			¥329,941	¥513,565	¥437,665
HARRIS, RICHARD	3	1	$5,216	$5,216	$5,216
			DM9,821	DM9,821	DM9,821
			£3,220	£3,220	£3,220
			¥551,328	¥551,328	¥551,328
HAWKES & SON	1	1	$2,950	$2,950	$2,950
			DM4,108	DM4,108	DM4,108
			£1,840	£1,840	£1,840
			¥249,408	¥249,408	¥249,408
HEBERLEIN	1	1	$2,875	$2,875	$2,875
			DM4,327	DM4,327	DM4,327
			£1,745	£1,745	£1,745
			¥321,368	¥321,368	¥321,368
HEBERLEIN, HEINRICH TH. (JR.)	1	1	$2,881	$2,881	$2,881
			DM4,813	DM4,813	DM4,813
			£1,725	£1,725	£1,725
			¥350,158	¥350,158	¥350,158
HEL, JOSEPH	1	0			
HESKETH, THOMAS EARLE	2	1	$10,060	$10,060	$10,060
			DM14,278	DM14,278	DM14,278
			£6,325	£6,325	£6,325
			¥933,886	¥933,886	¥933,886
HIGHFIELD	1	0			
HIGHFIELD, IAN	1	1	$1,892	$1,892	$1,892
			DM3,202	DM3,202	DM3,202
			£1,190	£1,190	£1,190
			¥234,479	¥234,479	¥234,479
HILL, JOSEPH	10	5	$5,036	$23,101	$11,539
			DM7,124	DM42,739	DM20,225
			£3,220	£13,800	£6,946
			¥511,365	¥3,078,642	¥1,461,385
HILL, JOSEPH (attributed to)	3	1	$16,373	$16,373	$16,373
			DM29,335	DM29,335	DM29,335
			£9,775	£9,775	£9,775
			¥1,901,238	¥1,901,238	¥1,901,238
HILL, JOSEPH & SONS	1	1	$3,887	$3,887	$3,887
			DM5,743	DM5,743	DM5,743
			£2,530	£2,530	£2,530
			¥414,247	¥414,247	¥414,247

Viola

Maker	Items		Selling Prices		
	Bid	Sold	Low	High	Avg
HILL, LOCKEY	1	1	$3,850	$3,850	$3,850
			DM7,123	DM7,123	DM7,123
			£2,300	£2,300	£2,300
			¥513,107	¥513,107	¥513,107
HILL, W.E. & SONS	4	0			
HILL, WILLIAM	1	1	$6,574	$6,574	$6,574
			DM9,244	DM9,244	DM9,244
			£4,140	£4,140	£4,140
			¥586,762	¥586,762	¥586,762
HOFMANN, MAX	1	1	$2,795	$2,795	$2,795
			DM5,020	DM5,020	DM5,020
			£1,725	£1,725	£1,725
			¥329,941	¥329,941	¥329,941
HOFNER, KARL	2	1	$144	$144	$144
			DM260	DM260	DM260
			£88	£88	£88
			¥17,356	¥17,356	¥17,356
HOING, CLIFFORD A.	2	1	$5,081	$5,081	$5,081
			DM7,155	DM7,155	DM7,155
			£3,220	£3,220	£3,220
			¥519,489	¥519,489	¥519,489
HOLLY, FLOYD	1	1	$895	$895	$895
			DM1,265	DM1,265	DM1,265
			£562	£562	£562
			¥79,443	¥79,443	¥79,443
HOLT, ROBERT	1	1	$230	$230	$230
			DM333	DM333	DM333
			£150	£150	£150
			¥23,288	¥23,288	¥23,288
HOMOLKA, FERDINAND AUGUST	1	1	$4,754	$4,754	$4,754
			DM8,940	DM8,940	DM8,940
			£2,990	£2,990	£2,990
			¥574,798	¥574,798	¥574,798
HORLEIN, KARL ADAM	1	0			
HOWE, ROBERT	1	1	$963	$963	$963
			DM1,781	DM1,781	DM1,781
			£575	£575	£575
			¥128,277	¥128,277	¥128,277
HUBER, JOHANN GEORG	1	1	$9,373	$9,373	$9,373
			DM16,215	DM16,215	DM16,215
			£5,750	£5,750	£5,750
			¥1,069,500	¥1,069,500	¥1,069,500
HUSSON	1	0			
HUSSON FAMILY (MEMBER OF)	1	1	$8,642	$8,642	$8,642
			DM14,438	DM14,438	DM14,438
			£5,175	£5,175	£5,175
			¥1,050,473	¥1,050,473	¥1,050,473
JACQUOT, CHARLES	2	0			
JACQUOT, CHARLES (attributed to)	2	1	$5,435	$5,435	$5,435
			DM7,676	DM7,676	DM7,676
			£3,450	£3,450	£3,450
			¥547,284	¥547,284	¥547,284
JAIS, ANTON	2	1	$1,610	$1,610	$1,610
			DM2,924	DM2,924	DM2,924
			£985	£985	£985
			¥199,930	¥199,930	¥199,930
JAIS, JOHANN	1	0			

Maker	Items Bid	Sold	Selling Prices Low	High	Avg
JAURA, WILHELM THOMAS	1	0			
JOHNSON, MOIRA	1	1	$1,134	$1,134	$1,134
			DM1,610	DM1,610	DM1,610
			£713	£713	£713
			¥105,274	¥105,274	¥105,274
JOHNSON, W.A.	1	1	$1,342	$1,342	$1,342
			DM2,052	DM2,052	DM2,052
			£863	£863	£863
			¥132,639	¥132,639	¥132,639
JOMBAR, PAUL	1	0			
JUZEK, JOHN (workshop of)	1	1	$920	$920	$920
			DM1,330	DM1,330	DM1,330
			£601	£601	£601
			¥93,150	¥93,150	¥93,150
KAUL, PAUL	1	1	$6,914	$6,914	$6,914
			DM12,834	DM12,834	DM12,834
			£4,140	£4,140	£4,140
			¥925,042	¥925,042	¥925,042
KENNEDY, T. (attributed to)	1	1	$2,342	$2,342	$2,342
			DM4,393	DM4,393	DM4,393
			£1,455	£1,455	£1,455
			¥281,523	¥281,523	¥281,523
KENNEDY, THOMAS	1	0			
KENNEDY, THOMAS (attributed to)	1	1	$3,887	$3,887	$3,887
			DM5,743	DM5,743	DM5,743
			£2,530	£2,530	£2,530
			¥414,247	¥414,247	¥414,247
KLOTZ, AEGIDIUS (I)	1	1	$5,290	$5,290	$5,290
			DM9,985	DM9,985	DM9,985
			£3,275	£3,275	£3,275
			¥559,682	¥559,682	¥559,682
KLOTZ, AEGIDIUS (II)	2	2	$4,801	$5,589	$5,195
			DM8,021	DM10,523	DM9,272
			£2,875	£3,450	£3,163
			¥583,596	¥590,709	¥587,153
KLOTZ, JOSEPH (attributed to)	2	1	$4,609	$4,609	$4,609
			DM7,700	DM7,700	DM7,700
			£2,760	£2,760	£2,760
			¥560,252	¥560,252	¥560,252
KLOTZ FAMILY (MEMBER OF)	1	0			
KOBERLING, JOHANN	1	0			
KONYA, LAJOS	2	1	$978	$978	$978
			DM1,673	DM1,673	DM1,673
			£578	£578	£578
			¥121,386	¥121,386	¥121,386
KRAUSS, KARL	1	1	$684	$684	$684
			DM1,045	DM1,045	DM1,045
			£437	£437	£437
			¥76,278	¥76,278	¥76,278
KUCZER, JOHN T.	1	1	$2,185	$2,185	$2,185
			DM3,155	DM3,155	DM3,155
			£1,392	£1,392	£1,392
			¥189,549	¥189,549	¥189,549
KUDANOWSKI, JAN	2	1	$2,744	$2,744	$2,744
			DM3,894	DM3,894	DM3,894
			£1,725	£1,725	£1,725
			¥254,696	¥254,696	¥254,696

Maker	Items		Selling Prices		
	Bid	Sold	Low	High	Avg
KUSTER, FREDERICK	1	1	$920	$920	$920
			DM1,574	DM1,574	DM1,574
			£544	£544	£544
			¥114,246	¥114,246	¥114,246
LABERTE, MARC	5	3	$489	$6,958	$2,712
			DM870	DM10,411	DM4,170
			£298	£4,140	£1,617
			¥67,897	¥776,167	¥311,940
LABERTE, MARC (workshop of)	1	1	$1,725	$1,725	$1,725
			DM2,596	DM2,596	DM2,596
			£1,047	£1,047	£1,047
			¥192,821	¥192,821	¥192,821
LABERTE-HUMBERT BROS.	2	1	$3,707	$3,707	$3,707
			DM5,689	DM5,689	DM5,689
			£2,415	£2,415	£2,415
			¥405,744	¥405,744	¥405,744
LABRAM, LEONARD	1	1	$1,502	$1,502	$1,502
			DM2,692	DM2,692	DM2,692
			£897	£897	£897
			¥174,467	¥174,467	¥174,467
LAMBERTON, JAMES	1	0			
LANARO, ALOISIUS	2	0			
LANARO, UMBERTO	6	2	$3,850	$4,355	$4,103
			DM6,133	DM7,123	DM6,628
			£2,300	£2,760	£2,530
			¥445,276	¥513,107	¥479,192
LANDOLFI, CARLO FERDINANDO	1	1	$131,541	$131,541	$131,541
			DM233,223	DM233,223	DM233,223
			£80,700	£80,700	£80,700
			¥15,553,311	¥15,553,311	¥15,553,311
LANGONET, ALFRED CHARLES	3	0			
LANT, ERNEST FRANCIS	2	1	$1,118	$1,118	$1,118
			DM1,178	DM1,178	DM1,178
			£690	£690	£690
			¥85,419	¥85,419	¥85,419
LANTNER, FERDINAND	1	1	$4,928	$4,928	$4,928
			DM9,359	DM9,359	DM9,359
			£3,042	£3,042	£3,042
			¥517,736	¥517,736	¥517,736
LASSI, ENZO (attributed to)	2	1	$3,386	$3,386	$3,386
			DM5,025	DM5,025	DM5,025
			£2,185	£2,185	£2,185
			¥366,599	¥366,599	¥366,599
LAURENT, EMILE	2	0			
LECLERC, JOSEPH NICOLAS	1	1	$10,592	$10,592	$10,592
			DM16,253	DM16,253	DM16,253
			£6,900	£6,900	£6,900
			¥1,159,269	¥1,159,269	¥1,159,269
LEE, PERCY	2	1	$5,654	$5,654	$5,654
			DM8,354	DM8,354	DM8,354
			£3,680	£3,680	£3,680
			¥602,541	¥602,541	¥602,541
LEONI, GUIDO	3	1	$1,490	$1,490	$1,490
			DM2,677	DM2,677	DM2,677
			£920	£920	£920
			¥175,968	¥175,968	¥175,968

	Items		Selling Prices		
Maker	Bid	Sold	Low	High	Avg

Maker	Bid	Sold	Low	High	Avg
LODGE, JOHN	1	1	$576 DM963 £345 ¥70,032	$576 DM963 £345 ¥70,032	$576 DM963 £345 ¥70,032
LONGMAN & BRODERIP	1	1	$2,037 DM3,267 £1,323 ¥231,728	$2,037 DM3,267 £1,323 ¥231,728	$2,037 DM3,267 £1,323 ¥231,728
LOVERI BROTHERS	1	1	$3,968 DM7,489 £2,456 ¥419,762	$3,968 DM7,489 £2,456 ¥419,762	$3,968 DM7,489 £2,456 ¥419,762
LOWENDALL	1	1	$1,427 DM2,025 £897 ¥132,442	$1,427 DM2,025 £897 ¥132,442	$1,427 DM2,025 £897 ¥132,442
LUCA, IOAN	1	1	$963 DM1,726 £575 ¥111,838	$963 DM1,726 £575 ¥111,838	$963 DM1,726 £575 ¥111,838
LUCCI, GIUSEPPE	4	1	$8,698 DM13,014 £5,175 ¥970,209	$8,698 DM13,014 £5,175 ¥970,209	$8,698 DM13,014 £5,175 ¥970,209
LUFF, WILLIAM H.	1	0			
LYE, HENRY	1	0			
MAAG, HENRY	2	1	$219 DM389 £133 ¥30,354	$219 DM389 £133 ¥30,354	$219 DM389 £133 ¥30,354
MACHOLD, OSKAR	1	1	$1,236 DM1,896 £805 ¥135,248	$1,236 DM1,896 £805 ¥135,248	$1,236 DM1,896 £805 ¥135,248
MAGNIERE, GABRIEL	1	1	$3,870 DM6,206 £2,513 ¥440,284	$3,870 DM6,206 £2,513 ¥440,284	$3,870 DM6,206 £2,513 ¥440,284
MANGIACASALE, SALVATORE	1	0			
MANTEGAZZA, PIETRO GIOVANNI	1	1	$85,170 DM158,100 £51,000 ¥11,395,440	$85,170 DM158,100 £51,000 ¥11,395,440	$85,170 DM158,100 £51,000 ¥11,395,440
MARAVIGLIA, FRANCESCO	1	1	$4,943 DM7,585 £3,220 ¥540,992	$4,943 DM7,585 £3,220 ¥540,992	$4,943 DM7,585 £3,220 ¥540,992
MARAVIGLIA, GUIDO	3	1	$2,422 DM4,560 £1,495 ¥255,974	$2,422 DM4,560 £1,495 ¥255,974	$2,422 DM4,560 £1,495 ¥255,974
MARCHETTI, ABBONDIO (attributed to)	1	0			
MARCHETTI, ENRICO	1	1	$21,379 DM37,065 £12,650 ¥2,669,150	$21,379 DM37,065 £12,650 ¥2,669,150	$21,379 DM37,065 £12,650 ¥2,669,150

| Maker | Items | | Selling Prices | | |
	Bid	Sold	Low	High	Avg
MARTINI, ORESTE	1	1	$4,252	$4,252	$4,252
			DM6,362	DM6,362	DM6,362
			£2,530	£2,530	£2,530
			¥474,324	¥474,324	¥474,324
MASTERS, JOHN	1	1	$1,725	$1,725	$1,725
			DM2,951	DM2,951	DM2,951
			£1,020	£1,020	£1,020
			¥214,211	¥214,211	¥214,211
MATTER, ANITA	1	1	$1,863	$1,863	$1,863
			DM3,508	DM3,508	DM3,508
			£1,150	£1,150	£1,150
			¥198,605	¥198,605	¥198,605
MAUCOTEL & DESCHAMPS	1	0			
MAUSSIELL, LEONHARD	1	0			
MELLONI, SETTIMO	2	1	$2,990	$2,990	$2,990
			DM5,412	DM5,412	DM5,412
			£1,824	£1,824	£1,824
			¥361,013	¥361,013	¥361,013
MENNESSON, EMILE	1	0			
MERRETT, H.W.	1	1	$542	$542	$542
			DM766	DM766	DM766
			£345	£345	£345
			¥46,258	¥46,258	¥46,258
MEYER, MAGNUS ANDREAS	1	1	$3,995	$3,995	$3,995
			DM6,759	DM6,759	DM6,759
			£2,513	£2,513	£2,513
			¥495,012	¥495,012	¥495,012
MILLOSLAVSKI, JOSEPH	2	0			
MILNES, JOHN	1	0			
MINO DA FIESOLE	1	0			
MOCHALOV, ALEXANDER	1	1	$3,266	$3,266	$3,266
			DM4,600	DM4,600	DM4,600
			£2,070	£2,070	£2,070
			¥333,957	¥333,957	¥333,957
MOLLER, MAX (II)	1	1	$12,721	$12,721	$12,721
			DM17,968	DM17,968	DM17,968
			£8,050	£8,050	£8,050
			¥1,135,348	¥1,135,348	¥1,135,348
MONK, JOHN KING	1	0			
MONNIG, KURT	1	1	$4,658	$4,658	$4,658
			DM6,532	DM6,532	DM6,532
			£2,990	£2,990	£2,990
			¥470,635	¥470,635	¥470,635
MORASSI, GIOVANNI BATTISTA	1	0			
MORETTI, EGIDO	1	0			
MORIZOT, RENE	1	1	$1,212	$1,212	$1,212
			DM2,101	DM2,101	DM2,101
			£717	£717	£717
			¥151,287	¥151,287	¥151,287
MOUGENOT, LEON (workshop of)	1	1	$1,725	$1,725	$1,725
			DM3,071	DM3,071	DM3,071
			£1,035	£1,035	£1,035
			¥229,390	¥229,390	¥229,390
MOZZANI, LUIGI	1	1	$7,079	$7,079	$7,079
			DM12,717	DM12,717	DM12,717
			£4,370	£4,370	£4,370
			¥835,850	¥835,850	¥835,850

| Maker | Items | | Selling Prices | | |
	Bid	Sold	Low	High	Avg
MUELLER, KARL	1	1	$345	$345	$345
			DM596	DM596	DM596
			£213	£213	£213
			¥43,724	¥43,724	¥43,724
NEBEL, MARTIN	2	1	$1,587	$1,587	$1,587
			DM2,995	DM2,995	DM2,995
			£982	£982	£982
			¥167,905	¥167,905	¥167,905
NEEDHAM, HOWARD	1	1	$2,070	$2,070	$2,070
			DM2,993	DM2,993	DM2,993
			£1,352	£1,352	£1,352
			¥209,588	¥209,588	¥209,588
NEUNER, LUDWIG	1	0			
NEUNER & HORNSTEINER	6	5	$1,265	$4,626	$2,646
			DM1,829	DM7,827	DM4,513
			£826	£2,910	£1,617
			¥128,081	¥573,172	¥319,801
NEUNER & HORNSTEINER (workshop of)	2	2	$633	$1,610	$1,121
			DM952	DM2,866	DM1,909
			£384	£966	£675
			¥70,701	¥214,098	¥142,399
NIGGEL, SYMPERT	1	1	$4,428	$4,428	$4,428
			DM8,192	DM8,192	DM8,192
			£2,645	£2,645	£2,645
			¥590,073	¥590,073	¥590,073
NIX, CHARLES WILLIAM	1	0			
NOLLI, FRANCO	2	1	$1,500	$1,500	$1,500
			DM2,301	DM2,301	DM2,301
			£977	£977	£977
			¥164,146	¥164,146	¥164,146
NOWAK, STEFFEN	1	1	$3,688	$3,688	$3,688
			DM5,135	DM5,135	DM5,135
			£2,300	£2,300	£2,300
			¥311,760	¥311,760	¥311,760
NUPIERI, GIUSEPPE	7	5	$1,030	$1,629	$1,287
			DM1,782	DM2,783	DM2,209
			£621	£1,058	£799
			¥117,552	¥204,043	¥154,771
NURNBERGER, WILHELM	1	1	$1,062	$1,062	$1,062
			DM1,909	DM1,909	DM1,909
			£632	£632	£632
			¥122,753	¥122,753	¥122,753
NUTI, CANO	2	1	$2,118	$2,118	$2,118
			DM3,251	DM3,251	DM3,251
			£1,380	£1,380	£1,380
			¥231,854	¥231,854	¥231,854
ODOARDI, GIUSEPPE	2	1	$3,618	$3,618	$3,618
			DM6,411	DM6,411	DM6,411
			£2,222	£2,222	£2,222
			¥441,186	¥441,186	¥441,186
ODOARDI, GIUSEPPE (ascribed to)	1	1	$17,285	$17,285	$17,285
			DM28,877	DM28,877	DM28,877
			£10,350	£10,350	£10,350
			¥2,100,947	¥2,100,947	¥2,100,947
ODOARDI, GIUSEPPE (attributed to)	1	0			

Maker	Items		Selling Prices		
	Bid	Sold	Low	High	Avg
ORNATI, GIUSEPPE	2	2	$24,705	$40,227	$32,466
			DM37,956	DM76,153	DM57,054
			£16,100	£25,300	£20,700
			¥2,704,623	¥4,821,927	¥3,763,275
ORZELLI, JOSEPH	1	0			
PADDAY, A.L.	1	0			
PADEWET, CARL	1	1	$1,273	$1,273	$1,273
			DM1,873	DM1,873	DM1,873
			£828	£828	£828
			¥135,096	¥135,096	¥135,096
PALLOTTA, PIETRO	1	1	$50,164	$50,164	$50,164
			DM70,347	DM70,347	DM70,347
			£32,200	£32,200	£32,200
			¥5,068,377	¥5,068,377	¥5,068,377
PALMER	1	0			
PANORMO, VINCENZO	1	0			
PANORMO, VINCENZO (attributed to)	2	1	$21,379	$21,379	$21,379
			DM37,065	DM37,065	DM37,065
			£12,650	£12,650	£12,650
			¥2,718,106	¥2,718,106	¥2,718,106
PARESCHI, GAETANO	1	0			
PAUL, ADAM D.	1	0			
PEAT, RICHARD	1	1	$782	$782	$782
			DM1,202	DM1,202	DM1,202
			£518	£518	£518
			¥83,434	¥83,434	¥83,434
PERRIN, E.J. (FILS)	1	1	$2,899	$2,899	$2,899
			DM4,094	DM4,094	DM4,094
			£1,840	£1,840	£1,840
			¥291,885	¥291,885	¥291,885
PERRY, L.A.	1	1	$880	$880	$880
			DM1,433	DM1,433	DM1,433
			£518	£518	£518
			¥103,541	¥103,541	¥103,541
PERRY, THOMAS	1	1	$6,900	$6,900	$6,900
			DM11,806	DM11,806	DM11,806
			£4,081	£4,081	£4,081
			¥856,842	¥856,842	¥856,842
PETERNELLA, JAGO	1	0			
PEVERE, ERNESTO (ascribed to)	1	1	$3,575	$3,575	$3,575
			DM6,048	DM6,048	DM6,048
			£2,248	£2,248	£2,248
			¥442,905	¥442,905	¥442,905
PFRETZSCHNER, CARL FRIEDRICH	1	1	$7,452	$7,452	$7,452
			DM13,340	DM13,340	DM13,340
			£4,600	£4,600	£4,600
			¥878,922	¥878,922	¥878,922
PFRETZSCHNER, E.R. (workshop of)	1	1	$374	$374	$374
			DM639	DM639	DM639
			£221	£221	£221
			¥46,412	¥46,412	¥46,412
PICCAGLIANI, ARMANDO	2	0			
PICKERING, NORMAN	1	1	$805	$805	$805
			DM1,360	DM1,360	DM1,360
			£483	£483	£483
			¥98,210	¥98,210	¥98,210

| Maker | Items | | Selling Prices | | |
	Bid	Sold	Low	High	Avg
PILLEMENT, FRANCOIS	1	0			
PINEIRO, HORACIO	1	1	$4,715	$4,715	$4,715
			DM8,534	DM8,534	DM8,534
			£2,876	£2,876	£2,876
			¥569,289	¥569,289	¥569,289
PIZZOLINI, MARIO	2	0			
PLOWRIGHT, DENIS G.	2	1	$895	$895	$895
			DM943	DM943	DM943
			£552	£552	£552
			¥68,335	¥68,335	¥68,335
PROCAK, MYRON	1	0			
PUSKAS, JOSEPH	1	0			
QUENOIL, CHARLES	1	1	$3,738	$3,738	$3,738
			DM6,395	DM6,395	DM6,395
			£2,211	£2,211	£2,211
			¥464,123	¥464,123	¥464,123
RACZ, LORAND	2	1	$3,726	$3,726	$3,726
			DM7,015	DM7,015	DM7,015
			£2,300	£2,300	£2,300
			¥397,210	¥397,210	¥397,210
RADIGHIERI, OTELLO	1	0			
RAYMOND, ROBERT JOHN	2	2	$642	$1,460	$1,051
			DM952	DM2,730	DM1,841
			£414	£920	£667
			¥69,461	¥172,785	¥121,123
REITER, JOHANN	1	1	$1,845	$1,845	$1,845
			DM2,569	DM2,569	DM2,569
			£1,150	£1,150	£1,150
			¥155,682	¥155,682	¥155,682
REMY, JEAN MATHURIN	1	1	$1,817	$1,817	$1,817
			DM2,567	DM2,567	DM2,567
			£1,150	£1,150	£1,150
			¥162,193	¥162,193	¥162,193
RENOUX, F.	1	0			
RICHARDSON, ARTHUR	4	1	$2,237	$2,237	$2,237
			DM2,356	DM2,356	DM2,356
			£1,380	£1,380	£1,380
			¥170,837	¥170,837	¥170,837
RINALDI, GIOFREDO BENEDETTO (ascribed to)	4	0			
RINALDI, MARENGO ROMANUS (ascribed to)	1	1	$17,250	$17,250	$17,250
			DM24,909	DM24,909	DM24,909
			£10,990	£10,990	£10,990
			¥1,496,438	¥1,496,438	¥1,496,438
RITTER, HERMANN	1	1	$460	$460	$460
			DM819	DM819	DM819
			£276	£276	£276
			¥61,171	¥61,171	¥61,171
ROBINSON, WILLIAM	5	4	$2,820	$4,225	$3,576
			DM4,658	DM7,076	DM5,918
			£1,725	£2,530	£2,185
			¥347,737	¥513,565	¥430,014
ROCCHI, S.	1	0			
RODENBERG, KOR	1	0			
RONIG, ADOLF	1	0			

Maker	Items		Selling Prices		
	Bid	Sold	Low	High	Avg
ROSADONI, GIOVANNI	2	1	$2,319	$2,319	$2,319
			DM3,470	DM3,470	DM3,470
			£1,380	£1,380	£1,380
			¥258,722	¥258,722	¥258,722
ROSSI, GIUSEPPE	2	1	$6,765	$6,765	$6,765
			DM10,122	DM10,122	DM10,122
			£4,025	£4,025	£4,025
			¥754,607	¥754,607	¥754,607
ROSSI, STELIO	2	2	$5,444	$5,819	$5,631
			DM7,666	DM10,983	DM9,325
			£3,450	£3,602	£3,526
			¥556,595	¥615,650	¥586,123
ROST, FRANZ GEORG	1	0			
ROTH, ERNST HEINRICH	5	3	$681	$1,119	$914
			DM1,278	DM1,582	DM1,405
			£423	£713	£582
			¥81,898	¥95,600	¥91,010
ROTH, ERNST HEINRICH (workshop of)	2	2	$920	$1,323	$1,121
			DM1,574	DM2,496	DM2,035
			£544	£819	£681
			¥114,246	¥139,921	¥127,083
RUDDIMAN, JOSEPH	1	1	$2,178	$2,178	$2,178
			DM3,066	DM3,066	DM3,066
			£1,380	£1,380	£1,380
			¥222,638	¥222,638	¥222,638
RUPING, HENRY	2	1	$403	$403	$403
			DM615	DM615	DM615
			£265	£265	£265
			¥42,424	¥42,424	¥42,424
RUTH, BENJAMIN WARREN	1	1	$2,300	$2,300	$2,300
			DM3,935	DM3,935	DM3,935
			£1,360	£1,360	£1,360
			¥285,614	¥285,614	¥285,614
SALF	1	0			
SANAVIA, LEONE	1	1	$7,605	$7,605	$7,605
			DM14,354	DM14,354	DM14,354
			£4,707	£4,707	£4,707
			¥804,604	¥804,604	¥804,604
SANDERSON, DERICK	2	1	$1,153	$1,153	$1,153
			DM1,787	DM1,787	DM1,787
			£690	£690	£690
			¥131,314	¥131,314	¥131,314
SAUNDERS, WILFRED G.	1	1	$3,266	$3,266	$3,266
			DM4,600	DM4,600	DM4,600
			£2,070	£2,070	£2,070
			¥333,957	¥333,957	¥333,957
SCARAMPELLA, STEFANO	1	1	$78,857	$78,857	$78,857
			DM111,382	DM111,382	DM111,382
			£49,900	£49,900	£49,900
			¥7,037,746	¥7,037,746	¥7,037,746
SCARAMPELLA, STEFANO (attributed to)	3	1	$1,075	$1,075	$1,075
			DM1,519	DM1,519	DM1,519
			£675	£675	£675
			¥95,416	¥95,416	¥95,416
SCHLOSSER, HERMANN	1	1	$754	$754	$754
			DM1,371	DM1,371	DM1,371
			£460	£460	£460
			¥91,075	¥91,075	¥91,075

| Maker | Items | | Selling Prices | | |
---	Bid	Sold	Low	High	Avg
SCHMITT, LUCIEN	1	1	$5,775	$5,775	$5,775
			DM10,685	DM10,685	DM10,685
			£3,450	£3,450	£3,450
			¥769,661	¥769,661	¥769,661
SCOLARI, GIORGIO	3	2	$6,530	$7,128	$6,829
			DM10,713	DM10,909	DM10,811
			£3,910	£4,255	£4,083
			¥793,691	¥793,817	¥793,754
SDERCI, IGINO	4	2	$6,900	$8,777	$7,838
			DM9,977	DM16,615	DM13,296
			£4,507	£5,520	£5,014
			¥698,625	¥1,052,057	¥875,341
SEGAMIGLIA, GIUSTINO	1	0			
SERDET, PAUL	1	1	$19,205	$19,205	$19,205
			DM35,650	DM35,650	DM35,650
			£11,500	£11,500	£11,500
			¥2,569,560	¥2,569,560	¥2,569,560
SGARABOTTO, GAETANO	1	1	$25,180	$25,180	$25,180
			DM35,618	DM35,618	DM35,618
			£16,100	£16,100	£16,100
			¥2,556,825	¥2,556,825	¥2,556,825
SGARBI, GIUSEPPE	1	0			
SICCARDI, SERGIO	1	0			
SIMONAZZI, AMADEO	6	1	$4,099	$4,099	$4,099
			DM7,717	DM7,717	DM7,717
			£2,530	£2,530	£2,530
			¥436,931	¥436,931	¥436,931
SIRLETO	1	0			
SIRLETO BROTHERS	1	1	$4,600	$4,600	$4,600
			DM8,326	DM8,326	DM8,326
			£2,806	£2,806	£2,806
			¥555,404	¥555,404	¥555,404
SMITH, ARTHUR E.	1	1	$16,740	$16,740	$16,740
			DM24,711	DM24,711	DM24,711
			£10,925	£10,925	£10,925
			¥1,779,693	¥1,779,693	¥1,779,693
SMITH, BERT	1	1	$3,353	$3,353	$3,353
			DM6,024	DM6,024	DM6,024
			£2,070	£2,070	£2,070
			¥395,929	¥395,929	¥395,929
SMITH, THOMAS	1	0			
SMITH, THOMAS (attributed to)	1	0			
SOFFRITTI, ETTORE	1	1	$14,904	$14,904	$14,904
			DM28,060	DM28,060	DM28,060
			£9,200	£9,200	£9,200
			¥1,575,224	¥1,575,224	¥1,575,224
SOLOMON, GIMPEL	1	1	$1,892	$1,892	$1,892
			DM3,202	DM3,202	DM3,202
			£1,190	£1,190	£1,190
			¥234,479	¥234,479	¥234,479
SOMNY, JOSEPH MAURICE	1	1	$2,796	$2,796	$2,796
			DM4,896	DM4,896	DM4,896
			£1,725	£1,725	£1,725
			¥338,014	¥338,014	¥338,014

Maker	Items		Selling Prices		
	Bid	Sold	Low	High	Avg
SONZOGNI, UMBERTO	1	1	$2,300	$2,300	$2,300
			DM3,517	DM3,517	DM3,517
			£1,513	£1,513	£1,513
			¥242,420	¥242,420	¥242,420
STADLMANN, MICHAEL IGNAZ	2	0			
STAINER, JACOB	1	1	$67,106	$67,106	$67,106
			DM113,531	DM113,531	DM113,531
			£42,205	£42,205	£42,205
			¥8,314,385	¥8,314,385	¥8,314,385
STEFANINI, GIUSEPPE	1	0			
STEFANINI, GIUSEPPE (attributed to)	1	0			
STELZNER, DR. ALFRED	1	1	$2,875	$2,875	$2,875
			DM4,157	DM4,157	DM4,157
			£1,878	£1,878	£1,878
			¥291,094	¥291,094	¥291,094
STORIONI, CARLO	2	1	$1,933	$1,933	$1,933
			DM3,372	DM3,372	DM3,372
			£1,150	£1,150	£1,150
			¥246,514	¥246,514	¥246,514
STORIONI, LORENZO	2	1	$70,073	$70,073	$70,073
			DM97,569	DM97,569	DM97,569
			£43,700	£43,700	£43,700
			¥5,923,448	¥5,923,448	¥5,923,448
STYLES, HAROLD LEICESTER	3	2	$487	$1,237	$862
			DM852	DM1,827	DM1,340
			£299	£805	£552
			¥57,572	¥131,806	¥94,689
TAYLERSON, PETE	2	0			
TAYLOR, ERIC	3	1	$1,126	$1,126	$1,126
			DM2,008	DM2,008	DM2,008
			£690	£690	£690
			¥147,405	¥147,405	¥147,405
THIBOUVILLE-LAMY, J.	11	9	$839	$4,206	$2,000
			DM884	DM7,115	DM3,317
			£518	£2,645	£1,233
			¥64,064	¥521,065	¥229,209
THIR FAMILY (MEMBER OF)	1	0			
THOMPSON, CHARLES & SAMUEL	3	1	$3,470	$3,470	$3,470
			DM4,879	DM4,879	DM4,879
			£2,185	£2,185	£2,185
			¥308,463	¥308,463	¥308,463
THOMPSON, CHARLES & SAMUEL (attributed to)	1	1	$11,433	$11,433	$11,433
			DM17,553	DM17,553	DM17,553
			£7,475	£7,475	£7,475
			¥1,247,854	¥1,247,854	¥1,247,854
THOMSON, GEORGE	1	1	$959	$959	$959
			DM1,799	DM1,799	DM1,799
			£596	£596	£596
			¥115,280	¥115,280	¥115,280
TRIBBY, SCOTT L.	1	1	$2,415	$2,415	$2,415
			DM4,174	DM4,174	DM4,174
			£1,492	£1,492	£1,492
			¥306,065	¥306,065	¥306,065
TRIMBOLI, PIETRO	1	0			

Maker	Items Bid	Sold	Selling Prices Low	High	Avg
TRIMBOLI, PIETRO (ascribed to)	1	1	$2,462 DM3,781 £1,610 ¥268,769	$2,462 DM3,781 £1,610 ¥268,769	$2,462 DM3,781 £1,610 ¥268,769
TURCSAK, TIBOR GABOR	1	1	$1,932 DM3,473 £1,150 ¥223,365	$1,932 DM3,473 £1,150 ¥223,365	$1,932 DM3,473 £1,150 ¥223,365
VACCARI, RAFFAELLO	1	0			
VAN DER GEEST, JACOB JAN (attributed to)	2	0			
VAN DER GRINTEN, JOOST	2	0			
VATELOT, ETIENNE	1	1	$16,068 DM30,451 £9,919 ¥1,696,801	$16,068 DM30,451 £9,919 ¥1,696,801	$16,068 DM30,451 £9,919 ¥1,696,801
VATILIOTIS, C.A.	1	1	$2,444 DM3,920 £1,587 ¥278,074	$2,444 DM3,920 £1,587 ¥278,074	$2,444 DM3,920 £1,587 ¥278,074
VAVRA, JAN BAPTISTA	1	1	$2,178 DM3,066 £1,380 ¥222,638	$2,178 DM3,066 £1,380 ¥222,638	$2,178 DM3,066 £1,380 ¥222,638
VETTORI, CARLO	2	1	$3,105 DM4,748 £2,043 ¥327,267	$3,105 DM4,748 £2,043 ¥327,267	$3,105 DM4,748 £2,043 ¥327,267
VETTORI, PAULO	1	0			
VETTORI, PAULO (attributed to)	1	1	$4,071 DM7,732 £2,513 ¥427,695	$4,071 DM7,732 £2,513 ¥427,695	$4,071 DM7,732 £2,513 ¥427,695
VICKERS, J.E.	3	2	$505 DM880 £311 ¥61,122	$827 DM1,269 £541 ¥90,229	$666 DM1,074 £426 ¥75,676
VILLA, LUIGI	2	1	$1,824 DM3,047 £1,092 ¥221,665	$1,824 DM3,047 £1,092 ¥221,665	$1,824 DM3,047 £1,092 ¥221,665
VILLAUME, GUSTAVE EUGENE	1	1	$3,884 DM5,959 £2,530 ¥425,065	$3,884 DM5,959 £2,530 ¥425,065	$3,884 DM5,959 £2,530 ¥425,065
VOIGT (attributed to)	2	0			
VOIGT, E.R. & SON	3	2	$2,650 DM3,916 £1,610 ¥282,441	$2,721 DM4,717 £1,725 ¥345,941	$2,686 DM4,317 £1,668 ¥314,191
VOIGT, PAUL	3	0			
VOIGT, WERNER (workshop of)	1	1	$2,530 DM3,658 £1,653 ¥256,163	$2,530 DM3,658 £1,653 ¥256,163	$2,530 DM3,658 £1,653 ¥256,163
VOLLER BROTHERS (attributed to)	1	0			

Maker	Items		Selling Prices		
	Bid	Sold	Low	High	Avg
VUILLAUME (workshop of)	1	1	$14,517	$14,517	$14,517
			DM20,443	DM20,443	DM20,443
			£9,200	£9,200	£9,200
			¥1,484,254	¥1,484,254	¥1,484,254
VUILLAUME, JEAN BAPTISTE	1	1	$20,298	$20,298	$20,298
			DM28,256	DM28,256	DM28,256
			£12,650	£12,650	£12,650
			¥1,712,506	¥1,712,506	¥1,712,506
VUILLAUME, NICOLAS FRANCOIS	1	1	$5,463	$5,463	$5,463
			DM9,833	DM9,833	DM9,833
			£3,278	£3,278	£3,278
			¥42,444	¥42,444	¥42,444
WALKER, JOHN	1	1	$2,444	$2,444	$2,444
			DM4,138	DM4,138	DM4,138
			£1,495	£1,495	£1,495
			¥283,297	¥283,297	¥283,297
WARD, ROD	2	2	$288	$743	$515
			DM520	DM1,197	DM859
			£175	£437	£306
			¥34,713	¥91,866	¥63,289
WELLER, FREDERICK (attributed to)	1	1	$1,224	$1,224	$1,224
			DM1,874	DM1,874	DM1,874
			£782	£782	£782
			¥136,475	¥136,475	¥136,475
WHEDBEE, WILLIAM	2	0			
WHITE, WILFRED	1	0			
WHITMAN, EUGENE	1	1	$546	$546	$546
			DM790	DM790	DM790
			£357	£357	£357
			¥55,308	¥55,308	¥55,308
WHITMARSH, E.	2	1	$904	$904	$904
			DM1,389	DM1,389	DM1,389
			£598	£598	£598
			¥96,413	¥96,413	¥96,413
WHITMARSH, EDWIN	1	0			
WHITMARSH, EMANUEL	1	1	$3,105	$3,105	$3,105
			DM4,365	DM4,365	DM4,365
			£1,955	£1,955	£1,955
			¥275,993	¥275,993	¥275,993
WILKINSON, JOHN	1	1	$7,079	$7,079	$7,079
			DM12,673	DM12,673	DM12,673
			£4,370	£4,370	£4,370
			¥834,976	¥834,976	¥834,976
WILLER, JOANNES MICHAEL	2	0			
WITHERS, GEORGE & SONS	1	0			
WOLFF BROS.	1	1	$482	$482	$482
			DM722	DM722	DM722
			£287	£287	£287
			¥53,807	¥53,807	¥53,807
WULME-HUDSON, GEORGE (attributed to)	3	0			
ZANI, ALDO	2	1	$4,600	$4,600	$4,600
			DM6,642	DM6,642	DM6,642
			£2,931	£2,931	£2,931
			¥399,050	¥399,050	¥399,050
ZANOLI, FRANCESCO	1	0			

Maker	Items		Selling Prices		
	Bid	Sold	Low	High	Avg

VIOLA BOW

Maker	Bid	Sold	Low	High	Avg
BALINT, GEZA	1	1	$529	$529	$529
			DM998	DM998	DM998
			£327	£327	£327
			¥55,968	¥55,968	¥55,968
BAUSCH	6	2	$293	$309	$301
			DM473	DM539	DM506
			£173	£184	£178
			¥36,263	¥39,442	¥37,853
BAUSCH, LUDWIG	1	1	$863	$863	$863
			DM1,535	DM1,535	DM1,535
			£518	£518	£518
			¥114,695	¥114,695	¥114,695
BAZIN	3	3	$1,529	$4,081	$3,153
			DM2,163	DM7,123	DM5,454
			£978	£2,415	£1,898
			¥155,236	¥513,107	¥392,636
BAZIN, CHARLES	2	2	$2,588	$2,990	$2,789
			DM4,324	DM4,373	DM4,348
			£1,553	£1,953	£1,753
			¥302,738	¥344,319	¥323,528
BAZIN, CHARLES NICHOLAS	2	1	$3,674	$3,674	$3,674
			DM6,177	DM6,177	DM6,177
			£2,300	£2,300	£2,300
			¥450,945	¥450,945	¥450,945
BAZIN, LOUIS	2	2	$2,359	$2,726	$2,542
			DM3,322	DM3,850	DM3,586
			£1,495	£1,725	£1,610
			¥241,191	¥243,289	¥242,240
BAZIN, LOUIS (ascribed to)	1	0			
BECHINI, RENZO	1	0			
BERNARDEL, LEON	1	1	$1,093	$1,093	$1,093
			DM1,984	DM1,984	DM1,984
			£669	£669	£669
			¥135,667	¥135,667	¥135,667
BEUSCHER, PAUL	1	1	$2,028	$2,028	$2,028
			DM2,824	DM2,824	DM2,824
			£1,265	£1,265	£1,265
			¥171,468	¥171,468	¥171,468
BLONDELET, EMILE (workshop of)	1	1	$1,840	$1,840	$1,840
			DM2,814	DM2,814	DM2,814
			£1,211	£1,211	£1,211
			¥193,936	¥193,936	¥193,936
BOUVIN, JEAN	2	2	$575	$748	$661
			DM830	DM1,079	DM955
			£366	£476	£421
			¥49,881	¥64,846	¥57,363
BRISTOW, S.E.	2	2	$745	$1,390	$1,068
			DM1,403	DM2,063	DM1,733
			£460	£897	£679
			¥79,442	¥150,499	¥114,970
BRISTOW, STEPHEN	1	0			
BRYANT	1	1	$1,930	$1,930	$1,930
			DM2,701	DM2,701	DM2,701
			£1,208	£1,208	£1,208
			¥163,270	¥163,270	¥163,270

| Maker | Items | | Selling Prices | | |
	Bid	Sold	Low	High	Avg
BRYANT, PERCIVAL WILFRED	2	1	$1,118	$1,118	$1,118
			DM2,105	DM2,105	DM2,105
			£690	£690	£690
			¥118,142	¥118,142	¥118,142
BULTITUDE, ARTHUR RICHARD	14	12	$875	$3,468	$2,461
			DM1,516	DM6,314	DM3,813
			£518	£2,070	£1,548
			¥109,193	¥386,181	¥258,020
BUTHOD, CHARLES LOUIS	1	1	$1,150	$1,150	$1,150
			DM1,758	DM1,758	DM1,758
			£757	£757	£757
			¥121,210	¥121,210	¥121,210
CHALUPETZKY, F.	1	0			
COCKER, L.	3	3	$460	$653	$529
			DM643	DM1,169	DM826
			£288	£403	£330
			¥38,874	¥77,001	¥52,751
COLAS, PROSPER	1	1	$2,300	$2,300	$2,300
			DM4,094	DM4,094	DM4,094
			£1,380	£1,380	£1,380
			¥305,854	¥305,854	¥305,854
COLLIN-MEZIN, CH.J.B. (III)	1	1	$2,544	$2,544	$2,544
			DM3,594	DM3,594	DM3,594
			£1,610	£1,610	£1,610
			¥227,070	¥227,070	¥227,070
CUNIOT-HURY	1	1	$2,743	$2,743	$2,743
			DM5,192	DM5,192	DM5,192
			£1,725	£1,725	£1,725
			¥328,768	¥328,768	¥328,768
CUNIOT-HURY, EUGENE	1	0			
DEBLAYE, ALBERT	1	1	$937	$937	$937
			DM1,622	DM1,622	DM1,622
			£575	£575	£575
			¥106,950	¥106,950	¥106,950
DITER BROTHERS	1	0			
DODD	3	2	$1,349	$1,676	$1,512
			DM1,908	DM2,574	DM2,241
			£863	£1,092	£977
			¥136,973	¥183,444	¥160,208
DODD, J.	3	1	$3,291	$3,291	$3,291
			DM6,231	DM6,231	DM6,231
			£2,070	£2,070	£2,070
			¥394,521	¥394,521	¥394,521
DODD, JOHN	1	0			
DODD FAMILY (MEMBER OF)	1	1	$2,530	$2,530	$2,530
			DM3,869	DM3,869	DM3,869
			£1,664	£1,664	£1,664
			¥266,662	¥266,662	¥266,662
DOE, ROGER	1	0			
DOLLING, HEINZ	1	1	$633	$633	$633
			DM967	DM967	DM967
			£416	£416	£416
			¥66,666	¥66,666	¥66,666
DOLLING, KURT	3	2	$730	$759	$744
			DM1,145	DM1,355	DM1,250
			£437	£460	£449
			¥86,020	¥97,643	¥91,832

Maker	Items		Selling Prices		
	Bid	Sold	Low	High	Avg
DOLLING, MICHAEL	1	0			
DORFLER, EGIDIUS	1	0			
DUGAD, ANDRE	1	1	$1,536	$1,536	$1,536
			DM2,567	DM2,567	DM2,567
			£920	£920	£920
			¥186,751	¥186,751	¥186,751
DUPUY, PHILIPPE	1	1	$1,636	$1,636	$1,636
			DM2,310	DM2,310	DM2,310
			£1,035	£1,035	£1,035
			¥145,973	¥145,973	¥145,973
DURRSCHMIDT, OTTO	2	2	$750	$1,422	$1,086
			DM1,329	DM2,560	DM1,945
			£460	£862	£661
			¥88,656	¥205,113	¥146,884
DURRSCHMIDT, WILLI CARL	1	1	$1,426	$1,426	$1,426
			DM2,300	DM2,300	DM2,300
			£828	£828	£828
			¥167,900	¥167,900	¥167,900
ENGLISH, CHRIS	1	1	$596	$596	$596
			DM1,124	DM1,124	DM1,124
			£369	£369	£369
			¥63,025	¥63,025	¥63,025
FETIQUE, JULES	1	1	$1,344	$1,344	$1,344
			DM2,496	DM2,496	DM2,496
			£805	£805	£805
			¥179,869	¥179,869	¥179,869
FETIQUE, VICTOR	5	1	$4,801	$4,801	$4,801
			DM8,596	DM8,596	DM8,596
			£2,875	£2,875	£2,875
			¥660,618	¥660,618	¥660,618
FINKEL, JOHANN S.	1	1	$3,304	$3,304	$3,304
			DM5,728	DM5,728	DM5,728
			£1,955	£1,955	£1,955
			¥412,505	¥412,505	¥412,505
FINKEL, JOHANNES S.	3	1	$2,743	$2,743	$2,743
			DM5,158	DM5,158	DM5,158
			£1,725	£1,725	£1,725
			¥331,614	¥331,614	¥331,614
FLEISHER, HARRY	1	1	$633	$633	$633
			DM1,093	DM1,093	DM1,093
			£391	£391	£391
			¥80,160	¥80,160	¥80,160
GAND & BERNARDEL	1	1	$3,693	$3,693	$3,693
			DM6,402	DM6,402	DM6,402
			£2,185	£2,185	£2,185
			¥461,035	¥461,035	¥461,035
GAUDE, PHILIPPE	1	1	$2,722	$2,722	$2,722
			DM3,833	DM3,833	DM3,833
			£1,725	£1,725	£1,725
			¥278,298	¥278,298	¥278,298
GEROME, ROGER	1	1	$1,725	$1,725	$1,725
			DM2,638	DM2,638	DM2,638
			£1,135	£1,135	£1,135
			¥181,815	¥181,815	¥181,815
GOTZ, CONRAD (workshop of)	1	1	$690	$690	$690
			DM998	DM998	DM998
			£451	£451	£451
			¥69,863	¥69,863	¥69,863

Maker	Items		Selling Prices		
	Bid	Sold	Low	High	Avg
GRANIER, DENIS	2	0			
HEL, PIERRE JOSEPH	1	0			
HERRMANN, EMIL	1	0			
HERRMANN, LOTHAR	3	3	$425	$1,348	$829
			DM742	DM2,493	DM1,462
			£253	£805	£491
			¥54,233	¥179,587	¥105,923
HILL, W.E. & SONS	44	37	$707	$5,962	$3,108
			DM1,044	DM11,298	DM5,040
			£460	£3,680	£1,931
			¥75,318	¥629,538	¥337,147
HUSSON, AUGUST	1	1	$3,177	$3,177	$3,177
			DM4,876	DM4,876	DM4,876
			£2,070	£2,070	£2,070
			¥347,781	¥347,781	¥347,781
KUN, JOSEPH	1	0			
LABERTE, MARC	3	2	$1,632	$2,181	$1,906
			DM3,029	DM3,080	DM3,054
			£977	£1,380	£1,179
			¥194,631	¥218,301	¥206,466
LAMY, ALFRED JOSEPH	1	1	$16,767	$16,767	$16,767
			DM31,775	DM31,775	DM31,775
			£10,350	£10,350	£10,350
			¥1,770,575	¥1,770,575	¥1,770,575
LAPIERRE	1	1	$1,567	$1,567	$1,567
			DM2,182	DM2,182	DM2,182
			£978	£978	£978
			¥132,498	¥132,498	¥132,498
LAPIERRE, MARCEL	7	5	$1,059	$3,092	$1,910
			DM1,627	DM4,627	DM2,921
			£690	£1,840	£1,178
			¥115,912	¥344,963	¥214,368
LAUXERROIS, JEAN-PAUL	1	1	$1,527	$1,527	$1,527
			DM2,449	DM2,449	DM2,449
			£991	£991	£991
			¥173,696	¥173,696	¥173,696
LEE, JOHN NORWOOD	1	1	$794	$794	$794
			DM1,498	DM1,498	DM1,498
			£491	£491	£491
			¥83,952	¥83,952	¥83,952
LIU, LLOYD	1	1	$1,265	$1,265	$1,265
			DM1,934	DM1,934	DM1,934
			£832	£832	£832
			¥133,331	¥133,331	¥133,331
LOTTE, FRANCOIS	4	2	$838	$853	$845
			DM1,287	DM1,587	DM1,437
			£517	£517	£517
			¥88,443	¥96,679	¥92,561
LOTTE, ROGER	8	7	$1,366	$2,178	$1,598
			DM2,160	DM3,066	DM2,484
			£859	£1,380	£999
			¥153,582	¥222,638	¥181,154
MAIRE (workshop of)	1	1	$3,571	$3,571	$3,571
			DM6,740	DM6,740	DM6,740
			£2,210	£2,210	£2,210
			¥377,785	¥377,785	¥377,785

| Maker | Items | | Selling Prices | | |
---	Bid	Sold	Low	High	Avg
MAIRE, N. (attributed to)	1	1	$4,960	$4,960	$4,960
			DM8,339	DM8,339	DM8,339
			£3,105	£3,105	£3,105
			¥608,776	¥608,776	¥608,776
MAIRE, NICOLAS	2	1	$18,453	$18,453	$18,453
			DM25,688	DM25,688	DM25,688
			£11,500	£11,500	£11,500
			¥1,556,824	¥1,556,824	¥1,556,824
MAIRE, NICOLAS (attributed to)	1	1	$3,176	$3,176	$3,176
			DM4,880	DM4,880	DM4,880
			£2,070	£2,070	£2,070
			¥347,737	¥347,737	¥347,737
MALINE, GUILLAUME	2	1	$4,099	$4,099	$4,099
			DM7,717	DM7,717	DM7,717
			£2,530	£2,530	£2,530
			¥433,187	¥433,187	¥433,187
MALINE, NICOLAS (attributed to)	1	1	$6,146	$6,146	$6,146
			DM10,267	DM10,267	DM10,267
			£3,680	£3,680	£3,680
			¥747,003	¥747,003	¥747,003
MANGENOT, PAUL	1	0			
MAW, JOHN	1	1	$1,065	$1,065	$1,065
			DM1,533	DM1,533	DM1,533
			£690	£690	£690
			¥108,151	¥108,151	¥108,151
METTAL, WALTER	1	1	$450	$450	$450
			DM798	DM798	DM798
			£276	£276	£276
			¥53,193	¥53,193	¥53,193
MILLANT, JEAN-JACQUES	1	1	$5,775	$5,775	$5,775
			DM10,685	DM10,685	DM10,685
			£3,450	£3,450	£3,450
			¥769,661	¥769,661	¥769,661
MOINEL, DANIEL	1	0			
MOINIER, A.	2	0			
MOINIER, ALAIN	2	1	$1,265	$1,265	$1,265
			DM1,904	DM1,904	DM1,904
			£768	£768	£768
			¥141,402	¥141,402	¥141,402
MOLLER, MAX	1	1	$1,921	$1,921	$1,921
			DM3,565	DM3,565	DM3,565
			£1,150	£1,150	£1,150
			¥256,956	¥256,956	¥256,956
MORIZOT	2	1	$1,762	$1,762	$1,762
			DM2,601	DM2,601	DM2,601
			£1,150	£1,150	£1,150
			¥187,336	¥187,336	¥187,336
MORIZOT, C.	1	0			
MORIZOT, LOUIS	8	7	$919	$3,479	$2,435
			DM1,286	DM5,205	DM3,692
			£575	£2,070	£1,525
			¥77,747	¥388,084	¥248,609
MORIZOT, LOUIS (attributed to)	1	1	$975	$975	$975
			DM1,686	DM1,686	DM1,686
			£598	£598	£598
			¥111,228	¥111,228	¥111,228

Maker	Items		Selling Prices		
	Bid	Sold	Low	High	Avg
MORIZOT, LOUIS (II)	2	2	$2,888	$3,785	$3,336
			DM5,342	DM6,404	DM5,873
			£1,725	£2,381	£2,053
			¥384,830	¥468,959	¥426,894
NEUDORFER	1	1	$978	$978	$978
			DM1,495	DM1,495	DM1,495
			£643	£643	£643
			¥103,029	¥103,029	¥103,029
NEUVEVILLE, G.C.	1	0			
NURNBERGER, ALBERT	9	8	$978	$2,875	$1,601
			DM1,495	DM4,327	DM2,612
			£632	£1,745	£989
			¥94,774	¥321,368	¥171,980
NURNBERGER, CHRISTIAN ALBERT	1	1	$2,103	$2,103	$2,103
			DM3,558	DM3,558	DM3,558
			£1,323	£1,323	£1,323
			¥260,533	¥260,533	¥260,533
NURNBERGER, FRANZ ALBERT (II)	1	1	$2,181	$2,181	$2,181
			DM3,080	DM3,080	DM3,080
			£1,380	£1,380	£1,380
			¥194,631	¥194,631	¥194,631
NURNBERGER, KARL ALBERT	3	2	$1,312	$2,996	$2,154
			DM2,270	DM4,422	DM3,346
			£805	£1,955	£1,380
			¥149,730	¥318,471	¥234,101
OUCHARD, JEAN-CLAUDE	3	1	$2,194	$2,194	$2,194
			DM4,126	DM4,126	DM4,126
			£1,380	£1,380	£1,380
			¥265,291	¥265,291	¥265,291
PAESOLD, RODERICH	2	2	$569	$1,328	$949
			DM859	DM2,004	DM1,432
			£345	£805	£575
			¥64,515	¥150,535	¥107,525
PAJEOT, ETIENNE	3	1	$2,819	$2,819	$2,819
			DM4,162	DM4,162	DM4,162
			£1,840	£1,840	£1,840
			¥299,738	¥299,738	¥299,738
PECCATTE, FRANCOIS	3	1	$5,589	$5,589	$5,589
			DM10,592	DM10,592	DM10,592
			£3,450	£3,450	£3,450
			¥590,192	¥590,192	¥590,192
PFRETZSCHNER, H.R.	3	2	$2,049	$2,291	$2,170
			DM3,382	DM3,884	DM3,633
			£1,265	£1,495	£1,380
			¥216,404	¥243,537	¥229,970
PIERNOT, MARIE LOUIS	2	0			
PRAGER, AUGUST EDWIN	3	3	$1,265	$2,213	$1,678
			DM1,934	DM3,081	DM2,570
			£832	£1,380	£1,044
			¥133,331	¥194,120	¥171,502
PRAGER, GUSTAV	1	1	$792	$792	$792
			DM1,169	DM1,169	DM1,169
			£517	£517	£517
			¥84,220	¥84,220	¥84,220
RAUM, WILHELM	1	0			
REICHEL, AUGUST	1	0			

| Maker | Items | | Selling Prices | | |
	Bid	Sold	Low	High	Avg
RETFORD, WILLIAM C.	1	1	$5,143	$5,143	$5,143
			DM8,648	DM8,648	DM8,648
			£3,220	£3,220	£3,220
			¥631,323	¥631,323	¥631,323
RICHAUME, ANDRE	1	1	$12,558	$12,558	$12,558
			DM20,930	DM20,930	DM20,930
			£7,475	£7,475	£7,475
			¥1,500,905	¥1,500,905	¥1,500,905
ROTH, ERNST HEINRICH	1	1	$305	$305	$305
			DM489	DM489	DM489
			£198	£198	£198
			¥34,659	¥34,659	¥34,659
SALCHOW, WILLIAM	3	3	$1,125	$1,725	$1,448
			DM1,994	DM2,494	DM2,258
			£690	£1,127	£933
			¥132,984	¥174,656	¥155,071
SARTORY, EUGENE	8	6	$4,610	$23,101	$11,794
			DM6,419	DM42,739	DM18,720
			£2,875	£13,800	£7,245
			¥389,701	¥3,078,642	¥1,264,127
SARTORY, EUGENE (workshop of)	1	1	$7,188	$7,188	$7,188
			DM10,393	DM10,393	DM10,393
			£4,695	£4,695	£4,695
			¥727,734	¥727,734	¥727,734
SCHICKER, HORST	2	1	$461	$461	$461
			DM856	DM856	DM856
			£276	£276	£276
			¥61,669	¥61,669	¥61,669
SCHMIDT, C. HANS CARL	1	1	$1,898	$1,898	$1,898
			DM2,864	DM2,864	DM2,864
			£1,150	£1,150	£1,150
			¥215,050	¥215,050	¥215,050
SCHMIDT, HANS KARL	1	1	$2,138	$2,138	$2,138
			DM3,706	DM3,706	DM3,706
			£1,265	£1,265	£1,265
			¥271,811	¥271,811	¥271,811
SCHUSTER, ADOLPH CURT	2	2	$1,255	$1,495	$1,375
			DM1,878	DM2,527	DM2,203
			£747	£897	£822
			¥140,048	¥182,390	¥161,219
SCHUSTER, ALBERT	1	1	$1,035	$1,035	$1,035
			DM1,842	DM1,842	DM1,842
			£621	£621	£621
			¥137,634	¥137,634	¥137,634
SEIFERT, LOTHAR	2	2	$576	$2,888	$1,732
			DM1,070	DM5,342	DM3,206
			£345	£1,725	£1,035
			¥77,087	¥384,830	¥230,959
SERDET, PAUL	1	1	$2,827	$2,827	$2,827
			DM4,177	DM4,177	DM4,177
			£1,840	£1,840	£1,840
			¥301,271	¥301,271	¥301,271
SIMON (workshop of)	1	0			
SIRDEVAN, JOHN	1	1	$546	$546	$546
			DM789	DM789	DM789
			£348	£348	£348
			¥47,387	¥47,387	¥47,387

| Maker | Items | | Selling Prices | | |
	Bid	Sold	Low	High	Avg
STAGG, JOHN W.	1	0			
SUSS, JOHANN CHRISTIAN	1	1	$2,363	$2,363	$2,363
			DM3,337	DM3,337	DM3,337
			£1,495	£1,495	£1,495
			¥210,850	¥210,850	¥210,850
TAYLOR, MALCOLM	3	2	$669	$1,944	$1,306
			DM987	DM2,872	DM1,929
			£437	£1,265	£851
			¥71,393	¥207,124	¥139,258
THIBOUVILLE-LAMY, J.	5	1	$1,219	$1,219	$1,219
			DM2,132	DM2,132	DM2,132
			£748	£748	£748
			¥144,027	¥144,027	¥144,027
THIBOUVILLE-LAMY, J. (workshop of)	1	0			
THOMACHOT, STEPHANE	1	0			
THOMASSIN, CLAUDE	3	2	$2,185	$4,025	$3,105
			DM3,160	DM5,812	DM4,486
			£1,427	£2,564	£1,996
			¥221,231	¥349,169	¥285,200
THOMASSIN, CLAUDE (attributed to)	1	0			
THOMASSIN, VICTOR	1	1	$3,529	$3,529	$3,529
			DM5,422	DM5,422	DM5,422
			£2,300	£2,300	£2,300
			¥386,375	¥386,375	¥386,375
TUA, SILVIO	2	0			
TUBBS (ascribed to)	1	1	$916	$916	$916
			DM1,353	DM1,353	DM1,353
			£598	£598	£598
			¥97,415	¥97,415	¥97,415
TUBBS, J.	1	1	$10,805	$10,805	$10,805
			DM19,410	DM19,410	DM19,410
			£6,670	£6,670	£6,670
			¥1,275,771	¥1,275,771	¥1,275,771
TUBBS, JAMES	12	12	$922	$18,173	$7,662
			DM1,711	DM25,669	DM11,834
			£552	£11,500	£4,795
			¥123,339	¥1,621,926	¥796,617
TUBBS, JAMES (attributed to)	1	0			
UEBEL, K. WERNER	1	1	$1,265	$1,265	$1,265
			DM1,934	DM1,934	DM1,934
			£832	£832	£832
			¥133,331	¥133,331	¥133,331
UEBEL, KLAUS W.	1	0			
VICTOR, T.	1	0			
VIDOUDEZ, PIERRE	2	1	$3,785	$3,785	$3,785
			DM6,404	DM6,404	DM6,404
			£2,381	£2,381	£2,381
			¥468,959	¥468,959	¥468,959
VIGNERON, ANDRE	1	1	$6,722	$6,722	$6,722
			DM11,230	DM11,230	DM11,230
			£4,025	£4,025	£4,025
			¥817,035	¥817,035	¥817,035
VIGNERON, ARTHUR	1	1	$6,179	$6,179	$6,179
			DM8,728	DM8,728	DM8,728
			£3,910	£3,910	£3,910
			¥551,455	¥551,455	¥551,455

	Items		Selling Prices		
Maker	Bid	Sold	Low	High	Avg

VIGNERON, JOSEPH ARTHUR	1	1	$6,722	$6,722	$6,722
			DM12,478	DM12,478	DM12,478
			£4,025	£4,025	£4,025
			¥899,346	¥899,346	¥899,346
VILLAUME, GUSTAVE EUGENE	1	1	$1,677	$1,677	$1,677
			DM3,177	DM3,177	DM3,177
			£1,035	£1,035	£1,035
			¥177,057	¥177,057	¥177,057
VITALE, GIUSEPPE	1	0			
VOIGT, ARNOLD	3	2	$358	$1,584	$971
			DM547	DM2,981	DM1,764
			£230	£978	£604
			¥35,370	¥167,368	¥101,369
WATSON, D.	1	1	$4,801	$4,801	$4,801
			DM8,021	DM8,021	DM8,021
			£2,875	£2,875	£2,875
			¥583,596	¥583,596	¥583,596
WEICHOLD, R.	1	1	$1,863	$1,863	$1,863
			DM3,508	DM3,508	DM3,508
			£1,150	£1,150	£1,150
			¥196,903	¥196,903	¥196,903
WEIDHAAS, PAUL	1	1	$1,262	$1,262	$1,262
			DM2,189	DM2,189	DM2,189
			£747	£747	£747
			¥157,617	¥157,617	¥157,617
WERNER, E.	2	1	$580	$580	$580
			DM1,012	DM1,012	DM1,012
			£345	£345	£345
			¥73,954	¥73,954	¥73,954
WILSON, GARNER	9	6	$894	$2,377	$1,578
			DM1,353	DM4,470	DM2,589
			£555	£1,495	£978
			¥97,570	¥287,399	¥174,559
WITHERS, EDWARD	1	1	$1,004	$1,004	$1,004
			DM1,877	DM1,877	DM1,877
			£633	£633	£633
			¥118,790	¥118,790	¥118,790
WITHERS, GEORGE & SONS	1	1	$2,758	$2,758	$2,758
			DM3,858	DM3,858	DM3,858
			£1,725	£1,725	£1,725
			¥233,242	¥233,242	¥233,242
WURLITZER, REMBERT	1	0			

VIOLIN

ACHNER, PHILIP (attributed to)	2	1	$4,596	$4,596	$4,596
			DM6,430	DM6,430	DM6,430
			£2,875	£2,875	£2,875
			¥388,737	¥388,737	¥388,737
ACOULON, A. (attributed to)	2	1	$2,049	$2,049	$2,049
			DM3,858	DM3,858	DM3,858
			£1,265	£1,265	£1,265
			¥218,466	¥218,466	¥218,466
ACOULON, ALFRED (attributed to)	5	2	$1,219	$2,050	$1,635
			DM2,132	DM2,160	DM2,146
			£748	£1,265	£1,007
			¥144,027	¥156,601	¥150,314

Maker	Items		Selling Prices		
	Bid	Sold	Low	High	Avg
AERTS	1	0			
AERTS, MARCEL	1	1	$2,527	$2,527	$2,527
			DM4,380	DM4,380	DM4,380
			£1,495	£1,495	£1,495
			¥321,231	¥321,231	¥321,231
ALBANELLI, FRANCO	7	3	$2,990	$5,901	$4,059
			DM4,916	DM8,216	DM6,062
			£1,794	£3,680	£2,476
			¥364,780	¥498,817	¥410,040
ALBANI, GIUSEPPE	1	1	$9,450	$9,450	$9,450
			DM13,348	DM13,348	DM13,348
			£5,980	£5,980	£5,980
			¥843,401	¥843,401	¥843,401
ALBANI, JOSEPH	1	1	$18,092	$18,092	$18,092
			DM32,057	DM32,057	DM32,057
			£11,109	£11,109	£11,109
			¥2,205,930	¥2,205,930	¥2,205,930
ALBANI, MATTEO	1	1	$16,822	$16,822	$16,822
			DM28,460	DM28,460	DM28,460
			£10,580	£10,580	£10,580
			¥2,084,260	¥2,084,260	¥2,084,260
ALBANI, MATTHIAS	2	2	$7,825	$8,411	$8,118
			DM14,828	DM15,817	DM15,323
			£4,830	£5,290	£5,060
			¥826,268	¥1,016,950	¥921,609
ALBANI, MATTHIAS (ascribed to)	1	1	$16,187	$16,187	$16,187
			DM22,897	DM22,897	DM22,897
			£10,350	£10,350	£10,350
			¥1,643,673	¥1,643,673	¥1,643,673
ALBANI, MATTHIAS (attributed to)	2	0			
ALBERT, CHARLES F.	4	0			
ALBERT, J.	2	2	$661	$1,610	$1,136
			DM1,248	DM2,783	DM2,015
			£409	£995	£702
			¥69,960	¥204,043	¥137,002
ALBERTI, FERDINANDO (attributed to)	1	0			
ALDRIC, JEAN FRANCOIS	1	1	$21,808	$21,808	$21,808
			DM30,803	DM30,803	DM30,803
			£13,800	£13,800	£13,800
			¥1,946,311	¥1,946,311	¥1,946,311
ALDRIC, JEAN FRANCOIS (attributed to)	6	1	$5,401	$5,401	$5,401
			DM8,269	DM8,269	DM8,269
			£3,450	£3,450	£3,450
			¥602,094	¥602,094	¥602,094
ALEKSA, JOHN	1	0			
ALF, GREGG	4	2	$9,200	$12,353	$10,776
			DM13,846	DM18,978	DM16,412
			£5,585	£8,050	£6,817
			¥1,028,376	¥1,352,311	¥1,190,344
ALLEN, JOSEPH S.	1	1	$3,335	$3,335	$3,335
			DM5,936	DM5,936	DM5,936
			£2,001	£2,001	£2,001
			¥443,488	¥443,488	¥443,488
ALLETSEE, PAULUS (attributed to)	1	1	$3,738	$3,738	$3,738
			DM5,715	DM5,715	DM5,715
			£2,459	£2,459	£2,459
			¥393,933	¥393,933	¥393,933

| Maker | Items | | Selling Prices | | |
	Bid	Sold	Low	High	Avg
ALLISON, JOHN L.	1	1	$518	$518	$518
			DM921	DM921	DM921
			£311	£311	£311
			¥68,817	¥68,817	¥68,817
ALTAVILLA, ARMANDO	9	5	$3,872	$13,122	$7,949
			DM5,392	DM22,701	DM13,185
			£2,415	£8,050	£4,960
			¥327,348	¥1,497,300	¥882,078
AMATI, ANTONIO & GIROLAMO	2	2	$94,581	$142,299	$118,440
			DM174,981	DM252,297	DM213,639
			£56,500	£87,300	£71,900
			¥12,604,585	¥16,825,329	¥14,714,957
AMATI, DOM NICOLO	4	3	$6,325	$42,251	$27,618
			DM9,672	DM75,647	DM50,093
			£4,161	£25,300	£16,874
			¥666,655	¥5,813,434	¥3,366,643
AMATI, GIROLAMO (II)	1	1	$26,503	$26,503	$26,503
			DM39,158	DM39,158	DM39,158
			£17,250	£17,250	£17,250
			¥2,824,412	¥2,824,412	¥2,824,412
AMATI, NICOLO	5	1	$207,360	$207,360	$207,360
			DM372,480	DM372,480	DM372,480
			£128,000	£128,000	£128,000
			¥24,482,560	¥24,482,560	¥24,482,560
AMATI FAMILY (MEMBER OF)	1	0			
AMEDO, SIMONAZZI	2	1	$7,314	$7,314	$7,314
			DM13,846	DM13,846	DM13,846
			£4,600	£4,600	£4,600
			¥876,714	¥876,714	¥876,714
AMIGHETTI, CLAUDIO	4	3	$1,660	$5,750	$4,310
			DM2,311	DM9,445	DM6,803
			£1,035	£3,491	£2,597
			¥140,292	¥685,474	¥489,500
ANASTASIO, VINCENZO	3	1	$3,504	$3,504	$3,504
			DM4,878	DM4,878	DM4,878
			£2,185	£2,185	£2,185
			¥296,172	¥296,172	¥296,172
ANCIAUME, BERNARD	1	0			
ANDERSON, A.	2	1	$300	$300	$300
			DM524	DM524	DM524
			£184	£184	£184
			¥35,429	¥35,429	¥35,429
ANDREWS, EDWARD	1	1	$374	$374	$374
			DM652	DM652	DM652
			£230	£230	£230
			¥45,276	¥45,276	¥45,276
ANDREWS, M.H.	1	1	$431	$431	$431
			DM738	DM738	DM738
			£255	£255	£255
			¥53,553	¥53,553	¥53,553
ANGARD, MAXIME	1	1	$855	$855	$855
			DM1,372	DM1,372	DM1,372
			£555	£555	£555
			¥97,326	¥97,326	¥97,326
ANGERER, FRANZ	1	1	$1,955	$1,955	$1,955
			DM3,379	DM3,379	DM3,379
			£1,208	£1,208	£1,208
			¥247,767	¥247,767	¥247,767

| Maker | Items | | Selling Prices | | |
	Bid	Sold	Low	High	Avg
ANTONELLI, G.	2	1	$1,131	$1,131	$1,131
			DM2,004	DM2,004	DM2,004
			£694	£694	£694
			¥137,871	¥137,871	¥137,871
ANTONIAZZI (workshop of)	1	0			
ANTONIAZZI, GAETANO	1	1	$11,684	$11,684	$11,684
			DM20,704	DM20,704	DM20,704
			£7,175	£7,175	£7,175
			¥1,424,663	¥1,424,663	¥1,424,663
ANTONIAZZI, GAETANO (attributed to)	1	1	$56,235	$56,235	$56,235
			DM99,705	DM99,705	DM99,705
			£34,500	£34,500	£34,500
			¥6,649,185	¥6,649,185	¥6,649,185
ANTONIAZZI, RICCARDO	9	7	$6,914	$21,416	$13,738
			DM11,551	DM39,177	DM22,201
			£4,140	£12,650	£8,477
			¥840,379	¥2,822,089	¥1,587,057
ANTONIAZZI, ROMEO	13	11	$4,900	$33,922	$19,218
			DM8,682	DM60,108	DM33,863
			£3,009	£20,829	£11,714
			¥597,439	¥4,136,119	¥2,253,445
ANTONIAZZI, ROMEO (ascribed to)	2	1	$7,991	$7,991	$7,991
			DM13,519	DM13,519	DM13,519
			£5,026	£5,026	£5,026
			¥990,024	¥990,024	¥990,024
ANTONIAZZI, ROMEO (attributed to)	1	0			
ANTONIAZZI, ROMEO (workshop of)	1	1	$10,925	$10,925	$10,925
			DM18,463	DM18,463	DM18,463
			£6,555	£6,555	£6,555
			¥1,332,850	¥1,332,850	¥1,332,850
APPARUT, G.	1	0			
APPARUT, GEORGES	9	7	$1,467	$4,686	$3,106
			DM2,422	DM8,107	DM5,220
			£897	£2,875	£1,886
			¥181,579	¥535,526	¥360,873
APPARUT, GEORGES (workshop of)	1	1	$1,583	$1,583	$1,583
			DM2,980	DM2,980	DM2,980
			£977	£977	£977
			¥167,282	¥167,282	¥167,282
ARASSI, ENZO	2	0			
ARASSI, ENZO (workshop of)	1	1	$3,738	$3,738	$3,738
			DM6,316	DM6,316	DM6,316
			£2,243	£2,243	£2,243
			¥455,975	¥455,975	¥455,975
ARBUCKLE, WILLIAM	1	1	$1,917	$1,917	$1,917
			DM3,551	DM3,551	DM3,551
			£1,150	£1,150	£1,150
			¥256,025	¥256,025	¥256,025
ARBUCKLE, WILLIAM (attributed to)	1	1	$283	$283	$283
			DM418	DM418	DM418
			£184	£184	£184
			¥30,127	¥30,127	¥30,127
ARCANGELI, LORENZO	2	1	$21,202	$21,202	$21,202
			DM31,326	DM31,326	DM31,326
			£13,800	£13,800	£13,800
			¥2,259,529	¥2,259,529	¥2,259,529

| Maker | Items | | Selling Prices | | |
	Bid	Sold	Low	High	Avg
ARCANGELI, ULDERICO	3	1	$22,770	$22,770	$22,770
			DM34,362	DM34,362	DM34,362
			£13,800	£13,800	£13,800
			¥2,580,600	¥2,580,600	¥2,580,600
ARCANGELI, ULDERICO (attributed to)	1	1	$6,146	$6,146	$6,146
			DM10,267	DM10,267	DM10,267
			£3,680	£3,680	£3,680
			¥747,003	¥747,003	¥747,003
ARDERN, JOB	12	6	$870	$2,415	$1,653
			DM1,517	DM3,593	DM2,664
			£518	£1,577	£1,043
			¥110,931	¥254,901	¥181,289
ARMBRUSTER, ADOLF	1	1	$730	$730	$730
			DM1,132	DM1,132	DM1,132
			£437	£437	£437
			¥83,165	¥83,165	¥83,165
ARTHUR & JOHNSON	1	1	$1,150	$1,150	$1,150
			DM2,082	DM2,082	DM2,082
			£702	£702	£702
			¥138,851	¥138,851	¥138,851
ASHFORD, LAWRENCE (attributed to)	2	1	$974	$974	$974
			DM1,496	DM1,496	DM1,496
			£644	£644	£644
			¥103,829	¥103,829	¥103,829
ASKEW, JOHN	2	2	$971	$1,589	$1,280
			DM1,491	DM2,438	DM1,965
			£633	£1,035	£834
			¥106,253	¥173,890	¥140,072
ASSUNTO, CARLONI	1	1	$1,128	$1,128	$1,128
			DM1,910	DM1,910	DM1,910
			£690	£690	£690
			¥130,752	¥130,752	¥130,752
ATKINSON, WILLIAM	16	7	$1,886	$4,250	$3,042
			DM3,253	DM7,247	DM5,318
			£1,150	£2,530	£1,844
			¥215,234	¥507,999	¥365,354
AUBRY, JOSEPH	3	1	$4,060	$4,060	$4,060
			DM6,230	DM6,230	DM6,230
			£2,645	£2,645	£2,645
			¥444,386	¥444,386	¥444,386
AUCIELLO, LUIGI	1	1	$4,470	$4,470	$4,470
			DM7,750	DM7,750	DM7,750
			£2,645	£2,645	£2,645
			¥558,095	¥558,095	¥558,095
AUDINOT, JUSTIN (attributed to)	1	1	$1,880	$1,880	$1,880
			DM3,106	DM3,106	DM3,106
			£1,150	£1,150	£1,150
			¥232,793	¥232,793	¥232,793
AUDINOT, NESTOR	7	5	$4,718	$21,425	$12,778
			DM6,644	DM40,601	DM22,528
			£2,990	£13,225	£7,935
			¥482,383	¥2,262,401	¥1,378,179
AUDINOT, NESTOR (ascribed to)	1	0			
AUDINOT, NESTOR (attributed to)	1	1	$4,673	$4,673	$4,673
			DM8,106	DM8,106	DM8,106
			£2,760	£2,760	£2,760
			¥592,324	¥592,324	¥592,324

Maker	Items		Selling Prices		
	Bid	Sold	Low	High	Avg
AUDINOT, VICTOR	1	1	$9,315	$9,315	$9,315
			DM16,733	DM16,733	DM16,733
			£5,750	£5,750	£5,750
			¥1,099,803	¥1,099,803	¥1,099,803
AZZOLA, LUIGI	2	0			
BAADER & CO., J.A.	1	1	$403	$403	$403
			DM729	DM729	DM729
			£246	£246	£246
			¥48,598	¥48,598	¥48,598
BAADER, J. (workshop of)	1	1	$546	$546	$546
			DM972	DM972	DM972
			£328	£328	£328
			¥72,640	¥72,640	¥72,640
BADALASSI, PIERO	1	0			
BADARELLO, CARLO	3	3	$5,962	$9,179	$7,349
			DM9,754	DM14,086	DM11,688
			£3,680	£5,980	£4,677
			¥616,332	¥1,004,700	¥750,374
BAILLY, CHARLES	5	2	$2,492	$2,926	$2,709
			DM4,617	DM5,502	DM5,059
			£1,495	£1,840	£1,668
			¥332,832	¥353,722	¥343,277
BAILLY, CHARLES (attributed to)	1	1	$2,512	$2,512	$2,512
			DM4,186	DM4,186	DM4,186
			£1,495	£1,495	£1,495
			¥300,181	¥300,181	¥300,181
BAILLY, CHARLES (workshop of)	2	2	$2,185	$2,760	$2,473
			DM3,889	DM4,996	DM4,442
			£1,311	£1,684	£1,497
			¥290,561	¥333,242	¥311,902
BAILLY, JENNY	6	4	$450	$1,942	$1,472
			DM814	DM2,980	DM2,209
			£276	£1,265	£946
			¥54,286	¥212,533	¥151,629
BAILLY, JENNY (attributed to)	1	1	$1,211	$1,211	$1,211
			DM2,280	DM2,280	DM2,280
			£748	£748	£748
			¥129,093	¥129,093	¥129,093
BAILLY, PAUL	29	18	$1,169	$10,755	$6,376
			DM1,635	DM18,636	DM10,560
			£731	£6,440	£3,919
			¥98,841	¥1,307,256	¥692,675
BAILLY, PAUL (attributed to)	4	3	$1,704	$5,249	$3,020
			DM2,618	DM9,499	DM5,341
			£1,127	£3,220	£1,871
			¥181,701	¥633,342	¥365,556
BAILLY, PAUL (workshop of)	1	1	$4,025	$4,025	$4,025
			DM6,887	DM6,887	DM6,887
			£2,381	£2,381	£2,381
			¥499,825	¥499,825	¥499,825
BAILLY, RENE	1	1	$1,380	$1,380	$1,380
			DM2,456	DM2,456	DM2,456
			£828	£828	£828
			¥183,512	¥183,512	¥183,512
BALAZS, ISTVAN	2	2	$1,610	$1,955	$1,783
			DM2,866	DM3,379	DM3,123
			£966	£1,208	£1,087
			¥214,098	¥247,767	¥230,932

Maker	Items Bid	Sold	Selling Prices Low	High	Avg
BALBO, FRANCESCO	1	1	$1,475	$1,475	$1,475
			DM2,054	DM2,054	DM2,054
			£920	£920	£920
			¥124,704	¥124,704	¥124,704
BALDANTONI, GIUSEPPE (ascribed to)	1	1	$20,088	$20,088	$20,088
			DM28,245	DM28,245	DM28,245
			£12,650	£12,650	£12,650
			¥1,785,838	¥1,785,838	¥1,785,838
BALDONI, DANTE	1	1	$8,166	$8,166	$8,166
			DM11,499	DM11,499	DM11,499
			£5,175	£5,175	£5,175
			¥834,893	¥834,893	¥834,893
BALESTRIERI, TOMMASO	8	2	$113,611	$125,961	$119,786
			DM175,345	DM196,554	DM185,950
			£69,700	£78,500	£74,100
			¥10,627,016	¥12,964,200	¥11,795,608
BALL, HARVEY	1	1	$1,150	$1,150	$1,150
			DM1,944	DM1,944	DM1,944
			£690	£690	£690
			¥140,300	¥140,300	¥140,300
BALLANTYNE, ROBERT	1	1	$714	$714	$714
			DM1,209	DM1,209	DM1,209
			£437	£437	£437
			¥82,810	¥82,810	¥82,810
BALLERINI, PIETRO	1	0			
BALTZERSON, PETER E.	1	0			
BANKS, BENJAMIN	12	6	$1,687	$10,870	$5,042
			DM2,919	DM15,351	DM7,929
			£1,035	£6,900	£3,220
			¥192,510	¥1,094,568	¥539,592
BANKS, JAMES & HENRY	4	2	$3,220	$12,483	$7,852
			DM5,566	DM23,173	DM14,369
			£1,990	£7,475	£4,732
			¥408,087	¥1,670,214	¥1,039,150
BARBE, F. (attributed to)	4	1	$1,118	$1,118	$1,118
			DM2,105	DM2,105	DM2,105
			£690	£690	£690
			¥119,163	¥119,163	¥119,163
BARBE, FRANCOIS	1	0			
BARBE, JACQUES (SR.)	1	1	$460	$460	$460
			DM795	DM795	DM795
			£284	£284	£284
			¥58,298	¥58,298	¥58,298
BARBE, TELESPHORE AMABLE	2	1	$4,801	$4,801	$4,801
			DM8,021	DM8,021	DM8,021
			£2,875	£2,875	£2,875
			¥583,596	¥583,596	¥583,596
BARBE FAMILY	1	0			
BARBE FAMILY (MEMBER OF)	2	0			
BARBIERI, BRUNO	4	3	$2,705	$9,131	$6,277
			DM4,864	DM12,839	DM9,944
			£1,610	£5,750	£3,833
			¥312,710	¥873,540	¥667,066
BARBIERI, BRUNO (attributed to)	2	1	$5,616	$5,616	$5,616
			DM7,931	DM7,931	DM7,931
			£3,565	£3,565	£3,565
			¥565,527	¥565,527	¥565,527

	Items		Selling Prices		
Maker	Bid	Sold	Low	High	Avg
BARBIERI, ENZO	5	1	$3,448	$3,448	$3,448
			DM4,855	DM4,855	DM4,855
			£2,185	£2,185	£2,185
			¥352,510	¥352,510	¥352,510
BARNBURNS, A.F.	1	1	$1,752	$1,752	$1,752
			DM2,439	DM2,439	DM2,439
			£1,093	£1,093	£1,093
			¥148,086	¥148,086	¥148,086
BARREL	1	0			
BARRETT, JOHN	7	4	$794	$3,518	$2,281
			DM1,123	DM5,401	DM3,361
			£506	£2,300	£1,465
			¥67,845	¥383,955	¥223,504
BARRI, ROBERT	2	1	$556	$556	$556
			DM855	DM855	DM855
			£368	£368	£368
			¥59,331	¥59,331	¥59,331
BARTON, GEORGE	4	3	$192	$3,882	$1,558
			DM357	DM5,964	DM2,457
			£115	£2,530	£1,004
			¥25,696	¥425,012	¥173,855
BARTON FAMILY	2	1	$940	$940	$940
			DM1,591	DM1,591	DM1,591
			£575	£575	£575
			¥108,960	¥108,960	¥108,960
BARZONI, FRANCOIS	12	6	$1,273	$2,009	$1,678
			DM1,873	DM2,824	DM2,549
			£828	£1,265	£1,073
			¥135,096	¥197,016	¥172,170
BARZONI, FRANCOIS (attributed to)	2	1	$1,390	$1,390	$1,390
			DM2,063	DM2,063	DM2,063
			£897	£897	£897
			¥150,499	¥150,499	¥150,499
BASILE, PIETRO	1	1	$2,824	$2,824	$2,824
			DM4,334	DM4,334	DM4,334
			£1,840	£1,840	£1,840
			¥309,138	¥309,138	¥309,138
BASSOT, JOSEPH	3	2	$2,899	$7,728	$5,314
			DM4,338	DM13,892	DM9,115
			£1,725	£4,600	£3,163
			¥323,403	¥893,458	¥608,431
BASSOT, JOSEPH (attributed to)	1	1	$2,920	$2,920	$2,920
			DM5,066	DM5,066	DM5,066
			£1,725	£1,725	£1,725
			¥370,202	¥370,202	¥370,202
BASTIEN, E.	1	0			
BATCHELDER, A.M.	1	1	$431	$431	$431
			DM729	DM729	DM729
			£259	£259	£259
			¥52,613	¥52,613	¥52,613
BAUER, JEAN	4	2	$4,252	$5,405	$4,829
			DM6,362	DM9,783	DM8,073
			£2,530	£3,297	£2,914
			¥474,324	¥652,600	¥563,462
BAUR, ADOLF	3	2	$4,590	$6,415	$5,502
			DM7,043	DM8,990	DM8,016
			£2,990	£4,025	£3,508
			¥502,350	¥565,452	¥533,901

Maker	Items		Selling Prices		
	Bid	Sold	Low	High	Avg
BAUR, MARTIN	1	1	$1,475	$1,475	$1,475
			DM2,054	DM2,054	DM2,054
			£920	£920	£920
			¥124,704	¥124,704	¥124,704
BAUR, T.	1	0			
BAZIN, GUSTAVE	1	0			
BAZIN, GUSTAVE (attributed to)	1	0			
BEARD, JOHN	1	1	$877	$877	$877
			DM1,233	DM1,233	DM1,233
			£552	£552	£552
			¥78,235	¥78,235	¥78,235
BEARE & SON	1	1	$3,089	$3,089	$3,089
			DM4,364	DM4,364	DM4,364
			£1,955	£1,955	£1,955
			¥275,727	¥275,727	¥275,727
BECCHINI, RENZO	2	0			
BECKER, ROBERT	1	1	$3,000	$3,000	$3,000
			DM4,609	DM4,609	DM4,609
			£1,955	£1,955	£1,955
			¥328,418	¥328,418	¥328,418
BEDOCCHI, MARIO	3	1	$10,350	$10,350	$10,350
			DM15,577	DM15,577	DM15,577
			£6,283	£6,283	£6,283
			¥1,156,923	¥1,156,923	¥1,156,923
BEEBE, E.W.	1	1	$748	$748	$748
			DM1,292	DM1,292	DM1,292
			£462	£462	£462
			¥94,734	¥94,734	¥94,734
BELLAFONTANA, LORENZO	4	2	$5,998	$8,085	$7,042
			DM10,378	DM14,959	DM12,668
			£3,680	£4,830	£4,255
			¥684,480	¥1,077,525	¥881,002
BELLAFONTANA, LORENZO (ascribed to)	1	1	$1,759	$1,759	$1,759
			DM2,700	DM2,700	DM2,700
			£1,150	£1,150	£1,150
			¥191,978	¥191,978	¥191,978
BELLAROSA, VITTORIO	4	2	$9,775	$11,485	$10,630
			DM16,520	DM16,968	DM16,744
			£5,865	£7,475	£6,670
			¥1,192,550	¥1,223,912	¥1,208,231
BELLAROSA, VITTORIO (attributed to)	1	1	$4,206	$4,206	$4,206
			DM7,115	DM7,115	DM7,115
			£2,645	£2,645	£2,645
			¥521,065	¥521,065	¥521,065
BELLIVEAU, LEANDER	1	1	$345	$345	$345
			DM498	DM498	DM498
			£220	£220	£220
			¥29,929	¥29,929	¥29,929
BELTRAMI, GIUSEPPE	3	2	$2,310	$12,483	$7,397
			DM4,274	DM20,855	DM12,565
			£1,380	£7,475	£4,428
			¥307,864	¥1,517,350	¥912,607
BELTRAMI, GIUSEPPE (attributed to)	1	0			
BENOZZATI, GIROLAMO	2	0			

Maker	Items		Selling Prices		
	Bid	Sold	Low	High	Avg
BENOZZATI, GIROLAMO (attributed to)	1	1	$1,885 DM3,339 £1,157 ¥229,784	$1,885 DM3,339 £1,157 ¥229,784	$1,885 DM3,339 £1,157 ¥229,784
BERGER, KARL AUGUST	1	1	$4,025 DM6,887 £2,381 ¥499,825	$4,025 DM6,887 £2,381 ¥499,825	$4,025 DM6,887 £2,381 ¥499,825
BERGONZI, MICHAEL ANGELO	1	1	$113,543 DM167,607 £74,100 ¥12,070,964	$113,543 DM167,607 £74,100 ¥12,070,964	$113,543 DM167,607 £74,100 ¥12,070,964
BERGONZI, RICCARDO	1	1	$4,991 DM8,050 £2,898 ¥587,650	$4,991 DM8,050 £2,898 ¥587,650	$4,991 DM8,050 £2,898 ¥587,650
BERINI, MARCUS	1	0			
BERNADELL, ERNEST	1	0			
BERNADEO, LEON	1	1	$4,057 DM5,649 £2,530 ¥342,936	$4,057 DM5,649 £2,530 ¥342,936	$4,057 DM5,649 £2,530 ¥342,936
BERNARD, ANDRE	1	1	$2,471 DM3,792 £1,610 ¥270,496	$2,471 DM3,792 £1,610 ¥270,496	$2,471 DM3,792 £1,610 ¥270,496
BERNARD, ANDRE (attributed to)	1	0			
BERNARDEL (attributed to)	1	1	$2,249 DM4,071 £1,380 ¥271,432	$2,249 DM4,071 £1,380 ¥271,432	$2,249 DM4,071 £1,380 ¥271,432
BERNARDEL (workshop of)	2	2	$3,565 DM6,025 £2,139 ¥434,930	$28,194 DM41,619 £18,400 ¥2,997,378	$15,880 DM23,822 £10,270 ¥1,716,154
BERNARDEL, AUGUST SEBASTIEN PHILIPPE	10	4	$19,550 DM33,815 £11,730 ¥2,435,370	$25,082 DM38,749 £16,100 ¥2,841,656	$22,473 DM35,634 £14,001 ¥2,602,743
BERNARDEL, AUGUST SEBASTIEN PHILIPPE (attributed to)	4	0			
BERNARDEL, AUGUST SEBASTIEN & ERNEST AUGUST	3	0			
BERNARDEL, GUSTAVE	1	0			
BERNARDEL, GUSTAVE (workshop of)	1	1	$546 DM944 £338 ¥69,229	$546 DM944 £338 ¥69,229	$546 DM944 £338 ¥69,229
BERNARDEL, GUSTAVE ADOLPHE	2	0			
BERNARDEL, LEON	17	12	$1,320 DM2,246 £805 ¥163,407	$6,295 DM9,626 £4,025 ¥700,316	$3,114 DM4,954 £1,920 ¥340,515

| Maker | Items | | Selling Prices | | |
	Bid	Sold	Low	High	Avg
BERNARDEL, LEON (attributed to)	4	2	$1,026	$1,118	$1,072
			DM1,571	DM2,105	DM1,838
			£656	£690	£673
			¥114,398	¥119,163	¥116,780
BERNARDEL, LEON (workshop of)	2	2	$1,150	$1,840	$1,495
			DM1,944	DM3,180	DM2,562
			£690	£1,137	£913
			¥140,300	¥233,192	¥186,746
BERNARDEL FAMILY (attributed to)	1	1	$2,999	$2,999	$2,999
			DM5,697	DM5,697	DM5,697
			£1,852	£1,852	£1,852
			¥315,144	¥315,144	¥315,144
BERTELLI, LUIGI	1	1	$1,382	$1,382	$1,382
			DM1,925	DM1,925	DM1,925
			£862	£862	£862
			¥116,842	¥116,842	¥116,842
BERTOLAZZI, GIACINTO	2	1	$5,654	$5,654	$5,654
			DM10,018	DM10,018	DM10,018
			£3,472	£3,472	£3,472
			¥689,353	¥689,353	¥689,353
BETTS	10	2	$332	$717	$525
			DM536	DM1,237	DM886
			£196	£437	£316
			¥41,098	¥81,789	¥61,443
BETTS, EDWARD	1	1	$1,075	$1,075	$1,075
			DM1,519	DM1,519	DM1,519
			£675	£675	£675
			¥95,416	¥95,416	¥95,416
BETTS, JOHN	18	12	$321	$16,124	$5,698
			DM583	DM22,612	DM8,416
			£196	£10,350	£3,605
			¥40,496	¥1,629,121	¥601,767
BETTS, JOHN (workshop of)	2	1	$8,824	$8,824	$8,824
			DM12,346	DM12,346	DM12,346
			£5,520	£5,520	£5,520
			¥746,376	¥746,376	¥746,376
BEUSCHER, PAUL (attributed to)	3	2	$1,188	$1,233	$1,211
			DM1,819	DM2,209	DM2,014
			£736	£759	£748
			¥132,461	¥143,152	¥137,806
BEUSCHER, PAUL (workshop of)	1	1	$1,725	$1,725	$1,725
			DM3,071	DM3,071	DM3,071
			£1,035	£1,035	£1,035
			¥229,390	¥229,390	¥229,390
BEYER, HERMANN	1	0			
BEYER, NEUMANN	1	0			
BIANCHI, CHRISTOPHER	1	0			
BIANCHI, NICOLO	1	1	$5,851	$5,851	$5,851
			DM11,003	DM11,003	DM11,003
			£3,680	£3,680	£3,680
			¥707,443	¥707,443	¥707,443
BIANCHI, PASQUALE	1	1	$863	$863	$863
			DM1,535	DM1,535	DM1,535
			£526	£526	£526
			¥119,818	¥119,818	¥119,818
BIGNAMI, OTELLO	2	0			

Violin

Maker	Items		Selling Prices		
	Bid	Sold	Low	High	Avg
BIMBI, BARTOLOMEO	2	0			
BIMBI, BARTOLOMEO (ascribed to)	1	1	$7,538	$7,538	$7,538
			DM13,357	DM13,357	DM13,357
			£4,629	£4,629	£4,629
			¥919,138	¥919,138	¥919,138
BIMBI, BARTOLOMEO (attributed to)	2	0			
BINI, LUCIANO	2	1	$2,062	$2,062	$2,062
			DM3,567	DM3,567	DM3,567
			£1,265	£1,265	£1,265
			¥235,290	¥235,290	¥235,290
BIRD, RICHMOND HENRY	7	4	$1,782	$4,713	$3,104
			DM3,115	DM8,932	DM5,819
			£1,093	£2,910	£1,914
			¥191,435	¥497,728	¥333,107
BISCH, PAUL (workshop of)	1	1	$1,725	$1,725	$1,725
			DM3,071	DM3,071	DM3,071
			£1,035	£1,035	£1,035
			¥229,390	¥229,390	¥229,390
BISIACH (attributed to)	1	0			
BISIACH (workshop of)	1	1	$14,752	$14,752	$14,752
			DM20,541	DM20,541	DM20,541
			£9,200	£9,200	£9,200
			¥1,247,042	¥1,247,042	¥1,247,042
BISIACH, CARLO	8	3	$21,942	$28,750	$25,273
			DM37,595	DM49,694	DM42,850
			£13,800	£17,765	£15,505
			¥2,652,912	¥3,643,631	¥3,033,123
BISIACH, LEANDRO	14	8	$7,161	$47,134	$24,352
			DM12,689	DM89,525	DM40,416
			£4,397	£29,095	£15,085
			¥873,181	¥4,952,260	¥2,657,816
BISIACH, LEANDRO (attributed to)	4	2	$8,228	$12,563	$10,396
			DM15,577	DM18,797	DM17,187
			£5,175	£7,475	£6,325
			¥986,303	¥1,401,413	¥1,193,858
BISIACH, LEANDRO (workshop of)	1	1	$25,300	$25,300	$25,300
			DM38,077	DM38,077	DM38,077
			£15,358	£15,358	£15,358
			¥2,828,034	¥2,828,034	¥2,828,034
BISIACH, LEANDRO & GIACOMO	4	1	$32,586	$32,586	$32,586
			DM52,265	DM52,265	DM52,265
			£21,160	£21,160	£21,160
			¥3,707,655	¥3,707,655	¥3,707,655
BISIACH, LEANDRO & GIACOMO (workshop of)	1	1	$26,450	$26,450	$26,450
			DM38,247	DM38,247	DM38,247
			£17,277	£17,277	£17,277
			¥2,678,063	¥2,678,063	¥2,678,063
BISIACH, LEANDRO (II) & GIACOMO	3	1	$26,565	$26,565	$26,565
			DM47,817	DM47,817	DM47,817
			£16,100	£16,100	£16,100
			¥3,830,995	¥3,830,995	¥3,830,995
BISIACH, LEANDRO (JR.)	1	1	$21,379	$21,379	$21,379
			DM37,065	DM37,065	DM37,065
			£12,650	£12,650	£12,650
			¥2,669,150	¥2,669,150	¥2,669,150

Maker	Items		Selling Prices		
	Bid	Sold	Low	High	Avg
BISIACH, LEANDRO (JR.) (workshop of)	2	1	$12,061	$12,061	$12,061
			DM21,372	DM21,372	DM21,372
			£7,406	£7,406	£7,406
			¥1,470,620	¥1,470,620	¥1,470,620
BISIACH FAMILY	1	1	$29,808	$29,808	$29,808
			DM53,360	DM53,360	DM53,360
			£18,400	£18,400	£18,400
			¥3,515,688	¥3,515,688	¥3,515,688
BISIACH FAMILY (MEMBER OF) (attributed to)	2	1	$13,138	$13,138	$13,138
			DM21,896	DM21,896	DM21,896
			£7,820	£7,820	£7,820
			¥1,570,178	¥1,570,178	¥1,570,178
BITTERER, JOSEPH	1	1	$460	$460	$460
			DM828	DM828	DM828
			£276	£276	£276
			¥3,574	¥3,574	¥3,574
BITTNER, ALOIS	1	1	$2,898	$2,898	$2,898
			DM5,210	DM5,210	DM5,210
			£1,725	£1,725	£1,725
			¥335,047	¥335,047	¥335,047
BLACK, JAMES	1	1	$462	$462	$462
			DM664	DM664	DM664
			£299	£299	£299
			¥46,865	¥46,865	¥46,865
BLANCHARD, PAUL	8	3	$11,454	$18,211	$14,596
			DM16,908	DM34,589	DM24,389
			£7,475	£11,241	£9,305
			¥1,217,685	¥1,913,373	¥1,558,917
BLANCHARD, PAUL (attributed to)	2	0			
BLANCHARD, PAUL (workshop of)	1	1	$6,997	$6,997	$6,997
			DM12,130	DM12,130	DM12,130
			£4,140	£4,140	£4,140
			¥873,540	¥873,540	¥873,540
BLANCHI, ALBERTO	5	4	$5,831	$12,908	$9,868
			DM10,109	DM21,344	DM15,608
			£3,450	£8,050	£6,153
			¥741,302	¥1,406,275	¥1,043,855
BLONDELET, EMILE	6	5	$1,424	$2,999	$2,125
			DM2,661	DM5,189	DM3,594
			£897	£1,840	£1,306
			¥168,466	¥342,240	¥244,834
BLONDELET, EMILE (workshop of)	1	1	$1,490	$1,490	$1,490
			DM2,806	DM2,806	DM2,806
			£920	£920	£920
			¥157,522	¥157,522	¥157,522
BLONDELET, H. EMILE	24	11	$1,155	$3,498	$2,126
			DM1,880	DM6,065	DM3,453
			£713	£2,185	£1,307
			¥123,135	¥444,781	¥236,983
BLONDELET, H. EMILE (attributed to)	1	1	$1,812	$1,812	$1,812
			DM2,559	DM2,559	DM2,559
			£1,150	£1,150	£1,150
			¥182,428	¥182,428	¥182,428
BLYTH, WILLIAMSON	3	1	$576	$576	$576
			DM882	DM882	DM882
			£368	£368	£368
			¥64,223	¥64,223	¥64,223

Maker	Items		Selling Prices		
	Bid	Sold	Low	High	Avg
BLYTH, WILLIAMSON (attributed to)	1	1	$452	$452	$452
			DM695	DM695	DM695
			£299	£299	£299
			¥48,206	¥48,206	¥48,206
BOCQUAY, JACQUES	1	1	$17,285	$17,285	$17,285
			DM32,085	DM32,085	DM32,085
			£10,350	£10,350	£10,350
			¥2,312,604	¥2,312,604	¥2,312,604
BOCQUAY, JACQUES (attributed to)	2	0			
BODOR, JOHN JR.	1	1	$2,875	$2,875	$2,875
			DM5,118	DM5,118	DM5,118
			£1,725	£1,725	£1,725
			¥382,317	¥382,317	¥382,317
BOERNER, LAWRENCE E.	2	0			
BOFILL, SALVATORE	1	1	$8,694	$8,694	$8,694
			DM15,629	DM15,629	DM15,629
			£5,175	£5,175	£5,175
			¥1,005,140	¥1,005,140	¥1,005,140
BOLLER, MICHAEL (ascribed to)	1	0			
BONDANELLI, CHIARISSIMO	1	1	$2,249	$2,249	$2,249
			DM3,892	DM3,892	DM3,892
			£1,380	£1,380	£1,380
			¥256,680	¥256,680	¥256,680
BONNAVENTURE, G. (attributed to)	1	1	$1,596	$1,596	$1,596
			DM2,770	DM2,770	DM2,770
			£943	£943	£943
			¥202,377	¥202,377	¥202,377
BONNEL, CHARLES	1	0			
BONNEL, EMILE	3	1	$2,540	$2,540	$2,540
			DM3,578	DM3,578	DM3,578
			£1,610	£1,610	£1,610
			¥259,745	¥259,745	¥259,745
BOOSEY & HAWKES (workshop of)	1	1	$1,233	$1,233	$1,233
			DM1,860	DM1,860	DM1,860
			£747	£747	£747
			¥139,689	¥139,689	¥139,689
BOOTH, WILLIAM (II)	1	1	$3,448	$3,448	$3,448
			DM4,855	DM4,855	DM4,855
			£2,185	£2,185	£2,185
			¥352,510	¥352,510	¥352,510
BOQUAY, JACQUES	2	2	$6,694	$15,456	$11,075
			DM9,867	DM27,793	DM18,830
			£4,370	£9,200	£6,785
			¥713,927	¥1,786,916	¥1,250,421
BORGHI, PIETRO	1	1	$5,807	$5,807	$5,807
			DM8,177	DM8,177	DM8,177
			£3,680	£3,680	£3,680
			¥593,702	¥593,702	¥593,702
BORRIERO, FRANCESCO	1	0			
BOSI, CARLO (attributed to)	2	1	$4,397	$4,397	$4,397
			DM6,751	DM6,751	DM6,751
			£2,875	£2,875	£2,875
			¥479,944	¥479,944	¥479,944
BOSSI, GIUSEPPE	2	0			

Maker	Items Bid	Sold	Selling Prices Low	High	Avg
BOSSI, GIUSEPPE (attributed to)	1	1	$4,801 DM8,021 £2,875 ¥583,596	$4,801 DM8,021 £2,875 ¥583,596	$4,801 DM8,021 £2,875 ¥583,596
BOTTOMLEY, THOMAS (attributed to)	2	1	$983 DM1,405 £621 ¥98,730	$983 DM1,405 £621 ¥98,730	$983 DM1,405 £621 ¥98,730
BOTTURI, BENVENUTO	2	1	$8,942 DM16,946 £5,520 ¥944,306	$8,942 DM16,946 £5,520 ¥944,306	$8,942 DM16,946 £5,520 ¥944,306
BOTTURI, BENVENUTO (ascribed to)	1	1	$704 DM1,080 £460 ¥76,791	$704 DM1,080 £460 ¥76,791	$704 DM1,080 £460 ¥76,791
BOULANGEOT, EMILE	6	4	$966 DM1,737 £575 ¥111,682	$5,624 DM9,729 £3,450 ¥641,700	$3,142 DM5,133 £1,940 ¥333,102
BOULANGEOT, EMILE (workshop of)	1	1	$2,049 DM3,858 £1,265 ¥216,593	$2,049 DM3,858 £1,265 ¥216,593	$2,049 DM3,858 £1,265 ¥216,593
BOULANGEOT, JULES CAMILLE	1	1	$3,671 DM6,118 £2,185 ¥438,726	$3,671 DM6,118 £2,185 ¥438,726	$3,671 DM6,118 £2,185 ¥438,726
BOULANGIER, C.	1	0			
BOULLANGIER, CHARLES	14	7	$3,265 DM6,061 £1,955 ¥436,825	$32,990 DM46,233 £20,700 ¥2,908,040	$12,388 DM19,748 £7,705 ¥1,323,594
BOULLANGIER, CHARLES (attributed to)	2	1	$2,340 DM3,583 £1,495 ¥260,907	$2,340 DM3,583 £1,495 ¥260,907	$2,340 DM3,583 £1,495 ¥260,907
BOULLANGIER, CHARLES (FILS)	1	1	$1,725 DM3,121 £1,058 ¥208,098	$1,725 DM3,121 £1,058 ¥208,098	$1,725 DM3,121 £1,058 ¥208,098
BOWLER, ARTHUR	2	2	$3,448 DM4,855 £2,185 ¥352,510	$4,725 DM6,674 £2,990 ¥421,701	$4,086 DM5,765 £2,588 ¥387,106
BOYES, ARNOLD	2	0			
BRAN, MARSINO	1	1	$1,410 DM2,081 £920 ¥149,869	$1,410 DM2,081 £920 ¥149,869	$1,410 DM2,081 £920 ¥149,869
BRANDNER, JOHANN	1	1	$529 DM780 £345 ¥56,201	$529 DM780 £345 ¥56,201	$529 DM780 £345 ¥56,201
BRAUND, FREDERICK T.	4	4	$756 DM1,155 £483 ¥84,308	$1,601 DM2,341 £1,035 ¥168,871	$1,362 DM1,973 £868 ¥136,931

Maker	Items		Selling Prices		
	Bid	Sold	Low	High	Avg
BRETON	6	4	$169 DM300 £104 ¥22,659	$3,091 DM5,152 £1,840 ¥369,454	$1,343 DM2,245 £802 ¥162,224
BRETON (workshop of)	4	3	$431 DM649 £262 ¥48,205	$633 DM952 £384 ¥70,701	$537 DM812 £335 ¥58,827
BRETON BREVETE	2	1	$187 DM332 £115 ¥22,164	$187 DM332 £115 ¥22,164	$187 DM332 £115 ¥22,164
BRETON, FRANCOIS (workshop of)	4	3	$460 DM664 £293 ¥39,905	$920 DM1,574 £544 ¥114,246	$690 DM1,144 £421 ¥80,533
BRETON FAMILY (MEMBER OF)	1	1	$1,588 DM2,769 £978 ¥192,421	$1,588 DM2,769 £978 ¥192,421	$1,588 DM2,769 £978 ¥192,421
BRIGGS, JAMES WILLIAM	9	4	$1,316 DM2,174 £805 ¥162,955	$5,092 DM8,787 £3,105 ¥581,132	$3,838 DM5,972 £2,415 ¥419,801
BRIGGS, MARTIN	1	1	$160 DM230 £104 ¥16,223	$160 DM230 £104 ¥16,223	$160 DM230 £104 ¥16,223
BROLIO, V. STEPHANO	2	0			
BROSCHI, CARLO	1	1	$2,638 DM4,675 £1,620 ¥321,698	$2,638 DM4,675 £1,620 ¥321,698	$2,638 DM4,675 £1,620 ¥321,698
BROWN, J.	4	3	$672 DM989 £437 ¥71,301	$1,759 DM2,700 £1,150 ¥191,978	$1,121 DM1,814 £721 ¥120,860
BROWN, JAMES	5	2	$1,829 DM3,439 £1,150 ¥221,076	$3,498 DM6,065 £2,070 ¥444,781	$2,663 DM4,752 £1,610 ¥332,928
BRUCKNER, E. (attributed to)	1	0			
BRUCKNER, ERICH (attributed to)	1	1	$790 DM1,304 £483 ¥97,773	$790 DM1,304 £483 ¥97,773	$790 DM1,304 £483 ¥97,773
BRUET, NICOLAS	1	0			
BRUGERE, CHARLES GEORGES	2	0			
BRUGERE, P.	1	1	$3,353 DM6,024 £2,070 ¥395,929	$3,353 DM6,024 £2,070 ¥395,929	$3,353 DM6,024 £2,070 ¥395,929
BRULLO, LORENZO R.	1	0			
BRUNEAU, SIMON	1	1	$2,185 DM3,777 £1,350 ¥276,916	$2,185 DM3,777 £1,350 ¥276,916	$2,185 DM3,777 £1,350 ¥276,916

Maker	Items		Selling Prices		
	Bid	Sold	Low	High	Avg
BRUNO, CARLO	4	1	$9,373	$9,373	$9,373
			DM16,215	DM16,215	DM16,215
			£5,750	£5,750	£5,750
			¥1,069,500	¥1,069,500	¥1,069,500
BRUNO, CARLO (workshop of)	2	2	$805	$1,265	$1,035
			DM1,162	DM1,827	DM1,495
			£513	£806	£659
			¥69,834	¥109,739	¥89,786
BRYANT, L.D.	1	1	$489	$489	$489
			DM826	DM826	DM826
			£293	£293	£293
			¥59,628	¥59,628	¥59,628
BUBENIK, JOHANN	1	1	$2,213	$2,213	$2,213
			DM3,081	DM3,081	DM3,081
			£1,380	£1,380	£1,380
			¥187,056	¥187,056	¥187,056
BUCCI, MARIANO	1	1	$11,322	$11,322	$11,322
			DM15,920	DM15,920	DM15,920
			£7,130	£7,130	£7,130
			¥1,006,563	¥1,006,563	¥1,006,563
BUCHSTETTER, GABRIEL DAVID	3	2	$1,380	$4,907	$3,143
			DM2,498	DM6,931	DM4,714
			£842	£3,105	£1,973
			¥166,621	¥437,920	¥302,271
BUCKMAN, GEORGE H.	3	2	$1,500	$1,632	$1,566
			DM2,301	DM3,029	DM2,665
			£977	£977	£977
			¥164,146	¥218,301	¥191,223
BULLARD, OLIN	1	1	$920	$920	$920
			DM1,555	DM1,555	DM1,555
			£552	£552	£552
			¥112,240	¥112,240	¥112,240
BUTHOD	3	3	$984	$1,641	$1,251
			DM1,505	DM2,951	DM2,106
			£633	£977	£767
			¥97,268	¥189,763	¥142,236
BUTHOD (workshop of)	1	1	$1,610	$1,610	$1,610
			DM2,783	DM2,783	DM2,783
			£995	£995	£995
			¥204,043	¥204,043	¥204,043
BUTHOD, CHARLES LOUIS	2	2	$357	$2,648	$1,502
			DM544	DM4,063	DM2,303
			£230	£1,725	£978
			¥39,583	¥289,817	¥164,700
BUTLER, AVA LUCILE	1	1	$2,645	$2,645	$2,645
			DM3,825	DM3,825	DM3,825
			£1,728	£1,728	£1,728
			¥267,806	¥267,806	¥267,806
BYROM, JOHN	1	1	$7,668	$7,668	$7,668
			DM14,205	DM14,205	DM14,205
			£4,600	£4,600	£4,600
			¥1,024,098	¥1,024,098	¥1,024,098
CAHUSAC	6	2	$1,062	$1,427	$1,244
			DM1,909	DM2,175	DM2,042
			£632	£920	£776
			¥122,753	¥158,332	¥140,543

| Maker | Items | | Selling Prices | | |
	Bid	Sold	Low	High	Avg
CAHUSAC (attributed to)	1	1	$1,604	$1,604	$1,604
			DM2,380	DM2,380	DM2,380
			£1,035	£1,035	£1,035
			¥173,652	¥173,652	¥173,652
CAHUSAC, THOMAS (SR.)	1	1	$2,471	$2,471	$2,471
			DM3,792	DM3,792	DM3,792
			£1,610	£1,610	£1,610
			¥270,496	¥270,496	¥270,496
CAIL, LOUIS	1	1	$920	$920	$920
			DM1,353	DM1,353	DM1,353
			£598	£598	£598
			¥97,570	¥97,570	¥97,570
CAIRNS, PETER	2	1	$338	$338	$338
			DM602	DM602	DM602
			£207	£207	£207
			¥44,221	¥44,221	¥44,221
CALACE, CAVALIERE RAFFAELE (attributed to)	1	1	$1,955	$1,955	$1,955
			DM2,827	DM2,827	DM2,827
			£1,277	£1,277	£1,277
			¥197,944	¥197,944	¥197,944
CALACE, GIUSEPPE	1	1	$4,255	$4,255	$4,255
			DM6,144	DM6,144	DM6,144
			£2,711	£2,711	£2,711
			¥369,121	¥369,121	¥369,121
CALACE, RAFFAELE	1	1	$3,618	$3,618	$3,618
			DM6,411	DM6,411	DM6,411
			£2,222	£2,222	£2,222
			¥441,186	¥441,186	¥441,186
CALCAGNI, BERNARDO	4	3	$22,356	$47,481	$31,849
			DM42,366	DM66,761	DM52,616
			£13,800	£29,900	£19,857
			¥2,360,766	¥4,221,073	¥3,098,907
CALCAGNI, BERNARDO (ascribed to)	1	1	$7,930	$7,930	$7,930
			DM11,705	DM11,705	DM11,705
			£5,175	£5,175	£5,175
			¥843,013	¥843,013	¥843,013
CALCAGNI, BERNARDO (attributed to)	1	1	$8,625	$8,625	$8,625
			DM12,472	DM12,472	DM12,472
			£5,634	£5,634	£5,634
			¥873,281	¥873,281	¥873,281
CALLIER, FRANK	1	1	$690	$690	$690
			DM1,228	DM1,228	DM1,228
			£414	£414	£414
			¥91,756	¥91,756	¥91,756
CALOT, JOSEPH	1	0			
CALOW, WILLIAM	1	1	$1,420	$1,420	$1,420
			DM2,030	DM2,030	DM2,030
			£897	£897	£897
			¥142,610	¥142,610	¥142,610
CALVAROLA, BARTOLOMEO	1	1	$2,865	$2,865	$2,865
			DM5,076	DM5,076	DM5,076
			£1,759	£1,759	£1,759
			¥349,272	¥349,272	¥349,272
CAMILLI, CAMILLO	7	5	$40,886	$134,435	$74,600
			DM70,929	DM224,595	DM124,358
			£24,150	£80,500	£45,760
			¥5,182,832	¥16,340,695	¥8,871,283

Maker	Items		Selling Prices		
	Bid	Sold	Low	High	Avg
CAMILLI, CAMILLO (attributed to)	4	2	$13,800	$16,000	$14,900
			DM24,840	DM27,040	DM25,940
			£8,280	£9,600	£8,940
			¥107,226	¥2,129,120	¥1,118,173
CANDI, CESARE	6	4	$12,702	$26,422	$21,333
			DM17,888	DM43,139	DM32,697
			£8,050	£17,250	£13,369
			¥1,298,723	¥2,818,133	¥2,195,839
CANDI, CESARE (attributed to)	1	0			
CANTOV, JULIUS (attributed to)	1	1	$845	$845	$845
			DM1,397	DM1,397	DM1,397
			£506	£506	£506
			¥98,822	¥98,822	¥98,822
CAPELA, ANTONIO	4	4	$5,589	$8,811	$7,165
			DM8,730	DM13,519	DM11,444
			£3,450	£5,750	£4,534
			¥529,993	¥990,024	¥761,851
CAPELA, D.	1	1	$5,756	$5,756	$5,756
			DM8,141	DM8,141	DM8,141
			£3,680	£3,680	£3,680
			¥584,417	¥584,417	¥584,417
CAPELA, DOMINGOS	1	0			
CAPELLINI, VIRGILIO	1	0			
CAPICCHIONI, MARINO	2	2	$13,800	$59,989	$36,894
			DM24,840	DM113,682	DM69,261
			£8,280	£37,030	£22,655
			¥107,226	¥6,334,722	¥3,220,974
CAPICCHIONI, MARINO (attributed to)	1	1	$12,650	$12,650	$12,650
			DM22,897	DM22,897	DM22,897
			£7,717	£7,717	£7,717
			¥1,527,361	¥1,527,361	¥1,527,361
CAPICCHIONI, MARIO	2	2	$9,603	$27,336	$18,469
			DM16,043	DM46,248	DM31,145
			£5,750	£17,193	£11,471
			¥1,167,193	¥3,386,923	¥2,277,058
CAPONNETTO, STEFANO (attributed to)	1	1	$1,930	$1,930	$1,930
			DM2,701	DM2,701	DM2,701
			£1,208	£1,208	£1,208
			¥163,270	¥163,270	¥163,270
CAPPA, GIOFFREDO	4	1	$50,253	$50,253	$50,253
			DM75,190	DM75,190	DM75,190
			£29,900	£29,900	£29,900
			¥5,605,652	¥5,605,652	¥5,605,652
CAPPA, GIOFFREDO (ascribed to)	1	0			
CAPPA, GIOFFREDO (attributed to)	1	1	$8,114	$8,114	$8,114
			DM11,297	DM11,297	DM11,297
			£5,060	£5,060	£5,060
			¥685,873	¥685,873	¥685,873
CARBONARE, ALAIN	1	1	$5,999	$5,999	$5,999
			DM11,368	DM11,368	DM11,368
			£3,703	£3,703	£3,703
			¥633,472	¥633,472	¥633,472
CARCASSI, LORENZO	5	3	$14,375	$40,176	$26,878
			DM26,105	DM56,490	DM43,900
			£8,798	£25,300	£16,733
			¥1,785,088	¥3,585,769	¥2,709,166

Maker	Items Bid	Sold	Low	Selling Prices High	Avg
CARCASSI, LORENZO & TOMMASO	12	9	$29,808	$55,890	$40,871
			DM51,543	DM105,915	DM71,137
			£18,400	£34,500	£24,972
			¥3,147,688	¥6,069,401	¥4,641,903
CARCASSI, LORENZO & TOMMASO (attributed to)	1	0			
CARCASSI, VINCENZO	1	1	$32,913	$32,913	$32,913
			DM61,893	DM61,893	DM61,893
			£20,700	£20,700	£20,700
			¥3,979,368	¥3,979,368	¥3,979,368
CARDI, LUIGI (ascribed to)	1	0			
CARDI, LUIGI (attributed to)	2	1	$4,481	$4,481	$4,481
			DM7,186	DM7,186	DM7,186
			£2,910	£2,910	£2,910
			¥509,803	¥509,803	¥509,803
CARDINET, D.	1	1	$1,321	$1,321	$1,321
			DM1,948	DM1,948	DM1,948
			£863	£863	£863
			¥140,907	¥140,907	¥140,907
CARESSA, ALBERT	3	1	$3,749	$3,749	$3,749
			DM6,785	DM6,785	DM6,785
			£2,300	£2,300	£2,300
			¥452,387	¥452,387	¥452,387
CARESSA & FRANCAIS	1	0			
CARLETTI, CARLO	8	3	$6,895	$10,563	$9,235
			DM9,711	DM19,418	DM15,592
			£4,370	£6,325	£5,673
			¥705,021	¥1,283,912	¥1,023,650
CARLETTI, CARLO (ascribed to)	1	1	$8,625	$8,625	$8,625
			DM14,908	DM14,908	DM14,908
			£5,329	£5,329	£5,329
			¥1,093,089	¥1,093,089	¥1,093,089
CARLETTI, CARLO (attributed to)	3	0			
CARLETTI, GABRIELE	1	0			
CARLETTI, GENUZIO	2	1	$4,744	$4,744	$4,744
			DM8,539	DM8,539	DM8,539
			£2,875	£2,875	£2,875
			¥684,106	¥684,106	¥684,106
CARLETTI, GENUZIO (ascribed to)	1	1	$4,888	$4,888	$4,888
			DM8,260	DM8,260	DM8,260
			£2,933	£2,933	£2,933
			¥596,275	¥596,275	¥596,275
CARLETTI, ORFEO	2	1	$14,621	$14,621	$14,621
			DM25,295	DM25,295	DM25,295
			£8,970	£8,970	£8,970
			¥1,668,420	¥1,668,420	¥1,668,420
CARLISLE, JAMES REYNOLD	1	1	$3,450	$3,450	$3,450
			DM5,192	DM5,192	DM5,192
			£2,094	£2,094	£2,094
			¥385,641	¥385,641	¥385,641
CARLONI, ASSUNTO	1	1	$3,220	$3,220	$3,220
			DM5,509	DM5,509	DM5,509
			£1,905	£1,905	£1,905
			¥399,860	¥399,860	¥399,860
CARMICHAEL, R.	1	0			

Maker	Items		Selling Prices		
	Bid	Sold	Low	High	Avg
CARROLL, JOHN	1	1	$531	$531	$531
			DM802	DM802	DM802
			£322	£322	£322
			¥60,214	¥60,214	¥60,214
CARSLAW, ROBERT	1	1	$559	$559	$559
			DM979	DM979	DM979
			£345	£345	£345
			¥67,603	¥67,603	¥67,603
CARTWRIGHT, CHARLES D.	4	2	$460	$690	$575
			DM703	DM1,249	DM976
			£303	£421	£362
			¥48,484	¥83,311	¥65,897
CARY, ALPHONSE	2	0			
CASELLA, MARIO	1	0			
CASINI, LAPO	2	0			
CASTAGNERI, ANDREA	5	3	$1,840	$8,797	$5,679
			DM2,814	DM12,329	DM9,059
			£1,211	£5,520	£3,585
			¥193,936	¥775,477	¥581,060
CASTAGNINO, GIUSEPPE	4	4	$9,220	$17,140	$12,871
			DM12,838	DM32,481	DM22,162
			£5,750	£10,580	£8,050
			¥779,401	¥1,809,921	¥1,312,429
CASTELLO, PAOLO	7	3	$5,750	$25,404	$13,835
			DM8,792	DM35,776	DM20,687
			£3,783	£16,100	£8,698
			¥606,050	¥2,597,445	¥1,488,732
CASTELLO, PAOLO (ascribed to)	1	1	$31,866	$31,866	$31,866
			DM55,131	DM55,131	DM55,131
			£19,550	£19,550	£19,550
			¥3,636,300	¥3,636,300	¥3,636,300
CATENARI, ENRICO	3	1	$49,450	$49,450	$49,450
			DM75,614	DM75,614	DM75,614
			£32,533	£32,533	£32,533
			¥5,212,030	¥5,212,030	¥5,212,030
CAUSSIN, F. (attributed to)	1	1	$4,713	$4,713	$4,713
			DM8,953	DM8,953	DM8,953
			£2,910	£2,910	£2,910
			¥495,226	¥495,226	¥495,226
CAUSSIN, F.N.	2	1	$2,422	$2,422	$2,422
			DM4,560	DM4,560	DM4,560
			£1,495	£1,495	£1,495
			¥255,974	¥255,974	¥255,974
CAUSSIN, FRANCOIS	4	2	$7,728	$9,673	$8,700
			DM13,892	DM16,365	DM15,128
			£4,600	£6,084	£5,342
			¥893,458	¥1,198,450	¥1,045,954
CAUSSIN, FRANCOIS (attributed to)	2	2	$960	$2,049	$1,505
			DM1,587	DM3,669	DM2,628
			£575	£1,265	£920
			¥112,298	¥241,704	¥177,001
CAUSSIN FAMILY (MEMBER OF)	2	1	$1,075	$1,075	$1,075
			DM1,812	DM1,812	DM1,812
			£667	£667	£667
			¥131,975	¥131,975	¥131,975

Maker	Items		Selling Prices		
	Bid	Sold	Low	High	Avg
CAVALAZZI, ANTONIO	3	1	$2,812	$2,812	$2,812
			DM4,865	DM4,865	DM4,865
			£1,725	£1,725	£1,725
			¥320,850	¥320,850	¥320,850
CAVALERI, JOSEPH	3	1	$24,705	$24,705	$24,705
			DM37,956	DM37,956	DM37,956
			£16,100	£16,100	£16,100
			¥2,704,623	¥2,704,623	¥2,704,623
CAVALLI, ARISTIDE	8	8	$1,960	$6,572	$3,638
			DM3,473	DM9,832	DM5,999
			£1,203	£3,910	£2,199
			¥238,976	¥733,047	¥420,010
CAVALLI, ARISTIDE (workshop of)	2	2	$1,255	$3,105	$2,180
			DM1,878	DM4,748	DM3,313
			£747	£2,043	£1,395
			¥140,048	¥327,267	¥233,657
CAVALLO, LUIGI	1	0			
CAVANI, G.	1	0			
CAVANI, GIOVANNI	1	0			
CAVANI, GIOVANNI (ascribed to)	1	1	$2,796	$2,796	$2,796
			DM2,945	DM2,945	DM2,945
			£1,725	£1,725	£1,725
			¥213,546	¥213,546	¥213,546
CAVANI, GIOVANNI (II)	1	0			
CAVANI, VINCENZO	3	1	$5,442	$5,442	$5,442
			DM9,435	DM9,435	DM9,435
			£3,220	£3,220	£3,220
			¥679,420	¥679,420	¥679,420
CAYFORD, FREDERICK	1	1	$3,187	$3,187	$3,187
			DM5,513	DM5,513	DM5,513
			£1,955	£1,955	£1,955
			¥363,630	¥363,630	¥363,630
CELESTINI, ANTONIO	1	0			
CELONIATO, GIOVANNI FRANCESCO	4	2	$30,925	$33,534	$32,229
			DM46,270	DM63,549	DM54,910
			£18,400	£20,700	£19,550
			¥3,449,632	¥3,541,149	¥3,495,391
CERMAK, JOSEF ANTONIN	1	1	$3,220	$3,220	$3,220
			DM4,846	DM4,846	DM4,846
			£1,955	£1,955	£1,955
			¥359,932	¥359,932	¥359,932
CERMAK, JOSEF ANTONIN (attributed to)	1	1	$530	$530	$530
			DM783	DM783	DM783
			£345	£345	£345
			¥56,488	¥56,488	¥56,488
CERRUTI, RICARDO	1	0			
CERUTI, ENRICO	6	3	$30,576	$61,851	$43,045
			DM43,250	DM116,311	DM75,190
			£19,550	£38,900	£26,767
			¥3,104,716	¥7,478,136	¥4,942,259
CERUTI, ENRICO (ascribed to)	2	2	$8,625	$31,688	$20,157
			DM14,908	DM52,940	DM33,924
			£5,329	£18,975	£12,152
			¥1,093,089	¥3,851,735	¥2,472,412

| Maker | Items | | Selling Prices | | |
	Bid	Sold	Low	High	Avg
CERUTI, GIOVANNI BATTISTA					
(attributed to)	2	2	$1,610	$7,680	$4,645
			DM2,721	DM14,442	DM8,581
			£966	£4,830	£2,898
			¥214,243	¥928,519	¥571,381
CERUTI, GIUSEPPE	1	0			
CERUTI FAMILY (MEMBER OF)	1	1	$40,572	$40,572	$40,572
			DM72,957	DM72,957	DM72,957
			£24,150	£24,150	£24,150
			¥4,690,655	¥4,690,655	¥4,690,655
CHADWICK, JOHN	1	1	$1,228	$1,228	$1,228
			DM1,735	DM1,735	DM1,735
			£782	£782	£782
			¥104,851	¥104,851	¥104,851
CHAMPION, RENE	2	1	$1,585	$1,585	$1,585
			DM2,337	DM2,337	DM2,337
			£1,035	£1,035	£1,035
			¥169,088	¥169,088	¥169,088
CHANNON, FREDERICK WILLIAM	1	1	$4,321	$4,321	$4,321
			DM7,219	DM7,219	DM7,219
			£2,588	£2,588	£2,588
			¥525,237	¥525,237	¥525,237
CHANOT	1	0			
CHANOT, FRANCOIS	1	0			
CHANOT, FREDERICK WILLIAM	3	3	$4,660	$7,486	$6,424
			DM4,909	DM12,769	DM9,596
			£2,875	£4,830	£3,987
			¥355,911	¥827,598	¥664,629
CHANOT, G.A.	4	4	$1,671	$5,511	$3,488
			DM2,565	DM9,266	DM5,530
			£1,093	£3,450	£2,199
			¥182,379	¥676,417	¥399,313
CHANOT, GEORGE	3	1	$40,331	$40,331	$40,331
			DM67,379	DM67,379	DM67,379
			£24,150	£24,150	£24,150
			¥4,902,209	¥4,902,209	¥4,902,209
CHANOT, GEORGE ADOLPH	7	2	$3,498	$7,065	$5,282
			DM6,065	DM9,978	DM8,022
			£2,070	£4,485	£3,278
			¥436,770	¥711,469	¥574,120
CHANOT, GEORGE ADOLPH (workshop of)	1	1	$4,600	$4,600	$4,600
			DM7,774	DM7,774	DM7,774
			£2,760	£2,760	£2,760
			¥561,200	¥561,200	¥561,200
CHANOT, GEORGES	8	8	$2,996	$32,200	$19,309
			DM4,422	DM58,475	DM33,402
			£1,955	£19,706	£11,737
			¥318,471	¥3,998,596	¥2,267,207
CHANOT, GEORGES (attributed to)	1	0			
CHANOT, GEORGES (II)	2	2	$1,925	$10,971	$6,448
			DM3,562	DM20,631	DM12,096
			£1,150	£6,900	£4,025
			¥256,554	¥1,326,456	¥791,505
CHANOT, GEORGES (III)	1	0			
CHANOT, JOSEPH ANTHONY	1	0			
CHANOT FAMILY (MEMBER OF)	1	0			

Maker	Items		Selling Prices		
	Bid	Sold	Low	High	Avg
CHAPPUY	5	5	$155	$1,844	$1,148
			DM270	DM2,568	DM1,731
			£92	£1,150	£713
			¥19,721	¥184,886	¥115,660
CHAPPUY (attributed to)	1	1	$679	$679	$679
			DM1,235	DM1,235	DM1,235
			£414	£414	£414
			¥85,756	¥85,756	¥85,756
CHAPPUY, A.	1	1	$1,266	$1,266	$1,266
			DM2,195	DM2,195	DM2,195
			£748	£748	£748
			¥160,421	¥160,421	¥160,421
CHAPPUY, AUGUSTINE	1	0			
CHAPPUY, N.	1	0			
CHAPPUY, N.A. (attributed to)	1	1	$2,142	$2,142	$2,142
			DM4,069	DM4,069	DM4,069
			£1,323	£1,323	£1,323
			¥225,103	¥225,103	¥225,103
CHAPPUY, NICOLAS	1	1	$3,214	$3,214	$3,214
			DM6,104	DM6,104	DM6,104
			£1,984	£1,984	£1,984
			¥337,654	¥337,654	¥337,654
CHAPPUY, NICOLAS AUGUSTIN	11	6	$1,315	$4,258	$2,400
			DM1,849	DM7,988	DM4,074
			£828	£2,645	£1,482
			¥117,352	¥511,860	¥282,700
CHAROTTE	2	2	$706	$923	$1,139
			DM971	DM1,345	DM1,718
			£437	£564	£690
			¥58,816	¥93,923	¥129,030
CHAROTTE, VICTOR JOSEPH	2	0			
CHAROTTE-MILLOT, JOSEPH	2	1	$1,102	$1,102	$1,102
			DM1,853	DM1,853	DM1,853
			£690	£690	£690
			¥135,283	¥135,283	¥135,283
CHAROTTE-MILLOT, JOSEPH (workshop of)	1	1	$575	$575	$575
			DM994	DM994	DM994
			£355	£355	£355
			¥72,873	¥72,873	¥72,873
CHERPITEL, GEORGE	1	0			
CHERPITEL, L.	2	0			
CHERPITEL, LOUIS	2	0			
CHERPITEL, N.E. (attributed to)	1	1	$2,999	$2,999	$2,999
			DM5,697	DM5,697	DM5,697
			£1,852	£1,852	£1,852
			¥315,144	¥315,144	¥315,144
CHEVRIER (ascribed to)	1	1	$282	$282	$282
			DM502	DM502	DM502
			£173	£173	£173
			¥36,851	¥36,851	¥36,851
CHEVRIER, ANDRE	1	1	$1,660	$1,660	$1,660
			DM2,311	DM2,311	DM2,311
			£1,035	£1,035	£1,035
			¥140,292	¥140,292	¥140,292
CHEVRIER, ANDRE (ascribed to)	1	0			

Maker	Items		Selling Prices		
	Bid	Sold	Low	High	Avg
CHEVRIER, CLAUDE	4	3	$1,093	$1,723	$1,360
			DM1,945	DM2,427	DM2,179
			£656	£1,092	£832
			¥145,281	¥176,175	¥159,514
CHIESA, CARLO	2	1	$2,823	$2,823	$2,823
			DM4,338	DM4,338	DM4,338
			£1,840	£1,840	£1,840
			¥309,100	¥309,100	¥309,100
CHIOCCHI, GAETANO	2	1	$6,085	$6,085	$6,085
			DM8,473	DM8,473	DM8,473
			£3,795	£3,795	£3,795
			¥514,405	¥514,405	¥514,405
CHIOCCHI, GAETANO (attributed to)	1	1	$12,184	$12,184	$12,184
			DM21,603	DM21,603	DM21,603
			£7,475	£7,475	£7,475
			¥1,440,657	¥1,440,657	¥1,440,657
CHIPOT, JEAN BAPTISTE	1	1	$4,032	$4,032	$4,032
			DM5,651	DM5,651	DM5,651
			£2,530	£2,530	£2,530
			¥355,427	¥355,427	¥355,427
CHIPOT, P. (attributed to)	1	1	$2,385	$2,385	$2,385
			DM3,524	DM3,524	DM3,524
			£1,553	£1,553	£1,553
			¥254,197	¥254,197	¥254,197
CHIPOT, PAUL	1	1	$4,844	$4,844	$4,844
			DM9,120	DM9,120	DM9,120
			£2,990	£2,990	£2,990
			¥511,948	¥511,948	¥511,948
CHIPOT-VUILLAUME	24	20	$677	$3,680	$1,840
			DM1,146	DM5,314	DM3,013
			£414	£2,345	£1,132
			¥78,451	¥319,240	¥208,815
CHIPOT-VUILLAUME (workshop of)	2	2	$1,380	$1,955	$1,668
			DM2,332	DM3,304	DM2,818
			£828	£1,173	£1,001
			¥183,637	¥238,510	¥211,073
CICILIATI, ALESSANDRO	1	1	$5,216	$5,216	$5,216
			DM9,370	DM9,370	DM9,370
			£3,220	£3,220	£3,220
			¥615,889	¥615,889	¥615,889
CIOFFI, A.	1	0			
CLARK, HOMER H.	1	1	$5,796	$5,796	$5,796
			DM10,419	DM10,419	DM10,419
			£3,450	£3,450	£3,450
			¥670,094	¥670,094	¥670,094
CLAUDOT, ALBERT	1	1	$4,945	$4,945	$4,945
			DM8,950	DM8,950	DM8,950
			£3,016	£3,016	£3,016
			¥597,059	¥597,059	¥597,059
CLAUDOT, AUGUSTIN	2	2	$3,046	$4,888	$3,967
			DM4,271	DM7,840	DM6,055
			£1,955	£3,174	£2,565
			¥307,723	¥556,148	¥431,936
CLAUDOT, CHARLES	4	2	$863	$3,416	$2,139
			DM1,491	DM5,154	DM3,323
			£533	£2,070	£1,301
			¥109,309	¥387,090	¥248,199

| Maker | Items | | Selling Prices | | |
	Bid	Sold	Low	High	Avg
CLAUDOT, CHARLES II	2	2	$1,131	$2,313	$1,722
			DM2,004	DM3,913	DM2,958
			£694	£1,455	£1,075
			¥137,871	¥286,586	¥212,228
CLEMENS, ROBERT	1	1	$1,380	$1,380	$1,380
			DM2,077	DM2,077	DM2,077
			£838	£838	£838
			¥154,256	¥154,256	¥154,256
CLEMENT, JEAN LAMBERT	1	1	$6,454	$6,454	$6,454
			DM8,987	DM8,987	DM8,987
			£4,025	£4,025	£4,025
			¥545,581	¥545,581	¥545,581
CLEMENT, JEAN LAMBERT (attributed to)	1	1	$4,099	$4,099	$4,099
			DM7,767	DM7,767	DM7,767
			£2,530	£2,530	£2,530
			¥432,807	¥432,807	¥432,807
CLOUGH, GEORGE	3	1	$1,272	$1,272	$1,272
			DM1,880	DM1,880	DM1,880
			£828	£828	£828
			¥135,572	¥135,572	¥135,572
COCCHIONI, ERALDO (ascribed to)	1	0			
COCKCROFT, W.	1	1	$825	$825	$825
			DM1,493	DM1,493	DM1,493
			£506	£506	£506
			¥99,525	¥99,525	¥99,525
COCKER, LAWRENCE	3	1	$2,113	$2,113	$2,113
			DM3,529	DM3,529	DM3,529
			£1,265	£1,265	£1,265
			¥256,782	¥256,782	¥256,782
COFFMANN, C.R.	1	0			
COINUS, ANDRE	1	1	$3,635	$3,635	$3,635
			DM5,134	DM5,134	DM5,134
			£2,300	£2,300	£2,300
			¥324,385	¥324,385	¥324,385
COLAPIETRO, FRANCESCO	2	0			
COLE, JAMES	3	2	$1,590	$2,213	$1,902
			DM2,349	DM3,081	DM2,715
			£1,035	£1,380	£1,208
			¥169,465	¥187,056	¥178,260
COLEMAN, EDWARD E.	1	1	$1,265	$1,265	$1,265
			DM2,187	DM2,187	DM2,187
			£782	£782	£782
			¥160,320	¥160,320	¥160,320
COLIN, JEAN BAPTISTE	32	27	$863	$2,824	$1,686
			DM1,411	DM4,832	DM2,725
			£533	£1,840	£1,035
			¥89,135	¥313,145	¥185,147
COLIN, JEAN BAPTISTE (attributed to)	1	1	$1,078	$1,078	$1,078
			DM1,656	DM1,656	DM1,656
			£713	£713	£713
			¥114,953	¥114,953	¥114,953
COLIN, JEAN BAPTISTE (workshop of)	1	1	$633	$633	$633
			DM1,093	DM1,093	DM1,093
			£391	£391	£391
			¥80,160	¥80,160	¥80,160

Maker	Items		Selling Prices		
	Bid	*Sold*	*Low*	*High*	*Avg*
COLLENET, RAYMOND	1	1	$2,178	$2,178	$2,178
			DM3,066	DM3,066	DM3,066
			£1,380	£1,380	£1,380
			¥222,638	¥222,638	¥222,638
COLLIER & DAVIS	2	2	$1,252	$4,121	$2,686
			DM1,924	DM5,779	DM3,851
			£828	£2,645	£1,737
			¥133,494	¥416,331	¥274,913
COLLIN, J.B. (workshop of)	1	1	$690	$690	$690
			DM1,181	DM1,181	DM1,181
			£408	£408	£408
			¥85,684	¥85,684	¥85,684
COLLIN-MEZIN	1	1	$4,658	$4,658	$4,658
			DM8,769	DM8,769	DM8,769
			£2,875	£2,875	£2,875
			¥492,258	¥492,258	¥492,258
COLLIN-MEZIN (attributed to)	4	2	$2,249	$2,485	$2,367
			DM3,576	DM4,071	DM3,823
			£1,380	£1,610	£1,495
			¥252,351	¥271,432	¥261,892
COLLIN-MEZIN (workshop of)	5	4	$546	$2,523	$1,400
			DM835	DM4,269	DM2,281
			£359	£1,587	£869
			¥57,575	¥312,639	¥169,375
COLLIN-MEZIN, CH.J.B.	88	66	$734	$7,700	$3,773
			DM1,099	DM14,246	DM6,152
			£437	£4,600	£2,329
			¥81,929	¥1,026,214	¥425,168
COLLIN-MEZIN, CH.J.B. (attributed to)	8	6	$691	$3,710	$2,098
			DM1,205	DM6,212	DM3,455
			£426	£2,415	£1,303
			¥83,760	¥402,615	¥233,044
COLLIN-MEZIN, CH.J.B. (workshop of)	5	4	$1,610	$2,875	$2,230
			DM2,721	DM4,996	DM3,758
			£966	£1,878	£1,391
			¥177,213	¥333,242	¥249,492
COLLIN-MEZIN, CH.J.B. (FILS)	16	13	$884	$5,467	$3,379
			DM1,301	DM9,250	DM5,664
			£575	£3,439	£2,075
			¥93,817	¥677,385	¥389,207
COLLIN-MEZIN, CH.J.B. (FILS) (attributed to)	2	1	$1,407	$1,407	$1,407
			DM2,460	DM2,460	DM2,460
			£863	£863	£863
			¥166,171	¥166,171	¥166,171
COLLIN-MEZIN, CH.J.B. (II)	10	5	$1,586	$2,648	$2,178
			DM2,341	DM4,063	DM3,352
			£1,035	£1,725	£1,411
			¥168,603	¥289,817	¥241,151
COLLIN-MEZIN, CH.J.B. (III)	7	3	$872	$2,467	$1,935
			DM1,232	DM3,723	DM2,865
			£552	£1,610	£1,219
			¥77,852	¥279,565	¥206,563
COLLINS, GLEN	1	1	$27,852	$27,852	$27,852
			DM52,781	DM52,781	DM52,781
			£17,193	£17,193	£17,193
			¥2,941,121	¥2,941,121	¥2,941,121

| Maker | Items | | Selling Prices | | |
	Bid	Sold	Low	High	Avg
COLOMBO, CAMILLO	2	0			
COLT, E.W.	1	0			
COMBS, JOHN	1	1	$230	$230	$230
			DM416	DM416	DM416
			£140	£140	£140
			¥27,770	¥27,770	¥27,770
COMSTOCK, WILMER E.	1	0			
CONANT, WILLIAM A.	4	3	$374	$1,035	$700
			DM572	DM1,789	DM1,184
			£246	£640	£437
			¥39,393	¥131,171	¥86,004
CONE, GEORGES (workshop of)	1	1	$1,610	$1,610	$1,610
			DM2,755	DM2,755	DM2,755
			£952	£952	£952
			¥199,930	¥199,930	¥199,930
CONE, GEORGES & FILS	1	1	$3,353	$3,353	$3,353
			DM6,024	DM6,024	DM6,024
			£2,070	£2,070	£2,070
			¥395,929	¥395,929	¥395,929
CONIA, STEFANO	7	4	$1,651	$7,376	$4,947
			DM2,863	DM11,397	DM7,863
			£977	£4,600	£3,012
			¥206,147	¥820,971	¥541,207
CONNELAN, MICHAEL	1	1	$384	$384	$384
			DM635	DM635	DM635
			£230	£230	£230
			¥44,919	¥44,919	¥44,919
CONTAVALLI	1	0			
CONTAVALLI, LUIGI	1	1	$3,392	$3,392	$3,392
			DM6,011	DM6,011	DM6,011
			£2,083	£2,083	£2,083
			¥413,612	¥413,612	¥413,612
CONTAVALLI, PRIMO	2	1	$16,822	$16,822	$16,822
			DM28,460	DM28,460	DM28,460
			£10,580	£10,580	£10,580
			¥2,084,260	¥2,084,260	¥2,084,260
CONTI, IVANO	1	1	$2,950	$2,950	$2,950
			DM4,108	DM4,108	DM4,108
			£1,840	£1,840	£1,840
			¥249,408	¥249,408	¥249,408
CONTINO, ALFREDO	7	7	$8,050	$22,356	$16,208
			DM11,640	DM42,090	DM27,566
			£5,258	£13,800	£10,037
			¥815,063	¥2,736,425	¥1,861,952
CONTINO, ALFREDO (attributed to)	1	1	$5,451	$5,451	$5,451
			DM9,457	DM9,457	DM9,457
			£3,220	£3,220	£3,220
			¥691,044	¥691,044	¥691,044
CONTRERAS, JOSE	2	2	$14,117	$25,310	$19,714
			DM21,689	DM43,908	DM32,799
			£9,200	£14,950	£12,075
			¥1,545,499	¥3,208,420	¥2,376,959
COOPER, HUGH W.	1	1	$805	$805	$805
			DM1,164	DM1,164	DM1,164
			£526	£526	£526
			¥81,506	¥81,506	¥81,506

| | *Items* | | *Selling Prices* | | |
Maker	Bid	Sold	Low	High	Avg
CORATTI, IVANO	1	1	$6,561	$6,561	$6,561
			DM11,351	DM11,351	DM11,351
			£4,025	£4,025	£4,025
			¥748,650	¥748,650	¥748,650
CORDANO, GIACOMO FILIPPO	3	1	$24,967	$24,967	$24,967
			DM41,711	DM41,711	DM41,711
			£14,950	£14,950	£14,950
			¥3,034,701	¥3,034,701	¥3,034,701
CORNELLISSEN, MARTEN	2	1	$6,392	$6,392	$6,392
			DM8,987	DM8,987	DM8,987
			£4,025	£4,025	£4,025
			¥568,221	¥568,221	¥568,221
CORSBY, GEORGE	4	0			
CORSINI, GIORGIO	1	0			
COSSU, FRANCESCO	2	0			
COSTA, FELIX MORI	1	1	$10,051	$10,051	$10,051
			DM15,038	DM15,038	DM15,038
			£5,980	£5,980	£5,980
			¥1,121,130	¥1,121,130	¥1,121,130
COUCH, C.M.	1	1	$345	$345	$345
			DM614	DM614	DM614
			£207	£207	£207
			¥45,878	¥45,878	¥45,878
COURTIER, LOUIS	1	0			
COUTURIEUX	1	1	$553	$553	$553
			DM770	DM770	DM770
			£345	£345	£345
			¥46,764	¥46,764	¥46,764
COUTURIEUX, M.	3	3	$768	$932	$835
			DM1,283	DM1,754	DM1,476
			£460	£575	£511
			¥93,375	¥102,022	¥97,950
CRAIG, JOHN	1	1	$1,546	$1,546	$1,546
			DM2,778	DM2,778	DM2,778
			£920	£920	£920
			¥178,692	¥178,692	¥178,692
CRAMOND	4	2	$402	$710	$556
			DM751	DM1,238	DM994
			£253	£437	£345
			¥47,516	¥86,023	¥66,770
CRAMOND, CHARLES	1	0			
CRASKE, GEORGE	37	25	$1,383	$7,498	$5,162
			DM1,978	DM13,294	DM8,542
			£874	£4,600	£3,179
			¥138,954	¥886,558	¥585,625
CRAY, PHILLIP	1	1	$2,437	$2,437	$2,437
			DM3,445	DM3,445	DM3,445
			£1,553	£1,553	£1,553
			¥208,161	¥208,161	¥208,161
CREMONINI, VIRGILIO	1	0			
CROSS, NATHANIEL	1	1	$1,932	$1,932	$1,932
			DM3,473	DM3,473	DM3,473
			£1,150	£1,150	£1,150
			¥223,365	¥223,365	¥223,365

| Maker | Items | | Selling Prices | | |
	Bid	Sold	Low	High	Avg
CROSS, NATHANIEL (attributed to)	2	1	$4,481	$4,481	$4,481
			DM7,186	DM7,186	DM7,186
			£2,910	£2,910	£2,910
			¥509,803	¥509,803	¥509,803
CROUT, THOMAS FARROW (attributed to)	1	1	$486	$486	$486
			DM744	DM744	DM744
			£311	£311	£311
			¥54,188	¥54,188	¥54,188
CUNAULT, GEORGES	4	3	$1,840	$12,617	$6,786
			DM2,769	DM21,345	DM10,777
			£1,117	£7,935	£4,244
			¥205,675	¥1,563,195	¥755,896
CUNAULT, GEORGES (workshop of)	1	0			
CUNIN, ALBERT (attributed to)	1	1	$1,594	$1,594	$1,594
			DM2,885	DM2,885	DM2,885
			£978	£978	£978
			¥192,363	¥192,363	¥192,363
CURLETTO, ANSELMO	3	1	$6,351	$6,351	$6,351
			DM8,944	DM8,944	DM8,944
			£4,025	£4,025	£4,025
			¥649,361	¥649,361	¥649,361
CURTIL, ANTOINE	1	1	$2,847	$2,847	$2,847
			DM4,787	DM4,787	DM4,787
			£1,783	£1,783	£1,783
			¥349,482	¥349,482	¥349,482
CURTIN, JOSEPH	2	2	$15,902	$25,709	$20,806
			DM23,495	DM48,721	DM36,108
			£10,350	£15,870	£13,110
			¥1,694,647	¥2,714,881	¥2,204,764
CURTIS, ROGER	1	1	$1,160	$1,160	$1,160
			DM1,735	DM1,735	DM1,735
			£690	£690	£690
			¥129,361	¥129,361	¥129,361
CUTHBERT, ROBERT	1	1	$9,143	$9,143	$9,143
			DM17,193	DM17,193	DM17,193
			£5,750	£5,750	£5,750
			¥1,105,380	¥1,105,380	¥1,105,380
CUYPERS, J.T. (attributed to)	2	1	$857	$857	$857
			DM1,628	DM1,628	DM1,628
			£529	£529	£529
			¥90,041	¥90,041	¥90,041
CUYPERS, JOHANNES	8	5	$28,756	$44,988	$36,880
			DM53,268	DM77,832	DM63,931
			£17,250	£27,600	£22,598
			¥3,376,541	¥5,133,600	¥4,211,353
CUYPERS, JOHANNES (attributed to)	1	1	$5,639	$5,639	$5,639
			DM8,324	DM8,324	DM8,324
			£3,680	£3,680	£3,680
			¥599,476	¥599,476	¥599,476
CUYPERS, JOHANNES FRANCIS	1	1	$19,205	$19,205	$19,205
			DM32,085	DM32,085	DM32,085
			£11,500	£11,500	£11,500
			¥2,334,385	¥2,334,385	¥2,334,385
CUYPERS, JOHANNES THEODORUS	3	3	$28,808	$32,712	$31,020
			DM46,204	DM53,363	DM49,232
			£17,250	£20,700	£19,263
			¥2,919,466	¥3,907,988	¥3,443,010

Maker	Items Bid	Sold	Selling Prices Low	High	Avg
CUYPERS FAMILY (MEMBER OF)	1	1	$10,588 DM16,267 £6,900 ¥1,159,124	$10,588 DM16,267 £6,900 ¥1,159,124	$10,588 DM16,267 £6,900 ¥1,159,124
CUYPERS FAMILY (MEMBER OF) (ascribed to)	1	1	$10,284 DM19,533 £6,348 ¥1,080,493	$10,284 DM19,533 £6,348 ¥1,080,493	$10,284 DM19,533 £6,348 ¥1,080,493
DAHLEN, FRANS WALDEMAR	2	2	$1,344 DM2,246 £805 ¥163,407	$2,113 DM3,529 £1,265 ¥256,782	$1,728 DM2,888 £1,035 ¥210,095
DAILEY, ISRAEL A.	1	1	$1,150 DM2,082 £702 ¥138,851	$1,150 DM2,082 £702 ¥138,851	$1,150 DM2,082 £702 ¥138,851
D'ALAGLIO, JOSEPH	1	1	$44,085 DM74,128 £27,600 ¥5,411,339	$44,085 DM74,128 £27,600 ¥5,411,339	$44,085 DM74,128 £27,600 ¥5,411,339
DAL CANTO, GIUSTINO	3	2	$2,313 DM3,913 £1,455 ¥286,586	$6,955 DM12,503 £4,140 ¥804,112	$4,634 DM8,208 £2,797 ¥545,349
DAL CANTO, GIUSTINO (attributed to)	1	1	$3,195 DM4,598 £2,070 ¥324,452	$3,195 DM4,598 £2,070 ¥324,452	$3,195 DM4,598 £2,070 ¥324,452
DALLA COSTA, PIETRO ANTONIO	3	2	$44,806 DM71,865 £29,095 ¥5,098,026	$56,925 DM85,905 £34,500 ¥6,451,500	$50,866 DM78,885 £31,798 ¥5,774,763
DALLA COSTA, PIETRO ANTONIO (attributed to)	1	1	$20,700 DM34,983 £12,420 ¥2,525,400	$20,700 DM34,983 £12,420 ¥2,525,400	$20,700 DM34,983 £12,420 ¥2,525,400
DALL'AGLIO, GIUSEPPE	3	0			
DALL'AGLIO, GIUSEPPE (ascribed to)	2	2	$26,082 DM49,427 £16,100 ¥2,754,227	$29,994 DM56,841 £18,515 ¥3,167,361	$28,038 DM53,134 £17,308 ¥2,960,794
DALLINGER, SEBASTIAN	1	0			
DARBEY, GEORGE	3	3	$2,888 DM5,342 £1,725 ¥384,830	$5,972 DM8,976 £3,565 ¥665,090	$4,243 DM6,753 £2,607 ¥490,757
DARBY	1	0			
DARCHE, HILAIRE	5	3	$6,427 DM12,208 £3,968 ¥675,308	$11,523 DM21,390 £6,900 ¥1,541,736	$8,483 DM15,631 £5,156 ¥1,034,534
DARCHE, NICHOLAS	1	1	$1,610 DM2,924 £985 ¥199,930	$1,610 DM2,924 £985 ¥199,930	$1,610 DM2,924 £985 ¥199,930

| Maker | Items | | Selling Prices | | |
	Bid	Sold	Low	High	Avg
D'ARIA, VINCENZO	1	1	$11,178	$11,178	$11,178
			DM20,079	DM20,079	DM20,079
			£6,900	£6,900	£6,900
			¥1,319,763	¥1,319,763	¥1,319,763
DARTE, A.	1	1	$2,785	$2,785	$2,785
			DM5,290	DM5,290	DM5,290
			£1,719	£1,719	£1,719
			¥292,634	¥292,634	¥292,634
DARTE, AUGUSTE	2	1	$3,957	$3,957	$3,957
			DM5,597	DM5,597	DM5,597
			£2,530	£2,530	£2,530
			¥401,787	¥401,787	¥401,787
DA RUB, ANGELO (attributed to)	1	1	$12,633	$12,633	$12,633
			DM21,902	DM21,902	DM21,902
			£7,475	£7,475	£7,475
			¥1,577,225	¥1,577,225	¥1,577,225
DAY, JOHN	1	1	$6,900	$6,900	$6,900
			DM11,806	DM11,806	DM11,806
			£4,081	£4,081	£4,081
			¥856,842	¥856,842	¥856,842
DAY, WILLIAM	2	0			
DEARLOVE, MARK	1	1	$5,403	$5,403	$5,403
			DM9,672	DM9,672	DM9,672
			£3,335	£3,335	£3,335
			¥637,218	¥637,218	¥637,218
DEARLOVE, MARK WILLIAM	1	0			
DEAS, WILLIAM	2	1	$282	$282	$282
			DM466	DM466	DM466
			£173	£173	£173
			¥34,919	¥34,919	¥34,919
DE BARBIERI, PAOLO	5	2	$17,986	$19,960	$18,973
			DM25,441	DM28,110	DM26,776
			£11,500	£12,650	£12,075
			¥1,826,304	¥2,040,850	¥1,933,577
DEBLAYE, ALBERT	9	7	$1,921	$2,981	$2,387
			DM3,066	DM5,612	DM4,061
			£1,150	£1,840	£1,481
			¥222,638	¥315,045	¥269,294
DEBLAYE, ALBERT (attributed to)	7	4	$1,034	$2,474	$1,637
			DM1,534	DM3,655	DM2,422
			£667	£1,610	£1,064
			¥111,909	¥263,612	¥173,499
DEBLAYE, ALBERT (workshop of)	1	1	$1,495	$1,495	$1,495
			DM2,558	DM2,558	DM2,558
			£884	£884	£884
			¥185,649	¥185,649	¥185,649
DE COMBLE, AMBROISE	1	1	$7,668	$7,668	$7,668
			DM14,205	DM14,205	DM14,205
			£4,600	£4,600	£4,600
			¥1,024,098	¥1,024,098	¥1,024,098
DE COMBLE, AMBROISE (attributed to)	1	1	$6,184	$6,184	$6,184
			DM9,137	DM9,137	DM9,137
			£4,025	£4,025	£4,025
			¥659,029	¥659,029	¥659,029
DECONET, MICHAEL	1	0			

| Maker | Items | | Selling Prices | | |
	Bid	Sold	Low	High	Avg
DEFAT, GEORGES	1	1	$9,087	$9,087	$9,087
			DM12,835	DM12,835	DM12,835
			£5,750	£5,750	£5,750
			¥810,963	¥810,963	¥810,963
DEGANI, DOMENICO (attributed to)	2	1	$7,590	$7,590	$7,590
			DM11,454	DM11,454	DM11,454
			£4,600	£4,600	£4,600
			¥860,200	¥860,200	¥860,200
DEGANI, EUGENIO	17	12	$17,087	$35,337	$28,608
			DM24,169	DM64,961	DM47,793
			£10,925	£23,000	£17,717
			¥1,734,988	¥4,069,269	¥3,223,357
DEGANI, EUGENIO (attributed to)	2	0			
DEGANI, GIULIO	15	9	$5,175	$30,360	$15,754
			DM7,701	DM45,816	DM26,103
			£3,198	£18,400	£9,562
			¥486,578	¥3,440,800	¥1,884,183
DE JONG, MATTHIJS	1	0			
DEL BUSSETTO, GIOVANNI MARIA	1	1	$248,711	$248,711	$248,711
			DM471,322	DM471,322	DM471,322
			£153,525	£153,525	£153,525
			¥26,263,522	¥26,263,522	¥26,263,522
DEL CANTO, GIUSTINO (attributed to)	1	0			
DELEPLANQUE, GERARD J.	2	2	$2,599	$5,654	$4,126
			DM4,808	DM8,354	DM6,581
			£1,553	£3,680	£2,616
			¥346,347	¥602,541	¥474,444
DELFOUR, DANIEL	1	0			
DEL HIERRO, JOSE	1	1	$3,562	$3,562	$3,562
			DM6,162	DM6,162	DM6,162
			£2,185	£2,185	£2,185
			¥406,410	¥406,410	¥406,410
DELIVET, AUGUSTE	2	1	$2,070	$2,070	$2,070
			DM3,578	DM3,578	DM3,578
			£1,279	£1,279	£1,279
			¥262,341	¥262,341	¥262,341
DELLA CORTE, ALFONSO	2	1	$9,692	$9,692	$9,692
			DM14,307	DM14,307	DM14,307
			£6,325	£6,325	£6,325
			¥1,030,349	¥1,030,349	¥1,030,349
DELLA CORTE, ALFONSO (attributed to)	2	0			
DEL LUNGO, ALFREDO	2	2	$1,783	$8,832	$5,307
			DM2,875	DM14,942	DM8,908
			£1,035	£5,555	£3,295
			¥209,875	¥1,094,237	¥652,056
DE MEGLIO, GIOVANNI	1	0			
DE MUZIO, FRANCESCO (attributed to)	1	1	$1,885	$1,885	$1,885
			DM3,339	DM3,339	DM3,339
			£1,157	£1,157	£1,157
			¥229,784	¥229,784	¥229,784
DENNIS, JESSE	1	0			
DENNY, JAMES GORRIE	1	1	$1,250	$1,250	$1,250
			DM1,749	DM1,749	DM1,749
			£782	£782	£782
			¥105,737	¥105,737	¥105,737
DENTI, ALBERTO	1	0			

Maker	Items		Selling Prices		
	Bid	Sold	Low	High	Avg
DE PLANIS, AUGUST	1	1	$38,823	$38,823	$38,823
			DM59,645	DM59,645	DM59,645
			£25,300	£25,300	£25,300
			¥4,250,122	¥4,250,122	¥4,250,122
DERAZEY, H.	7	5	$2,818	$8,694	$4,908
			DM4,155	DM15,634	DM8,529
			£1,840	£5,175	£3,042
			¥300,601	¥1,005,140	¥537,001
DERAZEY, HONORE	18	12	$1,410	$21,416	$8,338
			DM2,081	DM37,153	DM13,766
			£920	£12,650	£5,168
			¥149,869	¥2,714,817	¥975,047
DERAZEY, HONORE (workshop of)	2	1	$1,840	$1,840	$1,840
			DM3,110	DM3,110	DM3,110
			£1,104	£1,104	£1,104
			¥224,480	¥224,480	¥224,480
DERAZEY, JUSTIN	15	9	$2,540	$10,708	$4,904
			DM3,578	DM18,577	DM8,158
			£1,610	£6,325	£2,996
			¥259,745	¥1,357,408	¥578,874
DERAZEY, JUSTIN (attributed to)	4	0			
DERAZEY, JUSTIN (workshop of)	2	1	$1,051	$1,051	$1,051
			DM1,779	DM1,779	DM1,779
			£661	£661	£661
			¥130,266	¥130,266	¥130,266
DERAZEY FAMILY (MEMBER OF)	2	1	$3,936	$3,936	$3,936
			DM6,883	DM6,883	DM6,883
			£2,415	£2,415	£2,415
			¥465,008	¥465,008	¥465,008
DEROUX	1	1	$2,698	$2,698	$2,698
			DM3,816	DM3,816	DM3,816
			£1,725	£1,725	£1,725
			¥273,946	¥273,946	¥273,946
DEROUX, AUGUST S. (attributed to)	2	0			
DE RUB, A.	2	0			
DE RUB, ANGELO	1	0			
DESIATO, GIUSEPPE (attributed to)	3	3	$3,220	$4,776	$4,006
			DM5,732	DM8,031	DM7,126
			£1,932	£2,990	£2,484
			¥428,196	¥586,228	¥498,872
DESIATO, VINCENZO (ascribed to)	1	1	$1,472	$1,472	$1,472
			DM2,490	DM2,490	DM2,490
			£926	£926	£926
			¥182,373	¥182,373	¥182,373
DESIATO, VINCENZO (attributed to)	1	0			
DESIDERI, PIETRO PAOLO	1	1	$13,041	$13,041	$13,041
			DM24,714	DM24,714	DM24,714
			£8,050	£8,050	£8,050
			¥1,377,114	¥1,377,114	¥1,377,114
D'ESPINE, ALESSANDRO	4	1	$64,950	$64,950	$64,950
			DM91,739	DM91,739	DM91,739
			£41,100	£41,100	£41,100
			¥5,796,621	¥5,796,621	¥5,796,621
DE TOPPANI, ANGELO	2	2	$7,490	$12,633	$10,061
			DM12,513	DM21,902	DM17,207
			£4,485	£7,475	£5,980
			¥910,410	¥1,577,225	¥1,243,818

Maker	Items		Selling Prices		
	Bid	Sold	Low	High	Avg
DEULIN, JOSEF	1	1	$403	$403	$403
			DM689	DM689	DM689
			£238	£238	£238
			¥49,982	¥49,982	¥49,982
DE ZORZI, VALENTINO	5	3	$2,415	$29,390	$15,585
			DM3,492	DM49,419	DM26,507
			£1,577	£18,400	£9,649
			¥244,519	¥3,607,559	¥1,946,710
DE ZORZI, VALENTINO (workshop of)	1	1	$5,463	$5,463	$5,463
			DM9,346	DM9,346	DM9,346
			£3,231	£3,231	£3,231
			¥678,333	¥678,333	¥678,333
DICKENSON, EDWARD	2	1	$1,344	$1,344	$1,344
			DM2,496	DM2,496	DM2,496
			£805	£805	£805
			¥179,869	¥179,869	¥179,869
DICONET, MICHAEL (attributed to)	1	1	$3,620	$3,620	$3,620
			DM6,790	DM6,790	DM6,790
			£2,248	£2,248	£2,248
			¥435,081	¥435,081	¥435,081
DIDCZENKO, DIMITRO	1	0			
DIEUDONNE	2	2	$1,555	$3,123	$2,339
			DM2,696	DM5,251	DM3,973
			£920	£1,955	£1,438
			¥194,120	¥383,303	¥288,712
DIEUDONNE, A. (attributed to)	2	1	$1,863	$1,863	$1,863
			DM3,508	DM3,508	DM3,508
			£1,150	£1,150	£1,150
			¥198,605	¥198,605	¥198,605
DIEUDONNE, AMEDEE	18	12	$1,725	$9,462	$3,393
			DM2,657	DM16,009	DM5,623
			£1,035	£5,951	£2,116
			¥159,620	¥1,172,396	¥394,258
DIEUDONNE, AMEDEE (attributed to)	7	6	$1,847	$3,518	$2,479
			DM2,835	DM5,401	DM4,040
			£1,127	£2,300	£1,558
			¥201,576	¥383,955	¥268,800
DIGGNEY, CHARLES	1	1	$690	$690	$690
			DM998	DM998	DM998
			£451	£451	£451
			¥69,863	¥69,863	¥69,863
DI LELIO, ARMANDO	2	1	$5,467	$5,467	$5,467
			DM9,250	DM9,250	DM9,250
			£3,439	£3,439	£3,439
			¥677,385	¥677,385	¥677,385
DI SANTO CELLINI, MARCELLO	1	1	$2,291	$2,291	$2,291
			DM3,382	DM3,382	DM3,382
			£1,495	£1,495	£1,495
			¥243,537	¥243,537	¥243,537
DITER, JUSTIN	1	1	$6,325	$6,325	$6,325
			DM9,519	DM9,519	DM9,519
			£3,840	£3,840	£3,840
			¥707,009	¥707,009	¥707,009
DI VILONNI, ANGELO	1	1	$12,230	$12,230	$12,230
			DM17,300	DM17,300	DM17,300
			£7,820	£7,820	£7,820
			¥1,241,886	¥1,241,886	¥1,241,886

Maker	Items		Selling Prices		
	Bid	Sold	Low	High	Avg
DIX, DAVID	6	4	$511	$782	$615
			DM719	DM1,202	DM912
			£322	£518	£400
			¥45,637	¥83,434	¥60,519
DIXON, ALFRED THOMAS	1	1	$1,160	$1,160	$1,160
			DM1,735	DM1,735	DM1,735
			£690	£690	£690
			¥129,361	¥129,361	¥129,361
DOBBIE, WILLIAM	1	1	$937	$937	$937
			DM1,639	DM1,639	DM1,639
			£575	£575	£575
			¥110,716	¥110,716	¥110,716
DOBRETSOVITCH, MARCO	1	1	$17,986	$17,986	$17,986
			DM25,441	DM25,441	DM25,441
			£11,500	£11,500	£11,500
			¥1,826,304	¥1,826,304	¥1,826,304
DOBRITCHCOV, FILIP	1	1	$2,588	$2,588	$2,588
			DM4,373	DM4,373	DM4,373
			£1,553	£1,553	£1,553
			¥344,319	¥344,319	¥344,319
DODD, THOMAS	3	1	$12,710	$12,710	$12,710
			DM19,504	DM19,504	DM19,504
			£8,280	£8,280	£8,280
			¥1,391,123	¥1,391,123	¥1,391,123
DODD, THOMAS (attributed to)	1	1	$9,664	$9,664	$9,664
			DM14,460	DM14,460	DM14,460
			£5,750	£5,750	£5,750
			¥1,078,010	¥1,078,010	¥1,078,010
DOERFFEL	1	1	$504	$504	$504
			DM770	DM770	DM770
			£322	£322	£322
			¥56,205	¥56,205	¥56,205
DOLLENZ, GIOVANNI (attributed to)	1	1	$2,306	$2,306	$2,306
			DM3,574	DM3,574	DM3,574
			£1,380	£1,380	£1,380
			¥262,628	¥262,628	¥262,628
DOLLENZ, GIUSEPPE	2	1	$18,328	$18,328	$18,328
			DM25,685	DM25,685	DM25,685
			£11,500	£11,500	£11,500
			¥1,615,578	¥1,615,578	¥1,615,578
DOLLING, HERMANN	1	0			
DOLLING, HERMANN (JR.)	2	2	$1,291	$1,585	$1,438
			DM1,797	DM2,337	DM2,067
			£805	£1,035	£920
			¥109,116	¥169,088	¥139,102
DOLLING, ROBERT A.	2	2	$1,495	$1,495	$1,495
			DM2,286	DM2,527	DM2,406
			£897	£984	£940
			¥157,573	¥182,390	¥169,982
DOLLING, ROBERT A. (workshop of)	1	1	$1,093	$1,093	$1,093
			DM1,888	DM1,888	DM1,888
			£675	£675	£675
			¥138,458	¥138,458	¥138,458
DONI DE BONIS, ROCCO	1	0			
DONI DE BONIS, ROCCO (attributed to)	1	0			

Maker	Items		Selling Prices		
	Bid	Sold	Low	High	Avg
DOOLEY, J.W.	1	1	$1,404	$1,404	$1,404
			DM2,150	DM2,150	DM2,150
			£897	£897	£897
			¥156,544	¥156,544	¥156,544
DORELLI, GIOVANNI (ascribed to)	1	0			
DOTSCH, MICHAEL	1	1	$10,247	$10,247	$10,247
			DM18,406	DM18,406	DM18,406
			£6,325	£6,325	£6,325
			¥1,209,783	¥1,209,783	¥1,209,783
DOTSCH, MICHAEL (attributed to)	1	1	$4,298	$4,298	$4,298
			DM7,909	DM7,909	DM7,909
			£2,673	£2,673	£2,673
			¥506,964	¥506,964	¥506,964
DOW, WILLIAM HENRY	1	0			
DROUIN, CHARLES	1	0			
DROUIN, ETIENNE	1	1	$1,739	$1,739	$1,739
			DM3,126	DM3,126	DM3,126
			£1,035	£1,035	£1,035
			¥201,028	¥201,028	¥201,028
DROZEN, F.X.	2	1	$3,467	$3,467	$3,467
			DM6,212	DM6,212	DM6,212
			£2,070	£2,070	£2,070
			¥402,615	¥402,615	¥402,615
DUCHENE, NICOLAS	2	2	$690	$1,234	$962
			DM1,193	DM1,821	DM1,507
			£426	£805	£616
			¥87,447	¥131,135	¥109,291
DUCHENE, NICOLAS (ascribed to)	1	0			
DUERER, WILHELM	4	2	$154	$518	$336
			DM238	DM937	DM587
			£92	£316	£204
			¥17,509	¥62,483	¥39,996
DUERER, WILHELM (workshop of)	1	1	$259	$259	$259
			DM374	DM374	DM374
			£165	£165	£165
			¥22,447	¥22,447	¥22,447
DUKE, RICHARD	27	17	$1,105	$11,597	$5,413
			DM1,640	DM19,543	DM8,623
			£713	£6,900	£3,350
			¥119,627	¥1,407,370	¥609,977
DUKE, RICHARD (ascribed to)	2	1	$2,823	$2,823	$2,823
			DM4,338	DM4,338	DM4,338
			£1,840	£1,840	£1,840
			¥309,100	¥309,100	¥309,100
DUKE, RICHARD (workshop of)	1	1	$3,571	$3,571	$3,571
			DM6,740	DM6,740	DM6,740
			£2,210	£2,210	£2,210
			¥377,785	¥377,785	¥377,785
DUKE, RICHARD (JR.)	2	2	$1,660	$2,582	$2,121
			DM2,311	DM3,595	DM2,953
			£1,035	£1,610	£1,323
			¥140,292	¥218,232	¥179,262
DUKE, RICHARD (JR.) (attributed to)	1	0			
DUKE FAMILY	2	0			

| Maker | Items | | Selling Prices | | |
	Bid	Sold	Low	High	Avg
DUNLOP, JOHN	3	2	$357	$704	$531
			DM605	DM1,187	DM896
			£219	£437	£328
			¥41,405	¥86,466	¥63,936
DURRSCHMIDT, WILHELM	1	1	$2,415	$2,415	$2,415
			DM4,174	DM4,174	DM4,174
			£1,492	£1,492	£1,492
			¥306,065	¥306,065	¥306,065
DVORAK, CAREL BOROMAUS	2	1	$3,304	$3,304	$3,304
			DM5,728	DM5,728	DM5,728
			£1,955	£1,955	£1,955
			¥412,505	¥412,505	¥412,505
DVORAK, JAN BAPTISTA	7	5	$4,626	$6,110	$5,419
			DM7,155	DM9,972	DM8,943
			£2,910	£3,968	£3,404
			¥519,489	¥729,491	¥647,137
DVORAK, KARL	1	1	$2,300	$2,300	$2,300
			DM3,517	DM3,517	DM3,517
			£1,513	£1,513	£1,513
			¥242,420	¥242,420	¥242,420
DYKER, GEORGE	1	1	$2,390	$2,390	$2,390
			DM3,344	DM3,344	DM3,344
			£1,495	£1,495	£1,495
			¥202,143	¥202,143	¥202,143
DYKES, ARTHUR WILLIAM	2	1	$1,229	$1,229	$1,229
			DM2,031	DM2,031	DM2,031
			£736	£736	£736
			¥143,741	¥143,741	¥143,741
DYKES, GEORGE	1	1	$4,609	$4,609	$4,609
			DM7,700	DM7,700	DM7,700
			£2,760	£2,760	£2,760
			¥560,252	¥560,252	¥560,252
EATON, ERIC S.	1	1	$869	$869	$869
			DM1,300	DM1,300	DM1,300
			£517	£517	£517
			¥96,927	¥96,927	¥96,927
EBERLE, EUGENE	1	1	$3,286	$3,286	$3,286
			DM4,916	DM4,916	DM4,916
			£1,955	£1,955	£1,955
			¥366,523	¥366,523	¥366,523
EBERLE, JOHANN ULRICH	6	5	$2,990	$9,641	$7,011
			DM5,412	DM18,270	DM12,195
			£1,824	£5,951	£4,315
			¥361,013	¥1,231,457	¥781,085
EBERLE, TOMASO	5	5	$26,450	$65,297	$39,958
			DM43,378	DM109,089	DM65,383
			£16,373	£39,100	£24,780
			¥2,798,410	¥7,936,909	¥4,366,973
EBERLE, TOMASO (attributed to)	2	1	$2,513	$2,513	$2,513
			DM4,623	DM4,623	DM4,623
			£1,563	£1,563	£1,563
			¥296,379	¥296,379	¥296,379
ECKLAND, DONALD	3	2	$4,025	$4,364	$4,195
			DM6,957	DM8,238	DM7,597
			£2,487	£2,701	£2,594
			¥461,738	¥510,108	¥485,923

Maker	Items Bid	Sold	Selling Prices Low	High	Avg
EDREV, EDRIO	1	1	$2,178 DM3,066 £1,380 ¥222,638	$2,178 DM3,066 £1,380 ¥222,638	$2,178 DM3,066 £1,380 ¥222,638
EHRICKE, CHARLES	1	0			
EHRLICH	1	1	$4,252 DM6,362 £2,530 ¥474,324	$4,252 DM6,362 £2,530 ¥474,324	$4,252 DM6,362 £2,530 ¥474,324
EKSTRAND, GUSTAF	2	0			
ELLIOT, WILLIAM	2	2	$1,150 DM2,157 £714 ¥138,202	$2,600 DM4,659 £1,553 ¥301,961	$1,875 DM3,408 £1,133 ¥220,082
EMERSON, ELIJAH	1	1	$2,300 DM3,935 £1,360 ¥285,614	$2,300 DM3,935 £1,360 ¥285,614	$2,300 DM3,935 £1,360 ¥285,614
ERBA, PAOLO	1	0			
ERDESZ, OTTO	2	1	$3,738 DM6,765 £2,280 ¥451,266	$3,738 DM6,765 £2,280 ¥451,266	$3,738 DM6,765 £2,280 ¥451,266
ERDESZ, OTTO ALEXANDER	1	1	$3,220 DM4,924 £2,118 ¥339,388	$3,220 DM4,924 £2,118 ¥339,388	$3,220 DM4,924 £2,118 ¥339,388
ERMINIA, MALAGUTI (attributed to)	1	1	$3,677 DM5,144 £2,300 ¥310,990	$3,677 DM5,144 £2,300 ¥310,990	$3,677 DM5,144 £2,300 ¥310,990
ERTZ, NEIL	1	1	$1,491 DM1,571 £920 ¥113,891	$1,491 DM1,571 £920 ¥113,891	$1,491 DM1,571 £920 ¥113,891
ESPOSITO, RAFFAELE (attributed to)	1	1	$1,093 DM1,945 £666 ¥151,770	$1,093 DM1,945 £666 ¥151,770	$1,093 DM1,945 £666 ¥151,770
ESPOSTI, PIERGIUSEPPE	1	1	$1,840 DM2,657 £1,172 ¥159,620	$1,840 DM2,657 £1,172 ¥159,620	$1,840 DM2,657 £1,172 ¥159,620
EURSOLO, JOHANN GEORG	1	1	$2,898 DM5,211 £1,725 ¥335,047	$2,898 DM5,211 £1,725 ¥335,047	$2,898 DM5,211 £1,725 ¥335,047
EUSCHEN, KARL	1	1	$1,802 DM2,719 £1,092 ¥204,204	$1,802 DM2,719 £1,092 ¥204,204	$1,802 DM2,719 £1,092 ¥204,204
EVANS & CO., GEORGE	3	2	$544 DM767 £345 ¥55,660	$1,743 DM3,237 £1,058 ¥181,754	$1,144 DM2,002 £702 ¥118,707

Maker	Items		Selling Prices		
	Bid	Sold	Low	High	Avg
EWAN, D.	1	1	$225	$225	$225
			DM393	DM393	DM393
			£138	£138	£138
			¥26,572	¥26,572	¥26,572
EWAN, DAVID	1	0			
EWBANK, HENRY	1	1	$345	$345	$345
			DM614	DM614	DM614
			£207	£207	£207
			¥45,878	¥45,878	¥45,878
EYLES, CHARLES	1	1	$2,730	$2,730	$2,730
			DM3,904	DM3,904	DM3,904
			£1,725	£1,725	£1,725
			¥274,251	¥274,251	¥274,251
FABRICATORE, GENNARO	3	0			
FABRIS, LUIGI	2	1	$16,520	$16,520	$16,520
			DM28,641	DM28,641	DM28,641
			£9,775	£9,775	£9,775
			¥2,062,525	¥2,062,525	¥2,062,525
FABRIS, LUIGI (attributed to)	1	1	$8,777	$8,777	$8,777
			DM16,615	DM16,615	DM16,615
			£5,520	£5,520	£5,520
			¥1,052,057	¥1,052,057	¥1,052,057
FAGNOLA, ANNIBALE	7	4	$33,098	$55,890	$48,446
			DM57,418	DM100,395	DM85,346
			£19,550	£34,500	£29,593
			¥4,195,626	¥6,606,601	¥5,794,085
FAGNOLA, ANNIBALE (ascribed to)	1	1	$18,630	$18,630	$18,630
			DM35,075	DM35,075	DM35,075
			£11,500	£11,500	£11,500
			¥1,969,030	¥1,969,030	¥1,969,030
FAGNOLA, ANNIBALE (attributed to)	6	4	$12,121	$20,833	$16,348
			DM19,550	DM29,423	DM25,096
			£7,038	£13,225	£10,146
			¥1,427,150	¥2,097,921	¥1,700,588
FAGNOLA, H.	1	1	$72,979	$72,979	$72,979
			DM121,923	DM121,923	DM121,923
			£43,700	£43,700	£43,700
			¥8,870,663	¥8,870,663	¥8,870,663
FAGNOLA, H. (attributed to)	1	0			
FALISSE, A.	7	3	$3,299	$6,325	$4,504
			DM4,623	DM9,672	DM7,011
			£2,070	£4,161	£2,844
			¥290,804	¥666,655	¥480,920
FANTIN, DOMENICO	2	2	$4,523	$5,999	$5,261
			DM8,014	DM11,368	DM9,691
			£2,777	£3,703	£3,240
			¥551,483	¥633,472	¥592,477
FARINA, ERMINIO	2	2	$11,064	$17,699	$14,381
			DM15,406	DM31,792	DM23,599
			£6,900	£10,925	£8,913
			¥935,281	¥2,089,625	¥1,512,453
FARLEY, CHARLES E.	3	3	$529	$1,265	$790
			DM998	DM1,904	DM1,309
			£327	£768	£480
			¥55,968	¥141,402	¥91,278

Maker	Items		Selling Prices		
	Bid	Sold	Low	High	Avg
FAROTTI, CELESTE	3	3	$12,721	$19,435	$16,423
			DM17,968	DM33,695	DM26,421
			£8,050	£11,500	£9,829
			¥1,135,348	¥2,426,500	¥1,858,883
FAROTTO, CELESTE (attributed to)	1	1	$12,330	$12,330	$12,330
			DM18,177	DM18,177	DM18,177
			£8,050	£8,050	£8,050
			¥1,315,129	¥1,315,129	¥1,315,129
FAROTTO, CELESTINO	1	1	$31,050	$31,050	$31,050
			DM44,836	DM44,836	DM44,836
			£19,782	£19,782	£19,782
			¥2,693,588	¥2,693,588	¥2,693,588
FAWICK, THOMAS L.	1	0			
FEBBRARI, DIPENDENTE	2	0			
FENDT, BERNARD	1	0			
FENDT, BERNARD SIMON	2	1	$16,331	$16,331	$16,331
			DM22,999	DM22,999	DM22,999
			£10,350	£10,350	£10,350
			¥1,669,786	¥1,669,786	¥1,669,786
FENDT, BERNARD SIMON (attributed to)	4	2	$2,914	$11,178	$7,046
			DM4,814	DM20,079	DM12,446
			£1,783	£6,900	£4,341
			¥360,830	¥1,319,763	¥840,296
FENDT, FRANCOIS (attributed to)	1	0			
FENGA, GIULIANO (ascribed to)	2	1	$1,300	$1,300	$1,300
			DM1,837	DM1,837	DM1,837
			£828	£828	£828
			¥111,019	¥111,019	¥111,019
FENT, FRANCOIS	3	1	$4,235	$4,235	$4,235
			DM7,835	DM7,835	DM7,835
			£2,530	£2,530	£2,530
			¥564,418	¥564,418	¥564,418
FENT, FRANCOIS (ascribed to)	2	1	$3,795	$3,795	$3,795
			DM5,488	DM5,488	DM5,488
			£2,479	£2,479	£2,479
			¥384,244	¥384,244	¥384,244
FERRONI, FERDINANDO	1	1	$4,600	$4,600	$4,600
			DM7,034	DM7,034	DM7,034
			£3,026	£3,026	£3,026
			¥484,840	¥484,840	¥484,840
FERRONI, FERNANDO (attributed to)	1	1	$7,246	$7,246	$7,246
			DM10,234	DM10,234	DM10,234
			£4,600	£4,600	£4,600
			¥729,712	¥729,712	¥729,712
FETIQUE, EMILE (attributed to)	1	1	$5,570	$5,570	$5,570
			DM10,580	DM10,580	DM10,580
			£3,439	£3,439	£3,439
			¥585,267	¥585,267	¥585,267
FEYZEAU (attributed to)	2	1	$470	$470	$470
			DM776	DM776	DM776
			£288	£288	£288
			¥58,198	¥58,198	¥58,198
FICHTL, JOHANN ULRICH	3	2	$394	$1,620	$1,007
			DM602	DM2,476	DM1,539
			£253	£1,035	£644
			¥38,907	¥180,659	¥109,783

Maker	Items		Selling Prices		
	Bid	Sold	Low	High	Avg
FICHTL, JOHANN ULRICH (attributed to)	1	1	$730	$730	$730
			DM1,027	DM1,027	DM1,027
			£460	£460	£460
			¥65,196	¥65,196	¥65,196
FICKER, JOHANN CHRISTIAN	8	4	$2,037	$4,626	$2,711
			DM3,267	DM7,827	DM4,550
			£1,265	£2,910	£1,694
			¥231,728	¥573,172	¥331,006
FICKER, JOHANN GOTTLOB	7	6	$920	$3,856	$2,508
			DM1,407	DM7,325	DM4,344
			£605	£2,381	£1,559
			¥96,968	¥405,185	¥266,509
FIKER, JOHANN CHRISTIAN	1	1	$3,968	$3,968	$3,968
			DM7,489	DM7,489	DM7,489
			£2,456	£2,456	£2,456
			¥419,762	¥419,762	¥419,762
FILANO, LUIGI	1	1	$6,176	$6,176	$6,176
			DM9,489	DM9,489	DM9,489
			£4,025	£4,025	£4,025
			¥676,156	¥676,156	¥676,156
FILIPPI, VITTORIO	1	1	$3,080	$3,080	$3,080
			DM5,698	DM5,698	DM5,698
			£1,840	£1,840	£1,840
			¥410,486	¥410,486	¥410,486
FILLION, G.	1	0			
FIORINI, GIUSEPPE	7	4	$3,872	$47,134	$30,210
			DM5,392	DM89,525	DM49,466
			£2,415	£29,095	£19,090
			¥327,348	¥4,952,260	¥3,056,374
FIORINI, GIUSEPPE (ascribed to)	1	0			
FIORINI, PAOLO	2	2	$1,220	$2,138	$1,679
			DM2,063	DM3,706	DM2,885
			£767	£1,265	£1,016
			¥151,109	¥266,915	¥209,012
FIORINI, RAFFAELE	3	3	$2,444	$28,582	$13,036
			DM4,138	DM39,798	DM19,175
			£1,495	£17,825	£8,127
			¥283,297	¥2,416,143	¥1,230,506
FIORINI, RAFFAELE (attributed to)	1	1	$15,077	$15,077	$15,077
			DM26,715	DM26,715	DM26,715
			£9,258	£9,258	£9,258
			¥1,838,275	¥1,838,275	¥1,838,275
FISCHER	1	0			
FISCHER, CARL (workshop of)	1	1	$690	$690	$690
			DM996	DM996	DM996
			£440	£440	£440
			¥59,858	¥59,858	¥59,858
FISCHER, RAY	1	0			
FISCHER, ZACHARIAS	2	2	$74	$2,523	$1,299
			DM125	DM4,269	DM2,197
			£46	£1,587	£817
			¥9,102	¥312,639	¥160,870
FIVAZ, CHARLES	1	1	$2,687	$2,687	$2,687
			DM3,769	DM3,769	DM3,769
			£1,725	£1,725	£1,725
			¥271,520	¥271,520	¥271,520

Maker	Items Bid	Sold	Selling Prices Low	High	Avg
FIX, DAVID	1	1	$3,565 DM5,155 £2,329 ¥360,956	$3,565 DM5,155 £2,329 ¥360,956	$3,565 DM5,155 £2,329 ¥360,956
FLAMBEAU, PIERRE	1	1	$4,018 DM5,649 £2,530 ¥357,168	$4,018 DM5,649 £2,530 ¥357,168	$4,018 DM5,649 £2,530 ¥357,168
FLEURY, BENOIT	1	0			
FORBERGER, ROBERT	1	0			
FORD, JACOB	4	2	$3,286 DM4,916 £1,955 ¥366,523	$6,980 DM11,737 £4,370 ¥856,795	$5,133 DM8,327 £3,163 ¥611,659
FORD, JOSEPH W.	2	1	$425 DM742 £253 ¥54,233	$425 DM742 £253 ¥54,233	$425 DM742 £253 ¥54,233
FORST, HANS (workshop of)	2	1	$978 DM1,652 £587 ¥119,255	$978 DM1,652 £587 ¥119,255	$978 DM1,652 £587 ¥119,255
FORSTER, W.	1	0			
FORSTER, WILLIAM	6	2	$4,438 DM6,386 £2,875 ¥450,628	$7,298 DM12,192 £4,370 ¥887,066	$5,868 DM9,289 £3,623 ¥668,847
FORSTER, WILLIAM (II)	2	1	$3,226 DM4,868 £1,955 ¥365,585	$3,226 DM4,868 £1,955 ¥365,585	$3,226 DM4,868 £1,955 ¥365,585
FORSTER, WILLIAM (III)	1	0			
FOSCHI, GIORGIO	2	1	$5,005 DM9,260 £2,990 ¥667,039	$5,005 DM9,260 £2,990 ¥667,039	$5,005 DM9,260 £2,990 ¥667,039
FOUCHER, HENRI J. C. (attributed to)	1	1	$1,096 DM1,541 £690 ¥97,794	$1,096 DM1,541 £690 ¥97,794	$1,096 DM1,541 £690 ¥97,794
FOUGEROLLE, CLAUDE	1	1	$2,415 DM3,487 £1,539 ¥209,501	$2,415 DM3,487 £1,539 ¥209,501	$2,415 DM3,487 £1,539 ¥209,501
FOWERS, HERBERT	1	1	$395 DM552 £247 ¥33,398	$395 DM552 £247 ¥33,398	$395 DM552 £247 ¥33,398
FRACASSI, ARTURO	1	1	$10,046 DM18,066 £5,980 ¥1,161,495	$10,046 DM18,066 £5,980 ¥1,161,495	$10,046 DM18,066 £5,980 ¥1,161,495
FRANKE, PAUL	1	1	$3,728 DM3,927 £2,300 ¥284,729	$3,728 DM3,927 £2,300 ¥284,729	$3,728 DM3,927 £2,300 ¥284,729

Maker	Items		Selling Prices		
	Bid	Sold	Low	High	Avg
FRANOT, P.	1	1	$1,267	$1,267	$1,267
			DM2,268	DM2,268	DM2,268
			£782	£782	£782
			¥149,417	¥149,417	¥149,417
FRANOT, PATRICE	1	1	$1,380	$1,380	$1,380
			DM2,077	DM2,077	DM2,077
			£838	£838	£838
			¥154,256	¥154,256	¥154,256
FREDI, CONTE FABIO	1	0			
FREDI, RODOLFO	4	3	$4,235	$19,550	$12,634
			DM7,835	DM29,894	DM19,806
			£2,530	£12,862	£8,197
			¥564,418	¥2,060,570	¥1,390,162
FREDI, RODOLFO (ascribed to)	1	0			
FREDI, RODOLFO (attributed to)	3	1	$2,138	$2,138	$2,138
			DM3,706	DM3,706	DM3,706
			£1,265	£1,265	£1,265
			¥266,915	¥266,915	¥266,915
FREYER, WILLIAM	1	1	$1,180	$1,180	$1,180
			DM1,672	DM1,672	DM1,672
			£748	£748	£748
			¥121,843	¥121,843	¥121,843
FREYMADL, SEBASTIAN	1	0			
FRIEDRICH, JOHN & BROS.	2	1	$1,265	$1,265	$1,265
			DM1,904	DM1,904	DM1,904
			£768	£768	£768
			¥141,402	¥141,402	¥141,402
FRIEDRICH, JOHN & BROS. (workshop of)	3	3	$460	$1,610	$920
			DM692	DM2,325	DM1,357
			£279	£1,026	£586
			¥51,419	¥139,668	¥87,937
FUCHS, W.K. (workshop of)	1	1	$633	$633	$633
			DM915	DM915	DM915
			£413	£413	£413
			¥64,041	¥64,041	¥64,041
FULLER, HENRY	1	1	$1,592	$1,592	$1,592
			DM2,341	DM2,341	DM2,341
			£1,035	£1,035	£1,035
			¥168,871	¥168,871	¥168,871
FURBER	3	1	$3,666	$3,666	$3,666
			DM5,880	DM5,880	DM5,880
			£2,381	£2,381	£2,381
			¥417,111	¥417,111	¥417,111
FURBER (attributed to)	1	1	$134	$134	$134
			DM201	DM201	DM201
			£80	£80	£80
			¥14,998	¥14,998	¥14,998
FURBER, JOHN	3	2	$3,353	$3,385	$3,369
			DM5,590	DM6,003	DM5,797
			£2,070	£2,070	£2,070
			¥395,515	¥419,028	¥407,272
FURBER, JOHN (attributed to)	1	1	$1,372	$1,372	$1,372
			DM1,947	DM1,947	DM1,947
			£863	£863	£863
			¥127,348	¥127,348	¥127,348

Maker	Items		Selling Prices		
	Bid	Sold	Low	High	Avg
FURBER, MATTHEW	1	1	$6,184	$6,184	$6,184
			DM9,137	DM9,137	DM9,137
			£4,025	£4,025	£4,025
			¥659,029	¥659,029	¥659,029
FYDAL, M.H.	1	1	$546	$546	$546
			DM790	DM790	DM790
			£357	£357	£357
			¥55,308	¥55,308	¥55,308
GABOR, ANRISAK TIBOR	4	3	$1,270	$1,546	$1,409
			DM1,789	DM2,314	DM2,090
			£805	£920	£882
			¥129,872	¥172,482	¥152,301
GABRIELLI, GIOVANNI BATTISTA	7	5	$19,435	$50,531	$32,393
			DM33,220	DM87,607	DM52,956
			£11,500	£29,900	£19,780
			¥2,411,913	¥6,308,900	¥3,820,054
GABRIELLI, GIOVANNI BATTISTA (ascribed to)	3	1	$4,832	$4,832	$4,832
			DM7,230	DM7,230	DM7,230
			£2,875	£2,875	£2,875
			¥539,005	¥539,005	¥539,005
GADDA, GAETANO	4	3	$10,925	$19,435	$15,019
			DM19,774	DM28,716	DM24,400
			£6,664	£12,650	£9,505
			¥1,319,085	¥2,071,235	¥1,731,366
GADDA, GAETANO (attributed to)	4	1	$10,284	$10,284	$10,284
			DM19,533	DM19,533	DM19,533
			£6,348	£6,348	£6,348
			¥1,080,493	¥1,080,493	¥1,080,493
GAFFINO, ANDREA	1	1	$8,998	$8,998	$8,998
			DM17,052	DM17,052	DM17,052
			£5,555	£5,555	£5,555
			¥950,208	¥950,208	¥950,208
GAFFINO, GIUSEPPE (attributed to)	1	0			
GAFFINO, JOSEPH (attributed to)	1	0			
GAGGINI (ascribed to)	1	1	$2,898	$2,898	$2,898
			DM4,830	DM4,830	DM4,830
			£1,725	£1,725	£1,725
			¥346,363	¥346,363	¥346,363
GAGGINI, PIETRO	3	1	$7,475	$7,475	$7,475
			DM10,809	DM10,809	DM10,809
			£4,883	£4,883	£4,883
			¥756,844	¥756,844	¥756,844
GAGGINI, PIETRO (attributed to)	6	1	$2,049	$2,049	$2,049
			DM3,858	DM3,858	DM3,858
			£1,265	£1,265	£1,265
			¥216,593	¥216,593	¥216,593
GAGLIANO (workshop of)	1	0			
GAGLIANO, ALESSANDRO	4	3	$61,851	$230,575	$137,914
			DM116,311	DM435,210	DM259,886
			£38,900	£142,726	£85,975
			¥7,478,136	¥24,394,835	¥15,513,628
GAGLIANO, FERDINAND	11	8	$25,026	$75,266	$43,500
			DM43,638	DM105,994	DM65,931
			£14,950	£47,700	£27,056
			¥2,757,273	¥7,695,536	¥4,608,304

Maker	Items		Selling Prices		
	Bid	Sold	Low	High	Avg
GAGLIANO, FERDINAND (attributed to)	1	1	$44,850	$44,850	$44,850
			DM75,797	DM75,797	DM75,797
			£26,910	£26,910	£26,910
			¥5,471,700	¥5,471,700	¥5,471,700
GAGLIANO, GENNARO	2	2	$77,300	$125,632	$101,466
			DM111,776	DM187,974	DM149,875
			£50,492	£74,750	£62,621
			¥7,826,625	¥14,014,130	¥10,920,378
GAGLIANO, GENNARO (attributed to)	1	1	$65,702	$65,702	$65,702
			DM91,924	DM91,924	DM91,924
			£41,100	£41,100	£41,100
			¥5,557,254	¥5,557,254	¥5,557,254
GAGLIANO, GIUSEPPE	4	2	$54,050	$71,794	$62,922
			DM97,290	DM101,106	DM99,198
			£32,430	£45,500	£38,965
			¥419,969	¥7,340,606	¥3,880,287
GAGLIANO, GIUSEPPE & ANTONIO	4	1	$76,597	$76,597	$76,597
			DM117,539	DM117,539	DM117,539
			£49,900	£49,900	£49,900
			¥8,383,699	¥8,383,699	¥8,383,699
GAGLIANO, JOHANNES (attributed to)	1	1	$6,900	$6,900	$6,900
			DM12,282	DM12,282	DM12,282
			£4,140	£4,140	£4,140
			¥917,562	¥917,562	¥917,562
GAGLIANO, JOSEPH	2	0			
GAGLIANO, JOSEPH (attributed to)	1	0			
GAGLIANO, NICOLA	17	13	$71,445	$163,293	$112,266
			DM106,471	DM307,073	DM192,288
			£43,300	£102,700	£69,375
			¥6,465,640	¥19,743,048	¥12,584,428
GAGLIANO, NICOLA (attributed to)	2	2	$11,470	$25,026	$18,248
			DM17,622	DM46,300	DM31,961
			£7,475	£14,950	£11,213
			¥1,255,718	¥3,335,196	¥2,295,457
GAGLIANO, NICOLA (I)	1	1	$78,737	$78,737	$78,737
			DM110,883	DM110,883	DM110,883
			£49,900	£49,900	£49,900
			¥8,050,467	¥8,050,467	¥8,050,467
GAGLIANO, NICOLO (II)	2	0			
GAGLIANO, RAFFAELE & ANTONIO (II)	4	1	$23,826	$23,826	$23,826
			DM33,391	DM33,391	DM33,391
			£14,950	£14,950	£14,950
			¥2,100,251	¥2,100,251	¥2,100,251
GAGLIANO, RAFFAELE & ANTONIO (II) (attributed to)	1	1	$30,728	$30,728	$30,728
			DM51,336	DM51,336	DM51,336
			£18,400	£18,400	£18,400
			¥3,735,016	¥3,735,016	¥3,735,016
GAGLIANO FAMILY (MEMBER OF)	5	2	$34,652	$47,481	$41,067
			DM64,108	DM66,761	DM65,434
			£20,700	£29,900	£25,300
			¥4,221,073	¥4,617,963	¥4,419,518
GAGLIANO FAMILY (MEMBER OF) (attributed to)	1	1	$73,286	$73,286	$73,286
			DM108,279	DM108,279	DM108,279
			£47,700	£47,700	£47,700
			¥7,810,112	¥7,810,112	¥7,810,112

Maker	Items		Selling Prices		
	Bid	Sold	Low	High	Avg

Maker	Bid	Sold	Low	High	Avg
GAIANI, ROMANO	2	0			
GAIBISSO, GIOVANNI BATTISTA	7	4	$1,844	$10,971	$7,027
			DM2,568	DM20,769	DM11,458
			£1,150	£6,900	£4,370
			¥155,880	¥1,315,071	¥784,976
GAIDA, GIOVANNI	6	5	$11,682	$21,252	$18,496
			DM20,265	DM38,203	DM31,672
			£6,900	£12,650	£11,270
			¥1,480,809	¥2,457,010	¥2,011,478
GAIDA, SILVIO (attributed to)	1	0			
GAILLARD, CHARLES	7	2	$2,332	$2,899	$2,616
			DM4,043	DM4,338	DM4,191
			£1,380	£1,725	£1,553
			¥291,180	¥323,403	¥307,292
GAILLARD, CHARLES (attributed to)	4	1	$183	$183	$183
			DM341	DM341	DM341
			£115	£115	£115
			¥21,598	¥21,598	¥21,598
GALEAZZI, ADELINO	1	1	$1,055	$1,055	$1,055
			DM1,870	DM1,870	DM1,870
			£648	£648	£648
			¥128,679	¥128,679	¥128,679
GALIMBERTI, LUIGI	3	1	$9,436	$9,436	$9,436
			DM13,288	DM13,288	DM13,288
			£5,980	£5,980	£5,980
			¥964,765	¥964,765	¥964,765
GALLA, ANTON	4	4	$1,555	$5,479	$3,018
			DM2,696	DM7,703	DM4,853
			£920	£3,450	£1,852
			¥197,680	¥487,047	¥345,031
GALLINOTTI, PIETRO	1	0			
GAND, ADOLPHE CHARLES	2	1	$23,625	$23,625	$23,625
			DM33,370	DM33,370	DM33,370
			£14,950	£14,950	£14,950
			¥2,108,503	¥2,108,503	¥2,108,503
GAND, CHARLES	1	1	$13,609	$13,609	$13,609
			DM19,166	DM19,166	DM19,166
			£8,625	£8,625	£8,625
			¥1,391,489	¥1,391,489	¥1,391,489
GAND, CHARLES (attributed to)	1	1	$13,524	$13,524	$13,524
			DM24,311	DM24,311	DM24,311
			£8,050	£8,050	£8,050
			¥1,563,552	¥1,563,552	¥1,563,552
GAND, CHARLES FRANCOIS	3	2	$10,689	$23,000	$16,845
			DM18,532	DM41,630	DM30,081
			£6,325	£14,030	£10,178
			¥1,334,575	¥2,777,020	¥2,055,798
GAND BROS.	3	3	$10,626	$19,205	$15,267
			DM17,710	DM32,085	DM26,583
			£6,325	£11,500	£9,248
			¥1,269,997	¥2,334,385	¥1,841,286
GAND FAMILY (MEMBER OF)	1	1	$5,589	$5,589	$5,589
			DM10,592	DM10,592	DM10,592
			£3,450	£3,450	£3,450
			¥590,192	¥590,192	¥590,192

Maker	Items		Selling Prices		
	Bid	Sold	Low	High	Avg
GAND & BERNARDEL	13	10	$7,452 DM13,013 £4,600 ¥786,922	$17,250 DM27,209 £11,349 ¥1,964,200	$12,003 DM19,987 £7,408 ¥1,375,504
GAND & BERNARDEL (workshop of)	1	1	$3,353 DM6,314 £2,070 ¥354,425	$3,353 DM6,314 £2,070 ¥354,425	$3,353 DM6,314 £2,070 ¥354,425
GAND & BERNARDEL FRERES	1	1	$19,282 DM36,624 £11,903 ¥2,025,925	$19,282 DM36,624 £11,903 ¥2,025,925	$19,282 DM36,624 £11,903 ¥2,025,925
GARAVAGLIA, GARY	1	1	$2,530 DM3,658 £1,653 ¥256,163	$2,530 DM3,658 £1,653 ¥256,163	$2,530 DM3,658 £1,653 ¥256,163
GARDEN, JAMES	2	1	$874 DM1,249 £552 ¥87,760	$874 DM1,249 £552 ¥87,760	$874 DM1,249 £552 ¥87,760
GARIMBERTI, FERDINANDO	5	5	$9,436 DM13,288 £5,980 ¥935,281	$40,569 DM64,021 £25,300 ¥4,694,910	$26,313 DM39,760 £16,376 ¥2,720,382
GARIMBERTI, FERDINANDO (attributed to)	1	0			
GARTNER, EUGEN	2	1	$1,380 DM2,498 £842 ¥166,621	$1,380 DM2,498 £842 ¥166,621	$1,380 DM2,498 £842 ¥166,621
GASPARRI, MARIO	1	0			
GATTI, GEORGIO	5	2	$16,100 DM23,281 £10,517 ¥1,630,125	$21,583 DM30,530 £13,800 ¥2,191,564	$18,842 DM26,905 £12,158 ¥1,910,845
GEESMAN, EDWARD	1	0			
GEIGEN, TIM	1	1	$400 DM573 £253 ¥40,223	$400 DM573 £253 ¥40,223	$400 DM573 £253 ¥40,223
GEISSENHOF, FRANZ	14	8	$3,450 DM5,192 £2,094 ¥385,641	$20,165 DM34,512 £12,075 ¥2,451,104	$10,840 DM18,180 £6,608 ¥1,274,045
GEISSER, NICOLAUS	2	0			
GEMUNDER, AUGUST	2	2	$3,167 DM5,689 £1,955 ¥373,933	$5,175 DM8,854 £3,061 ¥642,632	$4,171 DM7,272 £2,508 ¥508,282
GEMUNDER, AUGUST & SONS	4	2	$575 DM1,024 £345 ¥76,464	$2,041 DM2,948 £1,300 ¥177,078	$1,308 DM1,986 £823 ¥126,771
GEMUNDER, AUGUST & SONS (workshop of)	2	1	$1,035 DM1,558 £628 ¥115,692	$1,035 DM1,558 £628 ¥115,692	$1,035 DM1,558 £628 ¥115,692

Maker	Items Bid	Sold	Selling Prices Low	High	Avg
GEMUNDER, GEORGE (SR.)	2	1	$13,973	$13,973	$13,973
			DM26,306	DM26,306	DM26,306
			£8,625	£8,625	£8,625
			¥1,476,773	¥1,476,773	¥1,476,773
GENIN, LOUIS (attributed to)	1	1	$1,391	$1,391	$1,391
			DM2,137	DM2,137	DM2,137
			£920	£920	£920
			¥148,327	¥148,327	¥148,327
GENOVA, GIOVANNI BATTISTA	1	0			
GENOVESE, RICCARDO	1	1	$16,608	$16,608	$16,608
			DM23,119	DM23,119	DM23,119
			£10,350	£10,350	£10,350
			¥1,401,142	¥1,401,142	¥1,401,142
GERARD, MICHEL	1	1	$1,198	$1,198	$1,198
			DM1,668	DM1,668	DM1,668
			£747	£747	£747
			¥101,254	¥101,254	¥101,254
GERMAIN, EMILE	4	3	$6,935	$8,998	$7,919
			DM12,424	DM17,052	DM14,768
			£4,140	£5,555	£4,842
			¥805,230	¥950,208	¥860,569
GERMAIN, EMILE (attributed to)	1	1	$3,271	$3,271	$3,271
			DM4,620	DM4,620	DM4,620
			£2,070	£2,070	£2,070
			¥291,947	¥291,947	¥291,947
GERMAIN, LOUIS JOSEPH (attributed to)	1	1	$3,968	$3,968	$3,968
			DM7,489	DM7,489	DM7,489
			£2,456	£2,456	£2,456
			¥419,762	¥419,762	¥419,762
GIAMBERINI, SIMONE	2	1	$18,925	$18,925	$18,925
			DM32,018	DM32,018	DM32,018
			£11,903	£11,903	£11,903
			¥2,344,793	¥2,344,793	¥2,344,793
GIANNINI, FABRIZIO	1	1	$6,542	$6,542	$6,542
			DM9,241	DM9,241	DM9,241
			£4,140	£4,140	£4,140
			¥583,893	¥583,893	¥583,893
GIANOTTI, ALFREDO	2	2	$3,680	$4,830	$4,255
			DM6,361	DM8,742	DM7,552
			£2,274	£2,946	£2,610
			¥466,385	¥583,174	¥524,780
GIBERTINI, ANTONIO	2	1	$36,347	$36,347	$36,347
			DM51,338	DM51,338	DM51,338
			£23,000	£23,000	£23,000
			¥3,243,851	¥3,243,851	¥3,243,851
GIBSON CO.	2	2	$794	$1,360	$1,077
			DM1,498	DM1,915	DM1,707
			£491	£862	£677
			¥83,952	¥139,068	¥111,510
GIGLI, GIULIO CESARE	1	1	$21,107	$21,107	$21,107
			DM37,400	DM37,400	DM37,400
			£12,961	£12,961	£12,961
			¥2,573,585	¥2,573,585	¥2,573,585
GILBERT, JEFFREY J.	2	1	$2,118	$2,118	$2,118
			DM3,253	DM3,253	DM3,253
			£1,380	£1,380	£1,380
			¥231,825	¥231,825	¥231,825

Maker	Items Bid	Sold	Selling Prices Low	High	Avg
GILBERT, JEFFREY JAMES	5	5	$1,126	$4,057	$2,524
			DM1,595	DM5,649	DM3,545
			£713	£2,530	£1,592
			¥116,219	¥342,936	¥243,160
GILCHRIST, JAMES	1	1	$1,127	$1,127	$1,127
			DM1,954	DM1,954	DM1,954
			£667	£667	£667
			¥143,318	¥143,318	¥143,318
GILKES, WILLIAM	1	1	$2,471	$2,471	$2,471
			DM3,796	DM3,796	DM3,796
			£1,610	£1,610	£1,610
			¥270,462	¥270,462	¥270,462
GIORDANI, ENRICO	1	0			
GIORGIS, NICOLAUS	1	1	$8,642	$8,642	$8,642
			DM15,473	DM15,473	DM15,473
			£5,175	£5,175	£5,175
			¥1,189,112	¥1,189,112	¥1,189,112
GIRARDI, MARIO	3	0			
GIUDICI, CARLO	1	0			
GLADSTONE, R.	1	1	$531	$531	$531
			DM780	DM780	DM780
			£345	£345	£345
			¥56,290	¥56,290	¥56,290
GLAESEL, EDMUND	1	1	$2,513	$2,513	$2,513
			DM4,743	DM4,743	DM4,743
			£1,555	£1,555	£1,555
			¥265,849	¥265,849	¥265,849
GLAESEL, ERNST	2	2	$751	$934	$843
			DM1,149	DM1,629	DM1,389
			£483	£575	£529
			¥74,278	¥113,189	¥93,733
GLAESEL, LUDWIG	1	1	$2,332	$2,332	$2,332
			DM4,043	DM4,043	DM4,043
			£1,380	£1,380	£1,380
			¥291,180	¥291,180	¥291,180
GLASS, FRANZ JOHANN	1	1	$2,523	$2,523	$2,523
			DM4,269	DM4,269	DM4,269
			£1,587	£1,587	£1,587
			¥312,639	¥312,639	¥312,639
GLASS, FRIEDRICH AUGUST	1	1	$403	$403	$403
			DM716	DM716	DM716
			£246	£246	£246
			¥55,915	¥55,915	¥55,915
GLASS, JOHANN	1	1	$3,335	$3,335	$3,335
			DM4,816	DM4,816	DM4,816
			£2,125	£2,125	£2,125
			¥289,311	¥289,311	¥289,311
GLASS, JOHANN (workshop of)	1	1	$2,070	$2,070	$2,070
			DM3,165	DM3,165	DM3,165
			£1,362	£1,362	£1,362
			¥218,178	¥218,178	¥218,178
GLENISTER, WILLIAM	13	7	$580	$3,030	$1,710
			DM1,042	DM4,496	DM2,751
			£345	£1,955	£1,065
			¥67,009	¥328,371	¥195,050

Maker	Items Bid	Sold	Low	Selling Prices High	Avg
GLIER, ROBERT	2	1	$1,495 DM2,661 £897 ¥198,805	$1,495 DM2,661 £897 ¥198,805	$1,495 DM2,661 £897 ¥198,805
GLIER & SOHN, C.G.	2	2	$1,863 DM3,531 £1,150 ¥196,731	$2,142 DM4,060 £1,323 ¥226,240	$2,003 DM3,795 £1,236 ¥211,485
GLIGA, VASILE	1	1	$963 DM1,825 £595 ¥101,710	$963 DM1,825 £595 ¥101,710	$963 DM1,825 £595 ¥101,710
GLOOR, ADOLF	3	2	$561 DM977 £345 ¥67,913	$635 DM1,108 £391 ¥76,968	$598 DM1,043 £368 ¥72,441
GOBETTI, FRANCESCO	1	1	$103,194 DM145,756 £65,300 ¥9,209,716	$103,194 DM145,756 £65,300 ¥9,209,716	$103,194 DM145,756 £65,300 ¥9,209,716
GOFFRILLER, MATTEO	2	1	$76,895 DM133,315 £45,500 ¥9,776,585	$76,895 DM133,315 £45,500 ¥9,776,585	$76,895 DM133,315 £45,500 ¥9,776,585
GOFFRILLER, MATTEO (ascribed to)	3	3	$21,942 DM41,262 £13,800 ¥2,652,912	$64,274 DM121,802 £39,675 ¥6,787,202	$47,369 DM89,660 £29,325 ¥5,114,010
GOFTON, ROBERT	1	1	$537 DM821 £345 ¥53,055	$537 DM821 £345 ¥53,055	$537 DM821 £345 ¥53,055
GOLL, CAROLUS	1	1	$7,452 DM14,122 £4,600 ¥786,922	$7,452 DM14,122 £4,600 ¥786,922	$7,452 DM14,122 £4,600 ¥786,922
GONZALEZ, FERNANDO SOLAR	1	0			
GORRIE, ANDREW	1	1	$730 DM1,365 £460 ¥86,393	$730 DM1,365 £460 ¥86,393	$730 DM1,365 £460 ¥86,393
GOSS, PHILIP (attributed to)	3	2	$624 DM926 £403 ¥67,531	$799 DM1,149 £518 ¥81,113	$711 DM1,038 £460 ¥74,322
GOSS, WALTER S.	5	5	$690 DM1,055 £454 ¥72,726	$2,645 DM3,825 £1,728 ¥276,916	$1,794 DM2,777 £1,140 ¥198,710
GOTTI, ANSELMO	3	3	$5,532 DM7,703 £3,450 ¥467,641	$16,100 DM29,141 £9,821 ¥1,943,914	$10,118 DM16,388 £6,264 ¥1,063,360
GOTTI, ORSOLO	3	2	$5,467 DM9,250 £3,439 ¥677,385	$6,708 DM10,294 £4,370 ¥734,204	$6,088 DM9,772 £3,904 ¥705,794

Maker	Items		Selling Prices		
	Bid	Sold	Low	High	Avg
GOTZ, C.A.	2	1	$207	$207	$207
			DM350	DM350	DM350
			£127	£127	£127
			¥23,971	¥23,971	¥23,971
GOTZ, CONRAD	1	0			
GOULD, JOHN ALFRED	2	0			
GOULD, JOHN ALFRED (workshop of)	1	1	$4,140	$4,140	$4,140
			DM5,978	DM5,978	DM5,978
			£2,638	£2,638	£2,638
			¥359,145	¥359,145	¥359,145
GOULDING	5	5	$394	$2,332	$1,351
			DM556	DM4,043	DM2,265
			£247	£1,380	£831
			¥34,915	¥296,521	¥158,116
GOULDING & CO.	3	2	$1,643	$2,318	$1,981
			DM2,866	DM3,864	DM3,365
			£978	£1,380	£1,179
			¥209,537	¥277,090	¥243,314
GOWAR, E. (attributed to)	5	1	$263	$263	$263
			DM469	DM469	DM469
			£161	£161	£161
			¥34,394	¥34,394	¥34,394
GRAGNANI, ANTONIO	6	5	$7,970	$64,136	$35,979
			DM14,345	DM116,311	DM64,535
			£4,830	£38,900	£21,971
			¥1,149,299	¥8,007,450	¥4,322,100
GRANCINO, FRANCESCO (attributed to)	1	0			
GRANCINO, GIOVANNI	9	5	$68,154	$207,725	$101,184
			DM101,633	DM393,651	DM174,032
			£44,400	£128,225	£63,515
			¥6,159,608	¥21,935,451	¥10,485,683
GRANCINO, GIOVANNI (attributed to)	1	0			
GRANDJON (attributed to)	1	1	$1,059	$1,059	$1,059
			DM1,627	DM1,627	DM1,627
			£690	£690	£690
			¥115,912	¥115,912	¥115,912
GRANDJON, J.	1	1	$2,332	$2,332	$2,332
			DM4,043	DM4,043	DM4,043
			£1,380	£1,380	£1,380
			¥296,521	¥296,521	¥296,521
GRANDJON, JULES (FILS)	2	1	$1,198	$1,198	$1,198
			DM2,154	DM2,154	DM2,154
			£713	£713	£713
			¥138,486	¥138,486	¥138,486
GRANDJON, JULES (FILS) (attributed to)	2	2	$2,049	$4,761	$3,405
			DM3,681	DM8,986	DM6,334
			£1,265	£2,947	£2,106
			¥241,957	¥503,714	¥372,835
GRANDJON, PROSPER GERARD	1	1	$1,495	$1,495	$1,495
			DM2,250	DM2,250	DM2,250
			£908	£908	£908
			¥167,111	¥167,111	¥167,111
GRANGEAUD, M.	1	1	$450	$450	$450
			DM689	DM689	DM689
			£288	£288	£288
			¥50,175	¥50,175	¥50,175

Maker	Items		Selling Prices		
	Bid	Sold	Low	High	Avg
GRANT, DANIEL P.	1	1	$518	$518	$518
			DM885	DM885	DM885
			£306	£306	£306
			¥64,263	¥64,263	¥64,263
GRATER & SON, T.	2	2	$660	$1,460	$1,060
			DM1,139	DM2,730	DM1,934
			£403	£920	£661
			¥75,332	¥172,785	¥124,059
GRATER, THOMAS	1	1	$787	$787	$787
			DM1,401	DM1,401	DM1,401
			£483	£483	£483
			¥105,743	¥105,743	¥105,743
GREENWOOD, GEORGE WILLIAM	1	1	$3,000	$3,000	$3,000
			DM4,609	DM4,609	DM4,609
			£1,955	£1,955	£1,955
			¥328,418	¥328,418	¥328,418
GRIFFIN, WOODBURY	1	1	$1,265	$1,265	$1,265
			DM2,164	DM2,164	DM2,164
			£748	£748	£748
			¥157,088	¥157,088	¥157,088
GROBITZ	1	0			
GRULLI, PIETRO	2	2	$5,901	$13,840	$9,870
			DM8,216	DM19,266	DM13,741
			£3,680	£8,625	£6,153
			¥498,817	¥1,167,618	¥833,217
GUADAGNINI, ANTONIO	1	1	$40,986	$40,986	$40,986
			DM77,165	DM77,165	DM77,165
			£25,300	£25,300	£25,300
			¥4,331,866	¥4,331,866	¥4,331,866
GUADAGNINI, ANTONIO (ascribed to)	1	0			
GUADAGNINI, CARLO (attributed to)	1	1	$44,158	$44,158	$44,158
			DM74,708	DM74,708	DM74,708
			£27,773	£27,773	£27,773
			¥5,471,183	¥5,471,183	¥5,471,183
GUADAGNINI, FELICE	2	1	$56,925	$56,925	$56,925
			DM102,465	DM102,465	DM102,465
			£34,500	£34,500	£34,500
			¥8,209,275	¥8,209,275	¥8,209,275
GUADAGNINI, FRANCESCO	5	2	$10,142	$45,230	$27,686
			DM14,122	DM80,144	DM47,133
			£6,325	£27,773	£17,049
			¥857,341	¥5,514,825	¥3,186,083
GUADAGNINI, GIOVANNI BATTISTA	12	5	$77,751	$401,775	$220,722
			DM134,514	DM606,315	DM336,359
			£47,700	£243,500	£134,540
			¥8,872,200	¥45,534,500	¥24,729,975
GUADAGNINI, GIOVANNI BATTISTA (attributed to)	2	1	$11,474	$11,474	$11,474
			DM17,607	DM17,607	DM17,607
			£7,475	£7,475	£7,475
			¥1,255,875	¥1,255,875	¥1,255,875
GUADAGNINI, GIUSEPPE	1	0			
GUADAGNINI, GIUSEPPE (attributed to)	4	1	$32,137	$32,137	$32,137
			DM61,040	DM61,040	DM61,040
			£19,838	£19,838	£19,838
			¥3,376,541	¥3,376,541	¥3,376,541

Maker	Items		Selling Prices		
	Bid	Sold	Low	High	Avg
GUADAGNINI, LORENZO	1	1	$123,865	$123,865	$123,865
			DM174,435	DM174,435	DM174,435
			£78,500	£78,500	£78,500
			¥12,664,562	¥12,664,562	¥12,664,562
GUADAGNINI FAMILY (MEMBER OF)	1	0			
GUADAGNINI FAMILY (MEMBER OF) (ascribed to)	1	1	$103,540	$103,540	$103,540
			DM172,980	DM172,980	DM172,980
			£62,000	£62,000	£62,000
			¥12,585,380	¥12,585,380	¥12,585,380
GUADAGNINI FAMILY (MEMBER OF) (attributed to)	3	1	$10,689	$10,689	$10,689
			DM18,532	DM18,532	DM18,532
			£6,325	£6,325	£6,325
			¥1,334,575	¥1,334,575	¥1,334,575
GUADO, LORENZO FRASSINO	2	2	$2,566	$3,795	$3,180
			DM3,596	DM6,831	DM5,213
			£1,610	£2,300	£1,955
			¥226,181	¥547,285	¥386,733
GUADO, LORENZO FRASSINO (attributed to)	1	0			
GUARNERI, ANDREA	7	4	$105,629	$162,640	$139,790
			DM195,421	DM308,213	DM255,337
			£63,100	£100,395	£85,074
			¥14,076,979	¥18,167,605	¥16,088,392
GUARNERI, ANDREA (attributed to)	1	1	$44,712	$44,712	$44,712
			DM84,180	DM84,180	DM84,180
			£27,600	£27,600	£27,600
			¥4,725,672	¥4,725,672	¥4,725,672
GUARNERI, GIUSEPPE (FILIUS ANDREAE)	2	1	$278,055	$278,055	$278,055
			DM464,535	DM464,535	DM464,535
			£166,500	£166,500	£166,500
			¥33,797,835	¥33,797,835	¥33,797,835
GUARNERI, GIUSEPPE (FILIUS ANDREAE) (ascribed to)	1	1	$4,600	$4,600	$4,600
			DM8,280	DM8,280	DM8,280
			£2,760	£2,760	£2,760
			¥35,742	¥35,742	¥35,742
GUARNERI, JOSEPH (DEL GESU)	2	1	$932,035	$932,035	$932,035
			DM1,615,895	DM1,615,895	DM1,615,895
			£551,500	£551,500	£551,500
			¥116,366,500	¥116,366,500	¥116,366,500
GUARNERI, PIETRO (OF MANTUA)	1	1	$64,800	$64,800	$64,800
			DM116,400	DM116,400	DM116,400
			£40,000	£40,000	£40,000
			¥7,650,800	¥7,650,800	¥7,650,800
GUARNERI, PIETRO (OF MANTUA) (ascribed to)	1	0			
GUARNERI, PIETRO (OF VENICE)	2	0			
GUARNERI FAMILY (ascribed to)	1	0			
GUARNERI FAMILY (attributed to)	1	1	$27,219	$27,219	$27,219
			DM38,331	DM38,331	DM38,331
			£17,250	£17,250	£17,250
			¥2,782,977	¥2,782,977	¥2,782,977
GUASTALLA, DANTE & ALFREDO	1	1	$13,414	$13,414	$13,414
			DM24,095	DM24,095	DM24,095
			£8,280	£8,280	£8,280
			¥1,583,716	¥1,583,716	¥1,583,716

Maker	Items		Selling Prices		
	Bid	Sold	Low	High	Avg

Maker	Bid	Sold	Low	High	Avg
GUASTALLA, DANTE & ALFREDO (attributed to)	2	0			
GUERRA, EVASIO EMILE	7	5	$14,904	$33,922	$20,497
			DM26,772	DM60,108	DM35,063
			£9,200	£20,829	£12,774
			¥1,759,684	¥4,136,119	¥2,505,406
GUERSAN, LOUIS	5	5	$822	$5,444	$3,581
			DM1,433	DM8,280	DM5,949
			£506	£3,450	£2,197
			¥35,742	¥556,595	¥288,616
GUERSAN, LOUIS (attributed to)	1	0			
GUICCIARDI, GIANCARLO	1	1	$18,262	$18,262	$18,262
			DM25,677	DM25,677	DM25,677
			£11,500	£11,500	£11,500
			¥1,629,895	¥1,629,895	¥1,629,895
GUIDANTE, FLORENO	1	1	$9,220	$9,220	$9,220
			DM12,838	DM12,838	DM12,838
			£5,750	£5,750	£5,750
			¥779,401	¥779,401	¥779,401
GUIDANTE, FLORENO (ascribed to)	1	1	$2,645	$2,645	$2,645
			DM4,867	DM4,867	DM4,867
			£1,645	£1,645	£1,645
			¥311,978	¥311,978	¥311,978
GUIDANTE, GIOVANNI FLORENO	2	1	$9,664	$9,664	$9,664
			DM14,460	DM14,460	DM14,460
			£5,750	£5,750	£5,750
			¥1,078,010	¥1,078,010	¥1,078,010
GUIDANTE, GIOVANNI FLORENO (ascribed to)	1	0			
GUIDANTE, GIOVANNI FLORENO (attributed to)	2	1	$24,967	$24,967	$24,967
			DM46,345	DM46,345	DM46,345
			£14,950	£14,950	£14,950
			¥3,340,428	¥3,340,428	¥3,340,428
GUILLAMI, JUAN	2	2	$14,531	$16,711	$15,621
			DM27,538	DM31,669	DM29,603
			£8,970	£10,316	£9,643
			¥1,534,498	¥1,764,673	¥1,649,585
GUINDON, H.	1	1	$298	$298	$298
			DM562	DM562	DM562
			£184	£184	£184
			¥31,513	¥31,513	¥31,513
GUTH, AUGUST	1	1	$2,915	$2,915	$2,915
			DM5,054	DM5,054	DM5,054
			£1,725	£1,725	£1,725
			¥363,975	¥363,975	¥363,975
GUTH, PAUL (attributed to)	1	1	$3,575	$3,575	$3,575
			DM6,048	DM6,048	DM6,048
			£2,248	£2,248	£2,248
			¥442,905	¥442,905	¥442,905
GUTTER, GEORG ADAM	1	0			
GUTTER, JOHANN GEORG	1	0			
GUTTER, JOHANN GEORG (attributed to)	2	2	$635	$1,291	$963
			DM1,108	DM2,312	DM1,710
			£391	£771	£581
			¥76,968	¥149,862	¥113,415

| Maker | Items | | Selling Prices | | |
	Bid	Sold	Low	High	Avg
GYULA, CSISZAR	1	1	$1,495	$1,495	$1,495
			DM2,558	DM2,558	DM2,558
			£884	£884	£884
			¥185,649	¥185,649	¥185,649
HAAHTI, EERO	1	1	$3,262	$3,262	$3,262
			DM3,436	DM3,436	DM3,436
			£2,013	£2,013	£2,013
			¥249,137	¥249,137	¥249,137
HADDEN, ROBERT	1	1	$690	$690	$690
			DM1,278	DM1,278	DM1,278
			£414	£414	£414
			¥92,169	¥92,169	¥92,169
HALL, GEORGE S.	1	1	$633	$633	$633
			DM1,093	DM1,093	DM1,093
			£391	£391	£391
			¥80,160	¥80,160	¥80,160
HALL, LOUIS HASTINGS	1	1	$546	$546	$546
			DM790	DM790	DM790
			£357	£357	£357
			¥55,308	¥55,308	¥55,308
HALL, R.G.	4	3	$920	$3,105	$2,262
			DM1,407	DM4,484	DM3,292
			£605	£1,978	£1,447
			¥96,968	¥269,359	¥201,919
HALL, WILLIAM	2	1	$309	$309	$309
			DM539	DM539	DM539
			£184	£184	£184
			¥39,442	¥39,442	¥39,442
HALLIDAY, R.L.	3	3	$360	$588	$492
			DM550	DM873	DM744
			£230	£380	£318
			¥40,147	¥63,673	¥53,804
HAMM, ALBAN (workshop of)	1	1	$518	$518	$518
			DM791	DM791	DM791
			£340	£340	£340
			¥54,545	¥54,545	¥54,545
HAMM, JOHANN GOTTFRIED	3	2	$1,150	$1,977	$1,564
			DM1,731	DM2,767	DM2,249
			£698	£1,237	£968
			¥128,547	¥167,258	¥147,903
HAMM, JOHANN GOTTFRIED (workshop of)	1	1	$173	$173	$173
			DM307	DM307	DM307
			£105	£105	£105
			¥23,964	¥23,964	¥23,964
HAMMETT, THOMAS	2	1	$910	$910	$910
			DM1,301	DM1,301	DM1,301
			£575	£575	£575
			¥91,417	¥91,417	¥91,417
HAMMIG, LIPPOLD	1	0			
HAMMOND, JOHN	2	1	$185	$185	$185
			DM312	DM312	DM312
			£115	£115	£115
			¥22,754	¥22,754	¥22,754
HANSEN, SVERRE	2	2	$1,583	$3,166	$2,375
			DM2,430	DM4,861	DM3,646
			£1,035	£2,070	£1,553
			¥172,780	¥345,560	¥259,170

Maker	Items		Selling Prices		
	Bid	Sold	Low	High	Avg
HARDIE, JAMES (attributed to)	2	0			
HARDIE, JAMES & SONS	1	1	$580	$580	$580
			DM1,042	DM1,042	DM1,042
			£345	£345	£345
			¥67,009	¥67,009	¥67,009
HARDIE, JAMES & SONS (attributed to)	3	1	$1,118	$1,118	$1,118
			DM1,178	DM1,178	DM1,178
			£690	£690	£690
			¥85,419	¥85,419	¥85,419
HARDIE, MATTHEW	5	2	$3,864	$5,677	$4,771
			DM6,440	DM9,605	DM8,023
			£2,300	£3,571	£2,935
			¥461,817	¥703,438	¥582,627
HARDIE, MATTHEW (attributed to)	4	2	$5,780	$8,554	$7,167
			DM8,686	DM13,720	DM11,203
			£3,450	£5,555	£4,502
			¥643,635	¥973,259	¥808,447
HARDIE, MATTHEW & SON	1	1	$5,216	$5,216	$5,216
			DM9,370	DM9,370	DM9,370
			£3,220	£3,220	£3,220
			¥615,889	¥615,889	¥615,889
HARDIE, MATTHEW & SON (attributed to)	1	0			
HARDIE, THOMAS	2	2	$973	$5,756	$3,364
			DM1,689	DM8,141	DM4,915
			£575	£3,680	£2,128
			¥123,401	¥584,417	¥353,909
HARDWICK, JOHN E.	2	2	$530	$707	$619
			DM783	DM1,044	DM913
			£345	£460	£403
			¥56,503	¥75,337	¥65,920
HARLOW, FRANK	4	1	$672	$672	$672
			DM989	DM989	DM989
			£437	£437	£437
			¥71,301	¥71,301	¥71,301
HARRIS, CHARLES	2	2	$6,185	$7,728	$6,956
			DM9,254	DM12,880	DM11,067
			£3,680	£4,600	£4,140
			¥689,926	¥923,634	¥806,780
HARRIS, CHARLES (II)	1	1	$3,416	$3,416	$3,416
			DM5,154	DM5,154	DM5,154
			£2,070	£2,070	£2,070
			¥387,090	¥387,090	¥387,090
HARRIS, GEORGE E.	1	1	$368	$368	$368
			DM514	DM514	DM514
			£230	£230	£230
			¥31,099	¥31,099	¥31,099
HARRIS, HENRY	1	1	$805	$805	$805
			DM1,457	DM1,457	DM1,457
			£491	£491	£491
			¥97,196	¥97,196	¥97,196
HARRIS, J.E.	1	0			
HART, GEORGE	1	1	$4,794	$4,794	$4,794
			DM6,676	DM6,676	DM6,676
			£2,990	£2,990	£2,990
			¥405,289	¥405,289	¥405,289

Maker	Items		Selling Prices		
	Bid	Sold	Low	High	Avg
HART & SON	5	5	$1,609	$4,285	$3,108
			DM3,026	DM7,697	DM5,384
			£1,012	£2,645	£1,925
			¥194,547	¥505,909	¥368,763
HART & SON (workshop of)	1	1	$1,898	$1,898	$1,898
			DM2,864	DM2,864	DM2,864
			£1,150	£1,150	£1,150
			¥215,050	¥215,050	¥215,050
HAUSMANN, OTTOMAR	1	1	$1,840	$1,840	$1,840
			DM3,180	DM3,180	DM3,180
			£1,137	£1,137	£1,137
			¥233,192	¥233,192	¥233,192
HAVEMANN, CARL FRIEDRICH	1	1	$210	$210	$210
			DM352	DM352	DM352
			£126	£126	£126
			¥25,577	¥25,577	¥25,577
HAWKES & SON	2	2	$943	$1,022	$983
			DM1,405	DM1,627	DM1,516
			£575	£633	£604
			¥85,128	¥107,617	¥96,373
HAYNES & CO.	1	1	$1,997	$1,997	$1,997
			DM3,378	DM3,378	DM3,378
			£1,256	£1,256	£1,256
			¥247,393	¥247,393	¥247,393
HAZELL, LEONARD W.	4	1	$186	$186	$186
			DM196	DM196	DM196
			£115	£115	£115
			¥14,236	¥14,236	¥14,236
HEATON, WILLIAM	4	3	$668	$1,096	$854
			DM1,026	DM1,541	DM1,327
			£437	£690	£537
			¥72,951	¥110,554	¥93,638
HEBERLEIN (workshop of)	3	3	$616	$1,497	$954
			DM909	DM2,210	DM1,400
			£402	£977	£622
			¥65,486	¥159,154	¥100,108
HEBERLEIN, ALBERT (JR.)	1	1	$3,306	$3,306	$3,306
			DM6,084	DM6,084	DM6,084
			£2,056	£2,056	£2,056
			¥389,972	¥389,972	¥389,972
HEBERLEIN, ALBERT AUGUST (JR.)	1	1	$1,874	$1,874	$1,874
			DM3,324	DM3,324	DM3,324
			£1,150	£1,150	£1,150
			¥221,640	¥221,640	¥221,640
HEBERLEIN, G.F. (JR.)	1	1	$978	$978	$978
			DM1,652	DM1,652	DM1,652
			£587	£587	£587
			¥119,255	¥119,255	¥119,255
HEBERLEIN, HEINRICH E. (JR.) (workshop of)	1	1	$518	$518	$518
			DM791	DM791	DM791
			£340	£340	£340
			¥54,545	¥54,545	¥54,545
HEBERLEIN, HEINRICH TH. (workshop of)	3	3	$978	$1,840	$1,323
			DM1,412	DM3,148	DM2,106
			£623	£1,088	£823
			¥84,798	¥228,491	¥144,833

Maker	Items		Selling Prices		
	Bid	Sold	Low	High	Avg
HEBERLEIN, HEINRICH TH. (JR.)	5	4	$805	$2,530	$1,557
			DM1,360	DM4,276	DM2,555
			£483	£1,518	£937
			¥98,210	¥308,660	¥187,618
HEBERLEIN, HEINRICH TH. (JR.) (workshop of)	14	12	$431	$2,300	$1,313
			DM665	DM3,542	DM2,083
			£255	£1,502	£818
			¥46,575	¥257,053	¥146,936
HEBERLEIN, L. FRITZ (attributed to)	1	1	$809	$809	$809
			DM1,449	DM1,449	DM1,449
			£483	£483	£483
			¥93,944	¥93,944	¥93,944
HEBERLEIN FAMILY (MEMBER OF)	1	0			
HEBERLIN, FRIEDRICH	2	1	$508	$508	$508
			DM815	DM815	DM815
			£330	£330	£330
			¥57,831	¥57,831	¥57,831
HECKEL, RUDOLF	1	1	$2,185	$2,185	$2,185
			DM3,155	DM3,155	DM3,155
			£1,392	£1,392	£1,392
			¥189,549	¥189,549	¥189,549
HECKEL, RUDOLF (attributed to)	1	1	$2,206	$2,206	$2,206
			DM3,087	DM3,087	DM3,087
			£1,380	£1,380	£1,380
			¥186,594	¥186,594	¥186,594
HEINEL, OSKAR BERNHARD	1	1	$805	$805	$805
			DM1,360	DM1,360	DM1,360
			£483	£483	£483
			¥98,210	¥98,210	¥98,210
HEINEL, OSKAR ERICH	3	1	$2,695	$2,695	$2,695
			DM4,986	DM4,986	DM4,986
			£1,610	£1,610	£1,610
			¥359,175	¥359,175	¥359,175
HEINICKE, MATHIAS	8	2	$3,353	$3,887	$3,620
			DM6,314	DM6,739	DM6,526
			£2,070	£2,300	£2,185
			¥354,425	¥485,300	¥419,863
HEL, J.	1	1	$16,324	$16,324	$16,324
			DM27,272	DM27,272	DM27,272
			£9,775	£9,775	£9,775
			¥1,984,227	¥1,984,227	¥1,984,227
HEL, JOSEPH	9	5	$3,540	$13,041	$9,149
			DM6,337	DM24,553	DM15,306
			£2,185	£8,050	£5,681
			¥417,488	¥1,378,321	¥1,011,230
HEL, JOSEPH (attributed to)	1	1	$16,295	$16,295	$16,295
			DM30,185	DM30,185	DM30,185
			£9,775	£9,775	£9,775
			¥2,176,208	¥2,176,208	¥2,176,208
HEL, JOSEPH (workshop of)	1	1	$431	$431	$431
			DM623	DM623	DM623
			£275	£275	£275
			¥37,411	¥37,411	¥37,411
HEL, PIERRE	1	1	$11,711	$11,711	$11,711
			DM21,967	DM21,967	DM21,967
			£7,274	£7,274	£7,274
			¥1,407,616	¥1,407,616	¥1,407,616

| Maker | Items | | Selling Prices | | |
	Bid	Sold	Low	High	Avg
HEL, PIERRE JEAN HENRI	4	3	$12,650	$18,211	$15,565
			DM19,343	DM34,511	DM27,954
			£8,322	£11,241	£9,780
			¥1,333,310	¥1,923,041	¥1,642,853
HEL, PIERRE JOSEPH	8	4	$14,404	$17,265	$15,743
			DM20,535	DM25,756	DM23,685
			£8,625	£10,925	£9,919
			¥1,297,540	¥1,835,280	¥1,606,110
HELLMER, JOHANN GEORG	1	1	$2,944	$2,944	$2,944
			DM4,981	DM4,981	DM4,981
			£1,852	£1,852	£1,852
			¥364,746	¥364,746	¥364,746
HELLMER, JOHANN GEORG (attributed to)	2	1	$3,187	$3,187	$3,187
			DM5,767	DM5,767	DM5,767
			£1,955	£1,955	£1,955
			¥384,529	¥384,529	¥384,529
HELLMER, KARL	1	1	$489	$489	$489
			DM836	DM836	DM836
			£289	£289	£289
			¥60,693	¥60,693	¥60,693
HEMPEL, JULIUS	1	1	$1,093	$1,093	$1,093
			DM1,888	DM1,888	DM1,888
			£675	£675	£675
			¥138,458	¥138,458	¥138,458
HENDERSHOT, JOHN C.	1	1	$345	$345	$345
			DM590	DM590	DM590
			£204	£204	£204
			¥42,842	¥42,842	¥42,842
HENDERSON, F.V.	1	1	$518	$518	$518
			DM921	DM921	DM921
			£311	£311	£311
			¥68,817	¥68,817	¥68,817
HENDERSON, HAROLD A.	1	1	$2,415	$2,415	$2,415
			DM3,635	DM3,635	DM3,635
			£1,466	£1,466	£1,466
			¥269,949	¥269,949	¥269,949
HENNING, GUSTAV	1	1	$690	$690	$690
			DM1,166	DM1,166	DM1,166
			£414	£414	£414
			¥84,180	¥84,180	¥84,180
HENRY	1	1	$7,321	$7,321	$7,321
			DM11,002	DM11,002	DM11,002
			£4,370	£4,370	£4,370
			¥815,272	¥815,272	¥815,272
HENRY, CHARLES	1	0			
HENRY, EUGENE	3	2	$2,028	$7,941	$4,985
			DM2,824	DM12,200	DM7,512
			£1,265	£5,175	£3,220
			¥171,468	¥869,343	¥520,406
HENRY, J.B.	1	1	$3,183	$3,183	$3,183
			DM4,683	DM4,683	DM4,683
			£2,070	£2,070	£2,070
			¥337,741	¥337,741	¥337,741
HENTSCHEL, JOHANN JOSEPH	1	0			
HERBRIG, CHARLES EDWARD	1	1	$805	$805	$805
			DM1,462	DM1,462	DM1,462
			£493	£493	£493
			¥99,965	¥99,965	¥99,965

Maker	Items		Selling Prices		
	Bid	Sold	Low	High	Avg
HERCLIK, FR.	1	1	$2,903	$2,903	$2,903
			DM4,089	DM4,089	DM4,089
			£1,840	£1,840	£1,840
			¥296,851	¥296,851	¥296,851
HERCLIK, LADISLAV	1	1	$1,802	$1,802	$1,802
			DM2,719	DM2,719	DM2,719
			£1,092	£1,092	£1,092
			¥204,204	¥204,204	¥204,204
HERMANN (workshop of)	1	1	$196	$196	$196
			DM348	DM348	DM348
			£119	£119	£119
			¥27,159	¥27,159	¥27,159
HERRMANN, HEINRICH (attributed to)	1	1	$530	$530	$530
			DM783	DM783	DM783
			£345	£345	£345
			¥56,488	¥56,488	¥56,488
HERRMANN, KARL (workshop of)	1	1	$1,150	$1,150	$1,150
			DM1,758	DM1,758	DM1,758
			£757	£757	£757
			¥121,210	¥121,210	¥121,210
HERTL, ANTON	3	1	$854	$854	$854
			DM1,516	DM1,516	DM1,516
			£518	£518	£518
			¥118,451	¥118,451	¥118,451
HESKETH	1	1	$4,993	$4,993	$4,993
			DM8,342	DM8,342	DM8,342
			£2,990	£2,990	£2,990
			¥606,940	¥606,940	¥606,940
HESKETH, THOMAS EARLE	12	10	$1,733	$7,342	$4,866
			DM3,205	DM13,197	DM7,928
			£1,035	£4,600	£3,013
			¥230,898	¥887,066	¥542,693
HEVELKA, SIMON JOANNES (attributed to)	1	1	$1,463	$1,463	$1,463
			DM2,077	DM2,077	DM2,077
			£920	£920	£920
			¥135,838	¥135,838	¥135,838
HEYLIGERS, MATHIJS	3	1	$7,750	$7,750	$7,750
			DM10,789	DM10,789	DM10,789
			£4,830	£4,830	£4,830
			¥653,866	¥653,866	¥653,866
HICKS, GEORGE HERBERT	1	1	$2,566	$2,566	$2,566
			DM3,596	DM3,596	DM3,596
			£1,610	£1,610	£1,610
			¥226,181	¥226,181	¥226,181
HILAIRE, PAUL	1	0			
HILAIRE, PAUL (workshop of)	1	1	$1,725	$1,725	$1,725
			DM2,982	DM2,982	DM2,982
			£1,066	£1,066	£1,066
			¥218,618	¥218,618	¥218,618
HILL, JOSEPH	10	8	$3,565	$8,066	$5,901
			DM6,265	DM13,476	DM9,315
			£2,175	£4,830	£3,654
			¥430,438	¥980,442	¥640,645
HILL, JOSEPH (attributed to)	5	4	$748	$7,750	$3,143
			DM1,303	DM10,789	DM4,509
			£460	£4,830	£1,984
			¥90,551	¥653,866	¥292,162

Maker	Items		Selling Prices		
	Bid	Sold	Low	High	Avg
HILL, LOCKEY	4	2	$1,270	$1,546	$1,408
			DM1,789	DM2,778	DM2,284
			£805	£920	£863
			¥129,872	¥178,692	¥154,282
HILL, W.E. & SONS	24	14	$5,436	$19,282	$10,281
			DM8,676	DM36,541	DM17,189
			£3,335	£11,903	£6,353
			¥524,257	¥2,036,161	¥1,112,129
HILL, W.E. & SONS (workshop of)	2	2	$2,251	$2,760	$2,505
			DM3,985	DM4,275	DM4,130
			£1,389	£1,758	£1,574
			¥236,456	¥239,430	¥237,943
HILL FAMILY (MEMBER OF)	5	2	$2,409	$3,479	$2,944
			DM4,060	DM5,205	DM4,633
			£1,495	£2,070	£1,783
			¥295,805	¥388,084	¥341,944
HJORTH, A.	1	0			
HJORTH, EMIL	3	1	$6,459	$6,459	$6,459
			DM8,991	DM8,991	DM8,991
			£4,025	£4,025	£4,025
			¥544,888	¥544,888	¥544,888
HJORTH, KNUD	2	1	$5,444	$5,444	$5,444
			DM7,666	DM7,666	DM7,666
			£3,450	£3,450	£3,450
			¥556,595	¥556,595	¥556,595
HOFFMANN, EDUARD	1	1	$1,058	$1,058	$1,058
			DM1,997	DM1,997	DM1,997
			£655	£655	£655
			¥111,936	¥111,936	¥111,936
HOFMANN, G. WILLIAM	1	1	$3,214	$3,214	$3,214
			DM6,104	DM6,104	DM6,104
			£1,984	£1,984	£1,984
			¥337,654	¥337,654	¥337,654
HOFMANN, GEORG PHILIP	1	0			
HOFMANS, MATHIAS (attributed to)	3	1	$1,679	$1,679	$1,679
			DM2,478	DM2,478	DM2,478
			£1,092	£1,092	£1,092
			¥178,843	¥178,843	¥178,843
HOFNER, KARL	2	2	$1,060	$1,263	$1,162
			DM1,566	DM2,190	DM1,878
			£690	£748	£719
			¥112,976	¥157,723	¥135,349
HOLDER, T.J.	2	2	$5,780	$8,457	$7,118
			DM8,686	DM11,832	DM10,259
			£3,450	£5,290	£4,370
			¥643,635	¥715,277	¥679,456
HOLDER, T.J. (attributed to)	3	0			
HOLDER, THOMAS	1	0			
HOLDER, THOMAS (attributed to)	3	0			
HOLLISTER, W.	1	0			
HOLST, JOHANNES (attributed to)	2	1	$883	$883	$883
			DM1,460	DM1,460	DM1,460
			£529	£529	£529
			¥103,314	¥103,314	¥103,314

	Items		*Selling Prices*		
Maker	Bid	Sold	Low	High	Avg
HOMENICK BROTHERS	1	1	$3,220	$3,220	$3,220
			DM5,566	DM5,566	DM5,566
			£1,990	£1,990	£1,990
			¥408,087	¥408,087	¥408,087
HOMOLKA, EMANUEL ADAM	1	1	$7,991	$7,991	$7,991
			DM13,519	DM13,519	DM13,519
			£5,026	£5,026	£5,026
			¥990,024	¥990,024	¥990,024
HOMOLKA, FERDINAND AUGUST	1	1	$7,951	$7,951	$7,951
			DM11,747	DM11,747	DM11,747
			£5,175	£5,175	£5,175
			¥847,323	¥847,323	¥847,323
HOMOLKA, FERDINAND JOS.	1	1	$1,034	$1,034	$1,034
			DM1,708	DM1,708	DM1,708
			£633	£633	£633
			¥128,036	¥128,036	¥128,036
HOPF	8	5	$212	$1,008	$545
			DM312	DM1,516	DM856
			£138	£633	£336
			¥22,516	¥109,193	¥58,789
HOPF (attributed to)	1	1	$691	$691	$691
			DM1,143	DM1,143	DM1,143
			£414	£414	£414
			¥80,854	¥80,854	¥80,854
HOPF, DAVID	1	1	$1,380	$1,380	$1,380
			DM2,332	DM2,332	DM2,332
			£828	£828	£828
			¥168,360	¥168,360	¥168,360
HOPF, L.	1	0			
HOPF FAMILY (MEMBER OF)	1	1	$1,536	$1,536	$1,536
			DM2,539	DM2,539	DM2,539
			£920	£920	£920
			¥179,676	¥179,676	¥179,676
HORNSTEINER	5	5	$394	$789	$565
			DM700	DM1,337	DM973
			£242	£483	£347
			¥52,872	¥91,527	¥68,146
HORNSTEINER (ascribed to)	1	1	$1,344	$1,344	$1,344
			DM2,246	DM2,246	DM2,246
			£805	£805	£805
			¥163,407	¥163,407	¥163,407
HORNSTEINER (attributed to)	1	0			
HORNSTEINER (workshop of)	1	1	$345	$345	$345
			DM614	DM614	DM614
			£210	£210	£210
			¥47,927	¥47,927	¥47,927
HORNSTEINER, J.	2	1	$489	$489	$489
			DM828	DM828	DM828
			£299	£299	£299
			¥56,659	¥56,659	¥56,659
HORNSTEINER, JOSEPH	2	1	$1,360	$1,360	$1,360
			DM2,359	DM2,359	DM2,359
			£805	£805	£805
			¥172,970	¥172,970	¥172,970
HORNSTEINER, JOSEPH (II)	3	3	$1,410	$3,866	$2,359
			DM2,081	DM5,784	DM3,528
			£920	£2,300	£1,437
			¥149,869	¥431,204	¥261,759

Maker	Items		Selling Prices		
	Bid	Sold	Low	High	Avg
HORNSTEINER, MATHIAS	2	1	$5,175	$5,175	$5,175
			DM8,854	DM8,854	DM8,854
			£3,061	£3,061	£3,061
			¥642,632	¥642,632	¥642,632
HORNSTEINER FAMILY	4	2	$309	$466	$388
			DM556	DM816	DM686
			£184	£288	£236
			¥35,738	¥56,336	¥46,037
HOWARD, CLARK	1	1	$1,725	$1,725	$1,725
			DM2,596	DM2,596	DM2,596
			£1,047	£1,047	£1,047
			¥192,821	¥192,821	¥192,821
HOWE, R.	1	1	$204	$204	$204
			DM344	DM344	DM344
			£127	£127	£127
			¥25,030	¥25,030	¥25,030
HOWE, ROBERT	2	0			
HOWELL, T.	1	1	$1,114	$1,114	$1,114
			DM1,727	DM1,727	DM1,727
			£667	£667	£667
			¥126,937	¥126,937	¥126,937
HOYER, ANDREAS	1	0			
HOYER, FRIEDRICH	2	2	$537	$1,380	$958
			DM994	DM2,361	DM1,678
			£322	£816	£569
			¥71,687	¥171,368	¥121,528
HUDSON, GEORGE	3	1	$1,883	$1,883	$1,883
			DM2,918	DM2,918	DM2,918
			£1,127	£1,127	£1,127
			¥214,479	¥214,479	¥214,479
HUDSON, GEORGE WULME	3	2	$8,942	$9,200	$9,071
			DM16,652	DM16,836	DM16,744
			£5,520	£5,612	£5,566
			¥945,134	¥1,110,808	¥1,027,971
HULINSKY, THOMAS	1	1	$3,887	$3,887	$3,887
			DM6,739	DM6,739	DM6,739
			£2,300	£2,300	£2,300
			¥485,300	¥485,300	¥485,300
HUMBERT	1	1	$1,211	$1,211	$1,211
			DM2,280	DM2,280	DM2,280
			£748	£748	£748
			¥129,093	¥129,093	¥129,093
HUME, ALEXANDER	3	2	$3,401	$5,286	$4,344
			DM4,758	DM7,804	DM6,281
			£2,128	£3,450	£2,789
			¥287,666	¥562,008	¥424,837
HUMS, ALBIN	1	1	$1,035	$1,035	$1,035
			DM1,842	DM1,842	DM1,842
			£621	£621	£621
			¥137,634	¥137,634	¥137,634
HUNGER, C.F.	1	1	$3,073	$3,073	$3,073
			DM5,134	DM5,134	DM5,134
			£1,840	£1,840	£1,840
			¥373,502	¥373,502	¥373,502
HURE, HARRY	2	1	$794	$794	$794
			DM1,498	DM1,498	DM1,498
			£491	£491	£491
			¥83,952	¥83,952	¥83,952

Maker	Items Bid	Sold	Selling Prices Low	High	Avg
HUSSON & BUTHOD	1	1	$1,089	$1,089	$1,089
			DM1,533	DM1,533	DM1,533
			£690	£690	£690
			¥111,319	¥111,319	¥111,319
IGNESTI, ROBERTO	1	1	$4,180	$4,180	$4,180
			DM5,904	DM5,904	DM5,904
			£2,645	£2,645	£2,645
			¥373,043	¥373,043	¥373,043
JACOBS, H.	1	1	$28,808	$28,808	$28,808
			DM48,128	DM48,128	DM48,128
			£17,250	£17,250	£17,250
			¥3,501,578	¥3,501,578	¥3,501,578
JACOBS, HENDRIK	4	4	$11,500	$24,369	$17,363
			DM20,815	DM43,206	DM29,846
			£7,015	£14,950	£10,790
			¥1,388,510	¥2,881,314	¥1,999,393
JACQUEMIN, RENE (attributed to)	2	0			
JACQUEMIN, RENE (workshop of)	1	1	$863	$863	$863
			DM1,535	DM1,535	DM1,535
			£518	£518	£518
			¥114,695	¥114,695	¥114,695
JACQUOT, CHARLES	4	4	$3,726	$8,942	$5,877
			DM6,670	DM16,946	DM10,236
			£2,300	£5,520	£3,651
			¥439,461	¥944,306	¥616,613
JACQUOT, CHARLES (ascribed to)	3	1	$4,771	$4,771	$4,771
			DM7,048	DM7,048	DM7,048
			£3,105	£3,105	£3,105
			¥508,394	¥508,394	¥508,394
JACQUOT, FERNAND	2	2	$2,820	$5,175	$3,998
			DM4,658	DM9,315	DM6,987
			£1,725	£3,105	£2,415
			¥40,210	¥349,190	¥194,700
JAIS, ANDREAS	1	0			
JAIS, ANTON	2	1	$5,636	$5,636	$5,636
			DM9,772	DM9,772	DM9,772
			£3,335	£3,335	£3,335
			¥703,685	¥703,685	¥703,685
JAIS, JOHANN (attributed to)	1	0			
JAMES, LESTER	1	1	$1,495	$1,495	$1,495
			DM2,159	DM2,159	DM2,159
			£952	£952	£952
			¥129,691	¥129,691	¥129,691
JAMIESON	1	0			
JAUCK, JOHANNES (ascribed to)	2	1	$2,876	$2,876	$2,876
			DM5,327	DM5,327	DM5,327
			£1,725	£1,725	£1,725
			¥384,037	¥384,037	¥384,037
JAY, HENRY (ascribed to)	1	1	$2,702	$2,702	$2,702
			DM4,837	DM4,837	DM4,837
			£1,668	£1,668	£1,668
			¥318,705	¥318,705	¥318,705
JIROUSEK, JOSEPH	1	1	$805	$805	$805
			DM1,164	DM1,164	DM1,164
			£526	£526	£526
			¥81,506	¥81,506	¥81,506
JIROWSKY, HANS	1	0			

Maker	Items		Selling Prices		
	Bid	Sold	Low	High	Avg
JOHNSON, GEORGE	2	1	$863	$863	$863
			DM1,476	DM1,476	DM1,476
			£510	£510	£510
			¥107,105	¥107,105	¥107,105
JOHNSON, JOHN	10	4	$920	$5,962	$3,463
			DM1,385	DM11,224	DM5,912
			£558	£3,680	£2,133
			¥102,838	¥630,090	¥386,897
JOHNSON, W.A.	1	0			
JOLLY, LEON	4	2	$597	$1,145	$871
			DM1,044	DM1,688	DM1,366
			£368	£748	£558
			¥72,110	¥122,119	¥97,114
JOLY, LOUIS	3	2	$763	$2,028	$1,396
			DM1,081	DM2,824	DM1,952
			£483	£1,265	£874
			¥78,729	¥171,468	¥125,099
JOMBAR, PAUL	5	1	$3,882	$3,882	$3,882
			DM5,964	DM5,964	DM5,964
			£2,530	£2,530	£2,530
			¥425,012	¥425,012	¥425,012
JOMBAR, PAUL (attributed to)	2	1	$2,881	$2,881	$2,881
			DM4,761	DM4,761	DM4,761
			£1,725	£1,725	£1,725
			¥336,893	¥336,893	¥336,893
JONES, WILLIAM H.	4	1	$820	$820	$820
			DM1,217	DM1,217	DM1,217
			£529	£529	£529
			¥88,756	¥88,756	¥88,756
JORIO, VINCENZO (ascribed to)	1	0			
JUZEK, JOHN	5	5	$431	$1,955	$1,340
			DM623	DM3,243	DM2,100
			£275	£1,208	£823
			¥37,411	¥236,746	¥153,001
JUZEK, JOHN (workshop of)	6	6	$431	$2,990	$1,442
			DM781	DM5,168	DM2,420
			£263	£1,848	£892
			¥52,069	¥378,938	¥171,286
KAGANSKY, VALERY	1	1	$2,999	$2,999	$2,999
			DM5,684	DM5,684	DM5,684
			£1,852	£1,852	£1,852
			¥316,736	¥316,736	¥316,736
KALTENBRUNNER, K. RICHARD	1	1	$5,750	$5,750	$5,750
			DM9,939	DM9,939	DM9,939
			£3,553	£3,553	£3,553
			¥728,726	¥728,726	¥728,726
KARNER, BARTHOLOMAUS	2	1	$960	$960	$960
			DM1,604	DM1,604	DM1,604
			£575	£575	£575
			¥116,719	¥116,719	¥116,719
KARNER, BARTHOLOMAUS (II)	3	0			
KAUL, PAUL	5	3	$2,990	$8,998	$6,853
			DM5,053	DM17,091	DM12,795
			£1,794	£5,555	£4,213
			¥364,780	¥945,431	¥738,391

Maker	Items Bid	Sold	Selling Prices Low	High	Avg
KEFFER, JOANNES (attributed to)	1	1	$1,740	$1,740	$1,740
			DM2,603	DM2,603	DM2,603
			£1,035	£1,035	£1,035
			¥194,042	¥194,042	¥194,042
KEMPTER, ANDREAS	1	1	$5,467	$5,467	$5,467
			DM9,250	DM9,250	DM9,250
			£3,439	£3,439	£3,439
			¥677,385	¥677,385	¥677,385
KEMPTER, ANDREAS (attributed to)	2	0			
KENNEDY (workshop of)	1	0			
KENNEDY, THOMAS	11	4	$1,259	$6,856	$4,880
			DM1,781	DM12,992	DM8,434
			£805	£4,232	£3,042
			¥127,841	¥723,968	¥509,486
KENNEDY, THOMAS (attributed to)	2	1	$2,236	$2,236	$2,236
			DM4,209	DM4,209	DM4,209
			£1,380	£1,380	£1,380
			¥238,326	¥238,326	¥238,326
KESSEL, M.J.H.	1	1	$2,313	$2,313	$2,313
			DM3,913	DM3,913	DM3,913
			£1,455	£1,455	£1,455
			¥286,586	¥286,586	¥286,586
KESSLER, JOHANN GEORG	1	1	$1,452	$1,452	$1,452
			DM2,044	DM2,044	DM2,044
			£920	£920	£920
			¥148,425	¥148,425	¥148,425
KESSLER, W. AUGUST (JR.)	1	1	$3,457	$3,457	$3,457
			DM6,417	DM6,417	DM6,417
			£2,070	£2,070	£2,070
			¥462,521	¥462,521	¥462,521
KINLOCH, WILLIAM	1	1	$946	$946	$946
			DM1,353	DM1,353	DM1,353
			£598	£598	£598
			¥95,074	¥95,074	¥95,074
KLEMM, GEORGE & AUGUST	1	1	$978	$978	$978
			DM1,412	DM1,412	DM1,412
			£623	£623	£623
			¥84,798	¥84,798	¥84,798
KLINTH, ALBERT W.	1	1	$431	$431	$431
			DM768	DM768	DM768
			£259	£259	£259
			¥57,348	¥57,348	¥57,348
KLOTZ, AEGIDIUS (I)	8	5	$1,660	$5,412	$4,040
			DM2,311	DM8,761	DM6,684
			£1,035	£3,220	£2,415
			¥140,292	¥642,461	¥483,547
KLOTZ, AEGIDIUS (I) (ascribed to)	1	1	$978	$978	$978
			DM1,412	DM1,412	DM1,412
			£623	£623	£623
			¥84,798	¥84,798	¥84,798
KLOTZ, AEGIDIUS (I) (attributed to)	1	1	$3,374	$3,374	$3,374
			DM5,982	DM5,982	DM5,982
			£2,070	£2,070	£2,070
			¥398,951	¥398,951	¥398,951
KLOTZ, AEGIDIUS (II)	5	3	$2,530	$4,255	$3,527
			DM4,579	DM7,191	DM6,200
			£1,543	£2,553	£2,132
			¥305,472	¥547,285	¥457,289

Maker	Items		Selling Prices		
	Bid	Sold	Low	High	Avg
KLOTZ, AEGIDIUS (II) (attributed to)	2	0			
KLOTZ, CARL FREDRICH (attributed to)	1	0			
KLOTZ, GEORG	8	6	$1,890	$5,498	$3,650
			DM2,888	DM7,706	DM5,534
			£1,208	£3,450	£2,264
			¥210,769	¥556,595	¥381,032
KLOTZ, GEORG (II)	10	4	$5,816	$19,282	$10,230
			DM8,214	DM36,541	DM17,462
			£3,680	£11,903	£6,311
			¥519,016	¥2,036,161	¥1,067,902
KLOTZ, JOHANN CARL	6	5	$2,476	$6,072	$3,850
			DM3,642	DM9,163	DM6,084
			£1,610	£3,680	£2,376
			¥262,688	¥688,160	¥429,550
KLOTZ, JOHANN CARL (ascribed to)	1	1	$2,181	$2,181	$2,181
			DM3,080	DM3,080	DM3,080
			£1,380	£1,380	£1,380
			¥194,631	¥194,631	¥194,631
KLOTZ, JOHANN CARL (attributed to)	1	1	$5,375	$5,375	$5,375
			DM7,537	DM7,537	DM7,537
			£3,450	£3,450	£3,450
			¥543,040	¥543,040	¥543,040
KLOTZ, JOSEPH	8	3	$4,237	$8,092	$6,283
			DM6,501	DM12,160	DM10,125
			£2,760	£4,830	£3,872
			¥463,708	¥901,090	¥711,553
KLOTZ, JOSEPH (attributed to)	1	1	$4,025	$4,025	$4,025
			DM6,802	DM6,802	DM6,802
			£2,415	£2,415	£2,415
			¥491,050	¥491,050	¥491,050
KLOTZ, MATHIAS (I)	3	1	$9,664	$9,664	$9,664
			DM14,460	DM14,460	DM14,460
			£5,750	£5,750	£5,750
			¥1,078,010	¥1,078,010	¥1,078,010
KLOTZ, MATHIAS (I) (attributed to)	3	1	$5,841	$5,841	$5,841
			DM10,133	DM10,133	DM10,133
			£3,450	£3,450	£3,450
			¥740,405	¥740,405	¥740,405
KLOTZ, MATHIAS (II)	1	0			
KLOTZ, MICHAEL	5	2	$1,273	$7,067	$4,170
			DM1,873	DM10,442	DM6,158
			£828	£4,600	£2,714
			¥135,096	¥753,176	¥444,136
KLOTZ, SEBASTIAN	9	5	$2,497	$27,945	$10,231
			DM4,470	DM52,613	DM17,770
			£1,495	£17,250	£6,392
			¥324,185	¥2,953,545	¥1,108,560
KLOTZ, SEBASTIAN (attributed to)	3	3	$2,300	$3,802	$3,247
			DM3,326	DM5,594	DM4,708
			£1,502	£2,473	£2,092
			¥232,875	¥403,413	¥333,985
KLOTZ, SEBASTIAN (II)	3	1	$3,457	$3,457	$3,457
			DM5,775	DM5,775	DM5,775
			£2,070	£2,070	£2,070
			¥420,189	¥420,189	¥420,189

FELIX MORI COSTA (attributed)
Milanese Violoncello: c. 1810
Skinner, May 9, 1999, Lot 90

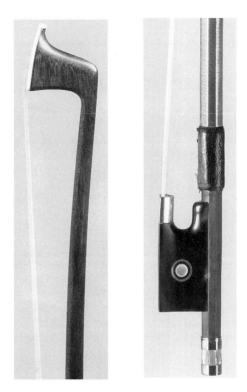

FRANCOIS XAVIER TOURTE
Gold and Tortoiseshell Violin Bow:
Paris, c. 1810
Sotheby's, November 16, 1999,
Lot 59

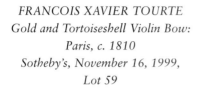

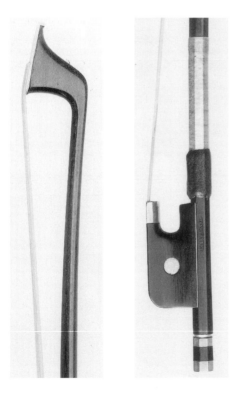

JOSEPH HENRY
Fine Silver Violoncello Bow:
Paris, c. 1860
Christie's, November 17, 1999,
Lot 181

JOSEPH MERLIN
Fine and Handsome English Violoncello:
London, c. 1780
Phillips, November 15, 1999, Lot 210

ORNATI
Very Fine Italian Viola: Milan, 1921
Bonhams, June 16, 1999, Lot 53

GIOVANNI GRANCINO
Violin: Milan, c. 1695
Sotheby's, November 16, 1999, Lot 37

CARL FRIEDRICH PFRETZSCHNER
Fine and Handsome German-School Viola:
Markneukirchen, c. 1790
Phillips, March 15, 1999, Lot 80

ROMEO ANTONIAZZI
Fine Italian Viola: Cremona, 1910
Skinner, November 7, 1999, Lot 90

TOMASO EBERLE
Rare Viola d'Amore: Naples, 1772
Skinner, May 9, 1999, Lot 25

Maker	Items		Selling Prices		
	Bid	Sold	Low	High	Avg
KLOTZ FAMILY (MEMBER OF)	25	18	$810	$8,118	$2,289
			DM1,238	DM12,146	DM3,676
			£518	£4,830	£1,400
			¥79,810	¥905,528	¥249,588
KNEDLER, VILMOS	1	1	$920	$920	$920
			DM1,385	DM1,385	DM1,385
			£558	£558	£558
			¥102,838	¥102,838	¥102,838
KNIGHT, FRANK R.	1	1	$1,724	$1,724	$1,724
			DM2,646	DM2,646	DM2,646
			£1,127	£1,127	£1,127
			¥188,138	¥188,138	¥188,138
KNILLING, JOHANN	1	1	$1,792	$1,792	$1,792
			DM2,512	DM2,512	DM2,512
			£1,150	£1,150	£1,150
			¥181,013	¥181,013	¥181,013
KNOPF, HENRY RICHARD	6	6	$1,725	$4,370	$3,115
			DM2,596	DM6,319	DM4,791
			£1,047	£2,854	£1,948
			¥192,821	¥442,463	¥349,534
KNOPF, W.	1	1	$1,397	$1,397	$1,397
			DM2,631	DM2,631	DM2,631
			£863	£863	£863
			¥147,677	¥147,677	¥147,677
KNORR, ALBERT	4	4	$1,495	$3,738	$2,455
			DM2,706	DM6,653	DM4,098
			£912	£2,243	£1,545
			¥180,506	¥497,013	¥290,955
KNUPFER, ALBERT	2	1	$936	$936	$936
			DM1,430	DM1,430	DM1,430
			£598	£598	£598
			¥104,381	¥104,381	¥104,381
KOBERLING, JOHANN	1	0			
KOCH, FRANZ JOSEPH	2	2	$1,150	$2,608	$1,879
			DM2,088	DM4,911	DM3,499
			£704	£1,610	£1,157
			¥142,807	¥278,047	¥210,427
KOCHLY, J. (attributed to)	1	0			
KONIG, PAUL & HERMANN	2	1	$2,915	$2,915	$2,915
			DM5,054	DM5,054	DM5,054
			£1,725	£1,725	£1,725
			¥363,975	¥363,975	¥363,975
KONYA, ISTVAN	1	0			
KRELL, ALBERT	3	2	$1,840	$2,070	$1,955
			DM2,989	DM3,110	DM3,049
			£1,104	£1,319	£1,211
			¥179,573	¥244,849	¥212,211
KREUTZINGER, ANTON (attributed to)	1	0			
KRIEGER, BOHUMIL J.	1	1	$748	$748	$748
			DM1,079	DM1,079	DM1,079
			£476	£476	£476
			¥64,846	¥64,846	¥64,846
KRIKUNOV	1	0			
KRILOV, ALESSANDRO	1	0			

Maker	Items		Selling Prices		
	Bid	Sold	Low	High	Avg
KRILOV, ALESSANDRO (attributed to)	2	1	$1,081	$1,081	$1,081
			DM1,139	DM1,139	DM1,139
			£667	£667	£667
			¥82,571	¥82,571	¥82,571
KRINER, HANS B.	2	2	$1,380	$2,122	$1,751
			DM2,498	DM3,122	DM2,810
			£842	£1,380	£1,111
			¥166,621	¥225,161	¥195,891
KRINER, JOSEPH	3	1	$1,139	$1,139	$1,139
			DM1,718	DM1,718	DM1,718
			£690	£690	£690
			¥129,030	¥129,030	¥129,030
KRIZ, FRANTISEK	1	0			
KRUMBHOLZ, LORENZ	4	3	$1,687	$7,298	$4,734
			DM2,991	DM12,192	DM8,335
			£1,035	£4,370	£2,875
			¥199,476	¥887,066	¥545,957
KUCHARSKI, B.	1	0			
KUDANOWSKI, JAN	12	7	$1,328	$3,575	$2,658
			DM2,359	DM6,048	DM4,444
			£805	£2,248	£1,635
			¥184,256	¥442,905	¥324,237
KULIK, JOHAN	2	2	$4,071	$8,625	$6,348
			DM7,732	DM14,757	DM11,245
			£2,513	£5,101	£3,807
			¥427,695	¥1,071,053	¥749,374
KULIK, JOHANN	1	1	$5,323	$5,323	$5,323
			DM9,985	DM9,985	DM9,985
			£3,306	£3,306	£3,306
			¥639,826	¥639,826	¥639,826
KUN, JOSEPH	1	1	$2,645	$2,645	$2,645
			DM3,981	DM3,981	DM3,981
			£1,606	£1,606	£1,606
			¥295,658	¥295,658	¥295,658
KUNTZE-FECHNER, MARTIN	1	1	$7,452	$7,452	$7,452
			DM14,030	DM14,030	DM14,030
			£4,600	£4,600	£4,600
			¥787,612	¥787,612	¥787,612
KUNZE, WILHELM PAUL	4	3	$1,179	$4,658	$3,218
			DM2,240	DM8,826	DM5,486
			£728	£2,875	£2,006
			¥123,904	¥491,826	¥318,778
KVAMME, MAGNE	1	1	$575	$575	$575
			DM1,024	DM1,024	DM1,024
			£345	£345	£345
			¥76,464	¥76,464	¥76,464
LABERTE	1	0			
LABERTE, MARC	8	5	$1,145	$5,435	$3,002
			DM1,690	DM7,676	DM4,659
			£747	£3,450	£1,898
			¥121,687	¥547,284	¥337,029
LABERTE, MARC (attributed to)	1	1	$1,519	$1,519	$1,519
			DM2,634	DM2,634	DM2,634
			£897	£897	£897
			¥192,505	¥192,505	¥192,505

Maker	Items Bid	Sold	Selling Prices Low	High	Avg
LABERTE, MARC (workshop of)	4	3	$863	$2,645	$1,993
			DM1,245	DM4,992	DM3,343
			£549	£1,637	£1,266
			¥74,822	¥279,841	¥208,386
LABERTE-HUMBERT BROS.	6	4	$1,128	$2,527	$1,669
			DM1,863	DM4,380	DM2,787
			£690	£1,495	£1,006
			¥139,676	¥315,445	¥200,953
LABERTE-MAGNIE	3	0			
LAFLEUR, J.	1	1	$937	$937	$937
			DM1,668	DM1,668	DM1,668
			£575	£575	£575
			¥125,885	¥125,885	¥125,885
LAIDLAW, JOHN W.	1	0			
LAJOS, KONYA	1	0			
LAMBERT	2	2	$3,080	$4,754	$3,917
			DM5,698	DM9,000	DM7,349
			£1,840	£2,990	£2,415
			¥410,486	¥569,864	¥490,175
LAMBERT, JEAN NICOLAS	2	1	$2,766	$2,766	$2,766
			DM3,851	DM3,851	DM3,851
			£1,725	£1,725	£1,725
			¥233,820	¥233,820	¥233,820
LAMBERTON, JAMES	1	0			
LANARO, UMBERTO	2	2	$4,725	$4,874	$4,799
			DM6,674	DM8,432	DM7,553
			£2,990	£2,990	£2,990
			¥421,701	¥556,140	¥488,920
LANDOLFI, CARLO FERDINANDO	6	4	$13,800	$78,857	$56,914
			DM24,978	DM111,382	DM82,523
			£8,418	£49,900	£36,142
			¥1,666,212	¥7,515,020	¥5,418,696
LANDOLFI, PIETRO ANTONIO	3	2	$46,261	$61,380	$53,821
			DM78,266	DM86,440	DM82,353
			£29,095	£38,900	£33,998
			¥5,731,715	¥6,275,815	¥6,003,765
LANDOLFI, PIETRO ANTONIO (attributed to)	2	1	$13,235	$13,235	$13,235
			DM20,333	DM20,333	DM20,333
			£8,625	£8,625	£8,625
			¥1,448,905	¥1,448,905	¥1,448,905
LANGE, H. FRANCIS	1	1	$748	$748	$748
			DM1,331	DM1,331	DM1,331
			£449	£449	£449
			¥99,403	¥99,403	¥99,403
LANGONET, EUGENE	5	3	$3,703	$6,706	$5,166
			DM6,989	DM10,302	DM8,160
			£2,292	£4,370	£3,294
			¥391,777	¥734,112	¥526,676
LANINI, LORIS	1	1	$2,657	$2,657	$2,657
			DM4,009	DM4,009	DM4,009
			£1,610	£1,610	£1,610
			¥301,070	¥301,070	¥301,070
LANTNER, FERDINAND MARTIN	1	1	$1,235	$1,235	$1,235
			DM2,316	DM2,316	DM2,316
			£767	£767	£767
			¥148,440	¥148,440	¥148,440

Maker	Items Bid	Sold	Selling Prices Low	High	Avg
LAPREVOTTE, ETIENNE	1	1	$3,835	$3,835	$3,835
			DM5,392	DM5,392	DM5,392
			£2,415	£2,415	£2,415
			¥342,278	¥342,278	¥342,278
LARCHER, JEAN	2	2	$1,344	$1,921	$1,632
			DM2,246	DM3,565	DM2,905
			£805	£1,150	£978
			¥163,407	¥256,956	¥210,181
LARCHER, JEAN (attributed to)	6	1	$604	$604	$604
			DM857	DM857	DM857
			£380	£380	£380
			¥56,033	¥56,033	¥56,033
LARGOWARD, RAYBURN	1	1	$796	$796	$796
			DM1,171	DM1,171	DM1,171
			£518	£518	£518
			¥84,435	¥84,435	¥84,435
LASSI, FRANCESCO	3	2	$2,194	$8,826	$5,510
			DM4,126	DM13,544	DM8,835
			£1,380	£5,750	£3,565
			¥265,291	¥966,058	¥615,674
LATTERELL, GEORGE	1	1	$1,380	$1,380	$1,380
			DM2,506	DM2,506	DM2,506
			£845	£845	£845
			¥171,368	¥171,368	¥171,368
LAUMANN, ROBERT	1	1	$6,355	$6,355	$6,355
			DM9,752	DM9,752	DM9,752
			£4,140	£4,140	£4,140
			¥695,561	¥695,561	¥695,561
LAURENT, EMILE	2	1	$7,682	$7,682	$7,682
			DM12,834	DM12,834	DM12,834
			£4,600	£4,600	£4,600
			¥933,754	¥933,754	¥933,754
LAURENT, EMILE (II)	1	1	$2,819	$2,819	$2,819
			DM4,162	DM4,162	DM4,162
			£1,840	£1,840	£1,840
			¥299,738	¥299,738	¥299,738
LAVEST, J.	1	1	$3,450	$3,450	$3,450
			DM5,903	DM5,903	DM5,903
			£2,041	£2,041	£2,041
			¥428,421	¥428,421	¥428,421
LAZZARO, GIOVANNI	1	1	$3,287	$3,287	$3,287
			DM4,622	DM4,622	DM4,622
			£2,070	£2,070	£2,070
			¥292,228	¥292,228	¥292,228
LEAVITT, F.A.	1	1	$518	$518	$518
			DM921	DM921	DM921
			£311	£311	£311
			¥68,817	¥68,817	¥68,817
LECCHI, ANTONIO	15	10	$654	$1,944	$1,224
			DM963	DM3,370	DM1,984
			£417	£1,150	£749
			¥69,425	¥247,101	¥141,004
LECCHI, BERNARDO GIUSEPPE	3	2	$8,473	$21,775	$15,124
			DM13,002	DM30,665	DM21,834
			£5,520	£13,800	£9,660
			¥927,415	¥2,226,382	¥1,576,898

Maker	Items		Selling Prices		
	Bid	Sold	Low	High	Avg
LECCHI, GUISEPPE	5	1	$13,251	$13,251	$13,251
			DM19,579	DM19,579	DM19,579
			£8,625	£8,625	£8,625
			¥1,412,206	¥1,412,206	¥1,412,206
LECCI, G. (attributed to)	1	0			
LECHI	1	1	$754	$754	$754
			DM1,371	DM1,371	DM1,371
			£460	£460	£460
			¥91,075	¥91,075	¥91,075
LECHLEITNER, CHRISTIAN (attributed to)	1	1	$2,571	$2,571	$2,571
			DM4,883	DM4,883	DM4,883
			£1,587	£1,587	£1,587
			¥270,123	¥270,123	¥270,123
LECLERC, JOSEPH NICOLAS	4	1	$3,601	$3,601	$3,601
			DM5,513	DM5,513	DM5,513
			£2,300	£2,300	£2,300
			¥401,396	¥401,396	¥401,396
LECYR, JAMES F.	1	1	$1,955	$1,955	$1,955
			DM3,345	DM3,345	DM3,345
			£1,156	£1,156	£1,156
			¥242,772	¥242,772	¥242,772
LEE, PERCY	1	1	$4,609	$4,609	$4,609
			DM7,700	DM7,700	DM7,700
			£2,760	£2,760	£2,760
			¥560,252	¥560,252	¥560,252
LEEB, JOHANN GEORG	2	2	$2,062	$9,589	$5,825
			DM3,567	DM13,352	DM8,459
			£1,265	£5,980	£3,623
			¥235,290	¥810,577	¥522,934
LEIDOLFF, JOHANN CHRISTOPH	2	0			
LEIDOLFF, JOSEPH FERDINAND	1	1	$1,651	$1,651	$1,651
			DM2,863	DM2,863	DM2,863
			£977	£977	£977
			¥206,147	¥206,147	¥206,147
LEMARQUIS, JEAN BAPTISTE	1	0			
LEMBOCK, GABRIEL	2	2	$5,295	$9,560	$7,427
			DM8,493	DM13,375	DM10,934
			£3,439	£5,980	£4,709
			¥602,494	¥808,574	¥705,534
LEONORI, PAOLO	1	1	$5,962	$5,962	$5,962
			DM11,224	DM11,224	DM11,224
			£3,680	£3,680	£3,680
			¥630,090	¥630,090	¥630,090
LE PILEUR, PIERRE	1	1	$3,652	$3,652	$3,652
			DM5,135	DM5,135	DM5,135
			£2,300	£2,300	£2,300
			¥325,979	¥325,979	¥325,979
LEWIS, WILLIAM & SON	1	0			
L'HUMBERT, E.	3	1	$6,178	$6,178	$6,178
			DM9,481	DM9,481	DM9,481
			£4,025	£4,025	£4,025
			¥676,240	¥676,240	¥676,240
LIESSEM, R.	2	2	$2,346	$4,803	$3,575
			DM4,183	DM7,445	DM5,814
			£1,438	£2,875	£2,156
			¥307,093	¥547,141	¥427,117
LINDORFER, WILLI	1	0			

Maker	Items		Selling Prices		
	Bid	Sold	Low	High	Avg
LINDSAY, DAVID	1	1	$1,234	$1,234	$1,234
			DM1,821	DM1,821	DM1,821
			£805	£805	£805
			¥131,135	¥131,135	¥131,135
LINDSAY, DAVID (attributed to)	1	1	$459	$459	$459
			DM679	DM679	DM679
			£299	£299	£299
			¥48,956	¥48,956	¥48,956
LIPPOLD, CARL FREDERICK (attributed to)	1	0			
LOGAN, JOHN	1	1	$1,069	$1,069	$1,069
			DM1,587	DM1,587	DM1,587
			£690	£690	£690
			¥115,768	¥115,768	¥115,768
LONDERO, RAFFAELE	1	0			
LONGIARU, GIOVANNI	2	2	$2,760	$3,042	$2,901
			DM3,991	DM5,741	DM4,866
			£1,803	£1,883	£1,843
			¥279,450	¥321,817	¥300,634
LONGMAN	4	2	$245	$566	$405
			DM423	DM1,029	DM726
			£150	£345	£247
			¥27,980	¥71,463	¥49,722
LONGMAN & CO.	1	1	$1,676	$1,676	$1,676
			DM2,576	DM2,576	DM2,576
			£1,093	£1,093	£1,093
			¥183,528	¥183,528	¥183,528
LONGMAN & BRODERIP	1	1	$3,281	$3,281	$3,281
			DM5,737	DM5,737	DM5,737
			£2,013	£2,013	£2,013
			¥387,603	¥387,603	¥387,603
LONGMAN, LUKEY & CO.	1	1	$768	$768	$768
			DM1,283	DM1,283	DM1,283
			£460	£460	£460
			¥93,375	¥93,375	¥93,375
LONGSON (attributed to)	1	1	$643	$643	$643
			DM900	DM900	DM900
			£403	£403	£403
			¥54,423	¥54,423	¥54,423
LORENZ FAMILY (attributed to)	1	0			
LO SCHIAVO, ANTONIO	1	1	$4,536	$4,536	$4,536
			DM6,389	DM6,389	DM6,389
			£2,875	£2,875	£2,875
			¥463,830	¥463,830	¥463,830
LOTT, JOHN	1	1	$31,706	$31,706	$31,706
			DM46,741	DM46,741	DM46,741
			£20,700	£20,700	£20,700
			¥3,381,759	¥3,381,759	¥3,381,759
LOTT, JOHN (ascribed to)	1	0			
LOTT, JOHN (attributed to)	1	0			
LOTT, JOHN (SR.)	2	1	$11,141	$11,141	$11,141
			DM16,390	DM16,390	DM16,390
			£7,245	£7,245	£7,245
			¥1,182,094	¥1,182,094	¥1,182,094
LOTT, JOHN FREDERICK	1	1	$45,540	$45,540	$45,540
			DM68,724	DM68,724	DM68,724
			£27,600	£27,600	£27,600
			¥5,161,200	¥5,161,200	¥5,161,200

| Maker | Items | | Selling Prices | | |
---	Bid	Sold	Low	High	Avg
LOTT, JOHN FREDERICK (ascribed to)	2	0			
LOTT, JOHN FREDERICK (attributed to)	1	0			
LOTT, JOHN FREDERICK (PERE) (attributed to)	1	1	$3,856 DM7,325 £2,381 ¥405,185	$3,856 DM7,325 £2,381 ¥405,185	$3,856 DM7,325 £2,381 ¥405,185
LOUGHTON, A.J.	2	1	$251 DM438 £150 ¥32,047	$251 DM438 £150 ¥32,047	$251 DM438 £150 ¥32,047
LOWENDALL	7	6	$256 DM363 £161 ¥23,772	$1,450 DM2,133 £943 ¥153,860	$674 DM1,043 £429 ¥73,353
LOWENDALL, HERMANN	1	1	$546 DM789 £348 ¥47,387	$546 DM789 £348 ¥47,387	$546 DM789 £348 ¥47,387
LOWENDALL, HERMANN (workshop of)	1	1	$1,265 DM2,164 £748 ¥157,088	$1,265 DM2,164 £748 ¥157,088	$1,265 DM2,164 £748 ¥157,088
LOWENDALL, L. (workshop of)	2	2	$345 DM499 £225 ¥34,931	$633 DM915 £413 ¥64,041	$489 DM707 £319 ¥49,486
LOWENDALL, LOUIS	16	13	$282 DM502 £173 ¥36,851	$2,508 DM3,517 £1,610 ¥253,419	$886 DM1,408 £552 ¥98,097
LOWENDALL, LOUIS (workshop of)	4	4	$230 DM394 £136 ¥28,561	$1,495 DM2,162 £977 ¥151,369	$955 DM1,518 £606 ¥95,718
LUCCA, ANTONIO	4	3	$5,216 DM9,254 £3,220 ¥551,328	$16,698 DM25,199 £10,120 ¥1,892,440	$9,366 DM14,758 £5,673 ¥1,044,565
LUCCI, GIUSEPPE	9	8	$7,512 DM13,459 £4,485 ¥872,333	$16,596 DM23,150 £10,350 ¥1,667,598	$11,325 DM18,609 £6,955 ¥1,266,974
LUCCI, GIUSEPPE (attributed to)	1	1	$5,463 DM9,442 £3,375 ¥692,290	$5,463 DM9,442 £3,375 ¥692,290	$5,463 DM9,442 £3,375 ¥692,290
LUDWIG, L. (workshop of)	1	1	$230 DM352 £151 ¥24,242	$230 DM352 £151 ¥24,242	$230 DM352 £151 ¥24,242
LUFF, WILLIAM H.	13	5	$3,167 DM6,002 £1,955 ¥334,442	$7,345 DM12,822 £4,370 ¥923,593	$5,245 DM9,296 £3,177 ¥600,435

Maker	Items		Selling Prices		
	Bid	Sold	Low	High	Avg
LUNN, W.J.	2	1	$457	$457	$457
			DM649	DM649	DM649
			£288	£288	£288
			¥42,449	¥42,449	¥42,449
LUPOT, FRANCOIS	1	0			
LUPOT, NICOLAS	7	3	$31,938	$134,769	$90,082
			DM59,909	DM225,153	DM152,681
			£19,838	£80,700	£54,179
			¥3,838,953	¥16,381,293	¥10,935,209
LUPOT, NICOLAS (attributed to)	2	0			
LUTHER, ANDREAS	1	0			
LUTZ, IGNAZ	1	1	$4,485	$4,485	$4,485
			DM7,580	DM7,580	DM7,580
			£2,691	£2,691	£2,691
			¥547,170	¥547,170	¥547,170
LUTZ, LOUIS (attributed to)	1	0			
LUZZATTI, GIACOMO	1	0			
LYE, HENRY	2	1	$2,297	$2,297	$2,297
			DM3,394	DM3,394	DM3,394
			£1,495	£1,495	£1,495
			¥244,782	¥244,782	¥244,782
LYON, U.	1	0			
MAAG, HENRY	7	5	$115	$460	$212
			DM205	DM819	DM380
			£70	£281	£129
			¥15,976	¥63,903	¥27,972
MACCARTHY, J.L.T.	1	0			
MACKINTOSH (attributed to)	1	1	$1,128	$1,128	$1,128
			DM1,614	DM1,614	DM1,614
			£713	£713	£713
			¥113,357	¥113,357	¥113,357
MACVEAN, ALEXANDER	1	0			
MADAY, EDWARD	1	1	$863	$863	$863
			DM1,491	DM1,491	DM1,491
			£533	£533	£533
			¥109,309	¥109,309	¥109,309
MAGGINI, GIOVANNI PAOLO	4	3	$17,020	$168,368	$75,931
			DM23,868	DM253,029	DM113,183
			£10,925	£100,500	£46,342
			¥1,719,628	¥18,749,381	¥8,329,356
MAGIALI, CAESAR	1	1	$5,798	$5,798	$5,798
			DM8,676	DM8,676	DM8,676
			£3,450	£3,450	£3,450
			¥646,806	¥646,806	¥646,806
MAGNIERE, GABRIEL	8	7	$1,344	$3,374	$2,315
			DM2,407	DM5,837	DM3,699
			£805	£2,070	£1,436
			¥184,973	¥385,020	¥265,132
MAGNIERE, GABRIEL (attributed to)	2	2	$2,308	$2,474	$2,391
			DM3,321	DM3,655	DM3,488
			£1,495	£1,610	£1,553
			¥234,326	¥263,612	¥248,969
MAGRINI, CESARE	1	1	$14,539	$14,539	$14,539
			DM20,535	DM20,535	DM20,535
			£9,200	£9,200	£9,200
			¥1,297,540	¥1,297,540	¥1,297,540

Maker	Items		Selling Prices		
	Bid	Sold	Low	High	Avg
MAICH, JOHN P.	1	1	$345	$345	$345
			DM596	DM596	DM596
			£213	£213	£213
			¥43,724	¥43,724	¥43,724
MAITRE, J. CHARLES (attributed to)	1	1	$2,166	$2,166	$2,166
			DM3,062	DM3,062	DM3,062
			£1,380	£1,380	£1,380
			¥185,032	¥185,032	¥185,032
MALAGUTI, ERMINIO	1	1	$3,439	$3,439	$3,439
			DM6,490	DM6,490	DM6,490
			£2,128	£2,128	£2,128
			¥363,793	¥363,793	¥363,793
MALAGUTI, ERMINIO (attributed to)	1	0			
MALIGNAGGI, PAUL	1	1	$633	$633	$633
			DM913	DM913	DM913
			£403	£403	£403
			¥54,869	¥54,869	¥54,869
MAAG, HENRY	7	5	$115	$460	$212
			DM205	DM819	DM380
			£70	£281	£129
			¥15,976	¥63,903	¥27,972
MACCARTHY, J.L.T.	1	0			
MACKINTOSH (attributed to)	1	1	$1,128	$1,128	$1,128
			DM1,614	DM1,614	DM1,614
			£713	£713	£713
			¥113,357	¥113,357	¥113,357
MACVEAN, ALEXANDER	1	0			
MADAY, EDWARD	1	1	$863	$863	$863
			DM1,491	DM1,491	DM1,491
			£533	£533	£533
			¥109,309	¥109,309	¥109,309
MAGGINI, GIOVANNI PAOLO	4	3	$17,020	$168,368	$75,931
			DM23,868	DM253,029	DM113,183
			£10,925	£100,500	£46,342
			¥1,719,628	¥18,749,381	¥8,329,356
MAGIALI, CAESAR	1	1	$5,798	$5,798	$5,798
			DM8,676	DM8,676	DM8,676
			£3,450	£3,450	£3,450
			¥646,806	¥646,806	¥646,806
MAGNIERE, GABRIEL	8	7	$1,344	$3,374	$2,315
			DM2,407	DM5,837	DM3,699
			£805	£2,070	£1,436
			¥184,973	¥385,020	¥265,132
MAGNIERE, GABRIEL (attributed to)	2	2	$2,308	$2,474	$2,391
			DM3,321	DM3,655	DM3,488
			£1,495	£1,610	£1,553
			¥234,326	¥263,612	¥248,969
MAGRINI, CESARE	1	1	$14,539	$14,539	$14,539
			DM20,535	DM20,535	DM20,535
			£9,200	£9,200	£9,200
			¥1,297,540	¥1,297,540	¥1,297,540
MAICH, JOHN P.	1	1	$345	$345	$345
			DM596	DM596	DM596
			£213	£213	£213
			¥43,724	¥43,724	¥43,724

Maker	Items		Selling Prices		
	Bid	Sold	Low	High	Avg
MAITRE, J. CHARLES (attributed to)	1	1	$2,166	$2,166	$2,166
			DM3,062	DM3,062	DM3,062
			£1,380	£1,380	£1,380
			¥185,032	¥185,032	¥185,032
MALAGUTI, ERMINIO	1	1	$3,439	$3,439	$3,439
			DM6,490	DM6,490	DM6,490
			£2,128	£2,128	£2,128
			¥363,793	¥363,793	¥363,793
MALAGUTI, ERMINIO (attributed to)	1	0			
MALIGNAGGI, PAUL	1	1	$633	$633	$633
			DM913	DM913	DM913
			£403	£403	£403
			¥54,869	¥54,869	¥54,869
MALINE	1	1	$3,477	$3,477	$3,477
			DM5,343	DM5,343	DM5,343
			£2,300	£2,300	£2,300
			¥370,818	¥370,818	¥370,818
MALINE FAMILY (MEMBER OF)	1	0			
MALVOLTI, PIETRO ANTONIO	1	1	$6,784	$6,784	$6,784
			DM12,022	DM12,022	DM12,022
			£4,166	£4,166	£4,166
			¥827,224	¥827,224	¥827,224
MANDELLI, CAMILLO	2	1	$23,000	$23,000	$23,000
			DM38,870	DM38,870	DM38,870
			£13,800	£13,800	£13,800
			¥3,060,610	¥3,060,610	¥3,060,610
MANGENOT, AMATI	4	2	$3,534	$3,597	$3,565
			DM5,088	DM5,221	DM5,155
			£2,300	£2,300	£2,300
			¥365,261	¥376,588	¥370,924
MANGENOT, PAUL	6	5	$811	$2,608	$1,576
			DM1,197	DM4,911	DM2,834
			£529	£1,610	£968
			¥86,175	¥275,664	¥177,465
MANSUY	2	1	$1,835	$1,835	$1,835
			DM3,300	DM3,300	DM3,300
			£1,093	£1,093	£1,093
			¥212,196	¥212,196	¥212,196
MANTEGAZZA, PIETRO GIOVANNI	2	1	$20,125	$20,125	$20,125
			DM34,011	DM34,011	DM34,011
			£12,075	£12,075	£12,075
			¥2,678,034	¥2,678,034	¥2,678,034
MANTEGAZZA, PIETRO GIOVANNI (attributed to)	1	0			
MARAVELLI	1	1	$920	$920	$920
			DM1,353	DM1,353	DM1,353
			£598	£598	£598
			¥97,570	¥97,570	¥97,570
MARAVIGLIA, FRANCESCO	1	0			
MARAVIGLIA, GUIDO	2	1	$2,706	$2,706	$2,706
			DM4,049	DM4,049	DM4,049
			£1,610	£1,610	£1,610
			¥301,843	¥301,843	¥301,843
MARCHAND, EUGENE	1	1	$7,123	$7,123	$7,123
			DM12,629	DM12,629	DM12,629
			£4,370	£4,370	£4,370
			¥842,230	¥842,230	¥842,230

Maker	Items Bid	Sold	Selling Prices Low	High	Avg
MARCHETTI, ENRICO	6	3	$5,290 DM9,575 £3,227 ¥638,715	$17,699 DM31,792 £10,925 ¥2,089,625	$10,724 DM18,937 £6,634 ¥1,285,234
MARCHETTI, ENRICO (attributed to)	1	0			
MARCHI, GIOVANNI (attributed to)	1	1	$13,605 DM23,587 £8,050 ¥1,729,704	$13,605 DM23,587 £8,050 ¥1,729,704	$13,605 DM23,587 £8,050 ¥1,729,704
MARCHI, GIOVANNI ANTONIO	2	1	$54,418 DM94,346 £32,200 ¥6,794,200	$54,418 DM94,346 £32,200 ¥6,794,200	$54,418 DM94,346 £32,200 ¥6,794,200
MARCONCINI, JOSEPH	2	1	$48,737 DM84,318 £29,900 ¥5,561,400	$48,737 DM84,318 £29,900 ¥5,561,400	$48,737 DM84,318 £29,900 ¥5,561,400
MARCONCINI, JOSEPH (attributed to)	1	0			
MARCONCINI, LUIGI ALOISIO	1	0			
MARDULA, FRANCISZEK & STANISLAW	2	1	$690 DM1,249 £421 ¥83,311	$690 DM1,249 £421 ¥83,311	$690 DM1,249 £421 ¥83,311
MARIANI (attributed to)	1	0			
MARIANI, ANTONIO	1	0			
MARISSAL, O. (workshop of)	1	1	$969 DM1,824 £598 ¥103,275	$969 DM1,824 £598 ¥103,275	$969 DM1,824 £598 ¥103,275
MARISSAL, OLIVIER	1	0			
MARISSAL, OLIVIER (workshop of)	1	0			
MARSHALL, JOHN (attributed to)	2	2	$3,309 DM4,630 £2,070 ¥279,891	$3,853 DM5,791 £2,300 ¥429,090	$3,581 DM5,210 £2,185 ¥354,491
MARSIGLIESE, BIAGIO	1	0			
MARTIN	1	0			
MARTIN, E.	1	1	$403 DM680 £242 ¥49,105	$403 DM680 £242 ¥49,105	$403 DM680 £242 ¥49,105
MARTIN, E. (workshop of)	13	12	$201 DM308 £132 ¥21,212	$575 DM894 £376 ¥65,585	$446 DM712 £276 ¥50,842
MARTINENGHI, MARCELLO G.B.	2	2	$9,176 DM14,098 £5,980 ¥1,004,574	$12,650 DM18,292 £8,263 ¥1,280,813	$10,913 DM16,195 £7,121 ¥1,142,693
MARTINI, ORESTE	2	2	$7,376 DM10,270 £4,600 ¥623,521	$7,984 DM11,244 £5,060 ¥816,340	$7,680 DM10,757 £4,830 ¥719,930

Maker	Items		Selling Prices		
	Bid	Sold	Low	High	Avg
MARTINI, ORESTE (attributed to)	1	1	$3,220	$3,220	$3,220
			DM5,566	DM5,566	DM5,566
			£1,990	£1,990	£1,990
			¥408,087	¥408,087	¥408,087
MARTINO, GIUSEPPE	1	1	$2,990	$2,990	$2,990
			DM5,168	DM5,168	DM5,168
			£1,848	£1,848	£1,848
			¥378,938	¥378,938	¥378,938
MASON, GEORGE	1	1	$451	$451	$451
			DM764	DM764	DM764
			£276	£276	£276
			¥52,301	¥52,301	¥52,301
MASON, WALTER	1	1	$3,523	$3,523	$3,523
			DM5,193	DM5,193	DM5,193
			£2,300	£2,300	£2,300
			¥375,751	¥375,751	¥375,751
MAST, JEAN LAURENT	1	0			
MAST, JEAN LAURENT (attributed to)	1	0			
MAST, JOSEPH LAURENT	3	2	$1,118	$1,285	$1,202
			DM2,118	DM2,436	DM2,277
			£690	£794	£742
			¥118,038	¥135,744	¥126,891
MATSUDA, TETSUO	1	1	$8,483	$8,483	$8,483
			DM11,811	DM11,811	DM11,811
			£5,290	£5,290	£5,290
			¥717,049	¥717,049	¥717,049
MATTER, ANITA	3	1	$934	$934	$934
			DM1,629	DM1,629	DM1,629
			£575	£575	£575
			¥113,189	¥113,189	¥113,189
MATTIUZZI, BRUNO	1	0			
MAUCOTEL, CHARLES	5	2	$13,041	$18,925	$15,983
			DM23,426	DM32,018	DM27,722
			£8,050	£11,903	£9,976
			¥1,539,724	¥2,344,793	¥1,942,258
MAUCOTEL, ERNEST (attributed to)	1	1	$9,743	$9,743	$9,743
			DM13,632	DM13,632	DM13,632
			£6,095	£6,095	£6,095
			¥824,123	¥824,123	¥824,123
MAULE, GIOVANNI (attributed to)	1	0			
MAURIZI, FRANCESCO	3	2	$14,980	$23,046	$19,013
			DM26,820	DM38,502	DM32,661
			£8,970	£13,800	£11,385
			¥2,061,127	¥2,801,262	¥2,431,194
MAWBEY, EDWIN	1	1	$542	$542	$542
			DM766	DM766	DM766
			£345	£345	£345
			¥46,258	¥46,258	¥46,258
MAYSON, WALTER H.	26	19	$730	$3,195	$1,570
			DM1,122	DM5,411	DM2,421
			£460	£1,955	£971
			¥77,872	¥370,465	¥164,371
MEDARD, NICOLAS (III)	1	1	$7,088	$7,088	$7,088
			DM10,011	DM10,011	DM10,011
			£4,485	£4,485	£4,485
			¥632,551	¥632,551	¥632,551

Maker	Items Bid	Sold	Selling Prices Low	High	Avg
MEDIO-FINO	1	1	$174	$174	$174
			DM303	DM303	DM303
			£104	£104	£104
			¥22,186	¥22,186	¥22,186
MEIER, KARL	1	1	$1,093	$1,093	$1,093
			DM1,671	DM1,671	DM1,671
			£719	£719	£719
			¥115,150	¥115,150	¥115,150
MEINEL, EUGEN (workshop of)	1	1	$1,380	$1,380	$1,380
			DM1,993	DM1,993	DM1,993
			£879	£879	£879
			¥119,715	¥119,715	¥119,715
MEINEL, FRIEDRICH WILHELM	1	1	$748	$748	$748
			DM1,279	DM1,279	DM1,279
			£442	£442	£442
			¥92,825	¥92,825	¥92,825
MEINEL, OSKAR	1	1	$920	$920	$920
			DM1,638	DM1,638	DM1,638
			£552	£552	£552
			¥122,342	¥122,342	¥122,342
MEISEL, FRIEDRICH WILHELM	1	1	$558	$558	$558
			DM854	DM854	DM854
			£357	£357	£357
			¥62,216	¥62,216	¥62,216
MEISEL, JOHANN GEORG	1	1	$575	$575	$575
			DM1,024	DM1,024	DM1,024
			£345	£345	£345
			¥76,464	¥76,464	¥76,464
MEISEL, KARL	1	1	$259	$259	$259
			DM437	DM437	DM437
			£155	£155	£155
			¥31,568	¥31,568	¥31,568
MEISEL, KARL (workshop of)	2	2	$633	$920	$776
			DM1,126	DM1,638	DM1,382
			£380	£552	£466
			¥84,110	¥122,342	¥103,226
MEISEL, LOTHAR	1	1	$1,265	$1,265	$1,265
			DM2,164	DM2,164	DM2,164
			£748	£748	£748
			¥157,088	¥157,088	¥157,088
MEISSNER, JOHANN FRIEDERICH	1	0			
MELEGARI, MICHELE & PIETRO	1	0			
MELZL, JOHANN GEORG	3	1	$1,024	$1,024	$1,024
			DM1,839	DM1,839	DM1,839
			£632	£632	£632
			¥120,883	¥120,883	¥120,883
MENICHETTI, MARTINO	2	0			
MENNEGAND, CHARLES (attributed to)	1	1	$2,999	$2,999	$2,999
			DM5,189	DM5,189	DM5,189
			£1,840	£1,840	£1,840
			¥342,240	¥342,240	¥342,240
MENNESSON, EMILE	12	7	$1,929	$4,979	$3,470
			DM3,243	DM6,933	DM5,343
			£1,208	£3,105	£2,183
			¥236,746	¥489,565	¥361,094

Maker	Items Bid	Sold	Low	Selling Prices High	Avg
MENNESSON, EMILE (attributed to)	1	1	$1,770 DM3,332 £1,093 ¥188,675	$1,770 DM3,332 £1,093 ¥188,675	$1,770 DM3,332 £1,093 ¥188,675
MENZINGER, GUSTAV	1	1	$1,380 DM2,456 £828 ¥183,512	$1,380 DM2,456 £828 ¥183,512	$1,380 DM2,456 £828 ¥183,512
MERCIOLLE, JULES (workshop of)	2	1	$2,415 DM4,299 £1,449 ¥321,147	$2,415 DM4,299 £1,449 ¥321,147	$2,415 DM4,299 £1,449 ¥321,147
MERLING, PAULI	1	1	$7,166 DM10,050 £4,600 ¥724,054	$7,166 DM10,050 £4,600 ¥724,054	$7,166 DM10,050 £4,600 ¥724,054
MERMILLOT, MAURICE	8	4	$3,457 DM6,417 £2,070 ¥462,521	$11,178 DM21,045 £6,900 ¥1,181,418	$7,215 DM13,022 £4,485 ¥788,175
MERRETT, H.W.	6	3	$128 DM182 £81 ¥11,886	$253 DM357 £161 ¥22,249	$196 DM287 £127 ¥18,574
MESSON, E.	1	1	$1,677 DM3,157 £1,035 ¥177,213	$1,677 DM3,157 £1,035 ¥177,213	$1,677 DM3,157 £1,035 ¥177,213
MEYER, KARL	3	2	$193 DM337 £115 ¥24,651	$1,005 DM1,807 £598 ¥116,150	$599 DM1,072 £357 ¥70,400
MEZZADRI, ALESSANDRO (ascribed to)	1	1	$5,796 DM10,419 £3,450 ¥670,094	$5,796 DM10,419 £3,450 ¥670,094	$5,796 DM10,419 £3,450 ¥670,094
MICELLI, CARLO	1	1	$230 DM414 £138 ¥1,787	$230 DM414 £138 ¥1,787	$230 DM414 £138 ¥1,787
MICHETTI, PLINIO	2	2	$7,475 DM12,633 £4,485 ¥911,950	$14,973 DM24,150 £8,694 ¥1,762,950	$11,224 DM18,391 £6,590 ¥1,337,450
MIGAZZI, LUIGI	1	1	$4,416 DM7,471 £2,777 ¥547,118	$4,416 DM7,471 £2,777 ¥547,118	$4,416 DM7,471 £2,777 ¥547,118
MILES, GEORGE	1	1	$3,861 DM5,401 £2,415 ¥326,539	$3,861 DM5,401 £2,415 ¥326,539	$3,861 DM5,401 £2,415 ¥326,539
MILES, ROLF	1	0			
MILITELLA, MARIANO	2	1	$3,565 DM5,148 £2,271 ¥309,264	$3,565 DM5,148 £2,271 ¥309,264	$3,565 DM5,148 £2,271 ¥309,264

Maker	Items		Selling Prices		
	Bid	Sold	Low	High	Avg
MILLANT, MAX (workshop of)	1	1	$1,553	$1,553	$1,553
			DM2,245	DM2,245	DM2,245
			£1,014	£1,014	£1,014
			¥157,191	¥157,191	¥157,191
MILLANT, R. & M.	1	1	$8,050	$8,050	$8,050
			DM11,624	DM11,624	DM11,624
			£5,129	£5,129	£5,129
			¥698,338	¥698,338	¥698,338
MILLANT, ROGER & MAX	1	0			
MILNE, PATRICK G.	1	1	$1,933	$1,933	$1,933
			DM2,892	DM2,892	DM2,892
			£1,150	£1,150	£1,150
			¥215,602	¥215,602	¥215,602
MILTON, LOUIS	1	1	$2,142	$2,142	$2,142
			DM4,069	DM4,069	DM4,069
			£1,323	£1,323	£1,323
			¥225,103	¥225,103	¥225,103
MINNOZZI, MARCO	1	1	$2,881	$2,881	$2,881
			DM5,158	DM5,158	DM5,158
			£1,725	£1,725	£1,725
			¥396,371	¥396,371	¥396,371
MIREMONT, CLAUDE AUGUSTIN	8	5	$4,801	$17,193	$10,174
			DM8,021	DM32,451	DM18,190
			£2,875	£10,642	£6,199
			¥583,596	¥1,818,967	¥1,186,777
MOCKEL, OSWALD	2	0			
MOCKEL, OTTO	3	1	$8,360	$8,360	$8,360
			DM11,808	DM11,808	DM11,808
			£5,290	£5,290	£5,290
			¥746,086	¥746,086	¥746,086
MODAUDO, G.	1	0			
MOENNIG, WILLIAM (workshop of)	1	1	$805	$805	$805
			DM1,212	DM1,212	DM1,212
			£489	£489	£489
			¥89,983	¥89,983	¥89,983
MOINEL, CHARLES	2	0			
MOINEL, DANIEL	1	1	$1,344	$1,344	$1,344
			DM2,496	DM2,496	DM2,496
			£805	£805	£805
			¥179,869	¥179,869	¥179,869
MOINIER, ALAIN	1	1	$3,672	$3,672	$3,672
			DM5,495	DM5,495	DM5,495
			£2,185	£2,185	£2,185
			¥409,644	¥409,644	¥409,644
MOINEL & CHERPITEL	3	1	$3,726	$3,726	$3,726
			DM6,693	DM6,693	DM6,693
			£2,300	£2,300	£2,300
			¥439,921	¥439,921	¥439,921
MOITESSIER, LOUIS	5	1	$999	$999	$999
			DM1,415	DM1,415	DM1,415
			£633	£633	£633
			¥103,098	¥103,098	¥103,098
MOLLER, MAX	1	1	$6,325	$6,325	$6,325
			DM9,146	DM9,146	DM9,146
			£4,131	£4,131	£4,131
			¥640,406	¥640,406	¥640,406

Maker	Items Bid	Sold	Selling Prices Low	High	Avg
MONK	1	1	$556	$556	$556
			DM855	DM855	DM855
			£368	£368	£368
			¥59,331	¥59,331	¥59,331
MONK, JOHN KING	4	3	$460	$812	$606
			DM781	DM1,148	DM916
			£276	£518	£380
			¥54,850	¥69,387	¥61,803
MONNIG, FRITZ	5	3	$933	$2,359	$1,832
			DM1,617	DM3,706	DM2,882
			£552	£1,495	£1,142
			¥118,608	¥270,567	¥210,122
MONTAGNANA, DOMENICO	1	0			
MONTEIRO, HENRIQUE	2	1	$3,304	$3,304	$3,304
			DM5,728	DM5,728	DM5,728
			£1,955	£1,955	£1,955
			¥412,505	¥412,505	¥412,505
MONTEVECCHI, LUIGI (attributed to)	1	1	$3,172	$3,172	$3,172
			DM4,682	DM4,682	DM4,682
			£2,070	£2,070	£2,070
			¥337,205	¥337,205	¥337,205
MONTEVERDE, CLAUDIO	6	3	$1,102	$4,332	$2,330
			DM1,853	DM6,374	DM3,641
			£690	£2,818	£1,476
			¥135,283	¥459,703	¥263,036
MONZANI (attributed to)	2	0			
MONZINO, ANTONIO	2	0			
MONZINO & FIGLI	2	1	$1,955	$1,955	$1,955
			DM3,151	DM3,151	DM3,151
			£1,150	£1,150	£1,150
			¥241,753	¥241,753	¥241,753
MOON, GEORGE	2	2	$655	$686	$671
			DM937	DM970	DM953
			£414	£437	£426
			¥58,593	¥65,820	¥62,207
MOORE, ALFRED	4	1	$1,501	$1,501	$1,501
			DM2,677	DM2,677	DM2,677
			£920	£920	£920
			¥196,540	¥196,540	¥196,540
MORARA, PAOLO	1	1	$1,312	$1,312	$1,312
			DM2,270	DM2,270	DM2,270
			£805	£805	£805
			¥149,730	¥149,730	¥149,730
MORASSI, GIOVANNI BATTISTA	3	2	$7,059	$11,945	$9,502
			DM10,845	DM17,951	DM14,398
			£4,600	£7,130	£5,865
			¥772,749	¥1,330,180	¥1,051,465
MORITZ, ALFRED	1	1	$730	$730	$730
			DM1,206	DM1,206	DM1,206
			£437	£437	£437
			¥85,346	¥85,346	¥85,346
MORIZOT, RENE	3	1	$3,450	$3,450	$3,450
			DM5,275	DM5,275	DM5,275
			£2,270	£2,270	£2,270
			¥363,630	¥363,630	¥363,630

Maker	Items		Selling Prices		
	Bid	Sold	Low	High	Avg
MORIZOT, RENE (attributed to)	1	1	$1,674	$1,674	$1,674
			DM2,394	DM2,394	DM2,394
			£1,058	£1,058	£1,058
			¥168,207	¥168,207	¥168,207
MORLOT	1	1	$1,031	$1,031	$1,031
			DM1,834	DM1,834	DM1,834
			£633	£633	£633
			¥138,473	¥138,473	¥138,473
MORLOT, NICOLAS	1	1	$575	$575	$575
			DM994	DM994	DM994
			£355	£355	£355
			¥72,873	¥72,873	¥72,873
MORRISON, ARCHIBALD	1	1	$926	$926	$926
			DM1,562	DM1,562	DM1,562
			£575	£575	£575
			¥113,771	¥113,771	¥113,771
MORSE, JOHN	1	1	$1,380	$1,380	$1,380
			DM2,361	DM2,361	DM2,361
			£816	£816	£816
			¥171,368	¥171,368	¥171,368
MORTIMER, JOHN WILLIAM	1	1	$430	$430	$430
			DM701	DM701	DM701
			£253	£253	£253
			¥50,620	¥50,620	¥50,620
MORTIN, LEON (attributed to)	1	1	$1,740	$1,740	$1,740
			DM2,503	DM2,503	DM2,503
			£1,127	£1,127	£1,127
			¥176,646	¥176,646	¥176,646
MOSCHELLA, SALVATORE	1	1	$1,586	$1,586	$1,586
			DM2,341	DM2,341	DM2,341
			£1,035	£1,035	£1,035
			¥168,603	¥168,603	¥168,603
MOSHER, ALEX H.	2	0			
MOSS, HENRY	1	1	$686	$686	$686
			DM970	DM970	DM970
			£437	£437	£437
			¥58,593	¥58,593	¥58,593
MOUGEL	1	0			
MOUGENOT, GEORGES	7	7	$2,125	$10,934	$4,402
			DM3,820	DM18,499	DM7,733
			£1,265	£6,877	£2,707
			¥245,701	¥1,354,769	¥546,620
MOUGENOT, GEORGES (attributed to)	1	1	$1,308	$1,308	$1,308
			DM2,281	DM2,281	DM2,281
			£805	£805	£805
			¥158,464	¥158,464	¥158,464
MOUGENOT, LEON	15	10	$1,529	$4,018	$2,565
			DM2,163	DM5,649	DM3,934
			£978	£2,530	£1,604
			¥155,236	¥393,406	¥261,992
MOUGENOT, LEON (attributed to)	4	4	$932	$4,529	$2,557
			DM1,754	DM6,396	DM4,097
			£575	£2,875	£1,581
			¥99,303	¥456,070	¥281,864
MOUGENOT, LEON (workshop of)	1	1	$920	$920	$920
			DM1,328	DM1,328	DM1,328
			£586	£586	£586
			¥79,810	¥79,810	¥79,810

Maker	Items Bid	Sold	Selling Prices Low	High	Avg
MOYA, HIDALGO	7	6	$1,641	$3,055	$2,516
			DM2,951	DM5,697	DM4,317
			£977	£1,984	£1,580
			¥189,763	¥347,593	¥283,170
MOYA, HIDALGO (attributed to)	1	0			
MOZZANI, LUIGI	12	8	$2,310	$8,570	$6,181
			DM4,274	DM16,240	DM10,620
			£1,380	£5,520	£3,860
			¥307,864	¥928,148	¥687,316
MOZZANI, LUIGI (attributed to)	3	1	$3,853	$3,853	$3,853
			DM5,791	DM5,791	DM5,791
			£2,300	£2,300	£2,300
			¥429,090	¥429,090	¥429,090
MOZZANI, LUIGI (workshop of)	1	0			
MUIR, HAROLD	2	0			
MULLER, JOSEPH	1	0			
MULLER, KARL	1	0			
MULLER, KARL (attributed to)	1	1	$1,212	$1,212	$1,212
			DM1,799	DM1,799	DM1,799
			£782	£782	£782
			¥131,204	¥131,204	¥131,204
MUMBY, ERNEST	1	0			
MUNCHER, ROMEDIO	4	4	$2,437	$6,900	$4,541
			DM4,216	DM10,385	DM7,325
			£1,495	£4,189	£2,806
			¥278,070	¥771,282	¥518,978
MUNCHER, ROMEDIO (attributed to)	1	1	$2,138	$2,138	$2,138
			DM3,706	DM3,706	DM3,706
			£1,265	£1,265	£1,265
			¥266,915	¥266,915	¥266,915
MUNCHER, ROMEDIO (workshop of)	1	0			
MURDOCH, JOHN	1	1	$1,156	$1,156	$1,156
			DM2,071	DM2,071	DM2,071
			£690	£690	£690
			¥134,205	¥134,205	¥134,205
MURRAY, THOMAS	1	1	$1,441	$1,441	$1,441
			DM2,234	DM2,234	DM2,234
			£863	£863	£863
			¥164,142	¥164,142	¥164,142
MUSCHIETTI, UMBERTO	2	1	$4,664	$4,664	$4,664
			DM8,087	DM8,087	DM8,087
			£2,760	£2,760	£2,760
			¥582,360	¥582,360	¥582,360
MUSCHKE, ANTON	1	1	$690	$690	$690
			DM971	DM971	DM971
			£437	£437	£437
			¥70,502	¥70,502	¥70,502
MUTTI, VITTORIO	3	0			
NAFISSI, CARLO (ascribed to)	1	1	$2,467	$2,467	$2,467
			DM3,642	DM3,642	DM3,642
			£1,610	£1,610	£1,610
			¥262,271	¥262,271	¥262,271
NALDI, A.	1	0			
NAMY, JEAN THEODORE	1	0			

Maker	Items		Selling Prices		
	Bid	Sold	Low	High	Avg
NATIONAL DOBRO CORP.	1	1	$1,150	$1,150	$1,150
			DM1,968	DM1,968	DM1,968
			£680	£680	£680
			¥142,807	¥142,807	¥142,807
NEBEL, HANS (attributed to)	1	1	$1,598	$1,598	$1,598
			DM2,299	DM2,299	DM2,299
			£1,035	£1,035	£1,035
			¥162,226	¥162,226	¥162,226
NEBEL, MARTIN	2	1	$2,415	$2,415	$2,415
			DM3,492	DM3,492	DM3,492
			£1,577	£1,577	£1,577
			¥244,519	¥244,519	¥244,519
NEMESSANYI, SAMUEL FELIX	2	2	$6,170	$6,325	$6,247
			DM8,688	DM9,133	DM8,911
			£3,910	£4,030	£3,970
			¥548,694	¥630,808	¥589,751
NEUBAUER, GERHARD	2	1	$1,725	$1,725	$1,725
			DM2,951	DM2,951	DM2,951
			£1,020	£1,020	£1,020
			¥214,211	¥214,211	¥214,211
NEUDORFER	1	1	$1,844	$1,844	$1,844
			DM2,568	DM2,568	DM2,568
			£1,150	£1,150	£1,150
			¥155,880	¥155,880	¥155,880
NEUDORFER, ALFRED	1	1	$1,218	$1,218	$1,218
			DM2,159	DM2,159	DM2,159
			£747	£747	£747
			¥143,969	¥143,969	¥143,969
NEUMANN, ADOLPH (workshop of)	1	1	$345	$345	$345
			DM614	DM614	DM614
			£207	£207	£207
			¥45,878	¥45,878	¥45,878
NEUNER (workshop of)	5	5	$403	$920	$673
			DM606	DM1,328	DM1,024
			£244	£586	£421
			¥44,991	¥94,734	¥68,513
NEUNER, LUDWIG	1	1	$364	$364	$364
			DM676	DM676	DM676
			£218	£218	£218
			¥48,710	¥48,710	¥48,710
NEUNER, MATHIAS	8	7	$345	$5,536	$1,580
			DM583	DM7,706	DM2,502
			£207	£3,450	£974
			¥42,090	¥467,047	¥158,726
NEUNER & HORNSTEINER	35	25	$81	$4,928	$966
			DM124	DM9,338	DM1,660
			£52	£3,042	£600
			¥9,033	¥520,352	¥109,020
NEUNER & HORNSTEINER (workshop of)	5	4	$288	$748	$561
			DM486	DM1,331	DM940
			£173	£454	£338
			¥35,075	¥99,403	¥69,801
NICOLAS	1	1	$2,999	$2,999	$2,999
			DM5,697	DM5,697	DM5,697
			£1,852	£1,852	£1,852
			¥315,144	¥315,144	¥315,144

Maker	Items		Selling Prices		
	Bid	Sold	Low	High	Avg
NICOLAS, DIDIER (L'AINE)	45	22	$489	$6,598	$1,653
			DM826	DM9,247	DM2,700
			£293	£4,140	£1,023
			¥59,628	¥590,117	¥183,306
NICOLAS, DIDIER (L'AINE) (attributed to)	1	1	$1,283	$1,283	$1,283
			DM1,904	DM1,904	DM1,904
			£828	£828	£828
			¥138,922	¥138,922	¥138,922
NICOLAS, DIDIER (L'AINE) (workshop of)	1	1	$1,093	$1,093	$1,093
			DM1,945	DM1,945	DM1,945
			£656	£656	£656
			¥145,281	¥145,281	¥145,281
NICOLAS, FRANCOIS FOURRIER	1	0			
NICOLAS, JOSEPH (II)	1	1	$1,633	$1,633	$1,633
			DM2,300	DM2,300	DM2,300
			£1,035	£1,035	£1,035
			¥166,979	¥166,979	¥166,979
NIEDT, KARL (attributed to)	1	1	$758	$758	$758
			DM1,072	DM1,072	DM1,072
			£483	£483	£483
			¥64,761	¥64,761	¥64,761
NOBILE, FRANCESCO (attributed to)	1	1	$4,620	$4,620	$4,620
			DM8,548	DM8,548	DM8,548
			£2,760	£2,760	£2,760
			¥615,728	¥615,728	¥615,728
NOEBE, LOUIS	3	3	$1,767	$3,271	$2,608
			DM2,611	DM5,290	DM4,174
			£1,150	£2,070	£1,646
			¥188,294	¥292,634	¥257,625
NOLLI, MARCO	1	1	$2,467	$2,467	$2,467
			DM3,723	DM3,723	DM3,723
			£1,495	£1,495	£1,495
			¥279,565	¥279,565	¥279,565
NORMAN, BARAK (ascribed to)	1	1	$963	$963	$963
			DM1,448	DM1,448	DM1,448
			£575	£575	£575
			¥107,273	¥107,273	¥107,273
NOSEK, VACLAV	3	0			
NOVELLI	1	0			
NOVELLI, NATALE	2	2	$7,633	$15,887	$11,760
			DM10,781	DM24,379	DM17,580
			£4,830	£10,350	£7,590
			¥681,209	¥1,738,904	¥1,210,056
NOVELLI, NATALE (ascribed to)	1	0			
NUNN, ERNEST S.	1	1	$1,006	$1,006	$1,006
			DM1,428	DM1,428	DM1,428
			£633	£633	£633
			¥93,389	¥93,389	¥93,389
NUPIERI, GIUSEPPE	5	4	$712	$1,495	$1,127
			DM1,232	DM2,527	DM1,907
			£437	£897	£679
			¥81,282	¥182,390	¥136,009
ODDONE, CARLO GIUSEPPE	8	5	$26,887	$45,230	$35,930
			DM44,919	DM80,144	DM56,056
			£16,100	£27,773	£22,115
			¥2,919,466	¥5,514,825	¥3,940,794
ODDONE, CARLO GIUSEPPE (ascribed to)	2	0			

Maker	Items		Selling Prices		
	Bid	Sold	Low	High	Avg
ODOARDI, GIUSEPPE	2	1	$3,276	$3,276	$3,276
			DM4,685	DM4,685	DM4,685
			£2,070	£2,070	£2,070
			¥329,101	¥329,101	¥329,101
ODOARDI, GIUSEPPE (attributed to)	2	2	$2,261	$3,241	$2,751
			DM4,007	DM4,962	DM4,484
			£1,389	£2,070	£1,729
			¥275,741	¥361,256	¥318,499
OETTL & HORNSTEINER	1	1	$4,140	$4,140	$4,140
			DM5,986	DM5,986	DM5,986
			£2,704	£2,704	£2,704
			¥419,175	¥419,175	¥419,175
OLDFIELD, W.	1	1	$162	$162	$162
			DM248	DM248	DM248
			£104	£104	£104
			¥18,066	¥18,066	¥18,066
OLIVER, FREEMAN ADAMS	1	1	$374	$374	$374
			DM540	DM540	DM540
			£244	£244	£244
			¥37,842	¥37,842	¥37,842
OLIVIER & BISCH	3	3	$2,305	$2,332	$2,318
			DM4,043	DM4,168	DM4,112
			£1,380	£1,380	£1,380
			¥268,037	¥317,096	¥293,885
OLIVIER & BISCH (attributed to)	1	1	$525	$525	$525
			DM950	DM950	DM950
			£322	£322	£322
			¥63,334	¥63,334	¥63,334
OLRY, J. (attributed to)	4	0			
OMOND, JAMES	2	1	$1,270	$1,270	$1,270
			DM1,789	DM1,789	DM1,789
			£805	£805	£805
			¥129,872	¥129,872	¥129,872
ORLANDINI, A.	2	1	$3,887	$3,887	$3,887
			DM6,739	DM6,739	DM6,739
			£2,300	£2,300	£2,300
			¥494,201	¥494,201	¥494,201
ORNATI, GIUSEPPE	7	3	$14,752	$40,986	$23,875
			DM20,541	DM77,165	DM40,695
			£9,200	£25,300	£14,950
			¥1,247,042	¥4,331,866	¥2,439,270
ORNATI, GIUSEPPE (attributed to)	1	0			
ORNATI, GIUSEPPE (workshop of)	3	1	$10,592	$10,592	$10,592
			DM16,253	DM16,253	DM16,253
			£6,900	£6,900	£6,900
			¥1,159,269	¥1,159,269	¥1,159,269
ORSELLI, ENRICO	2	2	$3,565	$6,061	$4,813
			DM5,451	DM9,775	DM7,613
			£2,345	£3,519	£2,932
			¥375,751	¥713,575	¥544,663
ORY, F.	3	1	$601	$601	$601
			DM1,019	DM1,019	DM1,019
			£368	£368	£368
			¥69,735	¥69,735	¥69,735
OSMANEK, A.	1	1	$1,057	$1,057	$1,057
			DM1,561	DM1,561	DM1,561
			£690	£690	£690
			¥112,402	¥112,402	¥112,402

| Maker | Items | | Selling Prices | | |
	Bid	Sold	Low	High	Avg
OTTO, C.W.F.	1	1	$2,209	$2,209	$2,209
			DM3,263	DM3,263	DM3,263
			£1,438	£1,438	£1,438
			¥235,368	¥235,368	¥235,368
OTTO, CARL AUGUST	1	1	$2,645	$2,645	$2,645
			DM4,787	DM4,787	DM4,787
			£1,613	£1,613	£1,613
			¥319,357	¥319,357	¥319,357
OTTO, WILHELM	1	1	$3,816	$3,816	$3,816
			DM5,391	DM5,391	DM5,391
			£2,415	£2,415	£2,415
			¥340,604	¥340,604	¥340,604
OTTO, WILHELM (workshop of)	1	1	$1,150	$1,150	$1,150
			DM1,661	DM1,661	DM1,661
			£733	£733	£733
			¥99,763	¥99,763	¥99,763
OWEN, JOHN W.	3	3	$1,342	$3,864	$2,709
			DM2,052	DM6,440	DM4,200
			£863	£2,300	£1,668
			¥132,639	¥461,817	¥284,738
PACHERELE, PIERRE	4	1	$26,887	$26,887	$26,887
			DM44,919	DM44,919	DM44,919
			£16,100	£16,100	£16,100
			¥3,268,139	¥3,268,139	¥3,268,139
PACHERELE, PIERRE (ascribed to)	2	2	$9,145	$15,902	$12,524
			DM12,980	DM23,495	DM18,237
			£5,750	£10,350	£8,050
			¥848,988	¥1,694,647	¥1,271,817
PACHERELE, PIERRE (attributed to)	3	2	$3,699	$3,761	$3,730
			DM6,211	DM6,417	DM6,314
			£2,185	£2,300	£2,243
			¥465,587	¥468,923	¥467,255
PAESOLD, RODERICH	1	1	$938	$938	$938
			DM1,673	DM1,673	DM1,673
			£575	£575	£575
			¥122,837	¥122,837	¥122,837
PAILLIOT	1	1	$1,686	$1,686	$1,686
			DM2,363	DM2,363	DM2,363
			£1,058	£1,058	£1,058
			¥148,633	¥148,633	¥148,633
PAINE, ARTHUR	1	1	$1,840	$1,840	$1,840
			DM3,275	DM3,275	DM3,275
			£1,104	£1,104	£1,104
			¥244,683	¥244,683	¥244,683
PAINE, THOMAS D.	2	1	$288	$288	$288
			DM512	DM512	DM512
			£173	£173	£173
			¥38,232	¥38,232	¥38,232
PAJEOT (FILS) (workshop of)	1	1	$932	$932	$932
			DM1,754	DM1,754	DM1,754
			£575	£575	£575
			¥98,452	¥98,452	¥98,452
PALLAVER, GIOVANNI	1	0			
PALLOTTA, PIETRO	3	1	$55,321	$55,321	$55,321
			DM77,028	DM77,028	DM77,028
			£34,500	£34,500	£34,500
			¥4,676,406	¥4,676,406	¥4,676,406

Maker	Items		Selling Prices		
	Bid	Sold	Low	High	Avg
PALMIERI, ALESSANDRO	1	1	$12,353	$12,353	$12,353
			DM18,978	DM18,978	DM18,978
			£8,050	£8,050	£8,050
			¥1,352,311	¥1,352,311	¥1,352,311
PAMPHILON, EDWARD	1	0			
PANORMO, GEORGE	3	2	$19,435	$35,958	$27,697
			DM33,695	DM50,068	DM41,882
			£11,500	£22,425	£16,963
			¥2,426,500	¥3,039,664	¥2,733,082
PANORMO, J. (attributed to)	1	1	$8,118	$8,118	$8,118
			DM12,471	DM12,471	DM12,471
			£5,290	£5,290	£5,290
			¥888,662	¥888,662	¥888,662
PANORMO, JOSEPH	1	1	$40,986	$40,986	$40,986
			DM77,165	DM77,165	DM77,165
			£25,300	£25,300	£25,300
			¥4,331,866	¥4,331,866	¥4,331,866
PANORMO, VINCENZO	7	5	$33,741	$48,364	$42,422
			DM58,374	DM81,823	DM70,133
			£20,700	£30,418	£26,128
			¥3,850,200	¥5,992,248	¥5,071,730
PANORMO, VINCENZO (ascribed to)	1	1	$18,745	$18,745	$18,745
			DM32,430	DM32,430	DM32,430
			£11,500	£11,500	£11,500
			¥2,139,000	¥2,139,000	¥2,139,000
PANORMO, VINCENZO (attributed to)	3	2	$18,975	$58,600	$38,788
			DM28,635	DM100,265	DM64,450
			£11,500	£34,660	£23,080
			¥2,150,500	¥7,276,948	¥4,713,724
PANORMO FAMILY (MEMBER OF)	1	0			
PANORMO FAMILY (MEMBER OF) (attributed to)	1	1	$16,376	$16,376	$16,376
			DM24,611	DM24,611	DM24,611
			£9,775	£9,775	£9,775
			¥1,823,634	¥1,823,634	¥1,823,634
PAOLETTI, SILVIO VEZIO	4	4	$3,618	$4,718	$4,298
			DM6,411	DM8,548	DM7,026
			£2,222	£2,990	£2,683
			¥441,186	¥615,728	¥500,751
PAOLO, ERBA (attributed to)	1	1	$8,457	$8,457	$8,457
			DM11,832	DM11,832	DM11,832
			£5,290	£5,290	£5,290
			¥715,277	¥715,277	¥715,277
PAQUOTTE, JEAN BAPTIST	1	1	$7,739	$7,739	$7,739
			DM12,413	DM12,413	DM12,413
			£5,026	£5,026	£5,026
			¥880,568	¥880,568	¥880,568
PARALUPI, RODOLFO (attributed to)	1	0			
PARESCHI, GAETANO	8	3	$4,592	$15,077	$9,581
			DM7,722	DM26,715	DM15,738
			£2,875	£9,258	£5,961
			¥563,681	¥1,838,275	¥1,109,872
PARKER, DANIEL	4	2	$5,089	$13,714	$9,401
			DM7,187	DM25,789	DM16,488
			£3,220	£8,625	£5,923
			¥454,139	¥1,658,070	¥1,056,105

Maker	Items		Selling Prices		
	Bid	Sold	Low	High	Avg
PARMEGGIANI, ROMOLA	2	1	$3,015	$3,015	$3,015
			DM5,343	DM5,343	DM5,343
			£1,852	£1,852	£1,852
			¥367,655	¥367,655	¥367,655
PARTL, ANDREAS NIKOLAUS II	1	1	$2,178	$2,178	$2,178
			DM3,066	DM3,066	DM3,066
			£1,380	£1,380	£1,380
			¥222,638	¥222,638	¥222,638
PASSAURO-ZUCCARO, RAYMOND	2	2	$805	$1,265	$1,035
			DM1,360	DM2,138	DM1,749
			£483	£759	£621
			¥98,210	¥154,330	¥126,270
PASTA, GAETANO	3	1	$20,407	$20,407	$20,407
			DM35,380	DM35,380	DM35,380
			£12,075	£12,075	£12,075
			¥2,547,825	¥2,547,825	¥2,547,825
PATOCKA, BENJAMIN	1	1	$1,938	$1,938	$1,938
			DM2,861	DM2,861	DM2,861
			£1,265	£1,265	£1,265
			¥206,070	¥206,070	¥206,070
PATOCKA, BENJAMIN (attributed to)	1	1	$2,120	$2,120	$2,120
			DM3,133	DM3,133	DM3,133
			£1,380	£1,380	£1,380
			¥225,953	¥225,953	¥225,953
PATZELT, FERDINAND (attributed to)	2	0			
PAUL, ADAM D.	1	1	$657	$657	$657
			DM924	DM924	DM924
			£414	£414	£414
			¥58,676	¥58,676	¥58,676
PAULI, JOSEPH	2	1	$1,265	$1,265	$1,265
			DM1,934	DM1,934	DM1,934
			£832	£832	£832
			¥133,331	¥133,331	¥133,331
PAULSEN, P.C.	2	1	$1,610	$1,610	$1,610
			DM2,325	DM2,325	DM2,325
			£1,026	£1,026	£1,026
			¥139,668	¥139,668	¥139,668
PAULUS, ALBIN LUDWIG	4	2	$1,059	$1,118	$1,089
			DM1,625	DM1,958	DM1,792
			£690	£690	£690
			¥115,927	¥135,206	¥125,566
PAULUS, KONRAD (attributed to)	2	0			
PAWLIKOWSKI, JAN	1	1	$1,725	$1,725	$1,725
			DM3,105	DM3,105	DM3,105
			£1,035	£1,035	£1,035
			¥13,403	¥13,403	¥13,403
PAYNE, ALAN	1	0			
PEARCE, WILLIAM	2	1	$1,739	$1,739	$1,739
			DM3,127	DM3,127	DM3,127
			£1,035	£1,035	£1,035
			¥201,028	¥201,028	¥201,028
PEDRAZZINI, GIUSEPPE	24	13	$12,775	$57,615	$30,165
			DM21,476	DM96,255	DM51,069
			£7,869	£34,500	£18,565
			¥1,396,675	¥7,003,155	¥3,564,453

| Maker | Items | | Selling Prices | | |
	Bid	Sold	Low	High	Avg
PEDRAZZINI, GIUSEPPE (ascribed to)	2	1	$13,630 DM19,252 £8,625 ¥1,216,444	$13,630 DM19,252 £8,625 ¥1,216,444	$13,630 DM19,252 £8,625 ¥1,216,444
PEDRAZZINI, GIUSEPPE (attributed to)	2	1	$5,511 DM9,266 £3,450 ¥676,417	$5,511 DM9,266 £3,450 ¥676,417	$5,511 DM9,266 £3,450 ¥676,417
PELLACANI, GIUSEPPE	3	2	$4,300 DM6,030 £2,760 ¥434,432	$6,325 DM9,133 £4,030 ¥548,694	$5,312 DM7,582 £3,395 ¥491,563
PELLACANI, GIUSEPPE (ascribed to)	1	0			
PELLACANI, GIUSEPPE (attributed to)	1	0			
PELLERANI, ANTONIO	1	1	$9,163 DM13,526 £5,980 ¥974,148	$9,163 DM13,526 £5,980 ¥974,148	$9,163 DM13,526 £5,980 ¥974,148
PELLIZON, ANTONIO (I)	2	2	$9,423 DM16,697 £5,786 ¥1,135,348	$12,721 DM17,968 £8,050 ¥1,148,922	$11,072 DM17,332 £6,918 ¥1,142,135
PERESSON, SERGIO	4	3	$18,463 DM30,665 £10,925 ¥2,226,382	$23,194 DM34,703 £13,800 ¥2,587,224	$21,144 DM32,459 £12,842 ¥2,372,927
PEROTTI, ENEA	1	0			
PERR, MICHAEL	1	0			
PERRY	2	1	$251 DM438 £150 ¥32,047	$251 DM438 £150 ¥32,047	$251 DM438 £150 ¥32,047
PERRY, JAMES	4	0			
PERRY, L.A.	1	1	$668 DM1,026 £437 ¥72,951	$668 DM1,026 £437 ¥72,951	$668 DM1,026 £437 ¥72,951
PERRY, THOMAS	8	4	$1,219 DM2,207 £748 ¥147,124	$2,760 DM3,991 £1,803 ¥279,450	$1,938 DM3,121 £1,228 ¥210,969
PERRY, THOMAS & WILKINSON, WM.	10	6	$772 DM1,080 £483 ¥65,308	$3,652 DM5,135 £2,300 ¥325,979	$1,654 DM2,362 £1,038 ¥154,045
PERRY & WILKINSON	9	5	$748 DM1,303 £460 ¥90,551	$4,025 DM7,309 £2,463 ¥499,825	$1,973 DM3,533 £1,194 ¥246,279
PERRY & WILKINSON (attributed to)	1	1	$1,013 DM1,816 £605 ¥117,673	$1,013 DM1,816 £605 ¥117,673	$1,013 DM1,816 £605 ¥117,673
PETERNELLA, JAGO	1	0			

Maker	Items		Selling Prices		
	Bid	Sold	Low	High	Avg
PETERS, WILLIAM L.	1	1	$1,610	$1,610	$1,610
			DM2,721	DM2,721	DM2,721
			£966	£966	£966
			¥196,420	¥196,420	¥196,420
PETERSON, P.A.	1	0			
PEVERE, ERNESTO	1	1	$3,872	$3,872	$3,872
			DM5,392	DM5,392	DM5,392
			£2,415	£2,415	£2,415
			¥327,348	¥327,348	¥327,348
PFRETZSCHNER	1	0			
PFRETZSCHNER, E.R.	1	1	$92	$92	$92
			DM164	DM164	DM164
			£56	£56	£56
			¥12,781	¥12,781	¥12,781
PFRETZSCHNER, G.A. (workshop of)	1	1	$201	$201	$201
			DM340	DM340	DM340
			£121	£121	£121
			¥24,553	¥24,553	¥24,553
PFRETZSCHNER, JOHANN GOTTLOB	1	1	$900	$900	$900
			DM1,375	DM1,375	DM1,375
			£575	£575	£575
			¥100,366	¥100,366	¥100,366
PICCAGLIANI, ARMANDO	1	1	$1,960	$1,960	$1,960
			DM3,473	DM3,473	DM3,473
			£1,203	£1,203	£1,203
			¥238,976	¥238,976	¥238,976
PICKARD, H.	1	1	$3,105	$3,105	$3,105
			DM5,367	DM5,367	DM5,367
			£1,919	£1,919	£1,919
			¥393,512	¥393,512	¥393,512
PICKSTONE, HARRY	2	2	$230	$332	$281
			DM381	DM542	DM461
			£138	£196	£167
			¥26,951	¥39,116	¥33,034
PIERCE, WILLIAM	1	1	$403	$403	$403
			DM680	DM680	DM680
			£242	£242	£242
			¥49,105	¥49,105	¥49,105
PIEROTTE, JULES	2	1	$559	$559	$559
			DM1,052	DM1,052	DM1,052
			£345	£345	£345
			¥59,071	¥59,071	¥59,071
PIERRAY, CLAUDE	4	4	$5,442	$10,870	$7,615
			DM9,435	DM15,351	DM11,579
			£3,220	£6,900	£4,715
			¥679,420	¥1,094,568	¥822,223
PILAR, KAREL	2	1	$1,360	$1,360	$1,360
			DM2,359	DM2,359	DM2,359
			£805	£805	£805
			¥169,855	¥169,855	¥169,855
PILAR, VLADIMIR	1	1	$2,467	$2,467	$2,467
			DM4,440	DM4,440	DM4,440
			£1,495	£1,495	£1,495
			¥355,735	¥355,735	¥355,735
PILAT, PAUL	4	4	$6,707	$11,903	$8,578
			DM12,710	DM22,466	DM15,828
			£4,140	£7,368	£5,324
			¥708,230	¥1,259,285	¥943,001

Maker	Items		Selling Prices		
	Bid	Sold	Low	High	Avg
PILLEMENT, FRANCOIS	3	2	$1,267	$2,277	$1,772
			DM2,268	DM3,436	DM2,852
			£782	£1,380	£1,081
			¥149,417	¥258,060	¥203,738
PINEAU, JOSEPH	1	1	$690	$690	$690
			DM1,228	DM1,228	DM1,228
			£414	£414	£414
			¥91,756	¥91,756	¥91,756
PIQUE, FRANCOIS LOUIS	1	1	$47,179	$47,179	$47,179
			DM66,441	DM66,441	DM66,441
			£29,900	£29,900	£29,900
			¥4,823,827	¥4,823,827	¥4,823,827
PIQUE, FRANCOIS LOUIS (attributed to)	1	1	$4,600	$4,600	$4,600
			DM7,871	DM7,871	DM7,871
			£2,721	£2,721	£2,721
			¥571,228	¥571,228	¥571,228
PIRETTI, ENRICO	3	2	$1,586	$8,625	$5,105
			DM2,341	DM12,472	DM7,406
			£1,035	£5,634	£3,334
			¥168,603	¥873,281	¥520,942
PIROT, CLAUDE	2	1	$17,250	$17,250	$17,250
			DM29,153	DM29,153	DM29,153
			£10,350	£10,350	£10,350
			¥2,295,458	¥2,295,458	¥2,295,458
PIVA, GIOVANNI	1	0			
PIZZAMIGHO, CARLO	1	0			
PLACHT, FRANZ	1	1	$699	$699	$699
			DM977	DM977	DM977
			£437	£437	£437
			¥59,088	¥59,088	¥59,088
PLATNER, MICHAEL	1	0			
PLOWRIGHT, DENIS G.	2	1	$765	$765	$765
			DM1,175	DM1,175	DM1,175
			£506	£506	£506
			¥81,580	¥81,580	¥81,580
PLUMEREL, CHARLES	1	1	$345	$345	$345
			DM498	DM498	DM498
			£220	£220	£220
			¥29,929	¥29,929	¥29,929
POEHLAND & FUCHS	2	2	$863	$3,450	$2,156
			DM1,491	DM5,275	DM3,383
			£533	£2,270	£1,401
			¥109,309	¥363,630	¥236,469
POGGI, ANSALDO	3	3	$29,956	$40,601	$34,904
			DM44,220	DM62,303	DM56,001
			£19,550	£26,450	£22,233
			¥3,184,715	¥4,925,565	¥4,184,715
POGGI, ANSALDO (attributed to)	1	1	$1,725	$1,725	$1,725
			DM3,105	DM3,105	DM3,105
			£1,035	£1,035	£1,035
			¥13,403	¥13,403	¥13,403
POIROT, A.	1	1	$1,131	$1,131	$1,131
			DM2,004	DM2,004	DM2,004
			£694	£694	£694
			¥137,871	¥137,871	¥137,871
POIROT, AINE	1	0			

| Maker | Items | | Selling Prices | | |
	Bid	Sold	Low	High	Avg
POIRSON, ELOPHE	1	1	$15,525	$15,525	$15,525
			DM27,635	DM27,635	DM27,635
			£9,315	£9,315	£9,315
			¥2,064,514	¥2,064,514	¥2,064,514
POLITI, ENRICO & RAUL	1	1	$14,576	$14,576	$14,576
			DM25,271	DM25,271	DM25,271
			£8,625	£8,625	£8,625
			¥1,819,875	¥1,819,875	¥1,819,875
POLITI, EUGENIO	1	0			
POLITI, RAUL	3	2	$6,641	$10,689	$8,665
			DM11,954	DM18,532	DM15,243
			£4,025	£6,325	£5,175
			¥957,749	¥1,334,575	¥1,146,162
POLLASTRI, GAETANO	9	5	$14,719	$42,757	$26,603
			DM23,411	DM74,129	DM43,230
			£9,258	£25,300	£16,227
			¥1,686,025	¥5,338,300	¥3,029,319
POLLASTRI, GAETANO (ascribed to)	4	3	$6,521	$10,925	$8,315
			DM12,357	DM19,447	DM15,338
			£4,025	£6,555	£5,070
			¥688,557	¥1,452,807	¥977,735
POLLASTRI, GAETANO (attributed to)	2	2	$8,384	$9,641	$9,012
			DM15,887	DM18,270	DM17,079
			£5,175	£5,951	£5,563
			¥885,287	¥1,018,080	¥951,684
POLLER, ANTON	1	1	$7,475	$7,475	$7,475
			DM10,794	DM10,794	DM10,794
			£4,762	£4,762	£4,762
			¥648,456	¥648,456	¥648,456
POSCH, ANTON	1	1	$5,216	$5,216	$5,216
			DM9,821	DM9,821	DM9,821
			£3,220	£3,220	£3,220
			¥551,328	¥551,328	¥551,328
POSTACCHINI, ANDREA	1	1	$7,161	$7,161	$7,161
			DM12,689	DM12,689	DM12,689
			£4,397	£4,397	£4,397
			¥873,181	¥873,181	¥873,181
POSTACCHINI, ANDREA (attributed to)	4	3	$4,388	$27,600	$16,796
			DM8,252	DM41,538	DM25,827
			£2,760	£16,755	£10,228
			¥530,582	¥3,085,128	¥1,890,821
POSTIGLIONE, VINCENZO	13	9	$10,350	$52,703	$30,249
			DM18,734	DM80,135	DM49,481
			£6,314	£33,350	£18,623
			¥1,249,659	¥5,772,454	¥3,240,830
POSTIGLIONE, VINCENZO (attributed to)	6	1	$31,719	$31,719	$31,719
			DM46,821	DM46,821	DM46,821
			£20,700	£20,700	£20,700
			¥3,372,051	¥3,372,051	¥3,372,051
POSTIGLIONE, VINCENZO (workshop of)	1	1	$15,882	$15,882	$15,882
			DM24,400	DM24,400	DM24,400
			£10,350	£10,350	£10,350
			¥1,738,686	¥1,738,686	¥1,738,686
POSTIGLIONE, VINCENZO & GIOVANNI PISTUCCI	1	0			

Maker	Items		Selling Prices		
	Bid	Sold	Low	High	Avg
POUZOL, EMILE (attributed to)	1	1	$1,971	$1,971	$1,971
			DM3,744	DM3,744	DM3,744
			£1,217	£1,217	£1,217
			¥207,095	¥207,095	¥207,095
POWERS, CLARK	2	1	$1,093	$1,093	$1,093
			DM1,580	DM1,580	DM1,580
			£714	£714	£714
			¥110,616	¥110,616	¥110,616
POWERS, LINCOLN	1	1	$374	$374	$374
			DM572	DM572	DM572
			£246	£246	£246
			¥39,393	¥39,393	¥39,393
POWLOSKI, PATRICIA	1	0			
POWLOSKI-BANCHERO, PATRICIA	1	1	$1,840	$1,840	$1,840
			DM3,275	DM3,275	DM3,275
			£1,104	£1,104	£1,104
			¥244,683	¥244,683	¥244,683
PRAGA, EUGENIO	5	3	$8,539	$48,438	$23,976
			DM15,370	DM91,195	DM42,727
			£5,175	£29,900	£14,947
			¥1,231,391	¥5,119,478	¥2,621,519
PRAILL, RONALD WILLIAM	5	1	$1,118	$1,118	$1,118
			DM1,178	DM1,178	DM1,178
			£690	£690	£690
			¥85,419	¥85,419	¥85,419
PRESSENDA, GIOVANNI FRANCESCO	7	5	$141,120	$197,063	$166,343
			DM220,720	DM289,523	DM253,024
			£84,000	£128,000	£104,790
			¥15,969,418	¥20,851,328	¥17,491,976
PRESTON, JAMES	1	1	$1,360	$1,360	$1,360
			DM2,359	DM2,359	DM2,359
			£805	£805	£805
			¥172,970	¥172,970	¥172,970
PRICE, REGINALD (attributed to)	2	1	$704	$704	$704
			DM995	DM995	DM995
			£449	£449	£449
			¥60,135	¥60,135	¥60,135
PRIER, PETER PAUL	1	1	$5,999	$5,999	$5,999
			DM11,368	DM11,368	DM11,368
			£3,703	£3,703	£3,703
			¥633,472	¥633,472	¥633,472
PRIESTNALL, J.	1	1	$1,060	$1,060	$1,060
			DM1,566	DM1,566	DM1,566
			£690	£690	£690
			¥112,976	¥112,976	¥112,976
PRIESTNALL, JOHN	1	1	$538	$538	$538
			DM998	DM998	DM998
			£322	£322	£322
			¥71,948	¥71,948	¥71,948
PRIMAVERA, ALFREDO (workshop of)	1	0			
PRINCE, W.B.	3	1	$1,316	$1,316	$1,316
			DM2,228	DM2,228	DM2,228
			£805	£805	£805
			¥152,544	¥152,544	¥152,544
PROCAK, MYRON	1	0			

| Maker | Items | | Selling Prices | | |
---	Bid	Sold	Low	High	Avg
PROCTOR, JOSEPH (attributed to)	2	1	$402	$402	$402
			DM571	DM571	DM571
			£253	£253	£253
			¥37,355	¥37,355	¥37,355
PROKOP, LADISLAV	3	3	$288	$6,856	$2,506
			DM497	DM13,022	DM4,722
			£178	£4,232	£1,547
			¥36,436	¥720,329	¥268,044
PROKOP, LADISLAV (II)	2	0			
PUGLISI, CONCETTO	1	0			
PUGLISI, MICHELANGELO	1	0			
PUGLISI, MICHELANGELO (attributed to)	1	1	$5,301	$5,301	$5,301
			DM7,832	DM7,832	DM7,832
			£3,450	£3,450	£3,450
			¥564,882	¥564,882	¥564,882
PUGLISI, REALE	3	3	$3,850	$5,356	$4,621
			DM7,123	DM10,150	DM8,700
			£2,300	£3,306	£2,827
			¥491,826	¥565,600	¥523,511
PULPANECK, FRITZ	1	0			
PUOZZO, EDSON	1	0			
PUPUNAT, FRANCOIS MARIE	3	1	$1,440	$1,440	$1,440
			DM2,201	DM2,201	DM2,201
			£920	£920	£920
			¥160,586	¥160,586	¥160,586
PURDAY, T.E.	1	1	$1,018	$1,018	$1,018
			DM1,633	DM1,633	DM1,633
			£661	£661	£661
			¥115,864	¥115,864	¥115,864
PUSKAS, JOSEPH	2	2	$2,875	$3,450	$3,163
			DM5,221	DM5,831	DM5,526
			£1,760	£2,070	£1,915
			¥357,018	¥459,092	¥408,055
PYNE, GEORGE	17	13	$1,999	$6,165	$4,143
			DM2,824	DM9,265	DM6,623
			£1,265	£3,910	£2,548
			¥178,412	¥686,544	¥466,765
QUAN, SHEN FEI ZHENG	1	1	$2,142	$2,142	$2,142
			DM4,060	DM4,060	DM4,060
			£1,323	£1,323	£1,323
			¥226,240	¥226,240	¥226,240
QUENOIL, VICTOR	2	0			
RACZ, LORAND	1	1	$4,255	$4,255	$4,255
			DM6,153	DM6,153	DM6,153
			£2,779	£2,779	£2,779
			¥430,819	¥430,819	¥430,819
RADIGHIERI, OTELLO	1	1	$2,185	$2,185	$2,185
			DM3,955	DM3,955	DM3,955
			£1,333	£1,333	£1,333
			¥263,817	¥263,817	¥263,817
RAE, JOHN	6	2	$559	$777	$668
			DM979	DM1,348	DM1,163
			£345	£460	£403
			¥67,603	¥97,060	¥82,331

Maker	Items		Selling Prices		
	Bid	Sold	Low	High	Avg
RAEBURN, JOHN	1	1	$1,348	$1,348	$1,348
			DM2,416	DM2,416	DM2,416
			£805	£805	£805
			¥156,573	¥156,573	¥156,573
RAMBAUX, CLAUDE VICTOR	2	2	$3,266	$4,229	$3,748
			DM4,600	DM6,243	DM5,421
			£2,070	£2,760	£2,415
			¥333,957	¥449,607	¥391,782
RAMIREZ, MANUEL (ascribed to)	1	1	$7,638	$7,638	$7,638
			DM13,674	DM13,674	DM13,674
			£4,715	£4,715	£4,715
			¥900,895	¥900,895	¥900,895
RAPOPORT, HAIM	1	0			
RASTELLI, LODOVICO	1	0			
RATHBONE, A. (attributed to)	1	1	$848	$848	$848
			DM1,253	DM1,253	DM1,253
			£552	£552	£552
			¥90,381	¥90,381	¥90,381
RAUCH, THOMAS (attributed to)	1	1	$368	$368	$368
			DM514	DM514	DM514
			£230	£230	£230
			¥31,099	¥31,099	¥31,099
RAUCHE (attributed to)	1	1	$686	$686	$686
			DM970	DM970	DM970
			£437	£437	£437
			¥58,593	¥58,593	¥58,593
RAVIZZA, CARLO	2	1	$4,893	$4,893	$4,893
			DM9,236	DM9,236	DM9,236
			£3,029	£3,029	£3,029
			¥517,706	¥517,706	¥517,706
RAVIZZA, CARLO (attributed to)	1	1	$6,642	$6,642	$6,642
			DM12,615	DM12,615	DM12,615
			£4,100	£4,100	£4,100
			¥697,818	¥697,818	¥697,818
RAYMOND, ROBERT JOHN	2	1	$468	$468	$468
			DM717	DM717	DM717
			£299	£299	£299
			¥52,181	¥52,181	¥52,181
REED, JOSEPH	2	1	$1,273	$1,273	$1,273
			DM1,873	DM1,873	DM1,873
			£828	£828	£828
			¥135,096	¥135,096	¥135,096
REGAZZONI, DANTE PAOLO	1	1	$3,187	$3,187	$3,187
			DM5,513	DM5,513	DM5,513
			£1,955	£1,955	£1,955
			¥363,630	¥363,630	¥363,630
REICHEL	1	0			
REICHEL, E.O.	1	1	$460	$460	$460
			DM777	DM777	DM777
			£276	£276	£276
			¥56,120	¥56,120	¥56,120
REICHEL, J.G. (attributed to)	1	0			
REICHEL, JOHANN GOTTFRIED	1	1	$278	$278	$278
			DM468	DM468	DM468
			£173	£173	£173
			¥34,131	¥34,131	¥34,131

Maker	Items		Selling Prices		
	Bid	Sold	Low	High	Avg
REICHERT, EDUARD	4	3	$316	$575	$441
			DM534	DM1,024	DM762
			£190	£345	£265
			¥38,583	¥76,464	¥55,886
REICHERT, EDUARD (workshop of)	2	2	$489	$748	$618
			DM870	DM1,081	DM975
			£293	£488	£391
			¥64,994	¥75,684	¥70,339
REITER, JOHANN	2	1	$1,610	$1,610	$1,610
			DM2,783	DM2,783	DM2,783
			£995	£995	£995
			¥204,043	¥204,043	¥204,043
REMENYI, MIHALY	1	1	$6,308	$6,308	$6,308
			DM10,673	DM10,673	DM10,673
			£3,968	£3,968	£3,968
			¥781,598	¥781,598	¥781,598
REMY, JEAN MATHURIN	3	1	$1,452	$1,452	$1,452
			DM2,044	DM2,044	DM2,044
			£920	£920	£920
			¥148,425	¥148,425	¥148,425
RESUCHE, CHARLES	1	1	$3,524	$3,524	$3,524
			DM5,202	DM5,202	DM5,202
			£2,300	£2,300	£2,300
			¥374,672	¥374,672	¥374,672
RESUCHE, CHARLES (attributed to)	2	1	$3,834	$3,834	$3,834
			DM7,102	DM7,102	DM7,102
			£2,300	£2,300	£2,300
			¥512,049	¥512,049	¥512,049
REUTER, GUNTHER	1	1	$4,313	$4,313	$4,313
			DM6,594	DM6,594	DM6,594
			£2,837	£2,837	£2,837
			¥454,538	¥454,538	¥454,538
RICARD, ALEXANDER	1	1	$920	$920	$920
			DM1,385	DM1,385	DM1,385
			£558	£558	£558
			¥102,838	¥102,838	¥102,838
RICE, JAMES	2	1	$1,349	$1,349	$1,349
			DM1,908	DM1,908	DM1,908
			£863	£863	£863
			¥136,973	¥136,973	¥136,973
RICHARD, ALEXANDER	1	0			
RICHARDSON, ARTHUR	13	10	$2,213	$7,767	$5,521
			DM3,081	DM12,834	DM9,096
			£1,380	£5,060	£3,462
			¥187,056	¥933,754	¥611,794
RICHARDSON, E.	1	1	$1,268	$1,268	$1,268
			DM1,791	DM1,791	DM1,791
			£805	£805	£805
			¥127,700	¥127,700	¥127,700
RICHARDSON, FRANK	1	1	$920	$920	$920
			DM1,407	DM1,407	DM1,407
			£605	£605	£605
			¥96,968	¥96,968	¥96,968
RICHELME, ANTOINE MARIUS	1	0			
RIEGER, GEORG	1	1	$2,028	$2,028	$2,028
			DM2,824	DM2,824	DM2,824
			£1,265	£1,265	£1,265
			¥171,468	¥171,468	¥171,468

| Maker | Items | | Selling Prices | | |
---	Bid	Sold	Low	High	Avg
RIEGER, PAUL	1	1	$1,677	$1,677	$1,677
			DM3,157	DM3,157	DM3,157
			£1,035	£1,035	£1,035
			¥177,213	¥177,213	¥177,213
RIEGER & FIORINI (attributed to)	2	1	$999	$999	$999
			DM1,549	DM1,549	DM1,549
			£598	£598	£598
			¥113,805	¥113,805	¥113,805
RINALDI, GIOFREDO BENEDETTO	2	2	$8,483	$22,908	$15,695
			DM11,811	DM33,815	DM22,813
			£5,290	£14,950	£10,120
			¥717,049	¥2,435,370	¥1,576,209
RINALDI, MARENGO ROMANUS (ascribed to)	1	1	$23,046	$23,046	$23,046
			DM38,502	DM38,502	DM38,502
			£13,800	£13,800	£13,800
			¥2,801,262	¥2,801,262	¥2,801,262
RIVA, CARLO "SEVERINO"	1	0			
RIVIERE & HAWKES	2	1	$677	$677	$677
			DM1,146	DM1,146	DM1,146
			£414	£414	£414
			¥78,451	¥78,451	¥78,451
RIVOLTA, GIACOMO	5	0			
ROBINSON	1	1	$296	$296	$296
			DM454	DM454	DM454
			£196	£196	£196
			¥31,519	¥31,519	¥31,519
ROBINSON, A.G.	2	2	$407	$608	$508
			DM598	DM935	DM767
			£265	£403	£334
			¥43,156	¥64,893	¥54,024
ROBINSON, STANLEY	1	0			
ROBINSON, WILLIAM	30	19	$533	$4,600	$2,588
			DM766	DM8,326	DM4,145
			£345	£2,806	£1,608
			¥54,075	¥564,418	¥288,806
ROBINSON, WILLIAM & STANLEY	1	1	$1,069	$1,069	$1,069
			DM1,587	DM1,587	DM1,587
			£690	£690	£690
			¥115,768	¥115,768	¥115,768
ROCCA, ENRICO	6	3	$29,900	$79,152	$47,598
			DM54,298	DM121,519	DM78,064
			£18,299	£51,750	£30,250
			¥3,712,982	¥8,638,990	¥5,400,724
ROCCA, ENRICO (ascribed to)	1	0			
ROCCA, ENRICO (attributed to)	1	0			
ROCCA, GIUSEPPE	5	3	$68,323	$165,773	$124,019
			DM96,217	DM234,147	DM175,076
			£43,300	£104,900	£78,500
			¥6,985,676	¥14,794,781	¥11,364,329
ROCCA, JOSEPH	1	1	$238,464	$238,464	$238,464
			DM452,934	DM452,934	DM452,934
			£147,200	£147,200	£147,200
			¥25,054,912	¥25,054,912	¥25,054,912

| Maker | Items | | Selling Prices | | |
	Bid	Sold	Low	High	Avg
ROCCA, JOSEPH (attributed to)	2	2	$25,709	$28,750	$27,230
			DM48,588	DM48,832	DM48,710
			£15,870	£17,250	£16,560
			¥2,701,233	¥3,825,763	¥3,263,498
ROCCA, JOSEPH (workshop of)	1	0			
ROCCHI, S.	1	0			
ROCCHI, SESTO	4	3	$8,642	$14,438	$11,140
			DM14,438	DM26,712	DM19,275
			£5,175	£8,625	£6,601
			¥1,050,473	¥1,924,151	¥1,397,300
ROCKWELL, JOSEPH H.	2	0			
ROGERI, GIOVANNI BATTISTA	1	1	$68,427	$68,427	$68,427
			DM96,650	DM96,650	DM96,650
			£43,300	£43,300	£43,300
			¥6,106,902	¥6,106,902	¥6,106,902
ROGERI, PIETRO GIACOMO	1	1	$132,158	$132,158	$132,158
			DM229,126	DM229,126	DM229,126
			£78,200	£78,200	£78,200
			¥16,500,200	¥16,500,200	¥16,500,200
ROMBOUTS, PIETER	2	0			
ROMBOUTS, PIETER (attributed to)	2	1	$9,058	$9,058	$9,058
			DM12,793	DM12,793	DM12,793
			£5,750	£5,750	£5,750
			¥912,140	¥912,140	¥912,140
ROMER, ADOLF	2	0			
ROOT-DUERER	1	1	$316	$316	$316
			DM563	DM563	DM563
			£193	£193	£193
			¥43,933	¥43,933	¥43,933
ROPE, A.J.	2	1	$1,317	$1,317	$1,317
			DM1,869	DM1,869	DM1,869
			£828	£828	£828
			¥122,254	¥122,254	¥122,254
ROPES, WALTER S.	1	1	$1,265	$1,265	$1,265
			DM1,934	DM1,934	DM1,934
			£832	£832	£832
			¥133,331	¥133,331	¥133,331
ROSADONI, GIOVANNI	1	1	$5,005	$5,005	$5,005
			DM9,260	DM9,260	DM9,260
			£2,990	£2,990	£2,990
			¥667,039	¥667,039	¥667,039
ROSCHER, CHRISTIAN HEINRICH WILHELM	1	1	$3,220	$3,220	$3,220
			DM5,732	DM5,732	DM5,732
			£1,932	£1,932	£1,932
			¥428,196	¥428,196	¥428,196
ROSSI, DOMENICO	3	0			
ROSSI, GIUSEPPE	4	2	$6,168	$6,182	$6,175
			DM9,104	DM11,117	DM10,111
			£3,680	£4,025	£3,853
			¥655,677	¥714,766	¥685,221
ROTH	1	0			
ROTH (attributed to)	1	1	$3,671	$3,671	$3,671
			DM6,118	DM6,118	DM6,118
			£2,185	£2,185	£2,185
			¥438,726	¥438,726	¥438,726

Maker	Items		Selling Prices		
	Bid	Sold	Low	High	Avg
ROTH, ERNST HEINRICH	28	22	$546	$6,388	$2,613
			DM822	DM11,982	DM4,421
			£332	£3,968	£1,605
			¥61,060	¥767,791	¥298,659
ROTH, ERNST HEINRICH (workshop of)	13	12	$460	$2,530	$1,246
			DM819	DM3,658	DM1,913
			£276	£1,653	£791
			¥60,693	¥256,163	¥127,478
ROTH, ERNST HEINRICH (II)	1	1	$2,213	$2,213	$2,213
			DM3,081	DM3,081	DM3,081
			£1,380	£1,380	£1,380
			¥187,056	¥187,056	¥187,056
ROTH & LEDERER	3	1	$518	$518	$518
			DM875	DM875	DM875
			£311	£311	£311
			¥63,135	¥63,135	¥63,135
ROUMEN, JOHANNES ARNOLDUS	1	0			
ROUMEN, L.W. (attributed to)	1	1	$4,285	$4,285	$4,285
			DM8,139	DM8,139	DM8,139
			£2,645	£2,645	£2,645
			¥450,205	¥450,205	¥450,205
ROVATTI, LUIGI	1	1	$5,216	$5,216	$5,216
			DM9,821	DM9,821	DM9,821
			£3,220	£3,220	£3,220
			¥551,328	¥551,328	¥551,328
ROVESCALLI, A.	3	1	$5,589	$5,589	$5,589
			DM10,523	DM10,523	DM10,523
			£3,450	£3,450	£3,450
			¥590,709	¥590,709	¥590,709
ROVESCALLI, MANLIO	1	0			
ROWINSKI, STANISLAV	2	0			
RUBUS, RIGART	2	2	$115	$288	$197
			DM205	DM440	DM337
			£70	£184	£127
			¥15,976	¥32,117	¥25,263
RUDDIMAN, JOSEPH	1	0			
RUFFE, CARL	1	1	$4,287	$4,287	$4,287
			DM4,516	DM4,516	DM4,516
			£2,645	£2,645	£2,645
			¥327,438	¥327,438	¥327,438
RUGGIERI, FRANCESCO	7	2	$111,356	$151,302	$131,329
			DM188,394	DM252,774	DM220,584
			£70,035	£90,600	£80,318
			¥13,796,895	¥18,390,894	¥16,093,895
RUGGIERI, FRANCESCO (ascribed to)	1	0			
RUGGIERI, FRANCESCO (attributed to)	1	0			
RUSHWORTH & DREAPER	6	5	$495	$2,608	$1,516
			DM731	DM4,685	DM2,604
			£322	£1,610	£938
			¥52,722	¥307,945	¥179,446
RUTH, BENJAMIN WARREN	1	1	$2,415	$2,415	$2,415
			DM4,132	DM4,132	DM4,132
			£1,428	£1,428	£1,428
			¥299,895	¥299,895	¥299,895

| Maker | Items | | Selling Prices | | |
---	Bid	Sold	Low	High	Avg
RUZIEKA, JOSEPHUS	1	1	$3,285	$3,285	$3,285
			DM6,142	DM6,142	DM6,142
			£2,070	£2,070	£2,070
			¥388,767	¥388,767	¥388,767
RUZIEKA, JOSEPHUS (attributed to)	1	1	$2,357	$2,357	$2,357
			DM4,476	DM4,476	DM4,476
			£1,455	£1,455	£1,455
			¥247,613	¥247,613	¥247,613
SACCANI, BENIGNO	1	1	$2,698	$2,698	$2,698
			DM3,816	DM3,816	DM3,816
			£1,725	£1,725	£1,725
			¥273,946	¥273,946	¥273,946
SACCANI, BENIGNO (workshop of)	1	1	$1,840	$1,840	$1,840
			DM3,180	DM3,180	DM3,180
			£1,137	£1,137	£1,137
			¥233,192	¥233,192	¥233,192
SACCONI, SIMONE FERNANDO	1	0			
SALOMON	2	2	$1,643	$6,388	$4,015
			DM2,458	DM11,982	DM7,220
			£978	£3,968	£2,473
			¥183,262	¥767,791	¥475,526
SALOMON, J.B.	2	2	$3,478	$7,728	$5,603
			DM5,796	DM12,880	DM9,338
			£2,070	£4,600	£3,335
			¥415,635	¥923,634	¥669,635
SALOMON, JEAN BAPTISTE DESHAYES	2	0			
SALSEDO, LUIGI	1	1	$2,743	$2,743	$2,743
			DM5,158	DM5,158	DM5,158
			£1,725	£1,725	£1,725
			¥331,614	¥331,614	¥331,614
SALVADORI, GIUSEPPE	1	0			
SALZARD, FRANCOIS	1	1	$863	$863	$863
			DM1,247	DM1,247	DM1,247
			£563	£563	£563
			¥87,328	¥87,328	¥87,328
SANNINO, V.	1	0			
SANNINO, VINCENZO	14	8	$7,621	$63,342	$32,501
			DM10,733	DM119,255	DM56,871
			£4,830	£39,100	£20,004
			¥779,234	¥8,237,033	¥3,828,398
SANNINO, VINCENZO (ascribed to)	1	1	$7,498	$7,498	$7,498
			DM12,972	DM12,972	DM12,972
			£4,600	£4,600	£4,600
			¥855,600	¥855,600	¥855,600
SANNINO, VINCENZO (attributed to)	3	1	$5,123	$5,123	$5,123
			DM7,731	DM7,731	DM7,731
			£3,105	£3,105	£3,105
			¥580,635	¥580,635	¥580,635
SANTAGIULIANA, GAETANO	1	0			
SANTAGIULIANA, GIACINTO	2	1	$14,517	$14,517	$14,517
			DM20,443	DM20,443	DM20,443
			£9,200	£9,200	£9,200
			¥1,484,254	¥1,484,254	¥1,484,254
SARACINI, ANTONIO (attributed to)	1	0			
SARFATI, GERARDO	1	0			

Maker	Items		Selling Prices		
	Bid	Sold	Low	High	Avg
SAUNDERS, S.	2	1	$544	$544	$544
			DM943	DM943	DM943
			£322	£322	£322
			¥69,188	¥69,188	¥69,188
SAUNIER	1	1	$748	$748	$748
			DM1,279	DM1,279	DM1,279
			£442	£442	£442
			¥92,825	¥92,825	¥92,825
SCARAMPELLA, GIUSEPPE	1	1	$48,438	$48,438	$48,438
			DM87,009	DM87,009	DM87,009
			£29,900	£29,900	£29,900
			¥5,718,973	¥5,718,973	¥5,718,973
SCARAMPELLA, STEFANO	9	6	$13,973	$53,903	$32,769
			DM26,479	DM99,723	DM58,111
			£8,625	£32,200	£20,360
			¥1,475,479	¥7,183,498	¥3,891,720
SCARAMPELLA, STEFANO (ascribed to)	2	2	$9,200	$10,904	$10,052
			DM15,401	DM16,376	DM15,889
			£5,520	£6,900	£6,210
			¥973,155	¥1,223,416	¥1,098,286
SCARAMPELLA, STEFANO (attributed to)	5	3	$4,713	$14,404	$10,634
			DM8,953	DM25,789	DM17,572
			£2,910	£8,625	£6,528
			¥495,226	¥1,981,853	¥1,204,507
SCARTABELLI, MAURO	2	2	$1,034	$1,357	$1,195
			DM1,751	DM2,404	DM2,077
			£633	£833	£733
			¥119,856	¥165,445	¥142,650
SCHAUPP, PAUL E.	3	2	$345	$374	$359
			DM528	DM572	DM550
			£227	£246	£236
			¥36,363	¥39,393	¥37,878
SCHAUPP, PAUL & CHARLES	1	0			
SCHETELIG, ERNST	2	0			
SCHEVERLE, JOANNES	1	1	$920	$920	$920
			DM1,574	DM1,574	DM1,574
			£544	£544	£544
			¥114,246	¥114,246	¥114,246
SCHILBACH, OSWALD A.	1	1	$920	$920	$920
			DM1,574	DM1,574	DM1,574
			£544	£544	£544
			¥114,246	¥114,246	¥114,246
SCHLEGEL, KLAUS	1	1	$1,687	$1,687	$1,687
			DM2,919	DM2,919	DM2,919
			£1,035	£1,035	£1,035
			¥192,510	¥192,510	¥192,510
SCHLEMMER, JOCHEN	1	1	$540	$540	$540
			DM827	DM827	DM827
			£345	£345	£345
			¥60,209	¥60,209	¥60,209
SCHLOSSER, HERMANN	3	3	$615	$1,262	$1,019
			DM1,027	DM2,189	DM1,628
			£368	£747	£621
			¥74,700	¥157,617	¥112,557
SCHMIDT, E.R. & CO.	7	4	$244	$368	$303
			DM389	DM514	DM444
			£150	£230	£190
			¥25,470	¥31,099	¥28,163

| Maker | Items | | Selling Prices | | |
	Bid	Sold	Low	High	Avg
SCHMIDT, ERNST REINHOLD	2	2	$2,070	$2,070	$2,070
			DM3,685	DM3,685	DM3,685
			£1,242	£1,242	£1,242
			¥275,269	¥275,269	¥275,269
SCHMIDT, ERNST REINHOLD (workshop of)	3	2	$518	$1,093	$805
			DM747	DM1,671	DM1,209
			£330	£719	£524
			¥44,893	¥115,150	¥80,021
SCHMIDT, REINHOLD	1	1	$1,150	$1,150	$1,150
			DM2,047	DM2,047	DM2,047
			£690	£690	£690
			¥152,927	¥152,927	¥152,927
SCHMIDT, REINHOLD (workshop of)	2	1	$546	$546	$546
			DM790	DM790	DM790
			£357	£357	£357
			¥55,308	¥55,308	¥55,308
SCHMITT, LUCIEN	2	1	$4,658	$4,658	$4,658
			DM8,769	DM8,769	DM8,769
			£2,875	£2,875	£2,875
			¥492,258	¥492,258	¥492,258
SCHOLL, H. (attributed to)	1	1	$366	$366	$366
			DM656	DM656	DM656
			£219	£219	£219
			¥42,498	¥42,498	¥42,498
SCHONFELDER, ADOLF (workshop of)	1	1	$431	$431	$431
			DM623	DM623	DM623
			£275	£275	£275
			¥37,411	¥37,411	¥37,411
SCHONFELDER, HERBERT EMIL	1	1	$978	$978	$978
			DM1,495	DM1,495	DM1,495
			£643	£643	£643
			¥103,029	¥103,029	¥103,029
SCHONFELDER, JOHANN GEORG	2	1	$1,058	$1,058	$1,058
			DM1,997	DM1,997	DM1,997
			£655	£655	£655
			¥111,936	¥111,936	¥111,936
SCHONFELDER, JOHANN GEORG (II)	1	1	$3,172	$3,172	$3,172
			DM4,682	DM4,682	DM4,682
			£2,070	£2,070	£2,070
			¥337,205	¥337,205	¥337,205
SCHROETTER, A.	3	2	$92	$316	$204
			DM164	DM476	DM320
			£56	£192	£124
			¥12,781	¥35,350	¥24,066
SCHULTZ, HENRY Y.	1	1	$2,185	$2,185	$2,185
			DM3,777	DM3,777	DM3,777
			£1,350	£1,350	£1,350
			¥276,916	¥276,916	¥276,916
SCHUSTER, EDOUARD	4	1	$1,926	$1,926	$1,926
			DM3,451	DM3,451	DM3,451
			£1,150	£1,150	£1,150
			¥223,675	¥223,675	¥223,675
SCHUSTER, HANS (workshop of)	1	1	$489	$489	$489
			DM706	DM706	DM706
			£311	£311	£311
			¥42,399	¥42,399	¥42,399

Maker	Items		Selling Prices		
	Bid	*Sold*	*Low*	*High*	*Avg*
SCHUSTER, MAX K.	2	2	$1,380	$3,850	$2,615
			DM2,456	DM7,123	DM4,790
			£828	£2,300	£1,564
			¥183,512	¥513,107	¥348,310
SCHUSTER BROS. (workshop of)	1	1	$1,495	$1,495	$1,495
			DM2,286	DM2,286	DM2,286
			£984	£984	£984
			¥157,573	¥157,573	¥157,573
SCHUSTER & CO.	2	2	$360	$662	$511
			DM550	DM926	DM738
			£230	£414	£322
			¥40,147	¥55,978	¥48,062
SCHUSTER & CO. (workshop of)	1	1	$546	$546	$546
			DM822	DM822	DM822
			£332	£332	£332
			¥61,060	¥61,060	¥61,060
SCHWAICHER, LEOPOLD	2	1	$2,899	$2,899	$2,899
			DM4,094	DM4,094	DM4,094
			£1,840	£1,840	£1,840
			¥291,885	¥291,885	¥291,885
SCHWAICHER, LEOPOLD (attributed to)	1	1	$1,118	$1,118	$1,118
			DM2,105	DM2,105	DM2,105
			£690	£690	£690
			¥119,163	¥119,163	¥119,163
SCHWARTZ, ANTON	2	1	$1,265	$1,265	$1,265
			DM1,934	DM1,934	DM1,934
			£832	£832	£832
			¥133,331	¥133,331	¥133,331
SCHWARZ, HEINRICH	1	1	$783	$783	$783
			DM1,371	DM1,371	DM1,371
			£483	£483	£483
			¥94,644	¥94,644	¥94,644
SCHWEITZER, JOHANN BAPTISTE	1	1	$15,968	$15,968	$15,968
			DM22,488	DM22,488	DM22,488
			£10,120	£10,120	£10,120
			¥1,632,680	¥1,632,680	¥1,632,680
SCHWEITZER, JOHANN BAPTISTE (attributed to)	1	1	$794	$794	$794
			DM1,460	DM1,460	DM1,460
			£494	£494	£494
			¥93,593	¥93,593	¥93,593
SCIALE, GIUSEPPE	1	1	$23,046	$23,046	$23,046
			DM38,502	DM38,502	DM38,502
			£13,800	£13,800	£13,800
			¥2,801,262	¥2,801,262	¥2,801,262
SCOGGINS, MICHAEL GENE	1	1	$2,415	$2,415	$2,415
			DM4,081	DM4,081	DM4,081
			£1,449	£1,449	£1,449
			¥294,630	¥294,630	¥294,630
SCOLARI, GIORGIO	2	2	$7,305	$7,311	$7,308
			DM10,271	DM12,648	DM11,459
			£4,485	£4,600	£4,543
			¥649,396	¥834,210	¥741,803
SDERCI, IGINO	5	2	$10,350	$13,444	$11,897
			DM14,966	DM22,460	DM18,713
			£6,761	£8,050	£7,405
			¥1,047,938	¥1,634,070	¥1,341,004

Maker	Items Bid	Items Sold	Selling Prices Low	Selling Prices High	Selling Prices Avg
SDERCI, LUCIANO	2	2	$10,592	$11,551	$11,071
			DM16,253	DM21,369	DM18,811
			£6,900	£6,900	£6,900
			¥1,159,269	¥1,539,321	¥1,349,295
SEAVER, GEORGE	1	1	$546	$546	$546
			DM790	DM790	DM790
			£357	£357	£357
			¥55,308	¥55,308	¥55,308
SEBASTIEN, JEAN	1	0			
SEIFERT	1	0			
SEIFERT, GEORGE	1	1	$1,853	$1,853	$1,853
			DM3,123	DM3,123	DM3,123
			£1,150	£1,150	£1,150
			¥227,543	¥227,543	¥227,543
SEIFERT, OTTO	4	2	$4,943	$5,089	$5,016
			DM7,187	DM7,585	DM7,386
			£3,220	£3,220	£3,220
			¥454,139	¥540,992	¥497,566
SEITZ, ANTON	2	1	$2,115	$2,115	$2,115
			DM3,121	DM3,121	DM3,121
			£1,380	£1,380	£1,380
			¥224,803	¥224,803	¥224,803
SEITZ, NICOLAS	1	1	$1,282	$1,282	$1,282
			DM2,333	DM2,333	DM2,333
			£782	£782	£782
			¥161,983	¥161,983	¥161,983
SERAPHIN, SANTO	6	3	$53,748	$135,999	$102,669
			DM75,372	DM257,727	DM181,843
			£34,500	£83,950	£63,817
			¥5,430,404	¥14,361,327	¥11,251,480
SERDET, PAUL	3	0			
SGARABOTTO, GAETANO	10	6	$26,450	$49,789	$34,793
			DM43,250	DM69,325	DM56,023
			£15,870	£31,050	£21,524
			¥3,104,716	¥4,882,164	¥3,898,267
SGARABOTTO, GAETANO (attributed to)	5	4	$5,796	$12,834	$9,624
			DM9,660	DM20,700	DM16,405
			£3,450	£7,452	£5,767
			¥692,726	¥1,511,100	¥1,145,495
SGARABOTTO, PIETRO	3	2	$13,840	$18,463	$16,151
			DM19,266	DM32,010	DM25,638
			£8,625	£10,925	£9,775
			¥1,167,618	¥2,305,175	¥1,736,397
SGARBI, ANTONIO	2	2	$3,795	$15,462	$9,629
			DM6,831	DM23,135	DM14,983
			£2,300	£9,200	£5,750
			¥547,285	¥1,724,816	¥1,136,051
SGARBI, ANTONIO (attributed to)	4	2	$3,177	$4,146	$3,661
			DM5,539	DM7,346	DM6,443
			£1,955	£2,546	£2,250
			¥384,842	¥505,526	¥445,184
SHAPIRO, OSCAR	1	0			
SHARLET, STACY	2	1	$920	$920	$920
			DM1,407	DM1,407	DM1,407
			£605	£605	£605
			¥96,968	¥96,968	¥96,968

Maker	Items		Selling Prices		
	Bid	Sold	Low	High	Avg
SHEARER, THOMAS	1	1	$661	$661	$661
			DM1,248	DM1,248	DM1,248
			£409	£409	£409
			¥69,960	¥69,960	¥69,960
SHELMERDINE, ANTHONY (attributed to)	1	1	$732	$732	$732
			DM1,311	DM1,311	DM1,311
			£437	£437	£437
			¥84,997	¥84,997	¥84,997
SHIPMAN, MARGARET	1	1	$2,300	$2,300	$2,300
			DM3,887	DM3,887	DM3,887
			£1,380	£1,380	£1,380
			¥306,061	¥306,061	¥306,061
SIEGA, ETTORE & SON	2	2	$7,825	$8,998	$8,411
			DM14,828	DM17,052	DM15,940
			£4,830	£5,555	£5,192
			¥826,268	¥950,208	¥888,238
SIEGA, IGINIO	2	1	$10,654	$10,654	$10,654
			DM17,914	DM17,914	DM17,914
			£6,670	£6,670	£6,670
			¥1,307,740	¥1,307,740	¥1,307,740
SIGNORINI, SERAFINO (attributed to)	1	0			
SILVESTRE, HIPPOLYTE	3	3	$9,087	$15,364	$13,020
			DM12,835	DM25,668	DM19,681
			£5,750	£9,200	£8,050
			¥810,963	¥1,867,508	¥1,325,754
SILVESTRE, HIPPOLYTE CHRETIEN	10	5	$6,361	$16,304	$13,496
			DM9,398	DM28,299	DM21,003
			£4,140	£10,350	£8,349
			¥677,859	¥1,834,135	¥1,432,231
SILVESTRE, HIPPOLYTE CHRETIEN (attributed to)	1	1	$6,613	$6,613	$6,613
			DM11,770	DM11,770	DM11,770
			£3,968	£3,968	£3,968
			¥879,330	¥879,330	¥879,330
SILVESTRE, PIERRE	5	3	$9,775	$26,503	$19,469
			DM17,595	DM39,158	DM29,188
			£5,865	£17,250	£12,305
			¥75,952	¥2,824,412	¥1,590,309
SILVESTRE, PIERRE (attributed to)	1	1	$26,450	$26,450	$26,450
			DM49,924	DM49,924	DM49,924
			£16,373	£16,373	£16,373
			¥2,798,410	¥2,798,410	¥2,798,410
SILVESTRE, PIERRE & HIPPOLYTE	7	4	$7,825	$28,513	$20,614
			DM14,828	DM45,732	DM33,250
			£4,830	£18,515	£12,880
			¥826,268	¥3,244,198	¥2,148,837
SILVESTRE & MAUCOTEL	4	2	$5,589	$6,613	$6,101
			DM10,523	DM11,119	DM10,821
			£3,450	£4,140	£3,795
			¥590,709	¥811,701	¥701,205
SIMEONI, GIANNANDREA (attributed to)	1	1	$4,240	$4,240	$4,240
			DM6,265	DM6,265	DM6,265
			£2,760	£2,760	£2,760
			¥451,906	¥451,906	¥451,906
SIMON, PIERRE	1	1	$8,570	$8,570	$8,570
			DM16,240	DM16,240	DM16,240
			£5,290	£5,290	£5,290
			¥904,960	¥904,960	¥904,960

Maker	Items		Selling Prices		
	Bid	Sold	Low	High	Avg
SIMONAZZI, AMADEO	5	3	$6,154	$18,400	$11,898
			DM10,281	DM26,606	DM19,349
			£3,685	£12,019	£7,527
			¥748,018	¥1,863,000	¥1,260,517
SIMONIN, CHARLES	2	2	$3,167	$7,305	$5,236
			DM5,689	DM10,271	DM7,980
			£1,955	£4,600	£3,278
			¥373,933	¥649,396	¥511,664
SIMONIN, CHARLES (attributed to)	6	1	$1,232	$1,232	$1,232
			DM1,740	DM1,740	DM1,740
			£782	£782	£782
			¥124,051	¥124,051	¥124,051
SIMOUTRE, NICHOLAS EUGENE	1	0			
SIMOUTRE, NICOLAS	2	2	$2,178	$3,693	$2,935
			DM3,066	DM6,402	DM4,734
			£1,380	£2,185	£1,783
			¥222,638	¥461,035	¥341,837
SIMPSON	1	1	$692	$692	$692
			DM989	DM989	DM989
			£437	£437	£437
			¥69,477	¥69,477	¥69,477
SIMPSON, JAMES & JOHN	2	2	$1,676	$2,588	$2,132
			DM2,576	DM4,373	DM3,474
			£1,093	£1,553	£1,323
			¥183,528	¥344,319	¥263,923
SIMS, BARRY	2	1	$692	$692	$692
			DM1,072	DM1,072	DM1,072
			£414	£414	£414
			¥78,788	¥78,788	¥78,788
SIRONI, AMBROGIO	2	2	$3,392	$12,061	$7,727
			DM6,011	DM21,372	DM13,691
			£2,083	£7,406	£4,744
			¥413,612	¥1,470,620	¥942,116
SIVORI	1	1	$1,014	$1,014	$1,014
			DM1,412	DM1,412	DM1,412
			£633	£633	£633
			¥85,734	¥85,734	¥85,734
SMALLEY, G.B.	1	1	$713	$713	$713
			DM1,272	DM1,272	DM1,272
			£437	£437	£437
			¥93,356	¥93,356	¥93,356
SMILLIE, ALEXANDER	3	3	$1,247	$4,993	$3,429
			DM2,084	DM8,342	DM5,546
			£747	£2,990	£2,127
			¥151,634	¥606,940	¥400,041
SMILLIE, ANDREW Y.	2	2	$1,461	$2,889	$2,175
			DM2,054	DM4,083	DM3,069
			£920	£1,840	£1,380
			¥130,392	¥246,709	¥188,550
SMITH, ARTHUR E.	2	2	$9,633	$12,721	$11,177
			DM14,477	DM18,796	DM16,636
			£5,750	£8,280	£7,015
			¥1,072,726	¥1,355,718	¥1,214,222
SMITH, BERT	3	2	$1,598	$2,236	$1,917
			DM2,640	DM4,016	DM3,328
			£978	£1,380	£1,179
			¥197,874	¥263,953	¥230,914

| Maker | Items | | Selling Prices | | |
	Bid	Sold	Low	High	Avg
SMITH, J.P.	2	1	$1,174	$1,174	$1,174
			DM1,659	DM1,659	DM1,659
			£748	£748	£748
			¥100,226	¥100,226	¥100,226
SMITH, JOHN	6	4	$1,134	$3,524	$1,961
			DM1,848	DM5,202	DM3,111
			£667	£2,300	£1,216
			¥133,453	¥374,672	¥223,288
SMITH, JOHN (attributed to)	1	1	$919	$919	$919
			DM1,357	DM1,357	DM1,357
			£598	£598	£598
			¥97,913	¥97,913	¥97,913
SMITH, THOMAS	2	2	$201	$2,119	$1,160
			DM340	DM3,796	DM2,068
			£121	£1,265	£693
			¥24,553	¥246,043	¥135,298
SMITH, THOMAS (attributed to)	4	3	$1,863	$3,936	$2,643
			DM3,508	DM6,883	DM4,795
			£1,150	£2,415	£1,629
			¥198,605	¥465,008	¥306,514
SMITH, WILLIAM (attributed to)	1	1	$2,889	$2,889	$2,889
			DM5,177	DM5,177	DM5,177
			£1,725	£1,725	£1,725
			¥335,513	¥335,513	¥335,513
SNEIDER, JOSEPH	1	0			
SNEIDER, JOSEPH (attributed to)	1	1	$16,100	$16,100	$16,100
			DM27,209	DM27,209	DM27,209
			£9,660	£9,660	£9,660
			¥2,142,427	¥2,142,427	¥2,142,427
SOFFRITTI, ALOYSIO LUIGI	1	0			
SOFFRITTI, ALOYSIO LUIGI (attributed to)	1	0			
SOFFRITTI, ETTORE	2	0			
SOFFRITTI, LUIGI	2	0			
SOFFRITTI, LUIGI (ascribed to)	1	1	$5,796	$5,796	$5,796
			DM10,419	DM10,419	DM10,419
			£3,450	£3,450	£3,450
			¥670,094	¥670,094	¥670,094
SOLFERINO, REMO	1	0			
SOLIANI, ANGELO	2	0			
SOLIANI, ANGELO (attributed to)	1	0			
SOLLNER, FRANZ JOSEF	3	1	$932	$932	$932
			DM982	DM982	DM982
			£575	£575	£575
			¥71,182	¥71,182	¥71,182
SORIOT & DIDION	1	1	$4,637	$4,637	$4,637
			DM8,338	DM8,338	DM8,338
			£2,760	£2,760	£2,760
			¥536,075	¥536,075	¥536,075
SORSANO, SPIRITO	1	1	$53,774	$53,774	$53,774
			DM96,278	DM96,278	DM96,278
			£32,200	£32,200	£32,200
			¥7,398,916	¥7,398,916	¥7,398,916
SORSANO, SPIRITO (attributed to)	1	1	$3,092	$3,092	$3,092
			DM4,627	DM4,627	DM4,627
			£1,840	£1,840	£1,840
			¥344,963	¥344,963	¥344,963

| Maker | Items | | Selling Prices | | |
	Bid	Sold	Low	High	Avg
SPATAFFI, GUERRIERO	1	0			
SPIDLEN, FRANTISEK F.	4	1	$10,573	$10,573	$10,573
			DM15,607	DM15,607	DM15,607
			£6,900	£6,900	£6,900
			¥1,124,017	¥1,124,017	¥1,124,017
SPIDLEN, OTAKAR FRANTISEK	5	3	$3,850	$6,948	$5,127
			DM6,763	DM13,066	DM8,984
			£2,300	£4,370	£3,220
			¥487,074	¥840,089	¥613,423
SPIDLEN, OTAKAR FRANTISEK (attributed to)	2	1	$8,333	$8,333	$8,333
			DM11,769	DM11,769	DM11,769
			£5,290	£5,290	£5,290
			¥839,169	¥839,169	¥839,169
SPIDLEN, PREMYSL OTAKAR	4	2	$5,479	$8,247	$6,863
			DM7,703	DM11,558	DM9,631
			£3,450	£5,175	£4,313
			¥488,968	¥727,010	¥607,989
SQUIER, JEROME BONAPARTE	3	3	$1,150	$3,795	$2,223
			DM1,663	DM5,803	DM3,319
			£751	£2,497	£1,449
			¥116,438	¥399,993	¥222,025
SQUIER, VICTOR CARROLL	2	1	$978	$978	$978
			DM1,690	DM1,690	DM1,690
			£604	£604	£604
			¥123,883	¥123,883	¥123,883
SQUIRE, V.C.	1	1	$374	$374	$374
			DM665	DM665	DM665
			£224	£224	£224
			¥49,701	¥49,701	¥49,701
STADLMANN, JOHANN JOSEPH	3	3	$1,093	$6,454	$3,758
			DM1,580	DM8,987	DM5,753
			£714	£4,025	£2,346
			¥110,616	¥545,581	¥365,372
STADLMANN, JOHANN JOSEPH (attributed to)	2	0			
STADLMANN, MICHAEL IGNAZ	1	1	$5,216	$5,216	$5,216
			DM9,370	DM9,370	DM9,370
			£3,220	£3,220	£3,220
			¥615,889	¥615,889	¥615,889
STAINER, JACOB	2	1	$57,615	$57,615	$57,615
			DM96,255	DM96,255	DM96,255
			£34,500	£34,500	£34,500
			¥7,003,155	¥7,003,155	¥7,003,155
STAINER, JACOB (attributed to)	2	2	$2,698	$7,194	$4,946
			DM3,816	DM10,177	DM6,996
			£1,725	£4,600	£3,163
			¥273,946	¥730,521	¥502,233
STANLEY, C.F.	2	2	$1,265	$1,840	$1,553
			DM1,829	DM3,275	DM2,552
			£826	£1,104	£965
			¥128,081	¥244,683	¥186,382
STANLEY, FREELAN OSCAR	1	1	$1,610	$1,610	$1,610
			DM2,328	DM2,328	DM2,328
			£1,052	£1,052	£1,052
			¥163,013	¥163,013	¥163,013

Maker	Items		Selling Prices		
	Bid	Sold	Low	High	Avg
STEFANINI, GIUSEPPE	4	4	$4,255	$10,106	$7,433
			DM7,355	DM17,521	DM12,733
			£2,629	£5,980	£4,464
			¥539,257	¥1,261,780	¥925,289
STEPHANINI	2	0			
STIEBER, ERNST	1	1	$2,812	$2,812	$2,812
			DM4,985	DM4,985	DM4,985
			£1,725	£1,725	£1,725
			¥332,459	¥332,459	¥332,459
STIRRAT, DAVID	3	1	$8,710	$8,710	$8,710
			DM12,266	DM12,266	DM12,266
			£5,520	£5,520	£5,520
			¥890,553	¥890,553	¥890,553
STONEMAN, HENRY (attributed to)	1	1	$989	$989	$989
			DM1,462	DM1,462	DM1,462
			£644	£644	£644
			¥105,445	¥105,445	¥105,445
STORIONI, CARLO	9	7	$668	$2,332	$1,654
			DM1,026	DM4,043	DM2,564
			£437	£1,380	£1,019
			¥72,951	¥291,180	¥186,005
STORIONI, LORENZO	2	1	$70,146	$70,146	$70,146
			DM126,003	DM126,003	DM126,003
			£43,300	£43,300	£43,300
			¥8,281,991	¥8,281,991	¥8,281,991
STOSS, IGNAZ GEORG	1	1	$1,348	$1,348	$1,348
			DM2,493	DM2,493	DM2,493
			£805	£805	£805
			¥179,587	¥179,587	¥179,587
STOTT, GEORGE T. (attributed to)	1	1	$684	$684	$684
			DM1,047	DM1,047	DM1,047
			£437	£437	£437
			¥76,265	¥76,265	¥76,265
STRAATEMEIER, BARTOLOME	1	1	$867	$867	$867
			DM1,225	DM1,225	DM1,225
			£552	£552	£552
			¥74,013	¥74,013	¥74,013
STRADIVARI, ANTONIO	10	6	$219,328	$1,582,325	$687,584
			DM308,872	DM2,937,250	DM1,131,349
			£139,000	£947,500	£420,867
			¥22,425,148	¥211,709,400	¥78,803,202
STRADIVARI, FRANCESCO	1	0			
STRADIVARI, OMOBONO	1	0			
STRAINER, J.	1	1	$348	$348	$348
			DM534	DM534	DM534
			£230	£230	£230
			¥37,082	¥37,082	¥37,082
STRAUB, JOSEPH	1	1	$5,377	$5,377	$5,377
			DM8,984	DM8,984	DM8,984
			£3,220	£3,220	£3,220
			¥653,628	¥653,628	¥653,628
STRELLINI	1	1	$3,354	$3,354	$3,354
			DM5,147	DM5,147	DM5,147
			£2,185	£2,185	£2,185
			¥367,102	¥367,102	¥367,102

| Maker | Items | | Selling Prices | | |
	Bid	Sold	Low	High	Avg
STRIEBIG, JEAN	1	1	$4,592	$4,592	$4,592
			DM7,722	DM7,722	DM7,722
			£2,875	£2,875	£2,875
			¥563,681	¥563,681	¥563,681
STRINKOVSKY, LEV	1	0			
STRNAD, CASPAR	1	1	$11,523	$11,523	$11,523
			DM19,251	DM19,251	DM19,251
			£6,900	£6,900	£6,900
			¥1,400,631	¥1,400,631	¥1,400,631
STROBL, MICHAEL	1	0			
STUMPEL, H.C.	1	1	$403	$403	$403
			DM716	DM716	DM716
			£242	£242	£242
			¥53,524	¥53,524	¥53,524
SUCHY, FRANZ	1	1	$1,043	$1,043	$1,043
			DM1,876	DM1,876	DM1,876
			£621	£621	£621
			¥120,617	¥120,617	¥120,617
SUZUKI	1	1	$104	$104	$104
			DM189	DM189	DM189
			£63	£63	£63
			¥13,102	¥13,102	¥13,102
SZEPESSY, BELA	9	5	$3,110	$8,050	$5,328
			DM5,391	DM14,571	DM8,593
			£1,840	£4,911	£3,305
			¥388,240	¥971,957	¥604,451
TARANTINO, GIUSEPPE	1	1	$6,417	$6,417	$6,417
			DM10,350	DM10,350	DM10,350
			£3,726	£3,726	£3,726
			¥755,550	¥755,550	¥755,550
TARASCONI, G.	1	1	$19,435	$19,435	$19,435
			DM33,695	DM33,695	DM33,695
			£11,500	£11,500	£11,500
			¥2,426,500	¥2,426,500	¥2,426,500
TARR, THOMAS	2	1	$1,176	$1,176	$1,176
			DM2,089	DM2,089	DM2,089
			£713	£713	£713
			¥163,199	¥163,199	¥163,199
TARR, WILLIAM	3	1	$2,415	$2,415	$2,415
			DM3,635	DM3,635	DM3,635
			£1,466	£1,466	£1,466
			¥269,949	¥269,949	¥269,949
TARTAGLIA, FRANCESCO	1	0			
TASSINI, MARCO	3	3	$2,181	$4,276	$3,440
			DM3,080	DM7,413	DM5,813
			£1,380	£2,530	£2,070
			¥194,631	¥533,830	¥391,730
TATEM	1	1	$817	$817	$817
			DM1,158	DM1,158	DM1,158
			£518	£518	£518
			¥84,353	¥84,353	¥84,353
TATUM, D.J.	2	2	$695	$1,403	$1,049
			DM986	DM1,991	DM1,489
			£437	£900	£669
			¥64,523	¥142,699	¥103,611

Maker	Items		Selling Prices		
	Bid	Sold	Low	High	Avg
TAUSCHER, EDUARD	3	2	$500	$720	$610
			DM774	DM1,103	DM938
			£299	£460	£380
			¥56,903	¥80,279	¥68,591
TAYLOR, GULIELMUS (attributed to)	2	2	$267	$2,827	$1,547
			DM397	DM4,177	DM2,287
			£173	£1,840	£1,006
			¥28,942	¥301,271	¥165,106
TAYLOR, JOSEPH	1	1	$1,004	$1,004	$1,004
			DM1,412	DM1,412	DM1,412
			£633	£633	£633
			¥89,644	¥89,644	¥89,644
TAYLOR, N.S.	1	1	$1,380	$1,380	$1,380
			DM1,993	DM1,993	DM1,993
			£879	£879	£879
			¥119,715	¥119,715	¥119,715
TECCHLER, DAVID	6	3	$23,005	$30,309	$27,506
			DM42,614	DM50,963	DM48,080
			£13,800	£18,975	£16,675
			¥3,072,294	¥3,720,295	¥3,498,204
TELLER, ROMAN (workshop of)	1	1	$863	$863	$863
			DM1,319	DM1,319	DM1,319
			£567	£567	£567
			¥90,908	¥90,908	¥90,908
TENUCCI, EUGEN	1	1	$3,657	$3,657	$3,657
			DM6,877	DM6,877	DM6,877
			£2,300	£2,300	£2,300
			¥442,152	¥442,152	¥442,152
TERRANA, GERLANDO	1	0			
TERRY, JOHN	1	1	$2,645	$2,645	$2,645
			DM4,572	DM4,572	DM4,572
			£1,634	£1,634	£1,634
			¥335,214	¥335,214	¥335,214
TESTORE, CARLO ANTONIO	12	8	$30,728	$66,548	$49,622
			DM51,336	DM117,128	DM79,738
			£18,400	£42,550	£30,906
			¥3,735,016	¥7,698,618	¥5,443,139
TESTORE, CARLO ANTONIO (attributed to)	3	2	$14,950	$16,324	$15,637
			DM25,841	DM27,272	DM26,557
			£9,238	£9,775	£9,506
			¥1,894,688	¥1,984,227	¥1,939,458
TESTORE, CARLO GIUSEPPE	1	1	$72,345	$72,345	$72,345
			DM136,045	DM136,045	DM136,045
			£45,500	£45,500	£45,500
			¥8,746,920	¥8,746,920	¥8,746,920
TESTORE, CARLO GIUSEPPE (ascribed to)	1	0			
TESTORE, PAOLO ANTONIO	4	2	$6,784	$15,771	$11,278
			DM12,022	DM26,681	DM19,351
			£4,166	£9,919	£7,042
			¥827,224	¥1,953,994	¥1,390,609
TESTORE, PAOLO ANTONIO (attributed to)	1	0			
TESTORE FAMILY (MEMBER OF)	4	3	$11,523	$32,258	$22,656
			DM21,390	DM48,680	DM34,662
			£6,900	£19,550	£13,992
			¥1,541,736	¥3,655,850	¥2,547,089

Maker	Items		Selling Prices		
	Bid	Sold	Low	High	Avg
THIBOUT, JACQUES PIERRE	4	2	$12,633	$23,421	$18,027
			DM21,902	DM37,566	DM29,734
			£7,475	£15,209	£11,342
			¥1,577,225	¥2,664,877	¥2,121,051
THIBOUVILLE-LAMY, J.	148	119	$134	$8,834	$888
			DM242	DM13,053	DM1,420
			£80	£5,750	£554
			¥15,538	¥941,471	¥97,561
THIBOUVILLE-LAMY, J. (workshop of)	11	10	$288	$2,185	$871
			DM492	DM3,155	DM1,377
			£170	£1,392	£542
			¥35,702	¥189,549	¥94,135
THIBOUVILLE-LAMY, JEROME	1	0			
THIER (attributed to)	1	1	$1,445	$1,445	$1,445
			DM2,588	DM2,588	DM2,588
			£863	£863	£863
			¥167,756	¥167,756	¥167,756
THIER, JOSEPH	3	3	$1,745	$2,467	$1,997
			DM2,934	DM3,723	DM3,245
			£1,092	£1,495	£1,227
			¥203,112	¥279,565	¥232,292
THIR, ANTON	2	0			
THIR, JOHANN GEORG	3	2	$1,555	$3,353	$2,454
			DM2,696	DM6,314	DM4,505
			£920	£2,070	£1,495
			¥194,120	¥354,425	¥274,273
THIR, MATHIAS	5	4	$1,150	$4,934	$3,210
			DM1,663	DM8,880	DM5,413
			£751	£2,990	£1,970
			¥116,438	¥711,471	¥412,038
THOMASSIN	1	1	$8,349	$8,349	$8,349
			DM15,028	DM15,028	DM15,028
			£5,060	£5,060	£5,060
			¥1,204,027	¥1,204,027	¥1,204,027
THOMPSON, CHARLES & SAMUEL	27	19	$205	$3,450	$1,285
			DM236	DM5,275	DM2,015
			£127	£2,270	£810
			¥17,084	¥363,630	¥138,928
THOMPSON, E.A.	1	1	$288	$288	$288
			DM512	DM512	DM512
			£175	£175	£175
			¥39,940	¥39,940	¥39,940
THOMPSON & SON	1	1	$1,955	$1,955	$1,955
			DM3,379	DM3,379	DM3,379
			£1,208	£1,208	£1,208
			¥247,767	¥247,767	¥247,767
THOUVENEL	1	0			
THOUVENEL, CHARLES	1	1	$559	$559	$559
			DM1,052	DM1,052	DM1,052
			£345	£345	£345
			¥59,581	¥59,581	¥59,581
THOUVENEL, HENRY	1	1	$863	$863	$863
			DM1,319	DM1,319	DM1,319
			£567	£567	£567
			¥90,908	¥90,908	¥90,908

Maker	Items		Selling Prices		
	Bid	Sold	Low	High	Avg
THUMHARD, JOHANN STEPHAN	1	1	$1,391 DM2,137 £920 ¥148,327	$1,391 DM2,137 £920 ¥148,327	$1,391 DM2,137 £920 ¥148,327
TIEDEMANN, JAKOB	3	1	$1,682 DM2,932 £1,035 ¥203,740	$1,682 DM2,932 £1,035 ¥203,740	$1,682 DM2,932 £1,035 ¥203,740
TILLER, C.W.	1	1	$375 DM669 £230 ¥49,135	$375 DM669 £230 ¥49,135	$375 DM669 £230 ¥49,135
TILLER, C.W. (attributed to)	1	1	$450 DM814 £276 ¥54,286	$450 DM814 £276 ¥54,286	$450 DM814 £276 ¥54,286
TILLER, WILFRED	1	1	$656 DM1,167 £403 ¥88,119	$656 DM1,167 £403 ¥88,119	$656 DM1,167 £403 ¥88,119
TIMTONE	1	1	$1,150 DM2,082 £702 ¥138,851	$1,150 DM2,082 £702 ¥138,851	$1,150 DM2,082 £702 ¥138,851
TINSLEY, CHARLES	1	1	$250 DM450 £149 ¥28,940	$250 DM450 £149 ¥28,940	$250 DM450 £149 ¥28,940
TIPPER, J.W.	1	1	$1,191 DM1,968 £713 ¥139,249	$1,191 DM1,968 £713 ¥139,249	$1,191 DM1,968 £713 ¥139,249
TIVOLI, ARRIGO	1	1	$6,179 DM8,728 £3,910 ¥551,455	$6,179 DM8,728 £3,910 ¥551,455	$6,179 DM8,728 £3,910 ¥551,455
TOBIN, RICHARD	1	1	$13,414 DM24,095 £8,280 ¥1,583,716	$13,414 DM24,095 £8,280 ¥1,583,716	$13,414 DM24,095 £8,280 ¥1,583,716
TOBIN, RICHARD (ascribed to)	1	0			
TOMASHOV, DANIEL	1	0			
TONONI, CARLO	3	1	$51,198 DM96,278 £32,200 ¥6,190,128	$51,198 DM96,278 £32,200 ¥6,190,128	$51,198 DM96,278 £32,200 ¥6,190,128
TONONI, GIOVANNI	4	2	$43,550 DM61,330 £27,600 ¥4,452,763	$43,884 DM82,524 £27,600 ¥5,305,824	$43,717 DM71,927 £27,600 ¥4,879,294
TONONI, GIOVANNI (attributed to)	1	0			
TONONI, JOANNES (attributed to)	1	1	$9,200 DM16,652 £5,612 ¥1,110,808	$9,200 DM16,652 £5,612 ¥1,110,808	$9,200 DM16,652 £5,612 ¥1,110,808

Maker	Items		Selling Prices		
	Bid	Sold	Low	High	Avg
TONONI FAMILY (MEMBER OF)	1	1	$94,190	$94,190	$94,190
			DM131,118	DM131,118	DM131,118
			£58,700	£58,700	£58,700
			¥7,946,571	¥7,946,571	¥7,946,571
TOOMEY, T.	1	1	$559	$559	$559
			DM589	DM589	DM589
			£345	£345	£345
			¥42,709	¥42,709	¥42,709
TOSELLO, BENITO	1	0			
TOSELLO, BENITO (ascribed to)	2	0			
TOTH, JOANNES	1	1	$2,990	$2,990	$2,990
			DM4,500	DM4,500	DM4,500
			£1,815	£1,815	£1,815
			¥334,222	¥334,222	¥334,222
TRAPANI, RAFFAELE	1	1	$35,397	$35,397	$35,397
			DM63,365	DM63,365	DM63,365
			£21,850	£21,850	£21,850
			¥4,174,880	¥4,174,880	¥4,174,880
TRAPP, HERMANN	1	0			
TRAUTNER, HANS	1	1	$4,285	$4,285	$4,285
			DM8,067	DM8,067	DM8,067
			£2,645	£2,645	£2,645
			¥456,791	¥456,791	¥456,791
TROIANI, CARLO	2	1	$3,651	$3,651	$3,651
			DM5,610	DM5,610	DM5,610
			£2,415	£2,415	£2,415
			¥389,358	¥389,358	¥389,358
TURCSAK, TIBOR GABOR	2	2	$1,730	$2,785	$2,258
			DM2,775	DM5,278	DM4,027
			£1,124	£1,719	£1,421
			¥196,868	¥294,112	¥245,490
TURNER, WILLIAM	1	1	$3,237	$3,237	$3,237
			DM4,579	DM4,579	DM4,579
			£2,070	£2,070	£2,070
			¥328,735	¥328,735	¥328,735
TURRINI, GAETANO	1	0			
TURRINI, GAETANO (ascribed to)	1	0			
TWEEDALE, CHARLES L.	6	3	$805	$949	$896
			DM1,212	DM1,685	DM1,508
			£489	£575	£546
			¥89,983	¥131,612	¥111,594
TYSON, HERBERT W.	2	1	$1,378	$1,378	$1,378
			DM2,036	DM2,036	DM2,036
			£897	£897	£897
			¥146,869	¥146,869	¥146,869
UDALRICUS, JOHANNES (attributed to)	1	0			
ULCIGRAI, NICOLO	1	0			
ULLMANN, GIORGIO	1	1	$13,122	$13,122	$13,122
			DM22,701	DM22,701	DM22,701
			£8,050	£8,050	£8,050
			¥1,497,300	¥1,497,300	¥1,497,300
URBINO, RICHARD ALEXANDER	1	0			
URFF, WILLIAM	1	1	$431	$431	$431
			DM729	DM729	DM729
			£259	£259	£259
			¥52,613	¥52,613	¥52,613

| Maker | Items | | Selling Prices | | |
	Bid	Sold	Low	High	Avg
UTILI, NICOLO	1	0			
VACCARI, ALBERTO	2	1	$3,046	$3,046	$3,046
			DM4,271	DM4,271	DM4,271
			£1,955	£1,955	£1,955
			¥307,723	¥307,723	¥307,723
VACCARI, GIUSEPPE	2	2	$2,126	$2,513	$2,320
			DM3,709	DM4,383	DM4,046
			£1,265	£1,495	£1,380
			¥271,165	¥320,468	¥295,817
VACCARI, RAFFAELLO	8	4	$9,226	$11,272	$10,619
			DM12,844	DM19,543	DM15,800
			£5,750	£6,900	£6,555
			¥778,412	¥1,407,370	¥1,023,258
VALENTIN, GEORG	1	0			
VAN DER GEEST, JACOB JAN	4	1	$3,091	$3,091	$3,091
			DM5,152	DM5,152	DM5,152
			£1,840	£1,840	£1,840
			¥369,454	¥369,454	¥369,454
VAN HOOF, ALPHONS	3	3	$4,658	$6,930	$5,996
			DM8,366	DM12,822	DM11,074
			£2,875	£4,140	£3,680
			¥549,901	¥923,593	¥749,087
VATELOT, MARCEL	2	0			
VAUTELINT, N. PIERRE	1	0			
VAUTRIN, JOSEPH	5	3	$1,035	$2,795	$2,076
			DM1,789	DM5,261	DM3,463
			£640	£1,725	£1,287
			¥131,171	¥295,355	¥209,723
VAVRA, JAN BAPTISTA	1	0			
VAVRA, KAREL (I)	4	2	$2,185	$4,536	$3,361
			DM3,341	DM6,389	DM4,865
			£1,437	£2,875	£2,156
			¥230,299	¥463,830	¥347,064
VENTAPANE, LORENZO	7	3	$50,232	$51,198	$50,632
			DM85,381	DM96,278	DM90,652
			£29,900	£32,200	£31,280
			¥5,807,477	¥6,252,780	¥6,083,462
VENTAPANE, LORENZO (ascribed to)	1	0			
VENTAPANE, LORENZO (attributed to)	3	2	$8,118	$16,584	$12,351
			DM12,146	DM29,386	DM20,766
			£4,830	£10,183	£7,507
			¥905,528	¥2,022,103	¥1,463,815
VENTAPANE, PASQUALE	3	1	$4,033	$4,033	$4,033
			DM6,738	DM6,738	DM6,738
			£2,415	£2,415	£2,415
			¥490,221	¥490,221	¥490,221
VENTAPANE, PASQUALE (attributed to)	1	0			
VENTAPANE, VINCENZO	1	0			
VENTAPANE, VINCENZO (attributed to)	1	1	$18,400	$18,400	$18,400
			DM28,135	DM28,135	DM28,135
			£12,105	£12,105	£12,105
			¥1,939,360	¥1,939,360	¥1,939,360
VENTURINI, LUCIANO	2	0			

| Maker | Items | | Selling Prices | | |
	Bid	Sold	Low	High	Avg
VETTORI, CARLO	7	6	$3,457	$8,218	$5,628
			DM5,775	DM12,022	DM8,705
			£2,070	£5,175	£3,568
			¥420,189	¥827,224	¥600,569
VETTORI, DARIO	1	0			
VETTORI, PAULO	4	4	$3,565	$5,047	$4,237
			DM5,451	DM8,538	DM6,955
			£2,345	£3,174	£2,689
			¥375,751	¥625,278	¥499,685
VICKERS	2	0			
VICKERS, E.	2	1	$320	$320	$320
			DM541	DM541	DM541
			£196	£196	£196
			¥37,046	¥37,046	¥37,046
VICKERS, J.E.	3	1	$375	$375	$375
			DM656	DM656	DM656
			£230	£230	£230
			¥44,287	¥44,287	¥44,287
VIDOUDEZ, ALFRED	1	0			
VILLA, LUIGI	4	3	$1,824	$3,073	$2,616
			DM3,047	DM5,134	DM4,096
			£1,092	£1,840	£1,591
			¥221,665	¥373,502	¥281,525
VILLAUME, G. (attributed to)	1	1	$2,899	$2,899	$2,899
			DM4,094	DM4,094	DM4,094
			£1,840	£1,840	£1,840
			¥291,885	¥291,885	¥291,885
VILLAUME, GUSTAVE EUGENE	4	2	$1,687	$3,110	$2,398
			DM2,919	DM5,391	DM4,155
			£1,035	£1,840	£1,438
			¥192,510	¥388,240	¥290,375
VINACCIA, GAETANO	1	0			
VINACCIA, GENNARO	3	2	$11,551	$31,740	$21,645
			DM21,369	DM59,909	DM40,639
			£6,900	£19,647	£13,274
			¥1,539,321	¥3,358,092	¥2,448,707
VINCENT, ALFRED	21	13	$1,096	$5,962	$3,747
			DM1,613	DM10,709	DM6,206
			£713	£3,680	£2,380
			¥116,333	¥703,874	¥407,521
VINCENT, ARTHUR	1	1	$6,936	$6,936	$6,936
			DM10,423	DM10,423	DM10,423
			£4,140	£4,140	£4,140
			¥772,363	¥772,363	¥772,363
VISTOLI, LUIGI	3	1	$9,718	$9,718	$9,718
			DM16,848	DM16,848	DM16,848
			£5,750	£5,750	£5,750
			¥1,213,250	¥1,213,250	¥1,213,250
VITERBO, AUGUSTO DA RUB	3	0			
VIVENET	1	1	$1,315	$1,315	$1,315
			DM1,849	DM1,849	DM1,849
			£828	£828	£828
			¥117,352	¥117,352	¥117,352
VLUMMENS, DOMINIC	1	1	$5,883	$5,883	$5,883
			DM8,231	DM8,231	DM8,231
			£3,680	£3,680	£3,680
			¥497,584	¥497,584	¥497,584

Maker	Items		Selling Prices		
	Bid	Sold	Low	High	Avg
VLUMMENS, DOMINIC (attributed to)	1	1	$3,461	$3,461	$3,461
			DM4,981	DM4,981	DM4,981
			£2,243	£2,243	£2,243
			¥351,489	¥351,489	¥351,489
VOGLER, JOHANN GEORG	1	1	$1,380	$1,380	$1,380
			DM1,995	DM1,995	DM1,995
			£901	£901	£901
			¥139,725	¥139,725	¥139,725
VOIGT, ARNOLD	4	4	$541	$1,610	$1,114
			DM944	DM2,423	DM1,734
			£322	£977	£681
			¥69,024	¥179,966	¥119,420
VOIGT, JOHANN CHRISTIAN (II)	1	1	$1,035	$1,035	$1,035
			DM1,873	DM1,873	DM1,873
			£631	£631	£631
			¥124,966	¥124,966	¥124,966
VOIGT, JOHANN GEORG	2	1	$768	$768	$768
			DM1,426	DM1,426	DM1,426
			£460	£460	£460
			¥102,782	¥102,782	¥102,782
VOIGT, PAUL	2	2	$900	$1,475	$1,187
			DM1,601	DM2,054	DM1,827
			£552	£920	£736
			¥120,849	¥124,704	¥122,777
VOIGT, WERNER	3	1	$1,926	$1,926	$1,926
			DM3,451	DM3,451	DM3,451
			£1,150	£1,150	£1,150
			¥223,675	¥223,675	¥223,675
VOLLER BROTHERS	1	0			
VRANCKO, JULIUS	1	1	$1,385	$1,385	$1,385
			DM2,598	DM2,598	DM2,598
			£860	£860	£860
			¥166,466	¥166,466	¥166,466
VUILLAUME (workshop of)	1	1	$5,216	$5,216	$5,216
			DM9,024	DM9,024	DM9,024
			£3,200	£3,200	£3,200
			¥595,200	¥595,200	¥595,200
VUILLAUME, GUSTAVE	1	0			
VUILLAUME, JEAN BAPTISTE	38	28	$3,749	$117,555	$51,103
			DM6,486	DM222,775	DM86,936
			£2,300	£72,565	£31,366
			¥427,800	¥12,413,695	¥5,740,270
VUILLAUME, JEAN BAPTISTE (attributed to)	3	1	$13,629	$13,629	$13,629
			DM23,643	DM23,643	DM23,643
			£8,050	£8,050	£8,050
			¥1,727,611	¥1,727,611	¥1,727,611
VUILLAUME, JEAN BAPTISTE (workshop of)	3	1	$25,126	$25,126	$25,126
			DM37,595	DM37,595	DM37,595
			£14,950	£14,950	£14,950
			¥2,802,826	¥2,802,826	¥2,802,826
VUILLAUME, NICOLAS	13	5	$2,504	$6,334	$4,694
			DM4,486	DM11,378	DM8,198
			£1,495	£3,910	£2,898
			¥290,778	¥747,866	¥516,980
VUILLAUME, NICOLAS (workshop of)	1	1	$5,025	$5,025	$5,025
			DM7,519	DM7,519	DM7,519
			£2,990	£2,990	£2,990
			¥560,565	¥560,565	¥560,565

Maker	Items		Selling Prices		
	Bid	Sold	Low	High	Avg
VUILLAUME, NICHOLAS & J.B.	1	1	$20,493	$20,493	$20,493
			DM36,685	DM36,685	DM36,685
			£12,650	£12,650	£12,650
			¥2,417,036	¥2,417,036	¥2,417,036
VUILLAUME, NICOLAS FRANCOIS	7	4	$7,258	$21,107	$14,547
			DM10,222	DM32,405	DM22,385
			£4,600	£13,800	£9,056
			¥742,127	¥2,303,731	¥1,623,529
VUILLAUME, SEBASTIAN	4	1	$8,551	$8,551	$8,551
			DM14,826	DM14,826	DM14,826
			£5,060	£5,060	£5,060
			¥1,067,660	¥1,067,660	¥1,067,660
WADE, H.F.	1	1	$690	$690	$690
			DM1,228	DM1,228	DM1,228
			£414	£414	£414
			¥91,756	¥91,756	¥91,756
WAGNER & GEORGE	2	2	$4,099	$4,713	$4,406
			DM7,767	DM8,932	DM8,350
			£2,530	£2,910	£2,720
			¥432,807	¥497,728	¥465,268
WALKER, JOHN	2	2	$2,250	$3,303	$2,777
			DM3,446	DM5,076	DM4,261
			£1,438	£2,185	£1,811
			¥250,873	¥352,277	¥301,575
WALMSLEY, P. (attributed to)	1	1	$2,062	$2,062	$2,062
			DM3,732	DM3,732	DM3,732
			£1,265	£1,265	£1,265
			¥248,813	¥248,813	¥248,813
WALMSLEY, PETER	4	1	$1,220	$1,220	$1,220
			DM2,175	DM2,175	DM2,175
			£748	£748	£748
			¥159,688	¥159,688	¥159,688
WALTERS, PHILIP	2	1	$552	$552	$552
			DM772	DM772	DM772
			£345	£345	£345
			¥46,648	¥46,648	¥46,648
WALTON, WILLIAM	1	1	$1,454	$1,454	$1,454
			DM2,054	DM2,054	DM2,054
			£920	£920	£920
			¥129,754	¥129,754	¥129,754
WAMSLEY, PETER	7	2	$1,025	$2,513	$1,769
			DM1,929	DM3,759	DM2,844
			£633	£1,495	£1,064
			¥108,297	¥280,283	¥194,290
WARD, GEORGE	1	1	$2,705	$2,705	$2,705
			DM4,864	DM4,864	DM4,864
			£1,610	£1,610	£1,610
			¥312,710	¥312,710	¥312,710
WARD, GEORGE (ascribed to)	1	1	$1,159	$1,159	$1,159
			DM1,766	DM1,766	DM1,766
			£747	£747	£747
			¥128,559	¥128,559	¥128,559
WARD, GEORGE (attributed to)	2	0			
WARD, ROBERT	1	0			
WARRICK, A.	1	1	$2,758	$2,758	$2,758
			DM3,858	DM3,858	DM3,858
			£1,725	£1,725	£1,725
			¥233,242	¥233,242	¥233,242

| Maker | Items | | Selling Prices | | |
	Bid	Sold	Low	High	Avg
WARWICK, A.	2	1	$1,191	$1,191	$1,191
			DM1,968	DM1,968	DM1,968
			£713	£713	£713
			¥139,249	¥139,249	¥139,249
WASSERMANN, JOSEPH	2	0			
WATSON, FRANK	1	1	$2,305	$2,305	$2,305
			DM3,850	DM3,850	DM3,850
			£1,380	£1,380	£1,380
			¥280,126	¥280,126	¥280,126
WATT, WALTER	3	2	$746	$1,440	$1,093
			DM1,067	DM2,405	DM1,736
			£472	£862	£667
			¥74,962	¥174,977	¥124,970
WEBB, R.J.	1	1	$6,569	$6,569	$6,569
			DM10,948	DM10,948	DM10,948
			£3,910	£3,910	£3,910
			¥785,089	¥785,089	¥785,089
WEBER, ROBERT E.	1	1	$920	$920	$920
			DM1,328	DM1,328	DM1,328
			£586	£586	£586
			¥79,810	¥79,810	¥79,810
WEBSTER, GEORGE	1	1	$1,212	$1,212	$1,212
			DM1,975	DM1,975	DM1,975
			£713	£713	£713
			¥142,657	¥142,657	¥142,657
WEICHOLD, RICHARD	1	0			
WEISS, EUGENIO	1	1	$2,412	$2,412	$2,412
			DM4,274	DM4,274	DM4,274
			£1,481	£1,481	£1,481
			¥294,124	¥294,124	¥294,124
WELLBY, CHARLES	1	0			
WELLER, FREDERICK	5	1	$1,632	$1,632	$1,632
			DM3,029	DM3,029	DM3,029
			£977	£977	£977
			¥218,301	¥218,301	¥218,301
WELLER, FREDERICK (attributed to)	4	1	$307	$307	$307
			DM476	DM476	DM476
			£184	£184	£184
			¥35,017	¥35,017	¥35,017
WELLER, MICHAEL	1	1	$2,300	$2,300	$2,300
			DM3,935	DM3,935	DM3,935
			£1,360	£1,360	£1,360
			¥285,614	¥285,614	¥285,614
WENGER, GREGORI FERDINAND	1	1	$5,816	$5,816	$5,816
			DM8,214	DM8,214	DM8,214
			£3,680	£3,680	£3,680
			¥519,016	¥519,016	¥519,016
WERLE, J. PAUL (attributed to)	1	1	$1,153	$1,153	$1,153
			DM1,787	DM1,787	DM1,787
			£690	£690	£690
			¥131,314	¥131,314	¥131,314
WERRO, JEAN	1	0			
WERRO, JEAN & HENRI	2	1	$2,485	$2,485	$2,485
			DM3,576	DM3,576	DM3,576
			£1,610	£1,610	£1,610
			¥252,351	¥252,351	¥252,351

Maker	Items		Selling Prices		
	Bid	Sold	Low	High	Avg
WESTON, A.T.	1	1	$863	$863	$863
			DM1,566	DM1,566	DM1,566
			£528	£528	£528
			¥107,105	¥107,105	¥107,105
WHEELER, A.H.	1	1	$805	$805	$805
			DM1,457	DM1,457	DM1,457
			£491	£491	£491
			¥97,196	¥97,196	¥97,196
WHITE, ASA WARREN	5	5	$489	$2,645	$1,696
			DM747	DM4,787	DM2,960
			£322	£1,613	£1,030
			¥51,514	¥319,357	¥204,548
WHITE, IRA	1	1	$1,725	$1,725	$1,725
			DM2,951	DM2,951	DM2,951
			£1,020	£1,020	£1,020
			¥214,211	¥214,211	¥214,211
WHITE, NEHEMIAH	1	1	$805	$805	$805
			DM1,212	DM1,212	DM1,212
			£489	£489	£489
			¥89,983	¥89,983	¥89,983
WHITE, WILFRED	1	1	$1,715	$1,715	$1,715
			DM2,424	DM2,424	DM2,424
			£1,093	£1,093	£1,093
			¥146,483	¥146,483	¥146,483
WHITMARSH, E.	3	3	$1,800	$1,932	$1,865
			DM2,751	DM3,474	DM3,163
			£1,150	£1,150	£1,150
			¥200,733	¥225,343	¥216,480
WHITMARSH, EDWIN (attributed to)	1	1	$1,759	$1,759	$1,759
			DM2,700	DM2,700	DM2,700
			£1,150	£1,150	£1,150
			¥191,978	¥191,978	¥191,978
WHITMARSH, EMANUEL	16	11	$874	$3,287	$1,858
			DM1,515	DM4,622	DM2,887
			£517	£2,070	£1,158
			¥111,088	¥296,162	¥203,225
WHITMARSH, EMANUEL (attributed to)	2	2	$2,226	$2,912	$2,569
			DM3,289	DM4,164	DM3,727
			£1,449	£1,840	£1,645
			¥237,251	¥292,534	¥264,892
WIDHALM, LEOPOLD	10	6	$5,750	$11,072	$8,171
			DM9,838	DM15,413	DM12,383
			£3,401	£6,900	£5,033
			¥714,035	¥934,094	¥850,814
WIDHALM, LEOPOLD (attributed to)	2	1	$1,820	$1,820	$1,820
			DM2,603	DM2,603	DM2,603
			£1,150	£1,150	£1,150
			¥182,834	¥182,834	¥182,834
WIDHALM, MARTIN LEOPOLD	2	2	$9,220	$9,603	$9,411
			DM12,838	DM16,043	DM14,440
			£5,750	£5,750	£5,750
			¥779,401	¥1,167,193	¥973,297
WIDHALM, MARTIN LEOPOLD (attributed to)	1	1	$3,540	$3,540	$3,540
			DM6,337	DM6,337	DM6,337
			£2,185	£2,185	£2,185
			¥417,488	¥417,488	¥417,488

| Maker | Items | | Selling Prices | | |
	Bid	Sold	Low	High	Avg
WIEBE, DAVID	1	1	$4,713	$4,713	$4,713
			DM8,932	DM8,932	DM8,932
			£2,910	£2,910	£2,910
			¥497,728	¥497,728	¥497,728
WIEGANET, A.G.	2	1	$1,035	$1,035	$1,035
			DM1,583	DM1,583	DM1,583
			£681	£681	£681
			¥109,089	¥109,089	¥109,089
WILD, ANDREA (ascribed to)	1	0			
WILD, FRANK	1	1	$144	$144	$144
			DM204	DM204	DM204
			£92	£92	£92
			¥12,335	¥12,335	¥12,335
WILKANOWSKI, W.	9	9	$460	$1,093	$712
			DM692	DM1,580	DM1,099
			£279	£714	£449
			¥44,893	¥110,616	¥75,461
WILKANOWSKI, WILLIAM	1	0			
WILKINSON (attributed to)	1	1	$3,428	$3,428	$3,428
			DM6,511	DM6,511	DM6,511
			£2,116	£2,116	£2,116
			¥360,164	¥360,164	¥360,164
WILKINSON, JOHN	2	1	$4,175	$4,175	$4,175
			DM6,300	DM6,300	DM6,300
			£2,530	£2,530	£2,530
			¥473,110	¥473,110	¥473,110
WILKINSON, JOHN (ascribed to)	1	1	$1,594	$1,594	$1,594
			DM2,885	DM2,885	DM2,885
			£978	£978	£978
			¥192,363	¥192,363	¥192,363
WILKINSON, JOHN (attributed to)	3	1	$1,789	$1,789	$1,789
			DM3,344	DM3,344	DM3,344
			£1,127	£1,127	£1,127
			¥211,662	¥211,662	¥211,662
WILLARD, ELI A.	1	1	$489	$489	$489
			DM826	DM826	DM826
			£293	£293	£293
			¥59,628	¥59,628	¥59,628
WILLIAMS, F.C.	1	1	$920	$920	$920
			DM1,555	DM1,555	DM1,555
			£552	£552	£552
			¥122,424	¥122,424	¥122,424
WILMET, F.J.	1	1	$2,444	$2,444	$2,444
			DM4,138	DM4,138	DM4,138
			£1,495	£1,495	£1,495
			¥283,297	¥283,297	¥283,297
WILSON, H.	1	0			
WINFIELD	1	1	$548	$548	$548
			DM770	DM770	DM770
			£345	£345	£345
			¥48,897	¥48,897	¥48,897
WINTER & SON (attributed to)	2	1	$927	$927	$927
			DM1,375	DM1,375	DM1,375
			£598	£598	£598
			¥100,332	¥100,332	¥100,332

| Maker | Items | | Selling Prices | | |
	Bid	Sold	Low	High	Avg
WINTERLING, GEORG	2	2	$6,765	$8,085	$7,425
			DM10,122	DM14,959	DM12,540
			£4,025	£4,830	£4,428
			¥754,607	¥1,077,525	¥916,066
WITHERS, EDWARD	2	2	$1,701	$2,722	$2,212
			DM2,386	DM3,833	DM3,109
			£1,092	£1,725	£1,409
			¥171,884	¥278,298	¥225,091
WITHERS, EDWARD (workshop of)	1	1	$2,178	$2,178	$2,178
			DM3,066	DM3,066	DM3,066
			£1,380	£1,380	£1,380
			¥222,638	¥222,638	¥222,638
WITHERS, GEORGE	4	2	$2,319	$5,294	$3,807
			DM3,470	DM8,133	DM5,802
			£1,380	£3,450	£2,415
			¥258,722	¥579,562	¥419,142
WITHERS, GEORGE (attributed to)	1	1	$1,739	$1,739	$1,739
			DM2,456	DM2,456	DM2,456
			£1,104	£1,104	£1,104
			¥175,131	¥175,131	¥175,131
WITHERS, GEORGE & SONS	3	2	$1,329	$3,467	$2,398
			DM2,166	DM6,212	DM4,189
			£782	£2,070	£1,426
			¥156,463	¥402,615	¥279,539
WITHERS, JOSEPH	3	2	$2,068	$5,356	$3,712
			DM3,416	DM10,173	DM6,795
			£1,265	£3,306	£2,286
			¥256,073	¥562,757	¥409,415
WITTMANN, ANTON	1	1	$4,934	$4,934	$4,934
			DM7,283	DM7,283	DM7,283
			£3,220	£3,220	£3,220
			¥524,541	¥524,541	¥524,541
WOLFF BROS.	24	19	$339	$3,291	$928
			DM503	DM6,189	DM1,494
			£219	£2,070	£580
			¥36,660	¥397,937	¥100,222
WOOD, OTIS W.	1	1	$431	$431	$431
			DM768	DM768	DM768
			£259	£259	£259
			¥57,348	¥57,348	¥57,348
WOOD, WILLIAM HOWARD	1	1	$1,125	$1,125	$1,125
			DM2,123	DM2,123	DM2,123
			£696	£696	£696
			¥118,993	¥118,993	¥118,993
WOODWARD, CECIL F.	1	1	$235	$235	$235
			DM332	DM332	DM332
			£150	£150	£150
			¥20,045	¥20,045	¥20,045
WORNLE, GEORG (attributed to)	1	1	$2,812	$2,812	$2,812
			DM4,985	DM4,985	DM4,985
			£1,725	£1,725	£1,725
			¥332,459	¥332,459	¥332,459
WOULDHAVE, JOHN	2	1	$728	$728	$728
			DM1,374	DM1,374	DM1,374
			£451	£451	£451
			¥77,017	¥77,017	¥77,017

Maker	Items		Selling Prices		
	Bid	Sold	Low	High	Avg
WULME-HUDSON, GEORGE	13	9	$3,866	$9,410	$6,725
			DM5,784	DM15,722	DM10,715
			£2,300	£5,635	£4,045
			¥431,204	¥1,143,849	¥787,642
WULME-HUDSON, GEORGE (attributed to)	1	1	$3,467	$3,467	$3,467
			DM6,212	DM6,212	DM6,212
			£2,070	£2,070	£2,070
			¥402,615	¥402,615	¥402,615
WURLITZER CO., RUDOLPH	1	1	$403	$403	$403
			DM716	DM716	DM716
			£242	£242	£242
			¥53,524	¥53,524	¥53,524
YOUNG, JOHN	1	1	$695	$695	$695
			DM1,069	DM1,069	DM1,069
			£460	£460	£460
			¥74,164	¥74,164	¥74,164
ZACH & CO., CARL	1	1	$7,788	$7,788	$7,788
			DM13,510	DM13,510	DM13,510
			£4,600	£4,600	£4,600
			¥987,206	¥987,206	¥987,206
ZAHN, UTE	2	1	$935	$935	$935
			DM1,621	DM1,621	DM1,621
			£552	£552	£552
			¥118,465	¥118,465	¥118,465
ZANI, ALDO	1	1	$7,211	$7,211	$7,211
			DM10,881	DM10,881	DM10,881
			£4,370	£4,370	£4,370
			¥817,190	¥817,190	¥817,190
ZANISI, FILIPPO	1	0			
ZANOLI, FRANCESCO	1	1	$2,734	$2,734	$2,734
			DM4,625	DM4,625	DM4,625
			£1,719	£1,719	£1,719
			¥338,692	¥338,692	¥338,692
ZANOLI, GIACOMO	2	1	$28,750	$28,750	$28,750
			DM51,750	DM51,750	DM51,750
			£17,250	£17,250	£17,250
			¥223,388	¥223,388	¥223,388
ZANOLI, GIACOMO (attributed to)	2	0			
ZARI BROTHERS	1	1	$3,738	$3,738	$3,738
			DM5,397	DM5,397	DM5,397
			£2,381	£2,381	£2,381
			¥324,228	¥324,228	¥324,228
ZIMMERMANN, JULIUS HEINRICH (attributed to)	1	1	$1,061	$1,061	$1,061
			DM1,561	DM1,561	DM1,561
			£690	£690	£690
			¥112,580	¥112,580	¥112,580
ZURLINI, NICOLO	1	0			
ZUST, J. EMILE	1	1	$3,286	$3,286	$3,286
			DM4,916	DM4,916	DM4,916
			£1,955	£1,955	£1,955
			¥366,523	¥366,523	¥366,523
ZWERGER, ANTON	2	1	$2,624	$2,624	$2,624
			DM4,549	DM4,549	DM4,549
			£1,553	£1,553	£1,553
			¥327,578	¥327,578	¥327,578

Maker	Items		Selling Prices		
	Bid	Sold	Low	High	Avg

VIOLIN BOW

Maker	Bid	Sold	Low	High	Avg
ACKERMANN, GOTTFRIED	1	1	$1,392 DM2,637 £859 ¥146,958	$1,392 DM2,637 £859 ¥146,958	$1,392 DM2,637 £859 ¥146,958
ADAM	1	0			
ADAM (attributed to)	2	1	$6,338 DM11,765 £3,795 ¥847,955	$6,338 DM11,765 £3,795 ¥847,955	$6,338 DM11,765 £3,795 ¥847,955
ADAM, J.D.	1	1	$10,247 DM19,291 £6,325 ¥1,082,967	$10,247 DM19,291 £6,325 ¥1,082,967	$10,247 DM19,291 £6,325 ¥1,082,967
ADAM, JEAN (attributed to)	2	1	$1,380 DM2,077 £838 ¥154,256	$1,380 DM2,077 £838 ¥154,256	$1,380 DM2,077 £838 ¥154,256
ADAM FAMILY (attributed to)	1	1	$2,062 DM3,732 £1,265 ¥248,813	$2,062 DM3,732 £1,265 ¥248,813	$2,062 DM3,732 £1,265 ¥248,813
ALLEN, SAMUEL	2	1	$3,657 DM6,877 £2,300 ¥442,152	$3,657 DM6,877 £2,300 ¥442,152	$3,657 DM6,877 £2,300 ¥442,152
ALLEN, SAMUEL (attributed to)	3	2	$5,654 DM8,354 £3,680 ¥602,541	$7,246 DM10,234 £4,600 ¥729,712	$6,450 DM9,294 £4,140 ¥666,126
ALVEY, BRIAN	1	0			
AMES, ROBERT	1	1	$2,415 DM4,371 £1,473 ¥291,587	$2,415 DM4,371 £1,473 ¥291,587	$2,415 DM4,371 £1,473 ¥291,587
ASHMEAD, RALPH	1	0			
AUBRY, JOSEPH	3	3	$525 DM908 £322 ¥59,892	$3,177 DM4,876 £2,070 ¥347,781	$1,554 DM2,463 £989 ¥174,797
AUDINOT, JACQUES	1	1	$1,155 DM2,137 £690 ¥153,932	$1,155 DM2,137 £690 ¥153,932	$1,155 DM2,137 £690 ¥153,932
AUDINOT, NESTOR	1	0			
BAILEY, G.E.	1	1	$971 DM1,491 £633 ¥106,253	$971 DM1,491 £633 ¥106,253	$971 DM1,491 £633 ¥106,253
BAILLY, CHARLES	2	2	$1,433 DM2,010 £920 ¥144,811	$1,646 DM3,095 £1,035 ¥198,968	$1,539 DM2,552 £978 ¥171,890
BALMFORTH, LEONARD PERCY	1	1	$2,028 DM2,824 £1,265 ¥171,468	$2,028 DM2,824 £1,265 ¥171,468	$2,028 DM2,824 £1,265 ¥171,468

Maker	Items		Selling Prices		
	Bid	Sold	Low	High	Avg
BARBE, AUGUSTE	1	1	$4,252	$4,252	$4,252
			DM6,362	DM6,362	DM6,362
			£2,530	£2,530	£2,530
			¥474,324	¥474,324	¥474,324
BASTIEN, E.	2	1	$1,348	$1,348	$1,348
			DM2,493	DM2,493	DM2,493
			£805	£805	£805
			¥179,587	¥179,587	¥179,587
BAUSCH	7	5	$122	$734	$264
			DM187	DM1,099	DM397
			£81	£437	£161
			¥12,382	¥81,929	¥28,272
BAUSCH (workshop of)	2	1	$575	$575	$575
			DM831	DM831	DM831
			£376	£376	£376
			¥58,219	¥58,219	¥58,219
BAUSCH, L.	1	1	$403	$403	$403
			DM729	DM729	DM729
			£246	£246	£246
			¥48,598	¥48,598	¥48,598
BAUSCH, L. (workshop of)	1	1	$518	$518	$518
			DM791	DM791	DM791
			£340	£340	£340
			¥54,545	¥54,545	¥54,545
BAUSCH, LUDWIG	3	3	$690	$894	$796
			DM1,228	DM1,606	DM1,431
			£414	£552	£486
			¥91,756	¥105,581	¥98,178
BAUSCH, LUDWIG & SOHN	5	3	$673	$949	$766
			DM1,167	DM1,708	DM1,373
			£402	£575	£464
			¥77,004	¥136,821	¥101,169
BAUSCH, LUDWIG (II)	1	1	$1,234	$1,234	$1,234
			DM1,821	DM1,821	DM1,821
			£805	£805	£805
			¥131,135	¥131,135	¥131,135
BAUSCH, LUDWIG CHRISTIAN AUGUST	1	1	$863	$863	$863
			DM1,491	DM1,491	DM1,491
			£533	£533	£533
			¥109,309	¥109,309	¥109,309
BAUSCH, LUDWIG CHRISTIAN AUGUST (workshop of)	1	1	$374	$374	$374
			DM562	DM562	DM562
			£227	£227	£227
			¥41,778	¥41,778	¥41,778
BAUSCH, OTTO	1	1	$805	$805	$805
			DM1,433	DM1,433	DM1,433
			£491	£491	£491
			¥111,831	¥111,831	¥111,831
BAUSCH, OTTO (workshop of)	1	1	$805	$805	$805
			DM1,377	DM1,377	DM1,377
			£476	£476	£476
			¥99,965	¥99,965	¥99,965
BAZIN	22	11	$232	$5,356	$1,462
			DM405	DM10,150	DM2,589
			£138	£3,306	£890
			¥29,582	¥565,600	¥168,891

Maker	Items		Selling Prices		
	Bid	Sold	Low	High	Avg
BAZIN (workshop of)	2	1	$2,113	$2,113	$2,113
			DM3,529	DM3,529	DM3,529
			£1,265	£1,265	£1,265
			¥256,782	¥256,782	¥256,782
BAZIN, C.	3	3	$2,332	$5,756	$3,802
			DM4,043	DM8,141	DM5,602
			£1,380	£3,680	£2,377
			¥280,584	¥584,417	¥385,394
BAZIN, CHARLES	21	16	$1,093	$5,412	$2,499
			DM1,945	DM8,097	DM3,805
			£656	£3,335	£1,564
			¥22,339	¥603,686	¥242,418
BAZIN, CHARLES (II)	2	1	$559	$559	$559
			DM1,004	DM1,004	DM1,004
			£345	£345	£345
			¥65,988	¥65,988	¥65,988
BAZIN, CHARLES ALFRED	1	1	$1,955	$1,955	$1,955
			DM3,539	DM3,539	DM3,539
			£1,193	£1,193	£1,193
			¥236,047	¥236,047	¥236,047
BAZIN, CHARLES NICHOLAS	26	17	$1,089	$6,521	$2,224
			DM1,533	DM11,713	DM3,595
			£690	£4,025	£1,377
			¥111,319	¥769,862	¥257,503
BAZIN, LOUIS	20	18	$518	$4,416	$1,918
			DM894	DM7,471	DM3,219
			£320	£2,777	£1,188
			¥65,585	¥547,118	¥216,211
BAZIN, LOUIS (workshop of)	1	1	$374	$374	$374
			DM673	DM673	DM673
			£224	£224	£224
			¥2,904	¥2,904	¥2,904
BAZIN, LOUIS (II)	5	3	$347	$1,396	$954
			DM641	DM2,646	DM1,802
			£207	£862	£586
			¥46,180	¥147,462	¥103,893
BAZIN FAMILY (MEMBER OF)	3	1	$1,612	$1,612	$1,612
			DM2,902	DM2,902	DM2,902
			£977	£977	£977
			¥232,477	¥232,477	¥232,477
BAZIN FAMILY (MEMBER OF) (attributed to)	1	0			
BEARE, JOHN & ARTHUR	6	5	$1,588	$5,442	$3,156
			DM2,440	DM9,435	DM5,064
			£1,035	£3,220	£1,897
			¥173,869	¥691,881	¥372,792
BERNARD, J.P.	1	1	$1,009	$1,009	$1,009
			DM1,708	DM1,708	DM1,708
			£635	£635	£635
			¥125,056	¥125,056	¥125,056
BERNARDEL, GUSTAVE (workshop of)	1	1	$3,680	$3,680	$3,680
			DM5,538	DM5,538	DM5,538
			£2,234	£2,234	£2,234
			¥411,350	¥411,350	¥411,350
BERNARDEL, GUSTAVE ADOLPHE	1	1	$1,518	$1,518	$1,518
			DM2,291	DM2,291	DM2,291
			£920	£920	£920
			¥172,040	¥172,040	¥172,040

Maker	Items		Selling Prices		
	Bid	Sold	Low	High	Avg
BERNARDEL, LEON	10	4	$412	$1,944	$874
			DM713	DM3,370	DM1,537
			£253	£1,150	£524
			¥47,058	¥242,650	¥108,768
BERNARDEL, LEON (workshop of)	2	2	$2,530	$4,025	$3,278
			DM3,808	DM6,058	DM4,933
			£1,536	£2,443	£1,990
			¥282,803	¥449,915	¥366,359
BETTS	1	1	$2,497	$2,497	$2,497
			DM4,635	DM4,635	DM4,635
			£1,495	£1,495	£1,495
			¥334,043	¥334,043	¥334,043
BETTS, JOHN	2	2	$1,786	$2,721	$2,254
			DM3,022	DM4,717	DM3,870
			£1,124	£1,610	£1,367
			¥221,339	¥339,710	¥280,525
BEYER, HERMANN	1	1	$633	$633	$633
			DM915	DM915	DM915
			£413	£413	£413
			¥64,041	¥64,041	¥64,041
BLONDELET, H. EMILE	2	2	$1,942	$2,207	$2,074
			DM2,980	DM3,734	DM3,357
			£1,265	£1,388	£1,327
			¥212,533	¥273,446	¥242,989
BOLLINGER, JOSEPH	1	1	$920	$920	$920
			DM1,555	DM1,555	DM1,555
			£552	£552	£552
			¥122,424	¥122,424	¥122,424
BOURGUIGNON, MAURICE	1	1	$878	$878	$878
			DM1,650	DM1,650	DM1,650
			£552	£552	£552
			¥106,116	¥106,116	¥106,116
BOUVIN, JEAN	2	1	$805	$805	$805
			DM1,162	DM1,162	DM1,162
			£513	£513	£513
			¥69,834	¥69,834	¥69,834
BOVIS, FRANCOIS	1	1	$878	$878	$878
			DM1,650	DM1,650	DM1,650
			£552	£552	£552
			¥106,116	¥106,116	¥106,116
BRAMBACH, P. OTTO	1	0			
BRISTOW, S.E.	4	2	$883	$1,065	$974
			DM1,305	DM1,533	DM1,419
			£575	£690	£633
			¥94,147	¥108,151	¥101,149
BRISTOW, STEPHEN	2	2	$777	$1,845	$1,311
			DM1,348	DM3,200	DM2,274
			£460	£1,092	£776
			¥98,840	¥234,638	¥166,739
BRUGERE FAMILY	1	1	$1,769	$1,769	$1,769
			DM3,178	DM3,178	DM3,178
			£1,092	£1,092	£1,092
			¥208,867	¥208,867	¥208,867
BRYANT	2	0			
BRYANT, PERCIVAL WILFRED	5	4	$1,057	$2,178	$1,393
			DM1,561	DM3,066	DM2,232
			£690	£1,380	£877
			¥112,402	¥222,638	¥152,558

Maker	Items		Selling Prices		
	Bid	Sold	Low	High	Avg
BULTITUDE, ARTHUR RICHARD	23	20	$453	$5,390	$2,572
			DM824	DM9,972	DM4,169
			£276	£3,335	£1,602
			¥57,171	¥718,350	¥294,495
BUTHOD	3	2	$155	$169	$162
			DM270	DM286	DM278
			£92	£104	£98
			¥19,613	¥19,721	¥19,667
BUTHOD, CHARLES LOUIS	6	3	$1,125	$2,204	$1,638
			DM2,001	DM3,706	DM2,683
			£690	£1,380	£1,035
			¥151,062	¥270,567	¥196,744
BYROM, H.	1	1	$691	$691	$691
			DM1,238	DM1,238	DM1,238
			£414	£414	£414
			¥95,129	¥95,129	¥95,129
BYRON, J.	2	1	$468	$468	$468
			DM715	DM715	DM715
			£299	£299	£299
			¥52,190	¥52,190	¥52,190
CALLIER, FRANK	4	4	$331	$863	$543
			DM583	DM1,319	DM874
			£205	£567	£349
			¥35,041	¥90,908	¥58,676
CALLIER, PAUL J.	1	1	$1,495	$1,495	$1,495
			DM2,286	DM2,286	DM2,286
			£984	£984	£984
			¥157,573	¥157,573	¥157,573
CAPELA, ANTONIO	1	0			
CARESSA, ALBERT	6	4	$1,024	$3,304	$1,926
			DM1,839	DM5,728	DM3,239
			£632	£1,955	£1,179
			¥120,883	¥412,505	¥226,108
CARESSA & FRANCAIS	3	2	$1,749	$3,354	$2,552
			DM3,033	DM5,147	DM4,090
			£1,035	£2,185	£1,610
			¥218,385	¥367,102	¥292,743
CARESSA & FRANCAIS (workshop of)	1	1	$2,300	$2,300	$2,300
			DM3,321	DM3,321	DM3,321
			£1,465	£1,465	£1,465
			¥199,525	¥199,525	¥199,525
CHALUPETZKY, F.	1	1	$1,057	$1,057	$1,057
			DM1,561	DM1,561	DM1,561
			£690	£690	£690
			¥112,402	¥112,402	¥112,402
CHANOT	1	1	$675	$675	$675
			DM1,167	DM1,167	DM1,167
			£414	£414	£414
			¥77,004	¥77,004	¥77,004
CHANOT (attributed to)	1	1	$12,523	$12,523	$12,523
			DM18,820	DM18,820	DM18,820
			£7,475	£7,475	£7,475
			¥1,394,543	¥1,394,543	¥1,394,543
CHANOT, G.A.	2	1	$2,298	$2,298	$2,298
			DM3,215	DM3,215	DM3,215
			£1,438	£1,438	£1,438
			¥194,369	¥194,369	¥194,369

| Maker | Items | | Selling Prices | | |
	Bid	Sold	Low	High	Avg
CHANOT, GEORGE ADOLPH	1	1	$3,995	$3,995	$3,995
			DM6,759	DM6,759	DM6,759
			£2,513	£2,513	£2,513
			¥495,012	¥495,012	¥495,012
CHANOT & CHARDON	4	2	$914	$1,490	$1,202
			DM1,719	DM2,806	DM2,263
			£575	£920	£748
			¥110,538	¥157,522	¥134,030
CHARDON, ANDRE	1	1	$1,579	$1,579	$1,579
			DM2,920	DM2,920	DM2,920
			£943	£943	£943
			¥210,374	¥210,374	¥210,374
CHARDON, JOSEPH MARIE	2	0			
CHIPOT, JEAN BAPTISTE	1	1	$1,198	$1,198	$1,198
			DM1,668	DM1,668	DM1,668
			£747	£747	£747
			¥101,254	¥101,254	¥101,254
CHIPOT-VUILLAUME	2	0			
CLARK, JULIAN B.	2	1	$972	$972	$972
			DM1,685	DM1,685	DM1,685
			£575	£575	£575
			¥121,325	¥121,325	¥121,325
CLASQUIN, G.	5	3	$1,508	$2,453	$2,048
			DM2,671	DM3,889	DM3,342
			£926	£1,552	£1,263
			¥183,828	¥290,561	¥231,093
CLAUDOT, ALBERT	1	0			
CLUTTERBUCK, JOHN	1	1	$1,058	$1,058	$1,058
			DM1,957	DM1,957	DM1,957
			£632	£632	£632
			¥140,993	¥140,993	¥140,993
COCKER, L.	2	1	$174	$174	$174
			DM303	DM303	DM303
			£104	£104	£104
			¥22,186	¥22,186	¥22,186
COCKER, LAWRENCE	2	0			
COLAS, PROSPER	5	3	$693	$1,762	$1,099
			DM1,282	DM2,601	DM1,780
			£414	£1,150	£694
			¥92,359	¥187,336	¥125,286
COLAS, PROSPER (attributed to)	2	0			
COLLENOT, LOUIS	1	1	$1,463	$1,463	$1,463
			DM2,751	DM2,751	DM2,751
			£920	£920	£920
			¥176,861	¥176,861	¥176,861
COLLIN-MEZIN	3	1	$2,113	$2,113	$2,113
			DM3,529	DM3,529	DM3,529
			£1,265	£1,265	£1,265
			¥256,782	¥256,782	¥256,782
COLLIN-MEZIN, CH.J.B.	5	5	$960	$2,915	$2,005
			DM1,604	DM5,054	DM3,139
			£575	£1,725	£1,224
			¥116,719	¥370,651	¥220,814
COLLIN-MEZIN, CH.J.B. (FILS)	1	0			
COLLIN-MEZIN, CH.J.B. (II)	2	0			
CONE, GEORGES & FILS	1	0			

| Maker | Items | | Selling Prices | | |
	Bid	Sold	Low	High	Avg
COROLLA	1	0			
CORSBY, GEORGE	1	1	$3,416	$3,416	$3,416
			DM5,154	DM5,154	DM5,154
			£2,070	£2,070	£2,070
			¥387,090	¥387,090	¥387,090
CUNIOT-HURY	8	6	$1,235	$2,113	$1,562
			DM1,883	DM3,922	DM2,643
			£805	£1,265	£956
			¥135,231	¥282,652	¥193,514
CUNIOT-HURY, EUGENE	21	16	$578	$1,610	$971
			DM998	DM2,577	DM1,564
			£357	£1,026	£600
			¥73,189	¥165,711	¥107,992
DARBEY, GEORGE	7	5	$838	$2,555	$1,306
			DM1,350	DM4,793	DM2,237
			£518	£1,587	£812
			¥95,989	¥307,116	¥144,577
DARCHE, HILAIRE	5	5	$214	$1,733	$1,173
			DM345	DM3,205	DM2,146
			£124	£1,035	£703
			¥25,185	¥232,477	¥159,382
DARCHE, NICHOLAS	1	1	$968	$968	$968
			DM1,430	DM1,430	DM1,430
			£632	£632	£632
			¥102,953	¥102,953	¥102,953
DELIVET, AUGUSTE	1	1	$2,467	$2,467	$2,467
			DM3,723	DM3,723	DM3,723
			£1,495	£1,495	£1,495
			¥279,565	¥279,565	¥279,565
DIDIER, PAUL	2	0			
DITER, PAUL FRANCOIS	1	0			
DITER BROTHERS	1	0			
DODD	13	7	$922	$1,944	$1,254
			DM1,284	DM3,370	DM2,019
			£575	£1,150	£764
			¥77,940	¥247,101	¥141,417
DODD (ascribed to)	1	1	$1,013	$1,013	$1,013
			DM1,411	DM1,411	DM1,411
			£632	£632	£632
			¥85,666	¥85,666	¥85,666
DODD (attributed to)	4	3	$700	$1,413	$1,117
			DM1,213	DM2,088	DM1,710
			£414	£920	£713
			¥87,354	¥150,635	¥123,265
DODD, J.	6	2	$556	$960	$758
			DM937	DM1,604	DM1,271
			£345	£575	£460
			¥68,263	¥116,719	¥92,491
DODD, JAMES	6	4	$1,150	$1,852	$1,570
			DM1,988	DM3,439	DM2,719
			£711	£1,152	£983
			¥145,745	¥221,076	¥183,408
DODD, JOHN	26	21	$651	$6,613	$2,774
			DM1,170	DM12,167	DM4,583
			£402	£4,113	£1,728
			¥76,891	¥779,944	¥316,914

Maker	Items		Selling Prices		
	Bid	Sold	Low	High	Avg
DODD, JOHN (attributed to)	1	1	$989	$989	$989
			DM1,462	DM1,462	DM1,462
			£644	£644	£644
			¥105,445	¥105,445	¥105,445
DODD, JOHN KEW	1	1	$2,116	$2,116	$2,116
			DM3,893	DM3,893	DM3,893
			£1,316	£1,316	£1,316
			¥249,582	¥249,582	¥249,582
DODD FAMILY	2	0			
DODD FAMILY (MEMBER OF)	1	0			
DOLLING, BERND	1	1	$740	$740	$740
			DM1,092	DM1,092	DM1,092
			£483	£483	£483
			¥78,681	¥78,681	¥78,681
DOLLING, HEINZ	10	8	$169	$1,845	$1,077
			DM300	DM2,569	DM1,753
			£104	£1,150	£671
			¥22,659	¥182,373	¥115,663
DORFLER, EGIDIUS	1	1	$1,150	$1,150	$1,150
			DM1,944	DM1,944	DM1,944
			£690	£690	£690
			¥153,031	¥153,031	¥153,031
DOTSCHKAIL, R.	1	0			
DUBOIS, VICTOR	1	1	$39	$39	$39
			DM67	DM67	DM67
			£23	£23	£23
			¥4,930	¥4,930	¥4,930
DUCHAINE	1	0			
DUCHENE, NICOLAS (II)	1	0			
DUGAD, ANDRE	4	2	$637	$1,996	$1,317
			DM1,103	DM2,811	DM1,957
			£391	£1,265	£828
			¥72,726	¥204,085	¥138,405
DUGAD, C.	1	1	$738	$738	$738
			DM1,027	DM1,027	DM1,027
			£460	£460	£460
			¥62,352	¥62,352	¥62,352
DUPUY	4	2	$1,760	$1,771	$1,765
			DM1,865	DM2,836	DM2,351
			£1,035	£1,093	£1,064
			¥135,246	¥217,578	¥176,412
DUPUY, GEORGE	2	1	$2,261	$2,261	$2,261
			DM4,007	DM4,007	DM4,007
			£1,389	£1,389	£1,389
			¥275,741	¥275,741	¥275,741
DUPUY, GEORGE (workshop of)	1	1	$1,725	$1,725	$1,725
			DM2,596	DM2,596	DM2,596
			£1,047	£1,047	£1,047
			¥192,821	¥192,821	¥192,821
DUPUY, PHILIPPE	1	0			
DURRSCHMIDT, OTTO	5	3	$500	$604	$544
			DM774	DM1,041	DM866
			£299	£368	£337
			¥56,488	¥68,875	¥60,755
DURRSCHMIDT, WOLFGANG	2	0			

Maker	Items		Selling Prices		
	Bid	Sold	Low	High	Avg
ENEL, CHARLES	4	4	$570	$1,567	$1,261
			DM920	DM2,625	DM2,056
			£331	£978	£773
			¥67,160	¥191,652	¥142,795
ENEL, PIERRE	1	1	$1,265	$1,265	$1,265
			DM1,829	DM1,829	DM1,829
			£826	£826	£826
			¥128,081	¥128,081	¥128,081
EURY, FRANCOIS (ascribed to)	1	1	$1,412	$1,412	$1,412
			DM2,167	DM2,167	DM2,167
			£920	£920	£920
			¥154,569	¥154,569	¥154,569
EURY, NICOLAS	4	3	$3,534	$10,541	$7,194
			DM5,221	DM14,888	DM11,333
			£2,300	£6,670	£4,485
			¥376,588	¥1,000,559	¥772,621
EURY, NICOLAS (ascribed to)	1	1	$3,693	$3,693	$3,693
			DM6,402	DM6,402	DM6,402
			£2,185	£2,185	£2,185
			¥461,035	¥461,035	¥461,035
FAROTTO, CELESTINO	1	0			
FERRON & KROEPLIN	1	0			
FETIQUE, CHARLES	3	2	$863	$4,081	$2,472
			DM1,442	DM7,076	DM4,259
			£517	£2,415	£1,466
			¥104,946	¥509,565	¥307,255
FETIQUE, JULES	5	4	$3,688	$7,348	$5,787
			DM5,135	DM12,355	DM9,048
			£2,300	£4,600	£3,594
			¥311,760	¥901,890	¥620,706
FETIQUE, MARCEL	9	7	$3,154	$5,905	$3,971
			DM4,924	DM8,220	DM6,197
			£1,984	£3,680	£2,480
			¥339,388	¥518,911	¥436,654
FETIQUE, V.	1	1	$2,743	$2,743	$2,743
			DM5,192	DM5,192	DM5,192
			£1,725	£1,725	£1,725
			¥328,768	¥328,768	¥328,768
FETIQUE, VICTOR	59	44	$910	$15,614	$4,688
			DM1,301	DM26,254	DM7,677
			£575	£9,775	£2,915
			¥91,417	¥1,916,516	¥514,024
FETIQUE, VICTOR (attributed to)	2	1	$4,844	$4,844	$4,844
			DM9,120	DM9,120	DM9,120
			£2,990	£2,990	£2,990
			¥511,948	¥511,948	¥511,948
FETIQUE, VICTOR (workshop of)	1	1	$978	$978	$978
			DM1,740	DM1,740	DM1,740
			£587	£587	£587
			¥129,988	¥129,988	¥129,988
FINKEL	3	1	$304	$304	$304
			DM539	DM539	DM539
			£184	£184	£184
			¥42,116	¥42,116	¥42,116
FINKEL, JOHANN S.	4	3	$1,079	$1,187	$1,121
			DM1,526	DM1,669	DM1,584
			£690	£748	£709
			¥101,879	¥109,578	¥105,800

Maker	Items		Selling Prices		
	Bid	Sold	Low	High	Avg
FINKEL, JOHANN S. (workshop of)	2	2	$316	$345	$331
			DM541	DM590	DM566
			£187	£204	£196
			¥39,272	¥42,842	¥41,057
FINKEL, JOHANNES S.	4	2	$2,695	$8,141	$5,418
			DM4,986	DM15,428	DM10,207
			£1,610	£5,026	£3,318
			¥359,175	¥859,712	¥609,444
FINKEL, SIEGFRIED	3	2	$1,304	$1,898	$1,601
			DM2,471	DM2,864	DM2,667
			£805	£1,150	£978
			¥137,711	¥215,050	¥176,381
FLEURY, H.	3	2	$169	$407	$288
			DM300	DM653	DM477
			£104	£265	£184
			¥22,659	¥46,346	¥34,502
FONCLAUSE, JOSEPH	3	1	$3,353	$3,353	$3,353
			DM6,355	DM6,355	DM6,355
			£2,070	£2,070	£2,070
			¥354,115	¥354,115	¥354,115
FORSTER, WILLIAM	1	0			
FORSTER, WILLIAM (II)	2	1	$2,846	$2,846	$2,846
			DM4,295	DM4,295	DM4,295
			£1,725	£1,725	£1,725
			¥322,575	¥322,575	¥322,575
FOURNIER, GEORGE	1	1	$1,844	$1,844	$1,844
			DM2,568	DM2,568	DM2,568
			£1,150	£1,150	£1,150
			¥155,880	¥155,880	¥155,880
FRANCAIS, EMILE	3	3	$600	$2,467	$1,463
			DM1,038	DM3,642	DM2,371
			£368	£1,610	£934
			¥68,448	¥262,271	¥162,236
FRANCAIS, LUCIEN	3	1	$1,921	$1,921	$1,921
			DM3,209	DM3,209	DM3,209
			£1,150	£1,150	£1,150
			¥233,439	¥233,439	¥233,439
FRITSCH, JEAN	2	2	$932	$1,071	$1,001
			DM1,765	DM2,030	DM1,898
			£575	£661	£618
			¥98,365	¥113,120	¥105,743
GAND BROS.	2	2	$525	$1,944	$1,234
			DM908	DM3,370	DM2,139
			£322	£1,150	£736
			¥59,892	¥242,650	¥151,271
GAND & BERNARDEL	15	9	$1,312	$5,301	$2,720
			DM2,270	DM7,832	DM4,313
			£805	£3,450	£1,687
			¥140,292	¥564,882	¥291,157
GAULARD	1	1	$5,053	$5,053	$5,053
			DM8,761	DM8,761	DM8,761
			£2,990	£2,990	£2,990
			¥630,890	¥630,890	¥630,890
GAUTIE, P. & SON	1	1	$581	$581	$581
			DM818	DM818	DM818
			£368	£368	£368
			¥59,370	¥59,370	¥59,370

Maker	Items		Selling Prices		
	Bid	Sold	Low	High	Avg
GERMAIN, EMILE	1	1	$9,315	$9,315	$9,315
			DM16,733	DM16,733	DM16,733
			£5,750	£5,750	£5,750
			¥1,099,803	¥1,099,803	¥1,099,803
GEROME, ROGER	7	6	$960	$2,185	$1,337
			DM1,783	DM3,955	DM2,351
			£575	£1,333	£812
			¥128,478	¥263,817	¥162,946
GILLET	2	0			
GILLET, LOUIS	3	3	$1,452	$1,928	$1,686
			DM2,044	DM3,654	DM2,959
			£920	£1,190	£1,048
			¥148,425	¥203,616	¥176,366
GOHDE, GREGORY	1	1	$540	$540	$540
			DM825	DM825	DM825
			£345	£345	£345
			¥60,220	¥60,220	¥60,220
GOTZ, CONRAD	3	2	$428	$745	$586
			DM741	DM1,339	DM1,040
			£253	£460	£357
			¥53,383	¥87,984	¥70,684
GOTZ, CONRAD (workshop of)	2	2	$201	$1,093	$647
			DM291	DM1,644	DM967
			£128	£663	£396
			¥17,458	¥122,120	¥69,789
GOULD, JOHN ALFRED	1	1	$920	$920	$920
			DM1,328	DM1,328	DM1,328
			£586	£586	£586
			¥79,810	¥79,810	¥79,810
GRAND ADAM	2	0			
GREEN, HOWARD	3	3	$691	$963	$795
			DM1,155	DM1,781	DM1,385
			£414	£575	£475
			¥84,038	¥128,277	¥100,340
GRIMM	2	2	$789	$1,880	$1,335
			DM1,337	DM3,183	DM2,260
			£483	£1,150	£817
			¥91,527	¥217,920	¥154,723
GRUNKE, RICHARD	3	3	$920	$1,765	$1,393
			DM1,555	DM2,709	DM2,171
			£552	£1,150	£870
			¥112,240	¥193,212	¥157,521
HART & SON	3	3	$706	$2,357	$1,665
			DM1,084	DM4,466	DM2,923
			£460	£1,455	£1,022
			¥77,285	¥248,864	¥185,686
HART & SON (workshop of)	3	2	$1,610	$1,840	$1,725
			DM2,423	DM2,657	DM2,540
			£977	£1,172	£1,075
			¥159,620	¥179,966	¥169,793
HAWKES & SON	1	1	$266	$266	$266
			DM472	DM472	DM472
			£161	£161	£161
			¥36,851	¥36,851	¥36,851
HEBERLEIN (workshop of)	1	1	$575	$575	$575
			DM830	DM830	DM830
			£366	£366	£366
			¥49,881	¥49,881	¥49,881

Maker	Items		Selling Prices		
	Bid	Sold	Low	High	Avg
HEBERLEIN, HEINRICH TH.	1	1	$1,049	$1,049	$1,049
			DM1,820	DM1,820	DM1,820
			£621	£621	£621
			¥131,031	¥131,031	¥131,031
HEL, PIERRE JOSEPH	1	0			
HENRI (attributed to)	1	1	$13,587	$13,587	$13,587
			DM19,189	DM19,189	DM19,189
			£8,625	£8,625	£8,625
			¥1,368,210	¥1,368,210	¥1,368,210
HENRY	1	1	$20,226	$20,226	$20,226
			DM36,237	DM36,237	DM36,237
			£12,075	£12,075	£12,075
			¥2,348,588	¥2,348,588	¥2,348,588
HENRY, E.	1	0			
HENRY, EUGENE	2	1	$914	$914	$914
			DM1,719	DM1,719	DM1,719
			£575	£575	£575
			¥110,538	¥110,538	¥110,538
HENRY, J.V.	2	0			
HENRY, JOSEPH	7	4	$2,645	$18,400	$9,603
			DM4,162	DM27,458	DM15,764
			£1,645	£11,723	£6,053
			¥299,738	¥1,596,200	¥936,760
HENRY, JOSEPH (attributed to)	3	1	$6,714	$6,714	$6,714
			DM9,920	DM9,920	DM9,920
			£4,370	£4,370	£4,370
			¥715,518	¥715,518	¥715,518
HERMANN, ADOLF	1	1	$334	$334	$334
			DM562	DM562	DM562
			£207	£207	£207
			¥40,958	¥40,958	¥40,958
HERMANN, EMIL	1	1	$1,265	$1,265	$1,265
			DM2,252	DM2,252	DM2,252
			£772	£772	£772
			¥175,734	¥175,734	¥175,734
HERNOULT, HENRI (attributed to)	1	1	$1,921	$1,921	$1,921
			DM3,209	DM3,209	DM3,209
			£1,150	£1,150	£1,150
			¥233,439	¥233,439	¥233,439
HERRMANN, A.	7	4	$293	$1,035	$584
			DM473	DM1,873	DM977
			£173	£631	£362
			¥36,263	¥124,966	¥68,159
HERRMANN, AUGUST FRIEDRICH	1	1	$1,147	$1,147	$1,147
			DM1,760	DM1,760	DM1,760
			£747	£747	£747
			¥125,503	¥125,503	¥125,503
HERRMANN, E.	2	2	$389	$773	$581
			DM572	DM1,390	DM981
			£253	£460	£357
			¥41,279	¥89,346	¥65,313
HERRMANN, EMIL	3	2	$690	$1,323	$1,006
			DM1,055	DM2,433	DM1,744
			£454	£823	£638
			¥72,726	¥155,989	¥114,357

| Maker | Items | | Selling Prices | | |
	Bid	Sold	Low	High	Avg
HERRMANN, EMIL (workshop of)	1	1	$1,380	$1,380	$1,380
			DM2,110	DM2,110	DM2,110
			£908	£908	£908
			¥145,452	¥145,452	¥145,452
HILL	2	2	$684	$1,565	$1,124
			DM1,045	DM2,213	DM1,629
			£437	£1,001	£719
			¥76,278	¥158,888	¥117,583
HILL, WILLIAM EBSWORTH	1	1	$1,380	$1,380	$1,380
			DM2,332	DM2,332	DM2,332
			£828	£828	£828
			¥168,360	¥168,360	¥168,360
HILL, W.E. & SONS	346	308	$327	$7,996	$2,432
			DM512	DM14,246	DM4,002
			£196	£5,060	£1,506
			¥36,486	¥1,026,214	¥271,267
HOUFFLACK, G.	1	1	$1,829	$1,829	$1,829
			DM3,383	DM3,383	DM3,383
			£1,093	£1,093	£1,093
			¥243,726	¥243,726	¥243,726
HOYER (attributed to)	1	1	$1,148	$1,148	$1,148
			DM1,697	DM1,697	DM1,697
			£748	£748	£748
			¥122,391	¥122,391	¥122,391
HOYER, ADOLF	1	1	$849	$849	$849
			DM1,249	DM1,249	DM1,249
			£552	£552	£552
			¥90,064	¥90,064	¥90,064
HOYER, C.A.	6	2	$58	$1,051	$555
			DM101	DM1,779	DM940
			£35	£661	£348
			¥7,395	¥130,266	¥68,831
HOYER, HERMANN ALBERT	2	2	$385	$472	$429
			DM546	DM669	DM608
			£247	£299	£273
			¥39,163	¥48,737	¥43,950
HOYER, OTTO	6	5	$493	$1,265	$1,036
			DM876	DM2,252	DM1,781
			£299	£759	£638
			¥68,438	¥168,220	¥125,754
HOYER, OTTO (workshop of)	1	1	$920	$920	$920
			DM1,574	DM1,574	DM1,574
			£544	£544	£544
			¥114,246	¥114,246	¥114,246
HOYER, OTTO A.	24	16	$387	$3,635	$1,161
			DM674	DM5,134	DM1,885
			£230	£2,300	£714
			¥49,303	¥324,385	¥131,616
HOYER, OTTO A. (workshop of)	1	1	$661	$661	$661
			DM1,248	DM1,248	DM1,248
			£409	£409	£409
			¥69,960	¥69,960	¥69,960
HUMS, ALBIN	3	2	$792	$794	$793
			DM1,169	DM1,218	DM1,194
			£517	£517	£517
			¥84,220	¥86,861	¥85,540

Maker	Items		Selling Prices		
	Bid	Sold	Low	High	Avg
HURY, CUNIOT	4	4	$406	$1,826	$1,226
			DM565	DM3,437	DM2,172
			£253	£1,127	£748
			¥34,294	¥194,633	¥139,261
HUSSON, AUGUST	4	3	$856	$3,474	$2,468
			DM1,380	DM6,533	DM4,349
			£497	£2,185	£1,507
			¥100,740	¥420,044	¥298,095
HUSSON, CHARLES CLAUDE	10	5	$713	$1,955	$1,386
			DM1,150	DM2,942	DM2,236
			£414	£1,187	£845
			¥11,616	¥218,530	¥126,188
HUSSON, CHARLES CLAUDE (attributed to)	2	1	$1,324	$1,324	$1,324
			DM1,957	DM1,957	DM1,957
			£862	£862	£862
			¥141,139	¥141,139	¥141,139
HUSSON, CHARLES CLAUDE (II)	2	0			
JOMBAR, PAUL	10	5	$1,164	$4,099	$1,922
			DM1,632	DM7,362	DM3,051
			£747	£2,530	£1,207
			¥117,580	¥483,913	¥201,393
KARON, JAN	1	1	$794	$794	$794
			DM1,498	DM1,498	DM1,498
			£491	£491	£491
			¥83,952	¥83,952	¥83,952
KAUL, PAUL	1	0			
KEY, ALBERT E.	1	1	$374	$374	$374
			DM639	DM639	DM639
			£221	£221	£221
			¥46,412	¥46,412	¥46,412
KITTEL (attributed to)	1	0			
KITTEL, NICOLAUS (ascribed to)	1	0			
KITTEL, NICOLAUS (attributed to)	3	3	$2,588	$95,013	$39,318
			DM4,699	DM180,056	DM74,442
			£1,584	£58,650	£24,266
			¥321,316	¥10,033,256	¥4,167,951
KNOPF	1	0			
KNOPF (workshop of)	1	1	$748	$748	$748
			DM1,331	DM1,331	DM1,331
			£449	£449	£449
			¥99,403	¥99,403	¥99,403
KNOPF, H.	1	1	$1,304	$1,304	$1,304
			DM2,343	DM2,343	DM2,343
			£805	£805	£805
			¥153,972	¥153,972	¥153,972
KNOPF, HEINRICH	6	5	$616	$2,812	$1,483
			DM1,140	DM4,865	DM2,658
			£368	£1,725	£902
			¥82,097	¥320,850	¥181,755
KNOPF, HENRY RICHARD	1	0			
KOLSTEIN, SAMUEL	2	2	$535	$1,714	$1,124
			DM1,013	DM3,248	DM2,131
			£330	£1,058	£694
			¥56,462	¥180,992	¥118,727

Maker	Items		Selling Prices		
	Bid	Sold	Low	High	Avg
KOUCKY, WILLIAM H.	1	1	$633	$633	$633
			DM1,093	DM1,093	DM1,093
			£391	£391	£391
			¥80,160	¥80,160	¥80,160
KOVANDA, FRANK	1	0			
KREUSLER, ERNST	1	1	$360	$360	$360
			DM550	DM550	DM550
			£230	£230	£230
			¥40,147	¥40,147	¥40,147
KUEHNL, EMIL	3	2	$115	$1,495	$805
			DM193	DM2,558	DM1,375
			£69	£884	£477
			¥14,006	¥185,649	¥99,828
KUHNLA, STEFFEN	1	1	$315	$315	$315
			DM532	DM532	DM532
			£198	£198	£198
			¥38,967	¥38,967	¥38,967
KUN, JOSEPH	1	1	$1,495	$1,495	$1,495
			DM2,558	DM2,558	DM2,558
			£884	£884	£884
			¥185,649	¥185,649	¥185,649
LABERTE	4	2	$745	$1,125	$935
			DM1,334	DM1,967	DM1,650
			£460	£690	£575
			¥87,892	¥132,860	¥110,376
LABERTE, MARC	10	7	$187	$1,762	$997
			DM334	DM2,601	DM1,535
			£115	£1,150	£631
			¥25,177	¥187,336	¥102,606
LABERTE, MARC (workshop of)	3	1	$115	$115	$115
			DM173	DM173	DM173
			£70	£70	£70
			¥12,855	¥12,855	¥12,855
LAFLEUR	1	0			
LAFLEUR, JOSEPH RENE	7	5	$1,997	$3,841	$3,190
			DM3,378	DM6,417	DM4,885
			£1,256	£2,404	£2,020
			¥247,393	¥466,877	¥344,210
LAFLEUR, JOSEPH RENE (attributed to)	1	1	$631	$631	$631
			DM1,067	DM1,067	DM1,067
			£397	£397	£397
			¥78,160	¥78,160	¥78,160
LAMBERT, N.	2	2	$1,518	$1,646	$1,582
			DM2,732	DM3,095	DM2,914
			£920	£1,035	£978
			¥198,968	¥218,914	¥208,941
LAMY, A.	13	9	$3,319	$12,483	$8,020
			DM4,622	DM20,855	DM13,283
			£2,070	£7,475	£4,875
			¥280,584	¥1,517,350	¥918,200
LAMY, A. (attributed to)	3	1	$749	$749	$749
			DM1,111	DM1,111	DM1,111
			£483	£483	£483
			¥81,038	¥81,038	¥81,038
LAMY, ALFRED	30	23	$920	$13,697	$4,607
			DM1,665	DM19,258	DM7,240
			£561	£8,625	£2,857
			¥111,081	¥1,217,617	¥494,364

Maker	Items		Selling Prices		
	Bid	Sold	Low	High	Avg
LAMY, ALFRED (attributed to)	1	1	$1,265	$1,265	$1,265
			DM2,297	DM2,297	DM2,297
			£774	£774	£774
			¥157,088	¥157,088	¥157,088
LAMY, ALFRED JOSEPH	44	37	$1,087	$14,576	$5,760
			DM1,881	DM25,271	DM9,699
			£667	£8,625	£3,545
			¥37,972	¥1,819,875	¥636,853
LAMY, HIPPOLYTE CAMILLE	1	0			
LAMY, JULES	2	0			
LAMY, LOUIS	3	2	$1,765	$3,872	$2,819
			DM2,709	DM5,392	DM4,050
			£1,150	£2,415	£1,783
			¥193,212	¥327,348	¥260,280
LAMY, LOUIS (attributed to)	1	1	$835	$835	$835
			DM1,260	DM1,260	DM1,260
			£506	£506	£506
			¥94,622	¥94,622	¥94,622
LAMY FAMILY (MEMBER OF)	1	0			
LANGONET, EUGENE	1	0			
LANGONET, EUGENE (workshop of)	1	1	$1,955	$1,955	$1,955
			DM2,942	DM2,942	DM2,942
			£1,187	£1,187	£1,187
			¥218,530	¥218,530	¥218,530
LA PIERRE	1	1	$633	$633	$633
			DM1,145	DM1,145	DM1,145
			£386	£386	£386
			¥76,368	¥76,368	¥76,368
LAPIERRE, MARCEL	6	6	$1,265	$3,172	$1,762
			DM1,915	DM4,682	DM2,740
			£759	£2,070	£1,098
			¥139,068	¥337,205	¥192,616
LATOUR, ARMAND	1	1	$905	$905	$905
			DM1,603	DM1,603	DM1,603
			£555	£555	£555
			¥110,297	¥110,297	¥110,297
LAURY, N.	2	1	$1,697	$1,697	$1,697
			DM3,088	DM3,088	DM3,088
			£1,035	£1,035	£1,035
			¥214,390	¥214,390	¥214,390
LAUXERROIS, JEAN-PAUL	2	2	$1,145	$1,453	$1,299
			DM1,690	DM2,610	DM2,150
			£747	£897	£822
			¥121,687	¥171,569	¥146,628
LAVEST, J.	1	1	$817	$817	$817
			DM1,154	DM1,154	DM1,154
			£517	£517	£517
			¥72,916	¥72,916	¥72,916
LAVEST, MICHEL	1	1	$551	$551	$551
			DM927	DM927	DM927
			£345	£345	£345
			¥67,642	¥67,642	¥67,642
LECCHI, BERNARDO GIUSEPPE	1	0			
LECLERC FAMILY (MEMBER OF)	1	0			

Maker	Items		Selling Prices		
	Bid	Sold	Low	High	Avg
LEE, JOHN NORWOOD	5	3	$1,380	$2,357	$1,706
			DM2,110	DM4,466	DM2,979
			£816	£1,455	£1,060
			¥145,452	¥248,864	¥188,561
LEICHT, MAX	3	3	$673	$1,210	$866
			DM1,210	DM2,174	DM1,543
			£402	£747	£533
			¥88,581	¥142,879	¥107,047
LE JEUNE	1	1	$1,924	$1,924	$1,924
			DM2,697	DM2,697	DM2,697
			£1,208	£1,208	£1,208
			¥169,636	¥169,636	¥169,636
LENOBLE, AUGUSTE	3	1	$7,498	$7,498	$7,498
			DM13,294	DM13,294	DM13,294
			£4,600	£4,600	£4,600
			¥886,558	¥886,558	¥886,558
LORANGE, PAUL	1	0			
LOTTE, FRANCOIS	16	12	$1,089	$2,305	$1,481
			DM1,533	DM3,850	DM2,479
			£690	£1,380	£903
			¥111,319	¥280,126	¥176,634
LOTTE, ROGER	4	2	$2,523	$7,731	$5,127
			DM4,269	DM11,568	DM7,918
			£1,587	£4,600	£3,094
			¥312,639	¥862,408	¥587,524
LOTTE, ROGER-FRANCOIS	8	5	$822	$3,055	$1,942
			DM1,546	DM4,900	DM3,345
			£517	£1,984	£1,195
			¥99,388	¥347,593	¥237,977
LOUIS, A.N.	1	1	$5,750	$5,750	$5,750
			DM8,315	DM8,315	DM8,315
			£3,756	£3,756	£3,756
			¥582,188	¥582,188	¥582,188
LUCCHI, GIOVANNI	1	0			
LUPOT	4	3	$845	$7,398	$3,514
			DM1,506	DM10,906	DM5,433
			£518	£4,830	£2,243
			¥110,554	¥789,077	¥401,897
LUPOT, F. (attributed to)	1	0			
LUPOT, FRANCOIS (attributed to)	1	0			
LUPOT, FRANCOIS (II)	6	4	$2,648	$5,831	$4,499
			DM4,063	DM10,109	DM6,880
			£1,725	£3,450	£2,789
			¥289,817	¥727,950	¥461,189
LUPOT, NICOLAS	1	0			
MAGNIERE, GABRIEL	1	0			
MAIRE (workshop of)	1	1	$2,999	$2,999	$2,999
			DM5,318	DM5,318	DM5,318
			£1,840	£1,840	£1,840
			¥354,623	¥354,623	¥354,623
MAIRE, N. (workshop of)	2	2	$676	$5,762	$3,219
			DM1,216	DM9,626	DM5,421
			£403	£3,450	£1,926
			¥78,178	¥700,316	¥389,247

| Maker | Items | | Selling Prices | | |
---	Bid	Sold	Low	High	Avg
MAIRE, NICOLAS	10	6	$4,725	$25,300	$14,406
			DM6,674	DM43,288	DM25,174
			£2,990	£14,964	£8,694
			¥421,701	¥3,141,754	¥1,770,183
MAIRE, NICOLAS (attributed to)	1	1	$11,645	$11,645	$11,645
			DM16,331	DM16,331	DM16,331
			£7,475	£7,475	£7,475
			¥1,176,587	¥1,176,587	¥1,176,587
MAIRE, NICOLAS (workshop of)	1	1	$3,877	$3,877	$3,877
			DM5,723	DM5,723	DM5,723
			£2,530	£2,530	£2,530
			¥412,140	¥412,140	¥412,140
MAIRE, NICOLAS (II)	1	1	$6,729	$6,729	$6,729
			DM11,384	DM11,384	DM11,384
			£4,232	£4,232	£4,232
			¥833,704	¥833,704	¥833,704
MALINE (workshop of)	1	1	$4,388	$4,388	$4,388
			DM8,252	DM8,252	DM8,252
			£2,760	£2,760	£2,760
			¥530,582	¥530,582	¥530,582
MALINE, GUILLAUME	10	7	$3,531	$25,126	$10,242
			DM5,418	DM37,595	DM16,823
			£2,300	£14,950	£6,232
			¥386,423	¥2,802,826	¥1,181,516
MALINE, GUILLAUME (attributed to)	1	0			
MALINE, GUILLAUME (workshop of)	1	0			
MARTIN, J. (attributed to)	2	1	$1,782	$1,782	$1,782
			DM3,224	DM3,224	DM3,224
			£1,093	£1,093	£1,093
			¥214,982	¥214,982	¥214,982
MARTIN, JEAN JOSEPH	11	7	$2,300	$5,486	$3,957
			DM4,261	DM10,316	DM6,455
			£1,380	£3,450	£2,489
			¥307,229	¥663,228	¥446,434
MAUCOTEL & DESCHAMPS	5	3	$347	$1,236	$895
			DM641	DM1,896	DM1,463
			£207	£805	£567
			¥46,180	¥135,283	¥105,570
MCGILL, A.	1	0			
MEINEL, F.	1	0			
MENNESSON, EMILE	2	0			
METTAL, WALTER	2	1	$690	$690	$690
			DM1,253	DM1,253	DM1,253
			£422	£422	£422
			¥85,684	¥85,684	¥85,684
MILLANT, B.	3	2	$2,899	$3,816	$3,358
			DM4,338	DM5,391	DM4,864
			£1,725	£2,415	£2,070
			¥323,403	¥340,604	¥332,004
MILLANT, JEAN-JACQUES	2	2	$2,329	$3,887	$3,108
			DM3,266	DM6,739	DM5,003
			£1,495	£2,300	£1,898
			¥235,317	¥485,300	¥360,309
MILLANT, M.	2	1	$1,360	$1,360	$1,360
			DM2,359	DM2,359	DM2,359
			£805	£805	£805
			¥169,855	¥169,855	¥169,855

Maker	Items		Selling Prices		
	Bid	Sold	Low	High	Avg
MILLANT, ROGER & MAX	5	3	$823	$2,657	$1,452
			DM1,558	DM4,009	DM2,409
			£518	£1,610	£893
			¥98,630	¥301,070	¥168,302
MILLANT, ROGER	1	1	$1,829	$1,829	$1,829
			DM3,439	DM3,439	DM3,439
			£1,150	£1,150	£1,150
			¥221,076	¥221,076	¥221,076
MIQUEL, E.	2	1	$1,160	$1,160	$1,160
			DM1,735	DM1,735	DM1,735
			£690	£690	£690
			¥129,361	¥129,361	¥129,361
MIQUEL FAMILY (MEMBER OF)	1	0			
MOHR, RODNEY D.	2	2	$546	$690	$618
			DM789	DM1,228	DM1,008
			£348	£414	£381
			¥47,387	¥91,756	¥69,572
MOINEL, DANIEL	1	1	$1,633	$1,633	$1,633
			DM2,300	DM2,300	DM2,300
			£1,035	£1,035	£1,035
			¥166,979	¥166,979	¥166,979
MOLLER, M.	1	1	$1,642	$1,642	$1,642
			DM2,457	DM2,457	DM2,457
			£977	£977	£977
			¥183,168	¥183,168	¥183,168
MOLLER & ZOON	2	1	$1,635	$1,635	$1,635
			DM3,026	DM3,026	DM3,026
			£977	£977	£977
			¥217,959	¥217,959	¥217,959
MONNIG, A. HERMANN	2	1	$450	$450	$450
			DM778	DM778	DM778
			£276	£276	£276
			¥51,336	¥51,336	¥51,336
MORIZOT	2	2	$922	$2,397	$1,660
			DM1,284	DM3,338	DM2,311
			£575	£1,495	£1,035
			¥77,940	¥202,644	¥140,292
MORIZOT (attributed to)	1	0			
MORIZOT, L.	2	2	$1,071	$1,671	$1,371
			DM2,035	DM3,174	DM2,604
			£661	£1,032	£846
			¥112,551	¥175,580	¥144,066
MORIZOT, LOUIS	36	26	$615	$3,635	$1,924
			DM884	DM5,134	DM3,010
			£368	£2,300	£1,203
			¥64,064	¥347,781	¥206,113
MORIZOT, LOUIS (attributed to)	1	1	$1,495	$1,495	$1,495
			DM2,706	DM2,706	DM2,706
			£912	£912	£912
			¥180,506	¥180,506	¥180,506
MORIZOT, LOUIS (II)	14	9	$1,218	$4,571	$2,634
			DM2,107	DM8,596	DM4,471
			£747	£2,875	£1,635
			¥138,942	¥552,690	¥312,152
MORIZOT (FRERES), LOUIS	3	3	$1,150	$1,344	$1,269
			DM2,047	DM2,326	DM2,206
			£690	£805	£767
			¥152,927	¥163,407	¥157,161

Maker	Items		Selling Prices		
	Bid	Sold	Low	High	Avg
MORIZOT FRERES	1	0			
MORIZOT FAMILY	7	6	$748	$2,530	$1,379
			DM1,353	DM4,503	DM2,457
			£456	£1,518	£835
			¥90,253	¥336,439	¥168,423
MOUGENOT, LEON	3	1	$794	$794	$794
			DM1,218	DM1,218	DM1,218
			£517	£517	£517
			¥86,861	¥86,861	¥86,861
MULLER, FRIEDRICH KARL	1	1	$1,928	$1,928	$1,928
			DM3,654	DM3,654	DM3,654
			£1,190	£1,190	£1,190
			¥203,616	¥203,616	¥203,616
NEHR, J.P.	1	0			
NEUDORFER	2	2	$233	$402	$317
			DM356	DM565	DM460
			£150	£253	£201
			¥22,991	¥35,858	¥29,424
NEUVILLE	1	1	$396	$396	$396
			DM605	DM605	DM605
			£253	£253	£253
			¥44,161	¥44,161	¥44,161
NOLDER, T.J.	1	1	$701	$701	$701
			DM976	DM976	DM976
			£437	£437	£437
			¥59,234	¥59,234	¥59,234
NURNBERGER	4	2	$719	$1,125	$922
			DM1,018	DM2,123	DM1,570
			£460	£696	£578
			¥73,052	¥118,993	¥96,023
NURNBERGER (workshop of)	1	1	$1,265	$1,265	$1,265
			DM2,252	DM2,252	DM2,252
			-	£759	£759	£759
			¥168,220	¥168,220	¥168,220
NURNBERGER, ALBERT	67	59	$288	$4,748	$1,525
			DM433	DM6,676	DM2,402
			£175	£2,990	£954
			¥32,137	¥422,107	¥165,519
NURNBERGER, ALBERT (attributed to)	3	1	$1,121	$1,121	$1,121
			DM1,955	DM1,955	DM1,955
			£690	£690	£690
			¥135,827	¥135,827	¥135,827
NURNBERGER, ALBERT (workshop of)	2	1	$805	$805	$805
			DM1,391	DM1,391	DM1,391
			£497	£497	£497
			¥102,022	¥102,022	¥102,022
NURNBERGER, AUGUST	1	1	$978	$978	$978
			DM1,412	DM1,412	DM1,412
			£623	£623	£623
			¥84,798	¥84,798	¥84,798
NURNBERGER, CH.	1	1	$575	$575	$575
			DM879	DM879	DM879
			£378	£378	£378
			¥60,605	¥60,605	¥60,605
NURNBERGER, CHRISTIAN ALBERT	6	4	$1,536	$2,523	$1,828
			DM2,567	DM4,269	DM3,129
			£920	£1,587	£1,133
			¥186,751	¥312,639	¥223,160

Maker	Items		Selling Prices		
	Bid	Sold	Low	High	Avg
NURNBERGER, FRANZ ALBERT	1	1	$3,811	$3,811	$3,811
			DM5,366	DM5,366	DM5,366
			£2,415	£2,415	£2,415
			¥389,617	¥389,617	¥389,617
NURNBERGER, KARL ALBERT	35	28	$865	$3,457	$1,737
			DM1,278	DM5,775	DM2,938
			£517	£2,070	£1,066
			¥92,766	¥420,189	¥205,451
NURNBERGER, KARL ALBERT (II)	1	1	$2,295	$2,295	$2,295
			DM3,521	DM3,521	DM3,521
			£1,495	£1,495	£1,495
			¥251,175	¥251,175	¥251,175
NURNBERGER-SUESS, AUGUST	1	1	$1,162	$1,162	$1,162
			DM2,011	DM2,011	DM2,011
			£713	£713	£713
			¥132,618	¥132,618	¥132,618
OUCHARD, B.	2	2	$3,785	$5,693	$4,739
			DM6,404	DM8,591	DM7,497
			£2,381	£3,450	£2,915
			¥468,959	¥645,150	¥557,054
OUCHARD, BERNARD	2	1	$3,540	$3,540	$3,540
			DM6,708	DM6,708	DM6,708
			£2,185	£2,185	£2,185
			¥373,788	¥373,788	¥373,788
OUCHARD, E.	2	1	$4,592	$4,592	$4,592
			DM7,722	DM7,722	DM7,722
			£2,875	£2,875	£2,875
			¥563,681	¥563,681	¥563,681
OUCHARD, EMILE	22	16	$1,068	$6,038	$3,333
			DM1,852	DM10,203	DM5,516
			£632	£3,680	£2,030
			¥135,798	¥736,575	¥385,625
OUCHARD, EMILE (FILS)	1	1	$6,856	$6,856	$6,856
			DM13,022	DM13,022	DM13,022
			£4,232	£4,232	£4,232
			¥720,329	¥720,329	¥720,329
OUCHARD, EMILE A.	15	13	$519	$12,855	$5,885
			DM960	DM24,360	DM10,278
			£310	£7,935	£3,623
			¥69,158	¥1,357,440	¥632,385
OUCHARD, EMILE FRANCOIS	16	14	$909	$23,590	$4,958
			DM1,283	DM33,220	DM8,112
			£575	£14,950	£3,099
			¥81,096	¥2,411,913	¥524,303
OUCHARD, J.CL. (ascribed to)	1	0			
OUCHARD, J.CL. (attributed to)	2	0			
OUDINOT	1	0			
PAJEOT	7	5	$5,901	$11,765	$8,813
			DM8,216	DM21,176	DM14,403
			£3,680	£7,130	£5,474
			¥498,817	¥1,696,584	¥1,007,463
PAJEOT, E.	1	0			
PAJEOT, ETIENNE	14	7	$2,291	$13,800	$6,901
			DM3,382	DM23,322	DM11,638
			£1,495	£8,280	£4,190
			¥243,537	¥1,683,600	¥833,700

Maker	Items		Selling Prices		
	Bid	Sold	Low	High	Avg
PAJEOT, LOUIS SIMON	8	4	$1,682	$13,926	$7,235
			DM2,846	DM26,390	DM13,301
			£1,058	£8,596	£4,512
			¥208,426	¥1,470,560	¥804,073
PAJEOT, LOUIS SIMON (attributed to)	1	0			
PANORMO, LOUIS	1	1	$960	$960	$960
			DM1,604	DM1,604	DM1,604
			£575	£575	£575
			¥116,719	¥116,719	¥116,719
PAQUOTTE, ALBERT	1	1	$5,452	$5,452	$5,452
			DM7,701	DM7,701	DM7,701
			£3,450	£3,450	£3,450
			¥486,578	¥486,578	¥486,578
PARISOT, A.	1	1	$1,272	$1,272	$1,272
			DM1,797	DM1,797	DM1,797
			£805	£805	£805
			¥113,535	¥113,535	¥113,535
PASSA, FRANK	1	1	$690	$690	$690
			DM1,055	DM1,055	DM1,055
			£454	£454	£454
			¥72,726	¥72,726	¥72,726
PATIGNY, PIERRE	4	3	$3,009	$5,570	$4,288
			DM4,969	DM10,556	DM7,882
			£1,840	£3,439	£2,641
			¥372,470	¥588,224	¥471,058
PAULUS, GUNTER A.	2	1	$1,344	$1,344	$1,344
			DM2,496	DM2,496	DM2,496
			£805	£805	£805
			¥179,869	¥179,869	¥179,869
PAULUS, JOHANNES O.	3	2	$726	$792	$759
			DM1,022	DM1,169	DM1,096
			£460	£517	£489
			¥74,213	¥84,220	¥79,216
PAULUS, OTTO	1	1	$792	$792	$792
			DM1,169	DM1,169	DM1,169
			£517	£517	£517
			¥84,220	¥84,220	¥84,220
PECATTE, C.	1	0			
PECATTE, CHARLES	1	1	$4,571	$4,571	$4,571
			DM8,654	DM8,654	DM8,654
			£2,875	£2,875	£2,875
			¥547,946	¥547,946	¥547,946
PECCATTE, CHARLES	7	6	$1,999	$14,097	$5,434
			DM2,824	DM20,809	DM8,484
			£1,265	£9,200	£3,488
			¥178,412	¥1,498,689	¥592,376
PECCATTE, CHARLES (ascribed to)	1	1	$1,291	$1,291	$1,291
			DM1,797	DM1,797	DM1,797
			£805	£805	£805
			¥109,116	¥109,116	¥109,116
PECCATTE, CHARLES (attributed to)	1	0			
PECCATTE, D. & HENRY, J.	1	1	$7,682	$7,682	$7,682
			DM13,754	DM13,754	DM13,754
			£4,600	£4,600	£4,600
			¥1,056,988	¥1,056,988	¥1,056,988

Maker	Items		Selling Prices		
	Bid	Sold	Low	High	Avg
PECCATTE, DOMINIQUE	8	4	$5,286	$29,153	$19,010
			DM7,804	DM50,543	DM31,897
			£3,450	£17,250	£11,788
			¥562,008	¥3,639,750	¥2,154,222
PECCATTE, DOMINIQUE (ascribed to)	2	1	$27,209	$27,209	$27,209
			DM47,173	DM47,173	DM47,173
			£16,100	£16,100	£16,100
			¥3,397,100	¥3,397,100	¥3,397,100
PECCATTE, FRANCOIS	2	2	$7,258	$27,852	$17,555
			DM10,222	DM52,781	DM31,501
			£4,600	£17,193	£10,896
			¥742,127	¥2,941,121	¥1,841,624
PECCATTE FAMILY (MEMBER OF)	1	1	$15,836	$15,836	$15,836
			DM28,445	DM28,445	DM28,445
			£9,775	£9,775	£9,775
			¥1,869,664	¥1,869,664	¥1,869,664
PENZEL	1	1	$367	$367	$367
			DM641	DM641	DM641
			£219	£219	£219
			¥46,838	¥46,838	¥46,838
PENZEL, E.M.	1	1	$863	$863	$863
			DM1,298	DM1,298	DM1,298
			£524	£524	£524
			¥96,410	¥96,410	¥96,410
PENZEL, K. GERHARD	2	1	$2,118	$2,118	$2,118
			DM3,251	DM3,251	DM3,251
			£1,380	£1,380	£1,380
			¥231,854	¥231,854	¥231,854
PERSOIS	4	2	$6,542	$20,165	$13,354
			DM9,241	DM37,433	DM23,337
			£4,140	£12,075	£8,108
			¥583,893	¥2,698,038	¥1,640,966
PERSOIS, JEAN-PIERRE-MARIE	1	1	$56,868	$56,868	$56,868
			DM107,337	DM107,337	DM107,337
			£35,201	£35,201	£35,201
			¥6,016,582	¥6,016,582	¥6,016,582
PFRETZSCHNER	2	1	$469	$469	$469
			DM834	DM834	DM834
			£288	£288	£288
			¥62,942	¥62,942	¥62,942
PFRETZSCHNER (attributed to)	1	1	$940	$940	$940
			DM1,553	DM1,553	DM1,553
			£575	£575	£575
			¥116,397	¥116,397	¥116,397
PFRETZSCHNER, C.F.	1	0			
PFRETZSCHNER, F.C.	1	1	$509	$509	$509
			DM719	DM719	DM719
			£322	£322	£322
			¥45,414	¥45,414	¥45,414
PFRETZSCHNER, G.A.	6	6	$460	$1,380	$743
			DM828	DM2,332	DM1,245
			£276	£828	£453
			¥3,574	¥183,637	¥84,273
PFRETZSCHNER, H.R.	43	34	$373	$3,785	$1,280
			DM649	DM6,404	DM2,153
			£230	£2,381	£795
			¥39,381	¥468,959	¥150,544

Maker	Items Bid	Sold	Low	Selling Prices High	Avg
PFRETZSCHNER, H.R. (workshop of)	1	1	$489 DM826 £293 ¥59,628	$489 DM826 £293 ¥59,628	$489 DM826 £293 ¥59,628
PFRETZSCHNER, HERMANN RICHARD	1	1	$1,736 DM3,265 £1,092 ¥209,926	$1,736 DM3,265 £1,092 ¥209,926	$1,736 DM3,265 £1,092 ¥209,926
PFRETZSCHNER, L.	3	1	$1,552 DM2,183 £978 ¥137,997	$1,552 DM2,183 £978 ¥137,997	$1,552 DM2,183 £978 ¥137,997
PFRETZSCHNER, L. (attributed to)	1	1	$1,007 DM1,488 £656 ¥107,328	$1,007 DM1,488 £656 ¥107,328	$1,007 DM1,488 £656 ¥107,328
PFRETZSCHNER, W.	1	0			
PFRETZSCHNER, W.A.	5	5	$280 DM497 £172 ¥33,150	$1,610 DM2,914 £982 ¥194,391	$821 DM1,404 £506 ¥97,498
PFRETZSCHNER, WILHELM AUGUST	1	0			
PILLOT	2	2	$1,728 DM3,066 £1,035 ¥222,638	$2,178 DM3,209 £1,380 ¥231,260	$1,953 DM3,137 £1,208 ¥226,949
POIRSON	2	0			
POIRSON, JUSTIN	8	3	$294 DM498 £185 ¥36,475	$2,363 DM3,439 £1,495 ¥221,076	$1,495 DM2,425 £943 ¥156,134
POIRSON, JUSTIN (attributed to)	1	1	$2,185 DM3,955 £1,333 ¥263,817	$2,185 DM3,955 £1,333 ¥263,817	$2,185 DM3,955 £1,333 ¥263,817
PRAGA, EUGENIO	1	0			
PRAGER, AUGUST EDWIN	15	14	$576 DM898 £345 ¥54,490	$2,310 DM4,274 £1,495 ¥307,864	$1,323 DM2,235 £804 ¥163,764
PRAGER, GUSTAV	8	5	$352 DM593 £219 ¥43,233	$829 DM1,469 £517 ¥101,105	$639 DM1,014 £403 ¥72,136
PRAGER, GUSTAV OSKAR	2	2	$922 DM1,540 £552 ¥112,050	$1,093 DM1,850 £688 ¥135,477	$1,008 DM1,695 £620 ¥123,764
PRELL, HERMAN WILHELM	8	5	$415 DM754 £253 ¥50,091	$1,114 DM1,642 £725 ¥118,209	$750 DM1,253 £463 ¥85,486
RAHM, WILHELM	1	1	$1,412 DM2,167 £920 ¥154,569	$1,412 DM2,167 £920 ¥154,569	$1,412 DM2,167 £920 ¥154,569

Maker	Items		Selling Prices		
	Bid	Sold	Low	High	Avg
RAPOPORT, HAIM (attributed to)	6	2	$338	$338	$338
			DM602	DM602	DM602
			£207	£207	£207
			¥44,221	¥44,221	¥44,221
RAU, AUGUST	6	5	$375	$1,687	$1,268
			DM665	DM2,991	DM2,044
			£230	£1,035	£702
			¥44,328	¥199,476	¥136,670
REICHEL	1	1	$226	$226	$226
			DM391	DM391	DM391
			£138	£138	£138
			¥25,828	¥25,828	¥25,828
REIDEL, E.	2	2	$316	$460	$388
			DM457	DM787	DM622
			£207	£272	£239
			¥32,020	¥57,123	¥44,572
RETFORD, WILLIAM C.	1	0			
RICHAUME, ANDRE	5	5	$3,348	$8,998	$6,325
			DM4,942	DM17,052	DM10,770
			£2,185	£5,555	£3,940
			¥355,939	¥950,208	¥676,352
ROBICHAUD	1	1	$1,536	$1,536	$1,536
			DM2,567	DM2,567	DM2,567
			£920	£920	£920
			¥186,751	¥186,751	¥186,751
ROCKWELL, DAVID BAILEY	1	1	$403	$403	$403
			DM689	DM689	DM689
			£238	£238	£238
			¥49,982	¥49,982	¥49,982
ROLLAND	1	1	$5,762	$5,762	$5,762
			DM9,626	DM9,626	DM9,626
			£3,450	£3,450	£3,450
			¥700,316	¥700,316	¥700,316
ROLLAND, BENOIT	3	2	$1,177	$1,380	$1,279
			DM2,231	DM2,385	DM2,308
			£727	£853	£790
			¥124,334	¥174,894	¥149,614
ROLLAND, S.	1	0			
ROTH, ERNST HEINRICH (workshop of)	1	1	$805	$805	$805
			DM1,212	DM1,212	DM1,212
			£489	£489	£489
			¥89,983	¥89,983	¥89,983
ROTH, EUGEN	1	1	$173	$173	$173
			DM244	DM244	DM244
			£109	£109	£109
			¥17,808	¥17,808	¥17,808
SANDNER, A.L.	1	0			
SARTORY, E.	3	2	$10,712	$18,630	$14,671
			DM20,347	DM33,465	DM26,906
			£6,613	£11,500	£9,056
			¥1,125,514	¥2,199,605	¥1,662,559
SARTORY, EUGENE	115	97	$734	$30,576	$8,513
			DM1,320	DM43,250	DM13,888
			£437	£19,550	£5,276
			¥84,879	¥3,104,716	¥964,796

Maker	Items		Selling Prices		
	Bid	Sold	Low	High	Avg
SARTORY, EUGENE (attributed to)	2	2	$2,689	$3,498	$3,094
			DM4,492	DM6,065	DM5,279
			£1,610	£2,070	£1,840
			¥326,814	¥436,770	¥381,792
SARTORY, EUGENE (workshop of)	2	2	$3,226	$3,658	$3,442
			DM4,868	DM6,767	DM5,817
			£1,955	£2,185	£2,070
			¥365,585	¥487,452	¥426,518
SCHAFFNER, M.	1	1	$1,283	$1,283	$1,283
			DM1,798	DM1,798	DM1,798
			£805	£805	£805
			¥113,090	¥113,090	¥113,090
SCHICKER, HORST	2	0			
SCHMIDT, HANS KARL	1	0			
SCHMITT, LUCIEN	1	1	$1,518	$1,518	$1,518
			DM2,732	DM2,732	DM2,732
			£920	£920	£920
			¥218,914	¥218,914	¥218,914
SCHUBERT, PAUL	4	3	$149	$863	$417
			DM282	DM1,221	DM612
			£92	£552	£265
			¥15,738	¥87,663	¥41,222
SCHULLER	1	1	$601	$601	$601
			DM885	DM885	DM885
			£391	£391	£391
			¥63,796	¥63,796	¥63,796
SCHULTZ, T.	1	1	$348	$348	$348
			DM534	DM534	DM534
			£230	£230	£230
			¥37,082	¥37,082	¥37,082
SCHUSTER, ADOLF	4	2	$920	$1,150	$1,035
			DM1,330	DM1,988	DM1,659
			£601	£711	£656
			¥93,150	¥145,745	¥119,448
SCHUSTER, ADOLPH CURT	4	4	$916	$1,490	$1,162
			DM1,353	DM2,824	DM1,869
			£593	£920	£734
			¥97,415	¥157,384	¥123,036
SCHUSTER, GOTHARD	3	3	$186	$1,210	$788
			DM326	DM2,278	DM1,447
			£115	£747	£479
			¥22,534	¥127,901	¥87,373
SCHUSTER, MAX K.	1	1	$1,035	$1,035	$1,035
			DM1,842	DM1,842	DM1,842
			£621	£621	£621
			¥137,634	¥137,634	¥137,634
SCHUSTER, WILHELM R.	1	1	$805	$805	$805
			DM1,212	DM1,212	DM1,212
			£489	£489	£489
			¥89,983	¥89,983	¥89,983
SCHWARZ	1	1	$258	$258	$258
			DM359	DM359	DM359
			£161	£161	£161
			¥21,823	¥21,823	¥21,823
SEIFERT, LOTHAR	16	9	$288	$2,999	$1,144
			DM440	DM5,697	DM2,032
			£173	£1,852	£698
			¥30,303	¥315,144	¥135,120

| Maker | Items | | Selling Prices | | |
	Bid	Sold	Low	High	Avg
SEIFERT, W.	1	1	$487	$487	$487
			DM748	DM748	DM748
			£322	£322	£322
			¥51,914	¥51,914	¥51,914
SERDET, PAUL	3	1	$575	$575	$575
			DM1,035	DM1,035	DM1,035
			£345	£345	£345
			¥4,468	¥4,468	¥4,468
SILVESTRE, HIPPOLYTE CHRETIEN	1	1	$4,057	$4,057	$4,057
			DM5,649	DM5,649	DM5,649
			£2,530	£2,530	£2,530
			¥342,936	¥342,936	¥342,936
SILVESTRE & MAUCOTEL	5	2	$2,422	$2,819	$2,621
			DM4,162	DM4,350	DM4,256
			£1,495	£1,840	£1,668
			¥285,949	¥299,738	¥292,843
SILVESTRE & MAUCOTEL (workshop of)	2	1	$1,725	$1,725	$1,725
			DM2,596	DM2,596	DM2,596
			£1,047	£1,047	£1,047
			¥192,821	¥192,821	¥192,821
SIMON, F.R.	1	0			
SIMON, PAUL	5	3	$2,118	$6,325	$4,079
			DM3,253	DM11,259	DM7,114
			£1,380	£3,795	£2,492
			¥231,825	¥841,098	¥540,069
SIMON, PAUL (ascribed to)	1	1	$4,664	$4,664	$4,664
			DM8,087	DM8,087	DM8,087
			£2,760	£2,760	£2,760
			¥582,360	¥582,360	¥582,360
SIMON, PAUL (attributed to)	1	1	$4,140	$4,140	$4,140
			DM7,369	DM7,369	DM7,369
			£2,484	£2,484	£2,484
			¥550,537	¥550,537	¥550,537
SIMON BROS.	3	1	$1,874	$1,874	$1,874
			DM3,243	DM3,243	DM3,243
			£1,150	£1,150	£1,150
			¥213,900	¥213,900	¥213,900
SIRDEVAN, JOHN	3	3	$575	$920	$709
			DM831	DM1,328	DM1,025
			£376	£586	£458
			¥58,219	¥79,810	¥67,356
SMITH, THOMAS	1	1	$4,071	$4,071	$4,071
			DM7,714	DM7,714	DM7,714
			£2,513	£2,513	£2,513
			¥429,856	¥429,856	¥429,856
STOHR, H.A.	1	1	$207	$207	$207
			DM377	DM377	DM377
			£127	£127	£127
			¥25,046	¥25,046	¥25,046
STOSS, ARNOLD	1	1	$1,323	$1,323	$1,323
			DM2,496	DM2,496	DM2,496
			£819	£819	£819
			¥139,921	¥139,921	¥139,921
STUBER, JOHANN	1	1	$1,234	$1,234	$1,234
			DM1,821	DM1,821	DM1,821
			£805	£805	£805
			¥131,135	¥131,135	¥131,135

Maker	Items		Selling Prices		
	Bid	Sold	Low	High	Avg
SUESS, AUGUST NURNBERGER	1	1	$410	$410	$410
			DM718	DM718	DM718
			£253	£253	£253
			¥49,575	¥49,575	¥49,575
SUSS	1	1	$1,100	$1,100	$1,100
			DM1,541	DM1,541	DM1,541
			£690	£690	£690
			¥96,935	¥96,935	¥96,935
SUSS, CARL	1	1	$632	$632	$632
			DM1,138	DM1,138	DM1,138
			£379	£379	£379
			¥4,911	¥4,911	¥4,911
TAYLOR, MALCOLM	7	3	$805	$1,996	$1,481
			DM1,212	DM2,811	DM2,160
			£489	£1,265	£910
			¥89,983	¥204,085	¥159,110
TAYLOR, MICHAEL J.	3	3	$626	$2,295	$1,571
			DM878	DM3,521	DM2,304
			£402	£1,495	£1,016
			¥63,276	¥251,175	¥165,155
TECHLER	1	1	$149	$149	$149
			DM204	DM204	DM204
			£92	£92	£92
			¥12,382	¥12,382	¥12,382
THIBOUT, JACQUES PIERRE	1	1	$3,001	$3,001	$3,001
			DM4,605	DM4,605	DM4,605
			£1,955	£1,955	£1,955
			¥328,460	¥328,460	¥328,460
THIBOUVILLE-LAMY, J.	16	11	$428	$1,646	$856
			DM741	DM2,784	DM1,496
			£253	£1,035	£533
			¥53,383	¥203,895	¥103,085
THIBOUVILLE-LAMY, J. (workshop of)	1	1	$1,610	$1,610	$1,610
			DM2,328	DM2,328	DM2,328
			£1,052	£1,052	£1,052
			¥163,013	¥163,013	¥163,013
THIBOUVILLE-LAMY, JEROME	4	2	$1,371	$1,677	$1,524
			DM2,577	DM3,177	DM2,877
			£862	£1,035	£949
			¥165,711	¥177,057	¥171,384
THOMA, ADOLF	1	1	$1,018	$1,018	$1,018
			DM1,633	DM1,633	DM1,633
			£661	£661	£661
			¥115,864	¥115,864	¥115,864
THOMA, ARTHUR	3	0			
THOMA, MATHIAS	1	1	$1,304	$1,304	$1,304
			DM2,455	DM2,455	DM2,455
			£805	£805	£805
			¥139,024	¥139,024	¥139,024
THOMASSIN	2	1	$1,068	$1,068	$1,068
			DM1,852	DM1,852	DM1,852
			£632	£632	£632
			¥133,352	¥133,352	¥133,352
THOMASSIN (attributed to)	1	0			
THOMASSIN, C.	*7	5	$1,059	$6,762	$3,021
			DM1,959	DM12,160	DM5,261
			£633	£4,025	£1,840
			¥141,104	¥781,776	¥345,046

Maker	Items		Selling Prices		
	Bid	Sold	Low	High	Avg
THOMASSIN, CLAUDE	37	28	$673	$5,532	$2,651
			DM1,138	DM9,616	DM4,383
			£414	£3,450	£1,636
			¥77,004	¥692,694	¥301,436
THOMASSIN, CLAUDE (attributed to)	1	0			
TILLOTSON, J.	1	1	$730	$730	$730
			DM1,365	DM1,365	DM1,365
			£460	£460	£460
			¥86,393	¥86,393	¥86,393
TOURNIER, JOSEPH ALEXIS	2	1	$3,416	$3,416	$3,416
			DM5,154	DM5,154	DM5,154
			£2,070	£2,070	£2,070
			¥387,090	¥387,090	¥387,090
TOURNIER, JOSEPH ALEXIS (workshop of)	1	1	$2,530	$2,530	$2,530
			DM3,808	DM3,808	DM3,808
			£1,536	£1,536	£1,536
			¥282,803	¥282,803	¥282,803
TOURTE, FRANCOIS	2	1	$76,684	$76,684	$76,684
			DM122,994	DM122,994	DM122,994
			£49,795	£49,795	£49,795
			¥8,725,080	¥8,725,080	¥8,725,080
TOURTE, FRANCOIS (ascribed to)	1	0			
TOURTE, FRANCOIS (attributed to)	1	1	$9,775	$9,775	$9,775
			DM14,711	DM14,711	DM14,711
			£5,934	£5,934	£5,934
			¥1,092,650	¥1,092,650	¥1,092,650
TOURTE, FRANCOIS XAVIER	8	6	$4,180	$68,372	$38,481
			DM5,904	DM129,569	DM68,641
			£2,645	£42,205	£23,891
			¥373,043	¥7,220,009	¥3,918,416
TOURTE, LOUIS (PERE)	3	3	$5,589	$20,353	$10,790
			DM10,592	DM38,571	DM20,447
			£3,450	£12,564	£6,660
			¥590,192	¥2,149,281	¥1,139,397
TOURTE, XAVIER (ascribed to)	2	1	$5,303	$5,303	$5,303
			DM8,971	DM8,971	DM8,971
			£3,335	£3,335	£3,335
			¥656,995	¥656,995	¥656,995
TOURTE, XAVIER (L'AINE) (ascribed to)	1	0			
TOURTE FAMILY	1	0			
TOURTE FAMILY (ascribed to)	1	0			
TUA, SILVIO	3	0			
TUBBS	2	2	$664	$1,312	$988
			DM1,179	DM2,335	DM1,757
			£403	£805	£604
			¥92,128	¥176,239	¥134,183
TUBBS (attributed to)	1	0			
TUBBS, ALFRED	2	1	$2,608	$2,608	$2,608
			DM4,685	DM4,685	DM4,685
			£1,610	£1,610	£1,610
			¥307,945	¥307,945	¥307,945
TUBBS, C.E.	3	1	$2,950	$2,950	$2,950
			DM4,108	DM4,108	DM4,108
			£1,840	£1,840	£1,840
			¥249,408	¥249,408	¥249,408

Maker	Items		Selling Prices		
	Bid	Sold	Low	High	Avg
TUBBS, EDWARD	1	1	$1,840	$1,840	$1,840
			DM3,330	DM3,330	DM3,330
			£1,122	£1,122	£1,122
			¥222,162	¥222,162	¥222,162
TUBBS, J.	4	2	$2,981	$3,353	$3,167
			DM5,612	DM6,024	DM5,818
			£1,840	£2,070	£1,955
			¥315,045	¥395,929	¥355,487
TUBBS, JAMES	129	97	$1,152	$43,616	$4,963
			DM1,849	DM61,606	DM8,145
			£690	£27,600	£3,071
			¥112,234	¥3,892,621	¥544,259
TUBBS, JAMES (attributed to)	5	4	$720	$3,470	$1,662
			DM1,103	DM4,879	DM2,541
			£460	£2,185	£1,029
			¥80,279	¥309,680	¥174,645
TUBBS, T. (attributed to)	4	2	$103	$1,397	$750
			DM171	DM2,631	DM1,401
			£63	£863	£463
			¥12,804	¥147,677	¥80,240
TUBBS, THOMAS	3	2	$2,248	$3,348	$2,798
			DM4,244	DM4,942	DM4,593
			£1,392	£2,185	£1,788
			¥237,865	¥355,939	¥296,902
TUBBS, WILLIAM	3	0			
TUBBS, WILLIAM (attributed to)	3	2	$2,109	$2,120	$2,114
			DM3,133	DM3,906	DM3,519
			£1,265	£1,380	£1,323
			¥225,953	¥281,627	¥253,790
UEBEL, K. WERNER	2	0			
ULLMANN, GIORGIO	3	1	$856	$856	$856
			DM1,380	DM1,380	DM1,380
			£497	£497	£497
			¥100,740	¥100,740	¥100,740
VAN DER MEER, KAREL	4	2	$91	$2,236	$1,163
			DM170	DM4,016	DM2,093
			£57	£1,380	£719
			¥10,958	¥263,953	¥137,455
VEDRAL, JOSEPH	2	2	$1,118	$1,285	$1,202
			DM2,118	DM2,436	DM2,277
			£690	£794	£742
			¥118,038	¥135,744	¥126,891
VICKERS, J.E.	4	2	$226	$244	$235
			DM382	DM428	DM405
			£138	£150	£144
			¥26,150	¥28,883	¥27,516
VICTOR, T.	1	1	$1,864	$1,864	$1,864
			DM3,264	DM3,264	DM3,264
			£1,150	£1,150	£1,150
			¥225,343	¥225,343	¥225,343
VIDOUDEZ, PIERRE	7	5	$480	$3,816	$2,149
			DM889	DM5,391	DM3,256
			£287	£2,415	£1,355
			¥64,027	¥344,319	¥229,614
VIGNERON, A.	16	11	$1,280	$7,079	$4,561
			DM2,423	DM13,329	DM7,708
			£805	£4,370	£2,865
			¥153,425	¥748,231	¥493,486

| Maker | Items | | Selling Prices | | |
---	Bid	Sold	Low	High	Avg
VIGNERON, A. (attributed to)	2	0			
VIGNERON, ANDRE	13	10	$841	$7,269	$4,170
			DM1,423	DM11,230	DM6,551
			£529	£4,600	£2,548
			¥104,213	¥817,035	¥472,332
VIGNERON, ARTHUR	2	2	$3,543	$8,694	$6,119
			DM5,004	DM15,629	DM10,316
			£2,242	£5,175	£3,709
			¥316,205	¥1,005,140	¥660,673
VIGNERON, JOSEPH ARTHUR	41	34	$589	$13,283	$4,600
			DM996	DM25,172	DM7,785
			£370	£8,200	£2,828
			¥72,949	¥1,402,688	¥523,516
VIGNERON, JOSEPH ARTHUR (attributed to)	1	1	$2,049	$2,049	$2,049
			DM3,681	DM3,681	DM3,681
			£1,265	£1,265	£1,265
			¥241,957	¥241,957	¥241,957
VOIGT, ARNOLD	10	7	$630	$1,320	$803
			DM890	DM2,402	DM1,345
			£402	£805	£492
			¥63,921	¥166,748	¥94,514
VOIGT, ARNOLD (workshop of)	1	1	$690	$690	$690
			DM996	DM996	DM996
			£440	£440	£440
			¥59,858	¥59,858	¥59,858
VOIGT, WERNER	1	1	$451	$451	$451
			DM764	DM764	DM764
			£276	£276	£276
			¥52,301	¥52,301	¥52,301
VOIRIN, F.N.	5	3	$5,962	$12,110	$8,995
			DM11,183	DM22,799	DM16,704
			£3,703	£7,475	£5,538
			¥716,605	¥1,279,870	¥1,024,190
VOIRIN, FRANCOIS NICOLAS	80	54	$1,009	$42,849	$7,284
			DM1,708	DM81,202	DM12,310
			£635	£26,450	£4,513
			¥125,056	¥4,524,802	¥809,574
VOIRIN, FRANCOIS NICOLAS (ascribed to)	1	0			
VOIRIN, FRANCOIS NICOLAS (attributed to)	1	1	$2,867	$2,867	$2,867
			DM4,020	DM4,020	DM4,020
			£1,840	£1,840	£1,840
			¥289,622	¥289,622	¥289,622
VOIRIN, J.	5	1	$1,031	$1,031	$1,031
			DM1,834	DM1,834	DM1,834
			£633	£633	£633
			¥138,473	¥138,473	¥138,473
VOIRIN, JOSEPH	9	5	$1,304	$4,590	$2,521
			DM2,471	DM7,043	DM4,217
			£805	£2,990	£1,611
			¥137,711	¥502,350	¥278,075
VUILLAUME (workshop of)	3	2	$2,560	$4,081	$3,321
			DM4,814	DM7,076	DM5,945
			£1,610	£2,415	£2,013
			¥309,506	¥509,565	¥409,536

	Items		Selling Prices		
Maker	Bid	Sold	Low	High	Avg
VUILLAUME, JEAN BAPTISTE	31	21	$1,059	$12,633	$6,604
			DM1,625	DM21,902	DM11,359
			£690	£7,935	£4,046
			¥115,927	¥1,606,153	¥773,287
VUILLAUME, JEAN BAPTISTE (workshop of)	4	4	$2,990	$6,900	$4,777
			DM5,412	DM9,964	DM7,419
			£1,824	£4,396	£2,995
			¥361,013	¥598,575	¥470,901
WATSON, WILLIAM	3	2	$1,344	$1,840	$1,592
			DM2,496	DM3,275	DM2,885
			£805	£1,104	£955
			¥179,869	¥244,683	¥212,276
WEICHOLD	8	6	$283	$863	$546
			DM515	DM1,442	DM925
			£173	£517	£332
			¥35,732	¥104,946	¥68,024
WEICHOLD, R.	1	1	$1,025	$1,025	$1,025
			DM1,929	DM1,929	DM1,929
			£633	£633	£633
			¥108,297	¥108,297	¥108,297
WEICHOLD, RICHARD	26	21	$489	$1,815	$1,043
			DM826	DM3,133	DM1,709
			£293	£1,150	£645
			¥57,575	¥214,211	¥119,887
WEIDEMANN, R.	1	1	$696	$696	$696
			DM1,251	DM1,251	DM1,251
			£414	£414	£414
			¥80,411	¥80,411	¥80,411
WEIDHAAS, PAUL	5	2	$1,415	$1,682	$1,548
			DM2,081	DM2,846	DM2,464
			£920	£1,058	£989
			¥150,107	¥208,426	¥179,267
WEIMER, CARL	1	1	$900	$900	$900
			DM1,705	DM1,705	DM1,705
			£555	£555	£555
			¥95,021	¥95,021	¥95,021
WEISCHOLD, R.	2	1	$495	$495	$495
			DM731	DM731	DM731
			£322	£322	£322
			¥52,722	¥52,722	¥52,722
WERNER, EMIL	2	1	$1,687	$1,687	$1,687
			DM2,991	DM2,991	DM2,991
			£1,035	£1,035	£1,035
			¥199,476	¥199,476	¥199,476
WERRO, HENRY	2	0			
WERRO, JEAN	1	1	$1,198	$1,198	$1,198
			DM1,668	DM1,668	DM1,668
			£747	£747	£747
			¥101,254	¥101,254	¥101,254
WILSON, GARNER	12	10	$684	$1,845	$1,284
			DM1,028	DM3,297	DM2,070
			£437	£1,150	£802
			¥62,273	¥187,818	¥132,148
WINKLER, F.	2	2	$205	$575	$390
			DM359	DM879	DM619
			£127	£378	£252
			¥24,788	¥60,605	¥42,696

| Maker | Items | | Selling Prices | | |
	Bid	Sold	Low	High	Avg
WITHERS, EDWARD	2	2	$576	$726	$651
			DM882	DM1,022	DM952
			£368	£460	£414
			¥64,223	¥74,213	¥69,218
WITHERS, EDWARD & SONS	1	0			
WITHERS, GEORGE	3	2	$705	$811	$758
			DM1,040	DM1,197	DM1,119
			£460	£529	£495
			¥74,934	¥86,175	¥80,555
WITHERS, GEORGE & SONS	4	3	$773	$1,829	$1,381
			DM1,157	DM3,461	DM2,460
			£460	£1,150	£843
			¥86,241	¥219,179	¥161,453
WITHERS, GEORGE & SONS (workshop of)	1	1	$1,380	$1,380	$1,380
			DM1,993	DM1,993	DM1,993
			£879	£879	£879
			¥119,715	¥119,715	¥119,715
WUNDERLICH, F.R.	1	1	$451	$451	$451
			DM764	DM764	DM764
			£276	£276	£276
			¥52,301	¥52,301	¥52,301
WUNDERLICH, FRIEDRICH	5	5	$690	$1,500	$1,112
			DM1,181	DM2,301	DM1,731
			£408	£977	£696
			¥85,684	¥164,146	¥125,909
WURLITZER, REMBERT	1	1	$651	$651	$651
			DM1,234	DM1,234	DM1,234
			£402	£402	£402
			¥68,770	¥68,770	¥68,770
YOUNG, DAVID RUSSELL	1	0			
ZABINSKI, ROGER ALFONS	2	2	$518	$546	$532
			DM921	DM972	DM947
			£311	£328	£319
			¥68,817	¥72,640	¥70,729
ZIMMERMANN, JULIUS HEINRICH	1	0			

VIOLINO D'AMORE

| Maker | Items | | Selling Prices | | |
	Bid	Sold	Low	High	Avg
BISIACH, LEANDRO	1	0			

VIOLONCELLO

| Maker | Items | | Selling Prices | | |
	Bid	Sold	Low	High	Avg
ALBERTI, FERDINANDO (attributed to)	2	1	$1,852	$1,852	$1,852
			DM3,407	DM3,407	DM3,407
			£1,152	£1,152	£1,152
			¥218,384	¥218,384	¥218,384
ALDRIC, NICOLAS (ascribed to)	1	1	$2,726	$2,726	$2,726
			DM3,850	DM3,850	DM3,850
			£1,725	£1,725	£1,725
			¥243,289	¥243,289	¥243,289
ALLETSEE, PAULUS	1	1	$15,882	$15,882	$15,882
			DM24,400	DM24,400	DM24,400
			£10,350	£10,350	£10,350
			¥1,738,686	¥1,738,686	¥1,738,686
ANTONIAZZI, RICCARDO (attributed to)	1	0			

	Items		Selling Prices		
Maker	Bid	Sold	Low	High	Avg
APPARUT, GEORGES (workshop of)	3	1	$9,315	$9,315	$9,315
			DM16,675	DM16,675	DM16,675
			£5,750	£5,750	£5,750
			¥1,098,653	¥1,098,653	¥1,098,653
ARCANGELI, ULDERICO	1	0			
ARDOLI, MASSIMO	1	0			
BAADER, J.A. (attributed to)	1	1	$2,608	$2,608	$2,608
			DM4,911	DM4,911	DM4,911
			£1,610	£1,610	£1,610
			¥278,047	¥278,047	¥278,047
BACZYNSKI, LADISLAUS	1	0			
BAILEY, G.E.	1	0			
BAILLY, CHARLES	1	1	$6,914	$6,914	$6,914
			DM11,551	DM11,551	DM11,551
			£4,140	£4,140	£4,140
			¥840,379	¥840,379	¥840,379
BAILLY, PAUL	2	1	$31,370	$31,370	$31,370
			DM43,669	DM43,669	DM43,669
			£19,550	£19,550	£19,550
			¥2,646,601	¥2,646,601	¥2,646,601
BANDINI, MARIO	2	2	$5,589	$6,738	$6,163
			DM10,040	DM12,465	DM11,252
			£3,450	£4,025	£3,738
			¥659,882	¥897,937	¥778,909
BANKS, JAMES & HENRY	2	1	$7,305	$7,305	$7,305
			DM10,271	DM10,271	DM10,271
			£4,600	£4,600	£4,600
			¥651,958	¥651,958	¥651,958
BANKS, STEPHENSON (attributed to)	2	1	$1,738	$1,738	$1,738
			DM2,672	DM2,672	DM2,672
			£1,150	£1,150	£1,150
			¥185,409	¥185,409	¥185,409
BARBE, F.J.	1	1	$46,575	$46,575	$46,575
			DM87,688	DM87,688	DM87,688
			£28,750	£28,750	£28,750
			¥4,922,575	¥4,922,575	¥4,922,575
BARKER	1	1	$1,217	$1,217	$1,217
			DM1,870	DM1,870	DM1,870
			£805	£805	£805
			¥129,786	¥129,786	¥129,786
BARRETT, JOHN	1	0			
BERNARDEL, AUGUST SEBASTIEN PHILIPPE	1	1	$61,289	$61,289	$61,289
			DM102,393	DM102,393	DM102,393
			£36,700	£36,700	£36,700
			¥7,449,733	¥7,449,733	¥7,449,733
BERNARDEL, GUSTAVE	5	1	$24,714	$24,714	$24,714
			DM37,924	DM37,924	DM37,924
			£16,100	£16,100	£16,100
			¥2,704,961	¥2,704,961	¥2,704,961
BERNARDEL, GUSTAVE (workshop of)	1	1	$20,700	$20,700	$20,700
			DM37,467	DM37,467	DM37,467
			£12,627	£12,627	£12,627
			¥2,499,318	¥2,499,318	¥2,499,318
BERNARDEL, GUSTAVE ADOLPHE	1	0			

Maker	Items		Selling Prices		
	Bid	Sold	Low	High	Avg
BERNARDEL, LEON	3	2	$15,576	$22,770	$19,173
			DM27,020	DM40,986	DM34,003
			£9,200	£13,800	£11,500
			¥1,974,412	¥3,283,710	¥2,629,061
BERNARDEL, LEON (workshop of)	1	1	$10,350	$10,350	$10,350
			DM14,966	DM14,966	DM14,966
			£6,761	£6,761	£6,761
			¥1,047,938	¥1,047,938	¥1,047,938
BETTS	2	2	$23,771	$34,983	$29,377
			DM45,000	DM60,651	DM52,825
			£14,950	£20,700	£17,825
			¥2,849,321	¥4,367,700	¥3,608,510
BETTS, JOHN	3	1	$3,353	$3,353	$3,353
			DM6,024	DM6,024	DM6,024
			£2,070	£2,070	£2,070
			¥395,929	¥395,929	¥395,929
BINA, J.	2	1	$6,165	$6,165	$6,165
			DM9,088	DM9,088	DM9,088
			£4,025	£4,025	£4,025
			¥657,564	¥657,564	¥657,564
BISIACH (workshop of)	1	1	$37,950	$37,950	$37,950
			DM68,310	DM68,310	DM68,310
			£23,000	£23,000	£23,000
			¥5,472,850	¥5,472,850	¥5,472,850
BISIACH, LEANDRO & GIACOMO	2	1	$34,983	$34,983	$34,983
			DM60,651	DM60,651	DM60,651
			£20,700	£20,700	£20,700
			¥4,447,809	¥4,447,809	¥4,447,809
BLANCHI, ALBERTO	1	1	$28,117	$28,117	$28,117
			DM48,645	DM48,645	DM48,645
			£17,250	£17,250	£17,250
			¥3,208,500	¥3,208,500	¥3,208,500
BOLINK, JAAP	1	1	$4,947	$4,947	$4,947
			DM7,309	DM7,309	DM7,309
			£3,220	£3,220	£3,220
			¥527,223	¥527,223	¥527,223
BONORA, GIUSEPPE (ascribed to)	1	1	$10,925	$10,925	$10,925
			DM18,693	DM18,693	DM18,693
			£6,462	£6,462	£6,462
			¥1,356,667	¥1,356,667	¥1,356,667
BOULLANGIER, CHARLES	1	0			
BOUSSU, JOSEPH BENOIT	1	1	$20,700	$20,700	$20,700
			DM37,467	DM37,467	DM37,467
			£12,627	£12,627	£12,627
			¥2,499,318	¥2,499,318	¥2,499,318
BRIGGS, JAMES WILLIAM	3	3	$15,674	$23,194	$18,432
			DM21,825	DM34,703	DM27,036
			£9,775	£13,800	£11,117
			¥1,324,982	¥2,587,224	¥1,914,941
BRIGGS, JAMES WILLIAM (attributed to)	1	0			
BRYANT, PAUL	1	1	$1,604	$1,604	$1,604
			DM2,380	DM2,380	DM2,380
			£1,035	£1,035	£1,035
			¥173,652	¥173,652	¥173,652
BUCHESTETTER, GABRIEL DAVID	1	1	$13,782	$13,782	$13,782
			DM20,362	DM20,362	DM20,362
			£8,970	£8,970	£8,970
			¥1,468,694	¥1,468,694	¥1,468,694

Maker	Items Bid	Sold	Selling Prices Low	High	Avg
BUTHOD, CHARLES LOUIS	5	5	$3,889 DM5,742 £2,530 ¥414,353	$21,202 DM31,326 £13,800 ¥2,259,529	$11,896 DM17,401 £7,590 ¥1,262,963
CALCAGNI, BERNARDO	2	2	$34,466 DM61,698 £21,275 ¥4,065,014	$156,500 DM284,204 £95,778 ¥19,434,170	$95,483 DM172,951 £58,527 ¥11,749,592
CARCASSI, LORENZO & TOMMASO	3	3	$73,220 DM112,357 £47,700 ¥8,014,077	$176,985 DM335,398 £109,250 ¥18,689,398	$134,702 DM246,468 £83,983 ¥14,318,375
CARCASSI, TOMMASO	1	0			
CATENI, PIETRO	1	0			
CAUSSIN, FRANCOIS	1	1	$6,176 DM9,489 £4,025 ¥676,156	$6,176 DM9,489 £4,025 ¥676,156	$6,176 DM9,489 £4,025 ¥676,156
CAVALLI, ARISTIDE	1	1	$14,059 DM24,926 £8,625 ¥1,662,296	$14,059 DM24,926 £8,625 ¥1,662,296	$14,059 DM24,926 £8,625 ¥1,662,296
CERUTI, GIUSEPPE (ascribed to)	3	1	$16,203 DM24,808 £10,350 ¥1,806,282	$16,203 DM24,808 £10,350 ¥1,806,282	$16,203 DM24,808 £10,350 ¥1,806,282
CHANOT, GEORGES (II)	2	1	$56,775 DM96,053 £35,708 ¥7,034,378	$56,775 DM96,053 £35,708 ¥7,034,378	$56,775 DM96,053 £35,708 ¥7,034,378
CHANOT, JOSEPH ANTHONY	1	1	$17,874 DM30,239 £11,241 ¥2,214,526	$17,874 DM30,239 £11,241 ¥2,214,526	$17,874 DM30,239 £11,241 ¥2,214,526
CHARDON & FILS	2	1	$9,373 DM16,963 £5,750 ¥1,130,968	$9,373 DM16,963 £5,750 ¥1,130,968	$9,373 DM16,963 £5,750 ¥1,130,968
CHARETTE, PIERRE	1	1	$2,300 DM4,163 £1,403 ¥277,702	$2,300 DM4,163 £1,403 ¥277,702	$2,300 DM4,163 £1,403 ¥277,702
CHAROTTE, VICTOR JOSEPH	1	1	$3,457 DM5,775 £2,070 ¥420,189	$3,457 DM5,775 £2,070 ¥420,189	$3,457 DM5,775 £2,070 ¥420,189
CHRISTA, JOSEPH PAULUS	1	0			
COCKER, LAWRENCE	1	1	$5,659 DM8,325 £3,680 ¥600,429	$5,659 DM8,325 £3,680 ¥600,429	$5,659 DM8,325 £3,680 ¥600,429
COLAS, PROSPER	1	1	$12,563 DM18,797 £7,475 ¥1,401,413	$12,563 DM18,797 £7,475 ¥1,401,413	$12,563 DM18,797 £7,475 ¥1,401,413

Maker	Items		Selling Prices		
	Bid	Sold	Low	High	Avg
COLLIN-MEZIN, CH.J.B.	7	5	$7,670	$26,422	$18,583
			DM10,784	DM38,951	DM28,206
			£4,830	£17,250	£11,891
			¥684,556	¥2,818,133	¥1,967,414
COLLIN-MEZIN, CH.J.B. (workshop of)	1	1	$4,888	$4,888	$4,888
			DM8,363	DM8,363	DM8,363
			£2,891	£2,891	£2,891
			¥606,930	¥606,930	¥606,930
COLLIN-MEZIN, CH.J.B. (FILS) (attributed to)	1	1	$7,316	$7,316	$7,316
			DM10,384	DM10,384	DM10,384
			£4,600	£4,600	£4,600
			¥679,190	¥679,190	¥679,190
COLLIN-MEZIN, CH.J.B. (III)	2	1	$2,305	$2,305	$2,305
			DM3,850	DM3,850	DM3,850
			£1,380	£1,380	£1,380
			¥280,126	¥280,126	¥280,126
CONIA, STEFANO	1	1	$16,740	$16,740	$16,740
			DM24,711	DM24,711	DM24,711
			£10,925	£10,925	£10,925
			¥1,779,693	¥1,779,693	¥1,779,693
COSTA, FELIX MORI (attributed to)	1	1	$57,500	$57,500	$57,500
			DM104,075	DM104,075	DM104,075
			£35,075	£35,075	£35,075
			¥6,942,550	¥6,942,550	¥6,942,550
CRASKE, GEORGE	7	4	$6,895	$17,087	$13,026
			DM9,711	DM26,056	DM19,797
			£4,370	£10,925	£8,136
			¥705,021	¥1,734,988	¥1,332,922
CUISSET, A.	4	1	$4,715	$4,715	$4,715
			DM8,136	DM8,136	DM8,136
			£2,875	£2,875	£2,875
			¥538,085	¥538,085	¥538,085
CURLETTO, ANSELMO	2	1	$11,385	$11,385	$11,385
			DM17,181	DM17,181	DM17,181
			£6,900	£6,900	£6,900
			¥1,290,300	¥1,290,300	¥1,290,300
CUYPERS, JOHANNES	1	0			
DARCHE, HILAIRE	3	1	$13,605	$13,605	$13,605
			DM23,587	DM23,587	DM23,587
			£8,050	£8,050	£8,050
			¥1,729,704	¥1,729,704	¥1,729,704
DEARLOVE, MARK WILLIAM	1	1	$9,853	$9,853	$9,853
			DM17,718	DM17,718	DM17,718
			£5,865	£5,865	£5,865
			¥1,139,159	¥1,139,159	¥1,139,159
DEARLOVE, WILLIAM	2	1	$2,768	$2,768	$2,768
			DM5,192	DM5,192	DM5,192
			£1,719	£1,719	£1,719
			¥332,709	¥332,709	¥332,709
DE COMBLE, AMBROISE	1	1	$3,532	$3,532	$3,532
			DM4,855	DM4,855	DM4,855
			£2,185	£2,185	£2,185
			¥294,079	¥294,079	¥294,079
DECONET, MICHAEL	1	0			
DECONET, MICHAEL (ascribed to)	1	0			

Maker	Items		Selling Prices		
	Bid	Sold	Low	High	Avg
DEGANI, EUGENIO	2	2	$32,200	$59,700	$45,950
			DM55,658	DM89,849	DM72,753
			£19,896	£36,241	£28,069
			¥4,080,867	¥6,673,266	¥5,377,067
DERAZEY, HONORE	1	1	$36,992	$36,992	$36,992
			DM64,173	DM64,173	DM64,173
			£21,850	£21,850	£21,850
			¥4,689,229	¥4,689,229	¥4,689,229
DERAZEY, JUSTIN	1	0			
DIEUDONNE, AMEDEE	1	0			
DODD, THOMAS	4	1	$34,776	$34,776	$34,776
			DM62,535	DM62,535	DM62,535
			£20,700	£20,700	£20,700
			¥4,020,561	¥4,020,561	¥4,020,561
DOLLENZ, GIOVANNI	2	0			
DOLLENZ, GIUSEPPE	1	0			
DOLLING, AUGUST	1	1	$4,658	$4,658	$4,658
			DM8,366	DM8,366	DM8,366
			£2,875	£2,875	£2,875
			¥549,901	¥549,901	¥549,901
DOLLING, HERMANN (JR.)	1	1	$2,846	$2,846	$2,846
			DM5,123	DM5,123	DM5,123
			£1,725	£1,725	£1,725
			¥410,464	¥410,464	¥410,464
DUKE, RICHARD (attributed to)	2	2	$7,284	$16,376	$11,830
			DM13,836	DM24,611	DM19,223
			£4,497	£9,775	£7,136
			¥765,349	¥1,823,634	¥1,294,492
DYKES, GEORGE L. (workshop of)	1	1	$5,463	$5,463	$5,463
			DM9,887	DM9,887	DM9,887
			£3,332	£3,332	£3,332
			¥659,542	¥659,542	¥659,542
ELLERSIECK, ALBERT	1	1	$4,844	$4,844	$4,844
			DM8,701	DM8,701	DM8,701
			£2,990	£2,990	£2,990
			¥571,897	¥571,897	¥571,897
EMDE, J.F.C.	1	1	$1,945	$1,945	$1,945
			DM2,862	DM2,862	DM2,862
			£1,265	£1,265	£1,265
			¥206,397	¥206,397	¥206,397
EMERY, JEAN	1	1	$6,574	$6,574	$6,574
			DM9,244	DM9,244	DM9,244
			£4,140	£4,140	£4,140
			¥586,762	¥586,762	¥586,762
EMERY, JULIAN	1	1	$5,796	$5,796	$5,796
			DM9,660	DM9,660	DM9,660
			£3,450	£3,450	£3,450
			¥692,726	¥692,726	¥692,726
ENZENSPERGER, BERNARD (II)	1	1	$7,315	$7,315	$7,315
			DM13,534	DM13,534	DM13,534
			£4,370	£4,370	£4,370
			¥974,903	¥974,903	¥974,903
FANTIN, DOMENICO	1	0			
FARINA, ERMINIO	1	1	$32,649	$32,649	$32,649
			DM54,545	DM54,545	DM54,545
			£19,550	£19,550	£19,550
			¥3,968,455	¥3,968,455	¥3,968,455

Violoncello

Maker	Items		Selling Prices		
	Bid	Sold	Low	High	Avg
FAROTTI, CELESTE	1	1	$68,500	$68,500	$68,500
			DM121,930	DM121,930	DM121,930
			£41,100	£41,100	£41,100
			¥9,109,130	¥9,109,130	¥9,109,130
FAROTTO, CELESTE	1	1	$12,590	$12,590	$12,590
			DM17,809	DM17,809	DM17,809
			£8,050	£8,050	£8,050
			¥1,278,412	¥1,278,412	¥1,278,412
FENDT, BERNARD SIMON	1	1	$31,706	$31,706	$31,706
			DM46,741	DM46,741	DM46,741
			£20,700	£20,700	£20,700
			¥3,381,759	¥3,381,759	¥3,381,759
FORSTER, SIMON ANDREW	1	1	$38,410	$38,410	$38,410
			DM64,170	DM64,170	DM64,170
			£23,000	£23,000	£23,000
			¥4,668,770	¥4,668,770	¥4,668,770
FORSTER, WILLIAM	7	6	$26,384	$46,202	$33,020
			DM40,506	DM85,477	DM55,088
			£15,870	£27,600	£20,326
			¥205,517	¥6,157,284	¥3,425,701
FORSTER, WILLIAM (II)	2	2	$17,395	$30,728	$24,062
			DM26,027	DM51,336	DM38,682
			£10,350	£18,400	£14,375
			¥1,940,418	¥3,735,016	¥2,837,717
FRANCAIS, LUCIEN (attributed to)	1	1	$4,816	$4,816	$4,816
			DM8,628	DM8,628	DM8,628
			£2,875	£2,875	£2,875
			¥559,188	¥559,188	¥559,188
FRANKS, RAY	1	1	$4,194	$4,194	$4,194
			DM4,418	DM4,418	DM4,418
			£2,588	£2,588	£2,588
			¥320,320	¥320,320	¥320,320
FUCHS, WENZEL	1	1	$2,990	$2,990	$2,990
			DM5,322	DM5,322	DM5,322
			£1,794	£1,794	£1,794
			¥397,610	¥397,610	¥397,610
FURBER FAMILY	1	0			
GABOR, ANRISAK TIBOR	1	1	$3,448	$3,448	$3,448
			DM4,855	DM4,855	DM4,855
			£2,185	£2,185	£2,185
			¥352,510	¥352,510	¥352,510
GABRIELLI, GIOVANNI BATTISTA	1	1	$115,187	$115,187	$115,187
			DM162,213	DM162,213	DM162,213
			£73,000	£73,000	£73,000
			¥11,777,236	¥11,777,236	¥11,777,236
GAGLIANO, ALESSANDRO	1	1	$125,723	$125,723	$125,723
			DM176,305	DM176,305	DM176,305
			£80,700	£80,700	£80,700
			¥12,702,422	¥12,702,422	¥12,702,422
GAGLIANO, GENNARO	1	1	$409,860	$409,860	$409,860
			DM771,650	DM771,650	DM771,650
			£253,000	£253,000	£253,000
			¥43,318,660	¥43,318,660	¥43,318,660
GAGLIANO, JOSEPH	1	0			
GAGLIANO, RAFFAELE & ANTONIO (II)	2	2	$74,924	$115,968	$95,446
			DM132,759	DM173,514	DM153,137
			£46,006	£69,000	£57,503
			¥9,135,428	¥12,936,120	¥11,035,774

| Maker | Items | | Selling Prices | | |
	Bid	Sold	Low	High	Avg
GAGLIANO FAMILY (MEMBER OF)	1	0			
GALIMBERTI, LUIGI	1	1	$20,700	$20,700	$20,700
			DM37,260	DM37,260	DM37,260
			£12,420	£12,420	£12,420
			¥160,839	¥160,839	¥160,839
GALLA, ANTON	2	2	$3,353	$3,856	$3,605
			DM6,355	DM7,308	DM6,832
			£2,070	£2,381	£2,225
			¥354,115	¥407,232	¥380,674
GAND BROS.	4	0			
GARINI	2	2	$1,025	$1,259	$1,142
			DM1,781	DM1,795	DM1,788
			£633	£805	£719
			¥123,938	¥127,841	¥125,890
GATTI, ERNESTO	1	1	$13,609	$13,609	$13,609
			DM19,166	DM19,166	DM19,166
			£8,625	£8,625	£8,625
			¥1,391,489	¥1,391,489	¥1,391,489
GEISSENHOF, FRANZ (attributed to)	1	1	$13,973	$13,973	$13,973
			DM26,306	DM26,306	DM26,306
			£8,625	£8,625	£8,625
			¥1,476,773	¥1,476,773	¥1,476,773
GIANOTTI, ALFREDO (attributed to)	1	1	$3,082	$3,082	$3,082
			DM5,522	DM5,522	DM5,522
			£1,840	£1,840	£1,840
			¥357,880	¥357,880	¥357,880
GILBERT, JEFFREY J.	2	1	$7,342	$7,342	$7,342
			DM13,202	DM13,202	DM13,202
			£4,370	£4,370	£4,370
			¥848,785	¥848,785	¥848,785
GILBERT, JEFFREY JAMES	1	0			
GLENISTER, WILLIAM	1	1	$4,285	$4,285	$4,285
			DM8,139	DM8,139	DM8,139
			£2,645	£2,645	£2,645
			¥450,205	¥450,205	¥450,205
GLOOR, ADOLF	4	2	$1,028	$2,504	$1,766
			DM1,792	DM4,486	DM3,139
			£633	£1,495	£1,064
			¥124,508	¥290,778	¥207,643
GOATER, MICHAEL	1	0			
GODDARD, CHARLES (attributed to)	1	1	$784	$784	$784
			DM1,164	DM1,164	DM1,164
			£506	£506	£506
			¥84,897	¥84,897	¥84,897
GOTZ, C.A.	1	1	$1,230	$1,230	$1,230
			DM1,296	DM1,296	DM1,296
			£759	£759	£759
			¥93,960	¥93,960	¥93,960
GOULDING & CO.	2	2	$4,830	$14,801	$9,815
			DM8,685	DM26,641	DM17,663
			£2,875	£8,970	£5,923
			¥558,411	¥2,134,412	¥1,346,411
GRANCINO, FRANCESCO & GIOVANNI (ascribed to)	1	1	$4,025	$4,025	$4,025
			DM6,887	DM6,887	DM6,887
			£2,381	£2,381	£2,381
			¥499,825	¥499,825	¥499,825

Maker	Items		Selling Prices		
	Bid	Sold	Low	High	Avg
GRANCINO, GIOVANNI	4	1	$307,280	$307,280	$307,280
			DM513,360	DM513,360	DM513,360
			£184,000	£184,000	£184,000
			¥37,350,160	¥37,350,160	¥37,350,160
GRANDJON, J. (attributed to)	1	1	$10,601	$10,601	$10,601
			DM15,663	DM15,663	DM15,663
			£6,900	£6,900	£6,900
			¥1,129,765	¥1,129,765	¥1,129,765
GRULLI, PIETRO	1	1	$27,553	$27,553	$27,553
			DM46,330	DM46,330	DM46,330
			£17,250	£17,250	£17,250
			¥3,382,087	¥3,382,087	¥3,382,087
GUADAGNINI, FRANCESCO	1	0			
GUADAGNINI, GIOVANNI BATTISTA	1	1	$259,390	$259,390	$259,390
			DM363,753	DM363,753	DM363,753
			£166,500	£166,500	£166,500
			¥26,207,600	¥26,207,600	¥26,207,600
GUERRA, ALBERTO	1	1	$16,100	$16,100	$16,100
			DM23,248	DM23,248	DM23,248
			£10,257	£10,257	£10,257
			¥1,396,675	¥1,396,675	¥1,396,675
GUERSAN, LOUIS	2	1	$2,277	$2,277	$2,277
			DM3,436	DM3,436	DM3,436
			£1,380	£1,380	£1,380
			¥258,060	¥258,060	¥258,060
HAIDE, JAY	1	0			
HAMMIG, JOHANN CHRISTIAN	1	1	$2,147	$2,147	$2,147
			DM3,283	DM3,283	DM3,283
			£1,380	£1,380	£1,380
			¥212,222	¥212,222	¥212,222
HAMMIG, W.H.	2	1	$7,825	$7,825	$7,825
			DM14,055	DM14,055	DM14,055
			£4,830	£4,830	£4,830
			¥923,834	¥923,834	¥923,834
HARDIE, MATTHEW	2	2	$15,685	$18,354	$17,019
			DM21,834	DM30,590	DM26,212
			£9,775	£10,925	£10,350
			¥1,323,300	¥2,193,631	¥1,758,466
HARRIS, CHARLES	4	4	$4,228	$13,216	$7,364
			DM5,916	DM19,509	DM11,747
			£2,645	£8,625	£4,629
			¥357,638	¥1,405,021	¥790,374
HAUSMANN, OTTOMAR	1	1	$3,910	$3,910	$3,910
			DM6,758	DM6,758	DM6,758
			£2,416	£2,416	£2,416
			¥495,534	¥495,534	¥495,534
HEELEY, JOHN LINACRE (attributed to)	1	1	$2,927	$2,927	$2,927
			DM4,154	DM4,154	DM4,154
			£1,840	£1,840	£1,840
			¥271,676	¥271,676	¥271,676
HEINICKE, MATHIAS	1	1	$7,452	$7,452	$7,452
			DM14,030	DM14,030	DM14,030
			£4,600	£4,600	£4,600
			¥794,420	¥794,420	¥794,420
HEL, JOSEPH	1	1	$67,012	$67,012	$67,012
			DM100,708	DM100,708	DM100,708
			£40,000	£40,000	£40,000
			¥7,462,440	¥7,462,440	¥7,462,440

| Maker | Items | | Selling Prices | | |
	Bid	Sold	Low	High	Avg
HEL, PIERRE JOSEPH	1	1	$11,474	$11,474	$11,474
			DM17,607	DM17,607	DM17,607
			£7,475	£7,475	£7,475
			¥1,255,875	¥1,255,875	¥1,255,875
HELLMER, JOHANN GEORG (ascribed to)	1	1	$2,497	$2,497	$2,497
			DM4,171	DM4,171	DM4,171
			£1,495	£1,495	£1,495
			¥303,470	¥303,470	¥303,470
HERRMANN, KARL (workshop of)	1	1	$1,610	$1,610	$1,610
			DM2,423	DM2,423	DM2,423
			£977	£977	£977
			¥179,966	¥179,966	¥179,966
HILL, HENRY LOCKEY	1	0			
HILL, JOSEPH	7	5	$14,383	$36,599	$26,223
			DM20,027	DM65,572	DM42,525
			£8,970	£23,000	£16,284
			¥1,215,866	¥4,249,825	¥2,849,326
HILL, JOSEPH (ascribed to)	1	1	$6,641	$6,641	$6,641
			DM11,954	DM11,954	DM11,954
			£4,025	£4,025	£4,025
			¥957,749	¥957,749	¥957,749
HILL, LOCKEY	6	3	$6,002	$25,266	$13,246
			DM9,210	DM43,804	DM22,895
			£3,910	£14,950	£7,973
			¥656,919	¥3,154,450	¥1,646,735
HILL, WILLIAM EBSWORTH	1	0			
HILL FAMILY (MEMBER OF)	1	1	$2,823	$2,823	$2,823
			DM4,338	DM4,338	DM4,338
			£1,840	£1,840	£1,840
			¥309,100	¥309,100	¥309,100
HOFNER, KARL	1	0			
HORNSTEINER	1	1	$3,961	$3,961	$3,961
			DM7,206	DM7,206	DM7,206
			£2,415	£2,415	£2,415
			¥500,243	¥500,243	¥500,243
HORNSTEINER, JOSEPH (attributed to)	1	1	$13,449	$13,449	$13,449
			DM20,846	DM20,846	DM20,846
			£8,050	£8,050	£8,050
			¥1,531,996	¥1,531,996	¥1,531,996
HUSSON & BUTHOD	1	1	$1,270	$1,270	$1,270
			DM1,789	DM1,789	DM1,789
			£805	£805	£805
			¥129,872	¥129,872	¥129,872
JONES, EDWARD B. (attributed to)	1	1	$2,721	$2,721	$2,721
			DM4,717	DM4,717	DM4,717
			£1,610	£1,610	£1,610
			¥339,710	¥339,710	¥339,710
JORIO, VINCENZO	1	0			
JUZEK, JOHN	3	2	$1,455	$2,777	$2,116
			DM2,746	DM5,242	DM3,994
			£900	£1,719	£1,310
			¥153,913	¥293,833	¥223,873
KAUL, PAUL	1	1	$18,630	$18,630	$18,630
			DM33,465	DM33,465	DM33,465
			£11,500	£11,500	£11,500
			¥2,199,605	¥2,199,605	¥2,199,605

Maker	Items		Selling Prices		
	Bid	Sold	Low	High	Avg
KENNEDY, THOMAS	12	10	$13,490	$46,092	$26,023
			DM19,081	DM77,004	DM43,896
			£8,625	£27,600	£16,310
			¥1,369,728	¥5,602,524	¥2,918,426
KENNEDY, THOMAS (ascribed to)	1	0			
KENNEDY, THOMAS (attributed to)	1	1	$5,630	$5,630	$5,630
			DM10,040	DM10,040	DM10,040
			£3,450	£3,450	£3,450
			¥737,024	¥737,024	¥737,024
KLIER, OTTO JOSEPH	1	1	$1,518	$1,518	$1,518
			DM2,291	DM2,291	DM2,291
			£920	£920	£920
			¥172,040	¥172,040	¥172,040
KLOTZ, AEGIDIUS (I)	1	1	$3,465	$3,465	$3,465
			DM6,411	DM6,411	DM6,411
			£2,070	£2,070	£2,070
			¥461,796	¥461,796	¥461,796
KLOTZ, SEBASTIAN (II) (attributed to)	1	0			
KLOTZ FAMILY (MEMBER OF)	1	0			
KOBERLING, JOHANN	1	0			
KRUMBHOLZ, LORENZ	1	0			
LABERTE	1	0			
LABERTE, MARC (attributed to)	2	1	$6,167	$6,167	$6,167
			DM10,751	DM10,751	DM10,751
			£3,795	£3,795	£3,795
			¥747,046	¥747,046	¥747,046
LABERTE-HUMBERT BROS.	2	1	$9,673	$9,673	$9,673
			DM16,365	DM16,365	DM16,365
			£6,084	£6,084	£6,084
			¥1,198,450	¥1,198,450	¥1,198,450
LAJOS, KONYA	1	1	$4,658	$4,658	$4,658
			DM8,338	DM8,338	DM8,338
			£2,875	£2,875	£2,875
			¥549,326	¥549,326	¥549,326
LAMBERT, JEAN NICOLAS	1	1	$18,330	$18,330	$18,330
			DM29,399	DM29,399	DM29,399
			£11,903	£11,903	£11,903
			¥2,085,556	¥2,085,556	¥2,085,556
LANG, BENEDIKT	4	2	$1,826	$2,138	$1,982
			DM2,568	DM3,706	DM3,137
			£1,150	£1,265	£1,208
			¥162,349	¥266,915	¥214,632
LANG, RUDOLF	1	1	$2,827	$2,827	$2,827
			DM4,177	DM4,177	DM4,177
			£1,840	£1,840	£1,840
			¥301,271	¥301,271	¥301,271
LECAVELLE, FRANCOIS	1	1	$5,377	$5,377	$5,377
			DM8,984	DM8,984	DM8,984
			£3,220	£3,220	£3,220
			¥653,628	¥653,628	¥653,628
LE LIEVRE, PIERRE	2	1	$9,718	$9,718	$9,718
			DM14,358	DM14,358	DM14,358
			£6,325	£6,325	£6,325
			¥1,035,618	¥1,035,618	¥1,035,618

Maker	Items		Selling Prices		
	Bid	Sold	Low	High	Avg
LONGMAN & BRODERIP	4	3	$752	$6,219	$4,348
			DM1,242	DM10,930	DM7,651
			£460	£3,680	£2,607
			¥93,117	¥875,656	¥581,751
LONGMAN, LUKEY & CO.	3	1	$6,400	$6,400	$6,400
			DM12,035	DM12,035	DM12,035
			£4,025	£4,025	£4,025
			¥773,766	¥773,766	¥773,766
LOTT, JOHN FREDERICK (attributed to)	1	0			
LOWENDALL	1	1	$5,475	$5,475	$5,475
			DM10,236	DM10,236	DM10,236
			£3,450	£3,450	£3,450
			¥647,945	¥647,945	¥647,945
LOWENDALL, L.	1	1	$4,637	$4,637	$4,637
			DM8,338	DM8,338	DM8,338
			£2,760	£2,760	£2,760
			¥536,075	¥536,075	¥536,075
LOWENDALL, LOUIS	1	1	$1,540	$1,540	$1,540
			DM2,849	DM2,849	DM2,849
			£920	£920	£920
			¥205,243	¥205,243	¥205,243
MAGNIERE, GABRIEL	1	1	$2,981	$2,981	$2,981
			DM5,612	DM5,612	DM5,612
			£1,840	£1,840	£1,840
			¥315,045	¥315,045	¥315,045
MANGENOT WORKSHOP	1	0			
MARCHETTI, ENRICO (attributed to)	1	0			
MARTIN, E. (workshop of)	1	1	$1,955	$1,955	$1,955
			DM3,379	DM3,379	DM3,379
			£1,208	£1,208	£1,208
			¥247,767	¥247,767	¥247,767
MAYNARD, BRIAN	1	0			
MAYSON, WALTER H.	1	1	$8,692	$8,692	$8,692
			DM13,358	DM13,358	DM13,358
			£5,750	£5,750	£5,750
			¥927,044	¥927,044	¥927,044
MEINEL, OSKAR	1	1	$2,875	$2,875	$2,875
			DM5,118	DM5,118	DM5,118
			£1,725	£1,725	£1,725
			¥382,317	¥382,317	¥382,317
MEINEL, PAUL	1	1	$15,523	$15,523	$15,523
			DM21,826	DM21,826	DM21,826
			£9,775	£9,775	£9,775
			¥1,379,966	¥1,379,966	¥1,379,966
MEISEL, JOHANN GEORG	1	1	$3,587	$3,587	$3,587
			DM5,066	DM5,066	DM5,066
			£2,277	£2,277	£2,277
			¥361,207	¥361,207	¥361,207
MELEGARI, ENRICO CLODOVEO	1	1	$47,945	$47,945	$47,945
			DM66,758	DM66,758	DM66,758
			£29,900	£29,900	£29,900
			¥4,052,885	¥4,052,885	¥4,052,885
MERIOTTE, CHARLES (attributed to)	1	1	$1,607	$1,607	$1,607
			DM2,260	DM2,260	DM2,260
			£1,012	£1,012	£1,012
			¥143,431	¥143,431	¥143,431

Maker	Items		Selling Prices		
	Bid	Sold	Low	High	Avg
MERLIN, JOSEPH	1	1	$27,852	$27,852	$27,852
			DM52,901	DM52,901	DM52,901
			£17,193	£17,193	£17,193
			¥2,926,335	¥2,926,335	¥2,926,335
MERLING, PAULI	1	1	$10,310	$10,310	$10,310
			DM17,837	DM17,837	DM17,837
			£6,325	£6,325	£6,325
			¥1,176,450	¥1,176,450	¥1,176,450
MESSORI, PIETRO	3	1	$3,018	$3,018	$3,018
			DM5,491	DM5,491	DM5,491
			£1,840	£1,840	£1,840
			¥381,138	¥381,138	¥381,138
METHFESSEL, GUSTAV	1	1	$11,500	$11,500	$11,500
			DM16,606	DM16,606	DM16,606
			£7,327	£7,327	£7,327
			¥997,625	¥997,625	¥997,625
METHFESSEL, GUSTAV (attributed to)	1	0			
MILNES, JOHN	2	2	$2,616	$3,018	$2,817
			DM4,283	DM4,561	DM4,422
			£1,610	£1,898	£1,754
			¥280,166	¥316,929	¥298,547
MORASSI, GIOVANNI BATTISTA	3	3	$16,436	$23,005	$20,156
			DM23,109	DM42,614	DM33,766
			£10,350	£13,800	£12,458
			¥1,466,906	¥3,072,294	¥2,381,508
MORRISON, JOHN	1	0			
MOUGENOT, LEON	5	4	$5,624	$11,202	$8,791
			DM9,971	DM17,966	DM13,778
			£3,450	£7,274	£5,672
			¥664,919	¥1,274,506	¥964,267
MUELLER, KARL (workshop of)	1	1	$748	$748	$748
			DM1,081	DM1,081	DM1,081
			£488	£488	£488
			¥75,684	¥75,684	¥75,684
MULLER, KARL	1	1	$3,941	$3,941	$3,941
			DM5,527	DM5,527	DM5,527
			£2,530	£2,530	£2,530
			¥398,230	¥398,230	¥398,230
NEUNER & HORNSTEINER	9	7	$759	$9,179	$3,832
			DM1,348	DM14,086	DM6,427
			£460	£5,980	£2,399
			¥105,289	¥1,004,700	¥443,904
NILSSON, GOTTFRIED	1	1	$6,940	$6,940	$6,940
			DM9,757	DM9,757	DM9,757
			£4,370	£4,370	£4,370
			¥619,360	¥619,360	¥619,360
NORMAN, BARAK	7	3	$3,018	$24,398	$10,681
			DM5,491	DM43,505	DM18,941
			£1,840	£14,950	£6,567
			¥381,138	¥3,193,769	¥1,382,693
NURNBERGER, ALBERT	1	1	$1,265	$1,265	$1,265
			DM2,164	DM2,164	DM2,164
			£748	£748	£748
			¥157,088	¥157,088	¥157,088
OTTO, C.W.F. (attributed to)	1	1	$3,310	$3,310	$3,310
			DM5,742	DM5,742	DM5,742
			£1,955	£1,955	£1,955
			¥419,563	¥419,563	¥419,563

| Maker | Items | | Selling Prices | | |
---	Bid	Sold	Low	High	Avg
OWEN, JOHN W.	3	1	$9,364	$9,364	$9,364
			DM13,836	DM13,836	DM13,836
			£6,095	£6,095	£6,095
			¥997,959	¥997,959	¥997,959
PADDAY, A.L.	1	0			
PADEWET, JOHANN II	2	1	$4,276	$4,276	$4,276
			DM7,413	DM7,413	DM7,413
			£2,530	£2,530	£2,530
			¥533,830	¥533,830	¥533,830
PANORMO, VINCENZO	1	0			
PANORMO, VINCENZO (attributed to)	2	2	$7,668	$59,821	$33,745
			DM14,205	DM106,063	DM60,134
			£4,600	£36,700	£20,650
			¥1,024,098	¥7,073,191	¥4,048,645
PARESCHI, GAETANO	1	1	$16,871	$16,871	$16,871
			DM29,187	DM29,187	DM29,187
			£10,350	£10,350	£10,350
			¥1,925,100	¥1,925,100	¥1,925,100
PARMEGGIANI, ROMOLA	1	1	$26,432	$26,432	$26,432
			DM39,018	DM39,018	DM39,018
			£17,250	£17,250	£17,250
			¥2,810,042	¥2,810,042	¥2,810,042
PARRAMON, RAMON	1	0			
PEDRAZZINI, GIUSEPPE	2	2	$61,456	$62,978	$62,217
			DM92,964	DM102,672	DM97,818
			£36,800	£41,100	£38,950
			¥6,695,231	¥7,470,032	¥7,082,632
PEDRAZZINI, GIUSEPPE (attributed to)	2	0			
PELLIZON FAMILY (MEMBER OF)	2	0			
PETERNELLA, JAGO	1	0			
PFRETZSCHNER (workshop of)	2	2	$575	$1,380	$978
			DM972	DM2,332	DM1,652
			£345	£828	£587
			¥70,150	¥168,360	¥119,255
PFRETZSCHNER, C.G.	1	1	$2,645	$2,645	$2,645
			DM3,825	DM3,825	DM3,825
			£1,728	£1,728	£1,728
			¥267,806	¥267,806	¥267,806
PIATTELLINI, A.	1	1	$57,615	$57,615	$57,615
			DM96,255	DM96,255	DM96,255
			£34,500	£34,500	£34,500
			¥7,003,155	¥7,003,155	¥7,003,155
PICCAGLIANI (workshop of)	1	0			
PICCAGLIANI, ARMANDO	1	1	$15,447	$15,447	$15,447
			DM21,819	DM21,819	DM21,819
			£9,775	£9,775	£9,775
			¥1,378,637	¥1,378,637	¥1,378,637
PICKARD, H.	1	1	$4,325	$4,325	$4,325
			DM7,143	DM7,143	DM7,143
			£2,645	£2,645	£2,645
			¥535,425	¥535,425	¥535,425
POGGI, ANSALDO	2	2	$59,821	$79,850	$69,835
			DM106,063	DM147,727	DM126,895
			£36,700	£47,700	£42,200
			¥7,073,191	¥10,641,393	¥8,857,292

Maker	Items		Selling Prices		
	Bid	Sold	Low	High	Avg
POGGI, ANSALDO (attributed to)	1	1	$17,336	$17,336	$17,336
			DM31,060	DM31,060	DM31,060
			£10,350	£10,350	£10,350
			¥2,013,075	¥2,013,075	¥2,013,075
POLLASTRI, CESARE FEDERICO	1	0			
POSCH, ANTON	3	1	$17,193	$17,193	$17,193
			DM31,634	DM31,634	DM31,634
			£10,694	£10,694	£10,694
			¥2,027,855	¥2,027,855	¥2,027,855
POSTIGLIONE, VINCENZO	2	0			
PRENTICE, RONALD	2	1	$3,374	$3,374	$3,374
			DM6,107	DM6,107	DM6,107
			£2,070	£2,070	£2,070
			¥407,148	¥407,148	¥407,148
PRESSENDA, GIOVANNI FRANCESCO	1	1	$343,170	$343,170	$343,170
			DM634,885	DM634,885	DM634,885
			£205,000	£205,000	£205,000
			¥45,733,450	¥45,733,450	¥45,733,450
PRESTON, JOHN	1	0			
PRINCE, W.B.	1	1	$5,775	$5,775	$5,775
			DM10,685	DM10,685	DM10,685
			£3,450	£3,450	£3,450
			¥769,661	¥769,661	¥769,661
PROKOP, LADISLAV	1	1	$4,313	$4,313	$4,313
			DM6,236	DM6,236	DM6,236
			£2,817	£2,817	£2,817
			¥436,641	¥436,641	¥436,641
REGAZZONI, DANTE PAOLO	1	1	$3,850	$3,850	$3,850
			DM7,123	DM7,123	DM7,123
			£2,300	£2,300	£2,300
			¥513,107	¥513,107	¥513,107
REITER, JOHANN	2	0			
RENAUDIN, LEOPOLD	3	2	$12,357	$14,517	$13,437
			DM18,962	DM20,443	DM19,703
			£8,050	£9,200	£8,625
			¥1,352,481	¥1,484,254	¥1,418,367
RICHARDSON, ARTHUR	2	1	$5,403	$5,403	$5,403
			DM9,672	DM9,672	DM9,672
			£3,335	£3,335	£3,335
			¥637,218	¥637,218	¥637,218
RIECHERS, AUGUST (attributed to)	2	1	$3,259	$3,259	$3,259
			DM6,037	DM6,037	DM6,037
			£1,955	£1,955	£1,955
			¥435,242	¥435,242	¥435,242
RIVOLTA, GIACOMO (attributed to)	1	1	$49,933	$49,933	$49,933
			DM83,421	DM83,421	DM83,421
			£29,900	£29,900	£29,900
			¥6,069,401	¥6,069,401	¥6,069,401
ROADWATER, HORROBIN	1	1	$1,638	$1,638	$1,638
			DM2,342	DM2,342	DM2,342
			£1,035	£1,035	£1,035
			¥164,551	¥164,551	¥164,551
ROBINSON, WILLIAM	1	0			
ROSSI, GIOVANNI	1	1	$33,922	$33,922	$33,922
			DM60,108	DM60,108	DM60,108
			£20,829	£20,829	£20,829
			¥4,136,119	¥4,136,119	¥4,136,119

| Maker | Items | | Selling Prices | | |
	Bid	Sold	Low	High	Avg
ROTH, ERNST HEINRICH	1	1	$6,146	$6,146	$6,146
			DM10,267	DM10,267	DM10,267
			£3,680	£3,680	£3,680
			¥747,003	¥747,003	¥747,003
ROUGIER, MAURICE	2	0			
RUBIO, DAVID	1	0			
RUGGERI, FRANCESCO	1	1	$193,281	$193,281	$193,281
			DM289,191	DM289,191	DM289,191
			£115,000	£115,000	£115,000
			¥21,560,200	¥21,560,200	¥21,560,200
RUNNACLES, HARRY E.	2	2	$2,120	$2,130	$2,125
			DM3,065	DM3,133	DM3,099
			£1,380	£1,380	£1,380
			¥216,301	¥225,953	¥221,127
SACQUIN, CLAUDE	1	1	$21,202	$21,202	$21,202
			DM31,326	DM31,326	DM31,326
			£13,800	£13,800	£13,800
			¥2,259,529	¥2,259,529	¥2,259,529
SALSEDO, LUIGI	1	1	$7,590	$7,590	$7,590
			DM11,454	DM11,454	DM11,454
			£4,600	£4,600	£4,600
			¥860,200	¥860,200	¥860,200
SANDNER, ANTON	1	1	$4,588	$4,588	$4,588
			DM7,049	DM7,049	DM7,049
			£2,990	£2,990	£2,990
			¥502,287	¥502,287	¥502,287
SANNINO, VINCENZO	2	1	$31,227	$31,227	$31,227
			DM52,507	DM52,507	DM52,507
			£19,550	£19,550	£19,550
			¥3,833,032	¥3,833,032	¥3,833,032
SANTAGIULIANA, GAETANO	1	0			
SCAPPIO, FRANCESCO	2	2	$11,178	$12,855	$12,016
			DM21,183	DM24,360	DM22,772
			£6,900	£7,935	£7,418
			¥1,180,383	¥1,357,440	¥1,268,912
SCARAMPELLA, GIUSEPPE (ascribed to)	2	0			
SCARAMPELLA, STEFANO	1	0			
SCARAMPELLA, STEFANO (ascribed to)	2	1	$14,628	$14,628	$14,628
			DM27,508	DM27,508	DM27,508
			£9,200	£9,200	£9,200
			¥1,768,608	¥1,768,608	¥1,768,608
SCARAMPELLA, STEFANO (attributed to)	1	0			
SCHUSTER, JOSEF	2	1	$1,739	$1,739	$1,739
			DM3,126	DM3,126	DM3,126
			£1,035	£1,035	£1,035
			¥201,028	¥201,028	¥201,028
SCHWARZ BROS.	1	1	$10,514	$10,514	$10,514
			DM18,239	DM18,239	DM18,239
			£6,210	£6,210	£6,210
			¥1,332,728	¥1,332,728	¥1,332,728
SCIORILLI, LUIGI	1	1	$2,113	$2,113	$2,113
			DM3,529	DM3,529	DM3,529
			£1,265	£1,265	£1,265
			¥256,782	¥256,782	¥256,782

Maker	Items		Selling Prices		
	Bid	Sold	Low	High	Avg
SILVESTRE, HIPPOLYTE CHRETIEN	2	1	$36,800	$36,800	$36,800
			DM65,504	DM65,504	DM65,504
			£22,080	£22,080	£22,080
			¥4,893,664	¥4,893,664	¥4,893,664
SMILLIE, ALEXANDER	2	1	$3,093	$3,093	$3,093
			DM5,395	DM5,395	DM5,395
			£1,840	£1,840	£1,840
			¥394,422	¥394,422	¥394,422
SMITH, ARTHUR E.	1	1	$18,529	$18,529	$18,529
			DM28,467	DM28,467	DM28,467
			£12,075	£12,075	£12,075
			¥2,028,467	¥2,028,467	¥2,028,467
SMITH, THOMAS	9	6	$2,555	$16,764	$8,849
			DM4,777	DM25,756	DM14,898
			£1,610	£10,925	£5,601
			¥302,374	¥1,835,280	¥930,041
SMITH, THOMAS (attributed to)	4	2	$2,632	$8,060	$5,346
			DM4,348	DM14,588	DM9,468
			£1,610	£4,945	£3,278
			¥325,911	¥972,632	¥649,271
SMITH, WILLIAM	1	1	$1,874	$1,874	$1,874
			DM3,243	DM3,243	DM3,243
			£1,150	£1,150	£1,150
			¥213,900	¥213,900	¥213,900
SMITH, WILLIAM EDWARD	1	1	$2,277	$2,277	$2,277
			DM3,436	DM3,436	DM3,436
			£1,380	£1,380	£1,380
			¥258,060	¥258,060	¥258,060
SPIEGEL, JANOS	1	1	$10,080	$10,080	$10,080
			DM14,127	DM14,127	DM14,127
			£6,325	£6,325	£6,325
			¥888,568	¥888,568	¥888,568
STEWART, C.G.	1	0			
STOSS, JOHANN MARTIN	2	1	$9,664	$9,664	$9,664
			DM14,460	DM14,460	DM14,460
			£5,750	£5,750	£5,750
			¥1,078,010	¥1,078,010	¥1,078,010
STRADIVARI, ANTONIO	1	1	$898,945	$898,945	$898,945
			DM1,593,835	DM1,593,835	DM1,593,835
			£551,500	£551,500	£551,500
			¥106,290,595	¥106,290,595	¥106,290,595
TARASCONI, CAROL	1	0			
TECCHLER, DAVID	1	0			
TECCHLER, DAVID (attributed to)	1	0			
TESTORE, CARLO ANTONIO	1	0			
TESTORE, CARLO ANTONIO (attributed to)	1	1	$66,993	$66,993	$66,993
			DM115,902	DM115,902	DM115,902
			£41,100	£41,100	£41,100
			¥7,644,600	¥7,644,600	¥7,644,600
TESTORE, CARLO GIUSEPPE	1	1	$158,650	$158,650	$158,650
			DM294,500	DM294,500	DM294,500
			£95,000	£95,000	£95,000
			¥21,226,800	¥21,226,800	¥21,226,800

Maker	Items		Selling Prices		
	Bid	Sold	Low	High	Avg
THIBOUT, JACQUES PIERRE	1	1	$19,384	$19,384	$19,384
			DM28,613	DM28,613	DM28,613
			£12,650	£12,650	£12,650
			¥2,060,698	¥2,060,698	¥2,060,698
THIBOUVILLE-LAMY, J.	32	26	$585	$6,402	$2,205
			DM831	DM10,808	DM3,507
			£368	£4,025	£1,365
			¥54,335	¥789,765	¥240,927
THIBOUVILLE-LAMY, J. (attributed to)	1	1	$4,907	$4,907	$4,907
			DM6,931	DM6,931	DM6,931
			£3,105	£3,105	£3,105
			¥437,920	¥437,920	¥437,920
THIBOUVILLE-LAMY, J. (workshop of)	1	1	$575	$575	$575
			DM1,024	DM1,024	DM1,024
			£345	£345	£345
			¥76,464	¥76,464	¥76,464
THIBOUVILLE-LAMY, JEROME	1	1	$1,280	$1,280	$1,280
			DM2,407	DM2,407	DM2,407
			£805	£805	£805
			¥154,753	¥154,753	¥154,753
THOMA, MATHIAS (workshop of)	1	1	$575	$575	$575
			DM984	DM984	DM984
			£340	£340	£340
			¥71,404	¥71,404	¥71,404
THOMPSON, ALFRED	1	0			
THOMPSON, ROBERT (attributed to)	1	1	$2,971	$2,971	$2,971
			DM5,504	DM5,504	DM5,504
			£1,783	£1,783	£1,783
			¥396,838	¥396,838	¥396,838
TOMAS, OTIS A.	1	1	$1,610	$1,610	$1,610
			DM2,783	DM2,783	DM2,783
			£995	£995	£995
			¥204,043	¥204,043	¥204,043
TOMASSINI, DOMENICO	1	0			
TRAPP, HERMANN	2	1	$2,610	$2,610	$2,610
			DM4,569	DM4,569	DM4,569
			£1,610	£1,610	£1,610
			¥315,480	¥315,480	¥315,480
UCHIYAMA, MASAYUKI	2	0			
UEBEL, ERHARD	1	1	$8,050	$8,050	$8,050
			DM11,640	DM11,640	DM11,640
			£5,258	£5,258	£5,258
			¥815,063	¥815,063	¥815,063
VALENCE (attributed to)	1	1	$10,530	$10,530	$10,530
			DM17,391	DM17,391	DM17,391
			£6,440	£6,440	£6,440
			¥1,303,643	¥1,303,643	¥1,303,643
VAN HOOF, ALPHONS	1	1	$11,454	$11,454	$11,454
			DM16,908	DM16,908	DM16,908
			£7,475	£7,475	£7,475
			¥1,217,685	¥1,217,685	¥1,217,685
VENTAPANE, LORENZO	2	2	$85,514	$87,458	$86,486
			DM148,258	DM151,628	DM149,943
			£50,600	£51,750	£51,175
			¥10,676,600	¥10,919,250	¥10,797,925
VENTAPANE, LORENZO (attributed to)	1	0			

Violoncello

Maker	Items Bid	Sold	Selling Prices Low	High	Avg
VERHASSELT, F.	1	1	$8,746	$8,746	$8,746
			DM15,163	DM15,163	DM15,163
			£5,175	£5,175	£5,175
			¥1,091,925	¥1,091,925	¥1,091,925
VERINI, ANDREA	1	1	$5,467	$5,467	$5,467
			DM9,250	DM9,250	DM9,250
			£3,439	£3,439	£3,439
			¥677,385	¥677,385	¥677,385
VETTORI, CARLO	1	0			
VICKERS, J.E.	1	0			
VILLA, LUIGI	1	0			
VOIGT, E.R. & SON	1	1	$3,947	$3,947	$3,947
			DM6,684	DM6,684	DM6,684
			£2,415	£2,415	£2,415
			¥457,633	¥457,633	¥457,633
VUILLAUME, JEAN BAPTISTE	6	5	$68,634	$115,187	$101,589
			DM126,977	DM173,541	DM157,347
			£41,000	£73,000	£62,507
			¥9,146,690	¥12,724,194	¥11,118,760
VUILLAUME, JEAN BAPTISTE (workshop of)	1	1	$39,982	$39,982	$39,982
			DM56,472	DM56,472	DM56,472
			£25,300	£25,300	£25,300
			¥3,568,236	¥3,568,236	¥3,568,236
VUILLAUME, SEBASTIAN	1	0			
WAMSLEY, PETER	5	3	$2,118	$9,373	$6,625
			DM3,251	DM16,215	DM11,508
			£1,380	£5,750	£4,102
			¥231,854	¥1,069,500	¥763,725
WEERTMAN, ROELOF	1	0			
WEIGERT, JOHANN BLASIUS	2	0			
WERNER, ERICH	6	1	$2,687	$2,687	$2,687
			DM3,769	DM3,769	DM3,769
			£1,725	£1,725	£1,725
			¥271,520	¥271,520	¥271,520
WHITAKER, MAURICE	1	1	$11,560	$11,560	$11,560
			DM17,372	DM17,372	DM17,372
			£6,900	£6,900	£6,900
			¥1,287,271	¥1,287,271	¥1,287,271
WHITE, ASA WARREN	1	1	$1,725	$1,725	$1,725
			DM3,122	DM3,122	DM3,122
			£1,052	£1,052	£1,052
			¥208,277	¥208,277	¥208,277
WHITMARSH, EMANUEL	2	1	$3,286	$3,286	$3,286
			DM4,916	DM4,916	DM4,916
			£1,955	£1,955	£1,955
			¥366,523	¥366,523	¥366,523
WITHERS, EDWARD	1	1	$11,645	$11,645	$11,645
			DM16,331	DM16,331	DM16,331
			£7,475	£7,475	£7,475
			¥1,176,587	¥1,176,587	¥1,176,587
WOLFF BROS.	3	2	$3,749	$5,025	$4,387
			DM6,486	DM7,519	DM7,002
			£2,300	£2,990	£2,645
			¥427,800	¥560,565	¥494,183
ZANI, ALDO	1	0			

Maker	Items		Selling Prices		
	Bid	Sold	Low	High	Avg
ZANOLI, GIACOMO	1	1	$67,815	$67,815	$67,815
			DM102,339	DM102,339	DM102,339
			£41,100	£41,100	£41,100
			¥7,685,700	¥7,685,700	¥7,685,700
ZANOLI, JOANNES BAPTISTA (ascribed to)	1	1	$26,979	$26,979	$26,979
			DM38,162	DM38,162	DM38,162
			£17,250	£17,250	£17,250
			¥2,739,455	¥2,739,455	¥2,739,455
ZIMMERMANN, JULIUS HEINRICH	1	1	$972	$972	$972
			DM1,685	DM1,685	DM1,685
			£575	£575	£575
			¥121,325	¥121,325	¥121,325
ZIMMERMANN, JULIUS HEINRICH (attributed to)	2	1	$4,124	$4,124	$4,124
			DM7,464	DM7,464	DM7,464
			£2,530	£2,530	£2,530
			¥497,626	¥497,626	¥497,626

VIOLONCELLO BOW

Maker	Items		Selling Prices		
	Bid	Sold	Low	High	Avg
ACOULON, ALFRED	1	0			
ADAM, JEAN DOMINIQUE	1	1	$2,950	$2,950	$2,950
			DM4,108	DM4,108	DM4,108
			£1,840	£1,840	£1,840
			¥249,408	¥249,408	¥249,408
ADAM, JEAN DOMINIQUE (attributed to)	1	0			
ALVEY, BRIAN	3	1	$274	$274	$274
			DM441	DM441	DM441
			£161	£161	£161
			¥33,845	¥33,845	¥33,845
BAILEY, G.E.	3	2	$743	$773	$758
			DM1,197	DM1,349	DM1,273
			£437	£460	£449
			¥91,866	¥98,606	¥95,236
BARBE, AUGUSTE	1	0			
BAUSCH	6	4	$56	$2,011	$707
			DM94	DM3,808	DM1,255
			£35	£1,265	£449
			¥6,826	¥241,096	¥82,151
BAUSCH, L.	1	1	$1,380	$1,380	$1,380
			DM2,361	DM2,361	DM2,361
			£816	£816	£816
			¥171,368	¥171,368	¥171,368
BAUSCH, LUDWIG	1	1	$2,049	$2,049	$2,049
			DM3,858	DM3,858	DM3,858
			£1,265	£1,265	£1,265
			¥216,593	¥216,593	¥216,593
BAZIN	3	3	$1,610	$3,936	$3,004
			DM2,755	DM6,810	DM5,325
			£952	£2,415	£1,812
			¥199,930	¥461,796	¥370,305
BAZIN (attributed to)	2	1	$2,236	$2,236	$2,236
			DM4,002	DM4,002	DM4,002
			£1,380	£1,380	£1,380
			¥263,677	¥263,677	¥263,677

| Maker | Items | | Selling Prices | | |
	Bid	Sold	Low	High	Avg
BAZIN (workshop of)	1	1	$1,765	$1,765	$1,765
			DM2,711	DM2,711	DM2,711
			£1,150	£1,150	£1,150
			¥193,187	¥193,187	¥193,187
BAZIN, CHARLES	3	2	$2,544	$3,401	$2,973
			DM3,594	DM5,897	DM4,745
			£1,610	£2,013	£1,811
			¥227,070	¥424,638	¥325,854
BAZIN, CHARLES NICHOLAS	13	10	$570	$4,404	$2,605
			DM920	DM7,059	DM4,297
			£331	£2,875	£1,610
			¥67,160	¥513,565	¥291,240
BAZIN, LOUIS	5	2	$1,062	$3,364	$2,213
			DM1,909	DM5,692	DM3,800
			£632	£2,116	£1,374
			¥122,753	¥416,852	¥269,803
BAZIN, LOUIS (workshop of)	2	1	$768	$768	$768
			DM1,270	DM1,270	DM1,270
			£460	£460	£460
			¥89,838	¥89,838	¥89,838
BAZIN, LOUIS (II)	1	1	$1,677	$1,677	$1,677
			DM3,177	DM3,177	DM3,177
			£1,035	£1,035	£1,035
			¥177,057	¥177,057	¥177,057
BEARE, JOHN & ARTHUR	3	2	$849	$3,055	$1,952
			DM1,544	DM4,900	DM3,222
			£518	£1,984	£1,251
			¥107,195	¥347,593	¥227,394
BEARE & SON	1	1	$1,155	$1,155	$1,155
			DM2,137	DM2,137	DM2,137
			£690	£690	£690
			¥153,932	¥153,932	¥153,932
BECHINI, RENZO	1	0			
BEILKE, MARTIN O.	1	1	$1,398	$1,398	$1,398
			DM1,473	DM1,473	DM1,473
			£863	£863	£863
			¥106,773	¥106,773	¥106,773
BERNARDEL, GUSTAVE	3	3	$1,462	$2,875	$2,107
			DM2,601	DM5,221	DM3,856
			£897	£1,760	£1,295
			¥196,380	¥357,018	¥254,426
BERNARDEL, GUSTAVE ADOLPHE	2	1	$637	$637	$637
			DM1,103	DM1,103	DM1,103
			£391	£391	£391
			¥72,726	¥72,726	¥72,726
BERNARDEL, LEON	4	2	$428	$1,733	$1,080
			DM690	DM3,205	DM1,948
			£248	£1,035	£642
			¥50,370	¥230,898	¥140,634
BOURGUIGNON, MAURICE	1	1	$2,118	$2,118	$2,118
			DM3,918	DM3,918	DM3,918
			£1,265	£1,265	£1,265
			¥282,209	¥282,209	¥282,209
BOUVIN, JEAN	1	1	$1,035	$1,035	$1,035
			DM1,495	DM1,495	DM1,495
			£659	£659	£659
			¥89,786	¥89,786	¥89,786

Maker	Items		Selling Prices		
	Bid	Sold	Low	High	Avg
BRISTOW, S.E.	1	1	$411	$411	$411
			DM717	DM717	DM717
			£253	£253	£253
			¥49,803	¥49,803	¥49,803
BRYANT, PERCIVAL WILFRED	2	2	$1,540	$1,792	$1,666
			DM2,512	DM2,849	DM2,681
			£920	£1,150	£1,035
			¥181,013	¥205,243	¥193,128
BULTITUDE, ARTHUR RICHARD	10	7	$705	$4,832	$2,338
			DM1,039	DM7,230	DM3,688
			£460	£2,875	£1,446
			¥75,150	¥539,005	¥255,155
BUTHOD	2	1	$87	$87	$87
			DM134	DM134	DM134
			£58	£58	£58
			¥9,270	¥9,270	¥9,270
BUTHOD, CHARLES	1	1	$787	$787	$787
			DM1,396	DM1,396	DM1,396
			£483	£483	£483
			¥93,089	¥93,089	¥93,089
BUTHOD, CHARLES LOUIS	2	2	$1,633	$1,892	$1,763
			DM2,300	DM3,202	DM2,751
			£1,035	£1,190	£1,113
			¥166,979	¥234,479	¥200,729
BUTHOD, CHARLES LOUIS (workshop of)	1	1	$1,380	$1,380	$1,380
			DM2,110	DM2,110	DM2,110
			£908	£908	£908
			¥145,452	¥145,452	¥145,452
BYROM, GEORGE	1	1	$970	$970	$970
			DM1,489	DM1,489	DM1,489
			£632	£632	£632
			¥106,182	¥106,182	¥106,182
BYROM, H.	1	0			
CARESSA, ALBERT	1	1	$1,152	$1,152	$1,152
			DM1,925	DM1,925	DM1,925
			£690	£690	£690
			¥140,063	¥140,063	¥140,063
CHANOT & CHARDON	1	0			
CHERPITEL, MOINEL	1	0			
CLUTTERBUCK, JOHN	1	1	$1,106	$1,106	$1,106
			DM1,541	DM1,541	DM1,541
			£690	£690	£690
			¥93,528	¥93,528	¥93,528
COCKER, L.	2	2	$348	$463	$406
			DM534	DM688	DM611
			£230	£299	£265
			¥37,082	¥50,166	¥43,624
COCKER, LAWRENCE	1	1	$1,149	$1,149	$1,149
			DM1,691	DM1,691	DM1,691
			£748	£748	£748
			¥121,962	¥121,962	¥121,962
COLAS, PROSPER	9	5	$475	$2,319	$1,473
			DM894	DM3,470	DM2,463
			£299	£1,380	£894
			¥57,480	¥258,722	¥176,372

Maker	Items		Selling Prices		
	Bid	Sold	Low	High	Avg
COLLIN-MEZIN (workshop of)	1	1	$3,450	$3,450	$3,450
			DM5,963	DM5,963	DM5,963
			£2,132	£2,132	£2,132
			¥437,236	¥437,236	¥437,236
COLLIN-MEZIN, CH.J.B.	1	0			
COLLINS, ROY	1	1	$442	$442	$442
			DM653	DM653	DM653
			£288	£288	£288
			¥47,074	¥47,074	¥47,074
CUNIOT-HURY	5	2	$1,271	$3,105	$2,188
			DM2,278	DM4,365	DM3,321
			£759	£1,955	£1,357
			¥147,626	¥275,993	¥211,809
CUNIOT-HURY, EUGENE	1	0			
DABERT, J.F.	1	1	$1,953	$1,953	$1,953
			DM2,810	DM2,810	DM2,810
			£1,265	£1,265	£1,265
			¥198,276	¥198,276	¥198,276
DARCHE, HILAIRE	1	1	$1,938	$1,938	$1,938
			DM2,861	DM2,861	DM2,861
			£1,265	£1,265	£1,265
			¥206,070	¥206,070	¥206,070
DARTE, AUGUSTE (workshop of)	1	1	$2,990	$2,990	$2,990
			DM4,500	DM4,500	DM4,500
			£1,815	£1,815	£1,815
			¥334,222	¥334,222	¥334,222
DAVIS	1	1	$2,497	$2,497	$2,497
			DM4,635	DM4,635	DM4,635
			£1,495	£1,495	£1,495
			¥334,043	¥334,043	¥334,043
DODD	10	9	$1,031	$7,700	$4,448
			DM1,526	DM14,246	DM7,656
			£633	£4,600	£2,690
			¥109,578	¥1,026,214	¥540,616
DODD, EDWARD	1	0			
DODD, J.	2	1	$2,823	$2,823	$2,823
			DM4,338	DM4,338	DM4,338
			£1,840	£1,840	£1,840
			¥309,100	¥309,100	¥309,100
DODD, JAMES	2	2	$1,371	$4,355	$2,863
			DM2,577	DM6,133	DM4,355
			£862	£2,760	£1,811
			¥165,711	¥445,276	¥305,494
DODD, JOHN	8	8	$1,590	$7,498	$3,445
			DM2,349	DM13,294	DM5,762
			£977	£4,600	£2,144
			¥169,465	¥886,558	¥412,894
DODD, JOHN (attributed to)	2	0			
DODD FAMILY	1	1	$777	$777	$777
			DM1,348	DM1,348	DM1,348
			£460	£460	£460
			¥97,060	¥97,060	¥97,060
DOLLING, HEINZ	1	1	$1,055	$1,055	$1,055
			DM1,620	DM1,620	DM1,620
			£690	£690	£690
			¥115,187	¥115,187	¥115,187

Maker	Items		Selling Prices		
	Bid	Sold	Low	High	Avg
DUPREE, EMILE	1	1	$1,495 DM2,159 £952 ¥129,691	$1,495 DM2,159 £952 ¥129,691	$1,495 DM2,159 £952 ¥129,691
DUPUY, GEORGE	1	1	$1,612 DM2,902 £977 ¥232,477	$1,612 DM2,902 £977 ¥232,477	$1,612 DM2,902 £977 ¥232,477
DURRSCHMIDT, OTTO (workshop of)	1	1	$633 DM952 £384 ¥70,701	$633 DM952 £384 ¥70,701	$633 DM952 £384 ¥70,701
EURY, NICOLAS	1	0			
FETIQUE, MARCEL (attributed to)	1	0			
FETIQUE, VICTOR	13	11	$1,555 DM2,696 £920 ¥194,120	$8,066 DM13,476 £4,830 ¥980,442	$4,490 DM7,288 £2,776 ¥517,476
FETIQUE, VICTOR (ascribed to)	1	1	$1,210 DM2,278 £747 ¥127,901	$1,210 DM2,278 £747 ¥127,901	$1,210 DM2,278 £747 ¥127,901
FINKEL, JOHANN S.	3	2	$1,352 DM2,431 £805 ¥156,355	$1,944 DM2,872 £1,265 ¥207,124	$1,648 DM2,651 £1,035 ¥181,739
FINKEL, JOHANNES S.	2	0			
FINKEL, SIEGFRIED	2	2	$972 DM1,685 £575 ¥121,325	$1,433 DM2,010 £920 ¥144,811	$1,203 DM1,847 £748 ¥133,068
FORSTER	1	1	$3,887 DM5,743 £2,530 ¥414,247	$3,887 DM5,743 £2,530 ¥414,247	$3,887 DM5,743 £2,530 ¥414,247
FORSTER, WILLIAM (II)	1	1	$2,422 DM4,590 £1,495 ¥255,750	$2,422 DM4,590 £1,495 ¥255,750	$2,422 DM4,590 £1,495 ¥255,750
FORSTER, WILLIAM (III)	1	0			
FRANCAIS, EMILE	2	2	$1,502 DM2,778 £897 ¥200,112	$4,146 DM7,346 £2,546 ¥505,526	$2,824 DM5,062 £1,721 ¥352,819
FRITSCH, JEAN	1	1	$1,840 DM3,148 £1,088 ¥228,491	$1,840 DM3,148 £1,088 ¥228,491	$1,840 DM3,148 £1,088 ¥228,491
GAND BROS.	1	1	$2,496 DM4,025 £1,449 ¥293,825	$2,496 DM4,025 £1,449 ¥293,825	$2,496 DM4,025 £1,449 ¥293,825
GAND & BERNARDEL	4	3	$1,676 DM2,572 £1,092 ¥171,468	$3,529 DM5,422 £2,300 ¥386,375	$2,411 DM3,606 £1,552 ¥247,103

Maker	Items		Selling Prices		
	Bid	Sold	Low	High	Avg
GEROME, ROGER	2	2	$1,561	$1,725	$1,643
			DM2,625	DM2,915	DM2,770
			£978	£1,035	£1,006
			¥191,652	¥210,450	¥201,051
GILLET, LOUIS	3	2	$862	$5,762	$3,312
			DM1,492	DM9,626	DM5,559
			£529	£3,450	£1,990
			¥98,394	¥700,316	¥399,355
GOTZ	1	0			
GOTZ, CONRAD	1	1	$424	$424	$424
			DM624	DM624	DM624
			£276	£276	£276
			¥45,032	¥45,032	¥45,032
GRAND ADAM (attributed to)	1	0			
GRANDCHAMP, ERIC	1	1	$1,540	$1,540	$1,540
			DM2,849	DM2,849	DM2,849
			£920	£920	£920
			¥205,243	¥205,243	¥205,243
GRANIER, ANDRE	1	1	$3,220	$3,220	$3,220
			DM4,656	DM4,656	DM4,656
			£2,103	£2,103	£2,103
			¥326,025	¥326,025	¥326,025
GRUNKE	3	0			
HAMMIG, W.H.	1	1	$869	$869	$869
			DM1,300	DM1,300	DM1,300
			£517	£517	£517
			¥96,927	¥96,927	¥96,927
HART	1	1	$2,041	$2,041	$2,041
			DM3,538	DM3,538	DM3,538
			£1,208	£1,208	£1,208
			¥254,783	¥254,783	¥254,783
HART & SON	1	1	$526	$526	$526
			DM937	DM937	DM937
			£322	£322	£322
			¥68,789	¥68,789	¥68,789
HAWKES & SON	1	1	$1,068	$1,068	$1,068
			DM1,852	DM1,852	DM1,852
			£632	£632	£632
			¥135,798	¥135,798	¥135,798
HEBERLIN, FRIEDRICH	1	1	$1,412	$1,412	$1,412
			DM2,169	DM2,169	DM2,169
			£920	£920	£920
			¥154,550	¥154,550	¥154,550
HEL, PIERRE	1	0			
HEL, PIERRE JOSEPH (workshop of)	1	1	$1,093	$1,093	$1,093
			DM1,644	DM1,644	DM1,644
			£663	£663	£663
			¥122,120	¥122,120	¥122,120
HENDERSON, F.V.	1	0			
HENRY (attributed to)	1	0			
HENRY, EUGENE	1	0			
HENRY, JOSEPH	2	2	$9,436	$31,671	$20,553
			DM13,288	DM59,628	DM36,458
			£5,980	£19,550	£12,765
			¥964,765	¥3,347,351	¥2,156,058

| Maker | *Items* | | *Selling Prices* | | |
	Bid	*Sold*	*Low*	*High*	*Avg*
HERRMANN, EDWIN OTTO	2	2	$883	$1,938	$1,410
			DM1,354	DM2,861	DM2,108
			£575	£1,265	£920
			¥96,606	¥206,070	¥151,338
HERRMANN, EMIL	1	1	$1,725	$1,725	$1,725
			DM2,494	DM2,494	DM2,494
			£1,127	£1,127	£1,127
			¥174,656	¥174,656	¥174,656
HERRMANN, PAUL	1	1	$773	$773	$773
			DM1,390	DM1,390	DM1,390
			£460	£460	£460
			¥89,346	¥89,346	¥89,346
HILAIRE, PAUL	1	0			
HILL	3	2	$336	$1,191	$764
			DM494	DM1,670	DM1,082
			£219	£748	£483
			¥35,650	¥105,013	¥70,331
HILL, W.E. & SONS	87	72	$168	$5,479	$2,274
			DM293	DM9,985	DM3,642
			£104	£3,450	£1,407
			¥20,374	¥667,039	¥248,157
HURY, CUNIOT	1	0			
HUSSON, CHARLES CLAUDE	3	2	$2,236	$3,534	$2,885
			DM4,002	DM5,221	DM4,612
			£1,380	£2,300	£1,840
			¥263,677	¥376,588	¥320,132
JOMBAR, PAUL	1	1	$192	$192	$192
			DM321	DM321	DM321
			£115	£115	£115
			¥23,344	¥23,344	¥23,344
KOLSTEIN, SAMUEL	1	1	$1,380	$1,380	$1,380
			DM2,110	DM2,110	DM2,110
			£908	£908	£908
			¥145,452	¥145,452	¥145,452
LABERTE	1	1	$782	$782	$782
			DM1,401	DM1,401	DM1,401
			£483	£483	£483
			¥92,287	¥92,287	¥92,287
LABERTE, MARC	1	1	$1,234	$1,234	$1,234
			DM1,821	DM1,821	DM1,821
			£805	£805	£805
			¥131,135	¥131,135	¥131,135
LAFLEUR, JACQUES	1	0			
LAFLEUR, JACQUES RENE	1	1	$22,770	$22,770	$22,770
			DM34,362	DM34,362	DM34,362
			£13,800	£13,800	£13,800
			¥2,580,600	¥2,580,600	¥2,580,600
LAMY, A.	6	2	$3,688	$4,776	$4,232
			DM5,135	DM8,031	DM6,583
			£2,300	£2,990	£2,645
			¥311,760	¥586,228	¥448,994
LAMY, ALFRED	10	7	$2,300	$7,475	$4,623
			DM3,976	DM12,921	DM7,332
			£1,421	£4,619	£2,926
			¥291,491	¥947,344	¥515,999

Violoncello Bow

Maker	Items		Selling Prices		
	Bid	Sold	Low	High	Avg
LAMY, ALFRED JOSEPH	17	14	$2,236	$16,457	$5,928
			DM4,171	DM30,947	DM10,515
			£1,380	£10,350	£3,643
			¥236,077	¥1,989,684	¥709,200
LAMY, JULES	2	0			
LAPIERRE, MARCEL	2	1	$575	$575	$575
			DM1,041	DM1,041	DM1,041
			£351	£351	£351
			¥69,426	¥69,426	¥69,426
LAPIERRE, MARCEL (attributed to)	1	1	$2,889	$2,889	$2,889
			DM5,177	DM5,177	DM5,177
			£1,725	£1,725	£1,725
			¥335,513	¥335,513	¥335,513
LEE, JOHN NORWOOD	3	1	$1,265	$1,265	$1,265
			DM2,187	DM2,187	DM2,187
			£782	£782	£782
			¥160,320	¥160,320	¥160,320
LEWIS, WILLIAM & SON	2	2	$611	$1,096	$853
			DM980	DM1,541	DM1,260
			£397	£690	£543
			¥69,519	¥97,409	¥83,464
LOTTE, FRANCOIS	5	4	$428	$860	$655
			DM690	DM1,624	DM1,179
			£248	£532	£396
			¥50,370	¥107,752	¥77,256
LOTTE, ROGER-FRANCOIS	3	2	$2,689	$2,695	$2,692
			DM4,986	DM4,991	DM4,989
			£1,610	£1,610	£1,610
			¥359,175	¥359,738	¥359,457
MAIRE, NICOLAS	3	2	$2,899	$4,776	$3,837
			DM4,094	DM8,031	DM6,062
			£1,840	£2,990	£2,415
			¥291,885	¥586,228	¥439,057
MAIRE, NICOLAS (ascribed to)	1	1	$6,900	$6,900	$6,900
			DM9,977	DM9,977	DM9,977
			£4,507	£4,507	£4,507
			¥698,625	¥698,625	¥698,625
MALINE, GUILLAUME	3	0			
MARTIN, J.	1	0			
MARTIN, JEAN JOSEPH	5	4	$673	$7,499	$5,095
			DM1,245	DM14,210	DM9,636
			£402	£4,629	£3,144
			¥89,682	¥791,840	¥542,934
METTAL, WALTER	3	2	$96	$1,005	$550
			DM172	DM1,504	DM838
			£57	£598	£328
			¥11,071	¥112,113	¥61,592
MILLANT, MAX	1	0			
MILLANT, ROGER & MAX	2	2	$2,560	$10,971	$6,765
			DM4,814	DM20,631	DM12,722
			£1,610	£6,900	£4,255
			¥309,506	¥1,326,456	¥817,981
MOINEL & CHERPITEL	4	2	$712	$1,540	$1,126
			DM1,232	DM2,849	DM2,041
			£437	£920	£679
			¥81,282	¥205,243	¥143,262

Maker	Items		Selling Prices		
	Bid	Sold	Low	High	Avg
MORIZOT, LOUIS	4	3	$576	$2,248	$1,390
			DM1,070	DM4,137	DM2,567
			£345	£1,398	£849
			¥77,087	¥265,181	¥174,046
MORIZOT, LOUIS (II)	2	2	$1,328	$2,648	$1,988
			DM2,004	DM4,063	DM3,034
			£805	£1,725	£1,265
			¥150,535	¥289,817	¥220,176
MORIZOT (FRERES), LOUIS	2	0			
MORIZOT FAMILY	1	1	$1,380	$1,380	$1,380
			DM2,332	DM2,332	DM2,332
			£828	£828	£828
			¥168,360	¥168,360	¥168,360
NEUDORFER, RODOLF (II)	2	2	$894	$1,028	$961
			DM1,695	DM1,949	DM1,822
			£552	£635	£593
			¥94,431	¥108,595	¥101,513
NEUDORFER, RUDOLPH	2	1	$342	$342	$342
			DM607	DM607	DM607
			£207	£207	£207
			¥47,380	¥47,380	¥47,380
NEUVEVILLE, P.C.	1	0			
NEUVILLE	1	0			
NORRIS, JOHN	1	0			
NURNBERGER	1	0			
NURNBERGER, A.	1	1	$3,353	$3,353	$3,353
			DM6,314	DM6,314	DM6,314
			£2,070	£2,070	£2,070
			¥354,425	¥354,425	¥354,425
NURNBERGER, ALBERT	9	6	$690	$2,881	$1,531
			DM1,212	DM4,813	DM2,494
			£421	£1,725	£925
			¥83,311	¥350,158	¥179,508
NURNBERGER, CHRISTIAN ALBERT	1	1	$1,218	$1,218	$1,218
			DM2,107	DM2,107	DM2,107
			£747	£747	£747
			¥138,942	¥138,942	¥138,942
NURNBERGER, KARL ALBERT	3	2	$1,360	$1,544	$1,452
			DM1,915	DM2,181	DM2,048
			£862	£977	£920
			¥137,793	¥139,068	¥138,431
OUCHARD, E.	1	1	$3,523	$3,523	$3,523
			DM5,193	DM5,193	DM5,193
			£2,300	£2,300	£2,300
			¥375,751	¥375,751	¥375,751
OUCHARD, EMILE	4	4	$2,300	$5,750	$4,241
			DM3,935	DM8,854	DM6,960
			£1,360	£3,491	£2,531
			¥285,614	¥642,735	¥508,776
OUCHARD, EMILE (FILS) (attributed to)	2	1	$6,569	$6,569	$6,569
			DM10,948	DM10,948	DM10,948
			£3,910	£3,910	£3,910
			¥785,089	¥785,089	¥785,089
OUCHARD, EMILE A.	4	4	$1,542	$10,925	$5,951
			DM2,171	DM16,442	DM8,973
			£977	£6,632	£3,714
			¥157,621	¥1,221,197	¥657,695

| Maker | Items | | Selling Prices | | |
	Bid	Sold	Low	High	Avg
OUCHARD, EMILE F. & EMILE A.	1	1	$5,270	$5,270	$5,270
			DM7,444	DM7,444	DM7,444
			£3,335	£3,335	£3,335
			¥470,358	¥470,358	¥470,358
OUCHARD, EMILE FRANCOIS	5	3	$2,359	$4,023	$3,155
			DM3,322	DM7,565	DM5,077
			£1,495	£2,530	£1,993
			¥241,191	¥486,367	¥347,654
PAJEOT	1	1	$8,797	$8,797	$8,797
			DM12,329	DM12,329	DM12,329
			£5,520	£5,520	£5,520
			¥775,477	¥775,477	¥775,477
PAJEOT (FILS)	1	0			
PAJEOT, ETIENNE	2	2	$8,228	$12,334	$10,281
			DM15,473	DM22,201	DM18,837
			£5,175	£7,475	£6,325
			¥994,842	¥1,778,676	¥1,386,759
PAJEOT, LOUIS SIMON	1	0			
PANORMO (ascribed to)	2	1	$2,142	$2,142	$2,142
			DM4,034	DM4,034	DM4,034
			£1,323	£1,323	£1,323
			¥228,396	¥228,396	¥228,396
PANORMO (attributed to)	1	1	$2,364	$2,364	$2,364
			DM4,490	DM4,490	DM4,490
			£1,459	£1,459	£1,459
			¥248,396	¥248,396	¥248,396
PANORMO, LOUIS	3	1	$3,524	$3,524	$3,524
			DM5,202	DM5,202	DM5,202
			£2,300	£2,300	£2,300
			¥374,672	¥374,672	¥374,672
PAQUOTTE, PLACIDE	1	1	$2,497	$2,497	$2,497
			DM4,171	DM4,171	DM4,171
			£1,495	£1,495	£1,495
			¥303,470	¥303,470	¥303,470
PAULUS, GUNTER A.	3	2	$654	$978	$816
			DM926	DM1,413	DM1,170
			£414	£639	£526
			¥67,482	¥98,972	¥83,227
PAULUS, JOHANNES O.	2	1	$960	$960	$960
			DM1,783	DM1,783	DM1,783
			£575	£575	£575
			¥128,478	¥128,478	¥128,478
PECATTE, CHARLES	2	1	$10,563	$10,563	$10,563
			DM18,912	DM18,912	DM18,912
			£6,325	£6,325	£6,325
			¥1,453,359	¥1,453,359	¥1,453,359
PECCATTE, CHARLES	5	3	$1,792	$16,331	$8,602
			DM3,092	DM22,999	DM12,975
			£1,093	£10,350	£5,348
			¥204,472	¥1,669,786	¥936,004
PECCATTE, CHARLES (attributed to)	1	0			
PECCATTE, CHARLES & AUGUSTE LENOBLE (workshop of)	2	2	$5,589	$6,427	$6,008
			DM10,592	DM12,180	DM11,386
			£3,450	£3,968	£3,709
			¥590,192	¥678,720	¥634,456

Maker	Bid	Sold	Low	High	Avg
PECCATTE, DOMINIQUE	3	2	$10,689	$22,356	$16,523
			DM18,532	DM42,090	DM30,311
			£6,325	£13,800	£10,063
			¥1,334,575	¥2,362,836	¥1,848,706
PECCATTE, FRANCOIS	1	1	$15,005	$15,005	$15,005
			DM23,025	DM23,025	DM23,025
			£9,775	£9,775	£9,775
			¥1,642,298	¥1,642,298	¥1,642,298
PECCATTE, FRANCOIS (workshop of)	1	1	$3,073	$3,073	$3,073
			DM5,134	DM5,134	DM5,134
			£1,840	£1,840	£1,840
			¥373,502	¥373,502	¥373,502
PECCATTE, FRANCOIS & DOMINIQUE	1	1	$13,476	$13,476	$13,476
			DM24,931	DM24,931	DM24,931
			£8,050	£8,050	£8,050
			¥1,795,875	¥1,795,875	¥1,795,875
PENZEL, E.M.	1	1	$1,035	$1,035	$1,035
			DM1,558	DM1,558	DM1,558
			£628	£628	£628
			¥115,692	¥115,692	¥115,692
PFRETZSCHNER (workshop of)	1	1	$489	$489	$489
			DM885	DM885	DM885
			£298	£298	£298
			¥59,012	¥59,012	¥59,012
PFRETZSCHNER, CARL FRIEDRICH	1	1	$997	$997	$997
			DM1,404	DM1,404	DM1,404
			£632	£632	£632
			¥101,962	¥101,962	¥101,962
PFRETZSCHNER, CARL FRIEDRICH (III)	1	0			
PFRETZSCHNER, G.A.	1	1	$920	$920	$920
			DM1,574	DM1,574	DM1,574
			£544	£544	£544
			¥114,246	¥114,246	¥114,246
PFRETZSCHNER, H.R.	14	13	$489	$3,110	$1,789
			DM736	DM5,391	DM3,025
			£297	£1,840	£1,081
			¥54,632	¥388,240	¥220,597
PIERNOT, MARIE LOUIS	2	2	$1,725	$3,635	$2,680
			DM2,596	DM5,134	DM3,865
			£1,047	£2,300	£1,674
			¥192,821	¥324,385	¥258,603
POIRSON, JUSTIN	4	2	$570	$2,865	$1,717
			DM920	DM5,076	DM2,998
			£331	£1,759	£1,045
			¥67,160	¥349,272	¥208,216
PRAGER, AUGUST EDWIN	4	2	$637	$1,117	$877
			DM953	DM2,066	DM1,509
			£379	£667	£523
			¥71,055	¥148,801	¥109,928
PRAGER, GUSTAV	1	1	$705	$705	$705
			DM1,040	DM1,040	DM1,040
			£460	£460	£460
			¥74,934	¥74,934	¥74,934
REICHEL, AUGUST ANTON	1	1	$1,353	$1,353	$1,353
			DM2,024	DM2,024	DM2,024
			£805	£805	£805
			¥150,921	¥150,921	¥150,921

| Maker | Items | | Selling Prices | | |
	Bid	Sold	Low	High	Avg
RETFORD, WILLIAM C.	1	1	$4,813	$4,813	$4,813
			DM8,904	DM8,904	DM8,904
			£2,875	£2,875	£2,875
			¥641,384	¥641,384	¥641,384
ROLLAND, BENOIT	2	2	$2,852	$3,562	$3,207
			DM4,600	DM6,162	DM5,381
			£1,656	£2,185	£1,921
			¥335,800	¥406,410	¥371,105
ROTH, ERNST HEINRICH (workshop of)	1	1	$1,150	$1,150	$1,150
			DM1,731	DM1,731	DM1,731
			£698	£698	£698
			¥128,547	¥128,547	¥128,547
SARTORY, E.	1	1	$12,775	$12,775	$12,775
			DM23,964	DM23,964	DM23,964
			£7,935	£7,935	£7,935
			¥1,535,581	¥1,535,581	¥1,535,581
SARTORY, EUGENE	29	24	$3,287	$23,046	$11,055
			DM4,622	DM39,177	DM18,851
			£2,070	£13,800	£6,773
			¥292,228	¥2,822,089	¥1,265,897
SCHULLER, OTTO	1	1	$188	$188	$188
			DM318	DM318	DM318
			£115	£115	£115
			¥21,792	¥21,792	¥21,792
SCHUSTER, ADOLF	3	3	$944	$1,035	$986
			DM1,338	DM1,690	DM1,537
			£598	£681	£628
			¥97,474	¥123,883	¥110,149
SCHUSTER, GOTHARD	2	1	$805	$805	$805
			DM1,360	DM1,360	DM1,360
			£483	£483	£483
			¥98,210	¥98,210	¥98,210
SEIFERT, LOTHAR	2	0			
SEIFERT, W.	1	1	$155	$155	$155
			DM270	DM270	DM270
			£92	£92	£92
			¥19,721	¥19,721	¥19,721
SILVESTRE & MAUCOTEL	3	2	$1,845	$5,654	$3,750
			DM3,200	DM8,354	DM5,777
			£1,092	£3,680	£2,386
			¥234,638	¥602,541	¥418,590
SIMON (attributed to)	1	0			
SIMON BROS.	2	0			
SIMON, F.R.	2	0			
SIMON, F.R. (attributed to)	1	0			
SIMON, PAUL	5	3	$2,103	$7,452	$4,838
			DM3,558	DM13,386	DM8,690
			£1,323	£4,600	£3,002
			¥260,533	¥879,842	¥575,111
SIMON, PIERRE	3	1	$7,941	$7,941	$7,941
			DM12,200	DM12,200	DM12,200
			£5,175	£5,175	£5,175
			¥869,343	¥869,343	¥869,343
SOMNY, JOSEPH MAURICE	1	0			

Maker	Items		Selling Prices		
	Bid	Sold	Low	High	Avg
STENGEL, V.	1	1	$159	$159	$159
			DM283	DM283	DM283
			£98	£98	£98
			¥21,400	¥21,400	¥21,400
TAYLOR, DAVID	1	0			
TAYLOR, MALCOLM	2	1	$1,304	$1,304	$1,304
			DM2,455	DM2,455	DM2,455
			£805	£805	£805
			¥139,024	¥139,024	¥139,024
TAYLOR, ROBERT	1	0			
THIBOUVILLE-LAMY, J.	5	3	$1,383	$1,695	$1,493
			DM1,926	DM2,548	DM2,302
			£828	£1,012	£901
			¥116,910	¥188,800	¥161,136
THOMASSIN (attributed to)	1	0			
THOMASSIN, VICTOR	2	0			
TORRES, FRANK	1	0			
TOURNIER, JOSEPH ALEXIS	1	1	$989	$989	$989
			DM1,517	DM1,517	DM1,517
			£644	£644	£644
			¥108,198	¥108,198	¥108,198
TOURNIER, JOSEPH ALEXIS (workshop of)	1	1	$1,955	$1,955	$1,955
			DM2,942	DM2,942	DM2,942
			£1,187	£1,187	£1,187
			¥218,530	¥218,530	¥218,530
TOURTE, FRANCOIS XAVIER	1	0			
TOURTE, LOUIS (PERE)	1	0			
TUBBS, JAMES	6	4	$3,882	$9,218	$7,190
			DM5,964	DM15,401	DM11,027
			£2,530	£5,520	£4,428
			¥425,012	¥1,120,505	¥774,101
TUBBS, JAMES (attributed to)	1	1	$1,714	$1,714	$1,714
			DM3,068	DM3,068	DM3,068
			£1,058	£1,058	£1,058
			¥202,152	¥202,152	¥202,152
TUBBS, THOMAS	1	1	$10,018	$10,018	$10,018
			DM15,056	DM15,056	DM15,056
			£5,980	£5,980	£5,980
			¥1,115,635	¥1,115,635	¥1,115,635
TUBBS, THOMAS (attributed to)	2	1	$2,120	$2,120	$2,120
			DM3,133	DM3,133	DM3,133
			£1,380	£1,380	£1,380
			¥225,953	¥225,953	¥225,953
TUBBS, WILLIAM	1	0			
VAN DER MEER, KAREL	2	2	$1,006	$1,845	$1,426
			DM1,060	DM2,569	DM1,815
			£621	£1,150	£886
			¥76,877	¥155,682	¥116,280
VAN HEMERT, KEES	2	2	$575	$805	$690
			DM1,041	DM1,377	DM1,209
			£351	£476	£413
			¥69,426	¥99,965	¥84,695
VICKERS, J.E.	3	2	$201	$782	$492
			DM282	DM1,473	DM878
			£127	£483	£305
			¥17,929	¥82,699	¥50,314

Maker	Items Bid	Sold	Selling Prices Low	High	Avg
VIDOUDEZ, PIERRE	1	1	$3,353 DM5,151 £2,185 ¥367,056	$3,353 DM5,151 £2,185 ¥367,056	$3,353 DM5,151 £2,185 ¥367,056
VIGNERON, A.	2	1	$4,298 DM7,909 £2,673 ¥506,964	$4,298 DM7,909 £2,673 ¥506,964	$4,298 DM7,909 £2,673 ¥506,964
VIGNERON, ANDRE	2	0			
VIGNERON, JOSEPH ARTHUR	10	7	$1,035 DM1,583 £681 ¥109,089	$8,458 DM13,066 £5,520 ¥899,214	$4,945 DM8,215 £3,120 ¥551,394
VOIGT, ARNOLD	1	1	$1,089 DM1,533 £690 ¥111,319	$1,089 DM1,533 £690 ¥111,319	$1,089 DM1,533 £690 ¥111,319
VOIGT, CARL HERMANN	1	0			
VOIRIN, FRANCOIS NICOLAS	26	17	$748 DM1,353 £456 ¥90,253	$12,075 DM17,436 £7,693 ¥1,047,506	$4,952 DM7,844 £3,094 ¥523,046
VUILLAUME, JEAN BAPTISTE	10	5	$768 DM1,283 £460 ¥93,375	$13,714 DM25,789 £8,625 ¥1,658,070	$8,299 DM14,799 £5,101 ¥962,902
WANKA, HERBERT	1	0			
WATSON, W.D.	1	1	$2,981 DM5,354 £1,840 ¥351,937	$2,981 DM5,354 £1,840 ¥351,937	$2,981 DM5,354 £1,840 ¥351,937
WEICHOLD	1	0			
WEICHOLD, R.	2	0			
WEICHOLD, RICHARD	3	3	$431 DM738 £255 ¥53,553	$671 DM1,027 £437 ¥74,700	$572 DM919 £353 ¥66,602
WERNER, ERNST	1	1	$1,380 DM2,077 £838 ¥154,256	$1,380 DM2,077 £838 ¥154,256	$1,380 DM2,077 £838 ¥154,256
WERNER, FRANZ EMANUEL (workshop of)	1	0			
WERNER, KARL	1	1	$1,190 DM2,247 £737 ¥125,928	$1,190 DM2,247 £737 ¥125,928	$1,190 DM2,247 £737 ¥125,928
WERRO, JEAN	1	1	$248 DM364 £161 ¥26,269	$248 DM364 £161 ¥26,269	$248 DM364 £161 ¥26,269
WILSON, GARNER	7	6	$951 DM1,350 £598 ¥88,295	$2,062 DM3,567 £1,265 ¥235,290	$1,367 DM2,195 £849 ¥145,980

| Maker | Items | | Selling Prices | | |
	Bid	Sold	Low	High	Avg
WINKLER, FRANZ	1	1	$1,093	$1,093	$1,093
			DM1,580	DM1,580	DM1,580
			£714	£714	£714
			¥110,616	¥110,616	¥110,616
WITHERS, EDWARD	1	0			
WITHERS, GEORGE & SONS	4	1	$487	$487	$487
			DM852	DM852	DM852
			£299	£299	£299
			¥57,572	¥57,572	¥57,572
YAKQUSHKIN	1	1	$415	$415	$415
			DM716	DM716	DM716
			£253	£253	£253
			¥47,351	¥47,351	¥47,351

XYLOPHONE

Maker	Bid	Sold	Low	High	Avg
COSLEV	1	1	$556	$556	$556
			DM855	DM855	DM855
			£368	£368	£368
			¥59,331	¥59,331	¥59,331
PREMIER	2	2	$193	$789	$491
			DM289	DM1,120	DM704
			£115	£506	£311
			¥21,560	¥80,228	¥50,894
WARNE, REUBEN	3	1	$39	$39	$39
			DM67	DM67	DM67
			£23	£23	£23
			¥4,930	¥4,930	¥4,930

ZITHER

Maker	Bid	Sold	Low	High	Avg
KIENDL, A.	2	2	$194	$495	$345
			DM287	DM731	DM509
			£127	£322	£224
			¥20,712	¥52,722	¥36,717
KIENDL, KARL	1	1	$354	$354	$354
			DM520	DM520	DM520
			£230	£230	£230
			¥37,527	¥37,527	¥37,527
PUGH, JOHANNES	1	1	$476	$476	$476
			DM792	DM792	DM792
			£287	£287	£287
			¥55,489	¥55,489	¥55,489
SCHUSTER, CARL GOTTLOB (JR.)	1	1	$575	$575	$575
			DM1,065	DM1,065	DM1,065
			£345	£345	£345
			¥76,807	¥76,807	¥76,807
TIEFENBRUNNER, GEORG	2	2	$112	$271	$191
			DM195	DM383	DM289
			£69	£173	£121
			¥13,583	¥23,129	¥18,356

ZITHER-BANJO

Maker	Bid	Sold	Low	High	Avg
CAMMEYER, ALFRED D.	1	1	$339	$339	$339
			DM618	DM618	DM618
			£207	£207	£207
			¥42,878	¥42,878	¥42,878

Maker	Items		Selling Prices		
	Bid	Sold	Low	High	Avg
DALLAS	1	1	$63	$63	$63
			DM96	DM96	DM96
			£40	£40	£40
			¥7,026	¥7,026	¥7,026
GORDON, GERALD	1	1	$97	$97	$97
			DM169	DM169	DM169
			£58	£58	£58
			¥12,326	¥12,326	¥12,326
HUNT, H.H.	1	1	$104	$104	$104
			DM188	DM188	DM188
			£63	£63	£63
			¥12,523	¥12,523	¥12,523
WINDSOR	2	2	$50	$116	$83
			DM77	DM178	DM127
			£32	£75	£53
			¥4,952	¥11,495	¥8,224
WINDSOR, A.O.	2	2xj	$85	$115	$100
			DM154	DM166	DM160
			£52	£75	£64
			¥10,246	¥11,644	¥10.945

OTHER TITLES FROM
STRING LETTER PUBLISHING

Strings Magazine, 8 issues, $32.95
The leading periodical for string players and enthusiasts brings you global coverage of the string world through articles, interviews, reviews, transcriptions, profiles, letters, and lessons. With eight issues per year, Strings covers the personalities, music, news, events, instruments, and gear that matter. Each issue focuses on classical and new music while also exploring all musical genres in which string players are active.
For a free, no-risk copy of the latest issue, call (800) 827-6837 or visit www.stringsmagazine.com.

Commonsense Instrument Care Guide, 2nd edition, $9.95
Violin maker and dealer James N. McKean, past president of the American Federation of Violin and Bow Makers, has written the essential reference on maintaining the playability and value of violins, violas, and cellos and their bows.

THE *STRINGS* BACKSTAGE SERIES

21st-Century Violinists, Vol. 1, $12.95
21st-Century Violinists, Vol. 2, $12.95 (Fall 2000)
Some of today's leading violinists offer a rare glimpse into the fascinating life of the classical violin soloist. In these compelling profiles, each musician reveals the personal, technical, and psychological aspects of their lives in music: how they cope with isolation, how they approach and interpret their repertoire, and what kindles their passions and unites them with their audiences.

21st-Century String Quartets, Vol. 1, $12.95
In this collection of in-depth interviews, today's leading performers get to the heart of one of the most beloved forms of classical music; the string quartet. How they practice, how they come to consensus, their performance secrets and anxieties, what moves and inspires them—all this and more come to life in this series of revealing conversations.

For more information on books from String Letter Publishing, or to place an order, please call Music Dispatch at (800) 637-2852, fax (414) 774-3259, or mail to Music Dispatch, PO Box 13920, Milwaukee, WI 53213. Visit String Letter Publishing on-line at www.stringletter.com.